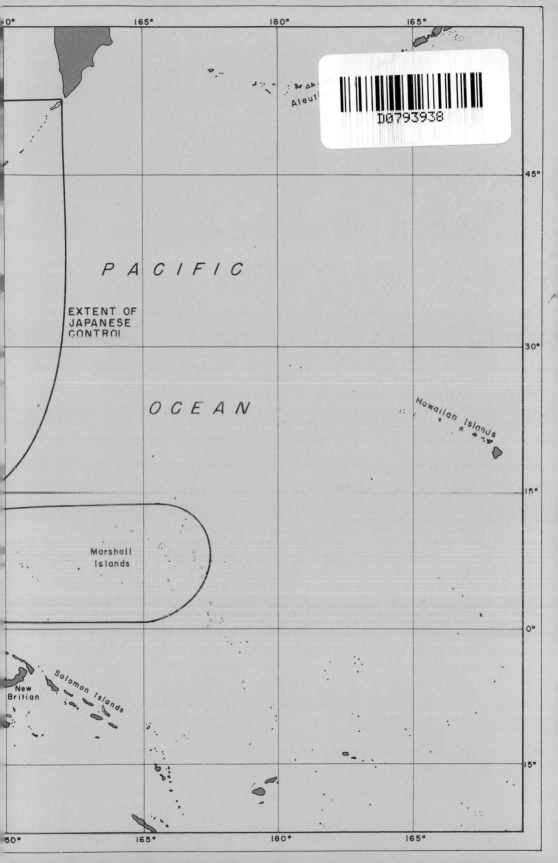

165°   180°   165°

Aleuti

45°

P A C I F I C

EXTENT OF
JAPANESE
CONTROL

30°

O C E A N

Hawaiian Islands

15°

Marshall
Islands

0°

Solomon Islands

New
Britian

15°

165°   180°   165°

Empires
in the
Balance

H. P. WILLMOTT

Empires
in the
Balance

JAPANESE AND ALLIED PACIFIC STRATEGIES
TO APRIL 1942

NAVAL INSTITUTE PRESS
Annapolis, Maryland

Library of Congress Cataloging in Publication Data

Willmott, H. P.
  Empires in the balance.

  Bibliography: p.
  Includes index.
  1. World War, 1939–1945—Japan. 2. World
War, 1939–1945—Pacific Ocean. 3. Japan—Foreign
relations—1926–1945. 4. Japan—History—1912–
1945. I. Title.
D767.2.W54   940.53′52   82-6475
ISBN 0-87021-535-3   AACR2

To and for
Pauline,
Gaynor, and Stephen

Men are seldom at their best in
dealing with insoluble problems.

Rear Admiral P. W. Brock, RN (Ret.)

Contents

Maps

Foreword

IN 1941 the two major Western powers in the Far East, in their different ways, sought to deter Japanese aggression. They attempted to do so from positions of military inferiority relative to Japan. Both Britain and the United States realized that, if their policies of deterrence failed, the defense of their interests and possessions in the Far East could be successful only if their ground forces were able to buy the time needed for reinforcements to make their way across the sea to the theater of operations.

Both the British in Malaya and the Americans in the Philippines employed policies of forward defense against an enemy with air superiority and superiority of numbers on the ground at the point of contact. This enemy possessed a sound and carefully developed battle doctrine based on mass, firepower, and armor, the latter being used in both reconnaissance and strike roles. British and American doctrines were based on infantry, and their infantry lacked an effective antitank weapon. The ground on which battles were fought was known to the defense, which had had years in which to conduct proper reconnaissance and prepare proper defensive positions.

In each case the defense was defeated. Chief among the many factors that contributed to their defeat was the fact that British and American ground forces were inadequate to fulfill the strategic tasks assigned to them in accordance with their nations' foreign policies. Foreign policy objectives and defense capabilities were out of alignment. The ground forces were outfought strategically and tactically, and the naval forces proved incapable of reinforcing ground forces on the scale needed to stem the tide of enemy conquest. This situation arose because neither the British nor the Americans possessed the margin of superiority that would have enabled them to secure command of the seas. As a result, Japanese doctrines of what would now be termed "sea denial" prevailed.

On this, the fortieth anniversary of the fall of Corregidor, one wonders how far the Maginot line mentality of 1941 might be applicable to the European and Atlantic theaters of operation today.

6 May 1982

Preface and Acknowledgements

ON MY APPOINTMENT to the staff of the Department of War Studies, Royal Military Academy Sandhurst, in December 1969, I was made responsible for a series of lectures, among which was one on the Pacific war, 1941–45. For some three years I delivered this lecture until departmental and syllabus changes led to its being dropped. It was not until early 1978 that I was forced to renew a "professional" interest in the Pacific.

In the intervening years, however, my casual interest in Japanese and Pacific matters had been maintained, though my immediate and practical attentions had been directed towards postwar insurgency in East and Southeast Asia. When in 1978 I began to pick up the threads of the Pacific campaign again, I was most forcibly struck by what seemed to me to be certain major omissions in accounts of the Pacific war. It appeared that there was no well-written single-volume account of the campaign that did justice to the subject, and I could not help but note what seemed to be two quite distinct features of most accounts. The first was the seemingly perfunctory manner in which Japan was handled in most works. The second was the way in which both American and British accounts tended to look at events in a rather narrow and nationalistic manner, at the expense of a wider Allied view.

I resolved to try to remedy this situation, but I soon saw that such was the complexity, and, indeed, grandeur, of this struggle that a single volume could never hope to do more than scratch the surface. I began to appreciate the extent of the problems that would face anyone who attempted to tackle the task of giving an account of the Pacific campaign. My attentions focused upon what seemed to me to be the crucial matter of the war, namely precisely why and for what objectives Japan went to war in 1941, and on what basis she could possibly envisage fighting a defensive war against the most powerful industrialized state in the world, the United States; the greatest of the imperialist powers, Britain; and the most populous state on earth, China, in what was the largest ocean of the world, the Pacific, whose size is greater than the total land surface of the planet.

Five years at the university had taught me a healthy skepticism of "turning points" and "critical battles." A wise critic of one paper I wrote commented, "For every complicated human problem there is a simple solution: neat, plausible, and wrong." The one matter that seemed to emerge from the Pacific campaign in the light of this comment was the danger in simplifying events and, in particular, in seeing the Battle of Midway, and the American victory then, as both decisive and inevitable—a paradoxical view. The more I looked at Midway the more I became convinced of an even deeper paradox. On the one hand was the immediate and tactical consideration pointing to the fact that since the stronger side was defeated in battle, the outcome of the action could hardly be considered "inevitable" or "predestined." On the other hand it was hard to resist the notion that the Japanese would not have encountered "a Midway" at some time or another somewhere in the Pacific.

The latter view, almost Marxist in its perspective, presupposed that, given the disparity between American and Japanese resources, Japan's defeat was unavoidable in the long term. In such a view Midway, for all the element of chance that played so large a part in the outcome of the battle, really marked the point when, perhaps for the first time in the Pacific conflict, the immutable factors of war—the drag of logistics; the demands of space, time, and distance; qualitative and quantitative factors of training, manpower, and materiel—began to impose their imprint on the conduct and outcome of operations. Rightly or wrongly, I became convinced of the correctness of this view and, as a result, of the opinion that all the ingredients of Japan's defeat were to be found, if not in the events of the decade of Japanese involvement in China before 1941, then certainly in the period of her greatest triumphs, in Southeast Asia in the period between December 1941 and April 1942. Here, to me, seemed the crux of the Pacific war.

By the process of elimination, therefore, my attentions became fixed upon this period of Japanese conquest, and I applied myself to the task of trying to give an account of the campaign from the Japanese point of view.

It seemed to me only logical to try to trace the course of events from the viewpoint of the side with the strategic initiative. It made little or no sense to try to portray events in a fragmented and piecemeal manner from the perspectives of the various Allied nations in Southeast Asia and the Southwest Pacific. But once this task had begun in earnest, two matters naturally demanded proper attention and consideration. First, the Allied responses and actions in the theater of operations were important in their own right, and they could not be simply dismissed as reaction to events. Second, once I began from the point of view of Japanese intentions and policy, then the totality of conflict throughout Burma, the Indies, Malaya, and the Philippines, on land, in the air, and at sea, demanded comprehensive treatment. I noted the British tendency to consider the campaign in Southeast Asia in terms of "Malaya and Singapore plus" and the American inclination to see events in terms of "Pearl Harbor, the Philippines, and other events." I noted the British and American neglect of the campaign in the Indies, even though possession of the resources of the Indies was perhaps the most important single factor that led Japan into war.

On the basis, therefore, that an account had to try to trace events throughout Southeast Asia and the Pacific from both Allied and Japanese viewpoints, I began to research and write. As I framed my terms of reference, six individuals were especially helpful in providing advice and encouragement. First, I am grateful to Dr. A. H. le Q. Clayton of the Department of Political and Social Studies, Royal Military Academy Sandhurst. As a keen naval historian with more than a passing interest in the Imperial Japanese Navy, he was an invaluable source of information and assistance. It was he who did so much to keep alive my interest in the Pacific between 1972 and 1978, and after I began to work seriously on my text he gave me every encouragement and the best of his knowledge. Second, on a dark and miserable night in the autumn of 1978, five of my colleagues in the Department of War Studies and International Affairs, namely Mr. N. C. de Lee, Dr. C. J. Duffy, Dr. P. G. Griffith, Mr. M. J. Orr, and Lieutenant Commander A. G. Thomas, RN (Ret.), attended a departmental War Discussion Group at which I talked about Southeast Asia and how I intended to try to handle the subject. The meeting helped to crystallize many issues and problems in a far more effective manner than I could have achieved by my own unaided efforts. For the insights of these friends and colleagues, and for their subsquent help and encouragement, I am most grateful.

Majors F. A. Godrey (Ret.) and Major R. d'A. Ryan (Ret.), both of the Department of War Studies and International Affairs, shared with me their knowledge of the Far East and closely scrutinized the text relating to operations in Hong Kong, Malaya, and Singapore. My thanks also extend to Mr. D. G. Chandler, head of the department, for his encouragement of the project, and particularly for his provision of material on oil and Japanese planning and for contacts in Japan.

Mr. J. R. F. de Klerk, Department of Military Technology, translated various Dutch material; Lieutenant Commander G. S. Stavert, RN, (Ret.), Department of Political and Social Studies, read several drafts, and Lieutenant Commander R. A. de S. Cosby, RN, read my final manuscript with a view to ensuring that all nautical matters were rendered in a style that should secure acceptance within the Royal Navy. I also appreciate deeply the efforts of Mr. M. G. H. Wright, deputy librarian at the academy, in completing the indexing of the book. Within the academy, two colleagues, Dr. T. A. Heathcote, curator of the Sandhurst Collection, and Mr. B. T. Jones, academic registrar, found themselves appointed as my proofreaders. In the course of twelve months they never showed any sign of dismay when yet one more tome, in need of their most careful and urgent attention, found its way to their desks. For the many hours that they have spent in working their ways through the script and then checking the various amended drafts, I am most indebted. But neither they nor anyone else who has helped me so much are responsible for what follows in the text.

From outside the academy, Mr. A. Corley, official historian to Burmah Oil; Mr. W. Duijnhouwer of K.M.A. at Breda; Dr. C. M. Schulten and Major H. L. Zwitzer of the Historical Branch of the Dutch General Staff; Vice Admiral Saburo Toyama, Professor of Military History at the Defense Academy at Yokosuka; Captain H. Kiryu at the Japanese Embassy in London; and Lieutenant Colonel Akihiko Kurushima from the Staff College at Camberley all were most helpful. I am equally grateful to the staffs of the various libraries in which I have worked: the British Museum, the Imperial War Museum, the Institute of Historical Research, the National Maritime Museum, the Royal Naval College Greenwich, the Royal United Services Institute, and the School of Oriental and African Studies. My deepest thanks, naturally, extend to the staffs of the libraries nearest home, the Staff College and Royal Military Academy Sandhurst. The staff of the academy library showed remarkable tolerance of my irregular working habits and obscure requests.

Those who have suffered in the preparation of the manuscript include successive departmental secretaries who contributed their time, attention, resources, and humor; and two departmental members who, at different times, had the misfortune to share an office with me. Majors A. Cain and T. Maley must have despaired on many occasions when they entered the office only to be greeted by scenes of wild disorder and furious endeavor. For their indulgence, not least when I "tried out" various lines of thought upon them, I am sincerely indebted.

My agent, Mrs. Herta Ryder of Hughes Massie, continued to work on the book when, on all too many occasions, the outlook seemed more than a little bleak. I appreciate the confidence the Naval Institute Press and Orbis Publishing Limited have shown in publishing the book, and am grateful for the sharp editorial pencil wielded by Judie Zubin. The maps were specially drawn for the book by Mr. W. M. Shannon. The photographs were supplied by: the Associated Press, Robert Hunt Library, Imperial War Museum, MacArthur Memorial Library, National Archives, Naval History, Orbis, Popperfoto, Royal Netherlands Army, Royal Netherlands Navy, U.S. Army, U.S. Naval Institute, and U.S. Navy.

My last and special debts are reserved for those who suffered most at the sharp end of my writing. My two dogs had to forego far too many walks while their master wrote, but it was the children, Gaynor and Stephen, and my wife, Pauline, whose lives were most affected by the domestic demands that the book made upon them. I can only hope that in the end they will feel the final product made everything worthwhile.

Standardization
of Names

IT IS ALWAYS DIFFICULT to settle upon the spelling of place names when usage, post-independence alterations, and transliteration from non-Roman scripts provide a variety of English-language options. To spell any place name in any given manner is to invite some form of criticism on the ground that some other form is more accurate or usual.

With certain specific exceptions, I settled upon retaining the original name of a place in the event of its being subsequently renamed, and therefore standardized other place names, where spellings have changed, to accord with those in use in 1941–42. Original names have been used because to use modern names would be anachronistic and in certain instances altogether wrong. It would be incorrect to refer to the Dutch in anything other than Batavia, since the city was renamed as part of the decolonization process. One exception to this general practice has been made. Thailand is the name given to the country that, before 1949, was known as Siam. Perhaps wrongly, I decided in this instance that the modern form and usage should prevail over strict historical accuracy.

I also, rather arbitrarily, settled the spelling of Java's second port in favor of the then-current Dutch rendering, Soerabaja. This place name probably caused more problems than any other. English-language texts are often weak on Dutch place names, with much confusion surrounding the use of the letter *u* for *oe* and *j* for *y*. Among the many versions Soerabaja was adopted for no other reason than that the Dutch had a warship of this name and spelling in the port. It seemed incongruous to have the *Soerabaja* being scuttled in Soerabaia, Surabaja, Soerabaya, or (present version) Surabaya.

With names and ranks, I settled upon current rank, irrespective of whether it was substantive, with the first forename, initial, and surname wherever possible. This American style has been applied to all Australian, British, Dutch, and American names, even though this may seem to jar with some British readers. Japanese names have been standardized with the family name given after the personal name rather than in the Japanese manner (the other way around). Because various alternate personal names exist, some of the names given in the text will be at variance with those normally given. For example, the commander of the Japanese 25th Army in Malaya is generally known in the West as Tomoyuki Yamashita (pronounced Yamashta); in Japan he is known as Yamashita Hobum, and he is referred to in this second manner, after reversal of order, in this text.

Military organizations have been standardized with all Japanese operational ground forces, from armies to battalions, being given in italics in order to differentiate them clearly from Allied forces. This was essential because in certain instances Allied and Japanese formations with the same name were in conflict with one another. All ship names, naturally, have been given in italics, regardless of nationality. Using current military definitions, the word *unit* has been applied to a force up to the size of a battalion and the word *formation* to any force larger than a unit. The word *regiment* has been standardized to the normal practice, not used in the British Army, of denoting a three-battalion formation. In British terms such a formation would be a brigade—which in the Dutch Indies army, but not in the Dutch army, was a section of about nineteen men. The normal use of the word in the Japanese army denoted more than one three-battalion regiment. The word *brigade* has been retained where it formed part of an operational command and where it refers to a formation larger than a regiment but less than a division. The British system of using names to denote arms of service has been discarded.

Where battalions from parent regiments have been named (e.g., the 1st Battalion of the 1st Infantry Regiment) I decided, in the absence of any common practice by the armies of the time, that the unit should be presented as the 1st/1st Infantry. This will probably find favor with few, but it will at least avoid accusations of national bias.

Finally, standard symbols have been used on the maps to identify specific military formations:

☐   Basic unit symbol

☒   Infantry

XXXXX	Army group
XXXX	Army
XXX	Corps
XX	Division
X	Brigade
|||	Regiment
||	Battalion
(+)	Overstrength unit or formation
(−)	Understrength unit or formation
⊓	Reinforced all-arms group based upon single unit.

Introduction: Context and Theater

To THE OVERWHELMING MAJORITY of Europeans the term *the Second World War* immediately conjures up memories or impressions of the conflict against Hitler's Germany. Perceptions of this war vary greatly from nation to nation. For example, the experiences of Poland and the Soviet Union, the great killing zones of the war, were very different from those of the countries of Western Europe that saw relatively few battlefield deaths. Even within the latter, the experience and perceptions of Britain, unde-feated and unoccupied, are very different from those of a France that was humbled by defeat in 1940. Even within a nation perceptions of the war vary. For France the war recalls the divide between Pétain, the embodiment of legitimacy, obedience, and service, and de Gaulle, the personification of honor and duty. To many Britons and Americans alike the land war would almost seem to have started in 1944, with the Normandy invasion. That Europeans should be Eurocentric in their view of events is natural. It is only to be expected that in the light of postwar developments and national vanity the wartime Allies should have taken great pains to decry the efforts of their erstwhile friends and to claim for themselves the credit for the defeat of the dictators. It is all the more important, therefore, to recall that the Second World War in fact consisted of two concurrent wars. There was a war fought by the United Nations in Europe and Africa, in the seas around and in the skies above these continents, against the totalitarian powers of Germany and Italy and their minor allies. There was also a war in Asia and the Pacific between the United Nations and Japan. It must be remembered, of course, that hostilities in the Far East began at least two years before the start of the European conflict, and still had to be finally resolved at the time of the German surrender in May 1945.

What is often forgotten about the war against Japan is that it was fought on a scale, in terms of time and distance, that dwarfs anything that took place in the European theater. It was a war in which the fifth most powerful nation on earth was not merely beaten but pulverized into defeat by what were virtually the unaided efforts of the greatest of the Allies. That Allied nation, the United States of America, allocated little more than one-quarter of her total war effort to the struggle against Japan. The contributions made to this struggle by the allies of the United States were negligible; the demands they imposed upon the Americans were on occasion considerable. This is not in any way to denigrate the efforts of the allies of the United States or to assert that they did not have their successes. British Empire forces at Kohima-Imphal inflicted on the Imperial Japanese Army what was up until that time the greatest defeat in its history; the Soviet intervention in August 1945 was a devastating psychological blow to Japan and a major factor in bringing about her surrender. But the war in the Far East is a conflict to which Europeans seemingly pay very little attention, perhaps in a subconscious effort to mitigate the humiliations of 1941–42. Undoubtedly the nature of these defeats touches a raw racial nerve. Yet the war in the Far East deserves the most serious consideration because it was to have vast repercussions in the shaping of the world in the two decades that followed the Japanese surrender on 2 September 1945. The defeat of the European empires in 1941–42 paved the way for the eventual independence of their colonies, while the defeats themselves had ramifications that were felt not only in those areas directly concerned in the Far East but throughout the whole of the empires. Moreover, the American victory in the Pacific was based on the rise to a position of preeminence of a navy that was for two decades not merely unchallengeable but the underwriter of the *pax Americana* and the freedom of Western democracy. It is only by understanding the scale and totality of American power and victory in this conflict, and the relative ease with which victory was bought, that one can comprehend the postwar failures of the Americans and their allies to realize the limitations of American power, only now becoming obvious in the aftermath of Vietnam.

This book is an attempt to explain certain aspects of the war in the Pacific. It is not an attempt to cover the whole of the conflict. It is concerned with trying to explain how and why the conflict broke out and the manner in which the various combatant nations devised their strategies. The text tries to give a rational and calculated critique of the deliberations and actions of the major powers and to follow the course of the critical first five months of the war. The author has set out his own views of the myths and realities of this war, and he has attempted to point out the one course of action that the Japanese could and perhaps should have pursued if they were to have had any chance of avoiding the ultimate defeat many Japanese commanders suspected was inevitable. That course of action was to have exposed their Pacific conquests to the worst that the Americans could have done in 1942 and smashed the British position throughout the Middle East.

From Amsterdam to Moscow is 1,579 miles; from Rome to Oslo, 1,624 miles. Europe, with an area of about 4,000,000 square miles the least of the continents, extends over 35 degrees of latitude and 70 degrees of longitude, being at its greatest extent about 2,400 miles from north to south and 3,000 miles from east to west. Much of the land surface of Europe was conquered by the Germans in the period 1938–42, and it took the forces of the Allies, infinitely more powerful than Germany in manpower, industrial, and financial resources, more than three years to accomplish the defeat of Hitler, once the flood tide of German conquest had been stemmed. Compared to the area of the Pacific, the decisive theater of the war in the Far East, Europe is a puny irrelevance. One-third of the earth's surface is covered by this ocean, which is bigger than the two Atlantic and Indian Oceans combined. The Pacific is larger in area 68,000,000 square miles if one includes the adjacent seas—than the total land surface of the planet. At its extremities it stretches some 9,600 miles from the Bering Strait to Antarctica and some 13,200 miles from Colombia to Malaya. Within its vast expanse the Pacific contains many thousands of diverse islands, the peoples of which differ distinctively. Approximately 7,000 islands make up the Philippines; Japan, surprisingly, consists of 3,000 islands. Indonesia contains perhaps as many islands as Japan and the Philippines together. In addition to these major concentrations many thousands of islands stretch across the Pacific, from the Ryukyus to far-away Easter Island, from the Aleutians to New Zealand. It was this ocean and these islands that formed the theater of operations for Japan and the Allies. Admittedly, not all the Pacific was a war zone. For the most part the conflict was confined, if that is the correct word, to the area west of Hawaii and north of the central Solomons group. But even this area is enormous. From Oahu to Yokohoma is 3,902 miles, while the Americans had to move war materiel across the whole expanse of the ocean. From Panama to Auckland is 7,496 miles; from Oahu to Panama is 5,424 miles. Even theaters of operation considered small by Pacific standards are vast. Guadalcanal and Australia are considered near by local standards, but the distance from the former to Sydney, via Noumea in New Caledonia, is about 2,500 miles. It was these vast distances that led Charles Darwin to write, "It is necessary to sail over this great ocean to comprehend its immensity . . . for weeks together . . . nothing but the same blue, profoundly deep ocean."

Direct European involvement in the Pacific dates from the first quarter of the sixteenth century when Europe, for centuries the victim of destructive invasions from Asia and Arabia, entered upon an expansionist phase that was largely dictated by increasing demographic pressures and growing strain on resources. But the immediate impetus to what was the European discovery and penetration of the East was the desire to secure the lucrative Arab monopoly in the spice trade. Pepper from throughout southern Asia, cinnamon from Ceylon, cloves from Tidore and Ternate, nutmeg and mace from Amboina were the major spices sought as condiments and preservatives, while luxury items such as Chinese silk, Arabian perfumes, Persian carpets, and Indian precious stones were similarly prized. It fell to the Portuguese to lead the way to the East when their new oceanic sailing ships worked their way southwards down both coasts of Africa before Vasco da Gama reached Calicut in India via the Cape of Good Hope in 1498.

Portugal's era of dominance of the trade with the East was to be short-lived. Scattered bases around Africa, South America, and India weakened rather than strengthened her and left her vulnerable to stronger, more vigorous opponents, while she had little success in establishing a presence east of Malacca, secured in 1511. Canton was visited for the first time in 1514 but it was not until 1557 that the Macao concession was secured. Native resistance in the Spice Islands proved too strong to be overcome. For a brief period Portugal enjoyed a very lucrative and privileged position in the spice trade, but this was shattered by the Dutch between 1601 and 1667.

The Dutch, in their war of liberation against Spain, carried their struggle to Spain's colonies. The Spaniards, having passed into the Pacific via the Straits of Magellan for the first time in 1520, had colonized Cebu and Luzon, and established a settlement at Manila in 1571. Spanish colonies survived Dutch depredations, but Portugal, united with Spain in the person of Philip II after 1580, could not withstand Dutch assaults. Beginning with the Battle of the Sunda Strait in 1601, the Dutch virtually destroyed Portuguese power in the Far East by 1667. The Dutch thereafter embarked upon a policy of annexation and colonization. Over the next 250 years they charted the islands of the Indies and subjugated them, in the process encountering fierce opposition from nature, the local inhabitants, and two other European powers.

The most important opposition came from Britain and France, but in fact the position of Dutch possessions in the Far East was to be barely affected by these two powers, each individually much more powerful than the Dutch. The two powers tended to cancel one another out, and in any case the British and Dutch, united in religious propinquity and their dislike and fear of France, were normally allies. The Anglo-French clash of interest was mainly centered in North America. Their territorial interests in the East, which were subordinate to their trading interests, were mainly directed towards the Indian subcontinent, and their struggle there was resolved in Britain's favor in the course of the Seven Years War (1756–63). For much of the period Britain was so powerful at sea that she could have taken what she wanted, but she sought to preserve the Netherlands as a barrier against French expansion and thus was indisposed to strip the Dutch of their possessions. Indeed, during the French Revolution and Napoleonic Wars, when the Dutch were overrun and forced into reluctant alliance with France, Britain took most Dutch possessions into "protective custody." By the terms of the Convention of London (1814) the British returned most of these possessions to the Netherlands, though they kept the Cape of Good Hope, Ceylon, and certain other minor possessions.

What Britain wanted in the East was a port through which her China trade could be channeled. Penang, secured in 1786, seemed a suitable port, but in 1819 Sir T. Stamford Raffles, British lieutenant governor of Java between 1811 and 1816, founded a settlement on the island of Singapore just off the coast of Johore. His action provoked a severe dispute with the Dutch, who had harbored ambitions of securing and consolidating possessions on both sides of the Strait of Malacca. There was no clear line of demarcation between overlapping British and Dutch settlements in the area, but in 1824 the dispute was settled by drawing a line through the straits: the Dutch abandoned their settlements in Malacca, the British theirs in western and northern Sumatra. This arrangement's effect was to break the Dutch grip on the trade routes to the Indies and to prevent Dutch domination of the Malayan peninsula. There British influence immediately became overwhelming. Thai incursions into northern Malayan vassal states that Bangkok always had regarded as within its sphere of influence resulted in an 1826 treaty through which the British assumed a position of great influence; thereafter the Thais were slowly but remorselessly excluded from the area. During the same year Britain obtained Arakan, Assam, and Tenasserim as a result of her first war with Burma, thereby securing India's eastern border. By the middle of the century, the British controlled lower Burma, though not until 1886 did they control the whole of Burma.

Thus, by the middle of the nineteenth century many areas of the Far East had been brought under European control of influence, but in a sense Europeans still had to reach their final destination—China. Trading contacts with the fabled Middle Kingdom had been established for three centuries, but European penetration of the most important of the eastern civilizations was far from complete. Indeed, contact remained minimal. But by the first half of the century a more ruthless attitude towards China had been evinced by the Europeans—most notably by the British in the Opium War of 1839–42—and this boded only ill for China.

By about 1850 the European powers stood poised on the brink of a second phase of expansion that was to prove infinitely more dynamic than their activities of the previous 350 years. Before 1850 the Spanish, Dutch, and British had established substantial colonial empires, the Portuguese and French lesser ones, yet except in India, their penetration of the Asian mainland had not been very great. This situation was to change dramatically under the impact of the Industrial Revolution. Though major colonizing efforts were not to be in the Far East, the growing economic and military power of European states allowed them to play an increasingly active and permanent role in the area. Concurrently, the European attitude towards imperialism underwent considerable change. In the first half of the century imperialism was decidedly unpopular; it seemed discredited, though states with colonies showed no real inclination to give them up. But France, Portugal, and Spain lost the greater part of their empires in the first quarter of the century without any apparent ill effects, and economists everywhere were well aware that after the New World secured its independence its trade with Europe had not lessened but greatly increased. It was the conservative Disraeli, not the liberal Gladstone, who denounced Britain's colonies as millstones around her neck, adding that in the very near future they would become independent in any case. But European attitudes were undergoing fundamental reevaluation, and a combination of factors led to a massive imperialist upsurge in the latter part of the century. The result was that virtually the whole of the Far East, with one vitally important exception, came under the control of nonindigenous forces.

Traditionally the flag had followed trade, but any attempt to interpret European activities in the Far East in the second half of the nineteenth century simply in terms of economic determinism is inadequate. Many factors were at work in the expansion of imperialism, a process that was not confined to the seaborne powers of western Europe but included the United States and czarist Russia. The desire to secure new markets for goods and capital and the need for raw materials *were* factors in late nineteenth-century imperialist expansion, but so were considerations of prestige and even national security. Religious and moral considerations, however muddled, were also present in many instances. For example, the French intervention in Indo-China was prompted by many factors, although the influence of the Catholic lobby with Napoleon III was perhaps the critical factor. Likewise, the American sense of mission, the fulfillment of a manifest destiny, and upholding the standards of decency and (white) civilization, were not mere devices; they were genuine, if wrong-headed, beliefs. They had been largely instrumental in bringing about the Spanish-American War of 1898, a conflict that resulted in the emergence of the United States as a major Pacific power. Some of those who claimed moral and Christian values as the basis of their actions knew that some of their professions were fraudulent, but the desire to promote Christianity and to bring order and civilization (as understood by white men) to backward areas *were* factors in the expansionist activities of various powers. The overall effect of this expansion, however, was to cause profound repercussions on the societies and politics of the Orient, and not in the way that the imperialists anticipated.

Imperialist expansion in the Far East was concentrated on three main areas. First, Russian overland expansion resulted in the annexation of Amur and Maritime provinces from China between 1858 and 1860. Further advances were made between 1854 and 1895 south of the Aral Sea and Lake Balkhash, but these had to be set against contraction of other interests. In 1867 the Russians sold Alaska to the United States and abandoned all their settlements on the American mainland. The Russians appreciated that they had overreached themselves and limited their objectives.

Second, the Pacific islands, now accurately located and charted, were gradually but systematically added to various empires, with Britain the main beneficiary. With Australia and New Zealand already secure as major areas of white colonization and both granted full internal self-rule in the 1850s, Britain was often under considerable pressure from Australasia to secure various island groups in the Southwest Pacific. To the island of Hong Kong, taken in 1842, and northern Borneo, formally secured in 1888, were added Fiji (1874), the Cook Islands (1888), and the Gilbert and Ellice islands (1886–92). Moreover, to these and other islands taken by Britain, an agreement with France established a joint Anglo-French dominion over the New Hebrides in 1887. The French, naturally, were active on their own account. They took Tahiti and the Society Islands in 1842 and New Caledonia, much to the chagrin of the British who were forestalled by a matter of hours, in 1853. In addition France acquired the Marquesas.

Britain's concern in the Southwest Pacific was to prevent the arrival of potential rivals in islands near Australia and New Zealand. Britain's initial suspicions were of France, but later there was fear of Germany, and, indeed, one of the features of the "scramble for the Pacific" was the late arrival on the scene of Germany and the United States. Germany in 1885 secured various islands off New Guinea, and the following year secured the division of New Guinea itself among the British, Dutch, and themselves. In 1885 she acquired the Marshalls and three years later Naura. But her main chance came in 1898–99 when she bought the remnants of Spain's colonial empire—the Marianas and Carolines—after the latter's defeat in the war of 1898. In that year the last of the unclaimed island chains, the Hawaiian Islands, was secured by the Americans, to go alongside their gains of the Philippines and Guam. By the turn of the century every island in the southern and central Pacific was under some form of European or American control.

The third area of imperialist expansion was on the Asian mainland between Vladivostok, founded in 1860, and the Thai-Malay border, and the offshore island group that made up the Japanese Empire. The main area of European and American interest and involvement was the ramshackle and decaying Chinese Empire which, despite its backwardness, presented a vast market for cheap manufactured goods and capital investment.

China, like Japan, for centuries chose to isolate herself from the outside world. Unavoidable contacts and trade were as circumscribed and tightly controlled as possible by a China that refused to treat with foreigners on a basis of equality. Used only to dealing with vassal states on the basis of tribute, China regarded dealings with foreign states as transactions between superior and inferior. Unfortunately for her, Europeans were not prepared to accept the position of inferiority thus conferred upon them, and they had the means to enforce their views.

It was Britain that forced China to open her doors to the outside world when, as a result of the Treaty of Nanking in 1842, she secured the island of Hong Kong, an indemnity (reversing the traditional Chinese role in the matter of cash transactions), the promise of full and equal diplomatic recognition, the abolition of import controls and the fixing of a low tariff rate, and the opening of five Chinese ports to British goods. The next year the British extracted the "most favored nation" clause whereby any concession granted by China to a third party automatically applied to Britain. The breach thus made in China's exclusiveness was widened in July 1844 when she was forced to conclude treaties with France and the United States, the latter agreement being the first of many that granted extraterritorial jurisdiction for foreign nationals.

China's problem was that the imperialists were not prepared to let matters rest at that point. They saw their gains not as ends in themselves but as the starting points for more concessions, and their chance to exploit the situation came as a result of a series of xenophobic incidents on the part of the Chinese. A joint Anglo-French intervention during the Arrow War resulted in easy victory for the two European powers, but when China tried to renege on the subsequent peace terms in 1859, their response was the capture of Peking and the destruction of the Summer Palace. The lesson of the futility of evasion, procrastination, and resistance was temporarily learned by China. Japan, watching the proceedings with interest, learned the lesson on a more permanent basis.

Two immediate consequences flowed from the war of 1857–60. First, full diplomatic recognition was accorded to foreign powers, and their nationals were given the undisputed right to reside in Peking. The loss of prestige these measures entailed for the imperial Chinese system was severe, and cannot be understated. Second, the paradox arose from the fact that while the successful penetration of China had depended on the weakness of the imperial system, the occidental powers, having recognized and been recognized by the Manchus, then had a vested interest in maintaining the regime: its continued existence was the guarantee of their rights and privileges.

In the 1860s there was much cooperation between China and the Western powers—the suppression of the T'ai p'ing Rebellion (1851–64) is an obvious example—but over a period of time a gradual disillusionment set in on both sides. The foreigners urged China to reform and modernize, but they came to doubt her capabilities and intentions. They suspected that China was intent only on a self-strengthening program whereby she intended to secure merely the means by which she could destroy the privileged European position in the country. Periodic demonstrations and rebellions that imperiled foreigners only substantiated these fears. China, on the other hand, was dismayed at the slow progress and painful consequences of change that seemingly only accelerated the fragmentation of society and did nothing to preserve her territorial integrity. As the nineteenth century drew to a close it seemed to China that the imperialists were gathering ever closer and that their intentions were ever more malign. Lands to the south and southwest that traditionally had been under her suzerainty were secured by Britain and France with relatively little difficulty, and China was forced to acquiesce in the loss of her vassal states, notwithstanding her initial attempts to encourage their resistance.

For all her alternation between modernization and procrastination, China at the turn of the century seemed on the brink of partition and destruction. As a result of her defeat in the war of 1894–95 there was a "scramble for China" among the imperialists. France secured a sphere of influence between Canton and Indo-China, Russia over northern Manchuria, Britain in the Yangtse valley. All the powers, even little Denmark, joined the rush to secure concessions and ports—all the powers, that is, except the United States. In 1899 and again in 1900 the Americans reaffirmed their commitment to the "Open Door" policy that gave all powers equal access to a sovereign China, and asked the other powers to reconfirm their earlier declarations to this effect. At the time all the powers were closing ranks to put down a rebellion against them stirred up by the imperial court, but though Russia was decidedly equivocal on the matter, the powers in the end admitted to a form of words that could be taken to mean recognition of China's integrity. Only after the Boxer Rebellion was suppressed did the rivalries of the powers resurface, and it was this division of interest and the sheer size of China, rather than Chinese resistance or American pronouncements, that saved China from dismemberment. Nevertheless, the beginnings of a conscious American moral commitment to China had been made, though by no stretch of the imagination was this commitment to the Open Door entirely altruistic. As the world's foremost manufacturing power, the United States had everything to gain from the policy and much to lose by the dismemberment of China.

The other area of imperialist interest in eastern Asia was Japan, but her response to the threat posed by Western powers was to be very different from that of China—after initial resistance had proved unavailing. Probably the most obvious reason for this was the example of China herself.

Though the Portuguese had reached Japan early in the sixteenth century, from 1598 Japan had deliberately adopted a policy of excluding herself from the outside world, mainly to insulate herself from the prospect of social upheaval that threatened to result from the aggressive proselytizing efforts of Catholic missionaries.* Thereafter, her only contacts were with China and the self-effacing Dutch, who were allowed to trade through Nagasaki. Over the centuries the Dutch became highly regarded for the scientific knowledge they could impart and as a source of intelligence about the outside world. By the nineteenth century the Dutch were giving Japan fair warning about the power of the major European states. It is no exaggeration to state that while very few Japanese ever questioned the wisdom or desirability of maintaining their self-imposed isolation, even before the arrival of the imperialist powers there was, among the ruling elite, a vague and undefined awareness of Japan's material inferiority to the outside world. There was grudging respect for the European achievement and the knowledge, from Dutch sources, of the dangerous temper of European powers when crossed.

Nevertheless, the 1844 warning that Japan would be well advised to treat with foreign powers was ignored. American attempts in 1846 and 1849 to break down Japanese isolation were rebuffed, but failure only made the Americans more determined. The great circle route between California and China brought American ships close to Japan's dangerous and inhospitable shores. Japan's exclusiveness, given America's need for coaling stations, was intolerable. In November 1852, therefore, the United States dispatched a squadron, including two steamers, from the Atlantic coast to Japan under Commodore Matthew Perry. Perry was granted extraordinary powers of discretion to force Japan to open her ports to American ships. The western European powers, distracted by other events, made no move, but the Russians, anxious not to be left out of any developments, sent a squadron to Japan from European waters in January 1853.

---

*The exclusion decrees were not systematically implemented until 1633, the same year that Galileo was forced to recant his alleged promotion of Copernican theories. These two acts had similar effects for Japan and Catholic southern Europe, since both tended to be excluded from the explosion of scientific knowledge and material advance that took place elsewhere from the middle of the seventeenth century onwards.

Perry and the Americans have been either credited or blamed for forcing Japan to open her doors to the West in the 1850s, but in fact it was a combination of American and Russian pressure, plus the knowledge that the British and French would appear sooner rather than later, that forced the Japanese to yield to American demands. American and Russian naval demonstrations in 1853 and 1854 convinced the Japanese, who heavily depended on a flourishing coastal trade, that resistance to the sea powers would be futile. On Perry's second visit in 1854 Japan was prepared to bow to the inevitable, and an American-Japanese treaty was signed at Yokohama. This allowed the Americans use of two small ports, Kakodate and Shimoda, and guaranteed good treatment of shipwrecked mariners. In reality the Americans did not obtain very much, but they made the all-important breach in Japan's isolation. The British and Russians promptly began to widen that breach, the Russians and Japanese dividing the Kuriles between them.

Despite the treaties forced upon Japan in 1854 and 1855, the imperialists' encroachments over the next thirteen years were not so great as might have been expected. European distractions elsewhere and America's Civil War shielded Japan from the full rigor of contact with the West. Yet even the effect of limited contact was profound, since it undermined a weakening political system. The shogunate was government by powerful clan interests, the very name *shogun* deriving from the title, "Great Resister of Barbarian Incursions." Failure to resist such incursions thus struck at the very credibility of the system, and a general uprising followed the 1858 decisions to open virtually all of Japan's ports to foreign trade and to fix very low tariffs on imports. While the shogunate rode out that particular storm, its power had been effectively and fatefully compromised, and in 1867 it was overthrown by a combination of new clans from western Japan and emergent merchant interests in the major ports. After the shogun's overthrow the emperor was plucked from the obscurity of an ornamental role and vested with the full prerogatives of a sovereign ruler.

The keynotes of Japanese policy in the post-1868 period were peace abroad and reconstruction at home. The Japanese sought to absorb Western techniques in order to escape European domination, but they were active diplomatically; caution did not imply passivity. Despite her relative backwardness, Japan asserted her claims over the Ryukyus in 1871 and the Bonins in 1873, with no opposition from foreign powers. Indeed, Britain and the United States waived their claims to the Bonins in Japan's favor. But Japan had other, more substantial, strategic interests. She wanted to secure Korea and Formosa, Korea for obvious reasons since the peninsula was the bridge between her and the mainland, Formosa because it lay across the route from the south from where the European powers had to come. Securing either or both was beyond her abilities, but in 1876, after her warships had bombarded the Kanghwa forts, Japan wrung from China acknowledgement that Korea was an independent state. This political neutralization of a Chinese vassal was the first step in the process of its being absorbed by Japan herself. Thus within twenty-five years of her first major contact with the imperialists, Japan had joined in their pastime of using force to extract concessions from an increasingly moribund China.

Such was the process by which various powers secured colonial territories and spheres of influence in the Pacific and Far East by 1900. It must be remembered, however, that even in areas where Europeans had been for centuries, there remained regions beyond their control. It was not until 1913, for example, that the Dutch, after a forty-year war, finally took Achin in northern Sumatra, scene of first contact between sixteenth-century Europeans and the Far East. Likewise, the small island of Bali was not secured until 1906. Many areas, often sheltering primitive peoples, proved beyond the reach of authority, in some cases until very recent times.

But what made these developments so important were two major considerations. First, there was the effect that these events had upon the indigenous societies; and second, there was the effect that these same events had upon the imperialists themselves.

The coming of the imperialists had a profoundly disruptive effect, ranging from venereal disease to social revolution, on all indigenous societies. After initial opposition, resistance to the superior organization and firepower of the newcomers collapsed. With very few exceptions societies in the Far East came under European domination or control, and only Japan proved capable of dealing with the problems posed by white supremacy. While the rest of Asia entered the world economy in a primary-producing straitjacket, Japan, despite the crippling terms of trade imposed on her, emerged as a manufacturing nation. Indeed, she showed a remarkable ability to adjust to the dictates of the political and social order in which she found herself. Nothing is more illustrative of Japan's adaptability than her trade figures. In the last quarter of the century her trade rose by 700 percent, but whereas in 1875 about 50 percent of her imports had been finished goods compared to 5 percent of her exports, by 1900 finished goods had fallen to 20 percent, while industrial raw materials accounted for one-half her imports. What was equally significant was that her rate of growth showed no signs of slackening. She still had a very long way to go before she began to draw level with the more powerful industrial states, but the basis of a strong economy was, seemingly, being laid.

The imperialists were naturally affected, both internally and externally, by the development of empire and interest in the Orient. The most important effect of occidental domination of the East was bringing into a rapidly growing world economy the wealth and diversity of the Far East. Such a gain, however, had to be balanced against the ever-growing commitment of political and psychological prestige to the maintenance of their interests. Moreover, to this there had to be added the problems posed by the dynamism of imperial expansion. These empires had been carved out in an area of relative primitiveness, but they had to be sustained in a polycentric world. Power was much more diverse. By the end of the nineteenth century even the most constant feature of world power over the last 230 years, British naval supremacy, was severely threatened. Britain's naval supremacy could no longer be guaranteed by her industrial power. New countries and modern industry were being built at a rate certain to relegate the Royal Navy to a position of primus inter pares within a very few years of the start of the century. Though at the time this fact was largely unappreciated, the whole of the imperialist position in the Far East was very similar to the situation of the Royal Navy vis-à-vis other parties. The very technology that had brought the imperialists to the Far East and later prompted them to establish themselves in the area on a permanent basis was certain to produce the circumstances that undermined their authority. The interplay of political, economic, and military factors in a world being shrunken by modern means of communication was certain to make the position of the imperialist possessions of the Far East ever more sensitive and vulnerable to developments elsewhere and to indigenous pressures created by native emulation of Western technique.

For the moment, however, the potential instability of the imperialists' position in the Far East went largely unappreciated. But what was realized, at least in some of the colonial adminstrations, was the moral imperative of acting on behalf of the subjected people brought under imperial control. While the immense strategic and economic value and importance of colonial possessions were clearly evident, the notion of "civilizing missions" imposed an obligation that went beyond the establishment of order. Lugard, in Nigeria, set down the principle that the only justification for one people to take control of the destiny of another was the enrichment and benefit of both. This concept was not a mere device, a meaningless concept to which lip service alone was paid. There was, moreover, a growing awareness among colonial adminstrators that the subjected people, their cultures, values, and institutions did have positive roles to play in shaping the future. This was a significant development from the earlier, easy assumption that the institutions of white rule could command the future and that there was no place for local factors in progress.

Notions of obligation and service, however, involved crippling inconsistencies. The most obvious of them was the fact that colonial administration tended to be cocooned, the ruling elements isolating themselves from the subject people and imparting their concepts with a paternalism that was ingratiating and often insulting because it was so often heavily imbued with racial overtones. Much of the good that moral and political enlightenment should have achieved was undone by this insensitivity. Moral endorsement in a metropolitan homeland did not quite make up for being treated as less than equal in a colony.

But this aspect of service and obligation, though important in its own right, was in fact part of a wider political development that in time was certain to bring about an impossible dilemma for all colonial authorities. In the course of the nineteenth century the process of democratization accelerated throughout Europe. Even in the less advanced countries of Europe, traditional rights and privileges of the old order were eroded. Increasing numbers of people became involved in the political process, while government itself was extended and took an increasingly active part not just in normal administration but in the regulation of many aspects of social existence. Subordinate colonial governments could not help but reflect the changing images of their home governments: the gradual democratization of Europe had to be paralleled, even in a modified form, by changes in the colonies. But while such changes could be expected to deal with many problems, they were certain to generate new complications and demands with which they could not deal. The more truly democratic colonial institutions became, the less they would be able to deal with local popular expectations of a specifically nationalist nature. Changes brought about by the extension of democracy and practice of government in the long term had to lead to the rise of nationalist demands for independence.

A British administrator might abstractly dwell on the vague notion that one day his charges might become independent, but he saw no good reason to expedite the process. Indeed, with the possible exception of the Americans with respect to the Philippines, none of the colonialists really came to grips with this problem. The French never even tried to do so, though the Dutch, in the Indies, did try to tackle at least certain aspects of the problem. In the course of the nineteenth century increasing numbers of Dutchmen became uncomfortably aware that much of their national prosperity stemmed from their exploitation and the wretchedness of the Indies. Under constant prodding from the Protestant churches and the Liberal party, in the latter part of the century the Dutch committed themselves to the enlightened, if unrealistic, "ethical policy." This envisaged a program of large-scale investment in the Indies to improve the lot of the masses and to create a new native elite that had assimilated Western culture and technique. The policy envisaged this elite bringing the Indies into a working partnership with the Netherlands, something on the lines of the dominions within the British Empire but more strongly bound together. The Dutch, for the most part, thought in terms of cooperation and partnership. Van Deventer, the one-time leader of the Liberals, was very much the exception in realizing that the ethical policy could well break rather than strengthen the links between the Indies and the Netherlands.

The most crippling inconsistency involved in the application of morality, however, lay in the clash between political and economic liberalism. When set against the often disastrous consequences of economic liberalism, political enlightenment lost much of its force. However much the notions of service and obligation might be pursued by administrations, laissez-faire doctrines and the belief that material progress itself was to everyone's ultimate advantage tended to reduce the impact of liberal attitudes. In all the colonies, moreover, plantation and settler interests took precedence over local wishes, and no imperial government was prepared to see the development of local manufactures that might prove inimical to domestic interests. The deliberate ruination of the Indian cotton industry during the nineteenth century in defense of Lancashire was an outstanding example of this phenomenon, yet this subordination of local to home interests was not unique to Britain and India. All the colonies were tapped for their wealth. For Britain India yielded coffee, jute, and tea. Malaya was the world's largest exporter of rubber and tin. Malaya, and various Pacific islands, and the Dutch East Indies, provided an impressive array of base ores, while Australia and New Zealand developed into Britain's dairy and also provided wool and meat for the mother country. Burma proved perhaps the richest of Britain's possessions. Her jungles yielded teak in abundance, and under British direction the ailing rice industry was revived to the extent that Burma emerged as the world's third largest exporter of the staple food of most Asians. Beans, coffee, grain, maize, millet, oilseed, sugar, and tea were among the major cash crops cultivated by British plantations; jute, rubber, and tobacco were scarcely less important. Amber, lead, rubies, silver, tin, tungsten, wolfram, and, most important of all, oil, were the major extractive industries whose success depended upon the sweated labor of a dispossessed and wretchedly abused population. France was even more rapacious in Indo-China. Salt, opium, and alcohol were monopolies of a state that imposed crippling per capita taxation rather than taxing on the basis of income, resources, or output. Forced labor, though supposedly illegal, was murderously enforced, and French plantation interests were encouraged by dispossessing and clearing the local population. In earlier times the Dutch in the Indies had been no less exploitive. The old "culture system" in Java had obliged the population to devote a part of the arable land to cultivating government-directed cash crops, yet even in a more enlightened time the Dutch finance and settler interests remained very powerful. In fact finance and settler interests were beginning to become rivals not merely in the Indies but in all the various empires. Everywhere local economies were being increasingly dominated by cartels and holding companies, with small-scale and individual enterprises being squeezed out of existence by major institutions.

The latent force of local feeling and the generally exploitive nature of European rule in the colonies and China were largely unrealized in the homelands. What was apparent in the homelands were the realities of better food, exotic goods, and splendidly clad native troops. These were not merely the benefits and manifestations of white rule in the Orient but the seeming security and guarantees of the permanence of the European position in Asia. At a very small cost to themselves in lives, money, and equipment, the Europeans secured huge colonial resources and spheres of influence, recognizing only the interests of other Europeans as restraints on their own acquisitiveness. Over the whole of eastern Asia and Oceania white power was dominant. Large forces were generally not deployed in the area because they were not normally necessary. The Indian subcontinent, for example, contained about 300,000,000 souls at the turn of the century, but in 1914 the area was garrisoned by 75,000 British troops and 125,000 sepoys. The colonies and spheres of influence were held more by prestige and the myth of white supremacy than by force of arms, though the Europeans showed on several occasions that they were willing and able to use force to maintain themselves. There was always the certainty of available force "over the horizon."

There was no immediate credible challenge to the European position from the indigenous population of the Far East. Chinese nationalism and xenophobia were forces to be reckoned with, but the relative ease with which the Boxer Rebellion was suppressed suggested a lack of stamina in the undisciplined and unorganized emotional reaction. The new forces of nationalism, channeled by the aping of European methodology, were not serious challenges by the turn of the century. The sole challenge to the imperialists' position would arise only if the Europeans exhausted themselves in fighting protracted wars with one another. Very few observers at the coronation of Edward VII in 1902 could have even guessed at the possibility that, within four decades, the whole European position in the Far East would be undermined to an extent that the empires were past recall, weakened in one world war, subverted by internal resistance thereafter, and defeated in a second conflict by the new power of the Far East—Japan, the one country that had managed to escape the shackles of white domination. Such was to prove the reality, but for the moment myths sufficed.

CHAPTER 1

The Emergence
of Japan

ON 18 JANUARY 1915 Hoiki Eki, the Japanese ambassador in Peking, presented to the president of the Republic of China, Yuan Shih-K'ai, a letter from the imperial government in Tokyo. Given the nature of diplomatic exchanges between states such an incident need not have attracted any undue attention, though the presentation of a note directly to a head of state is often an indication that the matter in hand is somewhat unusual. This note indeed was exceptional. It contained a series of Japanese requirements that, if accepted, would have effectively resulted in the total subjugation of China to the will of Japan. The note contained what were to become internationally infamous as the Twenty-one Demands.

For obvious political and strategic reasons, the island empire of Japan had always been deeply concerned with the affairs of the Asian mainland. Japan harbored hopes of aggrandizement on the continent. As early as the sixteenth century Hideyoshi Toyotomi had expounded the notion that Asia should be subjected to Japanese rule by the progressive conquest of first Korea and then China. This was a theme returned to in the mid-nineteenth century by the nationalist poet Shoin Yoshida. In neither instance, however, was anything forthcoming from what were, superficially, such extravagant notions of conquest. In neither era did Japan have the means to embark upon such plans, but that such ideas could be argued seriously was an indication of the view that Japan held regarding her own position and her

place in the world. According to Japanese mythology the eight islands of
Japan had been created by the god Izanagi and his wife Izanami. It was a
sacred land watched over by the lesser gods. Its people were semidivine,
and they were ruled by their *tenno*, or emperor, who was the direct
descendant of the greatest of the deities, the Sun Goddess Amaterasu. Her
grandson, Ninigi, had first peopled Japan. With such a basis for the
national ethic, it was no wonder that the Japanese, who saw death in the
service of their emperor as insufficient atonement for their obligation to
their homeland, considered themselves charged with a divine mission. That
mission was the domination of eastern Asia, and Toyotomi and Yoshida
were merely individuals who gave expression to assumptions and beliefs
widely prevalent in society.

Yet in the second half of the nineteenth century and the first three
decades of the present century a series of events within China and, above
all, on the wider international stage, conspired to place Japan in a position
whereby it was convenient for her to put into effect the basic provisions of
the Toyotomi-Yoshida doctrine. What was not so apparent at the time was
the fact that these events were paradoxically producing the very same
conditions that would prevent the realization of these objectives. Illusion
and reality were deeply and irrevocably intertwined, and only the march of
events over the passing years was to reveal the elements of contradiction in
the situation. And then, the revelation was only to be achieved at a cost in
blood and treasure of incalculable proportions, and at a price of releasing
dynamic forces that were to shape the destiny of eastern Asia in a manner
very different from the hopes and aspirations of the Japanese and all other
major parties originally involved in the situation.

As we have seen, the catalyst for what was to prove a simmering crisis in
eastern Asia was the penetration of the Far East by an alien culture that was
superior in technology and sophistication. The indigenous populations of
the area responded to that intrusion in a variety of ways. The impact of the
nineteenth-century penetration of the Far East by the European maritime
powers, the Russians, and the Americans was profound because the white
nations encountered and were opposed by moribund social and political
organizations incapable of offering effective resistance to the outsiders'
collective will and power. The nation to be most seriously affected was
China. The increasing enfeeblement of the imperial system, the tendency
towards diffusion of power, and the patent inadequacies of the Confucian
ethic, social organization, and political and military infrastructures were to
be ruthlessly exposed by the alternating Chinese acquiescence in and futile
opposition to white encroachments. The Chinese, with a supercilious
condescension born of a sinocentric view of the world, tried to ignore the
reality of white power. They sought to wield only those parts of Western
technique that would prove useful in preserving Chinese society as then
constituted. The Japanese were under no such illusions. The Japanese

realized that only profound change would enable them to escape domination. Thus the paths of China and Japan divided, the Chinese suffering the
growing humiliations of despoiled territorial integrity, usurped jurisdiction, and restricted sovereignty. The Europeans carved out for themselves
colonies (in Russia's case direct annexations) and spheres of influence,
ruthlessly plundering and exploiting China in the material interest of
egotistical calculation.

But Japan was not China, and the Japanese proved more adaptable than
the Chinese. Thus they escaped the worst of the humiliations that befell
China. At an early stage the Japanese came to realize the futility of attempting to resist the superior military power of Western nations. Admittedly, there was initial resistance, but the patently obvious superiority of
Western political, economic, and military organization, though distrusted
and disliked because of the position of inferiority it imposed on Japan,
commanded admiration, respect, and envy. It acted as a spur for the
Japanese: they wanted to possess those things that made other nations more
powerful than themselves. The Japanese recognized that the Western
elements of power and organization could be emulated and absorbed. The
Japanese clearly appreciated from what was happening to China that unless
the supreme compliment of imitation was paid, Japan would be made the
plaything of the powers.

Accordingly, the dominant themes in Japanese life in the period after
1868 were national regeneration, reform, and reconstruction. The aim of
these programs, to use the phrase often repeated in this period, was to
ensure that "the country will be able to rank equally with the other nations
of the world." The year 1868 was of utmost significance for Japan because it
was then that the shogunate, the system of rule by dominant clan interests
in the name of a figurehead emperor, was replaced by the Meiji (meaning
"enlightened government") Restoration. Under the rule of Emperor Mut-
suhito (1867–1912) the task of national reconstruction began in earnest.
Under the newly restored imperial system the old samurai caste system was
broken, its ethos being incorporated into a national conscript army, trained
initially by the French and then by the Germans. The Imperial Navy,
equally, looked to the West in its early formative years. For the first few
years of its development the navy looked to Britain for example and
method, but despite the fact that for some time afterwards Japan maintained very close links with Britain in such matters as placing warship
orders, the Japanese navy soon decided to go its own way. The Japanese
devised their own systems, particularly in the fields of officer and technical
training, where they felt that the methods employed by the Royal Navy
were inadequate and unscientific.

Japan was bent on emulating Western technology, for without it she
realized she could never escape Western domination. Yet the process of
industrialization was by its very nature slow and painful, and its progress

was not helped by the position of inferiority imposed upon Japan by the white powers with regard to trade and credit concessions. But gradually the "unequal treaties" were renegotiated, first with Britain in 1894 and then with the other powers. In 1894, however, an event of far greater importance than the Anglo-Japanese agreement took place. In that year the emerging Japan flexed her muscles for the first time. Her target was China, and, in accordance with the Toyotomi-Yoshida doctrine, the immediate issue of the war was the question of the control of Korea. Both China and Japan claimed suzerainty over the peninsula. Japan possessed considerable economic as well as immense and obvious strategic interests in Korea. The real issue of the war, however, was prestige. Japan sought to secure for herself the role of leading Asian power and, by implication, the status of equality with the leading European powers.

The war resulted in an easy Japanese victory, the only point of real significance of the war being that the Japanese started hostilities with the sinking of a Chinese troop transport rather than a formal declaration of war. In a short campaign the Japanese quickly crushed Chinese opposition on land and at sea, securing through the Treaty of Shimonoseki (17 April 1895) Formosa, the Pescadores, Port Arthur, the Liaotung peninsula, and the promise of a large indemnity. The Chinese, moreover, confirmed the principle of Korean independence, which by extension meant that China would not oppose any Japanese move to assert her control over the peninsula. The Japanese also secured the most favored nation clause that placed her on an equal economic footing with the European powers in terms of trade with the decaying Chinese empire.

Few Europeans had anticipated that Japan could have beaten China so quickly and so comprehensively; even the Japanese high command was surprised with its success because before the war started it thought that the struggle might well be long and difficult. The extent of Japanese gains, however, was of grave concern to the Europeans because they seemed to threaten both China and the European gains already established throughout the Far East. While they had no love for China, the Europeans were not willing to see Japan establish a position of dominance in the Far East. Accordingly, at the end of April 1895 a joint French, German, and Russian move "invited" Japan to "reconsider" her position in order to preserve "the peace of the Far East." Specifically, what became known as the Triple Intervention insisted upon a revision of the Shimonoseki provisions that covered Port Arthur and the Liaotung peninsula.

The war against China and the Triple Intervention were traumatic events for Japan. The growing self-confidence of the country had been shown to be justified by the successful prosecution of the war. Yet more important for the future was the fact that the war against China was the first occasion on which the Japanese were confirmed in their belief in their own

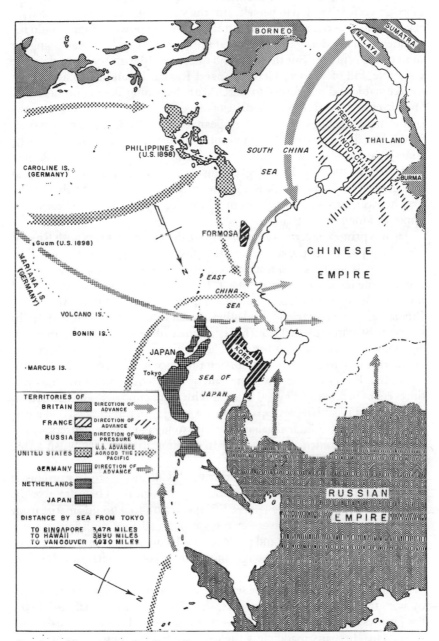

Strategic View of the Far East, from the Japanese Perspective, 1894–1900

ability to take on and defeat countries that at least on paper were infinitely
more powerful than Japan herself. But the strongest feeling engendered by
these events was the reaction against the European powers. Japan could see
no offense in her doing to China what the other nations had been doing for
most of the century. But there was no question of Japan trying to defy the
collective will of France, Germany, and Russia. Japan had to accept the
unacceptable and was forced to watch with deepening shame, humiliation,
and bitterness the almost immediate takeover of her relinquished conquests
by the imperialist powers. The European scramble for Chinese concessions
in the last five years of the nineteenth century was precipitated by the
Sino-Japanese war and the Triple Intervention. The Russians took over
Port Arthur and the Liaotung peninsula, while the Germans secured
Tsingtao. The French took Kwangchow Bay, while the British secured
Wei-hei-wei, across the bay from Tsingtao, and the New Territories
opposite Hong Kong island.

Japan's prime concern as a result of these developments was with Russia.
She alone possessed the forces and the physical presence in the Far East
both to challenge Japan's quest for control over Korea and to pose a genuine
threat to the Japanese homeland itself. Because of her obvious financial and
industrial weaknesses, Japan could not hope to challenge Russia. Moreover,
Russia had powerful friends and allies. Japan lacked allies—until 1902. In
that year Britain retreated from her egocentric illusion of splendid isolation
and joined Japan in an alliance. The British interest was to secure a
counterbalance to the growing Russian presence in Manchuria and northern China. For Japan there was the gain of British benevolent neutrality in
the event of her being involved in a war with another power, and the British
commitment to active participation in a war if Japan found herself in a war
with two powers. The real value of Britain to Japan in these matters was as
the counter to France, Russia's ally. In addition Britain gave Japan a free
hand over Korea.

Great though the material benefits from this alliance were—or promised
to be—for Japan its significance was psychological. That the world's
greatest empire, the proudest of the European nations, should emerge from
her self-proclaimed exclusiveness in favor of an alliance with Japan was a
source of great satisfaction and pride for the Japanese. It went some way to
offset the shame of 1895, though the final reckoning with the Russians
remained to be settled.

Events were to show that the settling of accounts could be resolved only
by war. In negotiations the Russians, showing an openly racial disdain for
the Japanese, demanded concessions that Japan could never seriously consider. The Russians made clear their demands for exclusive control over
Manchuria, where they already had extensive influence because of their

railway construction, and Korea. Korea was important to the Russians because it afforded good warm-water ports and would consolidate the Vladivostok-Port Arthur line. Russian intransigence and the Japanese determination to achieve at the very least the neutralization of Korea ensured that there had to be a recourse to arms. For this war Japan had behind her nine years of peace and preparation, and she was confident of success.

The Russo-Japanese war of 1904–5 was in many ways the most important event for Japan between her emergence in the 1860s and her going to war in 1941. This was mainly because it confirmed certain items of blind faith in the national consciousness and concealed weaknesses that national mythology and pride conspired to weave into a fabric that became grievously distorted in its final aspects. On 6 February 1904 the Japanese broke off negotiations with the Russians and on the eighth landed troops at Chemulpo (Inchon) and proceeded to occupy Seoul. Russian ships at Chemulpo were neutralized, but the main Japanese effort was made on the night of the eighth/ninth, when Japanese torpedo boats attacked the Russian fleet at its anchorage inside Port Arthur. Two Russian battleships and a cruiser were disabled and there were no Japanese losses. Only after this devastating success did Japan declare war. Ironically, in view of what was to be said in 1941, the Japanese attack before the formal declaration of war was greeted in many countries as an act of daring and the correct manner of waging war.

The Russo-Japanese war was to last until the Treaty of Portsmouth (New Hampshire) was signed on 5 September 1905. The basic pattern of Japanese success, established at the outset of the war, lasted throughout the conflict. At sea the Russian squadron at Port Arthur was contained by the close blockade the Japanese imposed upon the base, and on the few occasions when the Russians attempted to do battle, the Japanese had the better of brief and indecisive engagements. Russian naval units from Vladivostok were decisively routed at the battle of Ulsan when they attempted to join up with the Port Arthur squadron. The Russian naval forces inside the fortress were finally destroyed by land assault, Port Arthur falling after an epic five-month siege. The land war, on the other hand, witnessed a steady series of battles, gradually increasing in size, duration, and intensity. These battles, indeed, were some of the greatest and longest land battles fought to date, for this war was the first "modern war." It was fought with automatic long-range weapons and sustained by rail communications that combined to give the defense a considerable local superiority over the attack. In all the set-piece battles maneuver was limited and losses on both sides were enormous. But they were battles in which the Japanese prevailed, most notably before Port Arthur and Mukden. Only after the issue on land had been resolved in favor of Japan had the final act of the drama been played out at sea. On 27/28 May 1905 the Russian Baltic Fleet, having sailed around the world from St. Petersburg, was annihilated at the battle of Tsu-shima, the most momentous sea battle for one hundred years.

Thus in her second war the new Japan again defeated an enemy nominally far superior to herself. This was the picture that the Japanese people saw, but they were under certain illusions about the situation, illusions the authorities did nothing to dispell. The result was that myth hardened into fact with what was believed to have happened being more important than what did happen. The exhaustion of Japanese manpower reserves, industrial and financial resources, and Japan's desperate need for peace by mid-1905—a need almost as desperate as that of Russia—were largely unknown to and unsuspected by a population conscious only of successive victories. The moderation of the terms of peace was an indication of Japanese weakness, and this moderation made the government more unpopular in Japan. But, most important of all, the outcome of the Russo-Japanese war had fateful consequences on the evolution of Japanese strategic thinking. This war confirmed for the Japanese the wisdom of what may be termed a strategy of attrition within a framework of limited objectives, and this dominated Japanese strategic thought right up until 1941.

In both the Sino-Japanese and Russo-Japanese wars the Japanese had been able to achieve their limited objectives by a combination of localizing the conflict, securing and maintaining the initiative, and establishing an almost total supremacy at sea. In 1895, and to a lesser extent against the Russians, the Japanese were able to wage limited wars by securing an initial objective through an overwhelming concentration of force, and then fighting an attritional battle by exploiting their naval supremacy. In this battle of attrition the enemy's reserves, fed piecemeal at the end of a long and uncertain line of communication, were destroyed. Against both the Chinese and the Russians such a strategy was successful because both the Manchus and the Romanovs were willing to accept negotiated peace settlements rather than persist in wars that at best could only end in stalemate. The elimination of Chinese and Russian local naval power inevitably meant that the wars could not be taken to the Japanese homeland, that Japan could not be conquered. Moreover, to wrest from Japan the gains she had made at the outset of war was recognized by her enemies to be prohibitively expensive in time and resources.

But if the strategy the Japanese employed in both wars was vindicated, then the psychological and tactical aspects of the struggles were also validated. In both wars the Japanese placed heavy emphasis on their superior resolve and a reliance on human initiative and resources to overcome material deficits. In both wars, moreover, the Japanese secured supremacy at sea and, for the most part, maintained it without committing the battle fleet. The latter was husbanded most carefully. The cornerstone of

Japanese strategy in both wars was to preserve the battle fleet and use it only if and when its commitment was unavoidable. In the Russo-Japanese war the battle fleet was committed en masse only against the last despairing effort of the Baltic Fleet. In doing so the Japanese won the greatest naval engagement since Trafalgar; Tsu-shima fit into the classic "big-battle" concept beloved by all strategists before 1914. This concept was the linch-pin of Japanese strategy in the interwar period and it was what the Imperial Navy sought desperately in the period 1942–44. The active role of the battle fleet was relatively limited, the main effort of the war at sea devolving on light and expendable forces operating in the forward areas. The task of these forces was either to contain or defeat the enemy, or to inflict dispro-portionately heavy losses if containment or defeat proved impossible. The wars against China and Russia conformed to this basic pattern, and it was the strategic concepts embodied in these successful conflicts that dominated Japanese strategic doctrine right up until the start of the Pacific war. At least on the naval side—the example is less marked with the army—one can trace a direct line from these wars via the "big battleship program of 1915–22" to the *Yamato*-class battleships, the monstrous *STo* submarines, indeed the whole of Japanese naval rearmament in the thirties. One can see from Tsu-shima, the climax of the war at sea, the origins of the notion of the decisive battle against the Americans sought by the Japanese after the initial stages of the Pacific war. One can see in these events the acceptance of numerical inferiority and the reliance on human resources with "bigger and better" concepts. Where Japanese strategists of the Second World War totally erred, of course, was in their fundamental underestimation of American resolve, production, and means of transportation to the decisive theaters of war.

But these developments were to take time to unfold, and there was no ignoring the immediate fact that Japan had "emerged." She came through these wars with greatly enhanced prestige. Though many European pow-ers could point to local factors in Russia's defeat, and even play down the significance of a victory over the czar, no power could risk trying to treat Japan in the same cavalier manner that was the case in European dealings with China and, for that matter Japan, before 1900. The Western powers might try to deny the principle that an oriental power could be the equal of an occidental power, but that was the real lesson to be drawn from the war and there were others who were not slow to see this. In the Russo-Japanese war the Japanese showed that an oriental nation, armed with the same organization, techniques, and methods as the Europeans, could defeat Europeans in a stand-up war. The latter had often suffered local defeats, but until 1905 they had never lost such a war. In the Russo-Japanese war the Europeans lost the moral ascendancy that they had built over many decades of effortless, comfortable victories. Never again would Orientals see the Europeans in the same light as under pre-1904 circumstances, because in this war the Japanese revealed the myth of white supremacy for what it was—a myth. The subject peoples of the empires and China could not but be impressed, and it was to Japan that they looked for their example and model. Among those that looked to Japan, ironically, were many Chinese nationalists.

Between the end of the Russo-Japanese war and the signing of the Washington Naval Treaty in February 1922 a series of events conspired to place Japan in an ideal position to pursue an expansionist foreign policy. Many contrasting elements made up this favorable situation, but four main lines of development can be easily discerned. These elements were the collapse of the Manchu dynasty (1911–12) and the subsequent fragmentation of China, the decline of European power and influence in the Far East, the strengthening of Japan's economy, and the American reluctance to become deeply involved in the Far East situation. The catalyst, of course, was the First World War. This war effectively removed the European presence and left Japan with considerably strengthened industrial and financial infrastructures, mainly as a result of Japan taking over Asian markets that the Europeans could no longer supply. In addition, the war allowed Japan to make certain territorial gains that left her in a very strong position to dominate the Far East.

Chronologically, the first event in the series of happenings that led to this fortunate position for Japan was the reconciliation of Russian and Japanese interests and the secret convention of 30 July 1907 by which Russia and Japan divided Manchuria into spheres of influence. In addition to the accord over Manchuria, the two former enemies accepted Russia's "special position" in Outer Mongolia and Japan's equally "special interest" in Korea. In that year the Japanese grip on Korea tightened considerably when the Koreans were forced to accept Japanese advisers and officials in positions of control within the Korean adminstration. To his credit the Korean emperor refused to bow to Japanese demands and abdicated, but the Japanese were able to find pliable people to take the place of those who resisted their demands. It was not until 1910, however, that Korea was directly annexed to become part of the Japanese homeland. In this act were crystallized both the enlightenment and the total insensitivity of the Japanese towards the Koreans. To Japan there were obvious political and strategic benefits to accrue from the annexation of Korea, but the annexation was seen by the Japanese to be justified in terms of the mutual benefits that would come to both peoples. Japan saw herself as providing protection, leadership, and example to a weaker sister, but the rigors of Japanese military occupation, the condescension of Japanese officialdom, and the evident exploitiveness of Japanese economic activity in Korea ensured that the long-term reconciliation of the Koreans to Japanese rule could never be achieved. This was to be a pattern of events repeated in the conquered territories of Southeast Asia during the Second World War.

Also in 1910 Russia and Japan concluded a second secret convention that defined more closely their respective spheres of influence in Manchuria. In addition, the agreement guaranteed mutual support in excluding third parties from the area. This provision was mainly directed against the Americans, who in 1909 had proposed the internationalization of the Manchurian railway system, but the combination of Russia and Japan was successful in forestalling this proposal. Because of her agreement with Russia and her absorbing of Korea, Japan was able to consolidate and expand her economic interests on the Asian mainland, but her main chance came with the outbreak of war in Europe in 1914. For a victorious power war always offers the prospect of quick, cheap, and extensive gains, more plentiful in yield and precipitate in effect than the labors of diplomacy. Japan was such a victorious power. She entered the war on 23 August as an ally of Britain, though under the terms of the Anglo-Japanese alliance she was under no obligation to do so. She quickly overran the German-owned Pacific islands north of the equator—the Marshalls, Carolines, and Marianas—and with small British assistance captured the German fortress-port of Tsingtao on the Shantung peninsula. Subsequently, however, she made little active contribution to the war effort. She was to send destroyers to the Mediterranean but resolutely refused to send heavy units to Europe: destroyers were expendable, capital ships were not. The preservation of force to meet unforeseen circumstances was as much a part of Japanese strategy in the First World War as it had been in the Sino-Japanese and Russo-Japanese wars.

The Japanese conquest of German possessions in the Far East immediately raised two interrelated issues, the question of the legal ownership of those territories and the wider issue of Sino-Japanese relations. German territory on the Shantung peninsula had been leased from China, and by law it should have reverted to China after its conquest. But the Japanese had no intention whatsoever of relinquishing their control of Tsingtao, and they were fully aware of the fact that the European distraction gave them a splendid, and possibly unique, opportunity of wringing from China promises and concessions that might not otherwise be forthcoming. In this appreciation of the situation Japan was to be aided by internal events in China.

After a series of revolts against imperial authority in the last quarter of 1911 and the proclamation of a republic in December, the last of the Manchu emperors abdicated on 12 February 1912. On the fifteenth the provisional National Assembly, meeting in Nanking, elected Yuan Shih-K'ai as the provisional president. Yuan, the chief military commander of the Manchus, had been the most powerful single person in China before the anti-Manchu revolts, and his desertion of the emperor had been decisive in the collapse of the dynasty. The revolutionary elements in China had sought to use Yuan to bring about an end of the imperial system. They had promised to support his claims to the presidency if he overthrew the Manchus. But Yuan aspired to the imperial throne himself, and was prepared to use the revolutionaries and any method, fair or foul but mainly the latter, to facilitate that aim.

For China the fall of a ruling dynasty, weakened by years of corruption, inefficiency, and personal excess, was nothing new. Chinese history had been punctuated by the rise and fall of great dynasties, the territorial integrity and unity of China ebbing and flowing with the rise of new powerful emperors and their subsequent replacement by rulers under whom the empire declined. What was different about Yuan's attempt to attain the Dragon Throne was that both internal and external conditions in 1912 were unfavorable to the assumption of power by any single individual. The whole of the Confucian ethic, the official state philosophy, the Chinese social system, and the unquestioned permanency of the throne itself had been destroyed by a combination of growing demographic pressures, scarce resources, and the impact of Western civilization on China in the course of the previous century. China, moreover, was no longer in charge of her own destiny. Previous dynastic changes had taken place without regard to foreigners, but in 1911–12 the attitude of the Western nations was critically important. The foreign powers, despite their rivalries and quarrels, were aware that their prerogatives in China were dependent upon Chinese weakness and divisions. It was contrary to the interests of these countries to see a single man or an organization emerge with either the will or the means to unite the country. The internecine bickerings of the foreigners also depended on the weakness of the Chinese central government and the diffusion of power between Peking and local regional authorities. The policy of the outsiders in the collective sense was essentially one of divide and rule, that of the prison warder who stirred up the rivalries and hatreds of the prisoners so that they could be kept in some sort of order and subjugation. Such a policy automatically ran the risk of disaster if the prisoners reconciled their differences.

Initially, at least, the overthrow of the Manchus seemed to pose no threat to the foreign powers because the new republic was desperately dependent on foreign goodwill and credit. The latter was forthcoming—at very large discounts—but the former was in rather short supply. The majority of the Western countries withheld formal recognition of the Chinese republic until October 1913, by which time the first round of the power struggle inside China had been resolved in Yuan's favor. In this power struggle Yuan had managed to assert his personal ascendency over the parliament and various regional authorities, and he moved to establish and legitimize his personal rule when in December he performed the Worship of Heaven. This was an act that according to Confucian rites was accorded only to the emperor. The evident drift of Yuan's policies caused concern abroad, but it was not until December 1915 that the Allied powers—Britain, France, Italy, Japan, and Russia—collectively advised Yuan against assuming the imperial throne. This Allied action was instigated by Japan but was not supported by the United States.

Japan had become seriously alarmed by the implications of Yuan's attempt to establish a strong centralized authority in China because such a development could only lessen her own chances of expansion on the Asian mainland, as foreshadowed earlier in the year by the presentation of the Twenty-one Demands. The Japanese were also concerned by the fact that Yuan's ambitions and methods provoked severe opposition that threatened the security of the loans and investments Japan had made in China. In fact China was in the process of fragmenting, Yuan being opposed by powerful revolutionary organizations and self-interested warlords, both of whom were determined to resist any aggrandizement of the power of Peking at their expense. Yuan in fact never ascended to the Mandate of Heaven, since the opposition he provoked was too strong for him to overcome. He was forced to abandon his proposed coronation and died in 1916, a broken man. He left behind him a bitterly divided country, rent by his Machiavellian machinations and intrigues. He left a country that had unfulfilled expectations of genuine reform; he had gone a long way to discredit the institutions and practice of democracy and the republic. But he had also deeply disappointed Chinese nationalist aspirations as a result of his acquiescence in the Twenty-one Demands.

The Twenty-one Demands represented an extremely clumsy attempt on the part of the Japanese to extract concessions from China at a time of European weakness. By itself an action at a time of weakness on the part of others is part and parcel of diplomacy, but the extent of Japan's demands on China, the opportunism inherent in the move, and the suspicions aroused by Japan's action—plus the latent racial overtones implicit in the foreigners' attitudes to matters Japanese—made the events of February 1915 of utmost significance. Most importantly, the nature of Japanese demands revealed Japan to be as greedy, selfish, and self-interested as the worst of the Europeans, and without their arrogant finesse. By their action the Japanese forfeited much of the prestige and moral ascendency that they had created for themselves since 1895. No longer would most Chinese nationalists look to Japan not merely as a model or source of inspiration but for help; they saw Japan for what she was, an imperialist power bent on expansion.

The Twenty-one Demands were very extensive in scope and, had they been accepted, would have reduced China to the position of a Japanese protectorate. The demands fell into five main categories. They sought a

Chinese acceptance of Japan's conquests of German concessions in China; the granting of further concessions in Manchuria; a Chinese guarantee that no other power would secure any territorial concession in China; the granting to Japan of special rights in certain mining and metallurgical works in the Yangtse valley; and far-reaching concessions in specific railway development programs coupled with Chinese employment of Japanese officials in key financial, military, and police posts. In short, had the Japanese secured their demands, China would have been made totally dependent on the will of Tokyo.

Yuan knew full well that Japan was too powerful a foe to be defied openly, but he was equally aware that he could look neither to the foreigners nor to rival factions within China to support him in resisting the demands. Nevertheless, the demands represented a major psychological change in the Chinese situation because for the first time China received foreign sympathy and support (not altogether altruistic) rather than scorn. The Japanese, having clumsily shown their hand, were advised by their allies to moderate their demands. Yuan was forced to concede the principle of the demands in May, though the Japanese dropped the last group of requirements. This group related to the appointment of Japanese officials in the Chinese administration, but rather ominously Japan reserved her position in this matter and claimed the right to raise it in future discussions.

Foreign sympathy and support for China, given the circumstances of 1915, meant nothing in terms of immediate practical assistance in resisting Japan's demands. The Chinese did not possess the means to resist Japan's terms, and the war merely saw the consolidation and strengthening of Japan's position in China. But for Japan there was a price for her success. While none of the powers were in a position to help China in 1915, Japan never again enjoyed the full trust and confidence of these nations. Many neighbors were openly alarmed by the display of Japanese opportunism during the war, and the Allies were not slow to note Japan's attempt to exclude them from future gains in China. The Allies, however, promised to guarantee Japan's gains in undertakings made in January and February 1917, but when the question of invading the Netherlands was brought up by the Allies, Australia and New Zealand opposed the prospect because it would give the Japanese a chance to expand their power further southwards into the Indies. The Americans, likewise, were not impressed by Japanese actions, and their denunciation of the Twenty-one Demands was open and immediate. The United States was committed to the Open Door policy expounded in 1900 by Secretary of State John Hay, but the American moral position had been undermined by the recognition in 1908, reaffirmed in 1917, of Japan's special rights and interests in eastern Asia on account of Japan's "territorial propinquity." The Lansing-Ishii agreement of 1917 was clear in its recognition of Japan's special position in Manchuria and, by implication, on the Shantung peninsula.

What made these Allied, American, and Chinese promises all the more important was that by November 1917 Russia had ceased to exist as a power in the Far East. In the throes of revolution after March and having collapsed as a result of the intolerable strain imposed on her by the war against the Central Powers, the only major European power with a substantial land presence and power in the Far East was in eclipse. There was no force in the Orient that could possibly be used as a counterweight to Japan. By the end of 1917, with Russia to all intents and purposes out of the war, with Britain and France on the brink of collapse and disaster and the Americans increasingly committed to the war in Europe, Japan was in a position to cement still further her position of superiority in the Far East.

Yet the paradox of the Japanese position was still there for all to see. Japan in 1917 and 1918 was in a position to maintain and secure her gains as a result of the weakness of others; the war gave her virtually a free hand in the Far East. But the defeat of Germany, which in 1918 came as a surprise to Japan, had two practical results for Japan. It left her in final occupation of Germany's former possessions, and it meant that Japan was left to play a lone hand vis-à-vis allies who were more than a little suspicious of her intentions. Moreover, the victory of the democracies served to discredit militaristic adventurism and to strengthen democratic institutions in Japan. Certainly, for a period at least, the prestige of the army was in decline. There was little popular enthusiasm in Japan between 1917 and 1922 for the intervention in Siberia against the Bolsheviks, while the postwar slump dampened any schemes of expansion.

The paradox did not end there. Japan was ranked among the big five in the Allied camp, but, as with Italy, this was more an afterthought on the part of Britain, France, and the United States than a result of considering the merits of the situation or evaluating Japan in her own right. She was to be ranked as one of the great powers and she was to be granted a permanent seat on the council of the League of Nations. But the other powers, mainly under the remorseless prodding of the Australians, rejected Japan's insistence on a declaration of the principle of racial equality being incorporated into the covenant of the League. Like Orwell's animals, all animals were equal, but some were more equal than others, and the slight to Japan rankled most deeply. This was a festering wound, the infliction of which was not easily forgotten nor forgiven.

Even Japan's wartime gains, confirmed at the peace conference, were obtained at a price hardly commensurate with their value. China had declared war on Germany in order to try to recover at the peace table what she could not recover by force of arms. She was bitterly offended by the

Allied refusal to hand back Tsingtao to her, and as a result refused to sign
the Treaty of Versailles. The revelation of Allied double standards on the
issue of Tsingtao provoked a storm of dissent in China. Mostly this was
directed in the May Fourth Movement. In this anti-Japanese backlash—
which took the form of demonstrations and boycotts of Japanese goods—
can be seen the birth of various political movements among the Chinese
student and intellectual classes, movements that were to continue for many
years. Some of these were to be embryo nationalist and communist organizations whose subsequent development was to play such a profound role
in first precipitating and then frustrating Japanese aggression in the thirties.
Tsingtao cost the Japanese a great deal with regard to her relations with
China, but the port was also one of the issues that led the U.S. Senate to
refuse to ratify the Treaty of Versailles, imparting a further element of
jaundiced malevolence into Japanese-American relations. These were
already being soured by anti-Japanese immigration legislation and discrim-
ination inside the United States. On this issue, as with the question of the
covenant of the League of Nations, the Japanese were made to feel their
difference from and inferiority to the white nations, a feeling that was to be
rubbed in by the Washington Naval Treaty.

Japanese-American relations at the end of the First World War were
strained, with little goodwill on either side being much in evidence. The
suspicions aroused on both sides over the China, Siberia, and immigration
issues were inflamed by two further developments. These were the future
of the Anglo-Japanese alliance and the American-Japanese naval rivalry in
the Pacific. The two issues were interrelated, but the naval race between
the two leading Pacific powers was the more pressing because both Japan
and the United States had started after the war on construction programs
that placed them firmly on a collision course.

In 1914 the Japanese government decided, unofficially, that in order to
build up a navy commensurate with Japan's status and interests in the Far
East, it should authorize a policy of naval construction that became known
as the 8–8 Program. This was to be a building program of eight battleships
and eight battle cruisers, the active service life of capital ships being set at
eight years. The reality of Japan's financial and industrial strength, however, made the completion of such a program impossible. The Japanese
therefore trimmed the program, accepting an 8–4 Program in 1917 and an
8–6 Program in 1918. It was not until 1920, after Japan's industries had
been considerably strengthened as a result of the war, that the 8–8 Program
finally passed through the Diet. The building program was to be completed
by 1928, at which time the then-existing fleet would be constituted as a
second-line fleet. Because the new ships were intended not as replacements
for but as supplements to existing ships that were by no means obsolescent,
the program promised to build for Japan a battle fleet so powerful that no

nation could risk tackling it without fear of sustaining serious, perhaps crippling, damage.

That Japan could build modern, powerful battle units was unquestioned. The *Kongo* was the last major Japanese warship to be built abroad. After 1912, because of the growth of Japanese shipbuilding and armaments industries, there was no real need for Japan to look outside her own islands for the provision of warships. With the *Fuso* and *Yamashiro*, ordered in the 1911–12 program, the Japanese showed that they could build warships more powerful than those possessed by any other navy in the world. In the *Mutsu* and *Nagato* the Japanese in 1917–18 laid down two fast 16-inch-gun battleships as the first units in their (premature) 8–8 Program.

By that time, however, a chicken-and-egg situation vis-à-vis the Americans had developed. The Americans were not unaware of Japanese intentions; the 8–8 formula had first been aired as early as 1907. For some time the Americans had been determined to build a navy second to none, and by the act of 29 August 1916 Congress authorized the construction of ten battleships. Because of the wartime demand for the rapid construction of escorts, only one of these ships was laid down before the armistice. But the acts of 4 March 1917 and 11 July 1919, by authorizing on both occasions the construction of three capital ships, showed that the Americans were not prepared to confine themselves to "paper programs." With peace the Americans began to put their plans into action, and in time were to complete four of the ships they had ordered. Among the ships they intended to build were *Indiana*-class battleships (twelve 16-inch guns) and *Constellation*-class battle cruisers (eight 16-inch guns). With the world's greatest warship, the *Hood*, displacing 42,000 tons and carrying eight 15-inch guns, it was obvious that the world was beginning to enter a quantitative and qualitative arms race at least the equal to the prewar Anglo-German naval race.

This was precisely what many governments feared, particularly when in 1919 the Americans constituted their Pacific Fleet. The fear of many governments was that an unrestrained naval race between Japan and the United States, when set against the generally difficult nature of relations between the two countries, could easily lead to war. Of the powers most alarmed by this prospect the British had most to lose. Britain was allied to Japan, but she had no intention of becoming embroiled on the Japanese side in any American-Japanese dispute. The Anglo-Japanese treaty specifically excluded this possibility, and Britain knew that she would not have the support of any of her dominions if she tried to stand by Japan. Britain, moreover, was concerned by the threatening arms race on two further counts. First, the American and Japanese construction of a new generation of ships would force Britain into a massive construction program of her own unless she was prepared to see her traditional naval supremacy pass by default. Second, Britain was handicapped by the reality of obsolescence in design. She had been the first into the dreadnought race in strength. As a result, in 1918–19 she had a long tail of 12-inch-gun capital ships of low fighting value. Her naval supremacy rested on these ships because she was no longer automatically able to outbuild potential rivals. Her margin of superiority was in weak ships that had to be replaced. The Japanese and Americans, by being later into the dreadnought era and building fewer ships than the British, had fewer, but more powerful, older ships that were not in urgent need of replacement. The two Pacific powers therefore were for the most part adding to their strengths by fresh building; the British, if they built, were merely holding their position. Either way she looked at the problem, Britain would have to build, but financially weakened by the war, Britain was ill-prepared to embark upon massive construction. Faced with the reality of Japanese and American moves in 1921, Britain gave orders for the construction of four 48,000-ton battle cruisers.

With capital ships costing about $32 million apiece, Britain, Japan, and the United States by 1921 had committed themselves to capital ship construction programs—leaving aside cruisers and destroyers—that would have cost more than $1.1 billion. The ruinous nature of such prodigal expenditure was clear for all to see. Even the Americans, in the fortunate position of having the financial and industrial resources to outbuild any rival should the need arise, were to admit their difficulties in paying for the ships that they had ordered. Yet by 1921 another major consideration had begun to affect American resolve and led them to question the wisdom of the course on which they were embarked. This was the suspicion, which rapidly hardened into certainty, that the ships they planned would not necessarily be even the equal of those planned by the British and Japanese. With their dimensions limited by the size of the Panama Canal, American battleships were in danger of being totally outclassed by those of Japan (and to a lesser extent Britain). The Japanese, indeed, were committed to building "bigger and better" capital ships. With their 1920 program battle cruisers of 47,000 tons and ten 16-inch guns, the Japanese planned to outclass the American *Saratoga* and the British *Hood*. In 1921 the Japanese went a step further by ordering four battle cruisers each with eight 18-inch guns.

The fearful awareness of building ships that were inferior to those of other nations suddenly made the Americans very anxious to secure a treaty of limitation. By no stretch of the imagination was this desire guided by altruism; it was provoked mainly by the desire to restrict any potential threat to American security interests. Moreover, the Americans were determined to bring the Anglo-Japanese alliance to an end. Though they were aware that the alliance was not directed against them, the Americans were conscious that because of the alliance both the British and the Japanese derived a degree of freedom of maneuver relative to third parties, a freedom

THE EMERGENCE OF JAPAN

they would not otherwise possess. In their determination to end the alliance the Americans had the strong support of Canada, the more cautious support of Australia. The dominions supported the Americans on racial grounds and because they were concerned about the difficulties the alliance could cause for Anglo-American relations. Australia had mixed feelings about the Anglo-Japanese alliance because she realized that without it Britain could not act as a restraining influence on Japan, but in the end the Australians were prepared to support the Canadian view. Britain could not help but pay heed to the views of two of her dominions and the most important power in the world.

The Anglo-Japanese alliance was scheduled to lapse in July 1921, but both Britain and Japan were initially favorably disposed to its renewal. For the British the link with Japan was a not unhandy balance to the reality of American power, and it was seen, somewhat dishonestly, as a means of checking Japanese ambitions in eastern Asia. The British had mixed feelings towards Japan, and they felt that at this time they should maintain links that had served them well in the past. Britain felt that with question marks set against Japan's intentions it was better for her to be counted among Japan's friends rather than among her potential enemies. But the British link was crucial to Japan. It had been the cornerstone of Japanese foreign policy for two decades, and its maintenance was considered to be highly desirable. Japan appreciated that British interests in the Far East were mainly commercial and posed no strategic threat to her. Britain was a status quo power in the Far East and was anxious not to do anything to disturb the peace of the area.

Japan, though a revisionist power, was not particularly anxious to do something that might upset the Far East situation. She was aware that ending the Anglo-Japanese alliance would certainly lead to a British naval buildup in the Orient, a buildup that would have immense repercussions on Japan's strategic options. There were, in addition, three other considerations in Japan's desire to maintain the British connection. First, there was still the prestige and sense of fulfillment in being allied to Britain. The 1902 sense of gratitude towards Britain had passed, but the sense of achievement in the alliance was very deep. It was as if a nation still unsure of herself and conscious of her own weaknesses and differences with regard to the other powers saw the alliance as a seal of approval. Second, the Japanese were painfully aware that an abrogation of the treaty might lead to heightened racial antagonism towards them on the part of other nations. They knew that widespread racial antipathy existed already and were naturally perturbed by the prospect of isolation in a white-dominated world. Third, that isolation would be in a world dominated by the reality of American and British power. In this situation Japan's freedom of maneuver would be diminished. For all these reasons Japan was as anxious to maintain her only alliance as she was to continue the development of her fleet. For precisely these same reasons the United States was intent on ending the Anglo-Japanese alliance.

On both matters, alliance and construction, Japan was to suffer sore disappointment. Under American pressure the victorious Allies of the First World War assembled in November 1921 at Washington, and over the next three months concluded a series of agreements in what was a package deal that left the Japanese bruised and resentful.

Of the various agreements the best known and most important was the naval treaty of limitation. The main provisions of the treaty were to limit the battle fleets of the various powers and to fix the size of individual types of ships. Under the treaty's terms Britain was allowed a battle fleet of 580,000 tons, the United States 501,000 tons, Japan 301,000 tons, France 221,000 tons, and Italy 183,000 tons. Battleships were limited to 35,000 tons standard displacement, though the British, by special arrangement, were allowed a margin above this figure. Battleships could not be replaced within twenty years, and the largest guns they could carry were 16 inches. Certain provisions allowed for existing construction by various powers to be completed and for new construction—especially for France and Italy—to be started. Aircraft carriers were limited to 27,000 tons standard displacement. The upshot of these arrangements was to put an end to the race to build ever more, ever larger capital ships and to ensure, over a period of time, major scrapping of existing ships, especially by Britain.

The other agreements reached at the Washington Conference were of utmost significance. Britain, France, Japan, and the United States, in the Four-Power Treaty of 13 December 1921, agreed to respect one another's possessions and rights in the Far East and to consult together in the event of crisis, though the necessary machinery for doing so was not created. This guarantee of the status quo replaced the Anglo-Japanese alliance that was allowed to lapse in August 1923. But this device, backed up by platitudes regarding friendship and the League of Nations, left no one undeceived. The arrangement was manifestly fraudulent and empty, and left the Japanese resentful and hurt. The treaty was supplemented by the subsequent agreement by Britain and the United States not to build fleet bases at Hong Kong, Guam, and the Philippines. Britain undertook not to build naval facilities beyond Singapore and the Americans no further west across the Pacific than Hawaii. But Japan had to pay a high price in return for these guarantees of security because under American pressure and supervision she agreed to evacuate Shantung. She joined with China, Belgium, the Netherlands, Portugal, and her four major wartime allies in the Nine-Power Treaty. By this treaty all parties undertook to respect Chinese integrity and sovereignty and to maintain the Open Door policy beloved by Americans. In short, at the Washington Conference the Americans secured their way all along the line.

But if the Americans' will prevailed at Washington, virtually every other nation was less than overjoyed by the series of treaties. In Britain there was genuine regret that the link with Japan was broken, but this paled into insignificance with the implication of the treaties for British sea power. There was much criticism that the treaties had brought an end to Britain's traditional naval supremacy and that the limitation vis-à-vis the Americans left the British fatefully weak in their dealings with other powers. Though these feelings were genuinely held, there was not much substance in them. Without the treaties British naval supremacy would have been lost because of the superior resources of the Americans, and had there been no treaty of limitation Britain would not have been in a position to think in terms of powers other than the United States because Britain would have been forced to make provisions against the Americans. Anglo-American relations in the early twenties were somewhat fragile, and may not have survived British intransigence in 1921–22.

France was left bitterly resentful at the treatment accorded her. She had a long and proud naval tradition, even if she had had to play second best to Britain in all her wars at sea. She was distinctly unimpressed by being rated lower than Japan and felt grievously insulted by being paired with Italy.

But the most resentful party at Washington was Japan. She was deeply offended by the overt demonstration of her position of inferiority compared to Britain and the United States. Japan wrongly suspected that the Americans and British deliberately acted together in forcing on her unacceptable and unpalatable terms, but she was not wrong in harboring dark suspicions that racial considerations and a basic coolness towards Japan were never far from British and American considerations. Japan's main initial grievance lay in the 5:5:3 ratio foisted upon her by the treaties. She tried to hold out for a 70 percent strength compared to the British and Americans but was forced to accept a 60 percent standard. The 10 percent margin may not appear very much, but the difference was generally regarded by contemporary naval observers to be the difference between bare and comfortable margins of superiority for an attacking fleet. Japan sought a 10:10:7 margin rather than a 5:5:3 standard on the grounds that the former would give her more room for diplomatic maneuver and a greater degree of security than the latter. For precisely these reasons the Americans, and to a much lesser extent the British, were determined to insist on the lower standard of strength for Japan. Japan was forced to give way and accept the lower figure.

Japan felt that she had not secured much to comfort her from other provisions either; rather the reverse. The various treaties and declarations could not disguise Japan's new isolation and the basic unfriendliness of the outside world. The substitution of empty, meaningless treaties that were weakened rather than strengthened by the plethora of signatories, for the certainties of the Anglo-Japanese alliance could not hide the humiliating circumstances in which Japan was cut loose from an understanding in which she had so much pride. Just as the 1902 treaty had given cause for satisfaction in Japan, the ending of it was a bitter hurt, and the disillusionment was profound. The government of the day was savagely assailed for its "weakness" in giving way on so many matters involving national prestige and security, but in all truth it had very little alternative. Japan could not afford to defy the rest of the wartime Allies, and the Japanese leadership knew that Japan was unable to offer effective resistance in any form to American power. What went largely unappreciated in Japan at the time were the very real gains Japan secured at Washington.

The most positive asset for Japan was a degree of security in relation to the Americans, a security she could never have obtained had she trusted her own resources alone to provide for naval construction. The Japanese resented the limitations imposed upon their construction because they left them so markedly inferior to the Americans. The limitations imposed on American construction were not seen in relation to American resources, and Japan was so obsessed with her own situation that she failed to see the positions of Japan and the United States relative to one another and to their comparable resources. Grandiose though the 8–8 Program was, it could never have guaranteed Japan the degree of security relative to an unfettered United States that the 60 percent standard bestowed. This truth became obvious two decades later. But there was one other advantage that came Japan's way as a result of these treaties, and this was to have immense repercussions in the interwar period. Because of the European and imperial commitments of Britain and the two-ocean responsibilities of the United States, the Japanese were left with a clear local superiority in the Far East. Given the restrictions placed on British and American base construction in the Far East and Pacific, Japan was left in a position of total domination of the coast and approaches to China. An arrangement that had been intended to meet some of Japan's fears regarding her security achieved this, but at the cost of imposing such restrictions on other powers that they could not bring any form of real threat to bear against Japan. If either Britain or the United States wished to contest Japan's supremacy in the Orient, they would have to expose all their other interests and fight at great distances from their major bases in waters near Japan. Thus there was no conceivable threat to Japan and there was no possibility that either the Americans or the British could bring any form of military pressure to bear on Japan. In short, though the Washington treaties brought certain benefits to all three major naval powers, Japan was left in an extremely powerful position to exploit her interests on the Asian mainland. At this time, however, Japan was not disposed to embark upon a forward policy of aggrandizement.

CHAPTER 2

The Deepening Crisis, 1922–41

THE PERIOD BETWEEN the Washington Conference and the outbreak of the Pacific war was for Japan one of baffling contradictions that, taken together, resulted in a drift into war. It was a period that began with a policy of moderation and attempted reconciliation with China, but that was to finish with Japan totally committed to a war in China, a war she fought with nothing short of barbaric fury. It was, moreover, a period when Japan genuinely sought good stable relations with the Western powers and was anxious to secure peace throughout the Far East in order to expand her industries; but it was to be an era that ended with Japan on the brink of a major Pacific war largely, but not wholly, brought about by the need to secure resources and markets on which her industry and population depended. It was a time that seemed certain to witness in Japan the establishment of strong parliamentary democracy dominated by orthodox mass political parties, with firm legislative control of the executive and executive control of the bureaucracy and the major institutions of the state. It seemed certain in this period that Japan would see the firm establishment of the principles of political liberalism, the rights of the individual, and the development of consensus politics.

It was Japan's tragedy, and that of the Far East in general, that these hopes were to be unfulfilled. Liberalism and the concepts of Western democracy were to prove too fragile to withstand the development of more

powerful forces that came to dominate Japan. Chief among these forces was
a most powerful conservative and nationalist reaction, certainly anti-
Western but also to an extent anticapitalistic, that enforced conformity and
obedience to authority. This process saw the army emerge first as the
arbiter and then as the controller of government. It was a time that saw the
eclipse of civilian authority and its replacement by that of an army intent on
foisting on an all-too-willing nation its own narrow interpretation of national self-interest. Both the aim and the means of the army's actions were
disastrous for Japan. The dominant themes of the period, indeed, would be
the usurping of power by the growing army interest and the discrediting of
political and economic liberalism. In short, the two decades between the
Washington Conference and Pearl Harbor were ones when various
schizophrenic tendencies apparent in Japanese society were ultimately
resolved in favor of traditional antiliberal forces that plunged Japan into
war.

The origins of this confused situation lay in the fragmentation of the old
elitist control that the "oligarchy" of leading statesmen had possessed since
the time of the Meiji Restoration. The oligarchy, called the Genro, had
been able to unite and give leadership to a country that was traditionally
fragmented, divided, and faction-ridden. Japan had a long history of de-
volved power and blurred authority. As long as the old emperor was alive,
the Genro held the country together. But as members of the old Genro died
the continuity that had seen Japan emerge from her self-imposed isolation
was broken. Of the older, more authoritative Genro only Prince Kinmochi
Saionji survived into the thirties; Aritomo Yamagata, the most prestigious
of the elder statesmen, died in 1922. The Genro had provided gifted and
visionary leadership at a time when Japan's renewed contact with the
outside world threatened her very existence, but this had only been at the
expense of a narrow nationalist and traditionalist viewpoint and the imposition of a closed political system on the country. The narrowness of view,
however, was tempered by a shrewd appreciation of the realities of power.

With the gradual dying out of the Genro, the Japanese political system
became more open and less easily controlled because the vacuum caused by
their passing could not be properly filled. Power itself became more diffuse
as the old forces in Japanese society resurfaced, but the nationalism and
conservatism of the elder statesmen naturally survived. The old political
ethic of Japan, embodied in the Genro but drawn from beyond their time,
survived into an age of modern weapons and domestic political confusion.
The critical point to emerge from this situation was that Japanese politics in
the interwar period fragmented at two quite distinct, but interrelated,
levels because there took place a series of power struggles that took time to
be fully resolved. At one level there was the failure of the political parties to
develop into mass organizations or into the full political process. At the

other level the Imperial Diet failed to secure a position of control over government. Within governments ministers frequently failed to control their ministries. By their collective failures the parties and the Diet condemned themselves to final subservience to those factions that came to dominate the political process.

The body politic in the interwar period was essentially controlled by an establishment. This was a combination, often cemented by family relationships and marriage, of the old aristocracy, the *mombatsu* (the upper ranks of the civil bureaucracy), the leaders of the conservative parties that came to dominate the Diet, the *zaibatsu* (the major industrial combines that were closely associated with the conservative parties), and the upper echelons of the army. To these groupings must be added rural, and normally absentee, landlords, though many of these were businessmen who had expanded their interests into land. Within each and every group of this establishment, and within the latter itself, there were various factions constantly engaged in the struggle for power. As they cancelled one another out, the way was left clear for the emergence of the dominant army interest. There were, however, several groups within society that tried to challenge the establishment. The industrial workers, tenant farmers, and, briefly, the intellectual and growing professional classes formed powerful interest groups that could on occasion command mass support. But these groups—along with the social democrats, communists, syndicalists, and anarchists who temporarily gained in strength in the wake of the example of the Russian revolution—were never able to make inroads into the power of the establishment. The "opposition" political parties, those that might have developed genuine political appeal and have shown some degree of independence of spirit, were subject to police harassment, while the various economic interest groups never possessed the cohesion and sense of purpose that could have made them politically and socially formidable.

Perhaps the most important single factor in the failure of the democratic parties in Japan was the diffusion of working-class power. Neither urban nor rural workers were united, and neither developed political or economic institutions that were organized and strong. This situation arose from the peculiar development of the Japanese economy. A constantly rising cost of living index, largely resulting from a depression of living standards in order to raise profits and capital investment, made a prisoner of the urban and rural worker, reducing him to subservience and obedience.

Between 1910 and 1930 industrial production increased by over 200 percent and foreign trade doubled. A country with a rising population lost its place as a food exporter, but it was able to support its population to the extent that the per capita consumption of food and textiles rose in the course of the late nineteenth and early twentieth centuries. Japan, which began the First World War as a debtor nation running deficits on her annual trading account, emerged from the war with strong annual surpluses, major foreign reserves, and a dominant position in the textile markets of eastern Asia. Munitions production on behalf of the Allies helped stimulate and diversify the Japanese economy, while in the course of the war Japan's merchant fleet doubled in size to about 3,500,000 tons. Despite these very solid achievements—and in some ways because of them—the Japanese economy remained underdeveloped and very unbalanced.

Japan's economy was weak in that it was over-reliant on imported engineering machinery while heavy industry held a disproportionately large share of the gross national product. The banking system was, to say the least, precarious, lending money for fringe activities without holding sufficient reserve funds in hand. The banks were subject to all-too-frequent crashes in the twenties, and this did much to alienate small savers from the liberal politics with which many marginal entrepreneur businesses were associated. Japanese industry, moreover, was a curious combination of the great *zaibatsus* such as Yasuda, Sumitoho, Mistui, and Mitsubishi, and primitive, small-scale "cottage industries." While economic power came to be concentrated in fewer hands (i.e., the *zaibatsus*), the cottage industries absorbed surplus labor—but at the price of efficiency and low productivity and the depression of wage levels in a society suffering from the triple phenomena of rapid population growth, relative lack of industrialization, and a tendency towards capital-intensive as opposed to labor-intensive investment. There were several by-products of this situation. The consumer market never developed to any great extent; the majority of labor, except among the skilled, generally failed to secure advancing living standards at times when profits were high (in part resulting in a marked anticapitalist reaction); there were shortages and price rises that resulted in civil disturbances.

In addition to the industrial difficulties, there were considerable problems in agriculture, which remained primitive and inefficient. About 50 percent of all arable land was in holdings of less than 1.25 acres or in lease or both. The fragmented pattern of land-holding proved inimical to land improvement beyond very narrow limits because the system, plus a heavy taxation policy that insisted upon cash and not payment in kind, prevented capital accumulation. The use of fertilizers on a large scale and the reclamation of marginal land had reached the point of maximum yields. The growth of population in normal circumstances would have resulted in increasing profitability of farming. But the strain of population increase—Japan's population had reached 55,000,000 by 1920—had been concealed by imports, mainly from Formosa and Korea. This, of course, had not caused any drain on Japan's foreign reserves, but it had the effect of depressing commodity prices at considerable cost to the farmers. The price of agricultural produce rose, and rose steadily, but never to the point of being commensurate with rising farm costs. Moreover, by 1930 two further developments were beginning to make inroads into the agricultural sector of the economy. The land could neither produce any more food nor absorb any more labor, and for the family unit in the countryside the latter was catastrophic. In addition, in the twenties the price of raw silk fell by 75 percent. Again this collapse of price was disastrous for agriculture because many farmers were dependent on silkworms for income supplements.

These conditions were to have serious long-term consequences, mainly because in the interwar period the Japanese faced a series of acute dilemmas on the agrarian front, and this had implications for Japan's political and strategic options. After the end of the First World War, Japan was brought face to face with the realization that the era of unbridled imperialism and unrestricted capitalism was at an end. The Russian revolution, the devastation wrought by international war, and the establishment of the League of Nations all ushered in a new world order, largely devised by and geared to the benefit of the white nations. Satiated imperialist powers, Britain, France, and the United States, had as their main interest maintaining the status quo, which unmistakably worked to their advantage. Japan, in the twenties, found herself not merely in a world basically unfriendly to her on racial grounds, but working in a political and economic world order dictated by white imperialists. But Japan, being largely unaffected by the war in terms of squandered resources, had little or no real interest in maintaining the status quo. Indeed, her steady population growth, mounting pressure on her extremely scarce indigenous resources, and Japan's increased dependence on international trade pointed not merely to growing Japanese antipathy towards the privileged position of the Europeans in Asia but, more importantly, served as a powerful spur to throw aside the restrictive nature of the League of Nations. Moreover, as the terms of trade worsened for Japan during the twenties, there was a pressing incentive for her to look towards the Asian mainland and Southeast Asia to secure both the resources and the markets needed to extend her industries and thereby raise Japanese living standards, properly clothe and feed the population, and counter the twin scourges of unemployment and underemployment. The obvious long-term problem for Japan was that her increasingly difficult position and its implications were certain to bring her into conflict with entrenched Western interests.

In this gradually evolving situation—and it must be stressed that even in the financially troubled times of the twenties Japan did her utmost to observe the rules of a diplomatic game devised by the Western democracies—three factors were to play profound roles. First, in order to sustain her growing population and industrial requirements, Japan was totally dependent on the stability of the world economic system. This, of course, collapsed in the twenties. Japan, as with many present Third-World countries, lacked industrial diversification and was heavily dependent for her export earnings on raw silk (the price of which collapsed) and textiles (a very competitive market). These two commodities accounted for nearly 70 percent of all Japanese overseas earnings, but they were at the mercy of wild price fluctuations and protective policies in the interwar period. Second, Japan's deteriorating trading position reinforced the notion that with the recession and the white nations imposing restrictive tariffs on her, Japan had to secure markets in the Far East—for resources and colonization— even if this meant coming into conflict with the Western powers. Third, the prevalent discontent in rural Japan at the end of the twenties had an immense impact on the attitude and role of the army. Much of the rank and file of the army was drawn from the peasantry, largely as a result of the traditional family unit being unable to support sons on the land. The officer corps, particularly at the field level, could not help but be affected by the plight of their men's dependents.

Not unnaturally, the army shared many of the ultranationalist views concerning Japan's historic destiny widely held in society, but at work inside the military hierarchy was a series of pressures that were to have an immense impact on Japanese development during the interwar period. While many pressures were at work, three were of immediate relevance. These were the status enjoyed by members of the armed forces because of the privileged positions bestowed upon them by the constitution, the gradual breakdown of discipline within the army, and, last but by no means the least important, the spur to direct action brought about by the widespread rural distress already noted. When taken together and set against the army's abhorrence of moderate politics at home and abroad, these pressures provided the ingredients for two distinct but related developments. These were the increasing conviction within the army that it, rather than constituted authority, was the true custodian of national greatness and the interpreter of national interest—and that governments should be brought into line with army feeling in the event of their dissent from the views of the military; the second was the trend towards the growing militarization of society. The latter was of major, though indeterminate, importance because the Japanese army, like the French and German armies before 1914, claimed to be the "school of the nation." Brutal in a manner probably unknown elsewhere in the developed world—with the exception, of course, of the Soviet Union—the Japanese army secured at a most impressionable age the semiliterate products of a primitively developed capitalist society and within its ranks crushed out liberalism and individuality in favor of collectivist cohesion, based on the most narrow brand of nationalism. Even within the state secondary education system the army was to secure a major, indeed dominant, role by 1940. By this means society became increasingly regimented and organized to sustain, unquestioningly, an active and aggressive military policy in the Far East.

The extent of this militarization of society is something that is not easy to comprehend even though Europe experienced the concurrent rise of German and Italian fascism. The induction of the conscript into the army was an elaborate ceremonial process, but throughout the time the conscript served with the colors the cohesive nature of Japanese political, social, and religious ethos stressed obedience and maximum effort. The ultimate censure for failure was not so much individual disgrace but the fear of discrediting family and ancestors. These were vital considerations in a society where veneration of the family unit and ancestors was deeply ingrained. It was a small symptom of the manner in which moral factors as opposed to physical manifestations were stressed in the military manner of doing things. But when it came to nonconformity, then the physical realities could be very real indeed. To the fear of character assassination was added a very real fear of physical murder for leading civilians and soldiers who showed any degree of independent thought and doubts about beliefs in Japanese power and destiny that had become articles of faith.

But the key to the position of supremacy that the army secured for itself lay in the constitution. Two constitutional provisions were of paramount importance in this process, namely the unaccountability of cabinet government to the Diet and the provisions whereby the service ministries had to be headed by generals and admirals. The latter condition had not been an integral part of the constitution but had been added in the last years of the Meiji era. In that time and in the early twenties the provision had caused no problem, but in the course of the later twenties and the thirties the army increasingly used what was effectively the power of veto to encroach upon and then destroy civilian government. Because no general or admiral would consider serving as head of a service in the event of a colleague's resignation—despite the faction-ridden nature of the army's command hierarchy—the army was always able to block policies inimical to its own interest. But as time passed the army consistently used its position not simply to maintain its own vested interests but to bring down governments, to prevent the formation of new ones, and even, in the late thirties, to block individual ministerial appointments. During the thirties, indeed, prime ministers and governments, and their policies, increasingly had to be selected more or less on account of their acceptability to a boorish army.

Undesirable though this situation was, it was compounded by the growing lack of discipline in the middle and junior ranks of the army and the persistent manipulation of seniors by their juniors. The growing indiscipline in the army—it was less of a problem in the navy—and the army's division into contending factions, stemmed from a variety of causes. First, there was the weakness of control from Tokyo, especially marked in the case of Japanese army formations on the Asian mainland; second, there was resentment against civilian rule because of the effects of the depression, which was identified with Western values shown to be found wanting in the wake of the Wall Street crash. There was also another vitally important factor in promoting dissidence within the ranks of the army. This was the belief that Japan should act in order to take advantage of Chinese weakness. The importance of this was directly related to the question of the stability of the world economy. As long as world economic cooperation prevailed and Japan had ready access to resources and markets, there was no overwhelming need to resort to direct action. But with the depression there was an impetus towards conquest, and this urge was augmented by the fact that by the late twenties China was showing signs of pulling herself together and modernizing. As was the case after the fall of the Manchus, such a development could only threaten the present and future Japanese position in northern China.

The economic situation, therefore, was decisive in pushing the army to the fore in Japanese domestic politics and projecting Japan into an active military role on the Asian mainland. What the Wall Street crash did was to discredit Western capitalism. For the first time the Western capitalist system proved patently unable to function effectively, and in time this led the Japanese to write off the power and effectiveness of the democracies per se. It also served to strengthen the imperialist tendencies within Japan. Whereas in the West, imperialism was almost a dirty word—the mandate system applied by the League of Nations to former German and Turkish territories showed that overt imperialism was at an end—Japan had absolutely no incentive to abandon aggressive designs on the Asian mainland. Once the world economy began to founder, Japan was under intense pressure to move against Western interests in the Far East. Because of her relatively underdeveloped state and her reliance on primary products and textiles for overseas earnings, Japan was very exposed and vulnerable to slumps. The Great Depression struck Japan early, and with unanticipated ferocity. In this situation it was not unnatural that Japan should look to China as an area that could provide redress for her economic difficulties.

The period between the death of Yuan Shih-K'ai and 1928 was for China one of manifold complexities. In a way this state of affairs stemmed from the same factors that produced a similar situation in Japan, namely the diffusion of power. But the diffusion of power in China was different in its origins, nature, and results from the situation in Japan. Whereas in Japan the diffusion of power went hand in hand with continuity, expressed in the person of the emperor, in China this diffusion both resulted from and stimulated still further the disintegration of society.

The history of China, from the time of the first major white penetration of the empire in the first half of the nineteenth century to the latter part of the twenties, is one of consistent attempts to adopt minor changes in order to buttress the state. These merely hastened the increasingly rapid disintegration of Chinese society. For the greater part of the period Chinese efforts were directed to piecemeal attempts to reform and renovate the Confucian system. Even the overthrow of the Manchu dynasty can be seen in this light, but these attempts were uniformly unsuccessful either in preventing further foreign intrusions or in preserving the cohesion of the empire. The result of this situation was obvious. The rapaciousness of the imperialist powers grew with the realization of Chinese weakness, while power within China itself was contested ever more vigorously.

The power struggle inside China after the death of Yuan was extremely complicated because of the centrifugal nature of the situation. The writ of Peking was undermined by the realities of other sources of power—notably in Canton, but also in Shanghai and Nanking—that claimed exclusive national authority and legitimacy. There was also the emergence, normal after dynastic collapse, of extremely strong parochial interests, intent on preserving and maintaining their own local rights at the expense of national unity and cohesion. Moreover, the situation was aggravated by the opportunism of non-Chinese outlying areas such as Tibet, Sinkiang, Mongolia, and Manchuria, which tried to use Chinese weakness to consolidate their own local autonomy. Only Mongolia was to achieve a separate political identity.

The consequences of a baffling interplay of national, regional, and personality clashes, bedevilled by intrigue, backstabbing, and double-dealing of staggering dimensions, were ultimately not merely the increasing exasperation and despair of the ordinary peasantry, but the emergence of powerful radical and revolutionary forces that for a time seemed to be in control of the country. In this, there were to develop two quite distinct tragedies. First, the movement towards more militant extremist solutions came about because the more moderate democratic forces, which never recovered the ground they lost in the period 1912–24, were discredited. Second, the movement towards the radical solution was never consummated. This was to play a large part in the total disintegration of society, and was to be a chief ingredient in the final communist triumph in China between the years 1945 and 1949. But in the twenties, and in particular between 1924 and 1927, it seemed that national reunification, the necessary first step to rejuvenation, could be at hand. As events shaped up, it appeared that in the mid-twenties China was emotionally and intellectually prepared to embark upon the course taken by Japan six decades earlier. This could cause nothing but alarm in Japan.

Japan's position in China and the possibility of future aggrandizement rested on the weakness of China. As long as China remained weak there was the opportunity and the temptation for Japan to try to capitalize on the situation in the same manner as she had tried to turn Russian weakness after 1917 to her own advantage. As part of the Allied intervention in Siberia during the Russian civil war after 1918, the Japanese attempted to create a puppet state in northern Manchuria, the Mongolias, and central-eastern Siberia (including the Maritime Provinces). This scheme had come to grief because of the poor quality of the local personnel Japan tried to use as pawns. The Bolshevik victory of 1919–20—and the conquest of Mongolia in 1921—effectively brought an end to Japan's plans of expansion at Russian expense, but it was not until 1925 that the Japanese finally evacuated Sakhalien.

This inglorious episode, which attracted very little public enthusiasm and support, witnessed two developments with ominous implications for the future. In the Siberian fighting the Japanese army exhibited a barbarism well in tune with the nature of a civil war, with the obvious rider that Japan was not fighting a civil war and could have been expected to have maintained the extremely high standards she had exhibited in the Russo-Japanese war. Moreover, in its operations, the Japanese army experienced very slack control from Tokyo, and as a result of its experience, acquired a certain taste for local politics. It was this consideration that was to be so crucial in the thirties.

The politics pursued by the army on the mainland was considerably at variance with the official government line, which was to attempt a reconciliation with China. Japan was punctilious in her observation of the Shantung agreement signed at Washington, but a policy of moderation could not survive the fragile nature of Japanese domestic politics, the gradual emergence in southern China of a strong authority that threatened to unite the country, and the impact of the economic blizzard of the thirties.

The authority that began to emerge in China was the Kuomintang, a political party that was supported by Soviet arms and advisers. It was an uneasy coalition of radicals (including communists) and conservatives held together by their nominal commitment to the vague programs propounded by the dead founder of the Kuomintang, Dr. Sun Yat-sen. After much internal maneuvering, which saw the conservatives for the moment in the ascendency, the commander of the Kuomintang National Revolutionary Army, Chiang Kai-shek, in July 1926 initiated a series of military operations from Canton. These operations, called the Northern Expedition, resulted in the conquest of the provinces of Hunan, Hopei, Kiangsi, and Fukien by the end of the year. In March 1927 Shanghai and Nanking were taken, but there the march on the north effectively ended for the moment because of ferment in the rear of the advancing army. Hopei and Hunan were wracked by endemic peasant revolt, and the Yangtse industrialized areas were convulsed by a series of strikes and urban disturbances. The unrest in these most important areas of China was mainly instigated by the radicals and communists. The right, to which the Soviet connection was anathema, used the troubles as the pretext for crushing the left in a series of purges that began in March 1927. The clash between the left and the right within the Kuomintang culminated in a disastrous attempt by the communists to seize Canton in December of that year. The reality of the confused situation in 1927 was that Chiang Kai-shek and the right wing of the Kuomintang preferred to placate local interests in the north, and to come to a temporary alliance with them rather than enter into a genuine alliance with the radical element in Chinese society. Chiang's dealings with the northern interests were purely tactical, but he did show that the original option of the radical solution to China's problems counted for very little in the deliberations of the Kuomintang hierarchy.

With the communists and radicals curbed as a result of the actions of the right between April and December 1927, and with the south more or less pacified, in 1928 Chiang resumed the interrupted drive on Peking. He secured the old imperial capital in June 1928 and in October established a centralized and unified government at Nanking. The war against the warlords and against strongly entrenched local interests seemed at an end.

Chiang's administration was to survive even the disastrous Yangtse floods of 1931 that cost about 2,000,000 peasant lives, and it achieved certain impressive credits. The governmental administrative, monetary, and banking systems were overhauled, and new roads and railways were built. Industrial development was fostered and great stress was placed upon improvements and modernization of the state education system. Certain of the foreign concessions were recovered, thereby ensuring for China small recoveries of her lost sovereignty. But there were debits. The improvements in government were achieved only by further depression of already low standards of living in the countryside; the generally deplorable state of the peasantry definitely worsened in the period of Kuomintang rule. The unification of the nation was in many ways more nominal than real. Chiang had avoided any challenge emerging to his rule on a national scale, but he had had to compromise with local interests. He was really primus inter pares. Powerful local interests remained, though curbed and paying lip service to Chiang as head of state, but the real power in many areas was not held by Nanking. The communists, moreover, remained in the field, directly challenging the authority of Nanking with a policy that for the first time was moving into the realm of protracted rural militancy. And, here was the rub, the attitude of Japan was hardening.

As early as 1928, when Chiang's armies approached Peking, Japan made it patently obvious that she would not accept any nationalist attempt to reoccupy Manchuria. Conscious of Japanese power, if not of divisions on the ground at the time, Chiang took the prudent course of heeding the warning and did nothing that would provoke an open breach with Japan.

Of course, the logic of the nationalist position pointed to an eventual collision with entrenched Japanese interests in China. Many sections of the Japanese army, particularly in the field and lower staff ranks, argued that

because China's weakness was unlikely to prove permanent, it was in
Japan's interest to move openly and quickly against China. As the depression deepened and distress in the Japanese countryside became more widespread, there were growing demands for an aggressive foreign policy that
would enable Japan to secure new resources and markets.

The first real signs of the restlessness within the Japanese army in China
came in 1928, when members of the army were responsible for the murder
of the Manchurian warlord, Chang Tso-lin. Those responsible for the
murder planned to follow it up with a coup that would secure Mukden and
then the whole of the province. The latter part of the plan was forestalled by
the government in Tokyo, but such an action was merely delayed, not
averted. On 18 September 1931 the restlessness within the *Kwantung
Army** came to a head when, after the contrived Liutiaokon incident, the
Japanese army occupied Mukden. The government of Reijiro Wakatsuki,
warned from several sources that an incident was being planned, vainly
tried to forestall it; thereafter, the Wakatsuki administration also failed to
prevent the incident from escalating. It could not rein in the *Kwantung
Army*'s expansion of operations and was forced to dispatch fresh troops to
the Asian mainland to support the *Kwantung Army*. The forces on the
mainland presented Tokyo with a fait accompli so that public opinion,
thoroughly roused by the whole affair, made the position of the government impossible. The government could not repudiate the army's actions,
but at the same time, because of international opinion, it could not endorse
those actions. The Wakatsuki government, and its successor headed by
Tsuyoshi Inugai (December 1931 until May 1932), in the end could only
acquiesce in the *Kwantung Army's* occupation of the whole of Manchuria
and its reconstitution, under the last of the Manchu emperors, Pu Yi, as the
state of Manchukuo in February 1932. Tokyo could not repudiate the army
for fear of public feeling; it could not admit to foreign governments that it
could not control its armed forces.

The simple fact of the situation was that government in Tokyo was
totally unable to impose its will on an increasingly headstrong army. The
most obvious feature of the breakdown within the armed forces, mainly the
army, came in dramatic form. On 15 May 1932 Prime Minister Inugai was
murdered by a motley collection of naval officers and army cadets. This
action, plus other assassinations conducted by army officers and civilians in
the name of patriotism and to promote Japan's divine mission, effectively
spelled the end for orthodox party politics. In the vast majority of cases
where assassins were brought before the courts, the handling of trials was
lax and sentences were generally mild. The failure to enforce the law by
proper punishment naturally intimidated all sections of society, and made

*The Japanese army in Manchuria was so-called after the peninsula on which Port Arthur
stands.

the task of government virtually impossible. In desperation, the Genro advised the formation of a "national unity cabinet" after the assassination of Inugai; from this time dates the gradual domination of government by the armed services, in effect the army.

The army, as we have seen, came to dominate government to the point where it could effectively veto individual ministerial appointments. But equally and perhaps more important was the fact that formal discipline within the army could be maintained only by the pursuit of policies that the army demanded. Even this gradual development of the army's domestic power did not prevent several attempts at "direct action." The most notable of these attempts was the mutiny of February 1936 by army units in Tokyo, but this was a reflection of the power struggle being waged among various contending groups within the army itself. Nevertheless, the disputes within the army—basically resolved by mid-1936 in favor of hard-line conservative elements—never weakened the stance of the army in its dealings with civil authority. With time, the army was increasingly able to brush aside sporadic, futile, and ever-weakening attempts by the parties and Diet to reassert civil authority over it. In time the combination of an aggressive foreign policy with respect to China and the regimentation of society at home secured for the army a position of total control over the empire.

The whole tone of the thirties, especially the increasing militarization of Japanese society, was set by an event that preceded even the Wakatsuki and Inugai governments. In 1930 at the London naval disarmament conference the hated 5:5:3 ratio was again imposed upon Japan by the British and the Americans, while the ban on the construction of new capital ships was extended.* Despite the very real advantages that Japan secured from it, the treaty proved unpopular with the navy and the nation. Nevertheless, the government insisted on putting the treaty through, even to the point of accepting the resignation of the navy's chief of staff and infringing the accepted conventions of noninterference in operational aspects of policy. But the civil authorities, who had earlier cut down the strength of the army, had to make one vital concession in order to secure the treaty. The ratification of the treaty was accomplished only on the understanding within ruling Japanese circles that in the future Japan would be limited in her armaments only by her resources, not by treaties with other powers. (In this, the Japanese were as good as their word; in 1936 they deliberately wrecked the London disarmament talks, thereby freeing all nations from the restrictions that had governed naval construction since 1922.) Thus as

---

*The actual ratios for numbers of ships were: battleships and heavy cruisers 5:5:3, light cruisers and destroyers 10:10:7, submarines 1:1:1. Thus, the treaty gave the Japanese an unparalleled measure of security vis-à-vis the Americans, one that could not be justified by a comparison of resources. Though it gave Japan the ratios she wanted in Washington, the treaty caused immense resentment and upheaval within both Japan and the navy.

early as 1930 among the more moderate and cautious elements in Japan—the Genro, the Privy Council, and the leaders of government—there was evidence of Japanese distaste for any Anglo-American entente that left Japan inferior, isolated, and friendless. The events that followed merely confirmed and intensified Japan's estrangement from the democracies, beset as they were by economic problems at home and the rise of fascism in Europe.

The process of gradual alienation from the democracies and Japan's ever-closer links with Germany and Italy, ties that culminated in the Anti-Comintern Pact of December 1936, stemmed from the opposition of the democracies to Japan's actions against China. The opposition of the League of Nations—which Japan left in February 1933 after having been branded as an aggressor in Manchuria—and the United States only hardened nationalist resolve inside Japan. Moreover, the League and the Americans were discredited in Japanese eyes because they failed to back up their moral disapproval with action. Japan in this period seemed increasingly impervious to the dictates of world opinion.

The brazen bombing of Shanghai in February 1932 was evidence of the Japanese belief that world opinion was a self-imposed burden that Japan had no wish to shoulder. The irresolution of the democracies and the proven weakness of China permitted the Japanese penetration of the Great Wall and northern China in 1933, but it was not until July 1937 that serious fighting began to spread throughout China.

By that time, Japan had taken various measures that left her ideally placed to pursue her aims in China. Japan's recovery from the effects of the depression had been exceptionally rapid. The abandonment of the gold standard, ruthless devaluation, hard-sell marketing techniques, and the rigid suppression of home consumption and living standards resulted in a doubling of steel production in the course of the thirties and a vast growth of the heavy industry sector of the economy at the expense of goods and services. Massive investment in Manchuria ensured from China's richest province an enhanced level of production and the availability of raw materials that allowed Japan's armed services to take 70 percent of the country's entire budget in 1937. This, moreover, was only the beginning. In 1937 the armed forces drew up their plans for expansion, plans that over the next four years were applied consistently and remorselessly. Under the terms of the expansion programs the army grew from a strength of 24 divisions and 54 air squadrons in 1937 to 51 divisions, 9 armored regiments, and 133 squadrons (9 under strength) in 1941. In addition, the Anti-Comintern Pact, with its secret provisions for a defensive alliance against the Soviet Union, effectively checked any Soviet threat to Japanese movement southwards against China.

But the Japanese were aware by 1937 that time was not necessarily on their side. American naval rearmament plans were taking shape while the situation within China was changing. In December 1936 Chiang Kai-shek had been forced by recalcitrant Manchurian subordinates to abandon his attempts to exterminate Mao Tse-tung's communist forces in the face of the growing danger from Japan. Chiang's policy of "first pacification, then resistance" cut no ice with a Chinese nation very conscious of Japan's proximity and malevolence. To the Manchurians who had seen their homeland overrun, the policy was little short of treasonable. At Sian, Chiang was forced to barter his life, liberty, and position for a conclusion of a truce with the communists in order that a united national front could be presented to Japan. The Japanese clearly appreciated the danger to their position that this development posed, and they were determined to force the pace in order to achieve the complete domination of China.

Thus, when fighting broke out in northern China following the Marco Polo Bridge Incident of 7 July 1937, the Japanese army on the mainland was committed to forcing the pace, even though Tokyo initially intended to conduct only a small-scale operation designed to bring Chiang to his senses. But under the threat of the resignation of the war minister, the new government of Prince Fumimaro Konoe gave way, despite Foreign Office and Imperial Navy opposition to the army's demands for a widening of hostilities. With Japanese reinforcements rushed to the scene of conflict, the fighting rapidly spread after August 1937 into what the Japanese euphemistically called their "special undeclared war." China appealed ineffectively to the League of Nations. The Americans called for a conference of the signatories of the Nine-Power Treaty, but with the Japanese boycotting the proceedings, the ensuing Brussels Conference achieved nothing.

Japan had a free hand and quickly conquered vast tracts of Chinese territory, though Chinese resistance in certain places was bitter and sustained. Shanghai resisted Japanese assaults for three months before it fell in November, but elsewhere other cities quickly succumbed, Nanking being taken amidst scenes of mass murder, torture, rape, and pillage. With 1938 came even more success, culminating with the Japanese advance up the Yangtse and the fall of the Wuhan cities in November. In a little over seventeen months the Japanese were able to claim the conquest of nearly 700,000 square miles of northern and central China and a population of 170,000,000 for a cost of about 70,000 soldiers. The Chinese defeats, indeed, had been massive. The most modern and best equipped of the nationalist armies had been utterly defeated. Most of China's railways and industrial centers, virtually every port and almost all the coastline, and most of the areas that were major sources of revenue and resources had been secured by Japan. There was very little of value left for Japan to conquer.

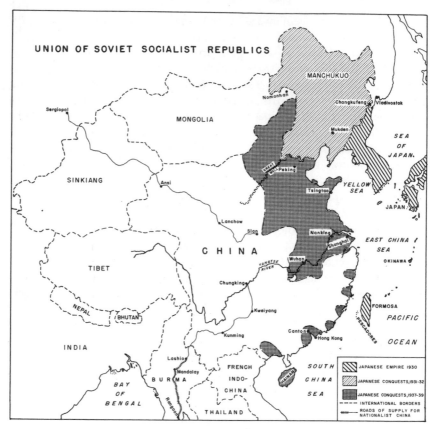

Japanese Conquests on the Mainland, 1931–39

It was under the impact of these successes that the Japanese, who not unnaturally began to confuse political, strategic, economic, and moral objectives, were led to proclaim the establishment of the "New Order of Eastern Asia"—a confederation of China, Manchukuo, Korea, and Japan under Japan's leadership. The defeats led to a series of defections from the ranks of the nationalist Chinese. These defectors despaired of China's ever being able to achieve anything by her own unaided efforts, and they were convinced that the only course open to China was wholehearted cooperation with Japan. The most important of the defectors to the Japanese cause was Wang Ching-wei, who was to head a puppet regime subsequently established by the Japanese in Nanking in March 1940. Even Wang, however, was more than a little sceptical about long-term Japanese intentions.

Great though the success of Japan had been in China, there were many facets to the reverse side of the coin. In order to sustain her effort Japan had

had to impose rationing domestically in 1938, and after March 1939 the country was for all intents and purposes ruled by decree. Virtually all production was geared to war, and there was no prospect of the war in China being brought to a speedy end. Defeat drove Chiang Kai-shek not to the conference table, as might be reasonably expected, but to the mountain fastness around Chungking. The Japanese, their overtures rejected, were left to rue the truth of the basic Clausewitzian dictum that, while it may be easy to conquer, it is difficult to occupy. By 1938 the Japanese had committed 1,500,000 troops to China—a total that represented one soldier for every hectare of ground conquered—in a war that was costing Japan $5 million a day.

The army, despite its gains, was bogged down in a war that it could not win. It did not have the strength to advance, and in any case there were no worthwhile objectives it could hope to secure. It could not force the "final battle" that would end the war. It could not properly pacify the areas it held. It was tied to the railways and major lines of communication, and was draining the industrial and financial resources of Japan without adequate compensation. The army had impaled itself in an impossible position, and had produced a disastrous situation for Japan herself. It had involved Japan in a war that could not be won and had secured gains that could not be dominated or consolidated. It had achieved the total mobilization of society under its own control, but had also mobilized world opinion against Japan.

Trouble from the rest of the world was in the offing, as both Chiang Kai-shek and Mao Tse-tung correctly anticipated. In 1937 a major confrontation with Britain and the United States was only narrowly averted after quite deliberate Japanese air attacks on various British and American positions in China. The most notable incidents were the attacks on the American gunboat *Panay* and the HMS *Ladybird*. A crisis was averted only by a prompt Japanese apology and restitution. The whole character of Japanese actions pointed to the fact that a clash with the democracies was inevitable at some time, but the first major conflict with a third party arose in an entirely different quarter.

In 1938 a major clash with the Soviets developed around Changkufeng, where Korea, Manchukuo, and the USSR converged. While some elements in the Japanese army seemed undismayed at the prospect of fighting the Soviets while continuing to wage the war in China, wiser counsels—backed by the personal intervention of a thoroughly exasperated emperor—prevailed. The conflict with the Soviets was allowed to die out, only to be resumed in full fury around Nomonhan in Mongolia during the short campaign season in 1939. In this battle, which began in May, the Japanese made many initial gains, but the Soviets, under the command of Georgi Zhukov, inflicted a total and humiliating defeat on the Japanese in August and September. In the course of their action, the Soviets, showing a total lack of squeamishness about their own losses, inflicted 11,124 casualties on the 15,140-strong *Komatsubara Force* the *Kwantung Army* used at Nomonhan. The effect of the battle was very salutary for the Japanese. Defeat at the hands of the Soviets in this relatively small engagement dampened the enthusiasm for a general war with the USSR. It showed that the Soviets had the ability to conduct offensive operations nearly 400 miles from their nearest rail base, and it showed that the Soviets were considerably superior to the Japanese in armor, artillery, and aircraft. It was after Nomonhan that the Japanese army really began to consider the development of an armor arm, projecting the ultimate creation of a total of ten tank divisions. None were to be complete before the outbreak of the Pacific war.

But there were other points to emerge from Nomonhan besides the military lessons and the conclusion that it was dangerous to underestimate Soviet power and determination. The Nomonhan experience cut the ground from beneath the feet of those who argued for a further expansion of Japan's commitment on the mainland. It strengthened the hands of the foreign ministry and the navy, both of which retained a healthy, if exaggerated, respect for Britain and the Royal Navy. As humiliating as the actual defeat was Germany's desertion of Japan at the time of Nomonhan. During August, when the battle was at its peak, the Germans had signed their infamous nonaggression pact with the USSR. At the time when their forces were being mauled, Japan felt that the treaty added insult to injury. The treaty had the effect of temporarily discrediting the Germans in Japanese eyes because it called into question their faithfulness as allies. Those members of the army who in 1938 and 1939 had urged an all-out alliance with Nazi Germany against the Soviets were undermined, the balance of opinion and concern tipping in favor of those who looked to the south for the resources Japan needed to survive. These people had good cause for concern. A month before the Nazi-Soviet pact, which was in its own right bad enough news for Japan, the Americans had served six months notice on Japan of the termination of the American-Japanese 1911 commercial treaty. The Americans, in short, were tiring of supplying Japan with the goods the latter needed to prosecute her war in China, where she was directly attacking American political, strategic, and economic interests.

For the first time in years Japan found herself in a position of confusion and irresolution in the autumn of 1939. The outbreak of war in Europe, indeed, gave Japan good reason to reconsider her whole position. Disillusionment with Germany was rife; respect for Soviet power was considerable. American economic power and antipathy towards Japan were factors with which Japan would have to take increasing account because of her heavy dependence on American iron, oil, certain raw materials, and shipping to meet her everyday needs. The respect for Britain and France increased because of their belated and fatalistic determination to stand up to

Hitler. With the outbreak of war in Europe the government of General Nobuyuki Abe declared Japan's neutrality.

It was clearly in Japan's interest to wait upon events in Europe and not to commit herself until matters unfolded. Japan could then be certain of either joining the winning side or being not too far on the wrong side of the victors. In reality, of course, an Anglo-French victory would be of no use to Japan. Such a victory would merely underwrite the status quo in the Far East and allow those countries and the United States to concentrate forces and attention on the area. Only a German victory in Europe offered Japan the prospect of major gains in eastern Asia. The Japanese were aware of this basic reality, but much of the reason for their hesitancy in the period between September 1939 and mid-1941 stemmed from their awareness of two other realities. First, they knew that they needed time to prepare for a major war. Detailed planning for a large-scale war was not nearly complete; indeed, in 1939 not even the general principle of a war in Southeast Asia had been fully conceded. The Japanese leadership, upon the insistence of the navy, knew that if there was to be a general war then it had to be delayed at least until the terms of the Third (1937) Replacement Program and possibly the Fourth (1939) Replacement Program (at least with regard to the light units) produced more ships for the navy. The navy, moreover, knew that it would take at least eight months to place the fleet on a full war footing. The tasks of recommissioning ships in reserve, working up all types of ships, requisitioning, converting, calling up fresh manpower, and training were necessarily slow, and the navy knew that it could not move quickly in the event of an action that might trigger a general war. Second, there were people in the leadership hierarchy who feared the consequences of seeking to expand the boundaries of the empire still further. There was no questioning the basic assumption that the Japanese, a semidivine people ruled by a divine emperor, were mandated to expand and be self-sufficient, but there were obvious reasons to fear the consequences if things went wrong.

The period between the outbreak of war in Europe and mid-1939 has as its main theme the growing determination of the Japanese navy to risk war and, in the end, the navy's successful campaign to convert the army to its point of view. The conventional wisdom regarding the outbreak of the Pacific war is that the navy reluctantly agreed to war in the face of an insistent army, the evidence for this being the well-known views of Isoroku Yamamoto.

This was not the case. The power of decision between 1939 and 1941 increasingly rested with the navy, and the navy's demands were not moderate. The navy was more realistic than most sections of the army in its appreciation of the realities of power and Japan's strength, but it came to the view that war was inevitable. This being the case, within limits, it was better that war came sooner rather than later. It was this view that the navy ultimately forced upon the army and the civilian leadership of Japan.

The navy had always wanted an advance to the south. As far back as the Shanghai incident in 1932 this had been made clear, and the navy's condemnation of the army's China venture was that it did little or nothing to meet Japan's basic strategic requirements. In the navy's view the basic Japanese requirement was the resources of Southeast Asia, without which Japan could not hope to survive. In 1936–39 the navy was restrained by the army. China was seen as the initial priority, and the army did not want to see complications arising in the south while operations in China were being pursued. The army, naturally, wanted to ensure that no trouble arose in the south while Soviet-Japanese relations were unresolved. The navy lost out in this round, but it resented being relegated to a position of mere support for army operations, and it knew that its views regarding Southeast Asia and the area's resources were basically irrefutable. The Japanese army, which had not been completely blind to the area's importance, came to support the navy's view but in a roundabout manner. Increasingly conscious that it could not win the war in China by direct military action, the army came to see the overrunning of Southeast Asia as the means of completing the isolation and encirclement of Chiang Kai-shek. By July 1940, the army was thinking in terms of securing Southeast Asia not for the area's resources but as a means of bringing to an end the interminable war in China.

Even before the war started in Europe the Imperial Navy made its first moves in the south. Implementing cabinet decisions made in the summer of 1938, the navy occupied Hainan Island in February 1939 and Spratly Island on 31 March, claiming at the same time jurisdiction over fourteen coral reefs in the South China Sea. The two moves brought Japan deeply into Southeast Asia, directly menacing French Indo-China, Malaya, and the Indies and all but completing the encirclement of the Philippines. The French, who had owned the Spratly group since 1930, could do nothing other than make futile protests.

With the outbreak of war in Europe the Imperial Navy was reorganized in order to take precautions against all possible eventualities. The most notable change was the formation of a southern task force, which was deployed to Palau in May 1940 to prevent any other nation from trying to take the Dutch East Indies into "protective custody" following the German invasion of the Low Countries. No nation, other than Japan herself, had either the wish or the means to do this, and the Japanese did not pursue the matter. But the collapse of the Netherlands, Belgium, and France and the patent weakness of Britain as a result of the debacle of May-June 1940 offered all sorts of glittering opportunities to Japan. It was obvious that not one of the European empires in the Far East was capable of defending itself. By the summer of 1940 the winning side seemed obvious. Only Britain remained opposed to Germany, and she was totally unable to contest the German mastery of the continental mainland. There seemed no good reason why Britain should not go down to defeat within a very short space of time. For Japan there was no good reason to suppose that the war would end in anything other than a German victory, notwithstanding the first American moves to succor Britain by all means short of war.

Within three months of the defeat of France Japan made a series of critically important decisions and moves that placed her firmly on the side of Germany and Italy, in the process clearing the decks for a general war. Three of Japan's moves were open and had immediate consequences, but they were made only as a result of a series of secret decisions by the army, navy, and heads of civilian government. The open moves were bringing irresistible pressure to bear on Britain to close Chiang Kai-shek's supply route along the Burma Road from Lashio to Chungking (8 and 27 July), forcing the Vichy government to accept the presence of Japanese bases in northern Indo-China (26 July), and signing the tripartite pact with Germany and Italy on 27 September. The latter was in many ways the most significant and the clearest possible indication of the nature of Japanese calculations. Japan bound herself to the future of Germany and Italy, but retained the freedom to choose the timing and objectives of her war effort.

The value and purpose of the treaty, as far as the Japanese were concerned, was in the anticipation that it would serve to check the Americans. The danger the pact posed for the Americans was that they would be caught with their attention and forces divided between two oceans and, as a result, be ineffective in both. This was what the Japanese hoped to achieve through the treaty, catching the Americans between two widely separated objectives. The Japanese premier, Prince Konoe, promised on 4 October that if the Americans accepted German-Italian domination of Europe and Japanese hegemony in Asia, then the three Axis powers would recognize American domination of the western hemisphere. If not, Konoe warned, Japan was prepared to fight to a finish. Three days later the Foreign Ministry announced that there was "no room for a basic readjustment of relations between Japan and the United States of America." This meant that the only basis for American-Japanese understanding was American acceptance of Japanese control over eastern Asia. Battle lines were being drawn, and the events of the next fourteen months were to show the observations of the Japanese Foreign Ministry to be correct, but not quite in the manner the Japanese intended.

The hardening of Japanese attitudes dated back to June 1940. As France fell to German arms the Japanese services, but particularly the navy, settled down to consider the problems that would be encountered if Japan moved against Southeast Asia. With the Royal Navy engaged in a desperate battle in the Atlantic and the Americans becoming increasingly embroiled in that ocean, the situation was one of great promise for Japan. Yet it quickly became obvious to the Japanese navy that any movement southwards was certain to involve war with Britain and the Netherlands, and almost certainly with the United States. The Japanese considered it impossible for the Americans to stand aside and abandon Britain, the Netherlands, and China to their collective fate. In July, as the navy pondered the implications of this conclusion, its view of the need to move against the south received support from an unexpected quarter—the army. Given the European situation, which for the moment neutralized the Soviet Union, the nakedness of the European empires in the Far East, and the intractability of the China war, the army was prepared to back the navy's demands for southwards expansion in order to isolate and then finish off Chiang and to achieve autarky. With the two services for once in full agreement, the army and navy combined to bring down the cautious Yonai government in July when it showed signs of hedging on the military's demands. Mitsumasa Yonai's successor, Prince Konoe, was allowed to form a government but only on terms that made him a hostage to the armed services. On 19 July Konoe was forced to agree to the demand for a treaty with Germany and Italy, the further buildup of the army, the signing of a nonaggression treaty with Moscow, and the adoption of a forward strategy in Southeast Asia. Konoe

The Japanese leadership in the summer of 1940. The cabinet brought to power when the army and navy combined to bring down the Yonai government was led by (left to right) Prime Minister Fumimaro Konoe, Foreign Minister Yosuke Matsuoka (to July 1941), Vice Admiral Zengo Yoshida (navy minister until September), and Lieutenant General Hideki Tojo (army minister and Konoe's successor in October 1941). Robert Hunt Library

was made painfully aware of the armed forces' view that the latter ran the risk of a breach and war with the United States.

Even after July 1940, it took a long time for the Japanese navy to absorb fully the fact that it had accepted the likelihood of war with the United States. But the navy's acceptance of the idea was based upon three incontrovertible arguments that the passing of time only strengthened. The Japanese navy always retained a healthy regard for the U.S. Navy. Before the war Japan's navy never fully divested itself of its mental reservations concerning the wisdom of tackling its American counterpart, but it also came to the conclusion that a war with the Americans was inevitable. The Japanese knew that probably never again would they find themselves in such an advantageous position as in 1940. In fact, 1941 proved an even better year. With mounting British losses, particularly in the Mediterranean in the second half of the year, 1941 confirmed Japan's position of strength. Everywhere in the Pacific Japan's potential enemies were desperately weak and dispersed while the Japanese, though not ready to strike, were concentrated. Moreover, the Japanese were aware that after the U.S. Congress passed the Two-Ocean Naval Expansion Act of June 1940 they were in a quandary. The long-term prospects of a naval victory over the Americans would be ended by the 1940 measure. To have even matched the American program of June 1940 Japan would have had to double the proposed construction program of 1942 (the Fifth Replacement Program), and already in 1940 there were doubts about whether Japan could fulfill the provisions of the current Fourth Program. The Fifth Program, as it stood, represented a major increase over its predecessor. The dilemma for Japan was obvious.

Thus, from June 1940 onwards, there was a powerful inducement for Japan to go to war. Although in the long term her prospects were worse than bleak, in the short term they were good. The major units of the Third Program and the smaller units of the next would be complete either in late 1941 or in early 1942. The first American construction under U.S. rearmament programs would be completed from 1943 onwards, and the provisions of the June 1940 act would be fulfilled only in the period 1946–48. Therefore, the Japanese had a brief period, no longer than two years and possibly not much more than one year, when they would stand at the peak of their strength relative to the Americans. Thereafter the level of American construction would take the U.S. Navy to a position of unassailable power. The Imperial Navy knew that time initially favored it, but in the long term inevitably doomed it: the Two-Ocean Naval Expansion Act doomed the Imperial Navy to second-class status, since the activities of American shipyards would be as catastrophic for Japanese aspirations as a disastrous naval battle would be. This was the argument that pushed Japan into war. The only chance that Japan had to avoid being relegated to the second rank to the sound of workmen's hammers and the roar of oxyacetylene torches was to fight in the near future and to achieve a decisive naval victory over the Americans in the opening stages of a war.

When the final arguments were unfolded in September 1941, the Imperial Navy estimated that the Americans were building three tons of warship for ever ton in Japanese yards. The navy estimated its own strength relative to the Americans would be 70 percent in late 1941. This would fall to 65 percent in 1942, to 50 percent in 1943, and to a disastrous 30 percent in 1944. At the very least the Japanese envisaged waging defensive attritional warfare, with battle in the Carolines-Marianas area, on a 50 percent margin. By the navy's calculation, a 50 percent margin was a strength below which it could not fall if defeat was to be averted. Unless there was a war, the Japanese strategic position would become hopeless by the end of 1943. It was this fear that haunted the Imperial Navy from the time Carl Vinson proposed the Two-Ocean Naval Expansion bill, and the fear spurred the Japanese on to secure the resources of Southeast Asia before it was too late.

On 1 August 1940 the navy made its first demand for the occupation of the whole of Indo-China. This it wanted to do in November when its plans would be finalized. The navy realized that the United States might take retaliatory measures, and concluded that the only way to escape the long-term consequences of American economic pressure would be to occupy the Dutch East Indies. The navy was confident that war would not result from any occupation of French Indo-China, but on 15 October it ordered the start of full war mobilization, scheduled to be completed in thirteen months.

What really pushed the navy on this course of action was not simply the desire to force the issue before it was too late, but the belief that the Americans could do no more to Japan than they were already doing or threatening to do. The economic argument reinforced the strategic logic that ultimately there was little if anything to lose by forcing the pace. It was patently obvious that little if any American goodwill towards Japan existed. As early as January 1940, at the time when the 1911 commercial treaty lapsed, there were calls in Congress for a total trade embargo against Japan. It was a clear sign of the way the wind was blowing in the United States, but the Roosevelt administration, in an election year with the president deciding to run for an unprecedented third term, was cautious. The administration was not to be rushed into precipitate action, but a series of trade restrictions imposed in July, September, and December 1940 and in January 1941 nevertheless had the effect of placing the American thumb firmly on the Japanese windpipe. The gentleness with which the hand was applied could not disguise the firmness of the grip. After the initial Japanese encroachment in Indo-China immediately after the fall of France, the United States banned the export of aviation fuel and high-grade scrap to

Japan.* It proved impossible for the Japanese to find an alternative source of supply for the latter commodity.† Subsequently the American embargo was extended to cover every major strategic material. In January 1941 the ban was extended to cover copper and brass, absolutely vital materials that Japan needed to survive.

Thus, after the Japanese secured northern Indo-China in November and the American grip tightened, the Imperial Navy found that it had placed Japan in the position of being part of a self-fulfilling prophecy. She needed expansion to secure the goods that the Americans denied her; the American denial justified expansion. When Japanese expansion was challenged by the United States, Japan's only option was to attempt a course of action designed to challenge, not accommodate, the American move. The navy used the American actions to justify claims for ever-larger appropriations being diverted into naval construction. What was a vicious circle was being closed, rapidly and with a vengeance.

Japan tried to break out of the closing net by dealing directly with the Dutch, but this proved singularly unrewarding. The Dutch refused even to try to meet Japanese requirements,‡ and they could hardly have been impressed by Japanese declarations in February 1941 that their possessions in the Indies were being allocated a place in the Japanese "New Order" in the Far East. But with their failure to secure from the Dutch sufficient resources to cover their needs, the Japanese and their navy had to move southwards, and in the course of 1941 Japan instigated a series of actions that brought about the final crisis with the Americans. In March Japan forced the Vichy government to accept the garrisoning of Saigon airport by

---

*The Japanese steel industry was heavily dependent on supplies of American scrap and the effect of the embargo is not to be underestimated. In 1939 Japan imported 2,515,000 tons of scrap, mostly from the United States. This total fell by nearly 50 percent, to 1,369,000 tons, in 1940 and continued to plunge dramatically over the next three years. In 1941 Japanese scrap imports stood at 199,800 tons, in 1942 at 38,385 tons, and in 1943 at 29,527 tons. Much of the difficulty that Japanese industry came to experience in building and repairing ships after 1941 stemmed from the lack of iron and steel imports.

†In 1940 the Japanese tried to secure supplies from the Dutch. They demanded increased oil supplies and certain prospecting rights on various islands in the Indies. The Dutch, though conscious of their vulnerability, never even answered the demands for mining concessions and put the Japanese off with an interim oil agreement that gave the Japanese less than half of what they demanded. By the end of 1940 it was obvious to Japan that she could not secure the resources of the Indies without a war, and she put down the failure of her diplomacy to American and British influence with the Dutch. She was correct. The Americans in particular put great pressure on the Dutch and the oil companies not to give in to Japanese demands. From the time of Japan's failure to get concessions from the Dutch dates her talk of being encircled by enemies.

‡But the Dutch had to make some concessions and the massive Japanese stockpiling effort in 1940 was mainly drawn from Dutch sources. Japanese imports from the Indies in 1940 rose dramatically. The amounts imported in 1940 from the Indies (with percentage increase over 1939) were bauxite 212,587 tons (28 percent), scrap iron 66,138 tons (43 percent), rubber 28,443 tons (33 percent), nickel ore 5,905 tons (400 percent), and tin 4,807 tons (337 percent).

Japanese troops and to turn over the whole of the Indo-China rice crop to Japan. In this move the Imperial Navy, not the army, was the pacemaker, and from June 1941 onwards the navy had an additional reason for haste. In that month the Japanese became aware of German preparations for an attack on the Soviet Union; after 22 June the invasion was an accomplished fact. As the German panzers bit deeply into European Russia, inflicting a series of massive defeats on the Soviet army, it seemed only a matter of time before Stalin's Russia collapsed. This prospect alarmed the navy because it feared that unless it moved immediately, the army might lose interest in the southern option. There were signs that the army might resume its old fascination with the prospects of a war with the Soviets, particularly under the conditions of a Soviet defeat in the West.

Just three days after the start of the German invasion of the USSR at an army-navy liaison meeting the two services settled matters by adopting the southwards expansion option before turning to face whatever situation arose as a result of the Nazi-Soviet conflict. This decision was formalized at an imperial conference on 2 July. The navy in effect had a free hand, and it was prepared to move quickly in order to prevent its being deflected from its chosen course. On 21 July the navy formally declared itself in favor of war with the United States in order to secure Southeast Asia, and four days later forced through the proclamation of a joint Franco-Japanese protecto-rate over Indo-China. The next day the United States, followed by Britain and the Netherlands, froze all Japanese assets in territories under their control and imposed what was in effect a total trade embargo. This natu-rally included all oil supplies.

For Japan this was the moment of truth. The Americans had committed themselves decisively. They saw Japan as an authoritarian power and a threat to peace, and believed that they had to force Japan to back down. The Japanese political, economic, and military leaders knew that without a resumption of trade they faced slow but certain economic strangulation. The army was forced to confirm the validity of the navy's case for war with the Americans in order to secure the resources of Southeast Asia. The Economic Mobilization Bureau of the War Ministry advised the army leaders that at the very most Japan had sufficient fuel reserves to sustain herself for about two years at her existing level of consumption. The bureau estimated that if Japan embarked upon a general offensive in the Pacific the armed forces had enough fuel for about a year of operations, the air forces for about six months of warfare. These estimations convinced the army that there was no alternative to the navy's arguments in favor of war.* The army and the civilian leadership recognized the validity of the argument that

---

*The Japanese oil problem and Japanese calculations on the matter of their reserves and expected consumption are dealt with in the section on the manner in which the need for resources determined the shape of Japanese war plans; see chapter 3.

unless Japan initiated action quickly she was certain to be dragged down to defeat by the sheer weight of the economic forces that would be brought to bear against her. The army also knew that the American terms for a resumption of trade—Japanese evacuation of China and Indo-China—were impossible to meet. At the very most Japan might be prepared to make cosmetic changes with regard to Indo-China and Southeast Asia, but she could not afford to forego the reality of her Chinese gains and the possibility of securing major concessions in the south. On 30 August the army formally endorsed the navy's demand, made two weeks earlier, for the start of hostilities at the end of October.

The civilian leadership of Japan dealt with the demands of the military on 25 September when it debated whether or not Japan should start hostilities at the end of November. The civilians had managed to win a "stay of execution" by insisting upon a last diplomatic effort to secure a compromise. Konoe managed to secure this respite, and he placed his hopes in a direct appeal for a summit conference between himself and Roosevelt. But the Americans quickly showed that Konoe's hopes would be disappointed. They rejected the proposal unless some form of prior agreement could be worked out between the two sides. This in effect meant that the Japanese had to concede the substance of American demands before holding talks that would place the seal on Japan's surrender. With the navy firmly in the hands of the hawks (Admiral Osamu Nagano as chief of the Naval General Staff after April 1941 and Admiral Shigareto Shimada as navy minister after September, when Admiral Kojiro Oikawa was forced to resign following some belated but rather rational second thoughts about the situation), Konoe had little option but to resign. He did so on 16 October, one day after the army-navy deadline for diplomatic efforts to find a way out of the impasse.

Konoe was replaced by General Hideki Tojo, the embodiment of hardline militarism. His appointment as premier marked the final, total triumph of the armed forces over the state they were supposed to serve. The armed services had mobilized the whole of society behind them and a war effort. The parties and the unions had been dissolved. Every aspect of Japanese political, economic, and social life had been subordinated to the military and regimented for the purpose of serving the war effort. There was no domestic opposition to the will of the armed forces. Through progressive capitulations the moderates had compromised with the extremists to the point where they and the extremists could not be told apart. At every stage the takeover of the state by the military and the military by the extremists had been characterized by the certainty of insubordination and indiscipline within the services unless the hardest of lines in foreign affairs was maintained. Had the leaders of Japan at any time shown the slightest degree of moderation, they would have faced the certainty if not of personal assassination then of mutiny and probably social revolution. Beside these certainties the hazards of foreign war presented fewer risks. In their acid test Japanese leaders were prepared to face the risks of war rather than those of social upheaval. This is hardly surprising. In similar circumstances most nations would have chosen the same course, to fight rather than face total humiliation and social discord.

Tojo knew, as well as any other member of the Japanese ruling hierarchy, that there was no way out of the impasse except war, but among his first acts was to extend the deadline for negotiations. The November deadline was put back until December, but there was little hope of success during these final, fruitless negotiations. The summer and autumn had revealed the depth of the divisions between Japan and the United States. In the last weeks of peace there was no chance of finding common ground that had been elusive for so long; in any case Japanese and American terms were mutually exclusive. Between them the Japanese and Americans had produced a situation from which there was no escape. Neither side was prepared to give way because too much was at stake. Too much effort and prestige, far too much of Japan's international standing, had been invested in the China venture for Japan meekly to evacuate the Asian mainland at American insistence, even when that demand was backed by power that the Japanese could not hope to match. Unless the Americans were prepared to resume normal economic relations, the Japanese would not even begin to consider concessions—and then only in Indo-China. Without prior concessions, the Americans would not contemplate the normalization of relations.

Both sides had made fundamental errors in their assessments of one another and of the realities of power. The Japanese had vastly overestimated the effectiveness of the tripartite pact in checking the Americans and had underestimated the resolve of the Americans in the course of 1941: at every stage their logic had been correct, but their ultimate conclusion had been wrong. The Americans, on the other hand, failed to appreciate the lack of options their demands left Japan, and they seemingly failed to realize the likelihood that Japan would be forced into war for want of an alternative. The Americans, and their associates, drastically underestimated the intentions and fighting effectiveness of the Japanese war machine. On 1 December the Japanese leadership finally and formally accepted that there could be no peaceful method of resolving Japanese-American problems and made the decision to go to war. By that time Japanese forces were at their battle stations and in certain cases were already moving on their initial objectives.

CHAPTER 3

The Japanese Situation

ONLY AFTER THE IMPOSITION of the Allied blockade in mid-1941 did the Japanese really face up to the twin realities that they had to contemplate a war with Britain, the Netherlands, and the United States and that such a war would come that year. Until mid-1940 the diffusion of power within the Japanese upper councils had led to the pursuit of two divergent objectives. The objective of the dominant army faction was the Asian mainland, specifically China but generally more widely, with the USSR figuring strongly in the army's list of options. The interest of the navy was in Southeast Asia. Though in early 1941 the two services had agreed to pursue the southwards option, it was not until the imposition of the trade embargo that the two armed forces studied the possible implications of the Allied move in detail. As a result of this study, they finalized plans that merged the army's and the navy's strategic considerations and intentions.

In 1944, British Minister of Production Oliver Lyttleton, in a moment of rare candor, admitted that the Japanese had been provoked into attacking the Americans at Pearl Harbor. Lyttleton's observation was based on his recognition that the economic pressure brought against Japan by the Allies left the Japanese with no option other than to fight, unless they were prepared to see their empire reduced to an Asiatic irrelevance at the beck and call of the Americans. But while it is generally recognized that economic factors were crucial in Japan's decision to go to war, what is not often realized is precisely why they were so important and the extent to which Japan's war plans had to be shaped by economic objectives.

Of all the Japanese needs, oil was the most critical. Japan had enough coal to support herself and, while considerations of securing other vitally needed raw materials and foodstuffs were important, it was concern about the security of her oil supplies that primarily molded Japanese strategy at the beginning of the war. In the summer of 1941 domestic crude and synthetic production accounted for 10 percent of Japanese needs. A similar amount was imported from the Dutch East Indies, while most of the balance was American-supplied. After the imposition of the Allied block-ade, therefore, Japan lost about 90 percent of her oil supplies and had to fall back on her reserves. Her domestic production could not cover even the relatively modest amounts used up after June, even though Japan tried to cut her consumption. In mid-1941 Japan's total reserves stood at about 58,000,000 barrels. During the Allied blockade the Japanese used up about 7,000,000 barrels from this reserve. Domestic production could not cover this loss even in a full year. Japanese production of crude oil totalled about 2,500,000 barrels in its peak year of 1937–38, while synthetic production added only half as much again to this total from indigenous sources. Even though the Japanese command rather optimistically assumed that domestic production of crude oil would rise to about 2,800,000 barrels in the coming year and that synthetic production would more than triple to account for 4,500,000 barrels within three years, there was no escaping the inevitable conclusion that Japan could not rely on her own resources to see her through the crisis her occupation of Indo-China had provoked.

If the Japanese were to break the grip of the Allied blockade they had to secure the oil fields of Borneo, Java, and Sumatra. These islands yielded enough oil to fulfill Japan's estimated need for about 37,800,000 barrels between September 1941 and September 1942. Together these islands produced about 65,000,000 barrels in 1940, with the Sumatran wells contributing just over 60 percent of this total. Clearly, if the Japanese could secure these islands quickly and get the oil wells back into action with the least possible delay, their problems of secure sources of energy would be solved. Japan had the technicians needed to work the fields and her re-fineries could process any amount of Indies oil. However, the question of secure sources was only part of Japan's overall oil problem. The Japanese did not have a sufficiently large tanker fleet to transport captured oil from the Indies to refineries in Japan. Normally Japan's oil had been mostly carried by nations now arrayed against her. The transportation problem was one without solution, and as time passed it gradually assumed chronic proportions. It was only partially relieved when Japan based her fleet in the south and fuelled directly from the Indies in the period 1942–44. This was a course of action for which the Japanese had made no allowance before the war, and, indeed, the Japanese had made no effort to think through their oil problem until war became inevitable.

But even if the Japanese managed to overrun the Indies quickly, one further obvious problem existed. It would take time to get the captured oil fields back into production, and in the meantime the Japanese would be using up their reserves without any commensurate increase in production. The joint army-navy committee that investigated the oil difficulty in June 1941 estimated that by the third year of the war, presuming hostilities began in the coming September, the Indies would yield about 17,730,000 barrels, but even that was of little comfort. By their own figures even if this was the case by the third year of the war the Japanese would need to find 28,000,000 barrels from production to meet an annual consumption of about 34,600,000 barrels. By that time the reserves would have been depleted to an extent that only about 6,600,000 barrels would be left, yet with production from all sources running at approximately 23,600,000 barrels, Japan would need just over 11,000,000 barrels from stocks to see her through the year. There was no possibility that this amount would be available. By their own calculations by September 1944 Japan would be about 4,400,000 barrels short—and this excluded the possibility of a major fleet engagement taking place in the first three years of war. For such an action the navy estimated that it would need about 3,150,000 barrels of oil. The overall deficit would therefore be (in the event of a naval action) about 7,500,000 barrels in September. By these calculations, the Japanese would run out of oil in June 1944.

JAPANESE ARMY-NAVY COMMITTEE ESTIMATES OF OIL NEEDS AND PRODUCTION
(TO NEAREST THOUSAND BARRELS)

	Estimated Reserve	Estimated Production	Estimated Consumption
September 1941/September 1942	61,045,000	5,035,000	37,760,000
September 1942/September 1943	28,320,000	12,901,000	34,613,000
September 1943/September 1944	6,608,000	23,600,000	34,613,000
September 1944	−4,405,000		

A subsequent review by the navy in August painted a more optimistic picture, but it was one that was based on the dubious premise that far greater yields would be secured in the first three years of war. This review envisaged the Indies producing about 15,400,000 barrels in year two of the war and a massive 30,000,000 barrels in year three. The naval command's glib assumption was that in the third year of war its operations would not be jeopardized by a shortage of oil. It believed that supplies would be forthcoming from various sources, but even in the August figures the navy saw a period of crisis during September 1943/September 1944. In that year stocks would fall to about 17,200,000 barrels in general reserve, and only 2,520,000 barrels in the operational reserve. Then rising production in the Indies would pull Japan clear of the danger zone.

JAPANESE NAVY AND PLANNING AGENCY
ESTIMATES OF OIL NEEDS AND PRODUCTION, 1941–44
(TO NEAREST THOUSAND BARRELS)

	Estimated Reserve	Estimated Production	Estimated Consumption
Estimates by the Navy Review, August 1941			
September 1941/September 1942	59,157,000	5,035,000	33,984,000
September 1942/September 1943	30,208,000	21,020,000	33,984,000
September 1943/September 1944	17,244,000	41,976,000	33,984,000
September 1944	25,236,000		
Estimates by the Japanese Planning Agency, December 1941			
December 1941/December 1942	52,863,000	5,349,000	32,725,000
December 1942/December 1943	25,487,000	16,362,000	31,466,000
December 1943/December 1944	10,383,000	33,354,000	29,893,000
December 1944	13,844,000		

It was a combination of these two reviews, and particularly the latter's observation on the mid-1944 operational reserve that made the navy in mid-1941 so insistent on war as soon as possible, and not later than October. With a projected monthly consumption of about 2,900,000 barrels, a single month's delay in beginning hostilities would wipe out the mid-1944 reserve. Although the two reviews varied considerably in their overall assessments, they almost agreed on the projected mid-1944 situation. Whereas the June review foresaw disaster, the August review envisaged a possible crisis of critical proportions. With or without war and with or without the Indies, the Japanese had problems—if their calculations were accurate.

It almost goes without saying, however, that their figures were wildly inaccurate. The Japanese vastly overestimated their own potential and drastically understated their requirements. The notion of a single major naval engagement showed that the navy really had no inkling of the kind of war it was going to have to fight. In the first year of war the navy used 60 percent more oil than it was allowed under any review or plan. Its operations consumed 30,520,000 barrels—80 percent of the assessed total *national* needs for 1941–42. Its declining needs thereafter reflected its losses, not its commitments. The Indies' maximum production was about 16,670,000 barrels in 1943, actually more than allowed for in the August review, but outflow to Japan fell 60 percent in 1944, mainly because of tanker losses and the direct fuelling of the navy in southern ports. Domestic production never exceeded 3,400,000 barrels in a year (1943).

ACTUAL JAPANESE OIL PRODUCTION AND CONSUMPTION
(TO NEAREST THOUSAND BARRELS)

	Reserve	Production	Consumption
December 1941/December 1942	52,863,000	12,524,000	51,919,000
December 1942/December 1943	13,468,000	20,076,000	41,661,000
December 1943/December 1944	− 8,117,000	9,629,000	29,452,000
December 1944	− 27,940,000		

From these figures can be seen just how and why the need to secure the Indies was so important to the Japanese. The islands had to be secured very quickly for their oil resources.

Although in mid-1941 oil was Japan's main concern, other economic factors entered into her calculations. She drew from the south a whole host of raw materials that were essential to a war effort and, indeed, without which she could not hope to survive. She was critically dependent on imports of iron, particularly from Malaya and the Philippines. Though Japan had extensively stockpiled and had a reserve of about 4,500,000 tons, this was a relatively small amount compared to her long-term needs. She needed rubber and tin as well as a variety of special materials vital to war production—bauxite, manganese, coal, cobalt, graphite, lead, nickel, phosphate, and potash—from Malaya and the Indies. None could be supplied from domestic resources. Nor could Japan clothe and feed her own population. One-fifth of Japanese rice and wheat needs, nearly all her sugar, and two-thirds of her soybean requirements had to come from abroad. The barren, mountainous homeland of Japan, with its few resources and backward agriculture, could not sustain its growing population and hungry industries. With the imposition of the blockade in 1941, the Japanese faced the stark alternatives of conquering or starving. The policies of the thirties had proved self-defeating.

The Japanese problem in 1941 was to secure the resources of Southeast Asia, the economic factor, as we have noted, being the consideration that shaped Japan's strategic deliberations and intentions. But two noneconomic factors were also present in Japanese thoughts, though in their separate ways even these tied in with economic considerations. First, though the Japanese objectives were mainly in the Dutch East Indies, Japan was aware that any move on her part was almost certain to provoke American intervention. The Americans had committed so much prestige in attempting to force the Japanese to back down in 1941 that it was inconceivable the United States would stand aside tamely and leave China and the European empires to their fate. Thus for Japan there was a powerful incentive to attempt the neutralization of American power at the outset of a conflict, particularly because the American positions in the Philippines lay astride Japanese lines of communication between the homeland and the intended area of conquest. The Japanese did not dare risk leaving the Philippines unreduced in their rear. On the islands were too many defense installations that, in the event of war, could be reinforced to menace Japanese sea communications. The American line of communication (Hawaii, Wake, Guam, Luzon, China) straddled Japanese lines of communication in the central and western Pacific, but this was not too great a threat. The Japanese, through their possession of the Marianas, Carolines, and Marshalls, held the superior geographical position in the area. Therefore, there was a need to strike at the Philippines, notwithstanding the islands' scarcity of resources and the overall lack of economic benefit likely to accrue from the occupation of the group. But the logic of the argument for attacking the Philippines led to another consideration that was important in its own right. The logic of the strategic situation dictated that Japan did not dare move southwards and leave the whole of her left flank, stretching across thousands of miles of sea, bared to an intact and alerted U.S. Pacific Fleet based at Pearl Harbor. The Pacific Fleet was the only force in the Pacific that could contest Japan's moves, and to strike an American possession without moving against the Americans per se was obviously illogical. These two strategic arguments thus reinforced the grand strategic argument in favor of an attack on the Americans in the light of the potential disparity of strength between the two nations from 1943 onwards.

Second, wherever Japan chose to strike the twin factors of speed and surprise were critical. Japan needed the raw materials of Southeast Asia quickly, urgently. Overall she had to force the issue of the war because the Japanese leadership knew that in a protracted struggle with the Americans the odds would lengthen considerably against them: conquest had to be turned to solid economic achievement and successful battle within a year or, at the outside, two years. But, in the short term, in the context of the first attacks, Japan was well aware of the need to strike at as many objectives as possible in order to make the greatest possible use of surprise and to keep the enemy nations off balance. The Americans and the British, in the east and west, had to be attacked simultaneously at the outset because if left unmolested they would be liable to increase their strengths and defenses to the point where there would be no hope of mounting a successful attack upon them. But these attacks had to be launched at the same time as those to secure the economic objectives of the campaign. Herein lay the crux of the problem for Japan. To prosecute a war over so large an area and in so many different directions at once, Japanese strength was only marginal to requirements.

The Japanese difficulty was threefold, but in fact boiled down to one very basic reality. They did not possess the necessary military, naval, and transport strengths for attacks across the whole of their intended area of conquest. The army's problem was basically the same as it had been since 1937; what precipitated the 1941 crisis in the first place was the army's overextension in Manchuria, China, and Indo-China. Manchuria swallowed up thirteen divisions and China twenty-three of Japan's fifty-one available divisions. When the requirements of home defense, Formosa, Korea, and Indo-China were taken into consideration, Japan only had eleven divisions available for service in Southeast Asia. Moreover, even though the army could genuinely point to its heavy commitment on the mainland as reason enough to explain its reluctance to earmark more forces for the south, it still harbored ambitions against and fears of the nation many of its members reckoned to be the real enemy—the USSR. Notwithstanding the events of 1938–39 and the Soviet-Japanese neutrality pact, the army wanted to be in a position to take advantage of a Soviet collapse that, in the autumn of 1941, seemed not merely a possibility but a near-certainty. On the other hand, the Japanese army was painfully aware of the danger of underestimating the Soviets and relying on Soviet good faith. The treaty of April 1941 did not result in the removal of a single regiment in Manchuria into the strategic reserve. But for the Japanese in the late summer and autumn of 1941 there was a bonus of a kind in this situation. The onset of winter would bring an effective end to the short campaign season in Siberia and Manchuria and would afford a reasonable degree of security to the Japanese if their drive on the south took place in that season.

The Japanese navy and the transport fleet faced similar problems with regard to strength, being inadequately prepared to prosecute a war over the vast expanses of the Pacific. The navy, already well established in the homeland, Formosa, Hainan, the Bonins, the Carolines, and the Marshalls, was ideally placed to attack in any direction. Indeed, one of the main initial targets, the Philippines, was all but surrounded by Japanese bases before the start of hostilities. But the strategic possibilities pulled the Imperial Navy in five different directions—towards Hawaii, Wake and Guam, the Dutch East Indies, Malaya, and lastly Burma, though the latter would be mainly an army operation with army-navy cooperation being restricted to just certain phases of the campaign. The Imperial Navy was uncomfortably aware of the fact that while tremendous opportunities presented themselves on many fronts, the navy and the transport fleets did not have the resources to tackle all possible objectives at once. Thus the navy insisted, and the army concurred, that attacks would have to be staggered.

In the summer and autumn of 1941, the Japanese army and navy came to an agreement over their long-term objectives and the means by which they were to be secured. The Japanese high command envisaged what was in effect a three-phase opening attack, the phases in certain respects being both merging and concurrent, depending on the theater of operations and the nature of the immediate objectives. The long-term aim, to be achieved after the end of the third phase, was to wear down enemy resolve and means of fighting until the enemy, tiring of struggle and losses, came to terms with the pointlessness of the conflict and the reality of Japanese conquests. The Japanese did not envisage being able to bring about the total defeat of Britain and the United States, but they calculated that the British and Americans, with their (in Japanese eyes) low resolve, would be forced to accept the fait accompli rather than fight on with little hope of success. This conclusion was not unreasonable given the seeming certainty of a German victory in Europe; indeed, the Japanese plan depended on it. In effect, the Japanese considered war in the Pacific in exactly the same light as the earlier wars against China and Russia around the turn of the century—a war that they could initiate and then limit in its conduct and aims. In global terms, the Japanese plans depended on the Anglo-Americans being engaged in two theaters, Europe and the Far East, and unable to mount effective responses in either area.

This state of affairs was to be achieved by securing a defensive perimeter around the area of Japanese conquests in each of the first three phases. In the first phase the Japanese planned to secure the first sector of their final perimeter defense between the southern tip of the Kamchatka peninsula and the Gilberts by eliminating opposition on Guam, Wake, and the Gilberts themselves. At the same time, the first phase was to be completed with the occupation of Thailand, northern Malaya, British Borneo and Sarawak, and the Philippines. From these positions the Japanese would be ideally poised to start the second phase of concurrent conquest and consolidation. This involved conquering Malaya and Singapore, taking southern Burma, and conquering the northern islands of the Dutch East Indies and the Bismarcks. In the final phase there would be a gigantic "straightening of the line" of continental proportions (some 3,000 miles) by the final reduction of Sumatra and the conquest of Java and Burma. When all this was achieved the Japanese would have been able to consolidate all their objectives behind a defensive perimeter that rested on the India-Burma border and stretched around the Nicobars and Andamans (actually added to the list of objectives after the start of the war) to pass between the Dutch East Indies and Australia and then through New Guinea and the Bismarcks and Solomons to the Gilberts and the Kuriles. The time allowed by Japanese strategic planners for the three-phase conquest of this vast area was five months.

The mechanics of the campaign were complicated, but were determined for the Japanese by the reality of American and British positions on the flanks. Dearly though the Japanese would have wished to have struck directly and immediately at the Dutch in order to secure the Indies, they could not trust to luck and hope that no Anglo-American reaction would be forthcoming. American power at Pearl Harbor and in the Philippines and the British presence at Singapore meant that the Japanese could not risk a full-scale drive in the center. In fact the Japanese never seriously considered the temptation of striking at the weak center while leaving alerted and intact enemy forces on their flanks and in the rear. Japanese commanders might wish that they could do so, and some hoped that if such a course was adopted the Americans would not move, but in the end such officers always had to come back to the unanswerable problem of the threat posed by the Americans. Similarly, the possibility of attacking the Philippines, Borneo, Java, Sumatra, and Malaya either in that or in reverse order was out of the question. Either way the Japanese might encounter in the final stages of a campaign an enemy too strong to be reduced. Thus the Japanese had to embark on a policy of first securing the outposts—such as Hong Kong, British Borneo, Brunei, and Sarawak—and clearing the flanks (Malaya, the Philippines, and Oceania) before converging on the coveted center (Java, Sumatra, and Dutch Borneo). Such a plan of campaign, however, did have the inestimable advantage of economy of effort because troops, ships, and aircraft earmarked for the initial assaults, on completion of their tasks, could be redeployed to subsequent more distant objectives. On the other hand, the scale of intended action dictated that for an assault on Pearl Harbor the main part of the Japanese naval strike force would be absent from the primary theater of operations. Such a division of force, in the face of enemies on paper stronger than Japan, was a risk of considerable proportions, but one that was shown to be well justified.

In the first phase of their operations the Japanese conceived a broad front offensive over six separate areas. These were the series of initial blows falling on Pearl Harbor in order to neutralize the U.S. Pacific Fleet; against central Thailand in order to facilitate concurrent operations against Malaya and subsequent operations against Burma; against southern Thailand and northern Malaya; against American air bases on the Philippines and a series of small-scale operations against Guam, Wake, and the Gilberts to break the American line of communications between Hawaii and Manila; and the reduction of Hong Kong. The initial assault had to be fixed for a Sunday morning in Pearl Harbor in order to catch the Americans there at their minimum degree of readiness, and then closely coordinated across some six time zones and the international date line in order to achieve maximum surprise. The impossibility of launching air strikes simultaneously from Pearl Harbor to Malaya was accepted. The initial strikes had to followed immediately by major land operations against the British and Americans because they alone might be in a position to dispute Japan's quest for supremacy in the area. The Japanese intended to follow up their air operations against the Philippines by seizing the two most important islands in the Commonwealth—Luzon and Mindanao. This would give the Japanese control of the Manila airfields and the seaplane base at Davao. These, along with the island of Jolo in the Sulu Sea (between Mindanao and Borneo) were to be the springboard for the attacks on the Dutch East Indies.

Concurrent with the Philippine operations were to be actions designed to secure British possessions on Borneo. The aim of these operations was both to secure the oil fields of the area and to secure Japanese sea communications with the south. Simultaneously, operations were to be carried out in order to eliminate Malaya and Singapore, the places from which Britain would have to operate if she was to challenge Japanese mastery of the area. During the second phase of operations, when Singapore was to be captured, the Japanese planned to secure the extremities—southern Burma and the Bismarcks. The flanks thus secured, the Japanese would then be in a position to develop their main effort in the center. This was to take the form of a three-pronged drive to burst asunder the Dutch position in the Indies, leaving the area to be conquered in detail. Driving from the South China Sea on eastern Sumatra, from the Makassar Strait on Dutch Borneo, and from the Molucca Passage on Celebes, Amboina, and Timor, the way was to be prepared for the reduction of Java and the remainder of Sumatra in the third and final phase of operations. At the same time the Nicobars, the Andamans, and the rest of Burma would be secured as the "long stop" line of defense against any British attempt to recover their losses by attacks from the Indian Ocean.

At the time of the outbreak of war the Imperial Japanese Navy consisted of 10 battleships, 6 fleet carriers, 4 light fleet carriers, 18 heavy and 20 light cruisers, 112 destroyers, and 65 submarines. In addition, the navy possessed a substantial number of smaller escorts, mine warfare vessels, auxiliaries, and tenders.

The whole of the navy, with the exception of those vessels detached for duty on the China station, came under the command of the Combined Fleet. Yamamoto was its commander after 1939. The Combined Fleet, however, was more nominal than real. For the purposes of administration and operations the fleet was never together but divided into a series of task forces. The great advantage of the Combined Fleet concept lay in its flexibility. From the various task forces (or fleets as they were sometimes called) the naval command was in a position to detach divisions from the subordinate commands to meet immediate strategic and tactical requirements.

The 1st Fleet, or Battle Force, consisted of the battleships. It was based on Hiroshima and was in effect the only part of Yamamoto's command under his immediate tactical control. Yamamoto's flagship was the *Nagato*, and later the *Yamato*. In mid-1941 the Battle Force consisted of ten battleships, four heavy cruisers, and two destroyer flotillas. Destroyer flotillas consisted of a light cruiser leader and a nominal destroyer establishment of between sixteen and twenty ships; in reality flotillas normally had about half that number of destroyers under command. The 2nd Fleet, or Scouting Force, under Admiral Shigeyoshi Inoue, was based on Hainan. This force consisted of eleven heavy cruisers and a destroyer flotilla. The 3rd Fleet, based on Formosa and under Vice Admiral Sankichi Takahashi, consisted of a single destroyer flotilla and a collection of various types of ships that enabled the fleet to live up to its alternative name, the Blockade and Transportation Force. The 4th Fleet, or Mandates Force, was based on Truk and consisted of three light cruisers and a destroyer flotilla. The 5th Fleet, or Northern Force, was a very weak detachment based on Maizuru in order to cover the waters of northern Japan. In fact, as far as the 5th Fleet was concerned, the title *Fleet* was bestowed for prestige rather than practical purposes. The 5th Fleet had been constituted in July 1939 at the height of the Japanese-Soviet confrontation. The 6th Fleet, based on Kwajalein and under Vice Admiral Shimizu, consisted of three submarine flotillas, about thirty submarines, and their tenders. In addition to the numbered fleets there was one other. This was the all-important Carrier Fleet, under Vice Admiral Chuichi Nagumo, at Kure.

For the opening operations the Combined Fleet was formed into four main task forces. What was known as the Main Body, effectively the Battle Force minus certain of its units, remained in home waters under the personal control of Yamamoto. Its role was to provide general though very distant support for the other operations though its noncommitment to battle accorded with the traditional Japanese practice of conserving main forces during hostilities. With the Main Body were the 16-inch-gun battleships *Nagato* and *Mutsu*; and the 14-inch-gun battleships *Fuso*, *Yamashiro*, *Ise*, and *Hyuga*. Two light cruisers from the 9th Cruiser Division and eight destroyers completed the Main Body.

The major part of the Combined Fleet's offensive power was formed into the Strike Force, which was to carry out the attack on Pearl Harbor. This force was formed around the 1st, 2nd, and 5th Carrier Divisions. The 1st consisted of Nagumo's flagship, the *Akagi*, and the *Kaga*; the 5th of the *Shokaku* and *Zuikaku*. The 2nd consisted of the light fleet carriers *Hiryu* and *Soryu*. In support of the carriers were two heavy seaplane cruisers, the *Tone* and *Chikuma*, from the 8th Cruiser Division; the fast battleships *Hiei* and *Kirishima* from the 3rd Battle Division; and the light cruiser *Abukuma* and nine destroyers from the 1st Destroyer Flotilla of Rear Admiral Sentaro Omori.

For the operations against Wake, Guam, and the Gilberts, Inoue was allocated the South Seas Force. This was centered on Truk under the tactical control of Rear Admiral Aritomo Goto. This force consisted of a light cruiser flagship; the heavy cruisers *Aoba, Kako, Furutaka,* and *Kinugasa* of the 6th Cruiser Division; the light cruisers *Tatsuta* and *Tenryu* of the 18th Cruiser Division; and the twelve destroyers of the 6th Flotilla. Nine submarines of the 7th Flotilla were also under Goto's command.

Numerically the greater part of the Combined Fleet was constituted into the Southern Force under Vice Admiral Nobutake Kondo. Basically this force consisted of the greater part of the 2nd and 3rd Fleets with elements of the 1st Fleet in support. The task of the Southern Force was to escort and cover the various landings in the Philippines, Malaya, Thailand, and the Dutch East Indies. The most important units with the Southern Force were the battleships *Kongo* and *Haruna* from the 3rd Battle Division and the light carriers *Zuiho* and *Taiyo* of the 4th Carrier Division. Twelve heavy cruisers from the 4th, 5th, and 7th Divisions; a light cruiser division; and four destroyer flotillas—in all four light cruisers and fifty-two destroyers—completed the surface units allocated to the southern drive. With this formidable array were three weak submarine flotillas totalling eighteen submarines. The forces under Kondo's command were entrusted with the task of securing the gains Japan had to make to have any chance of survival, but in carrying out these operations the Southern Force never acted as a unit. Instead it was divided to cover specific operations spread over thousands of square miles of ocean.

Four other groups completed the Japanese naval order of battle. There remained the naval units detached for service in China, some of which were deployed for operations against Hong Kong. A minute Northern Force of two light cruisers and two destroyers covered the waters that separated the USSR and Japan, while two light cruisers of the 3rd Carrier Division were detached for the all-important task of training replacement air crews for the Carrier Fleet. Finally, of course, there were the tenders, flagship, and the submarines of the Imperial Navy that had not been detached for service elsewhere. Thirty submarines were available to support Nagumo's strike on Pearl Harbor.

These thirty submarines were divided into three groups. First, there was a General Reconnaissance Element consisting of the *I-10* and *I-26*. These two submarines were assigned to scout the Pacific Fleet's alternative anchorages, the *I-10* at Samoa, the *I-26* in the Aleutians. Three submarines formed the second group, the Reconnaissance Element under Captain Kijiro Imaizumi. The *I-19, I-21,* and *I-23* scouted the route that Nagumo's Strike Force was to take on its way to Pearl Harbor. The third group was the Special Naval Attack Unit. This consisted of submarines from the 1st, 2nd, and 3rd Submarine Flotillas. The 1st Flotilla was made up of the *I-9, I-15, I-17,* and *I-25*. This Yokosuka-based force, under the command of

The Type B-1 scouting submarine *I-26*. She and her nineteen sisters were built and trained for fleet action, and were equipped with a single E14Y1 Glen reconnaissance seaplane or, occasionally, a Type A midget submarine, normally carried by Type C-1 attack submarines. The *I-26* was sunk in October 1944. Naval Institute Collection

Admiral Tsutomu Sato, was deployed to the north of the Hawaiian Islands, and it was joined on patrol by the three submarines from the Reconnaissance Element. To the east of Pearl Harbor were the seven submarines, *I-7*, *I-1*, *I-2*, *I-3*, *I-4*, *I-5*, and *I-6*, of Rear Admiral Shigeaki Yazazaki's Yokosuka-based 2nd Flotilla. Rear Admiral Shigeyoski Miwa's 3rd Flotilla from Kwajalein, with the *I-8*, *I 68*, *I-69*, *I-70*, *I-71*, *I-72*, *I-73*, *I-74*, and *I-75*, was deployed to the south of Oahu on patrol. There its nine submarines were to be joined on patrol by Captain Hanku Sasaki's Special Attack Unit. This unit consisted of the *I-16*, *I-18*, *I-20*, *I-22*, and *I-24*, all of which carried a midget submarine that the Japanese planned to use against Pearl Harbor. In fact these five submarines were to join the others without being able to recover their midgets, none of which registered any success.

The task of the submarines was threefold. First, they were to gather intelligence of American naval movements. One of them did scout the Pacific Fleet's alternative Hawaiian anchorage at Lahaina Roads off Maui on 6 December. Second, they were charged with rupturing American communications between the Hawaiian Islands and the mainland. Third, the submarines were to pick off American warships that attempted to break out of Pearl Harbor after Nagumo's attack. In all these roles the submarines were operating strictly in accordance with Japanese thinking on submarine warfare and, specifically, the use of light units on the forward edge of the battle area. The role of the submarines was to equalize the strength of the two sides by exacting a steady attrition of enemy ships; and within the Japanese naval command there were many officers who expected the submarines and the midget submarines to register greater success than Nagumo's aircraft.

From this summary of the Japanese naval deployment in late 1941 one can immediately appreciate one of the Imperial Navy's strengths and weaknesses at that time. For the opening of hostilities it was committed to the offensive, but at the expense of effectively emptying the strategic reserve. The Japanese navy committed its forces with an élan that came perilously close to rashness. The navy had to commit everything to a single roll of the dice, and such was its overcommitment that there was virtually no margin for error. That being said, it must be freely admitted that the Japanese navy had made very accurate calculations regarding its own and enemy forces in the opening phase of the war: it had the measure of its enemies and knew it.

Such was the deployment of the surface ships and submarines of the Imperial Navy at the outbreak of war. In their support operated the naval air forces, the effectiveness of which came as a very bad shock to enemies whose view of Japanese air power generally was colored by the crudest racism. Before the war, despite the freely available evidence of the China campaign, Japanese aviation was consistently denigrated in Western countries. Japanese aircrews and aircraft were considered utterly inferior to those of white nations. In fact they were superior, as the Japanese quickly demonstrated. The Imperial Navy deployed two air fleets. The 1st Air Fleet was the elite and served with the carriers. The other, the 11th Air Fleet, was a land-based expeditionary force that was divided between Formosa and French Indo-China. Two of the fleet's flotillas, the 21st and 23rd, were in Formosa to support operations against the Philippines, while the 22nd Flotilla was in Indo-China to carry out operations against Thailand, Malaya, and Burma. The 22nd, however, was reinforced before the outbreak of war by a group of aircraft from the 21st and by a special draft of aircraft that had been attached to headquarters, 21st Flotilla. This meant that with about 200 aircraft at its disposal in Indo-China, the 22nd was not much weaker than the two Formosa-based formations. Overall both the 1st and 11th Air Fleets totalled about 500 aircraft. Several small detachments were stationed in the Mandates and Japan.

For the invasion of Southeast Asia the Japanese army created the *Southern Army*, commanded by General Count Hisaichi Terauchi, with its headquarters at Saigon. The *Southern Army* had under its command four separate armies. The *14th Army* was detailed for the invasion of the Philippines; the *15th Army* was ordered to secure Thailand; the *16th Army* was earmarked for the conquest of the Dutch East Indies; and the *25th Army* was allocated to the Malayan venture. In addition to these armies the Japanese high command detailed the *38th Infantry Division* from Lieutenant General Takashi Sakai's *23rd Army* in southern China for the attack on Hong Kong and allocated Major General Tomitaro Horii's *55th Regimental Group*, from the *55th Infantry Division*, for operations against Guam, Wake, the Gilberts, the Bismarcks, and New Guinea. The latter formation consisted of the reinforced *144th Infantry Regiment* and was generally known as the *South Seas Detachment*.

The *14th Army*, under the command of Lieutenant General Masaharu Honma, consisted of the *16th Infantry Division*, based in the Ryukyus; the *48th Infantry Division* and the *65th Independent Infantry Brigade*, both stationed in Formosa; and the *56th Regimental Group*, which was divided between the Pescadores and Palau. Thus, for the attack on the Philippines, the Japanese were well placed with major formations to the north and east of the objective. In immediate support of the *14th Army's* operations were the *5th Air Division* and those parts of the 11th Air Fleet based on Formosa. The strength of the military air formation was about 300 aircraft.

The *25th Army*, under the command of Lieutenant General Hobum Yamashita, was made up of four divisions. Two divisions, the *5th Infantry Division* and the *18th Infantry Division*, were veterans of China, but the other two formations were untried. These were the *Imperial Guards Division*, which was in Indo-China, and the newly raised *56th Infantry Division*, which was in Japan. In fact Yamashita was so distrustful of the raw *56th Division* that he dispensed with its services altogether. As a result it did not see service in Malaya before it arrived in Burma to take part in the middle and final stages of the conquest of that country. But Yamashita was given the use of the *143rd Infantry Regiment* from the *55th Infantry Division*, part of the *15th Army*, to protect the rear and flank of his army's landings in the southern part of the Kra Isthmus. Air support for the *25th Army* was provided by the specially strengthened *3rd Air Division*, with about 450 aircraft, and the reinforced 22nd Air Flotilla. Yamashita was not given control of the operations against British Borneo; these were conducted under the direct control of the *Southern Army*.

The *14th* and *25th* were the only front-line armies under the command of the *Southern Army* at the time of the outbreak of war. The other two armies were really no more than cadres because their operations were largely dependent on the initial operations of Honma's and Yamashita's forces. The *15th Army*, based in Indo-China under the command of Lieutenant General Shojiro Iida, was to secure Thailand, but at the start of the war this formation consisted of only the *55th Infantry Division*, part of which was allocated to Yamashita while another part had been detailed for operations in the central Pacific. Nevertheless, in the course of the campaign the *15th Army* was reinforced for its operations in Burma by the *33rd Infantry Division* from China and then the *18th Infantry Division* (from Yamashita's *25th Army* in Malaya) and the scorned *56th Infantry Division*. The *5th Air Division* was to support the *15th Army* once the main American resistance in the Philippines was broken.

The task of reducing the Dutch East Indies was entrusted to Lieutenant General Hitoshi Imamura's *16th Army*. The *2nd Infantry Division* was earmarked for the *16th Army*, as were the *38th Infantry Division*, after it had taken Hong Kong; the *48th Infantry Division*, after it had taken Manila; and the *56th Regimental Group*, after it had secured Jolo. The *16th Army* deployed special reinforcements of marines and paratroopers. Air cover for its operations was to be provided by the 21st and 23rd Air Flotillas, after they broke the Americans in the Philippines. During the course of operations both light and fleet carriers were deployed to support the *16th Army*.

Both on paper and in reality the Japanese armed forces in December 1941 were formidable. Their quality was enhanced by the fact that they were grossly underrated by their potential enemies. The quality of the Imperial Navy, in particular, was extremely impressive. Indeed, it can be argued that qualitatively and in terms of fighting effectiveness the Imperial Navy was second to none in 1941. The Imperial Army, though lacking the sophistication and mechanization of Western armies, was long on battle experience, leadership, discipline, and morale. Nevertheless, as in any military forces, there were weaknesses, both in the armed services and in their supporting agencies; and these must be considered in conjunction with their strengths.

The first and most important of the various weaknesses was the latent division between the army and the navy. There was no genuine Ministry of Defense or joint planning organization whose task was to formulate policy and then supervise its implementation by the two services. Though the army and navy concurred in the strategy of 1941, there was no long-term coincidence of views between the continental-minded army and a navy that looked to the south and east. Relations between the two services were normally icily correct, rather than cordial. One gains the distinct impression that each service regarded the other, rather than the Americans, British, Chinese, and Dutch, as the real enemy. The navy was particularly scathing and disdainful of the army's China venture, which many naval officers felt to have needlessly brought Japan to a crisis of which they wanted no part. The navy despised the army as boorish and ignorant; the army was unimpressed by the navy's caution, conservatism, and insatiable demand for funds and steel. The differences between the two were to be concealed as long as the Japanese were on the offensive, as long as they were imposing their will on their enemies, but the divisions were to widen considerably under the impact of failure and defeat. It is worth noting that Tojo's initial reaction to the news of the Midway defeat was a waspish self-satisfaction that the navy had been defeated in an action that the army had opposed. Significantly, the navy failed to inform him of the full details of the defeat. With such touchy relations between the two services, it was a wonder that there was ever any cooperation between them.

If, however, the Imperial Navy was qualitatively most impressive, the problem for the navy was that quantity did not match quality. The navy was good as far as it went, but unfortunately for the Japanese that was not far enough. The Imperial Navy was so finely tempered that it was brittle.

In no aspect was this more true than with regard to the naval air force and particularly the carrier aviation. The air force of 1941 was of exceptionally high quality. The navy's aircrews were intensely trained and had combat experience from China. Its aircraft, similarly, were of outstanding quality. With the A6M2 Zero-sen fighter the Japanese had a carrier fighter that could at least match any land-based fighter in service with the Allies. Though time would reveal that it did have weaknesses in performance, the Zero-sen was superior in almost every respect to any British or American naval fighter. Yet there were neither men nor machines available to replace losses. There was to be no effective replacement for the Zero-sen, with the result that the A6M2, though changed slightly through a series of models, remained in service right up until the end of the war. All the subsequent models suffered debilitating problems during their development, and at the end of the war the Zero-sen was totally outclassed by American naval aircraft. Japan's aviation industry was never in a position to build aircraft in the numbers needed to meet demand.

Likewise, the training schools lacked the facilities to train pilots to a level of skill that would enable them to survive and inflict losses on the enemy. Even before the Battle of the Coral Sea Yamamoto was warned of the declining quality of replacement aircrews. Even in the initial stages of the war, when combat losses were relatively light, the naval training schools

The most numerous of Japanese fighters, the Zero-sen. In 1941–42 the Zero-sen swept aside all opposition in Southeast Asia. Shown in the foreground is a successor to the 1941 version, an A6M5 Model 52a from the 653rd Kokutai from the *Zuikaku*. Autumn 1944. U.S. Navy

simply lacked the facilities to cover losses. When American resistance in the air began to harden and Japan began to suffer the inevitable high loss rates, the result was disastrous. An indication of the pressure on resources and the resultant inadequate state of training can be gauged by the estimate that 60 percent of all air losses in 1941 and 1942 were sustained outside of combat, mainly in training and ferrying. The drastic qualitative decline of Japanese aircrews was becoming evident by the end of 1942; it was patently obvious by 1943. One of the major factors in Japan's recourse to suicide air attacks during 1944 was the simple fact that Japanese pilots were so poorly trained that only through such tactics could they hope to achieve any results whatsoever. The air fleets of 1941 were good, but there was not the strength in depth needed to fight a sustained campaign of attrition.

For the most part what the Japanese navy did possess in 1941 was superb. The quality of the navy's ships was most impressive, and the crews were well trained. Losses on exercises were heavy, mainly as a result of intensive use of rough seas in the northern Pacific. The losses were justified by a formidable standard of seamanship and fighting ability. The battleships were good, reliable ships, extensively modernized and refitted in the interwar period. The relatively small size of the navy meant that it had been able to rebuild its ships in a manner matched only by a few of the battleships in the British and American navies. In terms of quality, Japanese battleships were a match for their American and British counterparts, though with the new *Yamato* and *Musashi*, completed soon after the start of the war, the Japanese sought to offset American numerical superiority by a qualitative superiority that could not be challenged. This was achieved with ships with a deep load displacement of 75,500 tons. The two superbattleships carried a main armament of nine 18.1-inch guns, capable of firing a 3,000-pound shell nearly 27 miles. They carried a main armored belt up to 16-inches thick and turret face armor over 25-inches thick. Capable of steaming at 27 knots, these exceptionally graceful ships, complete with depressed forward turret, flared bow, clear lines, and elegant streamlining, were the most powerful battleships ever built. Yet they had their weaknesses, not least of which were the many exposed secondary and tertiary guns and the inadequate fire control arrangements. In the final analysis, these ships marked the point where perfection passed into obsolescence, because the design and building of such ships had been superseded by developments in naval aviation.

Japanese naval aviation was similarly impressive. Japanese carrier theory and practice in no way lagged behind that of the Americans, and was considerably in advance of that of the Royal Navy, though, like the Americans, the Japanese had not settled the vital questions of task force composition and defensive tactics for carriers. These were to prove crucial weaknesses at the Coral Sea and Midway. But the Japanese had developed

The 72,809-ton battleship *Yamato* on trials, 30 October 1941. Built on the "bigger and better" principle, she was intended to be larger and superior in armament, protection, and speed to any contemporary American battleship. She was sunk 7 April 1945 off Okinawa. National Archives 80-G-704702

an awesome array of formidable aircraft for specific tasks—fighters, bombers, and reconnaissance planes—that was superior to that of any other nation at the time. The *Shokaku* and *Zuikaku*, laid down in 1937 and completed in 1941 as direct counterparts of the *Yorktown* and *Enterprise*, were not surpassed until the middle of the Pacific war with the emergence of the *Essex* class. The Japanese carriers, each with between fifty-three and seventy-two aircraft, were formidable in both attack and defense.

With the lighter forces, both heavy and light cruisers and fleet destroyers, the Japanese consistently built extremely powerful, well-balanced ships, though their numbers were obviously limited by the lack of mass-production techniques. The 8-inch-gun heavy cruisers were uniformly ferocious beasts. These were fast, well-armed ships whose emphasis on speed and gun power was achieved at not too great a price in defensive power. The capacity of some of the cruisers to absorb punishment was quite outstanding. The *Aoba*, for example, was raked at the Battle of Cape Esperance in 1942 and utterly devastated, but she was able to escape and make her way to safety under her own power. Similar resilience was exhibited by the *Mogami*, which started as a light cruiser but was rearmed and improved in the course of her career to assume the dignity of heavy cruiser status. She survived almost crippling damage at Midway and was finally sunk by the Japanese themselves in 1944 during the Leyte action after she had been devastated by battleship and cruiser fire, bombing, and an accidental ramming. Japanese destroyers also exhibited certain outstanding features. As early as 1927 the Japanese had begun to equip their destroyers with enclosed dual-purpose main armament. Such equipment did not enter American service until well into the Pacific war. With the 3.9-inch dual-purpose gun first mounted in the *Akitsuki* class, the Japanese had a weapon that could outrange the contemporary American 5-inch gun.

The *Suzuya*, third ship of the *Mogami* class of light cruisers. Among the most heavily armed and fastest cruisers ever built by any nation, she and her sister ships were regunned with 8-inch main armament in 1939 and 1940. She was sunk 25 October 1944. Robert Hunt Library

Submarines, however, were not one of the strong points of the Imperial Navy. While the submarines that were built were generally satisfactory, too great an effort was made in diversification and experimentation. The wartime dalliance with the monstrous 6,500-ton *STo* class was a scandalous waste of precious resources. Moreover, with the emphasis on using submarines for deep reconnaissance and action against enemy battle units—in order to weaken the enemy's main force to a point where the main action could be fought on equal terms—Japanese submarine doctrine was grievously in error. Japanese submarines were forced to concentrate against enemy strength rather than weakness, and suffered heavily in doing so.

But while the quality of ships was at the very least good, certain aspects of weaponry and battle training were absolutely outstanding. The Japanese laid great stress on night fighting and were thoroughly prepared to engage in this most hazardous form of battle. Japanese optics and pyrotechnics were of very high quality, far superior to anything that the Americans and British possessed. But the most marked Japanese advantage was with the Type 93 torpedo, better known as the Long Lance, that entered service in 1933. This was a fearsome weapon, and subsequent modifications produced a torpedo (Type 95) never really to be equalled by NATO navies in the first twenty-five years of that alliance's existence. These torpedoes were fuelled by compressed oxygen and kerosene, making their research and development a decidedly dangerous process but one that reaped its reward in the form of a wakeless torpedo with a speed of up to 49 knots. With a half-ton warhead, the Long Lance had a range of 24 miles at 39 knots or 12 miles at 49 knots. Contemporary British and American torpedoes, with warheads of one-third of a ton, were pressed to cover 3.5 miles at 46 knots or 5 miles in 10 minutes. The revelation of the quality of Japanese equipment and fighting ability came as a nasty shock to the unsuspecting Allies in 1942.

Nevertheless, there were both material and doctrinal weaknesses in the Imperial Navy's position. Two of these weaknesses are of concern at this point. The first was the lack of research and development, particularly in such matters as replacement aircraft and, most seriously, in radar. The weaknesses with regard to the latter were to take time to show themselves. In the early part of the war Japanese warships without radar consistently outfought Allied warships with radar, particularly at night when first sighting should have given the Allies a distinct advantage. But thereafter the weakness of the Japanese in the radar field became increasingly pronounced as Japanese fighting efficiency declined with losses and American effectiveness increased with hard-won battle experience.

The second major weakness of the Imperial Navy was with respect to the supply fleet. The Japanese, like the Americans, had given considerable thought to and made great efforts in developing a supply fleet during the interwar period, but the Japanese interest had not been so marked as that of the Americans because they assumed that any campaign against the Americans would be fought in waters relatively near Japan. Until Yamamoto became commander of the Combined Fleet, the Japanese planned to fight in the Marianas-Carolines area. Yamamoto widened this area to include the Marshalls, and then extended the battle area to the Hawaiian Islands. The Japanese plan of campaign in 1941 of necessity envisaged a widening naval campaign fought further from Japan than anything that had been previously contemplated. This imposed intolerable strains on the capacity of Japan's very limited supply fleet. An indication of Japan's weakness on this count can be seen by the fact that she went to war with but ten oilers of the *Shiretoko* class—a total of about 140,000 tons. It was a measure of Japan's industrial weakness that in the course of the war only four more naval oilers were constructed or converted. Orders for forty-one oilers were given, but had to be cancelled. This, in a sense, was an accurate comment not merely on Japanese industry but also on the Imperial Navy: as with her air fleets, the navy lacked the strength in depth needed to sustain a major war effort prosecuted over a vast area and for a long duration.

The most crucial weaknesses of the Imperial Navy, however, lay in the sinews of maritime power, in elements often neglected and underrated when set against the more photogenic fighting ships, but nevertheless fully as crucial to the war effort. These elements of sea power were the mercantile fleet and the shipyards, both of which were alarmingly inadequate in terms of Japan's immediate and long-term requirements.

What is often not realized about the Pearl Harbor attack is that as a direct consequence of it (i.e., going to war) Japan effectively lost about 2,750,000 tons of merchant shipping. Japan, like Britain, is an island empire, totally dependent on the sea for survival. Transporting troops and materiel to theaters of war, feeding a large domestic population, and general trade all were utterly dependent on the sea and merchant shipping. Before the war Japan needed 10,000,000 tons of oceanic shipping of all types to meet her needs, but she had under her own flag only about 6,000,000 tons. About 40 percent of all Japan's requirements had to be carried in foreign bottoms, mainly in Allied ships. Except for those that she could capture or salvage, the Japanese lost the use of these ships. In the first six or seven months of the Pacific war Japan captured about 1,250,000 tons of Allied shipping. Thus the amount of merchant shipping available to Japan at the start of the war declined drastically at the very moment when her commitments and needs increased.

There was an added rider to this situation in that, at a time when not a single ship could be regarded as expendable, from her own resources Japan was in no position to make good even these losses; still less was she able to make good her subsequent losses. The Imperial Navy calculated that the annual merchantmen losses would be between 800,000 and 1,000,000 tons; it expected an annual construction program of 600,000 tons. In fact the situation was even more serious than these figures would suggest. Because Japanese shipyards were small and for the most part inefficient, Japan was not in a position to undertake large-scale construction and heavy refitting programs at the same time. The demands of new construction for the Imperial Navy meant that in December 1941 one ship in eight in the mercantile fleet was out of service because the shipyards lacked the means to attend to them. Other merchantmen therefore had to have their repairs and refits deferred, with the inevitable result that in time the number of merchantmen inoperative because of overdue maintenance rose considerably. By 1943 one merchantman in six was out of commission. Such a situation was tantamount to a wasting terminal illness, one without cure or even possibility of relief. From this basic circumstance stemmed one fundamental flaw in the argument for an extended perimeter defense. The lack of new construction and proper maintenance of vessels made the Japanese ability to sustain their scattered garrisons and, most critically, to transport substantial forces rapidly from one theater to another, very precarious. In time, as losses mounted, that ability was to become nonexistent, or nearly so.

The weaknesses of the merchant fleet and the shipyards were compounded by certain basic misunderstandings and confusion over priorities on the part of the Imperial Navy. These had immense repercussions because they led the navy to cling to dubious tactical doctrines at a time when mounting reverses should have prompted the search for fresh tactical initiatives in an effort to avert defeat. The most serious of these stemmed from the fact that the Imperial Navy was committed to a doctrine of the offensive battle with the U.S. Pacific Fleet. This state of affairs had two consequences, first, in the type of ship built for the navy, and second, in the degree of emphasis placed on escorts for merchant shipping.

The notion of offensive action and battle resulted in a basic focus on the battle fleet, but at the expense of a balanced force. The *Yamato*, *Musashi*, and later the giant carrier *Shinano* were built only at the cost of diverting resources from desperately needed construction in other fields, particularly small escorts on which the defense of trade depended. This, of course, was a reflection of the wider problem that the Japanese were attempting to do too much on too narrow an industrial base. It was also a reflection of the wider insoluble Japanese dilemma and the impossibility of her strategic situation in a war with the United States, but the fact that no destroyer escorts were launched between 1941 and 1943 by Japanese shipyards— compared to the 331 launched by the Americans, all but 25 in 1943—points to the utter neglect by the Japanese of this most vital aspect of their defenses. The importance of merchant shipping was simply not appreciated. The defense of merchantmen was held in very low esteem by a navy committed to offensive action. The result for Japan was ultimately disastrous, because the failure to provide adequate escort for merchantmen resulted in rising losses and falling imports. This in turn resulted in industry, particularly the steel industry, running short of raw materials, which in turn led to the shipyards being unable to build ships, even though the yards were working greatly under capacity. In this way the vicious circle was completed, because the lack of production of warships and merchantmen inevitably led to further drops in import and production levels. By 1943-44 Japanese industry was working at a vastly reduced capacity at the very time when every effort was needed to maintain the existing, though inadequate, strengths of the imperial and merchant fleets.

The Japanese army, on the other hand, possessed many attributes and strengths, but every point of strength in the final analysis went back to the hardness of the individual soldier. Much has been written about the ordinary Japanese soldier, and it is not proposed to add much to what has been set down elsewhere other than to observe that whether in attack or defense, the Japanese army showed a stolid insensitivity to suffering and losses, both its own and those of the enemy, that is difficult to comprehend even against the background of the Samurai-Bushido code.

The Western reader will have noted immediately from the Japanese army's order of battle in Southeast Asia that the corps does not appear in the Japanese military structure, the chain of command running directly from army to division. But equally apparent is the fact that the standard orga-

nization within the army was the infantry division and that there were no
armored, artillery, cavalry, and airborne divisions—a fact that reflected
Japanese strength in, and reliance upon, human as opposed to material
factors. Infantry was the backbone of the Japanese army, and it should be
noted, if only in passing, that armor languished and was by contemporary
standards unsophisticated and poorly equipped. Artillery, on the other
hand, was plentiful and of good quality, with emphasis on howitzers rather
than field guns. The support services—supply, transport, maintenance,
and medical—were run on a shoestring, and were barely adequate to meet
requirements, though the engineer branch was exceptionally well trained
and equipped.

There is one immediate problem in trying to give an outline of the
divisional organization within the Japanese army. That difficulty arises
from the fact that after 1937 major structural changes were introduced. As a
result, considerable diversity existed between divisions because the process
of change from square divisions with four infantry regiments to triangular
divisions with three formations was far from complete by 1941. In addition,
of course, though the basic foundation within the Japanese army was the
infantry division, there was the complication of specialist units, such as
mountain divisions, garrison divisions, and alternate establishments for the
standard infantry unit and formation. But, overall, the normal infantry
division committed to operations in Southeast Asia in 1941 and 1942
consisted of about 18,000 officers and men under the command of a major
general, though it was not unusual for a division to be commanded by a
lieutenant general. The most important part of a division was its infantry
group, commanded normally by a major general, with three regiments,
each with three battalions. Each battalion in a full-strength unit possessed
an organic artillery group of two 2.8-inch howitzers and four rifle companies and a machine-gun company. The group had under its command an
artillery unit of twelve 6-inch howitzers, while the division itself had an
artillery regiment of three battalions, its typical strength being twelve
3-inch field guns and twenty-four 4.2-inch howitzers. With each full-
strength infantry regiment numbering about 3,000 rifles and the equivalent
of five battalions of artillery in each division, the basic formation in the
Japanese army represented a formidable and well-balanced fighting force,
all the more so when it is remembered that every Japanese soldier, irrespective of branch and trade, was first and foremost an infantryman.

The support services within a Japanese division were minimal. One
example of the narrowness of Japanese administrative margins was the
unnecessary losses suffered in the Philippines campaign because of the
inadequate medical facilities at divisional and army levels. The administrative margins on which the Japanese worked were always precarious, but in
operations that were well planned, as in Malaya, both the infantry and the

supporting arms and services could perform extremely well. The Japanese engineers in the course of the Malayan campaign rebuilt 250 bridges, an average of 5 a day. This was an indication of the skill, application, and sufficiency of supporting arms—and of the planning and intelligence branches. The success of the engineers stemmed from the fact that their needs had been carefully considered in the light of detailed reconnaissance reports, but this type of preparation and success was very short-lived. One cannot ignore the simple fact that not a single operation planned after the start of the war met with success. The value of superb intelligence, more-over, was a wasting asset. Once Japan went to war most of the intelligence sources that had paved the way for the early victories were lost to her. Japan fought the final stages of the war with very little in the way of good intelligence.

The effectiveness of the Japanese army, and its intelligence and planning branches before the start of the war, can be gauged by the fact that a mere eleven of its divisions overran the whole of Southeast Asia, defeating and in the process humiliating forces much larger than themselves. That this should be so speaks highly of the army's state of preparation at the time of the outbreak of hostilities; in 1941 the Japanese army had taken the measure of its enemies. It had correctly assessed their strengths and weaknesses, and it had been thorough and painstaking in its preparations. Yet even in success it cannot be denied that the seeds of weakness and self-destruction were evident. The keys to success were the infantry and morale—the irresistible fury of *Nihon Seishin*. The infantrymen were superb. During the drive to the south the Japanese infantry proved outstanding in infiltration tactics, rapid movement, and camouflage. Its jungle craft, perfected since 1934 on Formosa in a school that combined training with the practical experience of exterminating primitive aboriginal tribes of the interior, was far beyond anything even considered possible on the Allied side. On the battlefield itself the Japanese army exhibited both a bravery and a barbarity that made it effective and feared. Many armies in the course of the Second World War were given orders to hold positions to the last man and last round. Only in the Japanese army were such orders superfluous; they were literally carried out as normal operational procedure. Yet the very morale that sustained the Japanese in the advance gave rise to a casual and blind cruelty at almost every turn, and these actions ensured a lasting enmity on the part of subject peoples who might have been won over with decent treatment. What made the Japanese such formidable conquerors prevented them from becoming effective consolidators. The Japanese army lived by the sword, and its problems were insuperable once the sword became blunted.

One of the great strengths of the Japanese military system was its curious combination of rigidity and flexibility. The rigidity stemmed from the

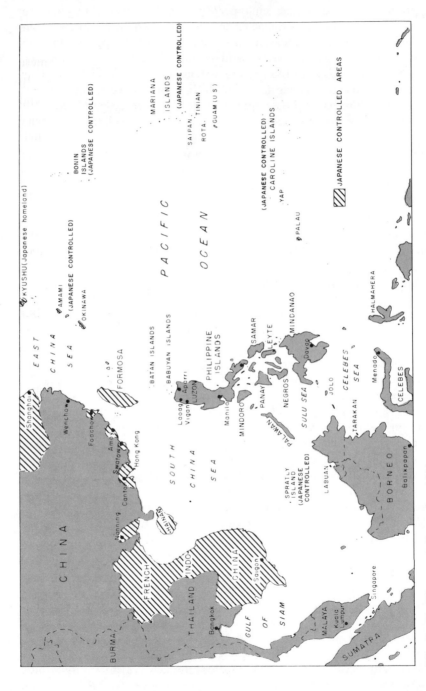

The Pacific Theater, 7 December 1941

selection of a given aim and the flexibility from the chain of command in carrying out orders. Devolution from above was very pronounced, with much initiative and discretion given to the middle and lower echelons with regard to the execution of orders. Forces were allotted to a task and left with a great deal of latitude as to how to fulfill the set objectives. The system worked well in the opening phase of the war, when the Japanese faced unprepared, and to be blunt poor, opposition. But when the tide of war began to change and then started to flow strongly against the Japanese, the weaknesses of the system became clearer. At every level of command there was a basic lack of realism and an unwillingness to concede defeat or a reverse, even at the cost of prolonging an effort and suffering casualties far in excess of the tactical or strategic value of an objective. The clearest example of this was to come in 1944 in the battles around Kohima and Imphal, where any sensible commander would have broken off battle rather than persist, at the price of ruining his forces, in an operation that simply could not bring about victory. Moreover, the novel notion of feeding an attacking army by making its initial objectives its enemy's messes has much to recommend it, but it is hardly the basis on which sustained campaigns can be fought.

The best single appreciation of the Japanese army, its strengths, and its weaknesses, is provided in *Defeat into Victory* by one of Britain's finest soldiers, Field Marshal Lord Slim. Slim suffered the humiliation of defeat at the hands of the Japanese in Burma in 1942. But with very few resources, great patience, and a superlative skill that was matched only by his humility, Slim was able to turn the tables. In 1944 he inflicted on the Japanese army what was until that time the greatest defeat in its history. He wrote,

> The Japanese . . . gained the moral ascendancy over us. . . . They bought that initiative, fairly and inevitably, by paying for it with preparation. . . . The Japanese were ruthless and bold as ants while their designs went well, but if their plans were disturbed or thrown out—ant-like again—they fell into confusion, were slow to re-adjust themselves, and invariably clung too long to their original schemes. This, to commanders with their unquenchable military optimism, which rarely allowed in their narrow administrative margins for any setback or delay, was particularly dangerous. The fundamental fault of their generalship was a lack of moral, as distinct from physical courage. They were not prepared to admit that they had made a mistake, that their plans had misfired and needed recasting. . . . Rather than confess that, they passed on to their subordinates, unchanged, the orders that they themselves had received, well knowing that with the resources available the tasks demanded were impossible. Time and again, this blind passing of responsibility ran down a chain of disaster. . . . It is true that in war determination by itself may achieve results while flexibility, without determination in reserve, cannot, but it is only the blending of the two that brings final success. . . . They scored highly by determination; they paid heavily for lack of flexibility.

The strength of the Japanese Army lay, not in its higher leadership, which, once its career of success had been checked, became confused . . . but in the spirit of the individual soldier. He fought and marched until he died. If five hundred Japanese were ordered to hold a position, we had to kill 495 before it was ours—and then the last five killed themselves. It was this combination of obedience and ferocity that made the Japanese Army, whatever its condition, so formidable.*

It is hard to find a shorter and more astute analysis of the Japanese army than these observations by the commander of the British 14th Army in Burma.

*Slim, *Defeat into Victory*, pp. 526–27.

The Situation and Strategy of the Allied Nations

AT THE OUTBREAK of the Pacific war the Allied nations did not possess, either individually or collectively, a defined and reasoned plan of campaign for dealing with Japanese aggression. In the place of a deliberately conceived strategy reigned confusion, unreality, and weakness, shrouded by wishful thinking. Of no nation was this more true than Britain. British policy can be defined as the three hopes: that war could be averted and matters would not come to a conflict; that if war did break out the Japanese would not do too much damage; and that if there was a war then the Americans would be able to pull the chestnuts out of the fire. The Americans were much more realistic, and they were quietly and correctly confident that if it came to a conflict they would win, but American strategy was nevertheless riddled with ambiguities and inconsistencies.

For the Allies the fundamental problem in 1941, as events began to assume an ominous hue, was essentially political. Neither the Americans nor the British were clear in their own minds whether their policy was one of deterrence or defense. The success of either was denied the Allies by one simple fact. The British and Dutch were belligerents; the United States was neutral. The United States naturally was set against binding commitments to belligerents at a time when she was at peace, and she was not prepared to enter into arrangements with the two nations in Southeast Asia. The Americans naturally wished to hold the power of making decisions regarding the Pacific and the Far East in their own hands; in the course of 1941 they failed to appreciate that their own actions allowed the power of making decisions to pass to Imperial General Headquarters in Tokyo. What the Americans were not prepared to do was enter into an open-ended commitment to the defense of British and Dutch possessions in Southeast Asia. The American public could never have swallowed an American underwriting of the imperialistic interests of the two European nations. Yet the only way to have deterred Japan, if indeed in 1941 Japan could have been deterred, would have been for the Americans to have endorsed publicly the status quo in the Far East and to have made its violation the casus belli. The only means of producing a viable policy of defense would have been to ensure proper coordination of American, British, and Dutch resources in order to conceal the weaknesses of individual states at that time. But neither of these courses was open to the Allied nations before the outbreak of war. By then, of course, deterrence had failed, and the chance of forming an effective defense had evaporated.

Nevertheless, the American failure to move decisively on these matters in 1941 cannot simply be dismissed as erroneous, unrealistic, and myopic. Two vital considerations governed American strategic deliberations during 1941, and time was to vindicate both. The most pertinent of these was the belief, first spelled out in November 1938 in staff assessments, that Germany posed the most serious long-term threat to the security of the United States. Subsequent events merely served to convince Americans of the gravity of the threat posed by a Europe under the heel of the German jackboot. The Americans were convinced, much to British relief, that if they were associated with Britain in a two-ocean war, their major effort and first priority had to be in the Atlantic and Europe. Even as the Pacific situation deteriorated with alarming rapidity, the Americans never wavered from this fundamental belief. Despite the Pacific situation, the American commitment in the Atlantic grew remorselessly during 1941. Had it not been for increasing American benevolence, Britain would have gone under in that year. This benevolent commitment, however, could only be made at a price. It would be achieved only at the expense of America's own rearmament programs and at the cost of not reinforcing those forces already in the Pacific on the scale needed to match the seriousness of the situation developing in the Far East.

The American concern and involvement in the Atlantic, at a time of deepening crisis in the Far East, is explicable only in the light of the second consideration. This was the certainty of being able to defeat Japan. Of this the Americans were absolutely convinced. In 1941 they thought in terms of standing on the defensive in the Pacific in the event of war. They were aware of their manifest inability to conduct offensive operations in the Atlantic and Pacific at that time. But the American high command was aware that such a time would come. The problem was that the provisions of the Two-Ocean Naval Expansion Act of June 1940 were not scheduled to be completed before 1946. At a cost of $4 billion, 7 battleships, 18 carriers, 27 cruisers, 115 destroyers, and 43 submarines would be added to the 358 major units already in commission and the 130 under construction. The Americans knew exactly what this meant, as, indeed, did the Japanese. It meant that in time the Americans would become too strong to be attacked by the Japanese—and this, of course, was a positive incentive for the Japanese to preempt such a situation. Chief of Naval Operations Admiral Harold N. Stark lived up to his name when he spoke of the certainty of American power. He warned the sober and pessimistic Japanese ambassador, Admiral Kichisaburo Nomura, that "While you may have your intitial successes due to timing and surprise, the time will come when you too will have your losses, but there will be this great difference. You will not only be unable to make up your losses but will grow weaker as time goes on; while on the other hand we will not only make up our losses but will grow stronger as time goes on. It is inevitable that we shall crush you before we are through with you."*

The real sadness of Stark's prophecy was that it was made to a man who knew its truth. Like many of his naval colleagues, Nomura was well aware of the power of the United States and feared the outcome of a conflict with the Americans. Unfortunately Nomura and his like-minded colleagues were not the people with the power of decision. Stark's comments, however, did nothing for the immediate situation. Statistics on the launchings of major naval units by the United States between 1 January 1930 and 2 September 1945 indicate the basis for Stark's confidence and the correctness of his judgment.

In the interwar period Britain did not have a defense policy for the Far East; after the outbreak of the European war she admitted as much. What masqueraded as a strategy or policy was a series of utterances characterized more by illusion than by any grip on reality. The illusions, procrastinations, and weaknesses of what was portrayed as policy became increasingly obvious with the passing of time.

British attention to the state of her Far East interests and defenses revived with the end of the First World War. For the duration of that war the British had been forced to rely on diplomacy and the power of their Japanese ally to safeguard British concerns in the Far East. The revelation of Japanese intentions towards China in 1915 and the open displays in wartime Japan of Anglophobia and pro-German sentiment naturally caused concern in Britain. Despite the existence of the Anglo-Japanese alliance and the British desire to maintain it, after the end of the war Britain

---

*Morton, *Strategy and Command*, p. 125.

NAVAL UNITS LAUNCHED BY THE UNITED STATES, 1 JANUARY 1930 TO 2 SEPTEMBER 1945

Year	Battleships	Battle cruisers	Fleet carriers	Light fleet carriers	Escort carriers	Heavy cruisers	Light cruisers	Destroyers	Destroyer escorts	Submarines
1930						3				1
1931						1				
1932						1				1
1933			1			5				2
1934								6		
1935			2			1		15		4
1936						1	3	17		5
1937						1	3	10		6
1938							3	15		6
1939			1					15		6
1940	2		1					17		10
1941	3				2		6	27		15
1942	3		3	3	15	2	8	119	25	41
1943	1	2	5	6	25	2	7	98	306	67
1944	1		9		35	3	12	61	105	78
1945			6	2	8	4	4	56		20

NOTE: The figures do not include American construction on behalf of various Allied navies and, of course, are only a reflection of the wider volume of American naval construction. In addition, it must be remembered that in March 1943 alone 140 7,157-ton Liberty Ships took to the water, each having taken an average of fifteen days to build.

began to examine two separate but related aspects of her defenses in the Far East.

The two issues that the British examined were the location of a fleet base in the Far East and the provision of a permanent fleet in the area. If Britain chose, or at some time was forced, to rely on only her own arms for the defense of her empire, trade, and dominions in the Far East, then by any standard both were essential. Australia and New Zealand, having been bled white by the war, both wanted the assurance of a British fleet in the Far East. If Britain was to provide an adequate force for the defense of her far-flung interests, then it could not be inferior to that of any possible rival. In fact it had to be considerably superior, particularly in light of the distance that separated it from its homeland.

But to provide for such a force Britain would have to maintain two fleets, one for home waters and one for the Far East. The new strategic reality of the situation was that Britain could no longer rely on the means that had secured her empire in bygone days. British overseas possessions could no longer be maintained and guaranteed by British naval supremacy in European waters choking any threat at the source. This notion had been invalidated by the emergence of extra-European powers. The threat posed by such powers had to be met in its own right. When it came to tackling the problems of the Far East, therefore, by any rational standard the uncertainties of the situation cried out for maintaining in the area a substantial British fleet. This, in its turn, necessitated the provision of a base. With Hong Kong denied on account of its vulnerability to land attack and its shallow harbor, the choice for such a site rested between Singapore and Sydney. The Australians pressed hard for the adoption of Sydney as the British base. The climate, white women, and the possibility of resettlement in Australia for British sailors were the obvious inducements and blandishments rejected by the British Admiralty. On 16 June 1921 the British cabinet formally endorsed the Admiralty's recommendation that Singapore, on the meeting point between the Indian and west Pacific oceans, would be the site of the new base. The main reason for the Admiralty's decision to recommend Singapore was that it was several thousands of miles closer than Sydney to the scene of any likely conflict.

There were two obvious problems. The provision of a fleet base and two battle fleets was beyond the straightened resources of a Britain exhausted by four years of European warfare. At a time of massive economies and cutbacks in force levels, the British did not have the means to provide for naval defense on the scale that would be needed. To compound this problem the phenomenon of obsolescence in design would have forced the British to undertake truly massive construction programs simply to replace their old dreadnoughts and thus allow Britain to have modern battle fleets equal to the newer American and Japanese navies. At the end of the war only the *Hood* was under construction, and many such ships would have to be built in order to replace the old ships then either obsolete or obsolescent.

The Washington Treaty, by effectively ending the construction of capital ships by the three major powers, eliminated the need for Britain to start massive building programs. But the treaty fixed the balance of strength among Britain, the United States, and Japan at such a level— 5:5:3—that Britain could not be strong in both European and Far Eastern waters. Allowing for ships out of commission and given the fact that Britain had to maintain a fleet in European waters that gave her a comfortable margin of superiority over any possible enemy, the provision of a Far East fleet at least the equal of Japan's was mathematically impossible. Britain simply did not have the resources. The British could not hope to match the Japanese in the Far East, yet given the ending of the Anglo-Japanese alliance this was essential. The problem of trying to do so, reconciling the irreconcilable, plagued sensible strategic deliberations in the whole of the interwar period.

It is tempting to make the uncharitable comment that in the interwar period the British hoped that by ignoring the problem posed by this situation it would never arise, and that if it did somehow the British would muddle through in their normal manner. This would imply that the British actually considered the problem, and some people might be prompted to deny even this. What in fact happened was not so much that the British never considered the nature of the problem but that they became trapped by their own propaganda. The inadequacies of British naval power to defend an empire secured, maintained, and succored by command of the seas was concealed by the repeated interwar assertion that, while the fleet would be based in European waters, it would be dispatched to the Far East in time of crisis. This was perhaps optimistic, but not wholly unrealistic, just as long as no threat from the European mainland materialized. If crises emerged simultaneously in Europe and the Far East, then by no standard would British naval strength be sufficient to meet the demands placed upon it. The Australasian dominions would have preferred the more substantial reality of a fleet in their waters or adjacent ones, but their governments were reassured by the British promise that the fleet would be dispatched, it was hoped in time to be in Far East waters before the outbreak of any hostilities but, if not, then very quickly afterwards. The general British view was that the fleet would be in Singapore within seventy days of the political decision being taken to send it. This became an article of faith in British defense planning in the interwar period.

The obvious flaw in the British reasoning lay in the assumption of stability in Europe. The European situation deteriorated rapidly, to Britain's considerable disadvantage, in the course of the thirties. The revival of German power under Hitler and the Anglo-German naval treaty of June

1935 that allowed the Germans to build up to 35 percent of the strength of the Royal Navy clearly pointed to the fact that Britain would have to hold back a considerable part of the fleet to face the resurgent *Kreigsmarine*. But as late as the Imperial Conference of 1937 Britain still held to the view that after Germany, Japan ranked above Italy on the list of possible enemy nations, and that the defense of the Far East ranked above that of the Middle East. The British Chiefs of Staff accepted the possible danger that might arise in the Middle East, but were confident that the French navy would be an effective check on the Italians in the Mediterranean. They considered the course of running down the Mediterranean requirement to be less fraught with risks than that of leaving the Far East undefended. By May 1939, however, the British had sufficiently backtracked on their hitherto bland assurances of "Main Fleet to Singapore," much to the alarm of the Australians. By that time it was no longer "possible to state how soon after Japanese intervention a Fleet could be despatched to the Far East . . . (or) to enumerate precisely the size of the Fleet that we could afford to send."*

The Australians were obviously concerned by the tone of the wording. For all the interwar period there had been talk of the fleet, or the overwhelming part of it, being sent east, but now the use of the indefinite article was significant. There was no guarantee of arrival before the start of a war, and indeed the whole tenor of the statement pointed to procrastination and an inadequate response to any developing situation in the Far East. If nothing else, the May 1939 statement was a very belated recognition of the inadequacy of British naval power in a world where British power was limited not simply against American standards but also by the standards of third parties. The statement, however, was not honest. It was a shallow deception of those dominions that had placed their faith in British declarations and now wanted the British to match their words with action.

In July 1939 the British made one further departure from what had been their declared intentions. This was the extension from seventy to ninety days of the time between the fleet (if there was one) leaving European waters (if it left at all) and its arrival in Singapore. In September the Chiefs of Staff informed the military authorities in Malaya that the time delay could be as long as six months. The British authorities in London, besides deceiving the dominions, could not be honest with their own subordinates. In May, during informal talks with the Americans over strategic intentions, the British had admitted the impossibility of sending even a single battleship to Singapore. Given the need to face Germany and keep a watch on the Italians, the British effectively went back on their 1937 position, without telling the dominions and the authorities in Malaya of the change. Perhaps this was a case of speaking for effect with the Americans and

*Kirby, *The War against Japan*, 1:19.

breaking the bad news to the Australians gently, but either way there was beginning to emerge a credibilty gap of staggering dimensions. The march of events revealed this. The fall of France in 1940 and Italy's entry into the war on the German side greatly increased the already wide responsibilities of the Royal Navy. These events made it perfectly obvious that, given the Royal Navy's overextension, there could be no possibility of sending significant forces to the Far East. This revelation, of course, came just at the time when the promises of two decades were being presented for honoring by Britain because the Japanese, as we have seen, were now prepared to show their hand.

The all-too-late recognition that it would be impossible to send a powerful British fleet to the Far East threw into the melting pot the whole question of the strategy Britain should employ to defend her interests now that the fleet, the very basis of British assumptions and planning, could not be deployed. For the first time there could be no possibility of a comfortable sheltering behind the myth that the fleet would be in position to defend the area or would arrive in time to secure the relief of Singapore. The British defense chiefs had to recognize the reality that in the absence of a fleet the defense of Malaya and Singapore had to be vested in the army and the Royal Air Force. These had to be able to hold out indefinitely, if the need arose. This was the inescapable conclusion, and it was a reality that was not faced.

While defense planning had labored under the comfortable illusion that the navy would be available to defend Malaya and Singapore, the role of the other two services was clearly secondary. But the twists and turns of strategy brought about by naval considerations were paralleled by interservice rivalries and a lack of coordination, priorities, and clarity of thought in assessing the threat to Malaya and Singapore. As a result there was no clear identification of the defense requirements of the commands in the Far East. These difficulties and problems seemed to increase, not lessen, as the threat began to emerge and time ran out.

The story of interservice disputes and lack of clear thought on the defense problems of the Far East was a long one. It stretched back to the time in 1921 when the decision was made to build the base at Singapore. It took the British four years—including the cancellation of the whole project in 1924 by the short-lived minority Labour government—to decide where on Singapore Island the base should be built. In February 1923 the Admiralty decided against building the base on the seaward side of Singapore Island because of the problem of such a base being located too near the commercial harbor. The question was settled in favor of a location on the Johore Strait, east of the causeway. By definition, therefore, the fortification requirements of the base entailed holding a perimeter defense on the mainland. This defense line had to be beyond the range of artillery from the base because the base and its ships had to be immune from land-based artillery attack. But despite all the evidence of the Japanese attacks on Port Arthur in two wars and on Tsingtao in 1914, the British were of the opinion that provision had to be made against an attack from the sea and not by land. All three attacks on these two fortresses in China had been successful within six months; Tsingtao in 1914 had succumbed within the magical seventy days. The British believed that the jungle of Johore and the southern and eastern part of the Malayan peninsula in itself afforded sufficient protection for the base from landward attack. The British reasoned that any attack from the north would take too long to be effective. This, by the standards of the time, was not an unrealistic conclusion. Therefore attention centered on the provision of defense against attack from the sea, and here the first signs of interservice dispute began to appear.

Both the navy and the army placed their confidence in permanent fixed defenses for covering the proposed naval base. Both of the two major services thought in terms of heavy artillery as the best means of defending Singapore Island against invasion. The Royal Air Force argued in favor of a balanced force of torpedo bombers, fighters, and reconnaissance aircraft supplementing the defenses. Of course there were some who regarded such a supplement as the thin end of the wedge, and such people were to be found in all three services. There were members of the air force who wanted to establish the principle in order to expand the role of the service to that of primus inter pares; there were members of the other services who feared this eventuality and were determined to prevent it. The whole question of the defense of Singapore called in the very vexed question of the role and capabilities of air power, and for much of the twenties this was an emotionally charged issue.

The case the Royal Air Force argued was that aircraft were greatly superior in range to artillery and that it was far more sensible to try to deal with any invasion force as far out to sea as possible than to deal with it when it arrived on the doorstep. Rigid linear defense on land, particularly in the form of immovable gun positions, was no counter to invading seaborne forces. The air force case was simply that the long sea passage of any invasion force should be the objective of a defensive effort. The airmen argued that aircraft were both more flexible and cheaper than permanent defenses, and that the necessary air power need not always be located on Singapore. Because of the superior speed of aircraft over ships, the rapid reinforcement of the Far East by aircraft was possible in the event of a crisis.

At the time when the Royal Air Force was arguing its case in the first half of the twenties it failed to make its views stick. Its failure came about on two counts. First, it was argued that there was no proof that aircraft by themselves could deal with surface units. This was an extremely fair point. Aircraft were relatively slow, poorly armed for offensive action, and of uncertain though improving performance. The American air experiments against surrendered German warships proved nothing other than if enough aircraft were allowed to bomb stationary hulks then these would ultimately sink. No responsible political or military authority was prepared to vest total or even substantial reliance in what was still a new element of power of unproved capabilities. The second count was more contentious. It was argued that the flexibility of air power might prove an illusion. It was contended that, when the time came, commitments elsewhere could result in the British air force being so stretched that it could not afford to deploy to the Far East. This again was a fair enough point, but it was one that could have been applied with equal validity to the Royal Navy. The logic of this does not seem to have been considered; the notion of "Main Fleet to Singapore" had become an unchallengeable sacred cow. The immediate issue of the defense of Singapore, therefore, was primarily vested in the artillery, and there was no change in this basic policy until the middle and late thirties.

In the thirties three considerations began to make increasing inroads into British thinking with regard to the defense of Singapore, though not to the point that they led to any revision of the notion that the main burden of the defense in the Far East still rested on the Royal Navy. First, there were the steady improvements in aircraft performance and the recognition that advance air bases, with reconnaissance aircraft operating well out to sea, were absolutely essential to the defense. This meant that a series of airfields had to be established in the north and along the east coast of Malaya. The result was that the Royal Air Force secured airfields on Kuantan, Kahang, and three around Kota Bharu. This, in its turn, led to the second consideration. In order to protect the airfields there had to be a forward deployment of the ground troops. This consideration was tied up with the third element, the first staff assessment by the military authorities in Malaya of an attack on Malaya and Singapore from the point of view of the Japanese. This assessment was made by the commander of the land forces, Major General William G. S. Dobbie, and his chief staff officer, a certain Brigadier Arthur E. Percival. In 1937 they calculated that the Japanese, after securing airfields in southern Thailand, would land in northern Malaya and southern Thailand and advance on Singapore along the whole length of the Malayan peninsula. What made this report so significant was that it came to the novel and highly unpleasant conclusion that the jungle would not pose an insurmountable obstacle to infantry. This raised all sorts of alarming possibilities. Unknowingly the two British officers had come to the same conclusion as the Japanese regarding the vulnerability of Singapore to an attack from the rear.

There was only one possible conclusion to be drawn if the findings of the staff assessment were accepted. This was that the land and air forces detailed for the defense of Malaya and Singapore had to be drastically increased. Once it was recognized that in addition to these considerations the fleet would either be very slow in arriving or would not arrive at all, then the need for greatly increased land and air forces became an absolute and urgent necessity. If the land and air forces could not rely on naval support, then they had to be entirely self-supporting and self-reliant in order to withstand what could easily become an indefinite siege. But by 1939, with war looming in Europe, the allocation of priorities for land and air forces was to France, the United Kingdom, and the Middle East. The events of the first year of war merely confirmed the commitment to the European and Middle East theaters. Singapore was starved of land and air reinforcements before war came to the Far East.

Once the inability of the navy to protect Malaya and Singapore was admitted, the main emphasis of the defense was placed upon the Royal Air Force. In a report in April 1940, Major General Lionel V. Bond suggested that, given the weakness of the army in Malaya, the air force should be built up in order to provide a formidable strike force against an invader, thereby lessening the need for a large number of ground troops who would otherwise be tied to a series of fixed locations to guard against invasions. Such troops would be strong nowhere but weak everywhere. The notion of making air power the cornerstone of Malayan defenses was accepted by London, but at this point incredulity begins to set in. The strengthening of the British air force in the Far East was deferred until the end of 1941. Given what was happening in Europe, perhaps this was inevitable, but in the interim London promised that the shortage of aircraft would be made good by the dispatch of more troops to Malaya. In this London was as good as its word: in 1940 just one division was deployed piecemeal to Malaya. In the whole of military history there can seldom have been a series of strategic decisions and actions that reached such a nadir as did those of the British at this point. For the defense of Malaya the British had placed their faith in warships. When they realized the bankruptcy of this notion they turned to air power in order to economize on troops, and in the end they sent troops to economize on aircraft.

Absurdity was not exhausted at this point; the question of how many aircraft should be deployed on Malaya still remained to be botched. Admittedly, the problem was complicated. Britain had very few aircraft and the French position in Indo-China, on which the British had relied up until 1940, was unclear. The Chiefs of Staff in London estimated the needs of the Royal Air Force to be 22 squadrons with 336 aircraft. This was a modest total when the assessment on which it was based pointed to the possibility of Japan having as many as 700 aircraft to throw against Malaya. The British air force in Malaya estimated its own needs to be 556 aircraft to defend against invasion, deny air bases in Borneo to Japan, and protect merchantmen in the general area. There were many who felt that even this total was too small. As it was, in 1940 the air force in Malaya mustered 8 squadrons with 88 aircraft, most of them obsolete. Four squadrons were equipped with Blenheims, two squadrons with the old—almost geriatric— Vildebeestes. The shocking state of British air defenses in the Far East can be gauged by the fact that even the homeless Dutch were able to deploy more aircraft in the Indies than the British in Malaya. The British commander in chief for the Far East was actually dependent on the Dutch and occasionally the Americans to provide him with a transport aircraft so that he could move around his vast command. Admittedly, Dutch aircraft were as poor in quality, if not worse, than those of the British, but at least there were 144 of them.

It has been noted that confusion characterized American interwar strategic deliberations but never to the extent of the unreality that gripped British policymaking. Throughout the interwar period American planners tried to grapple with the immense problems that a naval war in the Pacific presented; and, in many ways, despite the evident failures and half-measures, they achieved some remarkable results. The general soundness of interwar strategic, tactical, and material measures put through by the planning staffs and construction teams was to be shown by the experience of war. The tactical and material quality of the U.S. Navy was probably higher than that of any other navy and was to stand it in good stead in the days of defeat. These qualities were to provide the Pacific Fleet with the basis of recovery in the summer and autumn of 1942.

Much of the difficulty that confronted the services and planners stemmed from the state of domestic American politics in the interwar period. From the days following the American public's repudiation of the Democrats in 1920—of Woodrow Wilson, the Versailles treaty, and the League of Nations—the public mood was one of antagonism towards foreign entanglements and obligations. American opinion was profoundly isolationist. When Franklin D. Roosevelt became president, his awareness of the power of Congress and its determination to prevent any executive act that might lead to America's departure from her chosen path of exclusiveness, hampered his taking a firm line in foreign policy. Prevailing opinion was strongly isolationist right up until 1940, but even after the trauma of the fall of France the "America first" lobby was both powerful and vocal. American opinion was staunchly opposed to the behavior of the dictators in the thirties, but it was even more staunchly opposed to American involvement in war.

This isolationist attitude had obvious effects on defense expenditures, because there was no perception of any immediate threat to the United States. The Americans could not envisage any situation that would entail the use of their power, so the level of defense expenditures was low. This, combined with the limitations of the Washington treaties, had the effect of diminishing the offensive power of the United States. Roosevelt himself was acutely aware of the intimate relationship between the effectiveness of diplomacy and available military force, and the lack of available military clout was a factor in his restraint on issues where his internationalist tendencies would have led him into action. The passivity of American foreign policy, particularly in the thirties, was a reflection of the domestic political situation in the country at the time. A nation that was beset with economic and financial problems and a collapse of confidence in the American system was not interested in maintaining treaties to which it was a party or in taking prudent and precautionary measures in the event of those treaties lapsing or being broken. On many occasions moral utterances were substituted for policy and made the excuse for doing nothing.

With a background of public apathy and financial stringency to cheer them, the U.S. Navy and the planners had to try to come to grips with all sorts of problems of which two, arguably, were of prime importance. The first and most intractable was to decide between the respective merits of conflicting claims in the Atlantic and Pacific oceans, and to allocate inadequate resources to meet the needs of these two separated theaters. The dilemma became increasingly acute in 1940 with the American decision not to abandon Britain to her fate but to do everything possible, short of war, to sustain her. In 1940–41 the Americans, conscious of the threat posed to them by a German-conquered Europe and the provisions of the tripartite pact, were increasingly committed to supporting Britain in the Atlantic while they took on the task of restraining and intimidating Japan from a position of naval inferiority and weakness in the Pacific. It is hard to see what else the Americans could have done, other than to have abandoned either Britain or the Far East, but American policy in these years in stark military terms was nonsense. A policy of deterrence from a position of military inferiority is never likely to prove effective. The Japanese were alert to the inconsistencies of the American position in the last seventeen months of peace in the Pacific.

The second problem, tied in with the first, was the whole question of whether American interests in the Far East were best served by a policy of deterrence or one of defense. Since the Americans lacked adequate military force to underwrite their position, they relied on political and economic power either to force Japan to acquiesce to their demands or to buy time so that force levels could be built up. The deterrence policy proved a failure because the very instruments that the Americans applied proved self-defeating. The pressure that the Americans applied was positive inducement for Japan to go to war—the very opposite reaction to what was intended. The failure of deterrence resulted mainly from the failure to provide the means of defense. Here various difficulties beset American planning, among them the side effects of new technology; the immutable facts of time, space, and distance involved in Pacific operations; and tactical doctrine. These problems boiled down to three main issues. First, there was the tricky problem of whether American interests were best served by the strengthening or the abandonment of the Philippines. Second, there was the problem of how air power fit into American defense planning. Third, there was the whole question of the tactical aspects of amphibious operations in a war in the Pacific. The latter point tied in with such matters as the organization of amphibious forces, the provision of logistical support, the need to fight at great distances from fixed bases, and the place of battle in the tactical doctrine of the U.S. Navy. The real complexity of this situation lies in the fact that all these points were interrelated, with no clear lines of demarcation among the different issues involved. One of the matters under discussion, the defense of the Philippines, was fraught with political and strategic overtones, mainly as a result of the place played by the islands in the raison d'etre of the U.S. Navy as such.

The practical issue of the Philippines was in many ways at the heart of U.S. defense problems, and its influence was profound. The United States was a power in the Far East because she possessed the Philippines, even though her traditional and main interest was in China. The Philippines had been the reason why the U.S. Navy had developed into an oceanic force. Though the Americans had been the first of the white imperialists to open up Japan in the mid-nineteenth century, the United States did not become a major Asian power until the time of the Spanish-American War of 1898. In that year the Americans acquired a string of possessions across the Pacific, including the Hawaiian Islands, Guam, and, of course, the Philippines. It was the possession of these islands that justified the existence of a strong navy in the period 1898–1916 or, to be more accurate, was used to justify the claim that a strong navy was needed. By giving the United States a firm foothold in the western Pacific, and a point of access into China, the Philippines provided the rationalization from which the Americans drew their argument for a strong fleet, when really they aspired to a general world role that would result in the eclipse of British naval supremacy.

As early as December 1907, when under the orders of President Theodore Roosevelt the U.S. Navy's Atlantic Squadron (the Great White Fleet) began its famous world cruise, the Americans gave clear indication that they aspired to a worldwide oceanic role, but it was not until February 1916 that the formal commitment was made to attain such a status. In that month Woodrow Wilson enunciated the intention to build a fleet second to none. Congress gave Wilson's announcement its enthusiastic support. Nevertheless, as we have seen, first the American entry into the war and then the Washington treaties served to frustrate that aim. At Washington the Americans obtained statistical equality with the British and a 66 percent margin of superiority over the Japanese. They also succeeded in ending the Anglo-

Japanese alliance, maintaining the Open Door policy with regard to China, and stabilizing the situation on the lines of the status quo.

But for these successes the Americans had to pay a price, and while this price did not seem heavy at the time of the treaties, it was to prove so over the years. In order to compensate Japan for the loss of the British alliance and the denial of a 70 percent margin of strength, the Washington treaties included the critically important nonfortification provisions. These in the long run had a devastating impact on American strategic deliberations. Even before the Washington Conference American planners had concluded that the only means of guaranteeing the Philippines was by challenging and defeating any nation that posed a threat to the islands' security. This meant Japan. The Americans therefore accepted that in the event of war with Japan the U.S. Navy would have to move into the western Pacific basin in order to defeat Japan. The navy saw the only means of achieving this to be a combinaton of economic strangulation, which involved mining the Sea of Japan (technically impossible until 1945), and forcing a decisive battle in the waters off Japan.

To envisage the latter raised issues of crucial importance. Ever since the Spanish-American War and the emergence on the world stage of Mahan as *the* authoritative source on naval strategy, the U.S. Navy had been obsessed with the military aspects of sea power and the primacy of battle as the means of achieving command of the seas. After 1898 for the first time in their history the Americans possessed a battle fleet that, despite the very low quality of its ships, tactics, and battle drills, allowed them to pass from a strategy of commerce raiding to one of seeking to fight for command of the seas. Naturally the quality of the U.S. Navy improved out of all recognition in the first twenty years of the present century, but the twin realities of the nonfortification clauses of Washington and the problems caused by distance hamstrung the development of coherent strategic doctrine with regard to the defense of the Philippines. Given prevailing views concerning what might be termed the Clausewitzian concept of the diminishing force of the offensive with regard to fleets, the defense of the Philippines became problematical. Without a fortified base in the Philippines, the U.S. Navy could not hope to operate effectively in that area for extended periods, yet a sortie from Pearl Harbor via Guam to the Philippines left the American fleet dreadfully vulnerable to an attritional campaign during its passage. Japan held the dominant geographic position in the western Pacific on account of her possession of the Marianas and Carolines. The Americans were therefore left with an unpleasant choice. They either had to try to fight to retain the Philippines at the end of an extended line of communication, without a secure fleet base, and in a position of decided geographic inferiority; or they could abandon the Philippines and prepare to fight their way across the Pacific into a web of Japanese-owned islands.

No matter which way the U.S. Navy attempted to tackle the Philippines problem there were awesome difficulties. The natural difficulties of defending a coastline longer than that of the United States and thousands of miles from the nearest secure fleet base were bad enough in themselves, but they were compounded by political and interservice considerations. The political considerations centered upon the basic assumptions that guided the Hoover administration in its handling of Far Eastern matters. Hoover never believed that the United States had any interests in eastern Asia and the western Pacific that were worth a war. To Hoover the basic American stance in the Pacific had to be defensive and based on the Alaska, Hawaii, Panama triangle. This was not an unreasonable view, granted the few resources available for defense and the state of American public opinion, and it was a view that the Roosevelt administration could do little to change. Indeed, the idea of an active defense of the Philippines was somewhat weakened by the concession of the principle of independence for the Philippines under the terms of the Tydings-McDuffie Act of March 1934. The Philippines were to become an independent state after a ten-year transitional period in which time the Americans were to undertake the creation of Filipino armed forces; thereafter the Philippines were to be left to their own devices with regard to defense.

In light of the scheduled independence of the Philippines and the extreme isolationist view that any American force deployed there would be a hostage to fortune, the American reluctance to contemplate a major deployment to the islands was natural. This was the situation that Roosevelt inherited and with which he had to contend. But Roosevelt was confident that America could bring Japan to her knees by distant blockade, and events were to show that he was correct—in the long term. In the short term, however, blockade could do little or nothing to frustrate a Japan deliberately preparing to secure the means by which such a blockade could be overcome. Roosevelt's view, moreover, reinforced the tendency to remain in the eastern and central Pacific. The emphasis was as much on the word *distant* as on the word *blockade*. The president's view in turn was reinforced by the position of the U.S. Army. The army naturally saw the defense of the Pacific as primarily a naval affair. Being drastically understrength and woefully equipped, the army was totally unwilling to see itself put out on a limb in the Philippines and the Far East, waiting for a fleet that might never arrive. If the navy thought in terms of defending the Philippines, then carrying out a relief sortie had to depend on an adequate ground defense for the Philippines—a military task that the army was loath to accept. But for the army the alternative to the defense of the Philippines was equally dismal. Like the navy, the army was distinctly unimpressed by the thought of a deliberate campaign across the Pacific into a defensive Japanese mesh. Such a campaign would be time-consuming and costly in terms of manpower and materiel, which in the thirties were simply not available. The army's case, the concession in principle of independence to the Philippines, the politicians' faith in the effectiveness of a blockade mounted with minimal forces, and the basic lack of resources, all pointed to the Americans restraining themselves to the central Pacific.

To the navy, however, this was totally inadequate. The U.S. Navy had not fought the battle of Manila Bay in 1898 and had not created the Pacific Fleet in 1919 in order to play a secondary and passive role east of Hawaii. It did not believe that blockade would, in the long term, prove either politically acceptable or militarily effective. If it was to survive as an oceanic and worldwide force, the U.S. Navy had to plan for and secure the means to fight and win a war in the western Pacific. This, remarkably in view of its difficulties, is precisely what it achieved, at least in skeletal form, in the interwar period. This achievement found expression in three aspects of doctrine and organization (carrier aviation, amphibious operations, and logistical support), but not in materiel matters.

In the early twenties the U.S. Navy lagged behind those of Britain and Japan in aviation, and this state of affairs persisted well into the thirties. But by the time war broke out in Europe in 1939, the U.S. Navy had easily overtaken the Royal Navy and was possibly even ahead of the Imperial Navy in many aspects of naval aviation, except the number of carriers in service.

American carrier development began with the conversion of the naval collier *Jupiter* into the 11,000-ton carrier *Langley* in 1921. This small carrier was to be used for six years in testing carrier techniques and tactics before two heavy fleet carriers, the *Lexington* and *Saratoga*, entered service in 1928. Each of the latter displaced over 36,000 tons and carried between eighty and ninety aircraft. But the development of such large carriers, which were modifications of battle cruisers that otherwise would have been scrapped under the terms of the Washington treaties, was not universally popular within the U.S. Navy. With total U.S. carrier tonnage limited by treaty, there were many who felt that too much tonnage was worked into these two ships. Many felt that the fleet would have been better served by investment in smaller but more numerous carriers and that large carriers were excessively vulnerable. The upshot of this feeling was that there was a marked reaction in favor of moderate dimensions. When these arguments were combined with the tonnage left to the Americans under the terms of the Washington treaties, the result was the 14,000-ton *Ranger*, the first American purpose-built carrier. Though not much more than one-third the size of the *Lexington* or *Saratoga*, the *Ranger* carried as many aircraft, but she was considerably inferior to her older sisters. High speed had to be sacrificed to meet other essentials, and her length was not conducive to rapid flying operations. As a result, the *Ranger* was considered a reconnaissance carrier, not a fleet assault carrier. She was the only American carrier not to see service in the Pacific during the Second World War.

The *Ranger*, which joined the fleet in 1934, was the last American carrier built under treaty restrictions; thereafter the Americans were free to build any number of carriers of any displacement. Even before the *Ranger* entered service it was obvious that she had many weaknesses and that future American carriers would have to be developed on larger lines. The ideal size was considered to be around 20,000 tons. On this displacement the Americans estimated a carrier could deploy a complete air group without any compromise in speed, accommodations, protection, and armament. Thus, the next carriers to enter service, the *Yorktown* in 1937 and the *Enterprise* in 1938, displaced 19,900 tons, while the *Hornet*, which was commissioned in 1941, displaced 20,000 tons. Though there was a temporary aberration in favor of small dimensions with the *Wasp* (14,700 tons), by 1936–37 the Americans knew the optimal size for carriers, and by the time war broke out there were no less than ten of the slightly larger *Essex*-class carriers under construction. In terms of numbers, with only six carriers in commission at the outbreak of the Pacific war, the Americans were inferior to the Japanese, but they had evolved a successful design that was to prove so effective that not one of the *Essex* class then in the yards was to be lost in the course of the war.

The development of carrier design was related to the definition of aircraft requirements. For most of the interwar period the U.S. Navy was no better equipped than its British and Japanese counterparts, and it was slow to adopt monoplanes and specialized aircraft to meet specific functions. This was in large part deliberate. Given limited funds and rapid aircraft design obsolescence, the U.S. Navy was very reluctant to commit itself until suitable monoplanes, capable of further development, were available to fulfill the special roles of reconnaissance, fighting, dive-bombing, and torpedo-bombing. As a result, American carriers were not equipped with modern aircraft until 1938–41. These were good, though not quite as good as contemporary Japanese carrier aircraft. Nevertheless, the foundation of the massively successful series of carrier aircraft that were to dominate the Pacific in the period 1943–45 was laid by deferring orders in the interwar period.

Tactically, the U.S. Navy, like the other major navies, never resolved the issue of the use of air power, and particularly carrier aviation, in the interwar period. This was ironic in a way because the U.S. Navy in the interwar era showed far more imagination in the possible use of carrier aircraft than any other navy. In the fleet exercise of 1929 the *Saratoga* was deemed to have successfully destroyed objectives in the Panama Canal Zone. She left San Diego for the canal by a circumspect southern course that took her clear of the Galapagos Islands, thus ensuring surprise, and caught the defending air and naval units, including her sister ship, unprepared and on the wrong foot. The *Saratoga* was considered to have attacked her objectives successfully for the barest possible loss. The 1929 exercise hinted at the potential value of carriers, and this was brought home again nearly a decade later in the course of the 1938 fleet exercise. In that exercise Admiral Ernest J. King successfully attacked two shore installations, the first with the *Saratoga*, the second with both of the heavy carriers. In the first attack King chose to advance to contact behind the cover of a bad weather front, which defeated all efforts on the part of the defenders to locate him. He also chose to approach through waters not frequented very much by merchant shipping. The second attack, against the Mare Island Naval Yard near San Francisco, achieved complete surprise. The significance of these attacks was twofold. First, they showed the potential for carriers, operating with the choice of time and place for their attacks, to project offensive power deep into areas that in contemporary naval terms should have been commanded by enemy surface units. Second, the initial attack in the 1938 exercise had been on Pearl Harbor and the *Saratoga* had closed her objective from the northeast through the inhospitable waters of the northern Pacific.

In view of the results of these exercises it would have been reasonable to expect that the U.S. Navy would have recognized the offensive potential of carrier aviation. Both the 1929 and 1938 exercises revealed the flexibility, surprise value, and (supposed) offensive power of imaginatively used carriers and their aircraft. If nothing else, the carriers showed that their aircraft were far more flexible than land-based aircraft, and that at sea a fleet now had the ability to strike at targets well beyond the horizon. But, of course, carriers were unproved under war conditions and the U.S. Navy was no exception in that it had in its upper echelons admirals who, brought up in the age of the gun, retained their faith in the battleship as the arbiter of sea power. The battle line advocates still held sway despite the efforts of air enthusiasts, and carriers and their aircraft were seen primarily as adjuncts to the naval gun. The battleship was still regarded as the primary means of destroying an enemy, while aircraft were considered suitable to spot for the guns, to fight for air supremacy in order to defend the battle line, and to act in a deep reconnaissance role far beyond the range of cruisers. It was conceded, however, that aircraft might be used to attack a distant or fleeing enemy to ensure his being delivered up to the guns of the fleet.

The continued domination of the battle line school naturally had its effects on tactical doctrine. As early as 1930 a promising young lieutenant commander named Forrest B. Sherman advocated the adoption of a tactical formation that placed the carrier at the heart of the fleet. In the course of the thirties the Americans experimented with all sorts of task forces, essentially trying to find a blend of all types of ships. In this they were not particularly successful. There was always the problem of immediate priority for the escorts and there was the immense difficulty caused by the speed differential between the new fast carriers and old slow battleships. Carriers really demanded their own permanently assigned escorts in order that units would be trained to anticipate possible situations during the tricky phases of flying operations. Carriers needed sea room in order to turn into wind and work up speed; this could not be achieved safely with ad hoc escort formations and battleships in the way. Furthermore, the Americans never managed to decide whether a carrier task group should contain one or more carriers and whether the best counter to enemy air attacks was independent maneuver or concentration of ships and gunfire. By 1941 the Americans had left many matters unresolved, and the problems were becoming more urgent. With ever more carriers competing for scarce escorts there had to be an answer to the tactical fleet formation. But the Americans had done much of the spade work; the ground had been thoroughly prepared, and when the Japanese resolved the question of the relative merits of the battleship and carrier in no uncertain terms in December 1941, the U.S. Navy had its peacetime experience on which to draw. Neither the British nor the Japanese navies could match the Americans in this respect.

In amphibious operations the same unevenness that characterized the development of carrier doctrine repeated itself. The U.S. Marine Corps secured for itself the role of landing force in amphibious operations, and did much to settle such vexed questions as command structures, naval gunnery support, close air support, ship-to-shore movement, securing the beachhead, and logistics. These matters, indeed, were the six themes in the *Tentative Manual for Landing Operations*. Obviously not all the matters that the manual analyzed were necessarily resolved before the war; in fact it is probably accurate to state that most were not fully resolved even after eighteen months of war. Naval gunnery and close air support were not properly coordinated until the last year or so of the Pacific war, but the essential point was that before the start of the war the U.S. Marine Corps knew its problems and knew what type of war it wanted to fight. In the study of its problems the Marine Corps came up with the correct answer more often than not, and when men and materiel began to flow into the corps it knew exactly how to use them. Even strategically the Marine Corps had ideas of how to fight its way through the Japanese-held islands of the western Pacific.

As early as 1921 Lieutenant Colonel Earl H. Ellis of the Marine Corps produced a blueprint for operations and operational needs in the western Pacific that was largely borne out by events. It was not until 1938, however, that the concept of "island-hopping" was first formulated, and it was not until the experience of war brought empirical proof that this notion was accepted. This, indeed, was one of the most brilliantly imaginative parts of the American effort in the Pacific war. By focusing on positional advantage rather than the conquest of territory, the concept was the embodiment of the most intelligent form of warfare—attacking an enemy where it is not present. It was the island-hopping concept that was used with devastating success for the first time in the northern Solomons in 1943 and that was brilliantly deployed in the drive across the central Pacific in the course of 1944. Probably more than any other aspect of war, island-hopping upset Japanese calculations regarding the feasibility of a defensive, attritional campaign in the Pacific to wear down American resources and resolve. The groundwork for this concept of going around the back of the enemy's strength and leaving it to "wither on the vine" again was laid in the interwar period.

Yet logistically the U.S. Navy in the interwar period was something of a mess, largely because of the abolition of the Logistics Section of the Naval War College in the late twenties. As a result of service hostility and political indifference, the proper organization of logistical services languished, and had to be largely improvised when the war broke out. But in the interwar period three factors prevented the logistical side of naval activity from falling into total obscurity. The need to expand Pearl Harbor as a primary base forced the U.S. Navy into a major expansion of its transportation services; the adoption of oil as the fuel for warships allowed the development of a tanker fleet; and the practice of refuelling at sea became an almost standard feature of the U.S. Navy in the interwar period. The U.S. Navy had to cut away from its dependence on bases and had to be converted from a short-haul to a long-haul navy. Thoughtful Americans realized that, given the distances involved in a war with Japan, the fleet could not be tied to a major fixed base such as Pearl Harbor, Manila, or even Singapore; it had to take its base with it. Such a base had to be precisely that. It had to be complete in itself, capable of carrying out all but the most serious of repairs and maintenance tasks. Much of the study for such a supply fleet was carried out between the two wars.

Thus, by the approach of war the U.S. Navy was in many ways an unbalanced force. The Americans had ideas about how to organize and use their forces, but in no material respect were they ready for war. The basic organizational framework and doctrine were reasonably sound in such subjects as amphibious warfare, but this was not true of the tactical formations and logistics, while the tactical doctrine of carrier operations was far from settled. This state of affairs was largely responsible for the U.S. Navy urging the Roosevelt administration to delay the outbreak of hostilities for as long as possible. What was to redeem the unprepared state of the Americans was the massive expansion of American war production, which put flesh on the bare bones of the interwar experience.

Before we turn to examine Allied diplomacy and strategy in the last eighteen months of peace, two further *materiel* matters regarding the American fleet must be considered because they played major parts in forming

Allied policy—just as they affected Japanese deliberations. First, there must be consideration of the balance of power in the Pacific in 1941; and second, there must be reference to the state of American construction. On 7 December 1941 the Japanese possessed a clear-cut superiority over the forces of the three Allied nations in the Pacific, and a decisive margin of superiority over the Americans, particularly with regard to aircraft carriers.

NAVAL STRENGTH AS OF 7 DECEMBER 1941

	Capital ships	Aircraft carriers	Heavy cruisers	Light cruisers	Destroyers	Submarines
Britain and dominions	2		4	13	6	
Royal Netherlands Navy				3	7	15
U.S. Asiatic Fleet			1	2	13	29
U.S. Pacific Fleet	8	3	12	9	67	27
Total Allied strength	10	3	17	27	93	71
Imperial Japanese Navy	10	10	18	20	112	65
U.S. construction	15	11		54*	191	73

*Total of both heavy and light cruisers.

The bare statistics, particularly with regard to American construction, clearly indicate why the American navy wanted to delay and why the Imperial Navy wanted to hasten the outbreak of hostilities. But the figures show two other deficiencies very clearly. First, they show the utterly defenseless state of British and Dutch possessions in the Far East. Second, they show the extent of American inferiority to Japan and explain why the U.S. Navy resolutely turned against two moves that were politically essential and strategically desirable—though the latter point is debatable— if the policy of deterring or defeating Japan was to have any chance of success. These moves were the deployment of substantial forces either to reinforce the U.S. Asiatic Fleet or to reinforce Singapore. A move to Singapore was desperately sought by Britain in the course of 1941. The British knew that without an American force at Singapore Malaya was defenseless. For that very reason, because it was an open-ended commitment, such a move was politically unacceptable to the White House and strategically out of the question for the U.S. Navy. Given American inferiority in 1941, the U.S. Navy stressed the overwhelming importance of concentration and would not consider any strengthening of minor interests in the face of a superior enemy with the options of timing and direction of an assault.

Despite the U.S. Navy's numerical inferiority, its material quality was extremely high. By limiting competition in the number and size of capital ships and carriers, the Washington treaties had promoted rivalry among the powers in other fields, most notably in modernization and the battle efficiency of existing ships. (The initial result had been to produce a race in cruisers and to a lesser extent in other types of ships, but this rivalry was ended by subsequent limitation treaties.) The scrapping of older ships and limitations on the construction of new ones allowed for extensive modernization of the ships that remained in commission; a major effort to be made in electronics; and considerable attention to be paid to cruisers, submarines, and, as we have seen, integrated air services. In the fields of submarine development and radio communications the U.S. Navy quickly forged ahead of both the British and Japanese navies, and the all-around quality of its ships was very high. Ton for ton American battleships were every bit as good as those of any other nation; the cruisers, on which the brunt of surface actions fell in 1942 and 1943, proved tough in both taking and handing out punishment; the carriers, despite their lack of armored flight decks, proved remarkably difficult to sink, with none of the *Essex* class succumbing to enemy action, even though the *Franklin* almost ruined this record. The destroyers, after a shaky start, proved first the equals and then the masters of those of Japan.

The first negotiations among any of the nations that were to be attacked by Japan in December 1941 took place in 1938 in the aftermath of the Anti-Comintern Pact and the *Panay* Incident of December 1937. The fighting in and around Shanghai in September 1937 prompted angry Anglo-American reaction. The Americans began to contemplate seriously an economic blockade of Japan in cooperation with the British, Dutch, French, and Soviets, while the British urged a joint Anglo-American demonstration of force. Perhaps the British wanted a firm line in the Far East before the European situation, already very difficult, absorbed all Britain's attention and resources, and the sinking of the *Panay* at Nanking by Japanese naval aircraft seemed to play into their hands. For a brief moment it seemed as if the United States might bestir herself and join with Britain in some form of action, but a prompt Japanese apology defused the situation. By the time Anglo-American naval staff talks opened in January 1938, the heat had gone out of the crisis.

The January 1938 talks naturally achieved very little other than to make both the British and the Americans define the main features of their strategic intentions towards Japan. The Americans were forced to give their attention to the prospect of a two-ocean war in association with Britain, and both parties agreed that any basis of joint action against Japan had to be the presence of a British fleet at Singapore and of the U.S. Pacific Fleet at Hawaii. This remained the declared intention of both nations—declared to one another, that is—until May 1939. In that month, after the Americans had taken steps to reinforce their Pacific forces at the urging of Britain and France, the British advised the Americans that there could be no guarantee of their being able to send a fleet to the Far East. This forced the Americans to consider the awkward prospect of facing up to Japan alone, without Anglo-French support. The whole basis of American interwar thought about the Pacific had assumed British participation, yet at the first prospect of trouble this assumption had been shown to be false.

The events of May–June 1940 showed the fallacy of another American assumption, that of the permanency of French power. The Maginot line was as much the shield of the United States as France, and the fall of France to German arms was as much a threat to nonnegotiable American interests as it was to Britain. The defeat of France and Britain's truly desperate plight drew Britain and the United States together because the latter had already decided that the greatest threat to American security was posed by Germany. In 1940 Roosevelt was adamant that the United States had to support the last free nation fighting the dictatorships. This meant an increasing American commitment to the Atlantic in an effort to relieve the strain on Britain, but it did not mean a corresponding drawing together on Pacific matters.

In reality Anglo-American deliberations in 1940 and 1941 barely took the two nations beyond the point that had been reached in January 1938 and May 1939. The reason for this was obvious. The Americans and the British were pursuing totally diverging objectives. The Americans were seeking to establish common ground and areas of cooperation in the event of a Japanese attack. The British desperately wanted to know what the Americans would consider the casus belli, but the Americans could not and would not give Britain the definitions and undertakings she sought. The Anglo–Dutch–American negotiations at Singapore in April 1941 produced guidelines, but the British and Dutch were never sure whether Washington would act and under what circumstances. Britain was more interested in joint action than in joint planning because she knew that in reality joint action would be American action, which was certain to fulfill the primary British objective—the total commitment of the Americans either to war per se or to the defense of British interests that otherwise would have to be defended alone, which was impossible.

After Churchill became prime minister, the British had but one intention, to entangle the Americans in war, for the Americans were the only means of Britain's salvation. Every British effort after May 1940 was geared to that end, and the complete capitulation of British foreign policy with regard to the Pacific in 1941, when Churchill committed the British to support any American action in the area, was part of the process. In 1941 the British calculation was simply that if they passed their interests to

America for safekeeping, then the Americans would be obliged to defend them. Britain wanted the Americans to come out of the wings and onto the stage; the Roosevelt administration was naturally reluctant to do this, even though it increasingly committed itself to Britain's cause in Europe.

The roots of Roosevelt's problem in facing up to Japan in 1940 and 1941 were varied and complicated, and have been partially dealt with in earlier pages. It is essential to draw them together at this point because without some overview of the conflicting influences and pressures operating on the administration it is difficult to make sense of the events between June 1940 and November 1941.

First, Roosevelt had to contend with the country's strong isolationist sentiments, and these, combined with the fact that 1940 was an election year, made Roosevelt's search for a settled policy towards Japan most tortuous and devious. Second, Roosevelt's prime strategic concern was with Nazi Germany, not Japan. American attention and political, economic, and military endeavors were primarily directed towards Britain and the Atlantic, and the Roosevelt administration was naturally reluctant to face two problems at once when one might be averted or postponed. Third, under the urgings of his chiefs of staff Roosevelt wanted time in order to deal himself a stronger hand with regard to Japan. Fourth, the Roosevelt administration was by no means united with regard to the policy that should be adopted.

The administration had its hawks and its doves, but neither group knew for certain what impact various moves might have on Japan and whether or not Japan would go to war in response to American diplomatic or economic pressure. There were some who believed that any attempt to impose sanctions with bite would naturally force Japan to seek self-sufficiency through military action, but these were opposed by such able men as Stimson, who believed that in the end Japan would not pursue her policies in Asia in the face of American disapproval and economic threats. People like Stimson felt that the Japanese, when faced with the reality of American power, would back down; and for much of the time most members of the cabinet refused to believe that Japan would ever consider going to war before the battle of the Atlantic, and to a lesser extent the Nazi-Soviet conflict, were resolved. Roosevelt shared this view, at least for much of the time, but his cabinet tended to swing wildly between this view and the opinion, first stated publicly in October 1940, that the Axis could not be appeased or restrained under any circumstances. Perhaps the administration's most crucial problem was that it had no real idea of the likely consequences of its possible actions, and naturally this made the formulation of policy a task fraught with uncertainties.

The administration had four major options in its dealings with Japan, unless, of course, it reversed its position and allowed the Japanese a free hand in the Far East. Of the options one, a direct association with Britain and the Netherlands, was eliminated for political reasons, but the other three all carried inherent risks if they were applied in order to deflect Japan from her chosen course. The United States could choose to increase her support for Chiang Kai-shek in the hope that Japan would become so bogged down in China that she could not consider movement elsewhere— making China a permanent running ulcer on Japanese resources and freedom of action. The problem of following this course was that there was no means of knowing if it would be effective. China had difficulties enough in merely surviving, much less fighting and fighting effectively. The United States could attempt to strengthen her forces in the Far East. The danger of this was their resultant vulnerability and the fact that if forces were siphoned off to the Far East then it had to be at the expense of the Atlantic. Finally, the United States could impose sanctions, but this raised the problems of how, in what items, and to what extent—and for what purpose.

While these were the basic options on which various permutations could be devised, the administration was convinced of the need for military muscle to back up other forms of pressure. Because the necessary force was not available, there was a powerful incentive to be cautious. But the U.S. government also had one other difficulty. It is evident that the reason why the Roosevelt administration was unable and unwilling to commit itself on the subject of what it considered to be the casus belli in talks with Britain was that the administration simply did not know. It had no clear idea what Japanese action, if any, could constitute sufficient aggression to involve the United States in war. This was the critical point, particularly in Anglo-American dealings, and it is mainly this uncertainty that accounts for the seeming drift and irresolution of American policy between June and November 1941.

The Americans could not, and would not, commit themselves in advance to any given course of action. In this the influence of Secretary of State Cordell Hull was probably decisive. Hull was a person who believed in waiting upon events in the expectation that they would resolve themselves one way or another. Hull preferred to act upon events rather than seek to control them. He was keenly aware of the dangers inherent in any of the possible courses of action available to the administration, and this explains why he consistently opposed the idea of sanctions and shied away from taking a firm stance, even when he had strong personal feelings about Japanese behavior. Hull was a minimalist; he consistently sought to do the minimum necessary rather than the maximum possible, and he ended his opposition to sanctions on this basis.

In October 1940, when the administration first announced its position that it would not allow Japan to take control of the Indies and Singapore,

Hull considered the use of economic sanctions plus aid to Britain a policy that ensured as little risk to the United States as possible. Roosevelt, in the final analysis, went along with the Hull line, despite the twin dangers that the policy of waiting on events entailed. Both Roosevelt and Hull recognized that such a policy could be overtaken by events. If this happened, both men left themselves open to charges of mismangement, incompetence, and disingenuousness in their conduct of the nation's affairs. Nevertheless, granted the problems under which the administration labored, it is hard to see how Roosevelt could have departed from the Hull line, which, in the long term, served American interests remarkably well.

For the three major Allied nations there were two sets of bilateral talks—Anglo-Dutch and Anglo-American—and occasional multilateral talks involving all the Allies, including the British dominions and India. Anglo-American talks began to get under way seriously once the American presidential elections were over in November 1940; the first Anglo-Dutch discussions began in Batavia that same month. Before that time there had been some meetings, but it was only in late 1940 that the Allies tried to grasp the nettle of the defense of the Malay barrier and the Pacific. In these talks there was no political agreement and very little military cooperation, but the British were able to secure from the hapless Dutch what they could not secure from the Americans, namely, the recognition that retaining Singapore was an absolute priority and its defense had to take precedence over everything else in Southeast Asia. The Americans never moved from their position that the preservation of their fleet counted for more than the defense of a half-finished base that had proved incapable of repairing British warships damaged in the Mediterranean during the summer of 1941.

The Dutch had little option but to fall in with the British view. They clearly had much more to lose than anyone else in Southeast Asia and had far fewer forces than their future allies with which to defend themselves. The Dutch were absolutely dependent on Britain in political terms, and they looked to British and American political power to underwrite what they could not hold by force; their pathetically weak forces could not hope to resist Japan. But in this expectation of Anglo-American assistance the Dutch were to be disappointed. Once the Americans refused to take over the whole of the defense of Southeast Asia, first urged by Britain as early as May 1939, then the only possible source of support was Britain, and she specifically limited herself to the question of Singapore. There can be no doubt that when it came to the acid test the British regarded the Dutch not so much as a weak ally facing a common threat, an ally that should be helped, but as a source of support that could be tapped in an effort to buttress Britain's own position. It was not that the Dutch had very much that they could offer. In the Far East the Royal Netherlands Navy deployed three light cruisers, seven destroyers, and fifteen submarines. These forces were hopelessly inadequate to cover so vast an area as the Indies, and the Dutch had immense problems in trying to maintain even these forces. Nearly all her naval equipment and been supplied before the war, and with the German occupation of the Netherlands the supply of spare parts had dried up. Ships were being taken out of commission and used as material reserve in order to keep the others at sea, and there was no way in which the Dutch could replace those ships in commission and under construction that had been lost in May 1940. Among the ships under construction when the Netherlands had been overrun had been battle cruisers and a carrier. The plight of the air force was just as desperate. Apart from securing discarded aircraft from American sources, the Dutch had no means of building up their air power.

If the Dutch position was totally unenviable, that of the British was not much better. Such was the paucity of Anglo-Dutch naval and air strengths that there was only one hope of their survival. This was that some form of American naval action or presence might prevent the Japanese from using the sea for invasion purposes. At the very best this had been an extremely remote prospect before November 1940; thereafter this prospect disappeared entirely.

On 4 November, one day before Roosevelt's triumphant reelection, Stark drew up a celebrated paper that outlined the defense options that faced the United States. Stark laid out a series of choices the Americans faced in the defense of their interests and security. Once the elections were fought and won, the Roosevelt administration deliberated over Stark's suggestions and decided to adopt the fourth option, known as Plan Dog, as the best means of securing American interests. The broad outline of this plan was to stand on the defensive in the Pacific while undertaking major sea, land, and air operations in order to secure the defeat of Germany and Italy. In the course of the next six months the planners worked out in detail what this meant. In fact, when they began to put flesh on the bare bones it rapidly became clear that very little flesh was available to be added to the Pacific skeleton.

The planners accepted the loss of the Philippines. In doing so, they refused to consider reinforcing the Asiatic Fleet and the garrison or to contemplate any action on the part of the Pacific Fleet to relieve the islands. With the decision not to commit the fleet to the defense of the Philippines went the explicit refusal to use the fleet to help the British and Dutch. The American forces on the Philippines were there to buy time, the land forces, if need be, retreating into the Bataan peninsula in order to deny the Japanese use of the sea approaches to Manila. Naval resistance to the Japanese was vested in the Asiatic Fleet, but all the services, and particularly the navy's larger surface units, were to have the discretion to withdraw southwards to join either the British in the defense of Malaya or the Dutch in the defense of the Indies. In either of these eventualities American forces were to operate under the strategic direction of the local British or Dutch commanders. The planners accepted that naval units that withdrew to the south might in fact be forced to retire into the Indian Ocean—a very strong indication of the American faith in Singapore's powers of resistance. The task of offering resistance at sea to any invasion was therefore given to submarines and light patrol craft, but it was recognized that these could ward off neither invasion nor defeat, and they were regarded as expendable.

The task of the Pacific Fleet was seen not as attempting to force a fleet engagement but as securing its own lines of communication between the Americas and Hawaii. It was also to defend certain islands—Guam, Johnson, Midway, Palmyra, and Samoa—but the decision in February not to fortify Guam cut this totally unrealistic requirement. The Pacific Fleet was also required to cooperate with British and dominion naval units to defend the islands and line of communication in the area south of the equator and east of the meridian 155° east longitude (i.e., the east coast of Australia). Offensive operations were confined to diversionary attacks on the Marshalls designed to draw off Japanese pressure on the Indies and Malaya, but a systematic campaign across the Pacific was not to be attempted. American planners spoke of a subsequent fleet thrust across the western Pacific to "liberate" or "reconquer" the Philippines, a clear indication that the islands would fall and that much time would elapse between their fall and a serious American attempt to recover them.

In this form Plan Dog became known as Rainbow 5 (or W.P.L. 46) and was accepted by the chiefs of staff on 14 May. In essence the plan was basically unchanged from the staff assessments that preceded the Washington Conference twenty years before. But before three months were out the Roosevelt administration carried out an action that placed the United States firmly on the road to war and that forced it to overturn the whole of this plan. Indeed, such were the developments that planning began to focus on the questions of reinforcing the Philippines and holding the islands for a protracted, if not indefinite, period. This was what Rainbow 5 specifically sought to avoid.

The act that firmly placed the Americans on a collision course with Japan was the administration's freezing of all Japanese assets in the United States. This had the effect of ending all Japanese-American trade and came as a response to Japan's taking over eight air and two naval bases in southern Indo-China in July. The British and Dutch immediately followed the American lead. They could see that in forcing Japan either to compromise or to go to war they stood to benefit from the American move. Either war would be averted, or American involvement in war would be to their long-term advantage. The British, in particular, were quite clear about this.

Churchill would have preferred to avoid war with Japan, but an extension of the war to the Pacific was acceptable as long as the Americans were entangled in it. The freezing of assets, and the effective ending of trade, was an act that Stark, alone among the American political and military leaders, resolutely opposed. He clearly appreciated that such an action was certain to be counterproductive. Nothing could have been better calculated to drive Japan to war than this action, which was designed to prevent war. Stark believed that the U.S. Navy was simply unprepared to fight a war. In this belief Stark was correct. In the months that followed the freezing of Japanese assets, as negotiations between the two nations showed the utter impossibility of reconciliation, the Roosevelt administration realized that Stark was right. It also realized that American strength in the Pacific was totally inadequate to back up American demands. It finally began to dawn on the administration that it had managed to get into a position from which there was no retreat.

The American move in July had come in response to yet another Japanese encroachment into a hitherto unmolested area. But southern Indo-China was something different. It was 1,500 miles closer to Malaya and the Indies than to the Japanese homeland and the Japanese occupation of it was a direct and obvious menace to the peace and stability of the region. For the Americans in July 1941, southern Indo-China was the ne plus ultra line, to be defended if for no other reason than that otherwise further Japanese aggression would surely follow. But American imposition of economic sanctions on Japan miscarried. When sanctions were imposed, the administration was deliberately vague regarding their extent. Roosevelt and his advisers were imprecise, partly because they were genuinely unsure how far and how quickly to go, but mainly because they wanted to keep Japan on the end of a line. The administration intended to use the economic weapon as an extremely sensitive instrument of torture, to be applied or slackened depending on Japanese behavior. The Americans were prepared to turn the screw, but slowly and in a manner and at a time of their own choosing. By keeping matters vague, however, instead of keeping Japan in a state of uncertainty and leaving the Americans with the options of progressively increasing the extent of sanctions over a period of time, the Americans lost control of the situation. It was widely assumed that vagueness meant totality, and, perforce, so it became, from the outset. The embargo on Japanese trade thus became a cleft stick not only for the Japanese but also for the Americans; it established a position that was totally inflexible and nonnegotiable.

The imposition of sanctions on Japan went hand in hand with certain military decisions designed to strengthen the American position in the Far East. The decisions, however, had the effect of reversing the decisions made in May because they envisaged not abandoning the Philippines but rather attempting to defend the Commonwealth. Three measures were undertaken. First, all units of the American and Philippine armies in the islands were placed under a single operational command, the U.S. Army Forces in the Far East. In August U.S. Army Air Forces also were brought under this command. Second, the chief military adviser to the government of the Commonwealth, Field Marshal Douglas MacArthur, a former chief of staff of the U.S. Army, was recalled to active service, given the rank of major general, and appointed to the command of U.S. Army Forces in the Far East. Third, the decision was taken by Washington to provide the funds for the mobilization of the Philippine army. These decisions were made on 26 July, the day economic measures were taken against Japan. On 1 August U.S. Army Chief of Staff General George C. Marshall advised MacArthur that the Roosevelt administration would send reinforcements to the Philippines as quickly as possible. By mid-September the first reinforcements with armor, antiaircraft guns, and other heavy equipment had begun to arrive in the Philippines.

The reasons for this abrupt about-face are certainly both unclear and confused because it would appear that the Roosevelt administration was pursuing two separate but interrelated aims. First, it is evident that the administration came to appreciate the need for strong forces in the Philippines to underwrite the whole of the American position in the Far East. It saw that the policy of deterrence could work only if it was based on a position of strength. To make the policy of deterrence work the administration was pinning its faith in the 1941 version of the ultimate deterrent, the much-vaunted B-17 Flying Fortress. The B-17 could be effective in this role only if the Philippines were held in strength. Second, and here the element of confusion begins to arise, if the Japanese gave the Americans the time to deploy substantial forces to the Philippines, these forces would in turn perhaps provide the time the United States needed to build up her overall forces to a satisfactory level. The recall of MacArthur was vitally important in that it kindled the hope that the Philippines could be held. Under MacArthur the new command began to plan not for the token defense of central Luzon alone but for the fortification of the whole island group—in effect the eleven major islands that make up 96 percent of the Philippines—and the defense of the Commonwealth in depth.

It is not hard to see why these steps were taken, and it is easy to be both critical and sympathetic with the moves, but they hardly made for sound strategy. The Americans in the summer of 1941 for the first time became critically aware of the importance of time. They appreciated the overwhelming need to buy time to push through their preparations. The exposure of relatively small land, air, and sea forces on the Philippines station would be justified either if Japanese aggression was deterred or if the Japanese incurred disproportionately heavy losses. MacArthur, for all his idiosyncracies, radiated confidence; he was convinced that the Philippines could be held—and Washington was inclined to believe it. Just why it did so is unclear because it was a ludicrous concept. The coastline of the Commonwealth was longer than that of the United States, while the islands were all but surrounded by Japanese bases. Very few islands were worth taking and the Japanese were certain, if they attacked, to make their main effort against Luzon and, to a lesser extent, Mindanao. On Luzon the only worthwhile objectives could be in the central portion and the only sites for major landings were Lamon Bay and Lingayen Gulf. For the defense of the hilly and difficult terrain were ten reserve divisions, one from each of the military districts that made up the Philippines, and the Philippine Division. The latter was a regular division made up of American and Filipino troops. MacArthur hoped and believed that surface units of the Asiatic Fleet, the submarines, and the air forces on the islands could, if not prevent an invasion, at least deny the Japanese use of the seven major straits between the various islands. There was never any doubt about the ability of the Pacific Fleet to rise to the occasion if need be.

Of course, there were obvious dangers. Reinforcements for the Philippines might easily be going straight into prisoner-of-war camps if the Japanese moved before the Americans were ready. The forces were needed elsewhere, such as on Hawaii, where they would not be hostages to fortune. Furthermore, in number the forces were desperately small. At the end of November 1941 the total regular strength of the American and Philippine armies in the Commonwealth was 31,095 officers and men. Even with the assistance of ten reserve divisions of unproven worth, there was no rational standard by which such a small force could be expected to defend the beaches and the islands in depth, as MacArthur claimed. It was really far too late in the day to dispatch small-scale deterrent forces to any effect. In addition, no meaningful discussions and planning went on with the British and Dutch. Indeed, at this stage the Americans refused to undertake detailed political and military consultations and mutual commitments.

It was also far too late for the British to send small-scale deterrent forces to the Far East with any hope of success. As the situation deteriorated with alarming rapidity in September and October, the British began to cast around for a deterrent of their own. The fall of the Konoe government and its replacement by the Tojo administration was interpreted correctly as a clear pointer to war. This made the British government desperate to send a force to the Far East as much, if not more, for political as for strategic reasons.

There was indeed a desperate need for some force to be sent to the Far East. While in 1941 both the British army and the Royal Air Force in Malaya had been strengthened, both remained wretchedly understrength. Instead of the forty-eight infantry battalions and two armored brigades deemed necessary for the defense of Malaya, only thirty-three battalions were available in November 1941 and many of these were semitrained Indian units. These battalions were deployed in the defense of airfields scarcely used by the motley collection of 141 second-rate aircraft based on the peninsula. Of these a mere 44 were modern fighters, but even these Brewster Buffaloes were obsolescent. Possible troop and aircraft reinforcements had been squandered in the course of 1941 on the ill-judged Greek venture or sent to the USSR, so that by October neither the army nor the air force had any reserves that could be sent to Malaya. Greece and Russia between them cost Britain 600 first-line aircraft; these would have been beyond price in Malaya.

The only possible source of reinforcement was the Royal Navy. The Admiralty, indeed, was working towards a redeployment of the fleet. By late 1941 Australian naval units had been directed homewards, but the Admiralty's main plan was to work to a deadline of early 1942, when a strike force of three capital ships and two, possibly three, carriers would be based on Trincomalee and four old slow *Revenge*-class battleships would be assembled for escort duties in the Indian Ocean. The problem was that time was running out and the British could not afford to wait until the spring of 1942. Politically, moreover, all the ships earmarked for concentration in the Indian Ocean—and the proposed concentration on Ceylon and not Singapore was significant—were old and lacked glamor. None were a match for Japanese battleships. Churchill was attracted by the idea of a deterrent force, sent to the east to keep the Japanese quiet. Such a force had to be modern, fast, and powerful; the persuasiveness of Churchill's political arguments broke the resistance and better judgment of the Admiralty. With the old battle cruiser *Repulse* already in the Indian Ocean and thus available for use in a fast battle squadron, even though she was as old as the unglamorous battleships and in urgent need of a refit, the Admiralty compromised by ordering the battleship *Prince of Wales* to the cape. She was to be joined en route by the carrier *Indomitable*, then working up in the Caribbean. The situation when these two ships reached the cape would determine their subsequent deployment, but it was always Churchill's manifest intention that they proceed to Singapore.

The *Prince of Wales* slipped out of the Clyde on 25 October and arrived forty days later, on 4 December, at Singapore in the company of the *Repulse* and four destroyers, but no carrier. The *Indomitable* damaged herself in the West Indies, and in the desperate circumstances of November 1941, when the carrier *Ark Royal* (and the battleship *Barham*) was lost in the Mediterranean, the British simply did not have a carrier to replace her. The force that arrived at Singapore, therefore, was badly unbalanced. It lacked an integrated air arm and could not rely on the Royal Air Force in Malaya to provide overhead cover. It lacked cruisers and had but four destroyers as escorts, two of which, the *Encounter* and *Jupiter*, were of dubious value. They had been detached from the Mediterranean Fleet by its commander for precisely that reason. The *Prince of Wales* herself was not fully worked up, despite having already seen active service in May. Moreover, the personnel and command structure of the British arrangements left much to be desired. The commander of the British force, known as Force Z, was Vice Admiral Sir Thomas Philipps. Philipps had not been to sea during the war and had commanded neither a battleship nor a fleet. His only experience of command at sea was in cruisers and destroyers. He was contemptuous of air power and retained a complete faith in the ability of a battleship, if handled and fought properly, to withstand anything but possible action with an equal. This he believed in spite of the fact that of all the major units sunk to date in the war only one, the *Hood*, had been sunk in a direct artillery duel. In addition, on the outbreak of war Philipps was to take over from the local commander in chief, Vice Admiral Sir Geoffrey Layton, hardly an ideal arrangement.

The dispatch of Force Z was an act of bluff, and it was a shallow bluff in that the British tried to pretend that they had concentrated a more substantial force at Singapore than was in fact the case. Aided by its intelligence services, Tokyo was undeceived; only the British government and an uninformed public clung to their illusions. Philipps did not. After arriving in Ceylon he flew on ahead of his force, and then journeyed to Manila to confer with MacArthur and Admiral Thomas Hart, commander in chief, U.S. Asiatic Fleet. MacArthur boasted that in the event of a Japanese landing he would sweep them back into the sea; if the Japanese delayed he claimed he would prevent them landing at all. The talks with Hart were a little more realistic, but even some of these deliberations seem a bit fanciful. Philipps and Hart agreed that Singapore was indefensible, and concluded from that that British capital ships would be best deployed at Manila. But this was recognized to be impossible given the paucity of American air power in the Philippines. It was agreed therefore that the *Prince of Wales* and *Repulse* should be committed to the impossible task of trying to prevent an invasion of Malaya and the Indies and that Hart should begin to send his major units southwards. He promised to send four destroyers to (the indefensible) Singapore if the three British destroyers at Hong Kong were similarly redeployed. Hart and Philipps also agreed that the main Allied naval effort should be expended in maintaining lines of communication within the area bound by the Philippines, Malaya, Australia, and the Indies, but no overall command was established and the forces available for this mammoth undertaking were pathetically inadequate. The position of the Allies was one of extreme weakness and confusion.

On 6 December Philipps returned to Singapore to face the news that the Japanese were on the move. Immediately two potentially disastrous situations faced Philipps and, for that matter, all the Allied naval commanders. All prewar assumptions about Japanese aggression had been based on the belief that Japan lacked the strength to mount more than one invasion attempt at a time. This had been a very reasonable estimate, but as the evidence of Japanese movements mounted it became obvious that a grievous error of judgment had been made. No allowances had been made for Japanese recourse to land-based naval air power as the means of conferring flexibility and striking power deep into enemy territory in support of what otherwise would be badly overcommitted forces. Indeed, the special reinforcement of the air forces in Indo-China by a detachment of bombers sent to the 21st Flotilla Headquarters was carried out as a direct counter to the arrival in the Far East of Force Z. Moreover, the whereabouts of the Japanese carriers was unknown, and that was ominous. Of all the Allied leaders only one, Field Marshal Jan C. Smuts, the prime minister of South Africa, had caught a glimpse of the dangers in the situation. He warned Churchill of the glaring weakness of stationing at Singapore and Hawaii fleets that were inferior to a Japanese fleet holding the twin advantages of concentration and central geographic position. He intimated to the British prime minister, "If the Japanese are really nippy, there is here an opening for a first-class disaster." Just how disastrous, the Japanese were ready to demonstrate.

CHAPTER 5

The *Iai*:
The Initial Japanese
Attack

ALL THE JAPANESE FORCES earmarked for the opening attacks had to be deployed to their action stations in the last days of peace. While the greatest concentration of ships and men was in the south, the most important part of Japanese striking power had to move eastwards against Pearl Harbor. Before the final decision of whether or not to go to war was taken by the Japanese high command, Nagumo's Strike Force of six fleet carriers, two battleships, two heavy cruisers, and the ten escorts of the 1st Destroyer Flotilla slipped out of its anchorage in Tankan Bay, Etorofu, in the Kuriles. In order to be in a position to attack the Americans at their least degree of readiness on the morning of Sunday, 7 December, the Strike Force had to leave Japanese waters well before Japan finally committed herself. If Japan for any reason chose to pull back at the eleventh hour, Nagumo was to be recalled. If the Strike Force was compromised before 6 December, Nagumo was to abandon his mission. Under no circumstances was the world

The *iai* is a stroke in the repertoire of the traditional Japanese swordsman. It is a surprise blow struck at the outset of combat without the preliminary ritual or the customary exchange of courtesies. Delivered by a right-handed swordsman, the blow is struck in a single sweep as the sword leaves the scabbard, cutting up and through the opponent from the right hip to the left shoulder. The aim of the *iai* is to strike a surprise blow from which there can be no recovery by the opponent, and so to secure a first advantage that either destroys or totally incapacitates the enemy. The parallel between the *iai* and the Pearl Harbor raid is exact, except in execution.

to find out what the Japanese had planned if for some reason the attack was not executed.

When the Japanese force sailed on the morning of 26 November few, if any, could have realized that in attacking Pearl Harbor these twenty warships would unleash a war that not one of them was to survive.

The Strike Force steamed eastwards along the forty-third parallel into the stormy northern Pacific, seeking in those inhospitable waters the immunity from detection that was critical to the success of the operation. The price paid in storm damage, men washed overboard, and sheer crew fatigue was not light, but only one merchantman, fortunately Japanese, was encountered as the warships and their eight attendant oilers steamed slowly towards Hawaii. The international date line was crossed on 3 December, the Strike Force thereby gaining a day, by which time Nagumo had been given the code word to indicate that the operation should proceed as planned and not be abandoned. On the next day—the fourth by Japanese time but still the third for Hawaii—Nagumo's force began its turn to the southeast as part of the final closing of Oahu. By the evening of the sixth (Hawaii time) the carriers and their escorts were about 500 miles due north of Pearl Harbor, and throughout the night they steamed at high speed, to reach their flying-off position some 250 miles north of Oahu by dawn.

Fortune, and their own careful planning arrangements, favored the Japanese in that their approach was undetected, but it was to play them false with regard to the available targets. In undertaking the Pearl Harbor operation the Japanese carried out what was the greatest carrier operation in history up until that time. They were using their carrier aircraft to project offensive power deep into enemy-controlled waters. The only sensible objective of such an attack had to be the elimination of those ships with a similar capacity—the American fleet carriers. These, indeed, were the targets singled out for destruction by the Japanese. In mid-November the Japanese knew that four carriers were at Pearl Harbor and that a fifth, the *Saratoga*, then on the west coast, was scheduled to return to Hawaii. The Japanese might reasonably have hoped that all or at least most of the carriers would be at their moorings on the seventh.

Pearl Harbor was both an operational and a training base, and its broad routine was fixed. Exercises took place mostly from either Monday or Tuesday to Friday, and it was normal for the Americans to concentrate their fleet in the harbor over weekends. The Japanese were not to know that since mid-November two of the carriers had left for the Atlantic and that the *Saratoga* had not returned to Pearl Harbor. Yet as Nagumo's force closed on Oahu, the latest intelligence reports showed that none of the American carriers were in their base. The *Enterprise* and *Lexington* were both at sea, and their absence was a grave disappointment to the Japanese. There was some hesitation over whether or not to launch the attack, but the

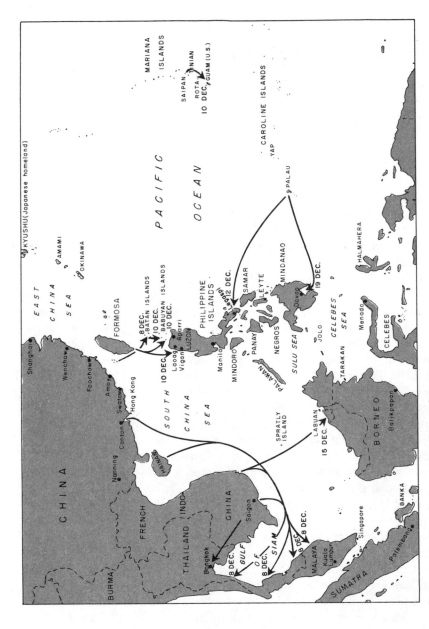

Japanese Strikes, 7 through 19 December 1941

tightness of the time schedule for the operation—because of its synchronization with other operations across the Pacific and in Southeast Asia—
made it impossible for the Strike Force to do anything other than proceed
with the attack. The general consensus was that eight battleships—one, the
Colorado, was undergoing repairs on the west coast—were too good a target
to miss. Nagumo's own view was that an operation could not be delayed on
account of ships that were not there.

Even as late as the sixth, Nagumo could reasonably hope that because
the cruisers normally with the *Enterprise* had returned to port, at least one of
the carriers might arrive back in time to be sunk. He should have been right.
The *Enterprise* should have tied up at about 0730 on the seventh, some thirty
minutes before the Japanese attacked, but she was delayed by refuelling
problems and was some 200 miles west of Pearl Harbor when the attack
materialized. Warned of the attack by some of her aircraft, which ran into
the first wave of Japanese attackers, the carrier disappeared westwards,
with the result that the Japanese never found her. Despite the absence of the
carriers, ninety-six warships, the major part of the Pacific Fleet, were in the
harbor, and there was no sign of any undue activity on the part of the
Americans. The situation seemed full of promise for the Japanese.

Just before dawn on the morning of the seventh, the Japanese carriers
began to turn eastwards into the wind to launch their aircraft. With a strong
southerly sea running, conditions for the launch were far from ideal, but
the first wave of forty-three Mitsubishi A6M2 Zero-sen fighters, eighty-
nine Nakajima B5N2 Kate level-altitude bombers, and eighty-one Achi
D3A2 Val dive bombers took to the air in record time. Only two aircraft
were lost during takeoff. The second wave, flown off a little less than an
hour later, was slightly smaller. It consisted of forty fighters, fifty high-
level Kates, and eighty Vals. Nagumo held back just eighty aircraft. Forty
were retained to combat air patrol and the remainder were either out of
service or held in reserve. The Japanese were to lose ten aircraft from the
first wave of attackers and nineteen from the second, though some of these
were to be lost when attempting to regain their carriers.

The attacks on Oahu began at 0755 and continued with only a brief lull
for about two hours. In that short time the Japanese smashed the U.S.
Pacific Fleet and American air power on the island into what appeared to be
smoking ruins. In fact, appearances were to prove deceptive, though the
losses themselves were very real. Most of the damage done to the Americans was inflicted in the first minutes of the attack, when resistance was
nonexistent and the Japanese objectives were not obscured by smoke. The
army air bases at Bellows, Hickam, and Wheeler Fields; the marine base at
Ewa; and the naval air stations on Ford Island and at Kaneohe were
mercilessly raked over, though the small army airfield at Haleiwa escaped
attention. By the time the Japanese finished with the airfields, 188 Amer-

ican aircraft out of the 394 on the island at the time of the attack had been destroyed and another 159 had been damaged.

In the attacks on the warships in the roads the Japanese scored heavily. In a matter of minutes four of the seven battleships at anchor were sunk. The *Arizona* was transformed from a battleship into a charred wreck when a bomb penetrated her forward magazine. The *California*, her double bottom opened up in readiness for an inspection the next day, settled on an even keel after two torpedo hits. The *Oklahoma*, the first of the battleships to be lost, capsized as a result of a series of torpedoes finding its mark, while the *West Virginia*, her port side gashed open by perhaps as many as six torpedoes and her upper three decks forward telescoped together and gutted by fire as a result of bomb damage, avoided turning turtle because of counterflooding and her retaining wires. Of all the battleships at anchor only the *Nevada* managed to get under way, but she was heavily damaged and was forced to beach herself in order not to sink in the channel and so prevent ships either entering or leaving the harbor. Only two battleships, the *Maryland* and *Tennessee*, moored inside less fortunate companions, escaped with relatively minor damage, while the fleet flagship, the *Pennsylvania*, which was drydocked, escaped with only a solitary bomb hit that did minor damage to her superstructure. The flagship was given much inaccurate attention by Japanese bombers in the second wave, but in missing the *Pennsylvania* they did wreck the destroyers *Cassin* and *Downes*, which were sharing the dock. The destroyer *Shaw*, in the floating drydock, lost her forward parts in a massive magazine explosion. Three light cruisers, the *Helena*, *Honolulu*, and *Raleigh*, were damaged, two of them quite severely, while the seaplane tender *Curtiss* and the repair ship *Vestal* were quite badly struck. The target battleship *Utah* and the ancient minelayer *Oglala*, however, were both lost and several other ships were shaken by near-misses.

Perhaps the most surprising feature of the whole attack was that only eighteen warships and auxiliaries were either sunk or badly damaged during the air attack. In view of the Pacific Fleet's evident unpreparedness and its defenseless state, the losses could have been much heavier. That losses were not heavier is explicable by three facts. First, the concurrent attack on the naval base by Japanese midget submarines failed to register a single success; second, Japanese aircraft tended to concentrate against the more obvious targets and thereby to ignore a plethora of smaller but no less important targets; and third, there was no attempt by Nagumo to resume the attack after the recovery of his carrier aircraft.

As recounted earlier, for the Pearl Harbor operation the Japanese committed twenty-eight submarines and five midget submarines to complement the air attack. Many Japanese officers, sceptical of the chances of the aircraft, placed great confidence in the submarine offensive, which was to be conducted thoroughly in line with Japanese submarine doctrine and

Battleship Row, Pearl Harbor, 7 December 1941. At the far end of the line is the *Oklahoma*, with the repair ship *Vestal* beside her, then the *West Virginia* and the *Arizona*. All three battleships, along with the *California* and *Nevada*, were sunk. Of the five, the *Oklahoma* and *Arizona* alone became total losses. U.S. Navy

training. The submarine offensive was a fiasco. Two of the midget submarines were sunk even before the air attack developed as they tried to enter the harbor, two were sunk inside the anchorage, and the last one was captured. The only partial success the fleet submarines achieved was on 11 January, when the *I-6* torpedoed but failed to sink the *Saratoga*. In return, on 10 December Japanese lost the *I-70* to aircraft from the *Enterprise* and later the *I-73* to an American submarine off Midway. The failure to achieve good results was a bad blow to the Japanese and led to a serious loss of face for the submarine arm. The decline of fortune for the submariners indeed dates from Pearl Harbor because the Japanese naval command never really regained its confidence in the submarines to achieve results. Diminishing faith was vested in the submarines as the war progressed and the service, despite its successes, ended up spending most of its time ferrying supplies to beleaguered Japanese garrisons in remote parts of the Pacific. Of all the submarines that were involved in the Pearl Harbor operation only the *I-21* survived the war.

The second factor involved in the Japanese failure to achieve better results was the fact that the aircrews naturally singled out the most prestigious targets for attack and failed to spread their efforts around the American fleet. Destruction, as we have seen, was therefore concentrated among the battleships, where proportionate losses were extremely severe. Five of the eight battleships in base at the time of the attack were lost, though in the end only two, the *Arizona* and *Oklahoma*, were destined to become total losses. The *Oklahoma* was later raised in order to clear the anchorage, but the *Arizona*, along with the *Utah*, still lies at Pearl Harbor. The other three battleships that were lost, the *California*, *Nevada*, and *West Virginia*, were recovered and all the battleships that were salvaged from Pearl Harbor took part in the Okinawa operation, thus participating in the final cornering of the Imperial Navy.

The third factor that prevented American losses from being far heavier was Nagumo's refusal to countenance a second strike. His pilots, once on board their carriers and with their aircraft rearmed and refuelled, wanted to return to Pearl Harbor to resume the pounding of the Americans. The strike leader, Commander Mitsuo Fuchida, was well aware that such an opportunity might never be repeated, and he pleaded with Nagumo to mount another attack to press home the Japanese advantage. Nagumo, however, was cautious. His orders had not contained instructions to attack shore installations and he felt no inclination to interpret orders liberally. Age and responsibility seem to have robbed him of the élan and vitality that he had displayed as a cruiser and destroyer commander and outspoken opponent of the 1935 disarmament conference. As a carrier admiral, a post for which he had no training or previous experience, he never showed flair or imagination. He had had little confidence in the plan of attack in the first place, and he was more than a little relieved that his force had not been compromised. Nagumo was alert to the critical importance of the carriers to Japan and it was he who had made the perceptive and ominous observation before the attack that carriers, with their massive and vulnerable flight decks, were wide open to dive-bombing attacks. These considerations, it must be admitted, made his position difficult. But in the final analysis, Nagumo placed the preservation and security of his force above the achievement of its strategic objectives. In rejecting the various calls for follow-up strikes, Nagumo acted more as a commander aware of having narrowly avoided decisive defeat than as one with total annihilating victory within his grasp. Fearful that to stay in waters near Hawaii would bring American aircraft against the carriers, Nagumo took the view that nothing more could reasonably be expected by continuing the attack. This being his conclusion, he hoisted the recall and turned for home. By this action he

Vice Admiral Chuichi Nagumo, commander of the carrier Strike Force that raided Pearl Harbor, Rabaul, Darwin, and Ceylon. Defeated at Midway, he was dismissed after the battle of Santa Cruz in October 1942. He committed suicide when the forces he commanded on Saipan were overrun in 1944. Orbis Collection

rejected a golden opportunity of turning what was a considerable success into a major victory. In failing to return to finish off the Americans at Pearl Harbor or to extend search operations for the elusive carriers to the south and west of Oahu, Nagumo left his task only half complete, with incalculable repercussions.*

Superficially the Japanese attack was an overwhelming victory. To a world that in 1941 was still accustomed to measuring sea power in terms of battleships, Pearl Harbor was a disastrous defeat for the Americans. On 6

---

*It is worth noting, if only en passant, the immediate consequences for the ships of his force of Nagumo's failure to press his advantage. For the attack the Japanese used twenty warships, eight oilers, and thirty submarines. One oiler and one submarine survived the war to surrender to the Allies. The result of leaving the attack unfinished was very quickly felt. The cream of Japanese naval aviation was mauled at the Coral Sea in May and annihilated at Midway in June. The Japanese losses in these battles were at the hands of the carriers missing from Pearl Harbor on 7 December 1941. American carrier aircraft ultimately accounted for ten of Nagumo's warships and shared two more with mines and gunfire. They also accounted for two submarines. Of all their sinkings perhaps the most appropriate and ironic was their last one—the heavy cruiser *Tone* on 24 June 1945. This warship, which had sailed halfway across the Pacific to take part in the Pearl Harbor attack, was sunk by American carrier aircraft in her home base of Kure. If it is correct to talk about poetic justice in war, then surely this must be a very good example.

December the U.S. Navy was the proud owner of seventeen battleships, more than any other nation in the world. By the end of the next day the Americans had a mere eight fit for operations, and several of these were old and could not hope to stand in the line against German or Japanese counterparts. For the loss of five Kates, fifteen Vals, and nine Zero-sens, plus five two-man midget submarines, the Imperial Navy appeared to have inflicted crippling damage on American sea power.

The reality of the situation was very different: Pearl Harbor was to prove just one more of the victories along the road that led Japan to decisive defeat. The utter finality of that defeat in large part stems from the bungled operation at Pearl Harbor. The extent of the American battleship losses tended to obscure the simple fact that the overwhelming part of the Pacific Fleet escaped unscathed, and, of course, only a very small part of the overall strength of the American navy was lost at Pearl Harbor. Both before and after the attack the U.S. Navy had eighteen heavy cruisers, twelve of them in the Pacific. Only three had been in Pearl Harbor at the time of the attack, and all escaped without a scratch. Three light cruisers had been damaged, but there still remained another fifteen in American possession, and their temporary loss did not result in the transfer to the Pacific of any of the eight light cruisers then in the Atlantic. After the attack the Americans still retained 168 destroyers and all 112 of their submarines. With destroyers in short supply, the loss of just one was undesirable, but the three that were lost could be absorbed. The carriers, of course, shared the submarines' immunity, and the significance of their remaining intact was not widely appreciated at the time. The carriers, indeed, had been fortunate to evade

The Achi D3A dive bomber, known as the Val, was the last fixed-undercarriage aircraft to serve with the Japanese carrier forces. Despite appearing obsolescent, the Val was the key strike aircraft of the Imperial Navy and sank more Allied ships than any other Axis aircraft. National Archives 80-G-196863

detection and destruction, but the fact was that six fleet carriers remained to the Americans after their Japanese counterparts turned for home.

What was lost at Pearl Harbor, therefore, was only the battle squadrons, but they were old and slow. None had been fast enough to keep up with the carriers, and none were a match for the new generation of ships then in service with the four major navies of the day. Irreverently, the battle squadrons have been dismissed as a collection of obsolescent scrap iron, but while this is an obvious overstatement, the comment recognizes the fact that the elimination of the battle line removed from the scene some ships of rather questionable value and forced the Americans to recast the whole of their tactical doctrine. The Americans were forced to jettison any lingering ideas of the battleship remaining the arbiter of sea power and, with the destruction of the battle line, were obliged to develop the war-winning concept of the fast carrier task force. After Pearl Harbor the Americans had to constitute their fleets around carriers for the simple reason that there were no battleships. It was one of the supreme ironies of Pearl Harbor that the Japanese settled the argument within the U.S. Navy over the relative merits and importance of battleships and carriers. For the Americans, moreover, the loss of the battleships had one other, unforeseen effect. In 1941 trained manpower in the U.S. Navy was in critically short supply. The loss of the battle line enabled the Americans to redeploy the survivors from sunken ships onto other warships. This meant that escort forces could be properly manned, and the carrier task forces could be properly constituted and balanced. This, in a very roundabout manner and at a cost of 2,403 dead servicemen and civilians, was one of the very positive advantages accruing to the Americans as a result of the Pearl Harbor operation.

Besides the carriers, one other type of warship escaped unscathed from the 7 December shambles. This was the submarine arm, and it was to this branch of the service that the task of carrying the immediate fight to the Japanese fell. For the moment there was no other force capable of undertaking offensive action against Japan. After Pearl Harbor the Japanese command of the seas could not be openly challenged; even before the attack the Imperial Navy possessed a marked numerical superiority over the Pacific Fleet in every type of warship, while after the attack the Americans had virtually no air power and, other than the carriers, no warship in the Pacific larger than a cruiser with which to undertake offensive operations. Thus, from the very start of the war, the Americans were forced to undertake unrestricted submarine warfare. By an ironic twist of history, this was the form of warfare that had brought the United States into the war against Germany in 1917 and to which the Americans objected in the Atlantic between 1939 and 1941.

In December 1941, however, the adoption of unrestricted submarine warfare was a reflex action, the tactical response to a lost strategic situation.

Yet, as we have noted, it was a form of warfare directed against one of the most critical weaknesses in the Japanese military and economic situation. The American submarines, necessarily slow to find their stride, were to impose a steady rate of attrition on Japanese commerce that in the end was to become unbearable. The full effect of this campaign was to be somewhat overshadowed by the totality of final victory, since in the last stages of the war the Allies were to be involved in continuous naval and air bombardment of the Japanese homeland. But the achievement of the submarine arm is not to be considered lightly. At the very small cost of 52 of their number, American submarines sank 1,152 Japanese merchantmen of 4,889,000 tons (more than aircraft, surface warships, mines, and natural causes combined) as well as many warships, including no less than seven carriers, including the 62,000-ton *Shinano*.*

The Americans could never have resorted to extensive use of their submarines and fast carrier task forces had the Japanese accounted for the crucially important Oahu base facilities, without which the Pacific Fleet could not have operated. About 4,500,000 barrels of oil had been painstakingly stockpiled at Pearl Harbor by the U.S. Navy in the previous eighteen months, and for the most part this had been stored above ground. This oil had been an easy and vulnerable target, but the Japanese had been obsessed with attacks on battle units. Even in their attacks on Battleship Row, the Japanese had attacked only battleships and ignored the *Neosho*, a tanker carrying high-octane aviation fuel. Had she been set on fire she might have incinerated as many as three battleships as effectively as any of the attacks on the battleships themselves. Similar dire consequences would have ensued from an attack on the oil dumps. Had these been attacked it is hard to see how the Americans possibly could have maintained their fleet at Pearl Harbor or, indeed, have offered even the weakest of defenses in the central Pacific. The position of the Pacific Fleet would have been untenable, and the fleet would have had to return to San Diego, from whence it had come in April 1940. Then it had been dispatched as a deterrent; had it had to retire in 1942, it would have done so in circumstances politically and strategically disastrous for the United States. The process of rebuilding the oil reserve could well have proved prohibitively expensive, at least in terms of time. Yet the dumps were untouched, and the Japanese failed to pay attention to the dockyards, power plants, and workshops that were essential to the maintenance of the fleet. Damage was inflicted on some of the shore installations, but only in passing. Had any of the permanent installations been destroyed, the American countermoves in the Pacific would have been held back for a period far longer than as a result of delays caused by damage to ships. Just as the Imperial Navy's obsession with battle led it to under-

*From Nagumo's force the submarines accounted for six warships and three submarines.

estimate the importance of defending commerce and to ignore the prospects of an offensive against American merchantmen, so this obsession led the Japanese navy to underestimate the importance of the Pearl Harbor facilities to the Americans. It was a fateful error of judgment.

In every material sense Pearl Harbor was a Japanese victory, but it was a victory in which every success had to be balanced against an omission or failure. If the mercantile balance is thrown on the scales, then the material consequences of the attack make the operation a serious Japanese defeat because five battleships sunk in return for 4,000,000 tons of merchant shipping lost was a ruinous rate of exchange for Japan. Yet the real loss to the Japanese was not material but psychological. The Japanese counted on their superior resolve to wear down the Americans in a war of attrition and thereby secure a negotiated peace. There can be no doubt that the Japanese belief in their moral supremacy over their enemies at all stages of the war never wavered. The use of kamikazi formations in the final stages of war is the ultimate proof of Japanese superiority in this one field. But just as the Japanese made fundamental miscalculations over the efficacy of their psychological primacy—and failed to realize that it could not overcome too severe a material handicap—their estimation of the effect of the Pearl Harbor attack on American attitudes was disastrously inept.

The Japanese deluded themselves into the belief that the attack would leave the Americans divided, confused, and dismayed. This was a miscalculation of monumental proportions and a total misunderstanding of American attitudes at the time. The attack had the effect of getting the Roosevelt administration off the hook; it no longer had to maneuver tortuously to check Japan while keeping one eye firmly on American isolationist strength. The attack did not impale the administration on a stake of public obloquy. Instead it cemented in a hitherto faction-ridden country a furious resolve to wage war by any means to the bitter end, and did so in a manner that no amount of creative domestic leadership could have achieved.

Rear Admiral Chuichi Hara, the gifted commander of the 5th Carrier Division, dryly commented after the war that for their attack on Pearl Harbor Roosevelt should have decorated the Japanese. If the Japanese were correct in their view that psychological rather than material factors were the decisive elements of war, then the Pearl Harbor attack ensured their defeat; the war was lost already. After 7 December the Americans would never have accepted anything less than either total victory over Japan or total defeat at her hands; after the attack there could never be any question of a compromise or a negotiated peace. The war had to be fought to a finish. The attack on Pearl Harbor did more than anything else, certainly more than Roosevelt could have done, to ensure that when he went before Congress the following day to ask for a declaration of war on Japan, it was as head of a united and resolute nation. He addressed a Congress already committed to final victory. Such a situation would have been impossible even a day before the attack. In their assessment of American psychology the Japanese made a fundamental and absolute error; Pearl Harbor was something not to mourn but to avenge.

Under the terms of the Japanese war plans the small concentration of forces based on Truk was earmarked to secure the various islands of the Southwest Pacific. In the first phase of operations the Gilberts, Guam, and Wake were to be secured, while in the second phase the Japanese were to move to secure the islands of the Bismarck Archipelago and certain positions in Papua, New Guinea. The account of the taking of these islands thus partially falls outside the scope of Japan's initial strikes, but for reasons of convenience and clarity the major part of these operations (at least from the Japanese side) needs to be considered at this point.

The main outline of events can be recounted quickly. The initial Japanese objectives were rapidly secured. Makin, in the Gilberts, and Guam were captured on 10 December. Subsequently Tarawa, also in the Gilberts, was taken without opposition, but minimal forces were left on the tiny atoll because the Japanese were content to deploy the major part of their forces in the Gilbert Islands on Makin. With flying boats based on Makin for the purpose of long-range reconnaissance, the Japanese were prepared to adopt a defensive stance in the islands and to rely on the rapid reinforcement of the island chain in the event of a developing threat against what was one of the main cornerstones of their defensive perimeter. The island of Wake was secured on 23 December.

After these first-phase attacks the Japanese developed their offensive, moving into the Bismarcks. Rabaul on New Britain was secured on 23 January 1942, and the next day Kavieng, the major settlement on the nearby island of New Ireland, was taken. But it was not until 9 February that Gasmata, the only place on Rabaul other than Rabaul to possess any strategic or tactical significance, was taken. A whole month elapsed before Japanese forces moved against New Guinea. Then, on 8 March, in the face of minimal and ineffective Australian resistance, Japanese forces secured Lae and Salamaua on the northern coast of the island. In all these operations minimal Japanese forces were employed and moved from one objective to another along interior lines of communication. The whole of the Japanese operations in this theater exhibited a beautiful economy of effort.

While all these operations were very small-scale affairs, they possess an interest quite out of proportion to the size of the forces engaged in them. First, they illustrate most graphically the great flexibility bestowed on the Japanese by their possession of the initiative and their dominance in sea power. Second, these operations contain the one and only instance in the whole of the Pacific war when a seaborne invasion attempt was defeated. At

Wake, on 11 December, at the cost of just one fatality, the Americans beat off a quite substantial Japanese force, without allowing a single Japanese soldier to get ashore. This success was never repeated in the war, by either side. Third, this was the area where the Americans were to launch some of their first counterattacks in the reconquest of the Pacific in the course of 1943. Fourth, and this point is beyond the scope of this chapter, the Japanese operations were contested by the Americans. In these phases, particularly in the second phase of operations, the Americans used their carriers to counter Japanese moves. No fleet action resulted until May, but there were several occasions when it seemed quite possible that a clash between the rival carrier forces would take place. These operations, therefore, bring into consideration the strategy employed by the Americans in this, their first, defensive, phase of the war.

Guam and Wake were two American possessions that were important as staging posts for aircraft between Hawaii and the Philippines, but there most of the similarities between the two islands ended. Guam is a large island, some 225 square miles in area, with an interior that is hilly and well vegetated. Wake is a desolate atoll of three islands and a shallow lagoon, the outside perimeter being about 20 miles in length. Though large enough to take a major garrison and base, Guam, as the most southerly of the major islands in the Marianas, to all intents and purposes was indefensible. It was hemmed in on all sides by Japanese possessions, particularly to the south in the Carolines. Wake, on the other hand, is "merely" 2,000 miles from Hawaii, and over 600 miles from the nearest Japanese base. Any major or prolonged Japanese attempt to secure Wake could result in a fleet engagement. This was an observation made before the war by Admiral Husband E. Kimmel, the ill-fated commander of the U.S. Pacific Fleet at the time of Pearl Harbor. But the possibility of such an action depended on timely intelligence and the ability of Wake to withstand an attack for a time. In the latter respect Wake was as poorly defended as Guam. Guam and Wake, both selected by the Japanese as targets in their opening offensive, were subjected to air attack within hours of the assault on Pearl Harbor.

Guam was the target of a two-day air offensive before the Japanese put ashore a 5,000-strong force shortly before dawn on the morning of 10 December. The tiny garrison of 365 marines and 300 native troops was overwhelmed inside an hour, the Americans surrendering in order to prevent the possibility of Japanese reprisals against the local population. In fact the Japanese assault force's treatment of its prisoners and the local population was correct. Yet, despite inducements, the local population did not collaborate but hid and supplied those few American servicemen who escaped into the interior.

Wake, however, proved a far harder nut to crack, and the Japanese seem to have been singularly careless in the preparations for their assault on the atoll. Very few troops—less than 450 men in the assault phase—were embarked for the attack, and the covering force consisted of three light cruisers (the flagship *Yubari*, and the *Tatsuta* and *Tenryu*) and six destroyers (the *Hayate*, *Kisaragi*, *Mochizuki*, *Mutsuki*, *Oite*, and *Yayoi*). The Japanese seem to have vastly underestimated the power and resolution of the garrison. This miscalculation may have stemmed from exaggerated reports of success from the raids carried out by aircraft, though it must be admitted that the damage inflicted during these softening-up operations had been considerable. The truth of the situation on Wake was that, though most of the F4F Wildcats flown in by the *Lexington* on 4 December had been destroyed and most of the installations on the islands had been flattened, none of the six 5.1-inch guns and twelve 3-inch antiaircraft guns had been touched. When on the eleventh the Japanese force closed in on the atoll, the marine gunners held their fire until the last possible moment. One of the transports, a converted destroyer, was crippled and later lost and another transport was damaged. In an effort to draw fire from the transports, three of the destroyers immediately closed in to engage the American batteries, the *Hayate* quickly being blown out of the water with no survivors. In the subsequent exchange with the shore batteries the *Oite* and *Yayoi* were both damaged, while four Wildcats struck lucky and accounted for the *Kisaragi*. She was destroyed by the detonation of her own depth charges, set off by the attacking aircraft. Without being able to put a single man ashore, the Japanese broke off the action and turned for Kwajalein. It is hard to resist the conclusion that this operation received its just deserts. Alone among the Japanese operations at this time it bears the imprint of being underprepared, undermanned, and ineptly executed.

The failure of the operation, however, ensured that the Japanese would renew their efforts with much greater force. Wake was essential to the Japanese. It was needed in order to complete their defensive perimeter across the width of the Pacific, and to prevent the atoll from being used by the Americans as a jumping-off point for future operations in the western Pacific. The possession of Wake, moreover, would facilitate any subsequent operation the Japanese might care to make against Midway and the western Hawaiian group. The failure of the operation of the eleventh, however, made a second operation hazardous because it presented the Americans with the chance to reinforce the atoll and deploy a task force to contest any Japanese invasion. This situation gave Kimmel a fleeting opportunity to retrieve something from the wreckage of his fleet and career. He ordered the reinforcement of Wake, instructing the *Saratoga* to give support to the atoll's garrison, and ordering the *Lexington* and *Yorktown* to stand by their sister carrier. Unfortunately for Kimmel the hand he hoped to deal himself failed to materialize.

The *Saratoga* was delayed in Pearl Harbor by refuelling problems and then lost two days topping up her destroyers at a time when the American task forces had to make all speed if they were to get into a position to cover Wake. But after the operation had been initiated, Kimmel was ordered to haul down his flag. Until the time that Admiral Chester W. Nimitz arrived to take over as commander of the Pacific Fleet, Kimmel's deputy, Vice Admiral William S. Pye, was in command. Pye's position was invidious. The abandoning of Wake after such a gallant defense was not an easy decision to make, but to hazard the carriers was unthinkable. There was a good chance that the American carriers could encounter a much inferior force and overwhelm it, but there was also the distinct possibility that, with the whereabouts of Nagumo's force unknown to the Americans, the three American carriers might find themselves up against a far superior force. The Americans suspected that the Japanese would use Wake as bait for a battle. In this they were wrong. Pye knew that, whatever happened, defeat and the loss of the carriers had to be avoided at all costs. For any new fleet commander Wake was expendable, the carriers were not. In the end, after much agonizing and in what seemed at the time to be deeply shaming circumstances, Pye decided against making an effort to relieve Wake.

While the American carriers east of Wake refuelled and their commanders fumbled for a decision, the Japanese renewed their attack. The assault force consisted of the survivors of the 11 December debacle, but in support were four heavy cruisers sent down specially from Guam, and the *Hiryu* and *Soryu* from Nagumo's Strike Force, and the seaplane tender *Chitose*. Returning home after the Pearl Harbor operation, Nagumo shed the two light fleet carriers in order to support the 24th Air Flotilla when it became clear that the operation of the eleventh had been a disaster. But even with these forces the Japanese were operating on dangerously narrow margins. In fact, in the general area of Wake at the time of the second assault, the Americans possessed superiority at sea. Had the Americans risked their carriers in the defense of Wake, it is quite possible that they could have overwhelmed the invasion force and the heavy cruisers without necessarily tangling with the Japanese carriers. This would have been a welcome tactical and strategic victory, and, more important, a major psychological triumph. As it was, through no fault of the unfortunate Pye, the chance of a victory was allowed to slip through American fingers, and Wake was abandoned to its fate.

The Japanese renewed their assault on the twenty-third, but their actions this time were more circumspect than they had been on the eleventh. The heavy cruisers prudently stayed outside the range of the shore batteries, while the assaulting troops were launched some 2 miles from the shore, and skillfully sought the security of dead ground for their landfall. Nevertheless, the ground fighting was severe, with savage hand-to-hand combat at the water's edge. But the odds were against the heavily outnumbered American garrison. Within a day and at the cost of 1,000 dead and wounded Japanese infantrymen, Wake passed into Japanese hands.

Two comments need to be made about the ill-starred Wake affair. On the Japanese side the whole of the operation had the hallmark of a botched-up job; the Japanese fielded their second team and it showed. Their losses were quite heavy, well deserved, and could have been worse. Indeed, they were lucky in escaping so lightly from a poorly conceived and badly conducted series of operations. On the American side it is difficult to be critical because of the command changes and the impossible situation in which Pye found himself. He was undoubtedly correct in not pressing on with the relief of Wake, humiliating though it undoubtedly was for the Americans to recall the carriers at the time when Wake was under attack. The outcome of any battle that might have resulted would have been close. The advantage should have been with the Americans, but had the *Saratoga* been caught by the dragon duet, then there would have been another disaster to set beside Pearl Harbor.

Nevertheless, Pye's caution, despite the anger it aroused in the fleet, was well in accord with American strategic thinking in the first month of the Pacific war. With the appointment of Ernest J. King as commander in chief, U.S. Fleet, and Nimitz as Pacific Fleet commander, American strategy in the Pacific had to be based on the realistic though necessarily harsh abandonment of minor interests to buy time in order that major interests could be secured. Interests that could not be maintained or quickly redeemed had to go, and Wake was such an interest. American naval strategy appreciated that the integrity of the Hawaii-Midway chain and the preservation of the line of communications between Pearl Harbor and the west coast were absolute considerations. These had to take precedence over everything else. American interests were therefore largely directed to the task of securing Pearl Harbor and its approaches. But the Americans also realized that Australia and New Zealand had to be preserved as bases for eventual offensive operations against Japanese conquests. The Americans recognized that neither of the Dominions could protect themselves and that the British could not be looked to for support. Thus the Americans had to hold open the lines of communication from Hawaii and Panama to Australasia, making certain that the Japanese could not break into the Fiji, Samoa, New Caledonia islands complex. At the same time, of course, the Americans had to provide bases across the Pacific in order to build up the forces and supplies needed to secure these islands and Dominions in the Southwest Pacific.

The Japanese plan of campaign against the American presence in the Philippines was very complicated and envisaged invasion after an air offensive designed to secure air supremacy over the islands. In order to secure command of the air, the Japanese would have liked to have synchronized their air strikes against the Philippines with the Pearl Harbor attack, but the time difference between Hawaii and Manila made this impossible. It was still dark in the Philippines when the Japanese carrier aircraft struck at Oahu. The Japanese, therefore, were forced to accept that the Americans on the Philippines were certain to be forewarned. The risk of any attack being met in the air had to be accepted. To complicate matters still further for the Japanese, two more problems existed. The army bombers on Formosa lacked the range to strike at the important airfields around Manila and in central Luzon. With no fleet carriers available and the small 10,600-ton carrier *Ryujo* detailed for operations against the American seaplane base at Davao on Mindanao, the Japanese were forced to rely on specially modified naval bombers from the 11th Air Fleet to provide the cutting edge for their air offensive. This, in its turn, necessitated army aircraft from the 5th Air Division flying close support for certain of the invasion forces. Moreover, the Japanese had to contend with the distinct possibility that the Americans would send their aircraft, particularly their Flying Fortresses, southwards on the outbreak of hostilities, well beyond the range of Japanese aircraft. Therefore, even by Japanese standards the margin for error in the opening strike against the Philippines was very narrow indeed.

On the morning of the opening attacks—8 December— the Japanese were faced with an additional problem that threatened the success of the whole venture. Early morning fog shrouded Formosa, grounding most aircraft. Only a few army bombers managed to sortie and strike targets in northern Luzon. With these mists Japanese fears increased because they were afraid of either an American retirement out of range or, more danger- ously, an American preemptive attack against Formosa itself. In fact, the Americans did neither, for something dangerously close to paralysis struck the American command on Luzon. Postwar research has failed to reconcile the conflicting claims of what various American commanders said they proposed and wanted to do on the eighth, but certain points seem to have emerged with reasonable clarity. The Americans appear to have assumed that they were reasonably secure in central Luzon. The obvious pres- ence of the Japanese carriers off Hawaii and the unsuspected range of naval bombers on Formosa implied that central Luzon was out of range for Japanese strike aircraft. The Americans were therefore content to confine themselves to defensive measures and to flying combat air patrols on the morning of the eighth in preparation for attacks on Formosa the following day. The Japanese never gave the Americans a chance to launch this attack. The main period of American alertness had passed by midday on the eighth, when most American aircraft were grounded, having been fuelled and parked. The aircraft were not dispersed but lined up in neat rows when at about 1215 some 192 Japanese aircraft, having sortied from Formosa once the early morning mists had lifted, appeared over central Luzon. The relative lateness of the hour, plus an untimely communications failure with the only operational radar set at this critical juncture, had the effect of achieving complete tactical surprise for the Japanese. By the end of the afternoon, for the loss of 7 Zero-sen fighters, the Japanese had destroyed 103 American aircraft, most of them on the ground and over half of them fighters. Many other aircraft and most of the base facilities at Clark Field and Nichols Field were damaged. The number of aircraft fit for service left to the Americans at the end of the first day of hostilities was about 50.

American air power on the Philippines ceased to pose a serious threat to the Japanese as a result of the first day's operations, but for five more days—with the exception of the eleventh, when the Japanese were regrouping their forces—the Japanese stepped up the tempo of their attacks with a series of ferocious raids mounted in slightly increasing strength. By the end of the thirteenth, the Japanese were virtually unopposed in the air, their attacks having almost totally annihilated American air power and having wrecked every major airfield. In addition, the Cavite Naval Yard on Manila Bay had been wrecked by a raid on the tenth, the Asiatic Fleet suffering a serious loss when its torpedo stock was destroyed. Such was the position in the air that on the fourteenth the decision was taken to send all major units of the Asiatic Fleet either southwards or to British and Dutch waters. The following day all heavy bombers were ordered to fly to northern Australia and to continue operations by staging through air strips in the southern Philippines. Such was the state of Japanese air supremacy that the surviving heavy bombers already had been ordered to spend as much time in the air as possible simply to lessen the risks of being caught on the ground.

American reconnaissance and bomber forces were flown out of Luzon to the relative safety of the southern islands or Australia between 14 and 17 December, and from that time onwards the Japanese enjoyed what was virtually an unchallenged supremacy in the air. Their merciless concentration against American air power had proved remarkably effective and, of course, it had the effect of making the position of the U.S. Asiatic Fleet completely untenable. Indeed, by the evening of the first day of the war all major units in the Philippines were ordered to clear Luzon, and by the tenth not a single major American warship remained in Philippine waters. The Japanese air concentration against American airfields, however, had two unforeseen results. First, a vast assembly of very valuable merchantmen and their cargoes in Manila Bay was allowed to escape southwards virtually unhindered. Second, the American warships themselves escaped more or less unscathed. The Japanese attack on Cavite reduced the base to a raging inferno and resulted in the destruction of the submarine *Sealion*, but the damage to other warships was largely irrelevant. The only American warship to draw fire on 8 December was not off Luzon but at Davao, where the tender *William B. Preston* managed to evade the four Japanese destroyers that tried to sink her after she had been attacked by aircraft from the *Ryujo*. With the decision to withdraw major surface units from Philippine waters, the Americans had to place their hopes in the submarines and what little remained of the bomber force to fend off Japanese invasion attempts.

In these circumstances the Japanese were able to mount their various invasions with some confidence. The main landings were to take place at Lingayen Gulf on 22 December and on Lamon Bay on the twenty-fourth, but before these took place the Japanese conducted a series of small-scale landings designed to achieve two main objectives. The landings in northern Luzon were conducted in order to secure airfields that could be used to project Japanese air power deep into central Luzon, while the other operations were designed to secure positions that could be used to get across American lines of communication or positions from which to pursue second-phase objectives. Nevertheless, the Japanese took what amounted to reckless risks in these small operations. These minor landings were undertaken with incredibly small forces—none bigger than three battalions—which were called upon to sustain themselves for up to two weeks in the face of a numerically superior and undefeated enemy. At the end of that time there was still no guarantee that these forces would be supported. Moreover, by parting with what was in effect just over two three-battalion regiments, the whole of the striking power of the *14th Army*—which consisted of two divisions, one brigade, and an infantry regimental group—was gravely reduced by these operations. Even among those at *14th Army* headquarters there was uneasiness over the operations.

The first of the minor landings was on the island of Batan, some 125 miles north of Luzon between the Bashi Channel and the Luzon Strait that separate Formosa from Luzon. Two transports carrying 450 men sailed from Formosa on 7 December in the company of the destroyer *Yamagumo*, two minesweepers, four torpedo boats, two gunboats, and nine submarine chasers. This force secured Batan on the eighth with no difficulty. The capture of the island was intended to provide airstrips from which army aircraft could cover landings on northern Luzon. The capture of the island of Camiguin, between Batan and Luzon, on the tenth, was similarly conceived. Because of the speed with which events on Luzon unfolded, however, taking these islands proved unnecessary.

While the first moves were being made from the north, the Japanese were closing in on the Philippines from the east, but not with the invasion of the islands immediately in mind. Fear of a possible American concentration of air power in the area of Davao on Mindanao prompted the Japanese to launch a small-scale strike against the seaplane base on the first day of the war. This operation, as has been related, was carried out by the carrier

Ryujo and an escorting force of destroyers. The raid proved something of an anticlimax. The Americans were not present in any strength and the *William B. Preston* evaded Japanese attention, but the base area was thoroughly raked over and the possibility of Davao being able to handle the staging of aircraft for use further north was all but eliminated.

With the Japanese in possession of the offshore islands, the initiative in the air over northern and central Luzon firmly in Japanese hands, and the

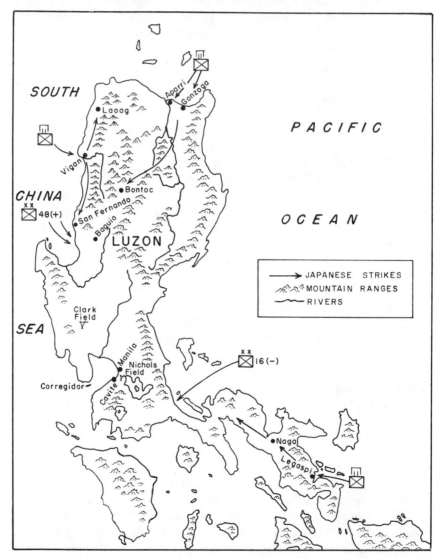

The Luzon Campaign, December 1941

base at Davao neutralized, the way was clear for the Japanese to begin their first landings on Luzon itself. The Japanese planned to make two landings on northern Luzon on the tenth. The airfields at Aparri and Padan were the objective, and the Japanese committed the *2nd Formosan Regiment* to this mission. Its three battalions were evenly divided between the two landings. The *Tanaka Detachment*, formed around the *2nd Battalion*, was used at Aparri, while the Padan operation was entrusted to the reinforced *3rd Battalion*, the *Kanno Detachment*.

The operations did not run very smoothly. The *Tanaka Detachment*, which sailed from Mako in the Pescadores on 7 December under the protection of the light cruiser *Natori*, six destroyers, three minesweepers, and nine submarine chasers (drawn largely from the 5th Destroyer Flotilla from the 3rd Fleet), encountered heavy seas off the intended landing beaches and was forced to disperse its effort between Aparri and Gonzoga. Despite the unanticipated problems with the seas—the landing craft were not up to the tasks set them—the 2,000-strong *Tanaka Detachment* established itself ashore with minimal opposition other than from nature. The Padan force did less well. The heavy seas forced the invasion force to move down the west coast to Vigan, and the landing force was unable to establish itself ashore with any degree of security until the eleventh. Both the Aparri invasion force and the slightly stronger Padan force—the light cruiser *Naka*, seven destroyers, six minesweepers, and nine submarine chasers (drawn in large part from the 4th Destroyer Flotilla from the 2nd Fleet)—were attacked by the depleted bomber force on Luzon. Each lost a single minesweeper (the *W-19* and *W-10*, respectively), while the Aparri force had two warships damaged and the Padan force had two of its transports more severely handled. Yet overall these losses were insignificant and the Japanese air forces had cause to be pleased. Though their control of the skies was not yet total and they could not prevent small raids that would inflict losses, the losses they had inflicted and were inflicting on the Americans were sufficient to ensure a very satisfactory margin of safety for invading forces when they were at their most vulnerable. All the same it was only natural that warships and transports alike showed a marked reluctance to loiter near the invasion beaches.

Once the two detachments were ashore, they immediately advanced on their objectives, the Laoag and Tuguegarao airfields. The *Kanno Detachment*, heading northwards, secured Laoag on the eleventh, and the next day part of the *Tanaka Detachment* captured Tuguegarao after advancing up the Cagayan valley. Virtually no resistance was encountered by the *Tanaka Detachment* as it moved deep inland. The one unit in the area, the 3rd/12th Infantry from the 11th Infantry Division of the Philippine army withdrew on Ilagan in the face of the Japanese advance. The 11th Infantry Division anticipated being able to hold the Japanese advance at the naturally strong position of the Balete Pass, at the head of the Cagayan valley, but in fact it never had the chance. With all their immediate objectives secured and their forces moving forward with commendable smoothness, the Japanese chose to reconcentrate the *2nd Formosan Regiment* in order to advance and link up with the forces detailed for the main landings on Lingayen Gulf. Accordingly, the *Kanno Detachment* began to advance southwards down the coast while the *Tanaka Detachment*, leaving the Cagayan valley, struck across country through Bontoc. The *2nd Formosan Regiment*, however, was not to be of much assistance to the main invasion effort; by the time it arrived on Lingayen Gulf the first invading elements were ashore.

Just as the Japanese had struck their first blows from the north and east, so their first landings were delivered from the same quarters. In addition to the four landings in the north, there was a landing at Legaspi in southern Luzon. This landing was made by the *Kimura Detachment*, formed from two battalions of the *33rd Infantry Regiment*, the *Kure 1st Special Naval Landing Force* and a battery from the *22nd Field Artillery Regiment*. It was no part of Japanese plans for victory either to wait upon events or to rely on a single blow or series of blows in one direction. Japanese operations were brilliantly planned to exact as much advantage from geographic position as possible and to use their forces to full effect. The Japanese plans were conceived as a series of attacks designed not merely to split enemy positions and allow for defeat in detail, but also to secure positions from which the next-phase objectives could be achieved even on other islands. On 12 December, therefore, the Japanese landed the 3,200-strong *Kimura Detachment* at Legaspi with the intention of denying the Americans any airfields south of Manila that could be used for staging attacks on the main force invasions. The possession of Legaspi, moreover, placed the Japanese across the line of American reinforcement and retreat, and threatened to break through the whole center of the Philippine position.

The importance of the Legaspi operation to the security of the pending operations may well have warranted the use of more than just two reinforced battalions, but even if the *Kimura Detachment* was a small one, it was afforded a scale of naval protection during its sea passage from Palau after 6 December that was seldom lavished on such efforts. Its seven transports were given the close support of a composite force consisting of the light cruiser *Nagara*, six modern destroyers, the two seaplane carriers *Chitose* and *Mizuho* of the 11th Carrier Division, and four other escorts. During its passage this force was met by the Davao strike force, the *Ryujo* and her nine destroyers, and by three heavy cruisers, the *Haguro*, *Myoko*, *and Nachi*, part of the 5th Cruiser Division. Four of the destroyers, headed by the light cruiser *Jintsu*, were detailed to support the mining of the San Bernardino and Surigao straits by the minelayers *Itsukushima* and *Yaeyama*. By laying about 350 mines in these waters the Japanese intended to seal off Luzon from reinforcements by sea from the south.

The *Kimura Detachment* landed and secured Legaspi without problems on 12 December and it rapidly began to develop its own offensive north-wards. The ease with which it did so proved the emptiness of MacArthur's vainglorious boast to Philipps of what he would do to the Japanese. There were no American or Philippine forces within 150 miles of Legaspi at the time of the Japanese attack, and the attempt to contain the Japanese at the narrow neck of the Bicol peninsula was certain to be no more than a temporary success because of the near-certainty of further landings behind any position the defenders tried to hold. Thus the *Kimura Detachment* quickly secured the airfield at Legaspi, then Naga, and finally Daet on 21 December. Thus, in a matter of a week the Japanese positions on Luzon were not merely secure but rapidly developing both in the north and in the south. Meanwhile, the American and Philippine land forces, despite their clear numerical superiority, had been totally unable to concentrate either to oppose an invasion or to counterattack those forces that were ashore. The knowledge that the main Japanese blows were yet to fall and that Lingayen Gulf was the obvious, indeed the only, target for a major landing, served to keep the Americans off balance. By their imaginative use of small bodies of troops the Japanese completely outmaneuvered the Americans, the level of their generalship being markedly superior to that of a defending force whose problems were immense and probably insoluble. With the land forces spread out and the air forces virtually eliminated, the only very slight hope of meeting an invasion lay with the submarine arm. While the submarines might be able to inflict losses, even considerable losses, on the enemy, they could not prevent an invasion. In short, after a week of war the Americans stood on the brink of disaster on Luzon.

By the time the Japanese from Legaspi secured Daet and made their main effort at Lingayen Gulf the following day, they had initiated the last parts of the first-phase offensive or, to put it another way, started on the first parts of their second-phase operations. These were the offensives aimed to complete the encirclement of the Philippines and to secure out-flanking positions whereby the Philippines themselves could be bypassed while still unreduced. In this manner the Japanese were able to develop their drive against the Dutch East Indies without having to wait for the elimination of resistance in the Philippines. The Japanese concepts of war were characterized by speed, surprise, and rapid exploitation—and econ-omy of force—and they were to employ all four to full effect in breaking open the American position in the southern Philippines.

Of all these elements in the Japanese manner of waging war, the opera-tions in the southern Philippines probably show economy of force to best effect. The bulk of those forces that had carried out the initial strikes on Davao were used to cover the Legaspi operation and then were redirected back to Davao to support operations designed to secure that town and its base—a very good example of the flexibility conferred on a combatant exercising command of the seas. The Davao operation was mounted from Palau again, with fourteen transports sailing on 16 December. The three heavy cruisers, the *Ryujo*, a seaplane carrier, and other escorts supported landings on both sides of the town on the night of 19/20 December. Opposition was minimal even though some 2,000 troops from the 2nd/101st Infantry Regiment from the Philippine army were in the sector where the landings took place. By the middle of the morning on the twentieth, the defenders had abandoned Davao and the Japanese had begun the simultaneous tasks of pushing inland and preparing the base for Japanese aircraft. The base was ready for use within twenty-four hours, but even by that time the Japanese were well on the way to completing their preparations for the further development of their offensive in the south. The next target was the island of Jolo in the Sulu Archipelago. This small island was to the Indies what Batan had been to Luzon, and its taking on Christmas Day by an understrength infantry battalion with the *Kure 2nd Special Naval Landing Force* in support was as painless to the Japanese as all the other landings. The way was clear for the *16th Army* to be activated and to begin the penetration of the Indies at the same time as the Americans were reeling under the impact of successive defeats. The first phase of operations on the Philippines was at an end, and while the Japanese operations may have run substantial risks, there is no denying the extremely impressive manner in which the Japanese planned and executed their opening moves.

By Christmas Day the Americans had been decisively beaten in the Philippines without having fought a major land battle. But they were to continue to operate in the field for several months, long after their Allies elsewhere in Southeast Asia had surrendered. Their generals were able to take advantage of Japanese mistakes by maneuvering to secure naturally strong defensive positions that a numerically inferior enemy could not break.

No such conditions or respite were afforded Britain's smallest colony in the Far East. On 25 December the governor of Hong Kong, Sir Mark Young, surrendered the colony to the commander of the attacking Japanese forces, Lieutenant General Taikaishi Saki. In the interwar period the British appreciated that in the event of war with Japan Hong Kong was indefensible. In purely military terms it would have been advisable to evacuate the colony, but for obvious political reasons this was impossible. The British had to attempt to deny Japan the use of the facilities of Hong Kong for as long as possible. But in 1940 only three battalions were available for the defense of the colony, and although this number had been doubled by the time war broke out, some 10,000 men was a pathetically inadequate force with which to try to hold off any Japanese attack from the positions they held in China. Equally, for a force that was certain to be written off, the deployment of six battalions was utterly unnecessary.

Nevertheless, with these forces the British drew up realistic plans to defend Hong Kong for as long as possible. The plans involved the use of three battalions to hold the New Territories while the destruction of mainland facilities, mainly in Kowloon, was carried out. The possibility of trying to hold the Japanese at the international frontier was not considered; the length of the frontier and the few forces available made this an impossible undertaking. The British plan rested on holding Gin Drinker's Line across the southern part of the New Territories. This was a much shorter and stronger line than the frontier, but the position lacked depth, good communications, and still remained a very long frontage for three battalions. The British, after the destruction of the facilities on the mainland, envisaged withdrawing the battalions earmarked for forward defense and regrouping all six battalions for a last-ditch defense of Hong Kong island.

The Japanese attack on Hong Kong opened on the morning of the eighth, some four hours after the attack on Pearl Harbor. The Japanese committed their *38th Infantry Division*. This formation consisted of three full-strength infantry regiments, the *228th*, *229th*, and *230th*, with specially reinforced artillery and engineer support. It took the Japanese less than two days to cover the country between the frontier and Gin Drinker's Line, during which time the minute Royal Air Force presence on Hong Kong was eliminated. On the night of 9/10 December the *3rd/228th Infantry*, in a surprise and unauthorized attack, secured the strong but undermanned Shing Mun position, levering apart the whole of the British defensive position on the western part of the line. Shing Mun was the key to the British defense, but there were simply not enough troops available for the counterattack. On the eastern part of the British position Japanese attacks were held, the British conceding very little ground, but only at the cost of suffering unacceptable attrition. The general officer commanding, Major General C. M. Maltby, was convinced that unless the evacuation of the three mainland battalions was undertaken immediately, then the means of offering serious and prolonged resistance on the island would be broken.

The British evacuation of the mainland was one of the more successful aspects of the defense of Hong Kong. The forces on the left and in the center were evacuated to the west of Kowloon, those to the right via the Lei U Mun channel. The denial of facilities on the mainland was thoroughly completed before the withdrawal, but much transport, particularly the mules, and ammunition, had to be abandoned. Successful though this phase of the operation was, the fact remained that resistance on the mainland lasted only five days. The forces remaining for the defense of the island were too few in number, low in morale, and somewhat disorganized. The Japanese, on the other hand, possessed total air supremacy and were naturally buoyed up by their success.

Nevertheless, the first Japanese attempt to launch an improvised crossing to the island on the night of 15/16 December was beaten off. The British

rejection of the Japanese demand for surrender on the seventeenth left the
Japanese with no option but to attempt a major set-piece attack. This took
the form of a six-battalion assault between North Point and Lei U Mun.
The aim of this attack was for all three regiments, when fully deployed on
the island, to develop their attacks westwards in order to take Victoria. The
assault phase proceeded smoothly enough, but thereafter events began to go
wrong for the Japanese. British resistance before Victoria around North

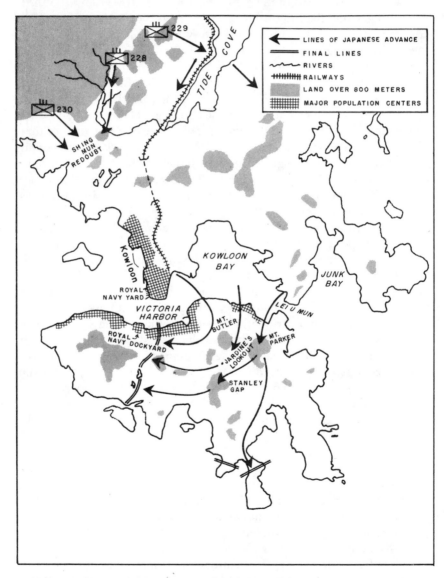

The Hong Kong Campaign, 8 through 25 December 1941

Point was desperate, and the Japanese were unable to make much progress. But the flexibility of the Japanese forces redeemed this situation. With command of the skies and by continuously inflicting a high loss rate on the defending British forces, by the nineteenth the Japanese were able to secure a major foothold that ran from Jardine's Lookout to the Lye Mun Gap via Mounts Butler and Parker. On the following day the Japanese broke through to the sea at Repulse Bay, thus splitting the defense in two. This success was hard earned, because British counterattacks on the mountain crests, around the Wong Nei Chong Gap, and in the vicinity of Jardine's Lookout were fierce and gallant. But in the end they were bound to be ineffective and suffered from the inescapable logic of weakening with every failure. The forces committed to holding and retaking these positions were inadequate in the first place; losses merely meant the weakening of successive attacks. In fact by the end of the twentieth the defense was becoming increasingly fragmented.

As serious as the manpower losses were the growing shortages of ammunition and water. It was a combination of these factors, plus the desire to avoid the massacre of prisoners and the civilian population, that prompted the governor's surrender on the afternoon of Christmas Day. At the time of the capitulation the British still held isolated positions on both sides of Stanley Bay and in the western part of the island, including Aberdeen and Victoria. But the position of the defenders was hopeless, with all units nearing exhaustion and all hope gone. Nearly half the garrison had been killed; the Japanese, in comparison, suffered nearly 3,000 casualties. Thus, after eighteen days of conflict, Hong Kong entered Japanese possession, suffering a lurid and violent sack as a result of its capitulation.*

---

*Since four British gunboats were lost at Hong Kong, the fall of the colony provides a good opportunity to recount the fate of certain of the European and American gunboats in the area. Before the war, of course, such warships were the very embodiment of white power, prestige, and influence in the Far East.

At Hong Kong the British lost the *Cicala*, *Moth*, *Robin*, and *Tern*. The Japanese salvaged the *Moth* and put her back into service as the *Suma*. She was striken in May 1945 after having been badly damaged two months earlier by a mine in the Yangtse. The American gunboat *Luzon*, sunk by Japanese artillery in May 1942 in Manila Bay, and the Italian gunboat *Ermanno Carlotto*, scuttled at Shanghai in September 1943 at the time of Italy's surrender, were similarly salvaged and put into Imperial Navy service as the *Karatsu* and *Narumi*, respectively. In 1943 the Japanese secured the Portuguese gunboat *Macau* and recommissioned her as the *Maiko*. This rather cosmopolitan trio shared a common fate. All survived the war to be surrendered to the Chinese Nationalists in 1945, and in 1949 they were surrendered to the Chinese Communists.

A similar fate befell the *Tatara*, though her surrenders in 1945 and 1949 completed a melancholy record of three capitulations in the course of her career. As USS *Wake* at Shanghai in December 1941 she surrendered, the only American warship during World War II to strike her colors.

Of the other British gunboats in the Far East, the *Falcon*, *Gannet*, and *Sandpiper* were trapped on the upper reaches of the Yangtse and turned over to the local Chinese Nationalists; the *Dragonfly*, *Grasshopper*, and *Scorpion* were lost at Singapore; and the *Mantis*, awaiting

British possessions on Borneo were vitally important to the Japanese, mainly because of their natural resources. The most important of these was oil from the wells at Miri and Seria. The position of the British territory on the South China Sea, across the sea route between Singapore and Japan, enhanced its value, and the seizure of Sarawak, Brunei, and British Borneo would enable the Japanese to develop their offensive against the Dutch. The British fully appreciated the importance of their possessions on Borneo, but in the straitened circumstances of 1941 they could allocate only one battalion, the 2nd/15th Punjab, to the defense of a vast area of virgin tropical jungle, coastal mangrove, swamps, and occasional settlements. British policy—it can hardly be dignified by use of the word *strategy*—was therefore directed towards the denial of the oil fields and the holding of the airfield at Kuching. This airfield was very important since it was only 350 miles from Singapore and close to the major Dutch airfield of Singkawang II. No attempt was made to hold Brunei, Labuan, and British North Borneo. The Japanese, anxious to secure the area and knowing it to be weakly held, detailed the *35th Infantry Brigade Headquarters* and the *124th Infantry Regiment*, part of the *18th Infantry Division* from Yamashita's *25th Army*, to secure these British possessions. These units came under the direct command of the *Southern Army*.

The British began the destruction of the oil fields on 8 December. The company of Punjabis detailed to cover this specialist task was evacuated by sea from Miri on the thirteenth. The same day the Japanese invasion force, supplemented by a marine battalion of about 1,200 troops, left Camranh Bay in the company of a battleship, a light carrier, three cruisers, and four destroyers. Ideally the Japanese would have liked to have moved against Borneo at the very start of the war, but the escort force had first to cover the operations in southern Thailand and northern Malaya. Only when these had been completed were the Japanese in a position to pay any attention to Borneo. Though the Borneo operation was therefore delayed, the attack showed once again the economy of effort the Japanese achieved in their opening series of attacks by the close phasing of objectives.

The Japanese reached Miri undetected on the fifteenth, and by the next day the air base and the oil fields were in Japanese hands. Having consolidated their position at Miri, the Japanese detached one battalion to occupy Brunei, Labuan, and British North Borneo. Labuan was occupied by the

---

disposal, and *Peterel* were lost at Shanghai. Six other British gunboats in the Far East escaped to safety.

Of all the losses, that of the *Peterel* alone was noteworthy. The 310-ton gunboat, with armament of two 3-inch antiaircraft guns and eight machine guns, fought rather than obey a Japanese call to surrender; she was sunk by the *Izumo*. The 10,305-ton Japanese ship, the flagship of the China Fleet, was armed with four 8-inch and eight 6-inch guns. Her last previous naval engagement had been at Tsu-shima. Ironically, the *Izumo* had been built in Britain between 1898 and 1901.

Japanese on New Year's Day, Jesselton a week later. The administrative capital of British North Borneo, Sandakan, was secured by the Japanese on 17 January; the British governor personally surrendered on the nineteenth.

While the reduction of the northern part of Borneo was thus in hand, the two remaining Japanese battalions were shipped south to take Kuching. But the Japanese did not have matters all their own way in the south as they had in the north. While British air and sea resistance was nominal and achieved absolutely nothing, Dutch resistance was more substantial and singularly unfortunate in not being better rewarded for some skillful and courageous attacks. Dutch naval aircraft attacked the Japanese shipping concentrations off Miri for three successive days before, on 19 December, accounting for the destroyer *Shinonome*. On 23 and 24 December Dutch submarines, one of which was subsequently lost, attacked the Japanese convoy en route to Kuching, sinking the destroyer *Sagiri* and two transports and damaging two other merchantmen. By the evening of the twenty-third, however, the major part of the invasion force was off Kuching, but a rather rash riverine approach was badly mauled by mortar and machine-gun fire before the single defensive platoon was overwhelmed. The British abandoned Kuching town without a fight, deciding instead to stand at the nearby airfield. Japanese infiltration tactics and movement through the jungle quickly made this intention unrealistic. On Christmas night the airfield was abandoned and the Punjabis began a withdrawal to Singkawang II. The main part of the battalion reached the Dutch base on the twenty-ninth, but the two companies detached as rear guard were all but annihilated. Their few survivors linked up with the main body on New Year's Day. The campaign in British Borneo was at an end.

Nevertheless, it was not the end of the campaign in western Borneo because a renewal of the Japanese offensive into Dutch territory was inevitable. Singkawang II was too important an air base to be left in Allied hands, and on 24 January the Japanese renewed their offensive with an overland advance from Kuching and an amphibious operation that secured Pamangkat on the twenty-seventh and Pontianak on the twenty-ninth. These pincer movements forced the Allies into a series of withdrawals, from Singkawang II on the twenty-seventh, from Ledo on the twenty-ninth, and from Ngabang on the thirty-first. Only at Singkawang II was serious resistance offered to the Japanese by two Punjabi platoons, which accounted for a couple of companies of Japanese infantry. Upon surrendering, the Punjabis were literally put to the sword.

With the few surviving forces left to the British and Dutch at Nanga-pinoh, it was decided that the only course open to the Allies was a withdrawal to the coast in the hope of securing ships that would allow their escape to Java. For over a month, therefore, the Allied columns struggled through the jungle to reach Pangkalanboeoen and Sampit, only to find that the Japanese, having moved around the south coast of Borneo from the east, had already taken the latter town on 6 March and that there were no means of escape for the exhausted Allied columns. To this cup of bitterness was to be added the news of the Allied surrender in the Indies. Realizing that further attempts to resist were out of the question and likely only to result in reprisals being taken by the Japanese, the Allied forces that had fought and marched for three months in the defense of northern and western Borneo surrendered on 9 March. This small campaign was therefore at an end, but

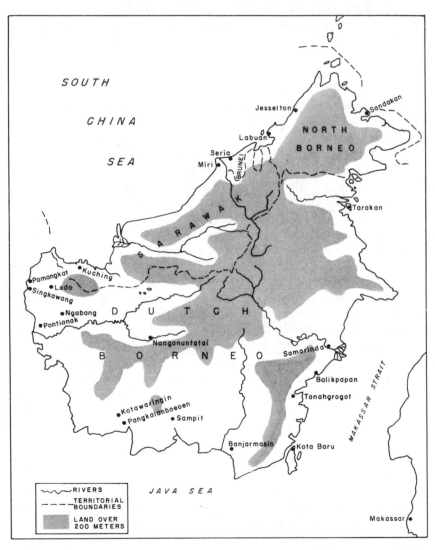

Borneo

its course had reflected highly on all the forces engaged. The simple fact of the matter for the British and Dutch was that the odds had been too heavily stacked against them in the first place.

The Japanese throughout the war persisted in complicated, interrelated plans that involved a rapid concentration of force over a wide area of operations in order to carry out subsequent offensives. There were considerable dangers inherent in such a fragmentation of force, as Midway and Leyte were later to prove, but in 1941, when faced by irresolute and weak enemies, Japanese arrangements prospered.

The Japanese plan of campaign in Thailand and Malaya was one of the more complicated operations carried out by the Japanese in the entire war. The complexity stemmed from several factors, namely, the need to preserve surprise and to deceive the enemy, for as long as possible; from the initial dispositions of the land forces; and the nature of the objectives Japan sought to attain. Added to these considerations were the problems caused by the need to stagger landings and operations because it was impossible to land simultaneously all the forces involved in the operations. Moreover, the constraints of shipping and the location of forces before December 1941 meant that the two armies earmarked for these operations, the *15th Army* in Thailand and the *25th Army* in Malaya, in effect had to borrow from one another in order to secure objectives that their own formations could not take. It was only after these objectives were taken and formations and units were fully deployed that the various forces could be disentangled and the proper command structures allowed to emerge.

For the operations against Malaya and Thailand the Japanese used elements from four divisions in the initial phase. These were the *5th* and *18th Infantry Divisions* and the *Imperial Guards Division* of the *25th Army*, and the *55th Infantry Division* of the *15th Army*. The latter division, in the assault phase, had only the *143rd Infantry Regiment* available for the task of securing the Kra Isthmus. In seven transports and escorted by a solitary light cruiser because no resistance was anticipated, this regiment sailed from Saigon on 5 December. The regiment's objectives were to secure Nakhorn (three transports), Bandon (one), Jumbhorn (two), and Prachuab (one) in order to accomplish three tasks. First, these landings were intended to secure the flank and rear of the *25th Army* as it developed its offensive down the Malayan peninsula. Second, the operations were designed to secure important airfields in southern Thailand; and third, the Japanese troops were under orders to develop their own offensive to the Indian Ocean coast and to secure Victoria Point. With this airfield in Japanese hands the British would be unable to attempt the reinforcement of Malaya from India by air.

To the north of this area the *Imperial Guards Division* was detailed to secure central Thailand by an overland advance from its bases in French

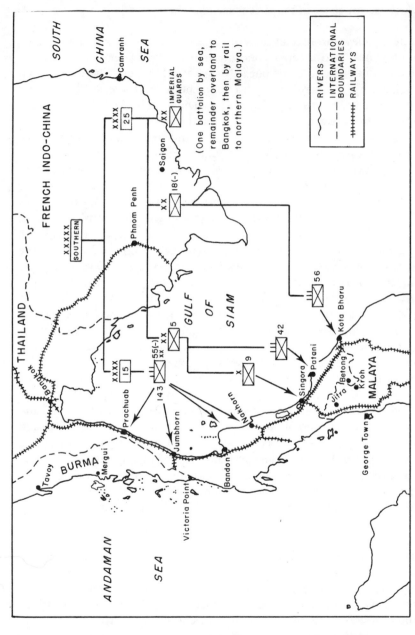

Initial Operations against Thailand, Malaya, and Burma, 8 December 1941

Within the figure:

SOUTH CHINA SEA

FRENCH INDO-CHINA

Camranh

XXXX 25

XX IMPERIAL GUARDS

Saigon

XX 18(-)

(One battalion by sea, remainder overland to Bangkok, then by rail to northern Malaya.)

RIVERS
INTERNATIONAL BOUNDARIES
RAILWAYS

XXXXX SOUTHERN

Phnom Penh

THAILAND

Bangkok

GULF OF SIAM

XXXX 15

55(-) XX
143

Prachuab

Jumbhorn

Bandon

Nakhorn

XX 5

42

x 9

56

Kota Bharu

Patani

Singora

Betong
Kroh
Jitra

MALAYA

George Town

BURMA

Tavoy

Mergui

Victoria Point

ANDAMAN SEA

Indo-China. One battalion was earmarked for transportation by sea to Bangkok in order to subdue the capital and force the Royal Thai government into submission. Only when the *33rd Infantry Division* began to deploy into Thailand from Indo-China as the first stage of its move against Burma was the *Imperial Guards Division* to pass southwards through the *143rd Infantry Regiment* to link up with the rest of the *25th Army* for subsequent operations in Malaya. The *143rd* was then to move northwards to join the *33rd Infantry Division* in central Thailand.

The main landings by the *25th Army* were carried out by the *5th Infantry Division*. The key areas of operations were Singora, where the *9th Infantry Brigade* went ashore; and Patani, where the Japanese committed the *42nd Infantry Regiment*. The left flank of the assault was covered by the *18th Infantry Division*, which detailed the *56th Infantry Regiment* for the task of taking Kota Bharu.

The forces for the invasion sailed in nineteen transports from Hainan on 4 December. The 26,640-strong force was protected by an escort composed of the heavy cruiser *Chokai*, a light cruiser, and thirteen destroyers. In close support were four more heavy cruisers and three destroyers. As the invasion force nosed south, under the distant cover of the fast battleships *Kongo* and *Haruna*, two heavy cruisers, and ten destroyers, which sailed on the fourth from the Pescadores, it was joined by transports from Camranh Bay, Saigon, and the Paulo Condore Islands, complete with small escort forces. These transports included two that carried airfield ground parties for the area of the *5th Infantry Division*'s operations.

With the great number of warships available to the Japanese in the general area of the South China Sea, it would have been expected that the Japanese would have thought to counter the presence of British warships with their surface units. This was not really the case. The Japanese were prepared to join battle with their surface units if the need arose, but the Japanese knew that Force Z outgunned their own battleships, which had to cover not only the Malayan operation but also those against Borneo and the Philippines. In the Japanese plan of campaign the check to the capital ships of the Royal Navy was the specially reinforced 22nd Air Flotilla, which received its extra aircraft as the counterweight to Force Z as the British ships neared Singapore. This aspect of Japanese naval policy was one imposed deliberately by Yamamoto, who almost alone within the Japanese naval command was sure that land-based naval aircraft could deal with any ships the British and American navies committed to battle. In a sense he had to follow this line because his carriers were "otherwise engaged," but it was a course for which the Allies were singularly ill-prepared.

After passing around the tip of Indo-China, the transports and their escorts steamed westwards into the Gulf of Siam. The Japanese hoped that the British would be misled into believing that Thailand, not Malaya, was to be the destination of their forces. This was what the British wanted to believe, and it was in the gulf that British reconnaissance aircraft found the Japanese. In order to preserve secrecy, Vice Admiral Jisaburo Ozawa, in command of the covering forces, ordered one shadowing aircraft shot down. This was carried out on 7 December, hours before the attack on Pearl Harbor. Fortunately for the Japanese the British did not attribute to Japanese action the fact that one of their aircraft was missing. Only at the last moment did the transports peel off at high speed and make their way to the invasion beaches. Three transports took the *56th Infantry Regiment* to Kota Bharu under the protection of a light cruiser and four destroyers; eight destroyers escorted five transports to Patani. All the air personnel and the ten remaining transports were sailed to Singora.

The immediate aim of the landings was to establish secure beachheads that were to include their airfields around Singora, Patani, and Kota Bharu. This would allow depth for the second echelons of the invasion force (scheduled to land after the thirteenth) and enable the leading elements of the air forces to be deployed into southern Thailand and northern Malaya. In addition, of course, the leading echelon was to develop its own offensive without waiting to consolidate its position. The *9th Infantry Brigade* was ordered to advance with its two regiments from Singora to the west coast in order to secure Alor Star in Kedah. The *42nd Infantry Regiment* was ordered to advance along the road from Patani to Kroh and Betong. Without these two advances the full deployment of the *25th Army* could not be completed. Most of the landing forces were to be directed through Singora and Patani. Though the leading elements of the *18th Infantry Division* were directed against Kota Bharu, with orders to proceed inland towards Machang and along the coast towards Kuantan, the main part of the division was scheduled to land not in northern Malaya but in southern Thailand in January, after the full deployment of the *5th Infantry Division* had been completed. From this position the Japanese had two options in the deployment of the *18th Division*. It could be pushed down the length of the peninsula in support of the main attack if it landed in southern Thailand, though there was always the chance of a landing around Kuantan or even further south if things went well. Or, in exceptionally favorable circumstances, it could be switched across the Strait of Malacca against Sumatra. The Japanese plans were nothing if not flexible.

The events that were to unfold on the Malayan peninsula make the initial Japanese operations there not merely the largest of the first-phase Japanese landings but by far the most significant. This significance was not merely strategic and material, though these features were present and important, but mainly psychological because of the ease with which the Japanese not merely defeated but humiliatingly routed the proudest of the European powers. To modern readers these events have lost almost all of their impact.

British arms on land, at sea, and in the air were overwhelmed in a series of total, unmitigated disasters, the effect of which was to shake the very foundations of the British Empire.

The whole of British credibility, power, and will were brought into question by events in the first week of war in the Far East. Before 8 December Britain's prestige was immense; her moral authority was awesome. Alone among the nations of Europe she had resisted the malevolent depredations of German power. For a year she had stood alone, sustained it is true by an increasingly benevolent United States, but supported only by her empire, by exiles from lands under enemy occupation, and by hope. Yet in the course of a ten-week campaign, British prestige and moral authority were torn to shreds. British nakedness, until then concealed by the cloak of prestige, was revealed for all to see as Japanese forces over, on, and around the Malayan peninsula moved from victory to victory. The process of degradation was to continue until the final humbling of 15 February 1942, but in truth the British cause was lost as a result of the events of the first five days of war. In those days there took place a series of disasters from which there was no recovery.

Before the war the British had concluded that their best chance of thwarting an anticipated Japanese invasion of Malaya lay in mounting an offensive to secure Singora and Patani in advance of any Japanese landings. But to put Operation Matador into effect two conditions had to exist. There had to be timely and unimpeachable evidence of Japanese intentions, and there had to be the will on the part of Britain to violate the sovereignty of a neutral country. The latter consideration was not a mere academic point; it was complicated by the overall British stance in the Far East. Britain could not justify violating a country's neutrality merely on the ground that its neutrality was going to be violated in any case by another country, though she had done so in 1940 with respect to Norway. In 1939, as she had in 1914, Britain championed the rights of small nations. The cause of first Belgium and then Poland Britain had made her own. In 1939 war in Europe had been brought about by the British and French refusals to abandon Poland. The British in March 1939 had been prepared to make the integrity and sovereignty of Poland the casus belli simply because it was obvious that Hitler intended to violate them. Britain could not afford to be seen to infringe the rights of a small neutral Asian country in 1941. The complication arose because it was not clear whether British policy in December 1941 was one of deterrence or effective defense. It was still official British policy to do everything possible to avoid a war with Japan, but the problem was that the choice was no longer in British hands. There was a fundamental contradiction between the desire not to do anything that might provoke hostilities and the need to take prudent measures that were essential if hostilities were unavoidable. The British were caught on the horns of a dilemma. To exacerbate the political problem, in the crucial last days of peace the necessary intelligence was not forthcoming. The Japanese transports were sighted to the south of Cape Cambodia before noon on 6 December, but there was no clear indication of their intended destination. Therefore the British frittered away the last hours before war started, and failed to put Operation Matador into effect. The result was that the Japanese landings at Singora and Patani were unopposed.

The British only began to put their plans into effect when the Japanese started to come ashore at Kota Bharu, about one hour before the first bombs fell on Pearl Harbor. Here rough seas hampered the Japanese, but the invaders' main problem was the fierce resistance put up by the 3rd/17th Dogras, part of the 8th Indian Brigade. The other units of the brigade were not in position to engage the Japanese during the assault phase, and the Dogras' resistance was sharp but short-lived as the Japanese broke through their center astride the Kulla Pa'ahat. A counterattack by the 1st/13th Frontier Force Rifles failed to dislodge the Japanese, who by the ninth had managed to advance some 15 miles inland, securing Mulong and Peringat in addition to Kota Bharu. By the eleventh the badly confused and disorganized Indian brigade had withdrawn south to Machang, where it was much better placed to cover its lines of communication—and its withdrawal. Much ground had been ceded, but little of real value had been lost. The airfields had been rendered irrelevant by Japanese air activity and what the Japanese had not destroyed the retreating forces demolished. Nevertheless, the Japanese had firmly established themselves in a major beachhead, and were ready to exploit their success. By then, however, there had been disasters for British arms elsewhere that made the events at Kota Bharu pale into insignificance.

These disasters had occurred impartially on land, at sea, and in the air, but the most spectacular and politically profound had taken place in the South China Sea. With Royal Air Force strength in northern Malaya slashed by more than half as a result of one day's operations—from more than 110 to less than 50 aircraft—there could be no question of British warships remaining idly at their berths while sister services were bled to death. The navy had to be committed. In the first desperate hours of the war, while the issue still remained in the balance, the Royal Navy, having failed to deter aggression, had to give battle. As custodians of a tradition of victory that reached back over the centuries, British naval officers were aware that they faced desperate odds. The chances of the *Repulse* and *Prince of Wales* achieving very much were slim and the risks they ran in attempting a high-speed dash to the invasion areas were very great. Any chance of success and immunity depended on an ability to reach the objective undetected. To be compromised in the face of an almost total enemy air superiority would be fatal. But the navy, which had risen to the challenge

The battle cruiser *Repulse* leaving Singapore, 8 December 1941. Two days later she was sunk by Japanese Nell and Betty bombers from Indo-China, the first capital ship to be sunk by air attack while at sea. Imperial War Museum

posed by enemy control of the skies in Norway, Greece, Crete, and at Dunkirk, had no option but to make the attempt. It was inconceivable that the force sent to secure Malaya from attack should not give battle when that attack materialized. British naval officers, however, were not to know that there was no real hope of catching any shipping concentrations off the invasion beaches. With the Japanese merchantmen and transports operating on the tightest of schedules, their turnaround had been extremely quick and many would be well clear of the danger zone by the time British warships arrived on the scene. But with the Japanese committed to a continuous flow of men and materiel into the beachheads (nearly forty transports were already in Camranh Bay with the second echelon), the Japanese could not afford to see a British battle division on the loose in the Gulf of Siam.

Late on 8 December the *Prince of Wales* and *Repulse*, in the company of four destroyers, slipped out of the harbor and steamed slowly down the Strait of Johore, bound for Singora. But despite the cover first of night and then of rain squalls and low clouds, the presence of Force Z on the open seas was quickly known to the Japanese. A few hours out of Singapore, when east of the Anamba Islands, the British force was sighted by a Japanese submarine, the *I 65*, though the submarine's report, being positionally incorrect, served to confuse rather than enlighten the Japanese command. Despite this problem, a Japanese reconnaissance aircraft from the heavy cruiser *Kumano* located the battle force. It was his awareness of having been found by aircraft that led Philipps to abandon the mission. With surprise lost there was no point in continuing the operation. After holding course for Singora in order to deceive the Japanese, the British turned around under cover of darkness. An unconfirmed report of Japanese landings at Kuantan prompted Philipps to set a course for that port, even though landings so far south at that time seemed unlikely. Arriving off Kuantan in the early hours of the tenth, the British ships suffered the bitter frustration of finding the port perfectly normal with no sign of Japanese activity anywhere. Philipps, who had maintained radio silence and had not intimated to Singapore that he would steer for Kuantan, made the inevitable decision to return to base and the certain disgrace of having failed in his mission. His radio silence, however, meant that for the return passage he would not obtain air cover, not that there was very much available.

On the ninth, as the sighting reports came in, the Japanese redeployed their forces across the South China Sea in order to counter the threat developing to their lines of communication. The transports and merchant-men in the general area were ordered to steer north in an effort to put as much distance as possible between themselves and the beachheads. The destroyers off the invasion areas were ordered southwards, being concentrated and grouped with the close covering force to stand between the beachheads and the approaching enemy. These forces were ordered to engage in night action, in which their numbers, training, and torpedoes could be used to best effect. The heavy units were to stand off to seaward, as all the Japanese forces closed up to give battle during the hours of daylight, when naval aircraft from Indo-China would be scouring the area for the British capital ships. With these arrangements the scene was set for a pell-mell action that was certain to be decisive, one way or another.

Matters never came to a gun-and-torpedo duel between the surface units. During the night of 9/10 and on 10 December the Japanese lost, found, again lost, and then for the last fatal time regained, contact with Force Z on its route first to Kuantan and then to Singapore. Having lost touch with the British forces after dark, the Japanese regained contact when the submarine *I-58* was almost run down on the surface by the British ships, which remained unaware of the submarine's presence. The *I-58* fired a spread of five torpedoes at the British ships, but none found their mark. Though contact could not be maintained, the submarine's sighting report enabled the Japanese to mount a ten-aircraft reconnaissance mission early on the tenth. In fact the area of search was too far to the east, but unfortunately for the British ships the flanking Japanese aircraft, on its homeward leg, found them through a break in the clouds just north of the Anambas.

The British force was discovered just after 1100 by Japanese aircraft operating some 400 miles from their base. This was a range far beyond that of any naval aircraft available to the Allies at that time, and the Japanese quickly demonstrated that their aircrews and weapons were every bit as good as their aircraft. The following engagement was an annihilating Japanese victory. For the loss of just three aircraft and another twenty-eight damaged out of a force of eighty-eight bombers and torpedo bombers sent from Indo-China, successive waves of Japanese naval aircraft concentrated first on the flagship *Prince of Wales*, crippling her with two torpedoes that wrecked her port screws and steering. Then, with clinical precision, they singled out the *Repulse* and conferred upon her the unsought distinction of becoming the first capital ship to be sunk on the open sea by air attack. She was simply overwhelmed by attacks from every quarter. Some fifty minutes later the *Prince of Wales* plunged to her final resting place in the South China Sea. With them the two ships took 840 members of their crews, including their admiral. The destroyers saved 2,072 seamen of the ships' companies.

The effect of losing the ships was shattering. The two capital ships, the epitome of British naval power and the symbols of a tradition of invincibility, had been sent to the Far East in a blaze of publicity. Yet their presence at Singapore had failed to deter an aggressor, and they had succumbed in their only action against an undervalued enemy, attacking at unprecedented ranges. What had been an act of political bluff by Churchill had been called, and when called had been found wanting. Nothing, absolutely nothing, was left in reserve. For the forces on the mainland the effect on morale was immediate and deadly. The loss of the warships was like the stone being moved into place over the tomb. This time there could be no hope of evacuation as there had been in Norway, at Dunkirk, off Greece, and at Crete. There was no navy other than the Japanese in the waters that washed Malaya, while in the air the Japanese were virtually unopposed. On land, moreover, the Japanese were poised to win the engagement that was to prove decisive in the outcome of the campaign.

When the original sighting of the Japanese convoys in the Gulf of Siam had been made on the sixth, the British army had been ordered to assume its "first degree of readiness." This meant that the 11th Indian Division was held, in torrential rains, on the border, but was not allowed to cross it. It was not until the Japanese landed at Kota Bharu that the British realized they were far too late to put Operation Matador into effect, and it was not for several more hours, until 1330, that the division received its first orders. Operation Matador was abandoned and the whole of the division was ordered to withdraw to and then hold the Jitra position. At the same time Krohcol, a formation of two Indian infantry battalions ordered to Kroh, was directed to advance into Thailand to take the critically important Ledge position. Both these moves proved to be minor disasters, which the Japanese, with characteristic drive and determination, turned into major debacles.

Krohcol crossed the frontier only to be met by light resistance from the Thai border police. But whereas this opposition should have been brushed aside with the disdain it deserved, the British advance almost stopped before it began. It hardly augured well for the first contact with the real enemy. A 3-mile advance was registered on 8 December. Betong was taken on the ninth, but the Ledge was never reached. The Japanese crossed the 75 miles from Patani to the Ledge before the British stirred themselves to make a serious effort to secure this critically important defensive position.

The first contact between the advancing 3rd/16th Punjab and the Japanese vanguard, which was supported by light tanks, immediately forced the Punjabis on the defensive. Yet the one solitary Punjab battalion—the rest of Krohcol was still at Betong—could not hope to check a full Japanese infantry regiment, especially when it had armor support. After sustaining quite heavy casualties on the eleventh, the 3rd/16th attempted to disengage on the morning of the twelfth. Unfortunately for the battalion, it made this effort at the very time that the Japanese mounted a major set-piece attack. The result was that the Punjabi position was reduced to debris, and the unit lost half its effective strength before it was able to gain the cover of the 5th/14th Punjab in the Betong-Kroh area. By the evening of the twelfth the 5th/14th was intact and holding for the moment, but the whole of the right flank of the 11th Indian Division was in danger of being swamped. The failure to secure the position of the Ledge forced the British to try to hold the Japanese in terrain less well suited for the defense, and with the small force available this attempt was doomed. The long-term implication of the dismal performance of Krohcol was very clear. With the right flank in danger of crumbling, the defense of the Jitra area would become untenable.

In a sense this did not matter very much: the Jitra position was being lost anyway without any reference to the failings of Krohcol. The defense of the Jitra position was so inept that it did not need the collapse of the right flank to force a withdrawal from the main position. The British position at Jitra deteriorated with alarming rapidity because of a combination of unpreparedness, tactical mishandling of units, and a lack of training and resolve on the part of certain units. The overall result was a disaster that was nothing short of shameful and a disgrace to British arms.

Jitra, it must be admitted, was not an ideal defensive position. It had a long and difficult frontage, but once the decision was made to try to hold the Japanese as far north as possible, then there was no other choice but to stand at Jitra. The good communications southwards from Alor Star and the concentration of airfields around the town meant that a defense had to be mounted north of Alor Star, and this could only mean at Jitra. But with the prewar emphasis in training placed on Operation Matador, very little had been done to prepare Jitra for defense. When the 11th Indian Division therefore withdrew from the border after the operation was cancelled, it returned to a position that was virtually unprepared. Few of the necessary defensive positions had been dug, and the rains had washed away most of those that had been constructed. Utter chaos prevailed.

Working feverishly to put together some form of defensive position at Jitra, the 11th Indian Division deployed three brigades. The 15th Indian Brigade stood on a 4-mile front astride the main road. Its right flank was unsecured, but its left flank was held by the 6th Indian Brigade. Its frontage was 12 miles of difficult country that reached to the sea. In reserve was the 28th Indian Brigade, but the handling of this formation by the divisional commander, Major General D.M. Murray-Lyon, was so singularly inept that whatever cohesion it had was dissipated even before battle was joined. Fed piecemeal to the enemy, the force that should have been held for the counterattack was squandered.

The advance of the *9th Infantry Brigade* from Singora was headed by two complete regiments, the *11th* and *41st*, with the *Reconnaissance Battalion*, supported by light tanks, in the vanguard. It was the latter that ran into and then over the covering force of the 1st/14th Punjab around Changlun and forced its withdrawal, but the Japanese turned this into a rout that extended to the shattering of the 2nd/1st Gurkhas at Asun. In the course of these actions the British lost their antitank guns, which were overrun by Japanese armor while the British gunners took shelter from the rain. The final insult during this disastrous phase came when the bridge at Manggoi was blown prematurely, with the British defenders on the wrong side of it. With all these events taking place on the eleventh, even before the main forces came into contact, the British had contrived to lose the equivalent of a whole brigade plus their reserve, and had lost or been forced to abandon most of their field and antitank guns.

With these successes behind them, the Japanese immediately began frontal and flanking assaults on the main British positions, and almost immediately two British weaknesses became apparent. Certain of the main defensive positions had been located in such a way that they could not provide mutual support, while the dissipation of the reserve began to make itself felt. On the right flank of the 15th Indian Brigade, the left and center of the 2nd/9th Jats were crushed; the right tenaciously held on though under ever-mounting pressure. The Japanese, however, could not open a gap between the 1st Leicesters and the 2nd/2nd Gurkhas. A British counterattack helped bring the Japanese to a standstill. Though the British were mauled, their position was not desperate, though quite clearly the full weight to the Japanese attack remained to be developed. But the brigade commander was not prepared to await a set-piece assault and urged a withdrawal behind the Rimba-Sungei Jitra-Sungei Bata line, which offered a natural obstacle to Japanese armor. Murray-Lyon, however, overruled this course in favor of a more precipitate withdrawal to the Alor Star position, where no defenses at all had been prepared. On the twelfth, contact with the Japanese was broken off, but only in a most haphazard manner. Some units moved along the coast, some by road, and some by the railway track. Other units did not receive orders to withdraw, and only became aware of the evacuation of the Jitra position when they found that their flanks were no longer held by their neighbors. What had been little more than a skirmish on the main defensive position at Jitra turned out to be decisive. The British withdrawal was totally disorganized, with morale, already low among raw Indian troops, plumbing new depths. On the other side, the Japanese secured guns, small arms, plentiful supplies of ammunition, rations, and gasoline with which to develop their offensive. The scene was therefore set for the second phase of Japanese operations on the Malayan peninsula, a campaign that was to take the *25th Army* deep into central-southern Malaya.

In the first two weeks of hostilities the Japanese secured a dominant position over their enemies. They were able to secure all their immediate objectives and were superbly placed to exploit their gains by a series of brilliantly imaginative thrusts that were to tear the Allies apart throughout Southeast Asia. In a series of audacious strikes the Japanese fought for and secured the strategic initiative and in the first days of the war achieved what was almost a total supremacy at sea and in the air.

The situation on land was also developing very favorably as far as the Japanese were concerned, the latter being well placed to maintain or increase the tempo of their land offensives in order to achieve the annihilation of their enemies. While there are many remarkable features about the Japanese performance in the opening weeks of the war, perhaps the most remarkable is that in their major land operations the Japanese were never numerically superior to the forces they opposed, except in the minor outpost campaigns. On the Malayan peninsula British forces decisively outnumbered the Japanese throughout the campaign: after Singapore surrendered Churchill informed a shocked House of Commons that the Japanese had been outnumbered three to one in Malaya and this estimate was near enough to be correct. On the Philippines the two Japanese divisions in the assault phase were outnumbered by an even greater extent by the Americans and Filipinos. The critical difference between the Japanese and the Allies was not in mass but in the concentration of the Japanese and in their possession of clear local superiority along the axes of advance compared to the widely dispersed Allied forces; in the homogeneity of Japanese units, their high standards of training, and their combat experience, compared to green Allied troops; and in the singleness of purpose and unity of command that the Japanese enjoyed compared to the total lack of coordination among the Americans, British, and Dutch, which meant that the Allies lacked the means of pooling their inadequate resources to meet the Japanese challenge. Moreover, of course, there were those differences pinpointed by Slim—the thoroughness of Japanese preparations and the superiority of the Japanese soldier over his Allied counterpart at this stage of the war. Through sound intelligence, careful planning, astute assessment of risks and of enemy morale, and the ruthless exploitation of the initiative against relatively weak enemies who discounted Japanese fighting abilities, there arose for the Allies a disastrous situation upon which the Japanese capitalized with savage satisfaction.

Of all the factors that went to make up Japan's dominant position in the last days of 1941, there is one that has been given very little attention in the course of these pages. It was in fact the most obvious manifestation of Japan's domination and, as it proved, it was the most transitory. This was in the air, where the A6M2 Zero-sen naval fighter was in the vanguard of the Japanese drive throughout the Pacific and Southeast Asia. The Zero-sen was a carrier aircraft with a performance that matched any Allied land-based fighter in service in 1941.

By any standard the Zero-sen was a remarkable aircraft. It first saw combat over China in August 1940 and it achieved devastating results against the heterogeneous collection of aircraft, known as the Chinese Air Force, that up until that time had been achieving quite respectable results against the Japanese. With an extremely long range designed for operations over the Pacific and a high degree of maneuverability, the Zero-sen combined good offensive with poor defensive powers. In this it reflected the whole of the Imperial Navy. It was devastating in the assault, where much of its impact was psychological rather than material, but it was to be found wanting in sustained operations, where rugged reliability, durability, and the ability to absorb punishment were needed. But in the opening phase of the war the Zero-sen was just what the Japanese needed, and the Allies were devastated by the appearance of a "super fighter." They need not have been.

Western observers in Japan and China, and the French in Indo-China, had reported the appearance of an exceptionally maneuvrable fighter with great powers of endurance. Photographs and sketches had been made available to Western governments and services. The American pilots with the Chinese Air Force had even devised tactics to try to take advantage of some of the aircraft's known weaknesses, not that these tactics had achieved very much. Such information was ignored. Western agencies chose to consider that Japanese fighters and pilots were, ipso facto, inferior to those of the West. The revelation of the quality of the Zero-sen was possibly the most psychologically damaging catastrophe to befall the Allies; Westerners simply could not understand that the Japanese could equal or surpass their own best efforts in various fields at certain times. At this time there were widely believed stories that German pilots flew Japanese aircraft; anything was done to deny the Japanese credit, to nurture the belief in white supremacy. There were stories that the designs of the Zero-sen had been drawn up but rejected by a Western power—normally given as the United States, but this varied. Nothing was further from the truth. In these ways were the Japanese aided even by their enemies. The failure to take the Japanese seriously before the war, the refusal to recognize that in the situation in which she found herself in late 1941 Japan was forced to go to war, and the inability to see the high quality of Japanese equipment and professionalism all combined to create for the Allies a situation that, in a matter of days after the start of hostilities, was pregnant with disaster.

CHAPTER 6

Contrasts and Paradox

MOST WESTERN ACCOUNTS of the campaign in Southeast Asia follow its course from a strictly national viewpoint, with the emphasis that is placed on one theater or aspect of the campaign being to the detriment of an overall view of the struggle. For the British the struggle in Southeast Asia concerned Singapore; a few other battles were fought on the Philippines and in the Indies at the same time. For the Americans the Luzon campaign overshadows all other aspects of the war in Southeast Asia. Little, if anything, is to be gained by such sectionalized accounts of the campaign. The events in the Indies, on Malaya, and in the Philippines were contemporaneous. Only through following the sequence of events in terms of Japanese moves throughout the area, moves against all the Allies, can the diverse aspects of the campaign be placed in a proper context and be readily understood. Factors that must be considered include the feebleness of Allied countermoves; the dynamic nature of the Japanese attack and its laudable economy, flexibility, and aggressiveness; and the mass of errors and miscalculations of *both* sides. One of the natural but unfortunate aspects of the many writings on the events in Southeast Asia between December 1941 and May 1942 is the fact that they are taken from the point of view of the defenders, though English texts tend to ignore the Dutch. Only by following the course of the campaign from the stance of the side with the strategic initiative can the full picture of the events be seen and understood.

In chapter 5 the initial Japanese attacks were treated together in order to show the extent and scope of Japan's opening moves and the nature of the problems that the Allied nations faced. In subsequent chapters the course of the campaign in Southeast Asia will be traced in the same general manner; the events will be followed not by theaters but by phases in order to show the progressive development of the Japanese attack and the gradual erosion of the Allied position. In recounting events in this manner it is clearly difficult to set dates to various phases of operations because there is an obvious continuity or theme in the course of events. Any choice in dividing the story is certain to be personal, to an extent arbitrary, and therefore open to question. Nevertheless, in recounting the phase of Japanese operations that followed the initial assaults in the first days of the war, the most suitable cutoff date can be considered to be 7 January 1942. By that Wednesday the question of victory and defeat in the Philippines had been settled. The final defeat of the Americans had been assured even though they had been successful in evading a double encirclement attempt and had withdrawn into the Bataan peninsula. On that day the official American defense of Bataan began, while across the South China Sea on the same day the British were forced to give battle in a disastrous engagement at the Slim River in central Malaya. This battle sealed the fate, if it had not been sealed before, of Malaya and Singapore.

Scarcely had the Americans completed their phased withdrawal into their semiprepared positions on Bataan and the British been savaged in central Malaya's jungles (and with weeks of fighting in these theaters still to come), than the Japanese began their initial moves in the next phase of their operations with a twin drive through the Makassar Strait and the Molucca Passage. In less than two months this offensive was to lead to the capitulation of the Indies—a surrender that predated by nearly nine weeks the end of American resistance in the Philippines. The Japanese occupation of Tarakan and Menado on 11 January, well before the Americans and British were finally crushed, was both a vivid example of the flexibility conferred on a nation possessing supremacy at sea and a prelude to operations that were to result in the Japanese severing Anglo-American communications by driving a 4,000-mile wedge between the British in the Indian Ocean and the Americans in the Southwest Pacific.

This basic outline would almost seem to imply that events moved with the smooth regularity of a well-maintained watch for the Japanese. One has to admit, with no very marked reluctance, that certain aspects of these operations, especially the small number of Japanese losses, would seem to confirm this view. Both in this and, particularly, the subsequent phase of operations, when a two-pronged simultaneous attack ripped open the Allied center and thereby prevented an effective Allied riposte to either thrust, the overall soundness of Japanese planning and preparation, training, and battle doctrine ensured that Japan's overall objectives were achieved, with remarkable economy. But the Japanese did not have everything their own way. Things did go wrong and the Japanese success was attained in a manner that the Japanese did not anticipate. In this phase of operations many paradoxes existed, underlining the truth of the dictum uttered by von Moltke the Elder that no plan ever survives the first contact of war.

Perhaps the most blatant paradox of the Southeast Asia campaign was the simple fact that, whereas on paper the Americans were the strongest of the Allies and the Dutch the weakest, the Japanese, even though their timetable was not so rigid as is often believed, allowed about fifty days for the conquest of the Philippines, approximately one hundred days for the British to be defeated in Malaya, and about five months for the overrunning of the Dutch East Indies. Though the determining factor in this timetable was obviously the geographic location of the various Allied territories in that before the war the Japanese believed that the Philippines had to be secured and American power had to be broken before the Indies could be assaulted, the odd fact is that American resistance proved longer-lasting than that of the British and Dutch. First to fall to the Japanese was the very symbol of white power in the Orient—Singapore, the invulnerable fortress. Singapore was taken in ten weeks; the Dutch lasted two months from the time of the first Japanese landings in the northern Indies to the final capitulation in Java in March. The Americans, with fewer troops than the British, fought on until May, but their continued operations in the field were a reflection less on the efficacy of their arms than on the fact that within a month of the outbreak of war the Japanese revised their priorities and concluded that taking the Philippines was not the prerequisite for the start of operations against the Dutch.

One of the ironies of the campaign, however, was that the gallantry and determination of the American garrison in the Philippines, which in no way was diminished or cheapened by Japan's strategic bypassing of the Philippines, did not buy time for the Americans or their Allies elsewhere in Southeast Asia. Japanese plans and intentions did not allow for a single check, reverse, or denial of total victory that could interrupt the flow of their operations. Though the Japanese had bypassed Americans points of resistance, strategically and tactically American resistance on Bataan had no appreciable effect on the development of Japan's offensive throughout Southeast Asia. The flexibility of Japanese plans ensured that, apart from the rather out-of-place operation that secured Zamboanga on Mindanao and the Jolo operation, no significant landings took place in the Philippines outside Luzon between 22 December and the time of the Dutch surrender in the Indies.

Equally strange was the manner in which the campaign on Luzon unfolded. The Japanese made brilliant use of their advantages of geographic position, time, surprise, and air and naval supremacy to see them successfully through the most difficult and dangerous phase of their operations on Luzon—the main force landings at Lingayen Gulf and Lamon Bay. These successful operations were full of resourcefulness, dash, and imagination. In the period before Christmas Day the Japanese completely outfought and outthought the Americans, thereby securing a position that ensured their final victory. But their hopes of a speedy conclusion to the Luzon campaign were to be confounded by a skilled and resourceful generalship that took full advantage of Japanese errors, miscalculations, and overconfidence. As a result, the Japanese were condemned to a debilitating four-month campaign on Bataan.

But the Japanese made no similar miscalculations in Malaya, where the insipid feebleness of British resistance contrasted badly with American resistance on Bataan, even allowing for the exaggerated praise that the latter attracted at the time. The British performance in Malaya was inept by any standard, however unexacting. A defending force that at the outset numbered nearly 90,000 soldiers was defeated by a combat force of three divisions totalling 50,197 officers and men. In what Churchill described as the worst defeat in British military history, the proudest of the imperial powers lost 138,708 men in an unavailing attempt to hold an empty naval base. For the British the humiliation of the loss of Singapore was total, with no redeeming or mitigating factors.

Yet this should not be allowed to obscure, as it so frequently does, the really outstanding nature of the Japanese success in Malaya. The simple fact of the campaign was that the British in Malaya were shattered by an enemy outnumbered at all times by at least two to one, an enemy whose only compensation for decided numerical inferiority was the initiative, for which it fought, and a realistic battle doctrine, which it secured by thorough preparation. What is so infrequently appreciated about the Japanese success in Malaya is that it was achieved by an army with no previous experience of major operations in the tropics or in jungle warfare. Yet in ten weeks and at a cost of 9,824 battle casualties, the Japanese shattered British power in Malaya and Singapore in what must rank as one of the most impressive and well-conducted campaigns in this or any other war.

But the greatest contrast between the two sides in the opening phases of the war was the simplicity of events on the Japanese side and the sheer extent of difficulties with which the Allied nations had to contend. Japan made her hard choices before she went to war; for at least three months after its start she had no real decisions to make because the campaign more or less ran itself. The Allied situation, on the other hand, verged on the chaotic. The prime and proper function of armed forces is to ensure in wartime national rights that automatically exist in times of peace. In the absence of hostilities the integrity of a nation's territory and her sea communications are secured automatically; in times of war the defense of the homeland and its surrounding waters naturally demands widening areas of interest, enhanced force levels, and the redeployment of resources and redefinition of priorities and policies designed to safeguard these rights and interests. The start of the Pacific war placed the Americans and British in fearsome difficulties because the strategic problems faced by both were expanded in terms of responsibilities, interests, manpower, and materiel requirements but simultaneously compressed in terms of the time available in which they could respond to a situation that was steadily running out of control.

The fact that the Pacific war came at a time of Japan's choosing and that the Japanese were able to dictate the tempo of the opening moves forced Britain and the United States into a series of decisions over whether or not to attempt to retain possessions that had been the immediate targets of Japanese aggression. Nations are naturally loath to cede voluntarily possessions of substantial political, economic, or military value before or at the outset of war. Even where the loss of such possessions is accepted in prewar calculations as inevitable, in the frenetic atmosphere of aggression such clinical, pragmatic, and dispassionate decisions are hard to adhere to. In purely military terms it can be argued that the Americans and British would have been well advised to have abandoned their possessions in the Philippines and Malaya, respectively, before the start of the war. In fact, in early 1941 the British government was advised that Malaya should be abandoned because Britain could not hope to defend it given the Middle East commitment. This advice came from the chief of the Imperial General Staff. But, of course, in devising strategy, military factors cannot have the final word.

If one accepts that the primary characteristic of war is its political nature and that war is, in accordance with Clausewitzian doctrine, an instrument of policy, then one must accept that political rather than military manifestations are the decisive elements in war, and that the effectiveness of military factors is dependent on political and psychological considerations. For the Americans and the British to have abandoned their Far East possessions before the war would have been impossible on political grounds. To have abandoned them during an armed attack and while it was still possible to reinforce them would have been extremely difficult and almost, but not quite, impossible, despite the inevitable military logic of the situation. This was the dilemma that the British and Americans faced in the opening days of the war. The Allies had been unable to prevent the start of war, and were then shown to be incapable of defending themselves and their possessions. Britain and the United States had to decide between attempting to reinforce their garrisons and thereby trying to retain their possessions, and abandoning garrisons and possessions alike to their fates. Only in the latter instance could the forces already in the Far East play a useful role because, once abandoned, they could attempt to buy time while not imposing demands of their own. Any attempt to reinforce them was certain to be prohibitively expensive in terms of time, manpower, and materiel, and almost certain not to result in any commensurate gain. Yet the response of the Americans and British to this situation and common problem differed considerably, though in the end both courses proved equally ineffective.

CHAPTER 7

From Lingayen Gulf to Bataan

With the opening of hostilities both Britain and the United States were too preoccupied with their own immediate peril to consider properly the wider issues of Allied cooperation and the pooling of resources. In the first crucial days of the war the two nations had to look to their own strengths, inadequate though they were, and fight what were uncoordinated actions against the common enemy. Both had to make immediate decisions on the future positions of their garrisons in the Far East, namely whether they were to attempt to reinforce their garrisons already under assault, and for what strategic purpose, or whether they were to abandon them. This was not a question that the Americans and the British had faced squarely before the start of the war. Their reliance upon a policy of deterring Japanese aggression had largely precluded serious and detailed consideration of strategy in the event Japan was not being deterred; what consideration and consultation had taken place on this problem had merely been tinkering with a possibility that became a certainty once war began. Only after London and Washington had made their initial decisions did Churchill and Roosevelt meet to discuss arrangements for the common direction of a global effort.

For the Americans the problem of defining their policy towards the Philippines was even more urgent than the British problem of Malaya because at the time of the outbreak of war a seven-ship convoy, under the protection of the heavy cruiser *Pensacola* and one other escort, was en route to the Philippines. This convoy, carrying pilots and aircraft, two artillery regiments, and diverse supplies, was west of Hawaii on the southern route to the Philippines. The questions of the safety of the convoy and whether or not it should proceed to its intended destination obviously assumed critical and immediate importance as it neared the combat zone. On the outbreak of war the convoy was ordered into Suva to await further instructions.

The forces carried by this convoy were part of the buildup that the Roosevelt administration had decided upon as part of its intention to create a deterrent force in the Far East. Before the outbreak of hostilities MacArthur's U.S. Army Forces in the Far East had been allocated priority for reinforcements, and the crux of the American problem on and after the start of war was that to divert the convoy was tacitly to accept the loss of the Philippines and its garrison. This, naturally, was something that Washington found very hard to stomach, even though the inescapable logic of Japanese superiority in the western Pacific pointed to the fact that reinforcements could not be fought through to the Philippines.

But when one is fighting in defense of what is regarded as home territory, military affairs cannot be the only consideration. The problem that confronted the Americans with regard to the Philippines was that the United States had a moral commitment to the islands that could not be dismissed lightly. For all the reality of the balance of power, it was desperately difficult for the Americans to appear to abandon in its hour of need a commonwealth they were leading to nationhood. The Americans knew that the whole of the Orient, indeed the world, looked for an American response to Japanese aggression, and they knew that the Philippines, in effect, were the litmus paper of American determination and resolve. Americans were aware of the importance of kudos in the east. They appreciated that failure to protect the Philippines could be redeemed by final victory over Japan, but they also knew that to appear not to lift a finger in defense of the Philippines would not be forgotten lightly.

The first weeks of the war saw Washington poised in agonized indecision between an acceptance of strategic reality and the hope that something might occur to get the administration off the hook. During the period the American leadership attempted to dodge the basic question of when it was to write off the Philippines and tell MacArthur this was the case. In a sense MacArthur was the key problem because, with the possible exception of General John J. Pershing, he was the most distinguished serving American general of the day and he was senior to all the officers who held power in Washington in 1941. It was very difficult for Washington within hours of the outbreak of war to tell any general, but particularly one of MacArthur's stature and authority, that his command, with all its political ramifications, was to be abandoned and written off. This was particularly difficult because of the prewar promises to reinforce the Philippines and because Washington had endorsed MacArthur's plans to wage a step-by-step defense of the Philippines. By his enthusiasm and confidence MacArthur had persuaded Washington—and even the sceptical commander of the Asiatic Fleet—that the Philippines should and could be defended, and by him. Against all the available evidence, men who should have known better allowed themselves to be convinced, and once they were converted to the MacArthur view, it was difficult for them to go back on their undertakings.

Disingenuousness characterized Washington's dealings with MacArthur between December 1941 and February 1942 because Washington never properly expounded three fundamental truths about the strategic position of the Philippines once Japan went to war. These were first, that the Philippines could play a significant strategic role only if abandoned to their fate; second, that the Americans did not have the means to aid the garrison; and third, that since the emphasis of all American prewar planning was directed towards Europe and not the Pacific, any attempt to relieve the Philippines involved a reversal of all American political and strategic priorities, a reversal the administration was not prepared to accept.

On the other side of the coin, MacArthur was equally disingenuous because these points should have been obvious to him. He was aware of the American intention to single out Germany and Italy as America's initial targets in a two-ocean war and to stand on the defensive in the Pacific. Even if he was not aware of this intention beforehand, he was certainly in possession of Rainbow 5 in October 1941. Moreover, it is inconceivable that the leading military intellect in the U.S. Army should not have appreciated the simple fact that the Philippines could play a strategic role in the prosecution of the war against Japan only if they were abandoned and left to tie down Japanese resources for as long as possible without making any further demands on American strength. But this was not how MacArthur viewed matters.

When MacArthur was framing his demands he was convinced that the Philippines theater was the place where the issue of victory or defeat would be resolved. He told his superiors in Washington that diversion to him of the entire aircraft production of the United States would be justified if the Philippines were retained. With incredible effrontery MacArthur casually informed Washington that "from my present position of vantage [in the Philippines] I can see the whole strategy of the Pacific perhaps clearer than anyone else." It was somewhat uncharacteristic of MacArthur to qualify his abilities by the use of the word *perhaps*. The simple fact was that MacArthur could see no further than the needs of his own command, and he was suffering from an acute attack of the familiar military disease known as "localitis."

In the autumn of 1941, Lieutenant General Douglas MacArthur, American commander in the Philippines, with his senior commander, Major General Jonathan M. Wainwright. Without the time needed to get extra troops and equipment to the islands, the gesture of defiance explicit in this publicity photograph never matured into more than a gesture. MacArthur Memorial Library

MacArthur's demands contained within them the insistence that he should settle the strategic direction of the war, ensuring as they did that the Pacific should become the Americans' main theater of operations—under MacArthur's personal direction. The megalomaniac streak in MacArthur, never far below the surface, demanded that Washington be subordinate to MacArthur's concepts of war-making. In a very real sense the disputes between MacArthur and Washington in 1941–42 were preliminary skirmishes to the battle that was to be fought out by MacArthur and President Harry S Truman over the conduct of the Korean conflict.

The key argument between MacArthur and Washington centered around MacArthur's needs and American resources. On 14 December MacArthur assessed his immediate needs to be 300 fighters, and he believed

that with 250 dive bombers he could *stabilize* the situation in the Philippines. He had yet to face the challenge of main-force landings. These
aircraft he specifically demanded and subsequently he suggested an attack
on the Japanese homeland by fleet units as a means of drawing Japanese
naval and air strength away from the south and west Pacific. He also
proposed that American carriers fly in aircraft to the Philippines, but this
expedient was rejected out of hand by a U.S. Navy with no intention of
risking its all-important carriers on such an operation.

It is hard not to feel sympathy for MacArthur in view of the impossible
situation in which he found himself; and, it must be admitted, in his idea for
an attack on Japan there was the seed of an operation that, when put into
effect in April, was to have fateful consequences for the whole of the Pacific
war. But the simple fact of the matter was that, given the slenderness of
American resources at that time with regard to transport, both generally
and in the Pacific specifically, there was never any question that aircraft in
the numbers demanded by MacArthur could have been deployed to the
Philippines. In a very real sense the sheer scale of MacArthur's reinforcement requirements pointed to the inescapable conclusion that the Philippines were as good as lost and that there was very little to be gained by
trying to sustain the U.S. Army Forces in the Far East. If MacArthur stood
in need of the reinforcements he demanded, then the Philippines were
doomed, and any attempt to relieve the islands would be no more than
throwing good coin after bad.

MacArthur's demands for aircraft were unrealistic not least because
there was no possibility of their being effective unless there was a substantial number of troops available to protect the airfields from which they
operated. Adequate numbers of troops were available neither in the Philippines nor in the reserve, while the problems of getting even the few
available aircraft to the Philippines were complex, and proved insurmountable. None of the seventy aircraft carried by the *Pensacola* convoy found
their way to the Philippines. The problems of distance and range, the lack
of available airfields in the southern Philippines and then on Luzon, and the
fact that none of the ground crews and essential supplies could go with the
aircraft all made the flying in of fighters impossible. The situation surrounding bomber reinforcements was no better. When war came to the
Pacific the Americans had just forty-seven B-17 Flying Fortresses divided
between Hawaii and the Philippines. In their initial attacks of the war the
Japanese destroyed five of the twelve at Pearl Harbor and fourteen in the
Philippines. In the weeks immediately after the start of the war the Americans made great efforts to send more Flying Fortresses to Southeast Asia.
This effort included sending fifty-three B-17Es from the 43rd Bombardment Group from the east coast via the Caribbean, Africa, and India. Of
these, forty-four actually reached Java and Australia, but none were able to

intervene in the Philippines and their effective contribution to the overall campaign in Southeast Asia was negligible. The aircraft were new, with no back-up facilities, while their crews were raw. The arrival of the Flying Fortresses was naturally spread over a period of time, with the result that they entered service as replacements for wastage and could never be concentrated en masse for any operation. Overall, the eighty B-17s that ultimately saw service in Southeast Asia and Australia flew 350 missions against Japanese forces and sank just two ships, while all but ten were lost to a variety of causes.

But if the prospects of getting air reinforcements into the Philippines were remote, then the chances of getting reinforcements and supplies to the islands, particularly Luzon, either by sea or by air, were even slighter. MacArthur's insistence on the Asiatic Fleet fighting convoys through to the Philippines with Australian and Dutch help—though what forces these two peoples could provide was far from clear—was absurd. With Japanese pincers reaching southwards around Mindanao and Jolo, the Japanese noose around the Philippines tightened from the first day of the war. Hart, commander of the U.S. Asiatic Fleet, knew this, and was castigated for stating the obvious. No blockade is ever total, and the Japanese blockade of the Philippines was never complete, but Hart knew that there could be no question of a slow and obvious convoy making its way to the Philippines. He knew that his "fleet" lacked the power to take on even a Japanese cruiser division, and that such a division was only a small part of the forces that the Japanese could bring against a convoy if they felt the need. The Japanese held far too many advantages—in the air, in the number of warships, in unity of command and geographical position—for the Americans to have any chance of getting significant reinforcements or resupply through to Luzon.

Submarines, long-range aircraft, and perhaps the occasional small ship, making their way towards Luzon stealthily and at night, were all that might be expected to run the Japanese blockade, yet there were obvious problems attached to getting such blockade runners through to the U.S. Army Forces in the Far East. Submarines and bombers could be used for getting supplies through to MacArthur only if they were diverted from their prime task of attacking the enemy's forces. Neither submarines nor bombers were capable of bringing in bulk items. They could bring in much urgently needed equipment (bombers, for example, brought in signal equipment and drugs), but their cargo loads were minute compared to the needs of the garrison. There was also the obvious difficulty of securing ships and crews to make the run into the Philippines. MacArthur might think that if sufficient effort and determination were put into getting ships through to the Philippines, the attempt would be successful, but ships' masters, crewmen of various nationalities, and ship and life insurers held very different views. MacArthur might berate the U.S. Navy for its "defeatism"—in the Philippines, at Pearl Harbor, and in Washington—and he might consider that the navy "refused" to help him, but the answer to these assertions was unwittingly provided by the refusal of seamen to succumb to large financial inducements to sail for Philippine ports. Ships did sail and arrive in the Philippines, but these were very few in number. The *Coast Farmer, Dona Nati,* and *Anhui* successfully ran the blockade, the former reaching Mindanao in February and the other two reaching Cebu in March, but then the Americans had the problem of transshipping the cargoes to small lighters in order to make the trip to Luzon or Corregidor. The coaster *Legaspi* made two successful runs from Panay before the she ran out of luck on her third voyage; the *Princessa* and *Elcano* also managed to get into Manila Bay, but between them they brought only about 1,000 tons of food (sufficient for the garrison for four days) and slightly greater amounts of ammunition and other supplies. The failure to get more through to the Philippines despite intense efforts by all concerned pointed to the fact that Hart was right, that the time for getting convoys through to Luzon ran out when Japan went to war. Thereafter it existed only in MacArthur's imagination.

But what was to the Philippines a matter of life and death was to Washington only one concern of many. The American Rainbow Plans had singled out Germany as the most dangerous threat to American security. Despite the nature and result of the Pearl Harbor attack, this fundamental conviction remained unshaken in Washington. The Roosevelt administration was utterly convinced that American security needs were inextricably tied up with the survival of Britain and the defeat of Hitler. No threat posed by Japan could compare to that posed by the swastika flag flying from the Urals to the Atlantic, from the North Cape to north Africa. The initial American problem, whereby the U.S. declaration of war on 8 December was only against Japan, was obligingly resolved for Roosevelt by the Germans and Italians themselves, when they declared war on the United States on 11 December.

In a two-ocean war Washington knew that it had to resist the natural demands (which in fact were not as intense as might have been expected) for immediate revenge by concentrating against Japan. Roosevelt and his advisers knew that first they had to give priority to the Atlantic and Europe. Desirable though it might have been to reinforce the Philippines or carry the war to Japan, the American leaders knew that such courses of action were possible only if they adopted an offensive policy in the Pacific and went on the defensive in the Atlantic. To do so was impossible: the situations in Russia, where the battle for Moscow was at its height, and in the Atlantic, were too dangerous to permit this. Reaffirmation of the "Germany first" principle in these initial days was the critical American decision of the war, and it was one that accepted the loss of the Philippines.

Unless the Roosevelt administration reversed the whole basis of its prewar strategic deliberations, which it had done once already, then there was no way in which the Philippines could be helped. American policy in the Pacific had to be defensive and the Americans had to make virtue of necessity. The Allied nations had to try to stem the flood of Japanese conquest by using their pathetically inadequate forces in the Far East to buy as much time as possible, but in strategic terms the Allies had to let the Japanese flood tide spend itself. For the Americans, once their fleet was broken at Pearl Harbor, and once the Philippines had been isolated by the fall of Guam and the breaking of the Malay barrier, then the security of defenseless northern Australia and the American lines of communication to Australia and Hawaii were the only real interests in the Pacific for which the Americans were prepared to fight—and these could not be subjected to sustained Japanese threat.

The logic of the situation was appreciated by one relatively junior brigadier general who at the start of the war was chief of staff to the 3rd Army. Because he had been MacArthur's chief of staff in the Philippines, and therefore, presumably, enjoyed MacArthur's confidence, U.S. Army Chief of Staff General George C. Marshall summoned the officer to Washington to ask for his assessment of the Pacific situation. After a few hours to think, the officer told Marshall that in his view the garrison in the Philippines clearly lacked the means to withstand a serious assault unless sufficient forces could be assembled by the Americans to make the relief of the islands even remotely possible. The Philippines, in effect, had to be written off, and the brigadier general concluded that American forces had to be deployed to secure northern Australia as a base for future offensive operations. The officer suggested that American efforts should be directed towards "defending the defensible," and this involved the sacrifice of interests that could not be sustained in order to devote resources to the defense of major interest that had to be retained.

This interview on 14 December made the career of the brigadier general in question. He was immediately posted as head of the Pacific Section of the War Plans Department and then to the head of the division itself during the shake-up of the general staff that Marshall put into effect in 1942. More glittering and prestigious posts were to come his way, including the highest of all elected offices, but this assessment made Eisenhower's reputation because it was in total accord with the views not just of Marshall but of Roosevelt and the U.S. Navy. But it was one thing to formulate such a view; it was quite another to put it into effect.

On the very first afternoon of the war Marshall signalled MacArthur to the effect that the latter would receive "all possible assistance within our power." The obvious escape clause in this promise seems to have been missed by MacArthur both in this message and in subsequent signals from

Washington. But on 9 December the service leaders met in Washington to decide upon the destination of the *Pensacola* convoy. Both the army and the navy leaders were in complete agreement that wherever it was sent, it was not going to the Philippines. While certain alarmist views were expressed and a very extremist demand for the recall of the convoy to the U.S. mainland was expounded, the joint board decided to divert the convoy to Hawaii, the security of which naturally, but wrongly, aroused misgivings after the events of 7 December. Given the unfolding of events in Southeast Asia, where the Japanese had revealed their hand with the invasions of Malaya and the Philippines, plus the opening attacks on Guam and Wake, which were the obvious harbingers of subsequent amphibious assaults in the Pacific, the Americans might have concluded that sustained Japanese operations against the Hawaiian Islands were out of the question and that little was to be gained by diverting the convoy to an area certain to be secured by default of main force operations. This, however, would have involved so wide and penetrating an analysis of the situation that it is hardly to be wondered that the Americans, in the midst of defeat and disaster, should have overlooked what seems now to be an obvious point. The decision to bolster the Hawaiian garrison was the natural, instinctive decision with which there could be no quarrel. The Americans, having been proved wrong on so many points between 6 and 9 December, can scarcely be upbraided for this decision, particularly in light of the shocked disbelief that gripped the United States at this time. To have attempted such a finesse as leaving Pearl Harbor bared after the events of 7 December would have required a superhuman nerve; the joint board's decision was the human and safe one.

Nevertheless, it was unacceptable to Roosevelt. The president wanted some move to the Far East to be made, and the following day the board, in deference to the wishes of the commander in chief, revised its decision, ordering the convoy to proceed to Brisbane. The reinforcement of the Hawaiian Islands was to be undertaken directly from the mainland. This was a far more sensible arrangement than the previous day's accord, yet in a very real sense it merely postponed a decision. At its very best it was an interim measure that recognized that the ultimate fate of the forces carried in the convoy was to be decided by circumstances largely beyond American control.

Once the convoy reached Australia it was to come under MacArthur's command. Both MacArthur and Washington thought in terms of getting as many aircraft, men, and supplies through to the Philippines as possible, but as the days passed with the convoy slowly making its way to Brisbane, it became clear to all but the demandingly persistent MacArthur that to get the convoy through from the south in the face of Japanese air and sea supremacy would be impossible. MacArthur's strained relations with the navy and Hart stemmed from the inability or the unwillingness, depending on viewpoint, of the navy to try to get this convoy through. It reached Australia on 22 December and most of the American forces went on to Darwin. One of the artillery battalions was shipped to Java, where it was forced to surrender in March. A few of the aircraft went on to the Indies but none went to the Philippines. The problem was that Washington never told MacArthur that these forces would not reach him. In January he was told that forces were being moved across the Pacific; he was not told that they were destined not for the Philippines but for various island garrisons. Marshall in several signals hinted that forces were being concentrated to relieve the Philippines when this was definitely not the case. Roosevelt, similarly, conveyed the impression that arrangements were in hand, but he did so ambiguously. His radio broadcast to the Philippines on 28 December definitely gave the impression that help, if not already on the way, was at hand. If not downright deceitful, the broadcast was certainly immoral.

Washington's pretense, however, could not be maintained indefinitely, and time quickly brought home to the American garrison in the Philippines that help would not be forthcoming. Messages of encouragement and promise were sent in December and January, but after mid-February there were no more: it was obvious that help would not be arriving. Washington could do no more than show its concern. But by that time the situation in the Philippines had stabilized, with American forces in the field holding the Japanese on the Bataan peninsula. Whether through calculation or accident, the abandonment of the Philippines by degrees, by the unfolding of events revealing the inability of Washington to affect the course of the battle, did prevent a collapse of morale in the first disastrous month of the war. By the time the realization of helplessness had sunk in, at least the army was safe for the moment and the troops had to fight because they had more than a shrewd idea of what would happen to them if they did not. If in the short term there were benefits to be gained by letting the helplessness of the situation permeate through to the defending forces, there were long-term dangers. There was certain to be a sense of abandonment and betrayal on the part of the garrison, particularly among the Filipinos, and at the time of the final American surrender on Luzon there were some ugly anti-American incidents. Fortunately for American-Filipino relations, however, the cracks were healed by the casual and unthinking brutality of the Japanese. But all this was for the future. Very slowly the realization dawned on the Philippines that no help would be arriving and that the U.S. Army forces had to fight on with what they had; the truth was that from the very first day of the war MacArthur's command was on its own.

On paper MacArthur's command in the Philippines, on land and in the air, was the strongest of the three Allied commands in Southeast Asia, while at sea the Asiatic Fleet, by virtue of its strong submarine component of twenty-nine boats and the relative closeness of the Philippines to Japanese sea lanes, was at least the equal as a threat to Japan as the more obvious challenge posed by the *Repulse* and *Prince of Wales*. The ground element involved in the defense of the Philippines consisted of twelve divisions, eleven of which were made up of Filipinos. Two divisions consisted of regulars: the Philippine Division, a mixed American-Filipino formation; and the 1st Infantry Division of the Philippine army. In January 1942 another regular division, the 2nd Infantry Division, was formed from the ranks of the paramilitary Philippine constabulary. The remaining divisions, the 11th, 21st, 31st, 41st, 51st, 61st, 71st, 81st, 91st, and 101st, were all reserve formations, each raised by one of the military districts into which the Philippines were divided. In the air the U.S. Far East command could put a grand total of 277 aircraft, but of these only 175 were fighters and merely 107 were modern P-40Es. The total bomber strength of the Americans was 74, of which 35 were Flying Fortresses. The Asiatic Fleet mustered a total of 1 heavy and 2 light cruisers, 13 destroyers dating from World War I, 12 gunboats and motor torpedo boats, a collection of auxiliaries, the submarines, and 32 reconnaissance aircraft.

Simple facts of geography pointed to these forces being totally incapable of defending the Philippines. The only way that the Philippines could be defended was by naval and air action that either prevented invasion or limited it to such small proportions that any invading force could be dealt with by the ground forces. The Philippines could not be defended effectively by ground forces, and the naval and air forces were totally inadequate to deter, limit, or defeat invasion.

The essential problem that faced land forces rested in the twin facts that the land area of the Philippines is relatively small and is fragmented. The Philippines, with an area of 114,834 square miles, are slightly smaller than the British Isles, but the 7,090 islands of the group have a total coastline longer than that of the United States. Two islands, more or less at either end of the group, between them account for 67 percent of the total land surface. Luzon, the most populous of the islands and the center of political, economic, and social life, is the largest island, with an area of 40,422 square miles. Mindanao, which has few areas of major settlement, is 36,539 square miles in area. Between these two islands lie the Visayans, of which the nine largest, ranging from Samar to Masbate, total 29,954 square miles or 26 percent of the total area of the Philippines. The remaining 7,079 islands, of which 4,306 are unnamed, average a little more than one square mile in area, though in fact only a couple hundred are larger than this.

This fragmentation, when combined with poor interisland and overland communications, a heavily indented coastline well suited to small-scale invasion attempts, and, paradoxically, the relative size and importance of Luzon, poses all kinds of headaches for a defender incapable of contesting

the sea passage of an invading force. Luzon is the natural and obvious target
for any invasion, but as the Americans themselves showed in 1944, the
possession of even one of the lesser islands—in the American case Leyte in
the Visayans—could tear apart even a quite strong defensive position in the
Philippines, leaving the attacker with all the advantages of choice regarding
future operations and the defender with a whole host of insoluble problems
in responding to an attack. The possession of such an island negates the
need to secure Luzon. In the narrow military sense an attacker need not
attack the largest and most important of the islands to secure control of the
islands, but the defender can do no other but hold Luzon in strength at the
expense of properly garrisoning the lesser islands. In 1944 the Americans
showed that the presence of major forces on Luzon availed nothing in the
Japanese defense of the Philippines. The Americans could have bypassed
Luzon if they had so wished, once the neutralization of Japanese air and sea
forces on the island had been achieved.

Luzon had to be held in strength because of its relative importance, but
the very size of the island made its holding all but impossible. Large
formations, with armor, could operate only in the area of the central plain,
bound in the north by Lingayen Gulf, in the south by Manila Bay, in the
west by the Zambales and Cabusilan mountains, and in the east by the
Sierra Madres. This plain, from north to south about 90 miles in length and
about half that distance from east to west, in 1941 contained about half the
15,000 miles of good roads in the Philippines. Yet Luzon itself measures
some 410 miles from the San Bernardino Strait to the most northerly
Mairaira Point, while about 140 miles of mountains and plains separate
Santa Cruz from Palanan Bay at northern Luzon's widest point. The size
and importance of the central plain made unity of command imperative for
the defense, but at the same time rendered it impossible. Manila is
approachable not merely from Lingayen Gulf but also from the south, from
Balayan and Batangas Bays. Command, therefore, had to be divided between the northern and southern approaches to the capital, and northern
and southern Luzon had to be covered by these commands. Northern
Luzon is large, and a military presence there was essential, notwithstanding
the absence from the area of places of significant strategic importance.
Southern Luzon similarly needed garrisoning if only as part of an attempt
to hold open communications with Samar and, via the Sibuyan Sea, the
other Visayans. But any attempt to hold the southern part of Luzon ran the
risk of encirclement by enemy landings in Lamon and Lopez bays. For the
defenders, there were immense problems of having to divide, disperse, and
then coordinate forces so that they could operate effectively. In addition,
the existence of so many inland seas and islands forced a further dispersal of
efforts and resources to hold both the passages from the open sea into these
seas and the islands themselves—hopeless tasks in the face of enemy air
supremacy.

Thus the geography of the Philippines in general and Luzon in particular threatened to pull the Americans in several different directions at one and the same time. In purely tactical terms, the Americans had to decide between trying to deny the Japanese the chance to get ashore by meeting an invasion on the beaches, and holding forces inland to wait until the Japanese

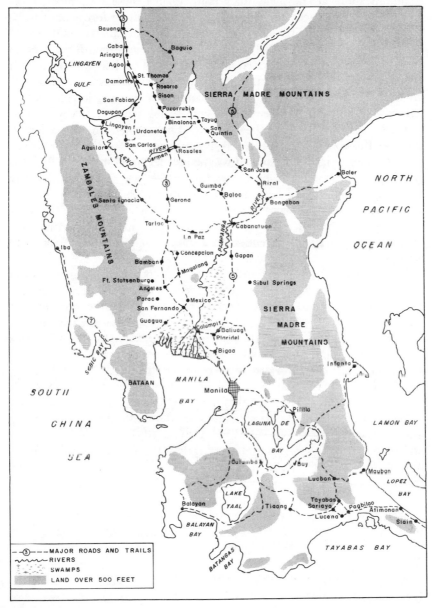

The Central Plain of Luzon

showed their hand before counterattacking to drive them back into the sea. Each course of action had its attractions and dangers. To fight on the coastline promised better chances since the most confused and vulnerable part of any amphibious assault is during the actual touchdown phase when the invading force is inevitably weak in artillery and armor and when communications are normally uncertain. Against these advantages, however, must be balanced the simple fact that defending forces have to be scattered to guard possible landing sites, with the inevitable result that at no one place is the defense likely to possess sufficient strength to meet an enemy certain to be concentrated for the assault. The defending forces not opposed to any landing effort, moreover, automatically are out of action. On the other hand, to stand inland demands the concentration of substantial, mobile, well-trained formations, with strong armor, artillery, and air support, to strike at enemy beachheads. The problem for the defender adopting this course is the speed of response to an invasion because once the crucial assault phase is negotiated by the invader, then it may well be too late for a counterattack to be successful. In the case of Luzon, the long coastline with its many bays gave an invader with assured air and sea supremacy so many choices of how, when, and where to make his effort that, through careful deception to ensure strategic and tactical surprise, the invaders could keep the defenders in a state of agonized indecision until after the latters' defeat was assured.

Before MacArthur's plan for the defense in depth of the Philippines was accepted by Washington in November, the Americans had decided against trying to hold any Japanese attack on the beaches. Under the terms of their plan, War Plan Orange-3 (WPO-3), the Americans set out to deny the Japanese use of Manila Bay as their primary strategic aim by retreating back into the Bataan peninsula. WPO-3 was a curious combination of the sound and the bizarre. The plan correctly recognized that use of Manila Bay was the major gain that the Japanese could hope to make in the Philippines. It envisaged a Japanese assault with about 100,000 men, an unrealistic estimate, on or even before a declaration of war. With little chance of obtaining advance warning of an invasion, WPO-3 envisaged abandoning the beaches and making a main effort only to buy time for troops and supplies to be moved into Bataan. The plan then involved a garrison of about 40,000 troops holding out for some six months until relief from the United States arrived to drive the Japanese back into the sea. The bizarre aspect of the plan lay in the fact that no plans existed for mounting the relief attempt, and the U.S. Navy estimated that two years would elapse before it managed to fight its way to Luzon. WPO-3 made no mention of what was to happen in the intervening eighteen months.

MacArthur branded WPO-3 as "defeatist" and "defensive." From the very start of his time in command he wanted to see American strategic policy assume a more active and aggressive role. The key to such a policy for MacArthur lay in air power, and under his schemes the defense of airfields was a priority second only to the defense of beaches, from which there was to be no withdrawal. MacArthur intended to fight the Japanese on the water's edge, and he concentrated the major part of his forces on Luzon because he anticipated that the main Japanese effort against the Philippines was certain to be directed against the island. All but three divisions of the Philippine army, the 61st, 81st, and 101st Infantry Divisions, were deployed on Luzon. These three divisions were constituted as the Visayan-Mindanao Force under Brigadier General William F. Sharp. Apart from headquarters elements this force had no regular army components. The 61st was initially on Panay but the main part of its original strength was to be siphoned off to join the 81st and 101st on Mindanao. The other two divisions raised outside Luzon, the 71st and 91st, were deployed on Luzon in a reserve role. The 71st Infantry Division was attached to Major General Jonathan M. Wainwright's North Luzon Force, but it was not to be used in support of the 11th, 21st, and 31st Divisions without MacArthur's expressed permission. The 41st and 51st Infantry Divisions were constituted as the South Luzon Force under Brigadier General George M. Parker, Jr. The 91st and the Philippine Division formed the Reserve Force under MacArthur's personal direction. At the time of the outbreak of war the 1st Infantry Division was in cadre form, and was established only in the second half of December by bringing it up to strength with reservists. It was sent to support Parker's South Luzon Force.

The deployment of these divisions reflected American concern for the security of the central plain. The Americans were convinced that the Japanese would make their main effort at Lingayen Gulf, and this consideration explains why so few forces were deployed in northern Luzon and why the U.S. Army command showed so little apparent concern with the Japanese landings on the Vigan coast and their operations up the Cagayan valley. Wainwright initially deployed the bulk of the 11th and 21st Infantry Divisions at the southern and eastern ends of Lingayen Gulf, with the 71st behind the Agno River in support and the 31st holding the coast south of Iba on the right flank. In the south the 41st Infantry Division was held in the Balayan Bay area, while the 51st was given the central-southern area of Luzon (bound by Batangas, Tayabas, and Lamon bays and by Lake Taal and Laguna de Bay) to defend.

Prudent though these deployments were, they failed to disguise several critical weaknesses. The most important of the weaknesses was the state of the Philippine army divisions. These were wretchedly unprepared and totally unfit to stand against a first-class enemy, especially so formidable and savage a foe as the Japanese. They were in the process of being formed, and by independence the Philippine army was to have a regular strength of about 10,000 and a reserve establishment of thirty divisions, each military district raising a corps. By 1941 these arrangements had progressed but slowly, and not even vastly increased expenditures in the last six months of peace could do much to remedy this situation. In theory every division should have had one field artillery and three infantry regiments with full transport and service support.* In reality very few divisions had even one properly constituted and trained regiment, and most units were either cadres or filled with untrained or partially trained levies. In every aspect of weaponry and equipment the reserve divisions were hopelessly deficient, though perhaps their most serious weakness lay in the linguistic and social divisions that plagued them. The task of training commissioned, noncommissioned, and warrant officers obviously was a long and difficult one, but mostly these people were drawn from the better-educated and more socially advanced classes who spoke mainly English or Tugalog, the chief native dialect of Luzon. With half the army drawn from outside Luzon, the difficulties were obvious. Many of the rank and file, who spoke Visayan, could not understand their officers and their fellow soldiers from different islands and areas.

There was one other crucial weakness with regard to the various divisions and this was that very few were properly concentrated. This was a general weakness, but it was one of particular importance when applied to the regular formations, particularly the Philippine Division, because they were the cutting edge of MacArthur's command. At the time of the outbreak of war the total strength of the U.S. Army in the Philippines was 31,095 officers and men. Headquarters elements accounted for 690 of all ranks. The service detachments and the air force totalled 4,268 and 5,609 of all ranks, respectively, while the Harbor Defense units mustered an additional 5,225. Combat units held the balance.

The Philippine Division totalled just over 10,000 men, with nearly 80 percent of its strength being made up of the regular Philippine Scouts. Only one formation, the 31st U.S. Infantry Regiment, was all-American; the Scouts manned the 45th and 57th Regiments and two field artillery regiments, the 23rd and 24th, which between them mustered three units. The Scouts also filled the ranks of four independent units, the 26th Cavalry, the 43rd Infantry, and the 86th and 88th Field Artillery Regiments. All four units were considerably under their authorized strengths.

The Philippine Scouts were good, but their obvious weakness was that there were far too few of them. The whole of the MacArthur concept for the defense of the Philippines might have enjoyed some success if all his divisions had been up to strength and trained to the level of the 10,000-

*Infantry regiments were numbered consecutively, the first regiment (and the artillery regiment) taking the divisional number. Thus the 11th Infantry Division deployed the 11th, 12th, and 13th Infantry Regiments and the 11th Field Artillery Regiment.

strong Scouts and the 31st U.S. Infantry Regiment. But as it was, the forces available to the U.S. Far East command were totally inadequate to hold the beaches or to launch serious counterattacks with much hope of success. With the Philippine Division scattered around the Manila area, the newly arrived 4th Marine Regiment condemned to guard duties (presumably because of MacArthur's long-standing dislike of the corps), and only the 26th Cavalry deployed at Pozorrubio in support of the North Luzon Force, the very real possibility existed that the better troops available to MacArthur would be fed into a battle in a piecemeal manner—if, indeed, the Japanese landed at Lingayen Gulf.

The Japanese did intend to land at Lingayen Gulf, but in typical fashion they chose to make more than one main-force effort in order to exploit their advantage of geographical position and so secure a double envelopment of American forces on Luzon. The Japanese envisaged a battle of encirclement in the Manila area; they did not suspect the American sidestep into Bataan despite the fact that American forces had practiced it as a peacetime maneuver. In order to achieve such an encirclement Honma's *14th Army* planned to use the *16th Infantry Division* of Lieutenant General Susumu Morioka and the *48th Infantry Division* of Lieutenant General Yuichi Tsuchibashi in a two-pronged invasion of Luzon at Lingayen Gulf and Lamon Bay.

The initial invasions of northern and southern Luzon had eaten away at the strength of both divisions, the *48th* having lost the *2nd Formosan* and the *16th* the *33rd Infantry*. Morioka's division was to lose more of its strength because, while it was to carry out the Lamon Bay operation, its *9th Infantry Regiment* was to support the *48th Infantry Division* in Lingayen Gulf. To assist the main formations two armored, one artillery, three engineer, and five antiaircraft units were attached, most of them to the Lingayen Gulf invasion force. The total strength of the two invasion forces was just under 35,000 soldiers (slightly more than the strength of the U.S. Army command's forces in the Philippines), of whom about 7,000 were bound for Lamon Bay.

The Japanese plan of campaign was simple and direct, with both invasion forces ordered to move immediately inland and to advance on Manila. The excellent road system in the coastal plain afforded easy access from the landing beaches on the gulf to Manila, but by the same token afforded the defenders the chance for a quick and perhaps decisive concentration against the invasion. The Japanese, therefore, decided upon consolidation of the beachhead by developing their offensive inland immediately rather than waiting for the armor and artillery to come ashore and be grouped properly for the advance. The Japanese intended to bypass resistance in the assault phase, allowing only the *9th Infantry Regiment* the luxury of systematic operations to secure blocking positions around Bauang on the Vigan and

Baguio roads as the left flank and rear protection for the *48th Infantry Division*'s drive southwards. Similarly, the forces at Lamon Bay, which were not expected to encounter resistance, were to exploit their assault directly inland towards Tayabas Bay, thus splitting Luzon at its narrowest point, before following Route 1 over the mountains to Manila—and battle. For its operations the *14th Army* was allowed fifty days, since Imperial General Headquarters and the *Southern Army* considered that the decisive battle would have been fought and won by that time. The *48th Infantry Division* was detailed to mop up scattered resistance and the various island garrisons of Manila Bay, but its main task after the battle was won was to be replaced in the line by the *65th Infantry Brigade* and move southwards for the operations against the Dutch East Indies. The task of reducing the Visayans and Mindanao was to be entrusted to the *16th Infantry Division*.

The Japanese planned to invade Luzon with their main forces as soon after the start of hostilities as possible, but they were wary of moving before the various detachments involved in the preliminary invasions had firmly established themselves ashore, and they were not prepared to commit transports and troops too far to the south before air supremacy had been secured. With an ease that both surprised and delighted the Japanese, these prerequisites were fulfilled within three or four days of the start of the war, and the Japanese prepared to move. In doing so they ensured a large measure of tactical surprise. The Americans on the Philippines not unnaturally doubted Japanese ability to conduct main-force landings on Luzon before January. With the Japanese heavily committed in Malaya and in the mid-Pacific, it seemed out of the question that the Japanese had the means to launch yet another main-force landing in the immediate future. Every day that passed without the Japanese landing in strength served to raise false American hopes on the Philippines that somehow or other the Japanese had miscalculated, that by some chance they would be met and defeated. No allowance was made for the speed of Japanese turnaround off various invasion beaches and loading of transports in home ports. Such was the effectiveness of Japanese arrangements that the first ships bound for Lingayen Gulf and Lamon Bay began to slip out of various ports on 17 December.

The Lingayen Gulf operation involved landings at three points on the eastern part of the gulf at Agoo, Caba and Bauang; the Japanese planned to stagger their landings from south to north over two hours on either side of dawn on 22 December. A total of eighty-two transports carried the troops involved in this operation in three distinct convoys, which linked up to enter the restricted waters of the gulf together in the correct order of disembarkation. From Takao on Formosa sailed twenty-seven transports carrying the understrength *47th Infantry* and *4th Tank Regiments* to Agoo; this force was escorted by the warships that had taken part in the landings at

Aparri. The *1st Formosan* and *7th Tank Regiments* sailed in twenty-eight transports from Mako in the Pescadores in the company of the warships from the Vigan venture, while twenty-seven transports carried the *9th Infantry Regiment*, which was well supported with more than two artillery regiments, from Kiran in Formosa to Bauang. This convoy was protected by the forces that had been used in the operation that secured Batan Island. Distant cover for the entire operation was drawn from two sources: the heavy units that had covered the Malayan operations, now released from those duties by the destruction of Force Z; and the warships that had covered the initial northern Luzon operations. These forces consisted of two battleships, four heavy cruisers, two seaplane tenders, and a flotilla with a leader and eight destroyers.

Though the Lamon Bay operation involved only the *20th Infantry Regiment*, it, too, planned for three sets of landings at Mauban, Atimonan, and Siain. The main effort was to be made in the center at Atimonan, where a regimental group composed of a reinforced *3rd Battalion* with one reconnaissance and two artillery units in support was to land with the intention of pushing through the Tayabas Mountains to Pagbilao. On either side battalion groups were to act as flank defenders, the *1st Battalion* at Siain being detailed to pass into the reserve as the Atimonan force developed its offensive towards Manila.

Honma in fact set little store in the landings at Lamon Bay. The force assigned to the operation was small, and the *16th Infantry Division* did not enjoy a good reputation within the Imperial Army. It had to cover some very difficult terrain on the way to Manila and, in any case, the whole of the Lamon Bay operation was something of a patched-up job as far as the Japanese were concerned. Initially the Japanese had planned to make a secondary landing at Balayan Bay, but a shortage of shipping and second thoughts about sending an invasion convoy across the mouth of Manila Bay—and the U.S. submarine base at Cavite—prompted the *14th Army* to switch its secondary effort to the east coast of Luzon. Thus it was that, without much faith being vested in it by Honma, the Lamon Bay force sailed in twenty-four transports from Amami O Shima on 17 December in the company of eight destroyers and minesweepers. As this force approached Lamon Bay it was to be given support by the warships that had operated off Legaspi.

When they planned the Lamon Bay operation the Japanese accepted the risks of bad weather and rough seas on Luzon's exposed east coast, but it was the operation at Lingayen Gulf that turned out to be the more seriously affected by inclement weather and seas. When these were combined with a navigational error by the lead ship, which overshot the landing beaches, there were all the ingredients of chaos, particularly because the roughness of the seas and the longer crossing to the beaches threatened to delay the landings until after dawn. The storms in fact overturned some assault boats and stranded others on the beaches, while the spray ruined many of the invaders' radio sets. It was the hardiness and initiative of the individual Japanese soldier that redeemed this situation because, with only a part of the armor and very little of the artillery able to get ashore on the first day, the Japanese infantry pushed inland and secured a position of reasonable depth by nightfall. The war was to show that if the Japanese were given time to establish a beachhead or a bridgehead then a couple of platoons would somehow multiply into battalions and then regiments, well dug in and prepared to resist a counterattack, within a matter of hours. In this situation nothing less than a carefully prepared full-scale attack, with armor, heavy artillery, and air support, could eliminate them. At Lingayen Gulf, of course, such a response was impossible, and the failure of the Americans to prevent the Japanese from getting off the beaches foreshadowed inevitable defeat. Once ashore, the Japanese were far too formidable to be halted by Philippine army formations whose frailties were quickly revealed. Some of the battalions that met the Japanese had only ten weeks of training to sustain them.

The Japanese came ashore at Bauang, Aringay, and on either side of Santo Thomas, but only at Bauang was their landing opposed, ineffectively, by units from the 12th and 71st Infantry Regiments. The latter had been ordered to move through the 11th Infantry Division's area of responsibility to meet the *2nd Formosan* as it came south from Vigan and the Cagayan valley, but instead of being able to establish a position in the San Fernando-Bauang area and crush the *2nd Formosan* against the sea with an attack against its left flank, the 71st was caught on its left flank by the *9th Infantry Regiment* as it overran the defenders of the 12th with little difficulty. From being the encircling force the 71st found itself in very real danger of being encircled by two Japanese regiments. In fact it was able to escape from its predicament, along with scattered units from the 11th, by moving off the road and into the interior. It was to pull back to Baguio, the summer capital, and it was given orders to make its way south, but subsequent events forced it to move eastwards and out of the battle. These small skirmishes therefore resulted in the *9th Infantry* and *2nd Formosan* linking up during the afternoon of the twenty-second, thus securing the rear for the *48th Infantry Division*'s drive southwards. At the same time as the link-up around San Fernando was made, the *3rd/9th Infantry* pushed up the twisting road to Baguio, which it secured on the twenty-fourth.

At Aringay and around Santo Thomas the Japanese, meeting no resistance, immediately moved off the beaches; the *1st Formosan* moved from Aringay along the coast road towards Damortis, while the *47th Infantry*, with supporting artillery, picked up the Agoo road that ran through the Aringay river valley to Rosario. To counter the landings around Santo

Thomas, Brigadier General William E. Brougher ordered a battalion from his 11th Infantry Division into the attack, but as it moved northwards from Damortis it met the *1st Formosan*, supported by the *4th Tank* and *48th Reconnaissance Regiments*, coming south. Not surprisingly the Filipinos scampered back to Damortis as quickly as possible, only to find that the elite 26th Cavalry, had taken possession of the town. In support of the Scouts were various oddments, including five tanks from Brigadier General James R. Weaver's Provisional Tank Group, but these forces could not hope to withstand an assault by units drawn from four regiments, supported by army aircraft. By late afternoon the Scouts had been forced out of Damortis and the town was completely in Japanese hands.

While these operations were taking place around Bauang and Damortis, both the Americans and the Japanese were making every effort to secure Rosario. With the Japanese landing on the east coast of the gulf and not in the extreme south near Lingayen itself, Rosario became the key to the first stage of the battle because it marked the border between the beachhead and the central plain. It was also linked to Baguio by road. On the afternoon of the twenty-second Brigadier General Clyde A. Selleck's 71st Infantry Division was ordered into Rosario and the 26th Cavalry was ordered to defend the Rosario-Baguio junction east of the town. Leading elements of the 71st occupied Rosario, but Selleck realized that with the Japanese pushing hard up the road from Damortis in pursuit of the Scouts and the *47th Infantry* closing the town from the north, the position of the 71st inside Rosario was untenable. In fact, the *48th Reconnaissance* caught the rear guard of the 26th Cavalry just west of Rosario, and the Filipino regulars barely managed to extricate themselves, with heavy losses, by blocking a small bridge with a burning tank. Even when the leading patrols of the 26th Cavalry entered Rosario they found the regiment's troubles were far from over because the *47th Infantry* had managed to fight its way into the center of the town. In fact both the Scouts and the 71st Infantry Division managed to escape from Rosario more easily than they might have expected, mainly because the *47th* was not in a position to press home its attack with all its strength. It had been ordered to send part of its strength all the way back to Agoo in readiness for an advance on San Fabian. This unimaginative move, ordered by the cautious Honma in order to clear the coastal batteries in the area so that he could move the tranports further south, could have been carried out far more easily and quickly by forces already in Damortis. But the order was obeyed, and with it slipped away a second chance of encircling and annihilating the 26th Cavalry.

Even if the Scouts had escaped, Rosario was secured by the Japanese late on the twenty-second, and by the end of the first day's operations there was no denying that the Japanese position was a good one. Though the day had been marred by the unavoidable failure to get most of the artillery and

Lieutenant General Masaharu Honma, commander of the *14th Army*, at his head-quarters at Baguio, summer capital of the Philippines. His failure to win a speedy victory resulted in eventual dismissal; his final success was the real reason for his conviction and execution after the war. Robert Hunt Library

armor ashore, the forces that had come ashore had done remarkably well. They had attacked along a 12-mile frontage and secured the whole of the narrow coastal plain, linking up with the *2nd Formosan* and securing in reasonable strength all the routes along which any counterattack, if it materialized, was certain to come. The Japanese were well poised to bite deeply into Luzon the following day.

The Japanese success on the twenty-second in fact precipitated the crisis of the battle, but the crisis was not so much on the battlefield as inside the U.S. command. MacArthur refused to begin the movement of men and stores into Bataan as a result of the initial landings at Vigan, Aparri, and Legaspi. He had told assembled and rather startled journalists, without any apparent awareness of the contradictions inherent in his words, that he was not going to be distracted by operations mounted for that purpose. Dismissing the notion that he could beat back every and any Japanese invasion effort (though this had been his declared intention before the war), MacArthur stated that it was his intention to hold back his forces in readiness to meet the main Japanese invasion. This was sound, but it would have been sounder still had MacArthur taken the proper precautions against the very distinct possibility that, whether he liked it or not, he might be forced to resort to WPO-3. Twelve precious days therefore had been wasted by MacArthur's refusal to consider what was prudent, and the events of 22 December cleared showed that, contrary to MacArthur's opinion, no very great faith could be placed in the Philippine army's divisions. Units from two divisions, the 11th and 71st, had broken; those from the 11th affected Brigadier General Mateo Capinpin's 21st Infantry Division as they fled toward Dagupan. The 26th Cavalry and the American tanks, the backbone of the North Luzon Force, had been worsted, and it was evident that the defenders, having been unable to check the Japanese with their full strength, would be unable to meet invaders who grew in strength as their forces disembarked. By the end of the twenty-second the whole of MacArthur's policy of forward defense, to which he had clung in the face of all the available evidence, was in ruins. The whole of the command, shorn of naval and air support, stood on the brink of disaster.

MacArthur was aware of the peril in which his command stood, for even on the twenty-second he told his chief of staff, Brigadier General Richard K. Sutherland, that WPO-3 would have to be put into effect. But he delayed giving the order until the following day, by which time the situation had deteriorated still further. During the previous night the 71st Infantry Division attempted to reorganize itself into a defensive position around Sison; the 91st Infantry Division (commanded by Brigadier General Luther R. Stephens) had been moved out of the strategic reserve and ordered to support the 71st. In fact, in its movement north, the 91st was delayed by a Japanese air strike that destroyed the bridge over the Agno River at Carmen, and its leading formations were unable to come to the support of the 71st, which was broken in an attack by the *4th Tank, 47th Infantry*, and *48th Reconnaissance Regiments* at Sison. The Japanese quickly secured the town and moved on to take Pozorrubio despite the resistance of the 91st during the night. These Japanese successes could only be the prelude to their clearing the area north of the Agno within a very short time, but from the twenty-third onwards their offensive was certain to coincide in many ways with the American intention to conduct a slow withdrawal from the general area.

The Americans, under the terms of WPO-3, had drawn up (on paper) a series of defensive positions through which they intended to fight a series of holding actions while the bulk of their forces moved into Bataan. Intention and strategic necessity therefore overlapped. Though the Americans intended to establish an interim line in front of the river, where they could regroup their badly disorganized forces, the weight of the Japanese attack forced them back towards the Agno. Despite fierce resistance by the 26th Cavalry, which was reduced to 450 men in the course of the fighting, on the twenty-fourth the Japanese secured Binalonan, forcing the remnants of the regiment eastwards towards Tayug behind the Agno. With the 91st in the area of the Rosales-Tayug road and the 71st in the general Tayug area, the right flank of the Americans, though mauled, was not in immediate danger. But in the center and left on the twenty-fourth the position was beginning to become ominous because the two divisions in the area, the 11th and 21st, were stretched over a wide front with their right flank in the air. The 11th was pulled back to the San Carlos-Urdaneta line and the 21st was forced to conform by pulling back from around Lingayen to positions on either side of the Agno River near Aguilar.

For the moment the American position was serious but not critical, though it could easily become so because the Japanese were well in control of the situation and were in a position to pick their line of advance. In simple terms two roads, on either side of the great Candaba Swamp, led southwards to Manila: Route 3 to the west from Carmen via Tarlac, Route 5 to the east from Rosales via Baloc. Only the 11th Infantry Division, with one armored unit in support, covered these roads. The 11th Infantry Regiment was in position around San Carlos, the 13th around Urdaneta, and neither could be expected to withstand a serious assault by the *48th Infantry Division*.

But of course under the arrangements of WPO-3 the 11th Infantry Division would not be called upon to fight a serious action. When MacArthur ordered the plan implemented there was little need to spell out the details to the North Luzon Force because these were well known to American officers as a result of prewar exercises. Wainwright's force knew exactly what was expected of it and this was to fall back slowly through a series of delaying positions. A series of lines was drawn up, spaced roughly a night's march apart. The North Luzon Force was to man these lines during the day in an effort to make the Japanese deploy for a systematic attack, thus slowing their advance. The aim was to avoid encounter battles but to force the Japanese into preparations for set-piece battles, which would then be avoided by timely withdrawals under cover of night, when all good Japanese aircraft were asleep. The positions that were drawn up were first on the Aguilar–Urdaneta–Tayug axis; then on the Agno River line itself; then on the Santa Ignacia, Gerona, Guimba, San Jose line; then roughly on the line of the lateral road that ran from Tarlac via La Paz and Carmen to Cabanatuan; and finally north of a rough line through Fort Stotsenburg, Mount Arayat, and Sibul Springs. The lines were neither prepared nor continuous since the Americans were intent on holding only the obvious axes of advance for a limited period—one day—until the last line.

The line running slightly north and on both sides of Mount Arayat was the critical one where the Americans were prepared to fight their main defensive battle before they drew back into the Bataan peninsula. Whatever happened the Japanese had to be held clear of two vital areas at least until 8 January because it was believed that the evacuation of men and supplies into Bataan could not be completed before that date. Any overland troop and logistics movement from Manila to Bataan had to pass through an extremely narrow bottleneck between the Candaba Swamp and the Pampanga delta, and hence the importance of the Mount Arayat line. On Route 5 the defenders had to stand in front of Gapan and Baliuag in order to keep the Japanese away from the vital Plaridel, Bigaa, Calumpit triangle, while on Route 3 the Americans had to keep the Japanese clear of San Fernando, where Route 7 left the major road to make its way across the neck of the Bataan peninsula to Iba. By the time that MacArthur and North Luzon Force drew up the timetable of withdrawal, however, they were aware that yet another threat was developing in the shape of the Lamon Bay invasion force. On the twenty-third its advance was compromised by an encounter with the submarine *Sculpin*, though without loss to either side, and by that evening the invasion force was drawing to anchor in the bay. In the first light of dawn on the twenty-fourth, the various groups from the *20th Infantry Regiment* began to come ashore.

Contrary to the expectations of Honma and his headquarters, the *20th* enjoyed considerable success on its first day ashore and continued in the same vein thereafter. At Mauban the Japanese came ashore under fire from a unit of the 1st Infantry Regiment, which had arrived the previous night and taken over from a battalion from the 52nd Infantry. But not even a unit from the 1st Infantry Division, albeit weakened by the reservists within its ranks, could stand up to a Japanese battalion group, and Mauban fell quickly and easily to the invaders. At Atimonan two companies from the 52nd held up the Japanese infantry as they came ashore but the *16th Reconnaissance Regiment*, when it landed, simply sidestepped the Filipinos and drove inland, leaving the infantry to sort out its minor difficulty by itself. At Siain the Japanese encountered no resistance and their companies divided to the north and south. Some followed the Atimonan force, others linked up with the *Kimura Detachment* coming up from Legaspi—and annihilated the Filipinos sent to delay the detachment but now encircled by the landings. Within the day and at a cost of about 250 killed and wounded, the Japanese broke through to Tayabas Bay and secured both Malicbay and Binahaan; the two battalions of Filipino infantry withdrew at night from the latter town before the Japanese mounted a serious assault.

The events around Lamon Bay added urgency to the implementation of WPO-3 because the first estimate of Japanese strength at Lamon Bay was wildly inaccurate, with supposedly one reinforced division coming ashore at Atimonan and a strong brigade group landing at Mauban. Though the direct route from the scene of the landings to Bataan was some 160 miles across very difficult country, it was obvious that the Americans faced a double envelopment, and that they had to move very fast indeed if they were to avoid being caught by either or both of the Japanese thrusts. On 24 December Parker was relieved of the command of the South Luzon Force by Jones and given the task of organizing the Bataan Defense Force, which was detailed to secure Bataan and begin to prepare positions there in readiness for the main forces as they fell back on the peninsula. When Parker arrived on Bataan on the twenty-fourth, as the flight of civilian officials and refugees and the movement of stores from Manila began to get under way, only elements from the Philippine Division were in position. This division had been denied Wainwright when the North Luzon Force commander requested it for a counterattack north of the Agno. Its deployment to Bataan was a clear indication of the flow of the battle. Other formations were not slow in arriving on the peninsula. On the twenty-sixth the 31st Infantry Division (Brigadier General Clifford Bluemel) completed its movement back down the coast from Iba, while on the twenty-eighth Brigadier General Vincente Lim's 41st Infantry Division, less its second regiment, reached Bataan after a four-day move from Balayan Bay. At the same time as these moves were taking place the rather battered 71st Infantry Division was ordered to pull out of its positions near Tayug and move to cover the vital San Fernando position on Route 3.

The 71st was ordered to move on Christmas Day and the next day the 26th Cavalry—or rather the little that was left of it—was ordered to Bataan in a reserve role. The first part of the phased withdrawal had gone well enough for the Americans, with only minor skirmishes developing as the defenders pulled back to the Agno. Patrols from the *48th Reconnaissance Regiment* closed up to the river during the late afternoon, and during the night a series of furious assaults brought the Japanese control of Tayug by dawn on the twenty-sixth. By these actions the Japanese mauled the 26th Cavalry and threatened to turn the whole of the American line. Twenty-four hours after the assault on Tayug began the *2nd Formosan Regiment* spearheaded an assault on Carmen. The defenders, the 11th Infantry Regiment with a battalion from the 21st in support, were quickly and roughly ejected from the town. By dawn on the twenty-seventh, therefore, the Japanese at two points had broken clear through the best defensive position in the central plain and roughly handled a number of enemy units in the process. The omens were inauspicious for the Americans.

The main Japanese advance beyond the Agno was not to be resumed until the morning of the twenty-eighth, though in the interim patrols probed various routes south for any sign of the American defenders. Honma spent the intervening couple of days consolidating on the line of the Agno, bringing the remainder of his forces ashore, allowing the *9th Infantry Regiment* to come up on his right flank, and distributing his forces for the main effort to the south. The *14th Army* planned a three-pronged drive to the south. On its right flank it planned to use the *9th Infantry Regiment* to advance along Route 3 from Carmen in the direction of Tarlac, while the *1st Formosan*, with artillery support, was to take the road from Rosales to Baloc, where it would converge with another force making its way from Tayug via San Jose. The latter force was more substantial since it consisted of three regimental groups, the *48th Reconnaissance*, the *47th Infantry*, and the understrength *2nd Formosan*. But the initial role of this force was the clue to Japanese intentions because in its move to San Jose it was only the second echelon of the Japanese advance. The first echelon was a force made up of the *4th* and *7th Tank Regiments* with the *1st/2nd Formosan* and a unit from the *48th Mountain Artillery* in support. Its task was to advance from San Jose not on the more obvious Route 5 but along the Rizal road and then across the Pampanga at Bongabon. It was then to swing westwards to come around the back of Cabanatuan as the rest of the *48th Division* came against the town from the north. By this maneuver the Japanese intended to lever apart the whole of the American defensive position between the Candaba Swamp and the Sierra Madre, and with Cabanatuan secured the Japanese intended to push a force, concentrated around the *2nd Formosan*'s main body, along the road to Tarlac. By this move the Japanese intended to secure the right flank of the main advance towards Gapan and Baliuag and, if possible, achieve the encirclement and annihilation of American forces in and north of Tarlac.

Such were the immediate tactical objectives that shaped the Japanese plan, but, of course, the somewhat curious and lopsided deployment of the *14th Army*'s forces coming south from the Agno was designed to ensure that the overwhelming part of the force moved on the direct route to Manila in order to fight the decisive encirclement battle in and around the capital. Honma deployed his forces with the whole weight of a reinforced *48th Infantry Division* on the eastern road and only the *9th Infantry Regiment*, strategically a flank defense force, on the western route. With such disparities in strength—between the two arms of the Japanese advance and between the opposing forces on Route 5—it is scarcely surprising that the main Japanese successes were registered on the axes of advance down which Tsuchibashi drove his division.

The main Japanese advance from the Agno began soon after dawn on the twenty-sixth and quickly cut through various positions that the Americans had abandoned or were abandoning. But by the next day the Japanese had closed up on the Americans sufficiently to allow them the chance to catch the 92nd Infantry Regiment in and around Cabanatuan. The armor, as planned, came around the open western flank, while the infantry closed the town from the north. Only demolitions delayed the Japanese for any time as their infantry secured the town, but almost the whole of the 92nd managed to escape from the town before the arms of the Japanese pincers closed. Then, with the *47th Infantry* leading, the Japanese pushed on to secure Gapan before nightfall on the thirtieth. The somewhat shaken 91st Infantry Division retreated back to Baliuag in order to reorganize as the momentum of the Japanese advance died away.

The advance of the *48th Infantry Division* to Gapan slightly outstripped that of the *9th Infantry Regiment* down Route 3, but the latter nevertheless managed to secure the heavily bombed town of Tarlac on the afternoon of

30 December. That afternoon produced mixed fortunes for the Japanese, however, because the *9th Infantry*'s attempt to exploit its success beyond the town ran into a well-sited defensive position manned by the 22nd Infantry. The Japanese suffered a sharp reverse and their regimental commander was killed. Simultaneously, the lunge down the road to Tarlac from Cabanatuan by a reinforced battalion group was stopped with sobering losses by the 11th Infantry Regiment, with tank support, around Carmen and La Paz. But by the end of the day the Japanese had managed to redeem their fortunes when the *9th Infantry*, attacking after dark, caught the 21st Infantry as it began to pull out of its positions in order to withdraw to the Mount Arayat line.

On paper the events of 28/30 December in the central plain constituted a massive Japanese success, and without doubt their gains were substantial and represented a serious threat to the Americans on the northern shore of Manila Bay. But the one thing that would have shown that the Japanese were winning was conspicuous by its absence: they had taken very few prisoners, and a large prisoner count generally is a yardstick of the success of a battle. Cynically it could be argued that the absence of prisoners stemmed from the Japanese disinclination to take any and that, in any case, the Filipinos deserted beforehand. This would be neither fair nor accurate. The absence of prisoners reflected the fact that the Japanese, as they pressed south, were pursuing not a defeated enemy, as Honma believed, but a foe that in fact was carrying out a withdrawal in reasonably good order. The American plan to fall back through a series of defense lines to the position on either side of Mount Arayat, notwithstanding the events on the eastern road, basically worked, though it was not without its nasty moments. Undamaged tanks had to be abandoned, without being destroyed, at both Moncada and Tarlac during the course of the retreat down Route 3; there were many desertions among the Filipinos; and several units were badly mauled. The gravity of the American position inevitably increased as the Japanese pushed southwards. But despite all these problems, by the night of 30/31 December the Americans were pulling back to the Mount Arayat line that they initially had intended to man on the thirty-first. They were back on their last line on schedule with formations and units that were reasonably intact, and, moreover, other forces were in position to cover the vital communications centers of San Fernando and Plaridel. The Japanese failed to appreciate that, despite their advance, they had failed to secure a single tactical victory of any great significance.

But this was not the only Japanese failure. The obsession with the idea of battle around Manila led Honma to overlook the significance of the American declaration on 26 December that Manila was an open city, and the massive movement of vehicles from the capital into Bataan. At first it appeared to the Japanese that the movements towards Bataan were simply those of flight, and they made no effort to interfere with the exodus. Literally miles and miles of vehicles built up periodically at various junctions and narrow bridges, but the Japanese aircraft made no attempt to interfere with the tightly packed traffic. Nor did Japanese aircraft attack the major bridge over the Pampanga at Calumpit, which the air staff of the *14th Army* did not consider a sufficiently worthwhile target. The bridge, or rather the two bridges, were virtually undefended, while the destruction of them would have left the Americans unable to cross a deep and fast-flowing river that could not be forded. Had the Japanese realized that a disorganized flight was in fact a planned withdrawal that was swelled by refugees, and responded by attacking and destroying the bridges, then the South Luzon Force would have been unable to retreat back into Bataan.

The South Luzon Force felt no sense of urgency when it received its orders to withdraw to Bataan on 24 December. With two weeks in which to get clear of Calumpit it had plenty of time in which to fight some neat and effective delaying actions. But as events unfolded, the opportunities for such actions failed to materialize. In the end the force had to carry out an effective demolition program to slow down the *20th Infantry Regiment* while it made good its escape into the temporary sanctuary of Bataan before the *48th Infantry Division* sealed off the road leading out of Manila to Bataan.

The Americans withdrew and the Japanese advanced along two main axes that came together near the town of Calamba on the southern shore of Laguna de Bay. Most activity took place on Route 1, the direct road between Atimonan and Manila running through Tayabas, Tiaong, and Santiago because it was on this road that most of the forces were deployed. Most of the activity on the American side was withdrawal and demolition, on the Japanese side unopposed advance or, at worst, light resistance to be overcome. The Japanese secured Pagbilao, Tayabas, Lucena, and Candalaria between 25 and 27 December, their main problem being how to rebuild the bridges that the Americans destroyed as they withdrew. To the north, on the minor axis, things were a little hotter. On Route 1 after 25 December the Japanese never came close to encircling the 51st Infantry Division or even fighting a major action against it, but to the north two quite brisk engagements were fought and for a day or so one Japanese battalion seemed poised to wipe out two battalions from the 1st Infantry Regiment.

This situation on the northern axis mainly arose because of the confusion that surrounded the various changes of command and rotation of units that plagued the force on 23 and 24 December. After a series of unfortunate and unauthorized withdrawals the 1st Infantry had uncovered Sampaloc and Piis; and on the twenty-sixth the Americans launched a counterattack, spearheaded by armor, to recover Piis. This was a badly managed affair. The Japanese decisively outfought the Americans, whose tanks attacked along a road off which they could not move. By using the standard tactic of knocking out the lead and rear tanks the Japanese broke up the attack and followed up hard, securing Lucban despite the presence in the American line of 300 retired Philippine Scouts. The Scouts stiffened the resistance of the 1st Infantry, but could not hope to deny Lucban to the Japanese. The Americans drew off towards Luisiana, thus leaving the Japanese with the options of wheeling south to Tayabas and thereby linking up with the rest of the *20th Infantry Regiment*, following the Americans north to Luisiana, or heading west along the rough tracks on the lower slopes of Mount Banahao.

The Japanese chose to advance to the north and west, thereby threatening to pin the 1st Infantry against the shores of Laguna de Bay if they managed to reach the Calauan, Bay, Los Banos area ahead of the 1st. In fact the 1st, by a forced march, managed to get back to Calauan before the Japanese came anywhere near the town, while the regiment's 3rd Battalion, still on Lamon Bay at Infanta, came south to hold Pililla just in case the Japanese tried to approach Manila by using the northern and eastern roads around the Laguna. On the main road, however, the Americans prepared to stand in the narrow defile at Tiaong. By this move the Americans hoped to allow the 42nd Infantry Regiment time to get clear of its positions at Balayan Bay while the 1st Constabulary Brigade moved into position to cover the withdrawal of the 51st after it had handed out a salutory lesson to the Japanese around Tiaong. In fact the South Luzon Force never had the chance to stand at Tiaong because the Japanese still had to reach the town when, on 28 December, the force received new orders to make certain that it cleared Calumpit by dawn on 1 January. Naturally fearing that things had gone badly wrong for the North Luzon Force, Jones's command did not tarry. Even though Manila had been declared an open city, units were moved through the capital and then into Bataan by 31 December.* In this retreat the *20th Infantry Regiment* was left far behind, still struggling to reach Santiago as the first of the South Luzon Force, the 42rd Infantry Regiment, entered the Bataan peninsula on 30 December. Two battalions of the 51st Infantry, plus a detachment of tanks, were left behind around Palilan to supplement the defenders of the 71st and 91st Infantry Divisions.

Some 14,000 men out of the South Luzon Force's original strength of about 15,000 reached Bataan. This was a considerable achievement, but the passing of most of the force over the Calumpit bridges ushered in another period of crisis for the Americans as the Japanese offensives along Routes 3 and 5 resumed their momentum. This crisis, however, was to prove not so serious as earlier ones in the central plain because the main thrust of the Japanese strike was to be away from the American forces and their line of retreat into the Bataan peninsula.

---

*The last American troops in Manila did not evacuate the capital until 31 December.

By 31 December the Americans had formed three defensive positions to cover the withdrawal into Bataan. These were in the Baliuag-Plaridel area, around Calumpit, and on the western part of the original Mount Arayat line. In and north of Baliuag the Americans had deployed the 71st and 72nd Infantry Regiments, supported by their divisional artillery and an armored company. In reserve behind Baliuag was the 91st Infantry Division, while the 2nd and 3rd Battalions, 51st Infantry, with an armored detachment in support at Bocaue, covered Plaridel. At Calumpit the 23rd Infantry, flotsam from various units, and most of an armored unit, were in position west of the river. The 21st Infantry Division's other two formations, the 21st and 22nd Infantry Regiments, were on Route 3 around Bamban, while the 11th Infantry Division held the area around Mount Arayat itself.

What is not immediately apparent from a map of these positions is the manner in which all of these forces depended on one another for survival. The key to this situation lay in the town of San Fernando, through which all these formations, with the exception of the 21st and 22nd, had to pass in order to reach Bataan. A Japanese attack either from the north or from the east always carried the threat that if a breakthrough was achieved on either axis, the Japanese would be able to force their way into San Fernando before the Americans could withdraw from the positions that still held firm. In this event the Americans ran the risk not only of having part of their defending force broken and the other part encircled, but also stood in danger of the Japanese immediately exploiting their success directly into Bataan before the defenders were ready.

What the Americans had to do was to draw back their defenders in an orderly manner that would prevent a Japanese breakthrough on either front, while leaving the 11th and 21st Infantry Divisions in position to cover the withdrawal from Route 3 to the Culo line. This was probably the most delicate American maneuver of the campaign to date. American resistance had to be strong enough to delay the Japanese but not too strong to prevent breaking contact while the positions lacked depth. Any panic on the part of any unit was likely to be infectious, and the Americans simply could not afford to see a *sauve qui peut* that resulted in a hopeless pileup of men and vehicles in San Fernando, easy prey to any Japanese advance. But in this phase of the defensive battle the Americans had one advantage. The weak spot in the defense was around Baliuag and Plaridel, but any attack by the *48th Infantry Division* through these towns was certain to be directed down Route 5 to Manila and therefore away from the American line of retreat. The real threat to the Calumpit-San Fernando area came not from the east of the Pampanga, but from the north. There, of course, the Japanese were weaker. Though the *9th Infantry Regiment* was reinforced after Tarlac by the arrival of the *3rd/2nd Formosan* and a leavening of artillery, it still remained a modest force. Yet unless the Japanese forces at

Gapan pushed across the Candaba Swamp along Route 10 to Arayat and then to Mexico and San Fernando, the *9th* was the only formation that could pose any real threat to the American withdrawal. At the very worst the Calumpit bridges could be blown without the evacuation being completed simply in order to deny the *48th Infantry Division* access across the Pampanga.

This situation never arose because on both Route 3 and Route 5 the Japanese were held for long enough to allow all the major American units to escape into Bataan. The Japanese forfeited their last chance of savaging the Americans while they were still outside Bataan by pausing to reorganize after having secured Tarlac and Gapan. By the time the *48th Infantry Division* and the *9th Infantry Regiment* resumed their attacks on 30/31 December and 31 December/1 January, respectively, their chances of catching the retreating American columns were slim.

Pushing down Route 5 the *48th* found its path blocked at Baliuag on the morning of the thirty-first. The defenders of the town did all that could be asked of them because, by holding onto the Agnat line when the Japanese tried to "bounce" the river, they forced the Japanese to deploy from column into line in order to carry out a set-piece assault on the town. The *48th*, frustrated by the demolition of the bridge in front of Baliuag, was forced to cross the river well to the east of the town and then fight its way into Baliuag, while the 91st Infantry Division, acting in the spirit if not to the letter of its orders, pulled back to Calumpit. As the Japanese massed for an assault, the 71st and 72nd Infantry withdrew, but their artillery and the armor fought a very successful spoiling action until well after nightfall, when in turn they began to break contact. At about 0300 the rear guard from Baliuag passed through Plaridel, where the 51st Infantry was still in position. An hour later the last defenders of Plaridel were subjected to Japanese small-arms fire as they pulled out, but being mechanized, unlike their attackers, the 51st was soon clear not only of Plaridel but also of Calumpit. By 0500 the whole of the 51st was on the west bank of the Pampanga, and with Japanese patrols advancing quickly up the river, the bridges at Calumpit were destroyed at 0615.

To the north serious contact between the 21st and 11th Infantry Divisions and the Japanese was established at about this time, and throughout New Year's Day the 21st comfortably held all Japanese attempts to get across the almost-dry Bamban riverbed. After nightfall the 21st began to pull back through Angeles and then to Porac, while the 11th, ineffectively attacked in the late afternoon by Japanese troops moving along the Concepcion to Magalang road, began to pull back through Magalang, Mexico, and San Fernando. The 11th followed the defenders of Plaridel and Calumpit through San Fernando to reach Guagua just as the covering force, the tanks from Baliuag, moved into San Fernando at about 0230. The armor blew the

San Fernando bridges behind them, thus affording themselves some respite, but in fact it was not until after dark that day, the second, that elements from the two Japanese formations—the *3rd/2nd Formosan* from the north and the *1st* and *2nd Battalions* of the same regiment from the east—linked up at San Fernando.

The unification of the *2nd Formosan* at San Fernando came at the end of a momentous day because on 2 January the Japanese occupied Manila and the *Southern Army* informed Honma that the *14th Army* would be losing the *48th Infantry* and *5th Air Divisions* in the immediate future. In fact 2 January marked a watershed in the campaign on Luzon, not only because of these events, important though they were, but also because the day marked all but the end of the movement phase in the Luzon campaign. A few more days of confusion and movement remained to run their course, but from this time distance was to be measured in terms of parts of miles or in single numbers of miles, not in the tens and scores of miles that had been the currency of the campaign to date.

Naturally all these elements of 2 January were interrelated. The fall of Manila was an event that, since it was predictable some days before it occurred, was a major factor in Imperial General Headquarters ordering formations of the *14th Army* to the Indies. Imperial General Headquarters and the *Southern Army* between them accepted that the move could well prolong the campaign on Luzon, but they considered the prospect of securing the Indies more rapidly to be well worth the temporary inconvenience of a lingering campaign in the Philippines. Where all the major commands involved in or affected by this decision—Imperial General Headquarters, the *Southern Army*, and the *14th Army*—fundamentally miscalculated was in believing that American resistance on Bataan would be weak. With the forcing of the Baliuag-Plaridel position and the advance on Manila, the *14th Army* realized the Americans had escaped into the peninsula, but this realization did not raise any doubts that what remained would be anything more than a minor mopping-up operation. Morioka, after the war, spoke of his belief that the American withdrawal into Bataan was like "a cat entering a sack," and the *16th Infantry Division* commander was not alone in his view. What the Japanese did not realize at this stage was that they had only managed to dock the cat's tail, not draw its claws; and, to pursue the analogy, the Japanese failed to remember that cats in sacks are seldom noted for their sociability.

Perhaps the Japanese should have seen the warning signs more quickly, but there was no getting away from the fact that, even with the small forces they had available for pursuing the Americans southeast of Route 3, the Japanese still managed to reach the Culo line by 6 January. The Americans took pride in this phase of operations, and rightly so. The Filipino units fought hard to hold their positions, and made Japanese eyes water on more than one occasion, but the greater achievement was that of the Japanese. American intelligence estimated that the Japanese had 120,000 men on Luzon, and that the formations that attacked them on the Porac-Guagua position on 2/3 January were the vanguard of this entire force. The Japanese had less than half that number on Luzon, and the forces that closed the American lines were literally all that the Japanese had available, for the moment.

The *9th Infantry Regiment*, supported by two understrength artillery formations, came down the road from Angeles to Porac in order to resume its contest with the 21st Infantry Division, while the regrouped *2nd Formosan*, backed by a battalion from the *47th Infantry*, an assortment of artillery units, and a company of tanks from the *7th Tank Regiment*, moved out of San Fernando in pursuit of the 11th Infantry Division, which had taken up a position in and around Guagua. Both the 11th and the 21st deployed virtually their full strengths in defense of the Porac-Guagua line, and they had two armored units and the reconstituted 26th Cavalry in support. The *9th Infantry Regiment* moved forward to make contact with the enemy during the afternoon of the second; the *2nd Formosan*, naturally later into its stride, only established contact with the 11th midway through the morning of the third.

What happened over the next two days can best be described as a confused series of brawls with fortune changing sides with impartiality. On neither front did the Japanese achieve a clear breakthrough of the American positions. On both axes they broke into the defense lines and mauled defending units, but they paid heavily for their limited and local successes, and the *2nd Formosan*, already having seen some fierce action since 10 December, was forced out of the operations because of its losses. But with the Japanese able to bring more reinforcements to the area (the *1st Formosan* replaced its sister formation) and the Americans not inclined to stand and fight it out in front of the Calo, the 11th and 21st Infantry Divisions were ordered back to the Gumain when, on the afternoon of the fourth, the Japanese appeared to be on the point of achieving a decisive result around Guagua. In considerable confusion because the Japanese forced the defenders of Guagua to make the long detour down Route 74 through the 21st Infantry Division's lines in order to get back to Santa Cruz, the Americans managed to get into position by dawn the next day. Though the Japanese sent patrols forward, no serious contact was reestablished before the American covering force began to draw back to the Calo. The final withdrawal was made amid scenes of incredible chaos (fortunately for the Americans not added to by the Japanese air force), as two divisions converged on the Layac bottleneck at the same time. Overall some 15,000 troops out of the North Luzon Force's original strength of 28,000 escaped into Bataan to join the 65,000 troops and 26,000 civilians already on the peninsula. Security

Roll call on Bataan. Members of the 228th Signal Operations and 252nd Signal Communications Companies on parade, 10 January 1942, at base camp "Mudhole" just after the withdrawal into Bataan and the start of the siege. U.S. Army

was only temporary as the Japanese were to follow up almost immediately, but by 6 January the war of movement died away with the Americans having avoided defeat in the field—so far.

The second stage of the Luzon campaign was at an end. By any standard it was for both sides a sprawling, untidy affair that lacked a clear-cut decision and from which neither side could really draw much satisfaction, though both sides had credits to their names. On the Japanese side there was the impressive achievement of two reinforced divisions establishing themselves on Luzon after difficult amphibious operations and then conducting a series of operations that within sixteen days secured Manila and brought them to the brink of victory. On the American side there was the striking tactical expertise that allowed partially trained, ill-equipped, and poorly disciplined Filipino divisions to fight a series of defensive battles and then brought them to the temporary safety of Bataan. But against these matters must be balanced the debits and the missed opportunities.

There can be no getting away from the fact that in the period 23 December to 6 January Honma's *14th Army* dissipated all the advantages of position, air and sea supremacy, and troop quality with which the Japanese began the campaign. These initial advantages had more than offset numerical inferiority. Yet the *14 Army*'s conduct of operations, particularly in the air, was inflexible, unimaginative, and at best no more than competent. Against a poor quality opposition the Japanese achieved nothing more than the ordinary, and achieved this in a way that condemned them to a debilitating three-month campaign on Bataan. The almost total inability to move away from a preconceived plan and to adjust to a changing tactical situation betrayed a wooden orthodoxy utterly unsuited to Japanese strategic and tactical requirements. For the Japanese it was a tragedy that there was only one Yamashita and that the more aggressive and colorful *25th Army* commander was in Malaya and not the Philippines. While accepting that Yamashita, had he been in the Philippines, might well have missed the significance of the American move into Bataan, it is hard to resist the notion that this more forceful commander would have achieved quicker and more decisive results than the more staid and dour Honma.

At least the Americans cannot stand accused of inflexibility, but their performance on Luzon is hard to assess, partly because it is inextricably bound up with the personality and professional reputation of MacArthur. Long after his death, MacArthur remains a subject of sharply divided opinions. There is also bound up with this question the matter of national prestige, and there is no escaping the simple truth that for the Americans the defeat on Luzon was a shameful humiliation. If the only justification for one people assuming control of another is the enrichment of both, then it follows that the lasting benefit the subjected people must secure as an inalienable right is the establishment and maintenance of order, and hence law, and protection from external aggression. In this the Americans failed the Philippines, and failed them lamentably.

Only by applying the sternest logic can any proper assessment of the movement into Bataan be assessed. What can be safely said is that the Americans' (i.e., MacArthur's) tactical handling of the situation after 23 December was far more sure than the policies that resulted in a disastrously inept initial deployment that invited, some would say deserved, defeat. Responsibility in both phases lies with MacArthur, and the censure that must be made on one matter must be balanced against the acclaim that the other commands.

Yet that acclaim can hardly extend to various praises that have been heaped upon the move into Bataan. In *American Caesar*, for example, William Manchester wrote, "MacArthur's sideslip into Bataan was, by any standard, a classic of its kind. Pershing called it 'a masterpiece, one of the greatest moves in all military history.' "* Patriotism warps perspective, both in praise and in condemnation.

WPO-3 was not MacArthur's plan. He scorned and rejected it, and cannot be credited with any part of it. He did everything to avoid having to implement it, yet he did so, and for that due regard must be given. Mental flexibility, an ability to discard ideas and intentions invalidated by events, is one of the highest attributes of generalship. MacArthur's change of policy

*Manchester, *American Caesar*, p. 218.

enabled the Americans on Luzon to roll with the punch, out of immediate danger, and thereby allowed his force to "live to fight another day." But if the plan to withdraw into Bataan was not MacArthur's and if such a move into the peninsula was inevitable at some time because of the lack of any alternative other than surrender, then it must follow that any attempt to credit MacArthur personally with implementing WPO-3 must rest either on the timing or on the conduct of his move. Delaying the implementation of the plan until 23/24 December—twelve days after MacArthur gave the chief executive of the Philippines a "warning order" to prepare to move to safety—ran the greatest possible risks in pursuit of the least possible gain. By no standard, however inexacting, can any claim to competence or genius be substantiated on the ground of timing.

Any claim that may be made on MacArthur's behalf with regard to the conduct of operations is equally hard to sustain because the operational aspects of the move, which were good, have to be balanced against the administrative arrangements, which were poor. The two aspects cannot be divorced any more than power and responsibility can be divided. They are sides of the same coin. MacArthur managed to get his army back to Bataan, but did so at the cost of neglecting sound administrative arrangements that alone would have enabled it to function effectively on the peninsula. Of course, in the long term there was nothing that MacArthur could have done that would have averted defeat on Bataan, and for that MacArthur cannot be censured. But material and supplies were abandoned on the central plain, provisions that would have been invaluable on Bataan. At Cabanatuan, for example, nearly 4,500 tons of rice, enough to feed the 105,000 mouths on Bataan for five months, were left to the Japanese, who also captured nearly 3,400,000 gallons of oil and gasoline and almost 500,000 rounds of artillery ammunition. All over Luzon warehouses and depots full of supplies ranging from food to clothing to drugs were left to looters, local and Japanese. The one week (24 to 31 December) that MacArthur's delay in implementing WPO-3 left for the evacuation of supplies to Bataan was totally insufficient for the peninsula to be stocked properly. By the time MacArthur made his belated decision to draw back into Bataan the movement of supplies had to fight with troop movements for road space and transport. Such was the extent of this administrative failure that the defenders of Bataan had to be placed on half-rations from the time they entered the peninsula. This situation had been avoidable, and the effects of delay were disastrous. As soon as the Americans were back over the Calo they had to turn to face not only Honma but also the three most successful generals in history, generals that had accounted for more armies and cities than mere human endeavor. Their names were Hunger, Disease, and Despair.

CHAPTER 8

The Fall of Northern and Central Malaya

WHILE THE AMERICANS were trying to grapple with the difficulties confronting them by the onset of war, the British were beset with their own problems, which in the end were to overwhelm them. If ever there was a story of self-inflicted wounds, then the campaign in Malaya and Singapore must surely be it. The problem that confounded the British was the same one that had plagued their interwar defense planning—the role of Singapore. From the time that the *Repulse* and *Prince of Wales* slipped to their final resting places on the bottom of the South China Sea, Singapore was useless to the British. Its only value was as a base for a fleet, and there was no fleet and no prospect that one would arrive. Indeed, there was a good argument that since the base had been unable to undertake major repairs on British warships damaged off Greece and Crete in May 1941, Singapore had been useless even before 8/10 December. Nevertheless, the British could not see that Singapore had no positive strategic value to them and that any attempt to hold or relieve it would involve an effort that was certain to be extremely costly in terms of the resources at hand—and probably beyond them—and unlikely to be successful. The nub of the Singapore problem was that the naval base in the interwar period, and particularly in the course of 1941, had become that most fateful of military phenomena—a symbol whose moral value outstripped all political and strategic significance. It was this symbolic value that served to prevent the full irony of the campaign from being realized either at the time or later. For ten weeks the British army attempted to stand in defense of a naval base that was bereft of any British fleet unit for all but one day of the war.

By December 1941 Singapore had become nothing less than a British virility symbol; its successful defense was something that would prove British resilience in the face of adversity and underpin a prestige somewhat tarnished by the disasters of that year, particularly in the Mediterranean theater. In light of the promises made in the interwar period to the Australians and New Zealanders, Malaya and Singapore had to be held, more for political than for sound strategic or economic reasons. These were the places where the British chose to make their stand in order to demonstrate their firmness, reliability, and good faith. There could be no question of a voluntary relinquishing of the peninsula and naval base, even though such a course of action might well have proved Britain's best option from the narrowly military point of view. Had the British chosen to abandon Malaya and Singapore and to concentrate forces on Ceylon, in India, and in Australia, then the undue and unnecessary loss of irreplaceable manpower and equipment would have been averted and the British might well have been left to play a major, not minor, part in rolling back Japanese conquests in 1943–44. In the context of 1941, however, such a line of action was never remotely possible.

We have seen in previous pages that much confusion surrounded the interwar deliberations over Singapore and the extremely low priority accorded Malaya by London in the course of 1941. Before the war British leaders, particularly Churchill, clung to the illusion that the Japanese could be deterred; once war broke out the new illusion that Singapore was a fortress that could be held took its place. The crux of the situation, however, was that Singapore never was and never could be a fortress. Churchill, indeed, after his folly of Force Z, was among the most guilty in holding onto the absurd notion that an island nearly 220 square miles in area with a civilian population of about 500,000 could be a fortress.

One of the major difficulties that always confronts reasoned discussion of fortresses is the fact that in literature their sieges are invariably epic and until they fall they are always considered to be impregnable. The British public out of ignorance, and leaders out of stupidity or dishonesty or both, had failed to appreciate the glaring deficiencies of Singapore and the true functions of a fortress in the conduct of war. A fortress is a fortified position, the prime purpose of which is to cover a route or territory coveted by a possible enemy. In denying the enemy uncontested access, the fortress serves to tie down disproportionately large numbers of enemy forces and to buy time for the defense to build up and concentrate resources for counter-offensive operations. Unless the ultimate loss of the fortress is acceptable, which indeed can be the case after it has served its purpose in delaying and inflicting loss upon the enemy, then it must be relieved because no fortress can be expected to survive a close and protracted siege. The sortie to relieve is one of the more difficult of all military operations, while adding sea and air dimensions to such an operation only complicates matters still further. But if relieved, a fortress then serves as a base for further offensive operations.

In the absence of a strong navy and an adequate air force that could prevent enemy landings, the minimal requirement for the successful defense of Singapore had to be a garrison capable of holding an attacker at arm's length from the naval base. Such a force may well have been available in Malaya in December 1941—though not as deployed by the British—but in every other aspect Singapore was manifestly unsuited to meet the requirements of being a fortress. For the most part the island was unfortified. It did not promise to tie down disproportionately large numbers of the enemy. In fact the reverse was the case, with the defense of Singapore acting as a greater drain on stretched British resources than the needs of an attack would have upon Japanese strength in the area. The base could not expect to be relieved because there was no prospect of sufficiently strong balanced forces being built up either in the Indian Ocean or on Australia in order to raise any siege. Moreover, because of its unpreparedness, Singapore could not serve as a base for future offensive operations.

Events were to show that the forces the British deployed in Malaya were incapable of holding the Japanese away from the naval base, and it is generally agreed that the major factor in this failing was the lack of numbers available to the defense. At the outbreak of war Malaya Command deployed in Malaya and Singapore the 3rd Indian Corps, consisting of two Indian divisions, the 9th and 11th; the 8th Australian Division; the 12th Indian Brigade; a reinforced battalion group on Penang; and the Singapore Fortress garrison. The latter consisted of two understrength Malay infantry brigades and assorted artillery units—coastal, heavy, and air defense—that between them accounted for about a division's worth of troops. In all, at the start of the war the British deployed about 90,000 troops in Malaya and Singapore. Of this total around 20,000 were British and about 15,000 were Australian; Indian army troops numbered approximately 37,000, and the balance, some 17,000 troops, consisted of locally recruited Asians from various parts of the Orient. This was not a very large force, and it was approximately 40 percent understrength. Much of the criticism of British strategy is correctly directed on this point, that Malaya was not held in the strength that London itself considered necessary. But a very good case can be made that, even allowing for the twin facts that the garrison was understrength and of low quality, the British situation in Malaya might have been redeemed had the force available been deployed in an intelligent and imaginative manner.

Three points must be made about the state of Malaya Command on 8 December 1941 in order to understand the events of the following ten weeks and to set in context the argument in favor of Malaya being held by a fresh strategic and tactical approach. First, Malaya Command was part of a command that was concerned not simply with Malaya but also with British Borneo (which was natural), with Hong Kong (which was not), and with Burma (which was incredible). It is hard to resist the conclusion that a Far East command structure that separated Burma from India, when the only conceivable threat to India was certain to come through Burma, merited defeat. Burma passed to India Command on 12 December, that is, after the start of hostilities and after the first Japanese moves into southern Burma. Incredible though it might sound, on receiving Burma, India Command was given instructions to move against Japanese forces in Thailand, if that was possible. It is hard to see how the British could have made matters worse for themselves even if they had deliberately set out to do so. Right up to the outbreak of war, therefore, Malaya Command was part of an organization that had far-flung and scattered interests and responsibilities that served to prevent proper concentrated attention on the main part of the theater—Malaya. Moreover, Malaya Command itself was grossly inadequate to discharge its tasks because the headquarters had been devised for a peacetime garrison in what was a backwater, and it had received, to put it bluntly, second-class officers who were neither trained nor in sufficient numbers to administer and control an operational command. Malaya Command was totally unfit to make the transition from a drowsy, soporific garrison to an active theater, which it had to do to meet the changing international situation. When these weaknesses are combined with the immense problems of having to coordinate military affairs first with London, which was singularly slow in responding to signals, and second with the local administration, which was complex because of the differing status and arrangements of the local Malay states, then it must be admitted that Malaya Command did have problems that might have been insoluble.

Second, the quality of troops inside Malaya was low, and the garrison was considerably understrength. By its own admission Malaya Command was at least seventeen units light. On its own calculations the command needed a garrison of forty-eight infantry battalions and two armored regiments, plus supporting arms and the necessary corps, divisional, and service troops. At the start of the campaign it mustered thirty-one battalions. To attempt to elaborate the qualitative weaknesses, however, is pointless because the deficiencies and shortages were virtually endless; only a very few of the more obvious ones can be pinpointed.

Among the most serious of the weaknesses was the quality of Indian units, the largest single part of the garrison. The seeds of the problem with Indian units lay in the fact that they were so numerous and that their

quality did not match their quantity. The prewar Indian army was an
all-regular elite force, drawn from what were regarded as the martial races
of the subcontinent. In many wars, particularly the Great War, Indian
units showed on many occasions that when properly commanded and
supported they were the equal of any unit in the British imperial forces,
with the possible exception of the Australians, who were in a class of their
own, in more ways than one. But the key to the effectiveness of Indian units
lay in the particularly close relationship that was developed during long
periods of peace between white and Indian officers, warrant officers, and
noncommissioned officers and the Indian rank and file. War was to show
that the effectiveness of Indian units fell drastically with the loss of known
and trusted white officers who were fluent in native dialects and ways. The
Indian units of the early years of the Second World War were often in this
situation, even before the start of action.

The massive contribution that India made to the Allied cause in the
Second World War is seldom recognized and still not fully and properly
appreciated, but the difficulties of the later years and the fact that at the
time of Kohima-Imphal the British had to deploy fifty-two battalions on
internal security duties are well known. The Indian contribution took
many forms, those of most immediate importance being the quadrupling in
the size of the Indian army between 1939 and 1941 and the employment of
very fine divisions in East Africa, North Africa, and the Middle East. Yet
the price paid by the use of good units in these operational theaters was the
obvious one. Milking established units by removing white officers to active
service with other units, important staff appointments, and critical training
establishments meant a general lowering of standards among newly raised
units. Even formations with so formidable a fighting record as the Gurkhas
were not immune to this problem. It was not unusual for a new unit to have
just two officers, a white commanding offficer and a senior Indian major, as
the link with a parent unit, while the junior appointments would be held by
officers conscripted for the duration and unfamiliar with Indian troops,
habits, and tongues.

Moreover, the level of training and equipment to which the new units
were subjected was inadequate in many cases. In 1941 not a single tank or
armored car existed in the whole of India; there was no tank and antitank
training worthy of the name in the whole of India Command. The situation
of the 3rd Indian Cavalry is a good example of the sort of problems such
deficiencies created. When the unit arrived in Singapore it had no troops
capable of operating armor, which was not really serious because there was
no armor for them to operate in Malaya in any case. The unit was in fact no
more than a motorized infantry battalion, but it lacked sufficient drivers for
its transport. When in the end it received sixteen armored cars, thoughtfully sent from South Africa without spares or even their machine gun

mountings, the regiment managed to write off all but three between the dockyards and the front line. The infantry were of equally poor quality. None of the divisions in Malaya in December 1941 had their third brigade, and very few of the units within a brigade had been trained up to formation attacks. None had been properly trained to work with their artillery, and some of the gunner units in Malaya had to wait until November for the guns with which they were to fight the campaign. The Indian formations had many soldiers who were at best only partially trained, and some were virtually untrained, while the British units were somewhat jaded. The Australians had a fearsome reputation and a general who was widely regarded as obnoxious commanding them, but not much more.

The third notable factor about the Malaya Command on 8 December 1941 was that the whole of the British strategic deployment within Malaya and Singapore must be questioned. At the time of the outbreak of war British forces in Malaya were scattered about the peninsula. In general terms the north, east, and center were entrusted to the 3rd Indian Corps, the 8th Australian Division held the south, the Singapore Fortress garrison was on Singapore Island, and the 12th Indian Brigade formed the command reserve, being deployed at Port Dickson.

The full deployment of the British forces in Malaya on 7 December 1941 was as follows. The 3rd Indian Corps, with its headquarters at Kuala Lumpur, deployed the 9th and 11th Indian Divisions. The 9th Indian Division deployed the overstrength 8th Indian Brigade in the general area of Kota Bharu, with some forces holding certain other east-coast ports and inland settlements, and the understrength 22nd Indian Brigade was at Kuantan. The 11th Indian Division deployed both of its brigades, the 6th and 15th, forward for the Operation Matador thrust. The corps reserve, the 28th Indian Brigade, was held at Ipoh, though part of it, as we have seen, was deployed well forward and was involved in the Jitra disaster. Krohcol came under the command of the 11th Indian Division, a highly unsatisfactory arrangement that was subsequently changed. Krohcol was composed of one battalion drawn from the 15th Indian Brigade with one battalion, drawn from the battalion group on Penang, in reserve. The 8th Australian Division was deployed in Johore, with its 22nd Brigade on the coast between Endau and Mersing, and the 27th Brigade covered the vital position of Kluang. The command reserve, as noted, was based on Port Dickson, while substantial formations remained on Singapore Island.

Before any detailed criticism may be made of the strategic deployment of these forces, a series of comments is in order concerning them. First, the antiaircraft capability of the field forces was practically nonexistent. Second, none of the forces were prepared in any way to deal with enemy armor. In the inevitable absence of plentiful antitank guns to send to Malaya, London had sent training manuals. Yet for months these lan-

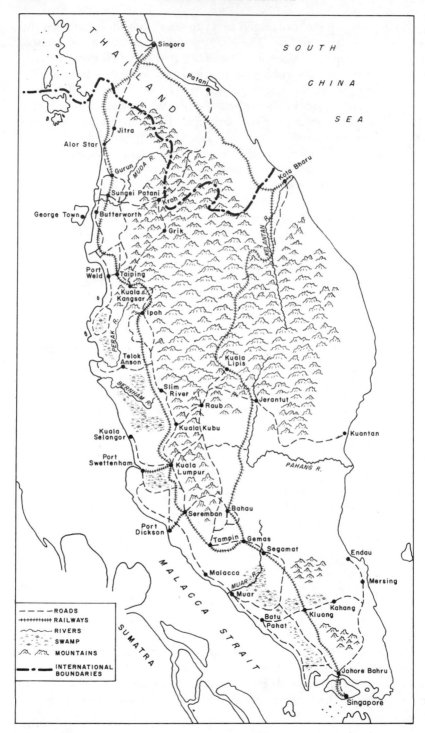

The Malay Peninsula

guished in an office, their existence unknown to or forgotten by a neglectful staff. They were discovered there at the end of November by a resourceful brigadier named Ivan Simson. Simson had the unfortunate habit of taking his responsibilities seriously and making pertinent remarks and suggestions about the defensive arrangements in Malaya, thereby making himself persona non grata with Malaya Command. Within the space of a week Simson heroically produced a synopsis, suitable for Indian troops, on various methods of tackling enemy armor. When on 6 December he sought to distribute his tract to units, permission was refused by Malaya Command for reasons that have never been properly established. Third, there was a dearth of prepared positions anywhere in Malaya. This was particularly serious around Jitra and Kota Bharu, where the first shock of an invasion would be met. But, in a failure of foresight, defensive positions were not prepared anywhere down the length of the peninsula, even though the indefatigable Simson, an engineer officer with specialist knowledge of defensive works, had consistently urged Malaya Command to authorize such construction. Malaya Command had refused to countenance such construction on the ground that it would be bad for morale: defensive preparations would be an admission that part of Malaya could not be defended. Malaya Command was not convinced that the Japanese would attack through the northeast monsoon, and was in any case not allowed to pay local labor more than 40 percent of the minimum rates the Malayan authorities considered were needed to attract workers from the rubber and tin industries. Fourth, none of the troops were trained in operations off the roads and few had any awareness of the importance of offensive action in order to spoil and smother Japanese preparations; there was a dangerous defensive mentality on the part of most units in Malaya. Fifth, and perhaps the most serious weakness, none of the forces in Malaya had any real idea of the character of the enemy. In the relaxed and easygoing Malayan atmosphere, of which Wavell was very critical when he visited Malaya in November, there was an all-pervading assumption, shared by Wavell himself, that Malaya for the moment was safe from attack by an enemy whose military reputation had been grossly exaggerated as a result of successes against poor-quality opposition in China. It was widely believed that the Japanese could be held by a first-class opponent, which the British, manifestly, were not, even though they assumed themselves to be.

When one begins to discuss the British deployment in Malaya in December 1941 one is immediately confronted by the galling fact that the defenders, who were numerically superior to the Japanese, correctly anticipated most aspects of Japanese strategic intentions, yet still managed to be decisively, humiliatingly beaten. While the major failing in the defense after the start of hostilities was tactical, it cannot be denied that the very disposition of British forces on 8 December 1941 all but ensured their ultimate defeat, not so much because the forces were inadequate but because they were deployed in so unimaginative and irrelevant a manner. The major strategic criticism of the British in Malaya should not be that the defenders were understrength and undertrained—though these points are not in dispute—but that Malaya Command failed to use what resources were available in the most intelligent manner possible.

The dominating factor in any deployment of forces in Malaya was certain to be geography. Malaya did not offer the Japanese the same military variation as the Philippines; in area about 49,000 square miles (the size of England), Malaya is only slightly larger than Luzon, but land and sea, climate and vegetation have conspired together to limit drastically the scope of operations on the peninsula.

The obvious feature of the peninsula is the high mountain ridge running down its length. The ridge reaches over 7,000 feet in several places—Gunong Tahan at 7,217 feet is Malaya's highest point—though it falls away to about 3,000 feet in the southern part of the country. The presence of the ridge has immediate effects on the vegetation, settlement, communications, and, therefore, the military characteristics of the area. It acts as a shield, between itself and the Strait of Malacca, for the western part of the peninsula, affording protection from the northeast monsoon just as effectively as the mountains of Sumatra shelter western Malaya from the full effects of the mid-yearly southwest monsoon. The western part of the peninsula therefore lies in two rain shadows. It has plentiful rainfall, at least 50 inches a year, but its precipitation is small compared to many parts of eastern Malaya, where the rainfall is upwards of 250 inches annually. To drain eastern Malaya of this vast amount of rainfall countless rivers make their way to the South China Sea, but even these become hopelessly clogged with the sheer weight of water coming off the mountains. The multitude of rivers and the waterlogged nature of the ground in the east make communication inland from the coast and among the various coastal settlements by land extremely difficult. Such settlements as Kuala Trennganu, Kuala Dungun, and Endau on the South China Sea are virtually cut off over land. The military significance of the ground of eastern Malaya is obvious.

While the heavy rainfall and extreme heat experienced by the whole of the peninsula give rise to luxuriant tropical jungle throughout the country, on the west coast the slightly easier climate has made the clearing of primeval jungle possible. Settlement, therefore, has been concentrated in the western part of the country with the major part of the road and rail systems, running between Singapore and the north, being concentrated in the west, mostly inland and away fron the swampy mangrove coast. One railway line, however, snakes its way through the interior to link Johore and Kota Bharu; its branching from the main lines makes Gemas in Negri Sembilan a communications center of major strategic importance.

The point of military importance that arises from Malaya's climate, terrain, and vegetation is that while 80 percent of the country is jungle uninhabited by anyone except primitive aborigines, military operations on the peninsula must be confined mainly to the all-important but very narrow strip of cleared and settled ground running over 400 miles the length of the country on its western side. This fact, plus the paucity of east-west communications, forced both the British and the Japanese to the conclusion that the only place for major landings had to be in Thailand, at Singora and Patani, with the aim of driving through to the west coast and then developing an attack down the length of the peninsula. There was no question of the Japanese being able to secure strategic surprise with an attack; they had none of the choice with regard to operations in Malaya as was the case with their operations in the Philippines. But they did retain certain advantages. They held the options with regard to timing, and here the British badly deluded themselves into the belief that the Japanese would not attack during the northeast monsoon, effectively from November to February, despite the evidence of Japanese amphibious assaults in China during the monsoon season. The Japanese had the advantage that, unlike the British, they had no scruples about violating Thailand. The Japanese, if and when they attacked, would hold the advantages of concentration and local superiority at the points of their attacks, since the British would be dispersed to an unnecessary extent throughout Malaya. Moreover, the Japanese possessed the incalculable advantage of a realistic battle doctrine based upon infantry movement through the jungle. For the Japanese the infantry was a mobile arm, but this was not the only thing to come as a shock to the British. The Japanese had learned the lesson of conventional warfare, that a shock force of light armor was needed with the reconnaissance and main battle forces. The whole essence of Japanese tactics was to use roads and tracks to advance to contact, but to move through the surrounding jungle to infiltrate, outflank, and encircle an enemy that was road-bound and reluctant to abandon conventional ideas. Whereas on Luzon the Americans were outfought mainly in strategic terms, in Malaya the British were outclassed tactically—and their initial strategic deployment could do nothing to redeem this situation.

The major weakness in the strategic deployment of land forces on the Malayan peninsula was that it was geared to achieve certain divergent objectives, most of which were irrelevant or of very dubious value. British forces were deployed to cover the airfields of eastern and northern Malaya and either to carry out Operation Matador or to hold a defensive position north of Alor Star. Certain very obvious points need to be made about these aims. First, the airfields of the north and east were only as valuable as the aircraft that used them. If there were no aircraft capable of either preventing an invasion or inflicting severe losses on a Japanese amphibious force coming out of the South China Sea, then there was no point whatsoever in deploying precious infantry in defense of these airfields. Second, with airfields available to the defense on Penang and near Butterworth, the airfields around Alor Star, a mere 40 miles away, were not absolutely essential to the British, particularly if in taking Victoria Point in southern Burma the Japanese severed the air link between India and Malaya. There was no imperative need for the British to try to make a stand north of Alor Star. Third, if, as was the case, the British lacked both the time and the forces needed to secure Singora and Patani in advance of a Japanese landing, there was very little point in trying to hold the northern part of the country unless either the Ledge or the Kroh-Betong area was held in strength. If the route through the mountains from Patani was not held by at least a brigade, in well-prepared defensive positions that could not be turned and that were covered by mines and antitank guns, then the whole policy of trying to retain the north, by standing at Jitra, was doomed.

A hard, dispassionate examination of the strategic realities of the situation in Malaya would seem to confirm certain basic conclusions, some of which were drawn at the time by India Command, and urged on but rejected by Malaya Command before the start of hostilities. First, the major part of the troops in Malaya were poorly trained and could not be expected to undertake major offensive operations. The aims of Operation Matador, simply from the point of view of the aptitude of the troops earmarked for the thrust, were totally unrealistic. The two brigades of the 11th Indian Division (three were considered necessary to hold Singora in the rainy season) were inadequate for a lunge into Thailand, while even their in-adequate training for offensive operations led to their neglecting both defensive training and their preparation of defensive positions. The state of confusion that surrounded the 11th Indian Division, torn between its offensive and defensive roles, ensured that it was never really able to prepare for either in a satisfactory manner. In retrospect it can be argued that, given the weakness of the 11th and the forces allocated for taking the Ledge position, plus the unlikelihood of having the early warning time that alone could ensure the success of Operation Matador, the British should have cut their losses with regard to operations into Thailand and staked everything on preparing the forces in the extreme north for defensive operations.

Second, the keynote of British preparations in eastern and northern Malaya never should have been defensive but rather the destruction and denial of facilities to the Japanese. With no navy and no air force to tackle the Japanese while at sea, the two brigades available in eastern Malaya could not hope to deny the Japanese either initial landing sites or ultimate control of their airfields. All that the infantry could hope to do was to defend the airfields just as long as there was no threat to them. There was nothing in the east of Malaya that could justify the deployment in the area of a whole infantry division, about one-quarter of the field forces available to the defense.

Third, while the British were still dealing with matters in the north, they absolutely had to hold Penang. If the Japanese took the island and its critically important port of George Town, the way was clear for them to attempt to turn the flank of any defensive position the British tried to establish. This they could attempt by small-scale landings along the coast of the Malacca Strait. Fourth, as long as Endau and Mersing were garrisoned and held in strength and blocking positions were established in the mountains on the route from Kuantan, there was no need to hold the general area of southern Malaya in strength, and there was no point in keeping substantial forces on Singapore Island. The much-reviled heavy coastal guns in fact were effective in that they did secure the seaward approaches to Singapore, and their presence should have been enough to free other forces in the south for other tasks elsewhere.

Fifth, to turn to a point made earlier and for once to exclude Malaya Command from criticism, if Malaya was so important that it had to be held—a debatable assumption because of the lack of a fleet and the inadequacies of the naval base—and if it was so undergarrisoned, then nothing was to be achieved by deploying six battalions, the backbone of two infantry brigades, on Hong Kong, the loss of which was accepted. If the token defense of Hong Kong was all that was required and could be expected, then the colony did not need 10,000 men. At the very most all that would be required was a company, bugler, a flag corporal, and a suave governor with a knighthood, double-barrelled name, stiff upper lip—and a tie from one of the lesser public schools. These six battalions could have been of utmost value in Malaya, and there is a good argument to suggest that even the single battalion earmarked for Borneo could have been used to better effect in Malaya. It is worth noting that the decision to reinforce Hong Kong was not made by Far East Command but in London, without consulting the commander in chief. When London took the decision to reinforce Hong Kong with two Canadian battalions it did so on the grounds that Malaya had been reinforced and was far better garrisoned than it had been. Be that as it may, with the Malaya garrison 40 percent under its authorized strength, this decision was amazing. The whole of London's strategic planning for the Far East exudes an air of total unreality and invites utter disbelief.

From these reasoned premises, and accepting the premise that Malaya and Singapore could not be abandoned, it can be argued that the best course available to the British was to have pursued the policy of abandoning eastern Malaya, leaving only demolition teams and small covering forces to wreck the airfields at Kota Bharu, Gong Kedah, and Machang. In the course of their withdrawal, such forces would have to destroy the railway track, roads, bridges, and all repair facilities, in order to impede any Japanese advance; then they would have to hold firm blocking positions on the routes that led from the east coast across the mountains. To have held such positions even on the western part of the peninsula would have been very acceptable in military terms because the Japanese would have secured very little of real military value in their unopposed occupation of eastern Malaya. The airfields of the area were of real significance and value only in that they covered the Gulf of Siam and the South China Sea; they were of relatively little value with regard to operations on the Malayan peninsula itself. Moreover, to hold blocking positions west of the mountains would have shortened British lines of communication and held British forces in a more central and concentrated position. It is even conceivable that some of the forces scattered throughout eastern Malaya would have been made available for operations elsewhere, though this is by no means certain.

If the east had been abandoned, and as long as the routes across the mountains could be denied to any Japanese forces that were pushed along them, the British reasonably could have hoped to establish and hold a main defensive line somewhere on the western part of the peninsula, without having to look continually over their shoulder to see whether or not the Japanese had turned their right flank. If they had done this, the British would still have retained a series of options, admittedly some of them rather difficult, but at least they might have been able to face the Japanese with more hope of success than was in fact the case. The basic problem would have been whether to make the main line of resistance somewhere in the north, in Kedah or Perak. Alternatively, they could have abandoned the whole of these areas and concentrated everything in an attempt to hold the Japanese either in the center of Malaya—north of Kuala Lumpur—or, ceding the federal capital, have stood in the Negri Sembilan, Malacca, northern Johore region, in the strategically vital area formed by the Seremban, Bahau, Gemas, Segamat, and Tampin complex. If the eastern coast of Johore was denied the Japanese and the routes over the mountains remained closed to the attacker, the defenders could hope to fight their main defensive battle in any of these three general areas with every hope of success, or at least of imposing severe losses on the Japanese in terms of time and manpower. Moreover, in any of these three cases, it would have been possible for the major part of the 8th Australian Division to have been properly deployed as the reserve for the 3rd Indian Corps. If the choice was to hold in the north or center, then the Australians, plus any other forces that could be stripped out of Singapore, could have been moved northwards. If the choice was to make the major defensive effort in the south, then the Indians could have been pulled back onto the Australian positions. Regardless of which option was chosen, a handily placed reserve, about one division strong, could have been deployed in a position where it could be used to maximum effect.

It is difficult to see which of these three courses would have served the British best. If the defense of Malaya per se was the all-important consideration, then the defenders had to think about holding the north, and here three major defensive positions recommended themselves. These were at Jitra, Gurun, and Taiping. Of the three Jitra was the worst, partly because of the length of front involved and partly because of the constant danger of the position being turned by a Japanese attack erupting out of Patani. The position at Gurun ran the same risk of being outflanked if the Japanese broke through at Kroh, but the frontage of Gurun, unlike that at Jitra, was narrow. The roads and railway converged in a bottleneck formed by the mountains between the Muda River and the sea. Holding the Taiping position, along the Port Weld, Taiping, Kuala Kangsar axis, would have placed the defenders in a strong position to face a frontal thrust down the west coast, and would have been adequate to block any attack developing along the Betong, Kroh, Grik axis.

But there were three major objections to the Taiping position. First, the positions at Jitra and Gurun covered the airfields in the north and these would have to be ceded if the British decided to hold at Taiping. If the British were to make a major effort in the air, then the best place to fight was in the north, where sufficient airfields could serve the Royal Air Force. In the central region, behind the Taiping position, there were relatively few suitable airfields, and there could be no denying the fact that the loss of all the northern airfields to the Japanese as part of an opening strategic deployment was bound to entail certain, perhaps major, strategic risks. Second, if the Japanese were held at Jitra or Gurun, then Penang would be covered, without the British necessarily having to deploy substantial forces on the island. Third, to hold in the extreme north would deny the Japanese total control of the rice-rich state of Kedah. Because the civil administration refused to authorize a dispersal program with regard to rice, nearly all the country's home-produced rice was in Kedah and Perlis. Moreover, if the British did stand on the Taiping position and accepted the loss of Penang and the north, the whole of the position along the Port Weld–Kuala Kangsar axis would be left vulnerable to an outflanking attack not from the east by land but from the west by sea. All the choices are difficult, but overall it is hard to resist the notion that if the British had chosen to stand in the north then their interests would have been served best by abandoning Perlis and northern Kedah and standing on the Gurun and Kroh positions in strength.

But if the defense of Malaya as a whole was not the prime strategic consideration, it is hard to resist the conclusion that to have abandoned the whole of the north and center would have been Britain's best course of action—if the aim was to buy time and try to hold part of the peninsula as either a "fortress" or a base for future offensive operations. If these more limited objectives were the ones that the British chose to pursue, then the greater part of Malaya could be surrendered without real loss. Kuala Lumpur had no intrinsic value; as the Americans on Luzon showed, capital cities do not have to be held as part of a strategically defensive policy. To have established the main line of resistance in Johore would have presented the Japanese with the formidable problem of having to mount a series of deliberate attacks against an enemy concentrated in a succession of strong defensive positions with very narrow fronts that could not be turned. To have held in the south would have drastically reduced the length of British lines of communication and, by definition, left reserves close to the front, ready to mount spoiling attacks to disrupt Japanese main-force preparations or to counterattack Japanese infiltration efforts. But against these considerations was the fact that northern Johore lacked depth as a defensive position and was really the last line of resistance available on the peninsula. It is not logical to make the last possible line of resistance the site of the main defensive effort. In addition, to have abandoned the whole of northern and central Malaya would have bared Sumatra, thus running the risk of a Japanese move against the western Indies and leaving Johore and Singapore strategically outflanked and isolated.

No matter which way the British turned there were problems, yet it is impossible to resist the notion that the British deployment in Malaya at the start of the war combined every conceivable weakness and played to no natural advantages. It is hard to believe that defeat was inevitable or, if it was, that the British could not have done better than was the case. The simple fact of the situation was that the British deployment at the outbreak of war left the defenders extremely vulnerable in the north, and after the initial defeat at Jitra, the mauled 11th Indian Division was literally harried from one unprepared position to another by an attacker that in the end deployed formations from three divisions in the line. Admittedly, one of the most difficult operations in war is to maintain forces intact during a retreat in the face of a superior and aggressive enemy. The Italians in North Africa in the course of the Five Day Raid, the Germans and Soviets at different times during the Nazi-Soviet conflict, and, later in the war, the Japanese in both Burma and the Philippines have provided examples of armies disintegrating under the pressure of a prolonged forced retreat. The 11th Indian Division was in good company. But, for all that, it is obvious that a ruthless stripping of forces from the unthreatened south and the marginally important north and east would have given the defenders much greater strength with which to meet the attackers, while a series of prepared positions through which the defense could have dragged the Japanese infantry in a series of meat-grinder operations could hardly have achieved a worse result than the one actually registered. The fact was that, as a result of operations in northern Malaya, Singapore was lost during the first four days of war; this should never have been the case.

After the Jitra disaster, unless there was a totally unforeseen and inexplicable collapse of the Japanese offensive for some unsuspected internal reason, only two things could redeem British fortunes on the peninsula. These were the combination of a speedy deployment of substantial reinforcements to Malaya and a period of inspired and brilliant generalship by Malaya Command in order to secure enough time for such reinforcements to arrive, become acclimated, and enter the line as effective fighting units.

With the start of the Pacific war the British Chiefs of Staff decided to reinforce their commands in the Far East. Initially London decided to limit reinforcements for Malaya to artillery units and aircraft, but the Jitra debacle forced the British to reconsider their initial decision to send the 18th British Division and the 17th Indian Division to Burma. On 17 December these two divisions were earmarked for Malaya as part of an overall arrangement that saw two infantry divisions, an armored regiment, and twelve fighter squadrons detailed for Burma and two infantry divisions allocated to the defense of the Dutch East Indies. To Malaya London decided to deploy not only these two formations but an armored brigade and eighteen air squadrons. In terms of numbers of ground troops London was as good as its word. Between 3 and 31 January 1942 the major part of the land forces promised by London arrived at Singapore. The first to arrive, the 15th Indian Brigade, part of the India-based 17th Indian Division, was followed on 13 January by the 53rd British Brigade, part of the 18th British Division, one antitank and two air defense units, and fifty-three crated Hurricanes. On 22 January the 44th Indian Brigade, sister formation of the 45th, arrived along with 7,000 replacements for the 11th Indian Division; and two days later an Australian machine gun battalion, plus 1,900 reinforcements, arrived to supplement the 8th Australian Division. On 29 January the headquarters element of the 18th British Division, plus its two remaining brigades, the 54th and 55th, disembarked at Singapore. Various small elements continued to arrive until 5 February. In addition to these forces the carrier *Indomitable* (whose absence from Force Z is regarded wrongly by many to have been the critical factor in the loss of the *Repulse* and *Prince of Wales*) on 26 January flew off forty-eight Hurricanes to Sumatra, their ultimate destination being Singapore. In fact these aircraft never completed their journey.

A whole host of comments, all of them bitter and jaundiced, can be made about the decisions that sent two divisions to Singapore in January of 1942 to no avail, but just three points need to be considered to reveal the bankruptcy of British strategic thought and policy at this time. First, one cannot but be struck by the fact that the forces promised by London and sent to Singapore were roughly equal to the extent by which the garrison in Malaya was understrength. It was strange how forces that were never available to the area before war were suddenly provided once hostilities began. Had these forces, promised by London in the opening days of the war, been deployed in Malaya before the start of the campaign, then both the land and air forces in Malaya would have been more or less at their established strengths. Malaya Command would have had sufficient forces, both of infantry and, critically, armor, to form a strong reserve for the counteroffensive, which was conspicuous by its absence throughout the actual campaign. Second, though on paper the forces sent to Singapore constituted a formidable addition to the strength of Malaya Command, it is difficult in the end to quarrel with the abrasive and acerbic conclusion of official British historian, Major General S. Woodburn Kirby, to the effect that reinforcements consisted of " . . . a physically unfit British division, two almost untrained Indian brigades, a number of partially trained Indian and Australian reinforcements and aircraft which could only be a wasting asset."*

The forces deployed to Malaya as reinforcements were worse than useless. They created feeding, billeting, and disciplinary problems without adding to the effectiveness of the defense because they were totally unfit to be deployed operationally on account of their woefully inadequate training and lack of acclimatization. The 18th British Division, for example, had been at sea for eleven weeks by the time it finally reached Singapore, and it had been trained for mechanized warfare, its original destination having been North Africa. Third, the whole strategic logic surrounding the arrival of these reinforcements is open to question. The forces arrived far too late to be effective, in large part because the forces already in Malaya patently failed to buy enough time for them to become properly operational. The major part of the unfortunate 18th British Division arrived just two days before the last units in Johore were withdrawn across the causeway into Singapore itself, at a time when Singapore was clearly known to be doomed. To have sent the formation to Singapore was tantamount to marching its soldiers straight off their ships into Japanese prisoner-of-war camps, thereby uselessly squandering irreplaceable manpower that would have been invaluable for operations elsewhere, possibly in Burma or northern Australia.

The strategic absurdity of this situation lay in the fact that Churchill and the Chiefs of Staff in London knew that Singapore was lost yet continued to pour men and materiel into the garrison. The only mitigation they could claim was a failure to realize just how quickly Singapore Island would succumb, and, from a distance, this was not easy to assess. Yet even

*Kirby, *Singapore: The Chain of Disaster*, p. 184.

allowing for this, the fact remains that the issue of the loss of Singapore was no more squarely faced in January 1942 than the whole question of the defense of Singapore had been properly tackled in the interwar period, particularly in 1940–41. Then Singapore had had to be defended for

A British soldier is made prisoner during the Malayan campaign. Such scenes took place more than 130,000 times between 7 December 1941 and 15 February 1942. Imperial War Museum

political reasons because the British failed to realize that, humiliating though the writing-off of Singapore would be without a major effort to hold it, even more humiliating would be the certainty of losing the base after a massive but unavailing effort to hold it, losing it, literally, at the point of a bayonet. Now, in January 1942, the same political fantasies gripped British decision-making and compounded the failure. Britain reinforced Singapore during the last week of January through fear of the accusation, made by the Australian government on 24 January, that failure to do so would constitute "an inexcusable betrayal" of interwar promises. London, moreover, was aware of the deplorable impression created by the ineffectiveness of the defense in Malaya, when set against events on Luzon. But the clinching argument was the political one that recognized that not to have reinforced Singapore at a time when communications with the port remained open would be an admission of defeat, certain to have incalculable political effects throughout the Far East and, indeed, the world. By 21 January, when an agonized London discussed whether or not to reinforce Singapore further even though it was evident that Johore would be lost, the question that faced Churchill and his military advisers was whether any more reinforcements could prolong the defense of Singapore Island for any commensurate gain, or whether they should be used to try to hold the Burma Road, then considered to be more important than the retention of Singapore itself.

The British decision to continue to reinforce Singapore, even though by late January its fall was seen to be inevitable, resulted from a total failure to recognize that with total humiliation already assured and unavoidable, to send more soldiers to Singapore would only add to the magnitude of the debacle. Throwing more troops into the caldron could do nothing to mitigate a disaster that was certain to be absolute. The failure on Churchill's part was one of moral courage in that he did not resist pressures that palpably had to be withstood. The Australian government's accusation was hysterical. A moment's sober reflection by the government of John Curtin would have brought home to it the obvious point that the security of Australia was not going to be enhanced one iota by continuing to dispatch irreplaceable forces to Singapore in the second half of January 1942. Moreover, nothing was to be gained by Churchill exhorting Malaya Command to fight to the last man, even in the ruins of Singapore, and to ensure, by the employment of scorched earth tactics, the denial of all facilities to the Japanese. This typically Churchillian bombast illustrates the limitations, some would say shallowness, of the prime minister's political and strategic thinking. An army cannot devastate the ground on which it is ordered to stand and fight to the last man; it simply cannot destroy the means by which it lives if it is ordered to continue operations for as long as possible. The orders were strategically contradictory, while politically they were inane.

It was inconceivable that a parliamentary democracy, even though an imperialist power, could consider fighting a battle of annihilation inside a city inhabited by a million subjects whom it was pledged to protect. The notion is grotesque, and totally immoral. Churchill was caught in a vice of unreality over Singapore just as firmly as his predecessors had been, but the difficulty of his immediate situation was largely of his own making. The Singapore episode for Churchill was a repeat of the errors that had been made over Greece. British forces, then on the point of achieving a major strategic victory in North Africa, were weakened to the extent that possible victory was snatched away from them in Libya by the dispatch of a totally inadequate force to Greece, where it could not possibly hope to achieve any lasting strategic success but would run the risk of utter annihilation. As a result, Britain was defeated in both Greece and Libya. There were obvious points of difference in the Singapore situation. Nowhere was there any prospect of victory that was ruined by the misuse of reserve forces. But in both the Mediterranean in the spring of 1941 and Singapore in December 1941 and January 1942 there was the same squandering of force in the pursuit of political aims that were totally unrealistic.

The reinforcements sent to Malaya certainly fell into the category of "too little, too late," because the inevitable consequence of the military situation in Malaya and the manner of their arrival in the theater certainly lessened any useful effect these forces might have had, even if they had been fit for service more or less on arrival. Anything other than the most shallow analysis of the situation in Malaya at the time when reinforcements were dispatched would have revealed that, if the three divisions—eight brigades—in the front line on 8 December could not hold the initial Japanese assault, then the arrival of five more formations could scarcely affect the outcome. The forces in the field in Malaya were not the equal of initial Japanese assaults made before the full strength of the invasion force was deployed in the line. The inescapable military logic of this situation was that, after the Jitra battle, any attempt to hold the Japanese, even when successful for a time, was certain to make inroads on British resources at a rate which reinforcements sent to Malaya, because they had to arrive and then deploy in a piecemeal manner, could not hope to cover. Given the mauling of the 11th Indian Division, any forces sent to Malaya would not be reinforcements per se, capable of adding to strength, but would be merely replacements for losses. The Japanese, on the other hand, unless they encountered some totally unforeseeable disaster, had merely to continue to exert pressure in order to achieve victory because, in the final analysis, reinforcements could be made available to sustain any attack if the need arose. By definition, the whole of British policy towards Malaya and Singapore in December 1941 and January 1942 was a lamentable strategic nonsense.

The reader will recall that the basis of prewar British planning for the defense of Malaya rested upon the army's defense of airfields and the implementation of Operation Matador to secure Singora and Patani in advance of any Japanese invasion. British army units were deployed accordingly. The main provisions north of Jitra were units from the two brigades of the 11th Indian Division and the corps reserve, and the 28th Indian Brigade, which was moved northwards on 8 December. There were also a weak brigade group at Kroh, a reinforced brigade at Kota Bharu, and an understrength formation at Kuantan. Command reserve, the 12th Indian Brigade, was at Port Dickson.

With the failure to carry out Operation Matador, British defense plans lay in ruins since nothing could prevent the Japanese from carrying the war into Malaya after they had secured Singora and Patani. If there was a chance of recovering anything from the strategic defeat created by the failure to implement Operation Matador, it had to be by a successful stand at Jitra and Kroh, while a rapid deployment of forces took place to meet the Japanese advance in the west. On 12 December the 12th Indian Brigade was placed under the command of the 3rd Indian Corps and moved northwards, though on the first day of the war, when the formation was initially moved to Ipoh, one of its units, the 4th/19th Hyderabad, was ordered to move forward to reinforce the 8th Indian Brigade at Kota Bharu. These moves in the first days of the war were totally inadequate to meet the Japanese challenge. Because Malaya Command quickly came to the conclusion that it faced an invasion force of four divisions*—one division each at Singora, Patani, and Kota Bharu, with another moving overland through Thailand—the initial British deployment and movement of reserves were essentially irrelevant to the dangers presented by the Japanese moves. If the 8th Indian Brigade really were faced by a Japanese division, then the deployment of a single additional battalion was utterly valueless. By definition, all the time delays involved in movement from the reserve into the line meant that the Hyderabad battalion could not reach the area of operations in time to be effective in any strategic sense, while the weakening of the 12th Indian Brigade might prove very unfortunate. Similarly, to leave a weakened 22nd Indian Brigade at Kuantan, where it was exposed to either assault from the sea or an advance overland from Kota Bharu, was asking for trouble. On the other hand, if the Japanese really did have two divisions at Singora and Patani with another division coming up, then it should have been evident to the British that the full strength of the 3rd Indian Corps had to be concentrated in the west to meet what was certain to be the most dangerous of the threats to the security of Singapore and Malaya. In a nutshell, if one Japanese division was operating in eastern Malaya then the

*This was a gross overestimation. At the time it faced four regiments.

scattered 8th Indian Brigade could do little to oppose it; if the 11th Indian Division faced three divisions in the west then it had to be supported.

This situation cried out for the immediate withdrawal of the 8th and 22nd Brigades and their concentration west of the mountain ridge after a thorough demolition of all installations and communications in eastern Malaya. This action was urged and requested on 11 December by the commander of the 9th Indian Division, Major General A. E. Barstow, and was endorsed by Lieutenant General Sir Lewis Heath, commander of the 3rd Indian Corps. But Malaya Command refused to sanction Barstow's proposal, reasoning that it was too early to contemplate such long withdrawals, that is, the adverse political and morale effects were deemed to outweigh the strategic gains of reconcentrating the division. But events at Jitra began to force the hand of the British command. Barstow was ordered to bring back his 8th Indian Brigade but to leave the 22nd at Kuantan. It was not until 2 January that the divisional commander was ordered to pull back his Kuantan formation to the Kuala Lipis-Jerantut area, where the 8th Brigade had been ever since its withdrawal from the Machang-Kuala Krai region between 19 and 22 December. By the time the 22nd Indian Brigade received its orders to withdraw, however, it was fully engaged by units from the *56th Infantry Regiment*. The retirement (which could and should have been carried out in an orderly manner because there was time to get clear without a rearguard action) was a shambles, with more than one battalion being destroyed.

Percival's slow reaction to the situation involving the 9th Indian Division was occasioned by his obsession with holding the airfields, in particular that at Kuantan. This was not unreasonable because the general officer commanding felt that the Japanese had to be held as far to the north as possible so that reinforcements could arrive in time to be effective. In particular, he sought to retain at least Kuantan in order to prevent the Japanese from using it as a base from which to attack troop convoys into Singapore, expected to arrive from mid-January onwards. These views were endorsed by the political leadership in Malaya and by an inter-Allied conference of British, Dutch, and Commonwealth representatives, held in Singapore on 18 December. Yet the facts remained that effective denial would have served the British better than the defense in the states of Kelantan and Trengganu, and that the delay in getting the two brigades back from their coastal positions resulted in unnecessary losses for both of them. Moreover, even with the concentration of the depleted division in the Kuala Lipis area, nothing was achieved in bringing help to the hard-pressed 11th Indian Division.

The situation facing the defenders on the western part of the peninsula was critical from the outset and its gravity only increased with the passing days. This situation arose partly because the forces assigned to the area, even after the arrival of most of the 12th Indian Brigade, were too thinly spread to be effective in any one area, partly because the initial positions at Jitra and Kroh were not mutually supporting and either could be turned by the Japanese breaking into the other. Both positions stood in danger of encirclement and annihilation. But these weaknesses were compounded by the twin facts that no defense in depth, involving prepared positions, had been envisaged and undertaken behind Jitra and that no assessment of Japanese strategic and tactical intentions had been made.

The Japanese, indeed, had completed a more thorough and perceptive staff assessment of the territory than the British. Prewar Japanese reconnaissance had established that the track from Kroh to Grik was passable to infantry but not to armor; between Grik and Kuala Kangsar the metalled road obviously posed no problem to movement. The British believed that the track between Klian Intan and Grik was passable to light motor traffic, but only in the dry season. The Japanese intended to make their main effort along the major roads down the west coast while using infantry from the *42nd Infantry Regiment* to push down the track to Grik and hence the Perak River in an attempt to outflank any British defensive position in northern Malaya near the coast. It was not until the Kroh to Grik track had been left exposed by the falling back of Krohcol to cover the Baling road—on the obvious route around the back of the Jitra position—that the British, belatedly, grasped its importance. They had manifestly failed to realize the truth of the old dictum that nature in itself poses no insurmountable obstacle to military movement and they had patently failed to conduct a proper reconnaissance of the route.

The Japanese, however, had not finished with flanking movements with the Perak line. They fully appreciated that with the road and railway closely hugging the mountains south of Kuala Kangsar, outflanking movements from the east were out of the question. But equally they realized that any British attempt to hold the main road from Kuala Kangsar through Ipoh, Kuala Kubu, and Kuala Lumpur to Tampin was hopelessly vulnerable to any outflanking movement from the west, particularly in southern Selangor, Negri Sembilan, and Malacca, where a good communications network offered a series of options for a southwards advance. Accordingly, among the equipment unloaded at Singora were assault boats, which were moved by road and rail across to the west coast of the peninsula, ready for use in operations designed to turn any British flank established on the Malacca Strait. Obviously the key to any Japanese amphibious operations was Penang. Its successful occupation would leave wide open to assault the whole of the coast south of Port Weld, where outflanking of main positions from the landward side would end. Overall, there can be no doubt that the Japanese did their homework in a most impressive manner.

Indeed, the Japanese had been most thorough in their planning of the Malayan campaign. Their planning had to be good because Imperial

Lieutenant General Hobum Yamashita, commander of the *25th Army*. Regarded as perhaps Japan's finest commander, the "Tiger of Malaya" ended the war on Luzon, where he conducted a rearguard action that did not end until Japan's final surrender. Yamashita was executed after the war. Robert Hunt Library

General Headquarters set Yamashita's *25th Army* the formidable task of overrunning Malaya and Singapore in just one hundred days. Given the facts that a direct assault on Singapore was out of the question and that the Japanese would have to land at Singora and Patani, Yamashita's command was given a stiff task, but it was one that never daunted the *25th Army*. Such was the confidence of Yamashita and his staff that not only did Yamashita decline the offer first of five divisions and then of four, using only three divisions, but one of his chief staff officers actually marked down 11 February 1942 as the date for the fall of Singapore.

Much of the reason for Yamashita's confidence stemmed from his knowledge that the British mustered about 90,000 troops in Malaya, less than half of whom were Caucasians. The presence of so many Indian and Asian troops in Malaya prompted Yamashita to observe that the Japanese task would be made very much easier because of the high proportion of non-whites in the defense. The Japanese had absolutely no regard for native troops; the idea of Asian troops offering effective resistance to the Japanese army was laughable to the Japanese. But Yamashita was aware not only of

British weakness but also of the strengths and merits of his own forces, which had been brought to a high state of preparedness through the efforts of his chief of operations and planning, Colonel Masanobu Tsuji.

The colonel enjoyed an extremely unsavory reputation even in an army hardly noted for its exacting standards of personal behavior. He was a henchman of Tojo, and was despised for his role as Tojo's stool pigeon, when the prime minister used him to report on the affairs and behavior of various generals. One of the reasons why Tsuji was on Yamashita's staff was that Yamashita and Tojo loathed one another intensely. Tsuji's unendearing traits combined extreme rudeness with irritability, but there was no disputing his industriousness, and equally there was no denying the fact that he achieved results. In January 1941 a new post was established for him as the second in command of the Taiwan Army Research Section, and head of the branch dealing with Malayan plans, at the jungle training school on Formosa. His task was to sort out all the problems of jungle warfare that the Japanese would have to face in Malaya. It was under the direction of this section that the main features of the strategy and tactics used in Malaya were devised. Under Tsuji's direction Major Terundo Kunitake of the consulate in Singapore undertook a detailed reconnaissance of Malaya that revealed, among other things, that the Kroh-Grik track was passable and that no less than 250 bridges—more than twice the original estimate by the section—carried the road from Singora to Singapore.

The discovery of so many bridges was important to the Japanese because their campaign therefore had to become primarily an engineer's operation. Kunitake's information led to each of the three divisions earmarked for the campaign being given a complete sapper regiment with yet another regiment held under the direct control of army headquarters. These regiments were lavishly equipped by Japanese standards, their needs having been assessed by Tsuji and his section as a result of the study of Kunitake's reports. Similarly, the infantry were given as much lightweight equipment as possible and trained intensively in the jungles and mountains of Formosa in flanking attacks through the jungle. For mobility the Japanese infantry were equipped with bicycles. It was Tsuji who devised the plans to turn any British positions in northern Malaya by use of the Kroh-Grik track and then use the sea to turn any defense in the central region. Much of the Japanese success in Malaya was owed to Tsuji who, despite the official "timetable" that set the crossing of the Perak for 23 December, earmarked 15 December as the approximate date for the Japanese to cross from northern into central Malaya.

Tsuji, therefore, gave just one week for Japanese forces to advance from Singora and Patani to the Perak, and the reasons for such haste are not hard to find. The Japanese sought to keep the British off-balance and secure the fall of Singapore before reinforcements arrived, thereby threatening to

Simple but effective. The key to the mobility and speed of the Japanese infantry in a theater where the British were road-bound was the bicycle. Here Japanese infantry, each laden with perhaps 100 pounds of equipment, advance down a Malayan road. Robert Hunt Library

involve the *25th Army* in a long, drawn-out siege. Moreover, from the very start of the campaign Yamashita was obsessed with the desire to annihilate his enemy; he saw no good reason to fight the same enemy more than once if it was possible to operate with such speed that the enemy could be annihilated in the opening encounters. In the course of the campaign Yamashita's diary became cluttered with bitter denunciations of his forces' failure to "crush" the enemy. Only by rapid movement and a relentless hounding of the British could Yamashita's forces fulfill their leader's wishes—and secure airfields that, when put back into service, would serve to project Japanese air power deep into central Malaya.

After Jitra the British enjoyed no such luxury as simplicity of aim because they had to engage in a fine balancing act among various divergent objectives. Their position was delicate and fraught with peril. If the Japanese could not be held in encounters on the frontier, serious delays had to be imposed upon them in order to carry out essential demolitions, prepare defensive positions in the rear, and carry out evacuations. But while vigorous delaying actions were fought to buy the time needed to carry out these tasks, it was vitally important not to become too deeply involved. British forces could not afford to become committed to major actions and risk not being able to break contact. After Jitra it was imperative to minimize losses and keep the four brigades in the north as effective fighting formations; this was as important as buying time for the defense to be reorganized and reinforcements to arrive. But it was obviously impossible for the depleted 6th, 15th, and 28th Indian Brigades and Krohcol, even when supported by one of the very few well-trained formations (Brigadier A.C.M. Paris's 12th Indian Brigade), to hold the Japanese assault.

The lack of prepared positions and the unfavorable terrain meant that it was impossible for the British to turn during a withdrawal in northern Malaya and fight a major defensive action with much hope of success. This course had to be avoided, yet above all else, this was what was desperately needed by the British after Jitra. Such an action was desirable on strategic and tactical grounds, but it was absolutely essential for reasons of morale. Routine garrison duties in peacetime had left Malaya Command and its units with a decidedly defensive mentality, and even before the war began morale was low. In the absence of offensive action a significant defensive success, one in which the Japanese were clearly seen to suffer badly, was utterly essential if the decline in morale, brought about by defeat and retreat, was to be checked.

The problem for the British in this respect was that somehow or other the front had to be stabilized, with the flanks anchored and secured, before a series of vigorous but small counterattacks could be mounted. But in the days that followed Jitra and Kroh it quickly became obvious that the prewar failure to appreciate the importance of the Grik trail was certain to exact a heavy price in keeping British forces north and west of the Perak off-balance. Although Malaya Command quickly deployed from its reserve a company of British infantry, supported by an armored car detachment, to secure Grik in front of the advancing Japanese, this force proved totally inadequate in slowing down attackers who secured Kuala Kenering on 17 December. Even when the British deployed a reinforced battalion on the Grik road, the Japanese, by moving along the river line and away from the road, were able to turn the British defensive positions with ease. By the twenty-second the Japanese advance had secured Kampong Sauk on the southern shore of Chenderoh Lake. The ease with which the Japanese *42nd Infantry* carried out its advance from Kroh to the Perak was one of the decisive factors in prompting the British to abandon their positions west of the river. Even though the position of the British forces west of the Perak was not under immediate threat on 21 December, when the 11th Indian Division was granted discretion to withdraw across the river, the fact was that the *42nd Infantry Regiment* was moving into a position whereby it would shortly be able to choose between advancing on the Perak bridges at Enggor or on the town of Sungei Siput. With very little with which to oppose the Japanese coming south from Grik, the British faced being caught in a pincer movement.

The British forces on the western part of the peninsula, facing the main Japanese assault, therefore found themselves in a precarious situation, with their right flank falling away, no reserve positions on which to fall back, and an aggressive enemy to their front. Dawn of 13 December found the 28th Indian Brigade as rear guard on the Kedah, with the brigades of the 11th Indian Division, somewhat the worse for wear, some miles to the south. But even though the Kedah line presented a natural obstacle and, in better circumstances, could have afforded the British a good position on which to make a stand, there could be no question of the British trying to hold the line, even though the initial Japanese probing assaults during the afternoon were easily held. During the night of 13/14 December the British retreat continued, though not without a repetition of the Jitra chaos with some of the defending units never receiving orders to fall back. Nevertheless, by noon on the fourteenth the British were back at Gurun, though without part of their transport, which was lost when the Kedah road bridge was blown with the transport on the wrong side of it. Moreover, the Kedah rail bridge resisted attempts to destroy it and had to be left more or less intact.

At Gurun the front was held by the 6th and 28th Indian Brigades, with the much-reduced 15th in reserve. The last of the defenders straggled back to Gurun just two hours before the initial Japanese attacks began. Despite the lack of prepared positions, these assaults were held with ease, but the main attack, launched soon after midnight, sliced through the 6th Indian Brigade before it was held by desperate and fierce resistance from units drawn from the 15th and 28th Brigades. With one battalion (the British East Surrey) ruined and another (the 1st/8th Punjab) forced to retreat by moving westwards to the coast road, there was no alternative but to continue the retreat.

The divisional commander, Murray Lyon, drew from this action the moral that his two brigades could not take a series of short withdrawals if they failed to make a clean break with the Japanese. Moreover, because he was aware of the developing threat to his lines of communication from the Japanese forces advancing from Grik, he urged Heath to authorize a withdrawal to the south of Kuala Kangsar. Heath agreed in principle, but Percival, correctly, refused to accept Heath's case for a stand on and south of the Perak. Percival's refusal to accept a withdrawal beyond the Muda was made on political grounds, but there were good military arguments to support his decision. With the 12th Indian Brigade in position at Baling and with the remnants of Krohcol under its command, there could be no question of a rapid withdrawal of the 6th, 15th, and 28th Indian Brigades behind Sungei Patani and the Muda. Moreover, time had to be bought for the evacuation of Penang and George Town and for carrying out essential demolitions at various installations in the north.

The 12th Indian Brigade was able to pull back safely, initially taking up position on the right flank of the British defenses on the Muda. The problem of trying to hold the river line was that, though the position itself was not unreasonable from the point of view of the defense, the area to the south was a relatively open one where armor could operate effectively. There was therefore a very real danger that if the Japanese broke through on the river their armor would be able to exploit a breach, thereby catching and annihilating the defenders in the open. The abandonment of the Muda line was thus inevitable, and on 16 December orders were given to pull back to the Krian River line, thereby laying bare Penang and the northern airfields not already lost.

By this time it can be seen that some confusion was beginning to engulf British decision-making because within a couple of days the decision to hold at or north of the Muda River was reversed in favor of a decision to hold a position 25 miles to the south. The truth was that, by the time the decision was made to retire to the Krian, the British were in the position of having to improvise in reacting to events that slowly but surely were beginning to slip out of their grasp and to acquire a momentum of their own. In this crisis Percival proved quite incapable of taking a grip on his forces and imposing his own will on events. He would not take the 11th Indian Division out of the line because he wanted to pull the 12th Indian Brigade back for the defense of the Grik trail, but he recognized that the 6th and 15th Indian Brigades would have to be taken out of the line in order to reorganize. He rejected Heath's suggestion for an immediate withdrawal to Johore and was intent on maintaining, if possible, a defense in the north, but, if not, then certainly in central Malaya. Yet on the seventeenth he gave permission for a withdrawal to the Perak line when Heath considered it necessary. Such a decision, at a time when British forces were still between the Muda and Krian rivers, was an explicit acceptance of the loss of northern Malaya, the defense of which had been considered the absolute priority before the war if Singapore was to be held. Granting permission to retire to—and hence behind—the Perak therefore accepted the projection of Japanese air power over central Malaya and it did something more; it represented a profound shift in the immediate tactical British priorities. What had been a concern for Kuala Kangsar and the whole of the Perak position was replaced by a concern for Kuala Kubu: the loss of Kuala Kangsar was implicit in granting permission to the 11th Indian Division to draw back to the Perak. Just as Kuala Kangsar had been the pivot for British operations on the Grik route and west and north of the Perak, Kuala Kubu was the pivot for the 9th and 11th Indian Divisions, separated as they were by the mountains. Any retirement of the former from eastern Malaya had to be channelled through either Kuala Kubu or Kuala Lumpur. As we have seen, however, the 9th Indian Division was authorized to pull back only the 8th Indian Brigade from the north and leave the 22nd at Kuantan.

Percival's decision at this time (16/18 December) not to pull back the whole of the 9th Indian Division was probably the critical one of the entire Malayan campaign because, with the ever-worsening situation on the west

Known to his subordinates as "Rabbit" because of his receding chin and protruding teeth, Lieutenant General Arthur E. Percival was a gentleman with all the appearance of an ineffectual fool. He lacked the presence and the ability to inspire that a general officer commanding, Malaya Command, needed if the omissions of two decades were to be made good. Popperfoto

coast, fresh battalions were absolutely essential if the Japanese advance was to be slowed and the four brigades in the west were to have any respite. After ten days of continuous movement, marching, digging, fighting, and losses, certain of the units, particularly from the 12th Indian Brigade, were beginning to weaken appreciably. In fact, at this time, the state of the 6th and 15th Indian Brigades led to their being reformed as a single brigade—the 6th/15th—while some of the battalions that had also suffered heavily were similarly reconstituted. These very actions pointed to the absolute need for the whole strength of the 3rd Indian Corps to be deployed to the western part of the peninsula; holding any position in the east would be of utter insignificance if the position in the west was broken asunder. As it was, Percival's decision condemned Heath's command to the worst of all worlds. The corps was prevented from retiring to the area in which it wanted to fight and denied the only forces that could possibly enable it to carry out its orders to retain a hold on central Malaya for as long as possible.

Heath's orders, in the absence of the long withdrawal and the sending of adequate reinforcements, were to conduct a series of defensive battles between Ipoh and Tanjong Malim. It was obvious that the Japanese had adopted the simple but extremely effective tactics of advancing with their main forces straight down the obvious routes and using infantry flanking attacks to lever the defenders out of their positions. The British correctly anticipated that in the next phase of operations in central Malaya the Japanese would use the main Ipoh–Kuala Lumpur road as the major axis of their advance. Heath and Percival therefore planned to make two major efforts to hold or slow down the Japanese by standing at Kampar and Tanjong Malim, where the narrowness of the front would not allow the Japanese to carry out their all-too-effective flanking attacks. As intermediate positions the British commanders chose to stand at Tapah, Bidor, and on the Slim River.

What Percival and Heath planned for was a series of stands and retreats, with units passing through one another to the fallback positions. Reserve forces for one position would act as rear guard when that position was abandoned, while demolitions along the routes would be used extensively in order to slow the Japanese advance. This, theoretically, should have allowed the defenders extra time in which to prepare themselves for the inevitable Japanese follow-up.

Such a plan might have worked, and it certainly would have had a better chance of success had Simson received any form of support from Percival, Heath, and Simmons (commander of Singapore garrison) in his attempt to construct prepared defensive positions for the troops to occupy as they retired. During Christmas week he made repeated efforts to get his superiors to start construction by impressing civilian labor. He alone seems to have grasped that the 3rd Indian Corps simply did not have the available manpower to prepare positions in the rear and that time was crucial. He knew that once Japanese aircraft began to appear over central Malaya civilian labor would disappear, but in all his efforts he met with blank—and bland—refusals on the ground that to start construction would be bad for morale. In the face of such stupifying imbecility Simson was helpless, and the troops of the 11th Indian Division were condemned to dig their own defensive positions after having fought and withdrawn, all in whatever time the Japanese were kind enough to grant them. The British plan to fight a slow rearguard action along the Ipoh–Kuala Lumpur road may have looked good on paper, but it certainly failed to take any account of the state of the troops called upon to fight such actions. It also failed to take proper account of Japanese intentions and capabilities.

Had the Japanese command been aware of the indecision, unreality, and downright stupidity of Malaya Command, it would have had good cause for satisfaction, but in fact Yamashita had some cause for concern about the situation in which he found himself. On the credit side was the fact that by 16 December the second echelon of the *5th Infantry Division* was put ashore at Singora. This division was the second strongest of the three available to the *25th Army*. The *4th* and *5th Regiments* of the *Imperial Guards Division*, moreover, were moving down through southern Thailand and would soon be in a position to reinforce the offensive, while the major part of the air forces allocated to the *25th Army* had been brought over to southern Thailand. On the thirteenth the British had abandoned Victoria Point and the Japanese occupation of the airfield on the eighteenth ensured that Malaya thereafter was cut off from reinforcements from India by air. On the other hand, Yamashita was more than perturbed by the failure to destroy enemy units. Though the British had been forced out of one position after another at Kota Bharu, Kroh, and Jitra, then the Kedah river, Gurun, and the Muda before the Krian River line—in no instance had a decisive tactical defeat been achieved. It was evident that the continuous rate of attrition inflicted on the British was severe. If unchecked, it would ultimately result in the loss of cohesion. Yet at no stage had the British forces been gripped and held to the extent that their encirclement and annihilation could have been accomplished.

But against this was to be balanced the simple fact that the British withdrawal had had to be quick in order to avoid envelopment. The very speed of the withdrawals had prevented the proper destruction of facilities in northern Malaya, destruction Percival's defense of the area had been designed to ensure. Just as the Japanese had suffered a serious strategic defeat in their failure to destroy installations at Pearl Harbor, so the British failure to carry out an effective scorched-earth policy in northern Malaya constituted a grave tactical defeat, possibly the equivalent of the loss of a division, certainly with regard to time and the tempo of operations.

While some 3,000 tons of tin proved more than a useful economic windfall with the taking of George Town, the overwhelming gains the Japanese made as a result of British negligence were of a military nature. When the British evacuated Penang (15/17 December), they failed to mine the harbor effectively and left intact a host of coastal vessels (motor vessels, barges, and junks) tailor-made to Japanese needs for their intended assaults along the Malacca Strait. The airfield at Kota Bharu was abandoned by the Royal Air Force in some confusion, not to say panic, with no attempt to destroy the runways, bomb and ammunition stores, or the fuel dumps; the latter were subsequently shelled to destruction by army gunners. The same situation prevailed at Sungei Patani airfield, though at Alor Star a thorough destruction of all stores and installations, other than the runway, was carried out. At George Town the small civilian airfield, considered by the prewar British air force to be unsuitable for military operations, was effectively wrecked. It was bad enough for the air force to have to abandon five of the six airfields in the north—three around Kota Bharu and two on the west coast—within two days of war beginning, but it was absolutely disastrous for many of them to fall virtually intact into enemy hands. By the simple expedient of using conscripted labor to repair bomb and demolition damage from captured stocks, the Japanese had the three critically important airfields of Alor Star, Sungei Patani, and Butterworth handling Japanese aircraft by 20 December. In the next two days the Japanese fought for and secured air supremacy over central Malaya, and on 23 December the Royal Air Force ceased to operate from Kuala Lumpur.

Thus, by the time the last British units were withdrawn behind the Perak and the road and rail bridges at Enggor and the pontoon bridge at Blanja were blown, one of the major British objectives in trying to hold central Malaya—retaining the airfields—had been rendered null and void. Though the Japanese were behind schedule in that they did not bridge the Perak until 26 December, they were on the point of making up for lost time by cruelly revealing the flaw inherent in Percival's plan to hold central Malaya by a series of roadblocks along the main road. When the 12th Indian Brigade, in defensive positions some 8 miles north of Ipoh, showed signs of fight and held the main Japanese thrust on 26/27 December, the Japanese were able to turn the position by an advance along the Perak valley to Blanja. The 28th Indian Brigade at Blanja was in no position to contest a flanking attack by two complete Japanese infantry regiments, the *41st* and *42nd*, and was forced to withdraw. The 11th Indian Division gave orders for the brigades to disengage, but both the 12th and 28th were very nearly caught by the Japanese pincers. They extricated themselves only with difficulty.

The Ipoh affair was only the start of the new outflanking problem for the British because, as we have seen, the Japanese intention to use a series of small-scale amphibious operations along the Malacca Strait was germane to their plans to overrun central Malaya. The weakness of the British positions at Kampar, Tapah, and Bidor was that they were vulnerable to the same outflanking movement from the sea by landings either at Kuala Selangor, with the intention of advancing on Rawang, or at Port Swettenham, where a good road system gave a Japanese commander with imagination and initiative a whole series of options for an inland or a coastal advance.

For the British there was a very real danger in this situation, for the 9th Indian Division still was not reconcentrated and available for operations. As a result, the plan to hold in northern and central Malaya at least until 14/15 January (by which time the first major troop convoy carrying reinforcements to Malaya should have arrived at Singapore) rested on the ability of exhausted brigades to withstand fresh enemy formations on the main road, while at the same time shedding parts of their strength to hold their own open flanks on the coast. The danger was that, with heavy losses being incurred and morale crumbling slowly, the 11th Indian Division was a wasting asset; its effectiveness inevitably was deteriorating. Even with the 45th Indian Brigade, which arrived at Singapore on 3 January, there was no real possibility that the gaps in ranks could be filled and fresh heart put into troops that, by 5 January, would have carried out a 225-mile retreat and lost 50 percent of their strength in a series of depressingly familiar defeats. The necessary dispersal of the brigades' remaining strengths ran the obvious risk that at some stage the demands of trying to counter the simultaneous threats on the main road and the coast would prove too much, and that the British would find themselves with inadequate forces on either or both fronts. Dispersal left the British open to defeat in detail, and it was virtually inevitable that at some time during the central Malaya campaign the Japanese would catch and overwhelm at least part of the defending forces.

At Kampar, however, success continued to elude the Japanese. The Kampar position was held by the 6th/15th and 28th Indian Brigades, with the 12th in reserve at Bidor, the first of the intermediate defensive positions. On New Year's Day the *25th Army* mounted a heavy assault with the *41st Infantry Regiment*, well supported by artillery and aircraft. The *42nd Infantry Regiment* was launched in a close outflanking move across the swamps of the Sungei Kampar to try to get around the back of the forward British positions. Fierce British resistance held the main attack, and the defenders even regained some of the ground lost on the first day in savage hand-to-hand fighting, while the *42nd Infantry* was never able to come up quickly enough and in sufficient strength to menace the British left flank. The problem of controlled movement through the extremely difficult ground, where an advance of 100 yards in an hour was fast, proved to be beyond the attackers. But wider flanking attacks by a battalion from the *4th Guards Regiment* down the Perak from Blanja and by a force one-and-one-half battalions strong from the *11th Infantry Regiment* from Port Weld to Utan Melintang between them secured Telok Anson (1/2 January). Even though British forces, masking Telok Anson after the town was lost, slowed the Japanese movement inland, the position at Kampar could not be sustained.

The British withdrawal from Kampar was orderly. The 6th/15th fell back to Bidor while its front was covered by the 28th and its left flank was held by the 12th. Both these brigades then passed through the 6th/15th to occupy positions on the Slim River; the rear guard then leapfrogged the position to retire into the main defensive position at Tanjong Malim. At this point British problems multiplied thick and fast. The Japanese plan was to advance with the *5th Infantry Division*, reinforced with an armored battalion, down the main road. The *42nd Infantry Regiment* was to lead, with the major part of the *11th Infantry Regiment* in the second echelon and the *41st Infantry Regiment* in reserve. The remaining part of the *11th Infantry*, along with the *4th Guards Regiment*, was detailed to sweep around the British flank from the sea, securing first Kuala Selangor and then Port Swettenham. The 11th Indian Division correctly anticipated a seaborne assault on Kuala Selangor and formed a scratch force, made up of units withdrawn from Telok Anson, locally recruited Malay forces, and, for the first time, a battalion and a battery from the 8th Indian Brigade, to hold Kuala Selangor. Realizing the danger of leaving so weak a force to try to hold the Japanese on the coast, though this was done on the second and third, the British sent more units from the 6th/15th Indian Brigade to Kuala Selangor and withdrew to Rawang what remained of the formation. Thus, they abandoned the second of the two major defensive positions in central Malaya at Tanjong Malim.

The two brigades at the Slim River were left rather exposed with no covered positions on which to fall back. They had but two days in which to prepare their defenses before they were attacked by the *42nd Infantry* and armor in the early hours of 7 January. For the British the result was catastrophic because virtually every conceivable error had been committed in organizing the defense. The reasons for this abysmal state of affairs were obvious. The two brigades involved had been pushed beyond the limits of their endurance and they made errors in siting the defenses, errors that can be explained only by sheer fatigue on the part of troops trying in just two days to prepare positions while under constant air attack. Virtually no antitank guns and mines were used to cover positions, though adequate numbers of both were available. The artillery was placed in reserve because it was wrongly believed that the restricted fields of fire available to the defense on the Slim River minimized the guns' effectiveness. The options the ground and vegetation presented to the attacker were simply not appreciated, and no steps were taken to ensure that the dead ground (formed by loops where the main road had been straightened) could be denied to the enemy. The 11th Indian Division, even when commanded by Paris, who had replaced Murray Lyon at the time of the withdrawal across the Perak, proved unequal to the task of properly supervising its two forward brigades. Paris, in effect, was playing simultaneous chess, with every board showing a losing position. It was inevitable that at some stage in the proceedings something would break, and it was perhaps predictable that the collapse, when it came, was on the main road where the Japanese strength was concentrated and where the British were at their weakest.

The Japanese advance to the Slim was characteristically dashing. Living up to the adage that time spent on reconnaissance is always wasted, the Japanese conducted their reconnaissance by drawing fire. At the Slim the notion of using a reconnaissance force strong enough to launch its own offensive off the line of march without having to pause to reorganize and mount deliberate assaults was triumphantly vindicated. The Japanese vanguard burst through four defended positions and caught two separate battalions in the open by the sheer speed and violence of its attack. It then captured the bridge over the Slim against opposition. This represented an advance against opposition of 17 miles in a little more than five hours. The devastating combination of skillful use of dead ground (the Japanese picked up the weaknesses of the road loops with no difficulty) and utter ferocity simply pulverized the British defenders, who had absolutely no time either to withdraw to rear positions or to bring up reserves in support. The speed of the assault was such that the reserve position of the forward formation, the 12th Indian Brigade, was unmanned when it was overrun, and its would-be defenders were annihilated in the open by a Japanese vanguard that covered some 6 miles in forty minutes in the breakthrough phase. In all, the two brigades at the Slim River could muster little more than a battalion between them by noon on the seventh, while the number of missing greatly exceeded the number of killed and wounded—always a bad sign for any army.

Even before the Slim River action was fought, Percival (in consultation with his senior commanders, Heath and Major General H. Gordon Bennett, general officer commanding the 8th Australian Division) had come to the conclusion that the loss of central Malaya was inevitable and that the good communications system and open flank on the sea in Selangor, Negri Sembilan, and Malacca would prevent the British from attempting to make a stand north of the state of Johore. The danger of trying to hold in any of the three central-southern states of Malaya was that Japanese armor, with the choice of several approach routes, might work its way around unsecured flanks while seaborne assaults, quickly striking inland, might secure the communications bottleneck at Tampin. In either eventuality the very real danger was that the defending forces—obviously most or all of the 11th Indian Division—would be surrounded and annihilated.

Clearly what was needed was fresh troops to man whatever positions the British chose to make their main line of resistance. On 4 January Gordon Bennett proposed that, if he was not given command of all forces in Johore (i.e., placed in control of Heath's 3rd Indian Corps) if and when it came to a retreat into that state, the 8th Australian Division should be given the task of holding western Malaya, while the much-depleted formations of Heath should be allocated eastern Malaya.

The merit of Gordon Bennett's plan was that it would have placed an intact and fresh division in the path of the main Japanese advance, but there were several obvious objections to such a proposal. The most pertinent was the fact that to switch the Australians from eastern to western Johore and to move them forward while at the same time switching the Indians from the west to the east in the course of their withdrawal promised problems of nightmarish proportions. Percival, correctly, rejected Gordon Bennett's suggestions, planning instead to reinforce the 3rd Indian Corps with the 45th Indian Brigade and to carry out a slow phased withdrawal of Heath's forces from Kuala Kubu (10 January) and Kuala Lumpur (14/15 January), to Tampin (24 January). Subsequently, on 7 January, Percival slightly amended his plan. In the three days following Gordon Bennett's initiative he had become increasingly convinced that the crucial period for the defense would come between the end of the withdrawal into Johore and the time when the promised reinforcements entered the line as effective fighting units, he hoped in mid-February. The defenders therefore had to hold for at least three weeks in Johore if there was to be any chance of saving Singapore. Percival thus settled upon taking the 27th Australian Brigade out of central Johore, replacing it with units from Singapore and from the 3rd Indian Corps as they came southwards. The Australian formation was to be deployed as the mobile force, detailed to mount aggressive counterof-fensives in an effort to smother and disrupt Japanese preparations. The wider arrangements whereby the overall security of Johore was divided between the Indians in the west and the Australians in the east were not altered.

Two events destroyed the basis of Percival's plan even as he drew it up on the morning of the seventh. The plan was founded on the assumption that the 11th Indian Division could hold the Japanese in a series of defensive actions and delay the Japanese arrival in northern Johore until late January. The first event, obviously, was the concurrent Slim River engagement. Even while Percival was devising his new plan, which arguably would have worked if it had been put into effect any time before 2 January, the Japanese destroyed the 11th Indian Division as an effective fighting force. It was evident that after the Slim River action there was no question of the British being able to delay the Japanese advance and hold the Japanese away from Johore until 24 January; the timing of the enemy arrival in Johore was no longer dependent on any factors over which the British had any control. Moreover, the 3rd Indian Corps, now shorn of most of the brigades with which it had tried to defend western Malaya, certainly lacked the means to hold western Johore for a month. The second event was unexpected—the personal intervention in the battle of the newly appointed Allied supreme commander in Southeast Asia, Wavell.

CHAPTER 9

Arcadia, ABDA, Anzac, and the Dutch

THE WAR WAS LESS than a few of days old when Churchill sought the permission of King George VI to visit Washington; he then invited himself to the United States by asking a rather startled Roosevelt for a meeting at the earliest possible opportunity. The reasons for Churchill's desire for a meeting and his haste were obvious. Though a certain basic framework for a joint Anglo-American strategy in a war against the Axis powers had already been established in talks before the start of the Pacific war, Churchill was anxious to discover at the first opportunity whether the extension of the war to the Pacific would in any way deflect the Americans from their intended "Germany first" policy. Churchill also had to discover the extent to which British supplies would be affected by the American entry into the war. Despite the American statement of principle that placed the European theater before the Pacific in the list of priorities, American policy was necessarily vague and ill-defined. So much American thought and effort had been directed towards arming the United States and her Allies that the Americans had never been able to devote much detailed attention to the strategy they would adopt in the event of war, the character of which the Americans could hardly be expected to gauge before they entered it.

In the grand strategic sense Churchill's talks with Roosevelt in December 1941 and January 1942 make the Arcadia Conference probably the most crucial meeting of Allied leaders during the Second World War, certainly in terms of Anglo-American relations. Its importance really stemmed from three decisions and actions that arose from the series of meetings between 22 December and 14 January. The first of these was the Declaration of the United Nations on 1 January 1942 by twenty-six Allied nations, which of course did not include France, that they adhered to the principles of the Atlantic Charter of 12 August 1941. The nations stated their intention to wage total war against the Axis powers and each undertook not to enter a separate peace with their enemies. The declaration foreshadowed the ultimate establishment of the United Nation organization and the formulation of the demand for unconditional surrender. The declaration thus served notice on the Japanese that they could not possibly hope to secure the objectives for which they went to war. The war was to be fought to a finish: both sides were fighting for their existence. Second, in the course of the conference various specifically military matters were tackled in committee by the American chiefs of staff and their British opposite numbers, both sides having their staffs with them.* What began as an informal working arrangement, brought about by necessity, in the course of the conference became formalized into a standing organization known as the Combined Chiefs of Staff, permanently based in Washington.† This was to be the firm basis of the generally cordial Anglo-American military cooperation that persisted throughout the war. Third, the British, much to their relief, found that despite Pearl Harbor and the increasingly serious situation in the Far East, the Americans had not gone back on their belief that if Germany was defeated, the conquest of Italy and Japan would quickly follow. The Americans still adhered to the policy of tackling the European theater before the Pacific.

In a very real sense the latter point was all that mattered to the British. With no doubts at all about the reality of American power or the backing behind an American promissory note, the British knew that in the end they would not be defeated. Much of the conference was devoted to European problems and to how the British and Americans should pursue the objective of defeating Germany. Shipping resources, allocation of production, the buildup and deployment of American troop levels all were examined. Underlying the discussions was a fundamental difference of opinion be-

*On the American side the leading personalities involved in the staff discussions were Admiral Ernest J. King for the navy, General George C. Marshall for the army, and General Henry H. Arnold for the army air forces. On the British side were Admiral of the Fleet Sir Dudley Pound, Air Chief Marshal Sir Charles Portal, and Field Marshal Sir John Dill. Pound and Portal were the heads of their respective services, Dill had been chief of the Imperial General Staff until 1 December 1941.

†A misnomer, of course, because the British chiefs were obviously in London. The Combined Chiefs of Staff consisted of the Americans meeting with a mission, headed by Dill, that represented the British Chiefs of Staff. This mission was in direct contact with London. The Combined Chiefs of Staff were presided over by Admiral William D. Leahy, presidental chief of staff, after July 1942.

The Atlantic Charter meeting, August 1941. The first meeting of President Frank-
lin D. Roosevelt and Prime Minister Winston Churchill on board the *Prince of Wales*.
Their advisers (left to right): Harry Hopkins, lend-lease administrator; W. Averell
Harriman, lend-lease coordinator in London; Admiral Ernest J. King, commander,
U.S. Atlantic Fleet; the two chiefs of staff, Generals George C. Marshall and Sir
John Dill; the two naval chiefs, Admirals Harold R. Stark and Sir Dudley Pound.
Associated Press

tween a nation, backed by limitless resources, that believed in overwhelming concentration at a single point and smashing through to victory, and a
nation whose straitened circumstances and strategic positioning inclined
her towards a more cautious and peripheral concept of war. The full extent
of this divergence, however, remained for the future. At this conference the
Americans were in no position to take exception to the broad lines of
strategy suggested by the British because they recognized that for the
immediate future their weaknesses prevented them from making any impact on the European theater.

The identification of Germany as the primary enemy necessarily resulted in the Pacific being designated a secondary theater. But with the
U.S. Pacific Fleet lying mauled at Pearl Harbor and Britain's Force Z on
the seabed long before Churchill even left Britain in the *Duke of York*, both
the Americans and the British had to define what they intended to do and
what they hoped to achieve in facing up to the Japanese challenge. In this
the Anglo-Americans had to adjust to the painful realities of the situation.
Strategy for the Americans and British alike was largely defined by
Japanese success, and all that the two could reasonably hope to achieve was

the retention of those positions they then held. For the British the places that had to be held in order to provide bases from which the Japanese could be rolled back were Dutch Harbor and Pearl Harbor in the Pacific; Java, Sumatra, and Singapore in Southeast Asia; and Rangoon and Ceylon in the Indian Ocean.

With this view the Americans were in entire agreement, but both the British and the Americans knew that it seemed unlikely the Japanese could be held in many of the combat zones. Roosevelt wanted the British to hold Singapore and reinforce the base if necessary and possible. He also wanted to hold onto the Philippines or, if that failed, to retain the Indies. But beyond the immediate defense of the mainland United States, the Hawaiian Islands, and the communications eastwards from Pearl Harbor, Roosevelt's overriding concern in the Pacific was the security of Australia. The Americans realized that Australia would have to serve as the base from which any countermove had to come. Thus, securing Australia and American lines of communication to Australia were absolute American priorities after the security of Pearl Harbor. The implications of this intent were not immediately apparent, but were nevertheless profound, because if the Americans were to move forces to Australia then they would have to provide naval escort right up to the Australian coastline. Neither the British nor the Australians could hope to provide naval forces for this task. The Americans, therefore, had to accept a commitment deep into the southern hemisphere, deep into the waters of the Southwest Pacific—something they had never previously considered seriously. The implication of this in terms of the world role of the United States and, more specifically, in relation to the course of the 1942 campaign in the islands of the Southwest Pacific, was to become obvious in the course of time.

But the immediate matter at hand was Southeast Asia, where the Allies had to face a Japanese onslaught already assuming daunting proportions. Both the British and the Americans realized that because of Japanese air and sea supremacy the enemy possessed the means to strike at will throughout the theater, and there was little they could do at the time to redress this state of affairs. They recognized, moreover, that the initial Allied requirement had to be to wrest general air supremacy from the Japanese. This they knew was unlikely in the short term, not so much because aircraft were unavailable as because they could not reach the combat zone and be concentrated in time to be effective. Indeed, some 301 American fighters reached the Southwest Pacific in the first two months of the war but for a variety of reasons, most of them technical, only 40 were able to get through to the Indies.

The immediate Anglo-American problem was that somehow or other the Japanese had to be held before they broke through the Allied positions in Southeast Asia. Just as the Australians in the interwar period had been persuaded that Singapore was their first line of defense, so the Americans and British were aware that unless they held the line of the Malayan Barrier—peninsular Malaya, Sumatra, Java, and the Lesser Sunda Islands—then they would not only lose resources vital to both themselves and the Japanese, but they also would be condemned to what was certain to be a long and difficult campaign of reconquest. In order to improve the prospects of holding this line, on 25 December Marshall proposed to the British that there should be a complete unity of command for all Allied land, sea, and air forces in Southeast Asia. The following day Roosevelt pressed the point on the reluctant British.

There were good supporting arguments for Marshall's proposals since the suggested theater of operations included no less than five distinct national commands: the Americans in the Philippines, the Dutch in the Indies, the Australians, and the British in Malaya and again in Burma. Churchill and his advisers were sceptical because, as Churchill rightly pointed out, the great distances within the area of operations rendered effective command and coordination extremely unlikely. In any case, the situation was such that every commander should be quite clear in his own mind what was expected of him. Yet Marshall's general view was correct: the existing command structure was the least efficient way of utilizing scarce resources to meet the common threat. The British, anxious to ensure a singleness of purpose in the Anglo-American war effort, could hardly hold out against the very first proposal for a single command structure in Southeast Asia.

What undoubtedly caused some cooling of the British reaction to the American proposal was the unexpected nomination by Marshall of General Wavell as the supreme commander for the area. By any standard Wavell was a remarkable soldier. He was fluent in Russian, read Greek and Latin, was an avid reader of classical literature and history, and even wrote poetry. Though most German generals found the latter decidedly peculiar, Rommel and Richenau were among Wavell's admirers, and to stand well in the eyes of the enemy is always a sign of marked ability. He had had experience commanding a vast operational theater with very few forces at his disposal, and had achieved both massive success against a numerically superior enemy and decisive defeat. Each experience would prove invaluable in what undoubtedly would be difficult days to come. Marshall was probably sincere in forwarding Wavell's name, though experience showed the Americans were never exactly forward in placing their forces under foreign command if there was any chance of glory. But the British were naturally somewhat alarmed by the prospect of American public opinion turning against them when, rather than if, American forces were involved in a disaster while under the command of a British officer. The British were under no illusions of what probably lay in store; they clearly anticipated defeat.

This was not the only British concern, though perhaps it was the most immediate. The Americans "suggested" that Burma be included in any command set up in Southeast Asia. This demand was reasonable in view of Burma's invasion and the fact that it offered the only link with Chiang Kai-shek's nationalist government in Chungking. But the British, with a clarity of logic that had proved elusive before the war, were reluctant to see yet another change of command for Burma so soon after the 12 December change. They argued against the proposed transfer on the ground that strategically and administratively Burma was part of India rather than Southeast Asia.

The British were also concerned about the terms of reference Marshall proposed for Wavell. Marshall proposed that Wavell should have no power to transfer ground forces from one area to another within his command, and he could deploy only the air forces the various national governments chose to make available to him. In addition, he could not relieve national commanders or interfere with their dispositions and the tactics of local forces, and he was not to have any control over the communications of his forces with their national commands. Marshall justified these stringent restrictions on the ground that, even if a supreme commander ended up being no more than an assessor of needs, this was an improvement on the existing situation. Marshall never favored putting American combat troops under foreign command; what he wanted was a collection of homogeneous national forces "under a supreme authority." It would seem that *direction* would have been a more suitable word than *authority*, because the proposals seem more cosmetic than substantive. Dill correctly pointed out that the terms of reference were so restrictive that they were certain to prevent the effective command that could be the only justification for creating a unified theater of operations in the first place.

Yet these points paled into insignificance when set against one consideration that, though not without its dangers, had certain attractions for the British. Despite his critical comments, Dill was one of the first to see that if the creation of a supreme command in Southeast Asia would inextricably commit the Americans to a given course of action, in effect denying them the unilateral right to alter deployments as circumstances changed, then such a command was highly desirable. Marshall insisted that "Suitable limitations could be imposed (on the powers of a supreme commander) to safeguard the interests of each nation."* This was Marshall's escape clause, but one that the British could reasonably hope need never arise. If Dill was correct then the Americans would have to consult on changes of policy, and

*Gwyer, *Grand Strategy*, 3: 368.

as far as the British were concerned, when Marshall spoke of each nation, what he really meant was both nations. What the British wanted above all else was to be sure that decision-making on the Allied side would be an Anglo-American prerogative. Notable by their absence from these talks were the four nations most directly affected by events in Southeast Asia— Australia, New Zealand, the Netherlands, and India. Because of the peculiar circumstances of British imperial arrangements and the Anglo-Dutch relationship, implicit in Anglo-American assumptions was the belief that Britain could speak on behalf of her commonwealth and the Dutch by virtue of the various liaison arrangements in London. Britain wanted to keep it that way. Direct Anglo-American talks were certain to be easier than multinational consultations, and the arrangement whereby Britain dealt directly with Washington implied a false sense of equality between the two nations, a "special relationship" in the making. If ensuring that Britain was at the heart of the decision-making process could be achieved only at the cost of deliberately excluding such people as the Dutch and Australians, this was fair enough as far as the British were concerned.

Not unnaturally, the New Zealanders, Australians, and Dutch suspected and resented what they thought was their deliberate exclusion from Allied decision making. The New Zealanders were the more circumspect in expressing their concern on this matter, but even they made the telling observation that they knew virtually nothing of British and American intentions. Their country was weak on land, at sea, and in the air, and most of the forces they did have were in the European and Middle East theaters. They recognized that in devising strategy their country was certain to be peripheral, but not so peripheral as to be excluded altogether. In one very vivid phrase the New Zealand government told Churchill that, even though it had very little knowledge of the intentions in the higher direction of the war, it "must have an eye, an ear and a voice whenever decisions affecting New Zealand are to be made."* Australia, on the other hand, was more forthright. The natural leadership that Britain had enjoyed within her empire during the First World War did not survive so easily into the Second World War. The fall of Singapore really killed any deference to Britain as far as the Australians were concerned. In the period 1939–41 Australia keenly resented her exclusion from British decision-making and was less than enamored by the fact that in 1941 in the Middle East heavy losses had been sustained by Australian troops in a series of operations of dubious strategic value. Naturally in the first weeks of the Pacific war the Australians became more than a little concerned by the very real prospect, rapidly hardening into certainty, that the whole basis of their security—the integrity of Singapore and the presence of the Royal Navy—no longer existed. Australians unashamedly began to look to the United States for the security

*Ibid., 3: 373.

that the British had promised but had been unable to discharge. In the first weeks of the Pacific war Australia insisted that, in the changed circumstances of the conflict, her forces in the Middle East had to come back to fight the Japanese and that she must be given her rightful place among the Allies.

The command that Marshall proposed, and to which the British agreed and the Dutch and Australians were admitted, was called ABDA (American, British, Dutch, Australian) Command. The directive to Wavell was that he command the defense of the ABDA area, which was defined as bound in the north by the Indian-Burmese border and then, via the Chinese frontier and coastline, to latitude 30° north. The northern boundary followed this parallel to the meridian 140° east. North of the equator this meridian formed the area's eastern boundary; south of the equator the boundary shifted one degree to the east until it reached the southern coast of New Guinea. There it again shifted eastwards, this time 138 miles, to follow the meridian 143° east to the northern Australian coast. The southern boundary followed the northern Australian coastline westwards to the meridian 114° east and then veered to the northwest to a position in latitude 13° south, longitude 92° east. This eastern meridian formed the western boundary of the ABDA area.

China, French Indo-China, and Thailand on the Asian mainland were excluded from the ABDA Command. Similarly, Australia was excluded from the ABDA area, and this situation immediately provoked a strong reaction from Canberra. The British and Americans might hope to override the claims for proper consultation made by their small Allies in the Far East, but they could not be indifferent to certain arguments they might raise. Australia was vitally important to the Allied war effort and both Washington and London had to give Canberra's views more than a cursory nod. They had to deal with a hypersensitive ally, one badly shaken by recent events but not too badly shaken to see a dangerous implication inherent in the establishment of the ABDA Command and the collapse of British sea power. The Australians realized that their island continent could not be included in ABDA Command, but they feared that its exclusion might result in Australia, as well as New Zealand and the small islands of the Southwest Pacific, falling into the void, between the British in the west and north and the Americans in the Pacific. The Australians were not mollified by a 29 December signal from Churchill indicating that the whole of the Pacific, up to the Australian coastline, was to be an American command area.

To meet these very real fears among the Australasians, the British and Americans, at King's suggestion, agreed to the creation of the Anzac area with an Anzac Force, drawn from the Allied navies, operating under the direction of the commander in chief, U.S. Fleet (King himself). The

ABDA and Anzac Areas

commander in chief was to exercise command through one or two American officers who worked in conjunction with one or more officers appointed by the Australian and New Zealand governments. The Australian government finally agreed on 27 January to the creation of the Anzac Command. The Anzac area was defined as bound in the north by the equator between the meridians 141° east and 170° east; in the east from the latter meridian to a position in latitude 20° south, longitude 175° west, and then due south. In the west, after sharing ABDA area's eastern border, the Anzac area extended to the northern Australian coast and the meridian 143° east, excluding land areas.

The creation and demarcation of the Anzac Command met at least one of Australia's political and strategic concerns, but the establishment of a command was not the same as having sufficient force at hand to reassure the Australians and New Zealanders. Initially the British promised to provide the near-useless light carrier *Hermes* for the Anzac Force, with the Americans undertaking to provide either a heavy or a new light cruiser and a couple of destroyers. The Australians had on station the heavy cruisers *Australia* and *Canberra*, the light cruiser *Adelaide*, the destroyers *Stuart* and *Voyager*, three armed merchant cruisers, and six small corvettes. Of the cruisers, however, only the *Australia* was in commission and immediately available for operations in the Anzac area. The remainder of the Royal Australian Navy, including the light cruisers *Hobart* and *Perth* and a number of minesweepers, was assigned to ABDA Command. The Royal New Zealand Navy was able to contribute virtually its total strength, the light cruisers *Achilles* and *Leander*, to the Anzac Force. The British Admiralty, however, withheld the *Hermes*, giving no explanation for its action. The naval units available for the Anzac Command were wretchedly inadequate. When the force was constituted at Suva in the Fiji Islands on 12 February, it consisted of the *Australia*, *Achilles*, and *Leander* and three American ships, the heavy cruiser *Chicago* and the destroyers *Perkins* and *Lamson*.

Time was to show that New Zealand's remoteness and Australia's vastness were their best guarantees against Japanese encroachment. The Dutch had no such protection. Their position in the Indies placed them directly in the path of the Japanese onslaught, primarily directed against them of course, with no hope that distance and their own power could hold the Japanese at bay for very long.

The Dutch were in a potentially disastrous situation from the very first day of the war, though this had not prevented their immediate association with the British and American declarations of war on Japan. It is, perhaps, a shock to realize that after Britain and France the Dutch at that time possessed the third largest colonial empire in the world, most of it in the Indies. All of it had been acquired in a long bygone age and was indefensible with the forces the Dutch then had at hand. It was not that the Dutch lacked the will to hold their empire. Just before the war they had embarked upon what for so small a nation was an ambitious and substantial naval rearmament program. Pride of place was allocated to three 28,000-ton battle cruisers armed with nine 11-inch guns. These cruisers, very similar in their characteristics to the *Gneisenau* and *Scharnhorst*, were envisaged specifically as counters to Japanese heavy cruisers. Yet the Dutch naval problem was obvious. The Netherlands had to divide her naval effort because she had to provide a substantial force for the defense of the homeland, particularly with regard to inshore ships, thus diverting resources from the Indies. Very little of the program had been completed before the outbreak of war in Europe, and the fall of the Netherlands in May 1940 obviously ended the hope that the Dutch would be able to provide major forces for their own defense. Critically, the fall of the

Netherlands ended the supply of ships and spares for those units already in the Indies.

What the Dutch had in the Far East was of little value. In stark terms, in 1941 the Dutch had in commission three light cruisers, the *de Ruyter*, *Java*, and *Tromp*; the destroyers *Banckert*, *Evertsen*, *Kortenaer*, *Piet Hein*, *Van Ghent*, *Van Nes*, and *Witte de With*; various small auxiliaries and defense ships; and the submarines *K-VII*, *K-VIII*, *K-IX*, *K-X*, *K-XI*, *K-XII*, *K-XIII*, *K-XIV*, *K-XV*, *K-XVI*, *K-XVII*, *K-XVIII*, *0-16*, *0-19*, and *0-20*. In terms of numbers this force was more than equal to anything that the British had in Southeast Asia after 11 December and was not far short of what the Americans were able to pull back from the Philippines to the Indies. (The antiaircraft cruiser *Jacob van Heemskerck* and the destroyer *Isaac Sweers* were to see service with the British Eastern Fleet in March and April 1942, but were not on the Indies station in the course of the Southeast Asia campaign.)

In quality the problem that many of these ships faced was that they were old. The *Java*, for example, was conceived at the time of Jutland and she was a good ship by the standards of the First World War's light cruisers. But with ten 5.9-inch guns in single turrets, giving a broadside of just seven guns, she was totally outclassed by Washington treaty cruisers. The *de Ruyter*, with seven guns, all on centerline, was similarly undergunned. All the Dutch ships, new and old alike, ran the problem that maintenance was becoming virtually impossible, with ships having to be put into reserve in order to provide parts for others. The air force was in the desperate position of being forced to rely on aircraft that other more powerful nations, particularly the United States, were prepared to make available. Not unnaturally, the only types of aircraft likely to come the Dutch way were those for which the Americans had no further use. The front-line Dutch bomber in the Indies was the B-10 Martin for which the B-17 Flying Fortress had been built as a replacement, the B-18 having had a short-lived and unsuccessful intervening career. With regard to reconnaissance aircraft the Dutch were scarcely better placed. They had five different types of American manufacture in their army air force, while the navy air force was equipped with Dornier Flying Boats. Maintenance and servicing must have been a nightmare.

The Dutch ground forces in the Indies were in an equally unenviable position. Most of the difficulties that surrounded the Royal Netherlands Indies Army (KNIL) stemmed from the fact that it functioned primarily as an adjunct to the civil power in policing the Indies rather than as an army organized to defend the islands against external aggression. Indeed, the "Principles of Defense" laid down in 1927 by the Hague government stated that the object of the forces in the Indies was first to maintain Dutch authority in the islands against possible unrest or rebellion by the "inland enemy" (i.e., the indigenous population), and second to fulfill Dutch obligations as a member of the community of nations. This was not a euphemism for an obligation under the terms of collective security but the maintenance of a strict Dutch neutrality in the event of war between other powers.

The dual function of the KNIL obviously prevented its reorganization and expansion on any significant scale during the thirties as the prospect of Japanese aggression grew and the need for such measures became ever more urgent. The KNIL was an all-professional force of about 38,000 officers and men of whom about 10,000 were Europeans or Eurasians. The latter, legally speaking, were considered Europeans and were eligible to fill the highest posts in the army and civil service. More than half of the remainder were Javanese, while Amboina and the Menadonese provided the bulk of the rest.

In support of the KNIL were members from two organizations. The first were from the militia. In Dutch terms the militia was the conscripted part of the army and the reserve. It did not exist as a separate operational organization, but its members were integrated with the regulars. Until November 1941 the militia was drawn only from the European population; too many question marks were set against the reliability of the indigenous civil population for the authorities to risk creating a general reserve drawn from the native populations. The initial recruitment of some 7,000 native militiamen in November was a case of too little, too late to meet the Japanese challenge. The second organization was the town guard. This was a paramilitary force, rather like the British Home Guard, that was drawn from the urban population. Its tasks included guarding important buildings, installations, and bridges. The guards were too few in number and short on training to have any practical significance other than to free the KNIL from some of its more tedious and static duties.

The KNIL therefore suffered from lack of numbers in facing anything other than the kind of internal threat that it traditionally had been called upon to counter. It had no experience of war against a first-class enemy, and it lacked the training, equipment, and an efficient and modern command organization that would enable it to face the test of war. The overall shortcomings of the KNIL can be illustrated by the command arrangements. The Dutch chain of command in the Indies ran from the governor-general, who was also the commander in chief, through the commander of the army, the legercommandant, to the commanders of the formations on Java, and the territorial commanders on the outlying islands. The latter commanded all the military forces in a given area, but had no authority over the police or the civil authorities. While some of the military forces at their disposal were unit-sized, most were "brigades." These brigades were independent operational subunits, in size the equivalent of a section that varied between fifteen and twenty men. Their function was to patrol the islands and inland areas as a demonstration of force to the local population. Their size, responsibilities, and dispersal therefore embodied every conceivable weakness when it came to oppose an external enemy. West Borneo, for example, was held by fifty brigades of fifteen men each, south Borneo by twenty-five brigades of nineteen men each. Elsewhere the story was much the same. Everywhere Dutch ground forces were few in number and dispersed. Even where the Dutch did deploy more substantial forces, their overall position was not much better. On Sumatra, for example, the Dutch deployed seven battalions on this massive and critically important island, but nearly all these units were deployed in an effort to maintain public order. In fact, after the start of the Pacific war the Dutch felt obliged to send reinforcements from Java to Sumatra just to try to stem the deteriorating internal security situation. Only one Dutch battalion was in southern Sumatra guarding the all-important oil fields at Palembang, Sungeigerong, and Pladju and the airfield near Prabumulih, while the five battalions in central Sumatra were not even constituted as a territorial command until February 1942. There was no overall command for the island.

Of course, Dutch weakness was compounded by geography. Even if more forces had been available, given the diversity of the Indies and the long coastlines of the islands, the Dutch position was hopeless. On Java, for example, the Dutch deployed the equivalent of two understrength divisions and a regiment, militia, town guards, and about 10,000 British, Australian, and American military personnel. Overall, in late February 1942, the Allies had perhaps 40,000 men under arms on Java. But the northern coast of the island on which an enemy might choose to land is about 700 miles long, and there was always the possibility of airborne landings against which precautions had to be taken. From the start, the Dutch position was without hope. Yet it is salutory to recall that in the defense of their empire the Dutch fought to destruction every one of their major surface warships, except the heavily damaged *Tromp*, as well as eight of their submarines. Two minesweepers and two minelayers were also lost in action and various other small warships and auxiliaries were lost to air attack while in harbor. It was not determination that the Dutch lacked but muscle.

It was precisely this lack of muscle that led to the Dutch being excluded from Anglo-American deliberations, much to their irritation. Indeed, Dutch feelings went beyond irritation because in formulating a unified command for Southeast Asia the Americans and British presented the Dutch, and the Australians and New Zealanders for that matter, with a fait accompli that allowed the small nations very little option but to do as they were told. Just as in March 1942 the Dutch had to bow to force majeure in the shape of the Japanese armed forces, so in December 1941 they had to bend the knee with regard to British and American wishes. Though before the war the Dutch had enjoyed a nominal equality of status with Britain and the United States, a week or so of war clearly brought home to them the fact that their two more powerful friends regarded them as unwelcome intruders on their own private conversations. The British were particularly clear about this, and from an examination of the record the irresistible conclusion would seem to emerge that, in their dealings with the Dutch, the British proved an ally as faithless politically as they were unreliable militarily, but the Dutch do not seem to have said so openly. The first of the wartime conferences went so well as far as the British were concerned that they were determined to ensure that third parties, who might otherwise infringe upon British standing vis-à-vis the Americans, did not gate-crash a club the British wanted to see remain very exclusive. The Americans simply refused even to talk to the Dutch in Washington. The voters of what had once been New Amsterdam weighed more heavily with the likes of Roosevelt than a people then on the point of embarking upon a nomadic existence.

The urgency and haste with which the Americans and British decided upon the establishment of ABDA Command to meet the Japanese threat precluded all but the barest possible consultation with the Dutch, Australians, and New Zealanders, as well as Wavell, before establishment of the command was announced publicly. As a result of these hurried arrangements many important loose ends remained to be tied up, more or less on a "muddling through" basis, when the command actually became functional. Some, inevitably, were never properly settled.

Wavell was given the least possible time to consider his appointment. Churchill signalled Wavell on 30 December of the intention to form ABDA Command and informed him that the Americans had nominated him as supreme commander. Duty forbade Wavell's declining the post and he accepted his appointment immediately, requesting that no public announcement be made until he was ready to take up command or, if that was impossible, until after he had received his instructions. Wavell's true feelings, however, were summarized aptly in his wire to Dill, indicating he felt that he had been left holding not the baby but quadruplets. The old adage that victory has many claimants but defeat is always fatherless was never more true than with ABDA Command. Wavell had no illusions about the seriousness of the situation in which the Japanese, showing exceptional bravery and an unanticipated tactical and strategic skill, already had inflicted grave defeats on the Allies. But Wavell could hardly have been prepared for sections of the Indian press, quoting reliable Australian sources, stating on 2 January that he was to take up the appointment of commander in chief, South West Pacific. The BBC "confirmed" his appointment the same day. It was not until the following day that Wavell received his instructions from Washington.

ABDA Command's first meeting in Batavia, 10 January 1942. At the head of the table are Colonel E. T. Kengen, KNIL, and (standing) Lieutenant Commander A.H.W. von Freytag Drabbe, RNN. Clockwise around the table from von Freytag are Group Captain Darvall, RAF; Major General Ian S. Playfair, Indian Army; Lieutenant General Sir Henry R. Pownall, chief of staff (hidden except for his hands); Wavell; Brett; Major General Lewis H. Brereton, USAAF; Air Commodore Hewitt, RNZAF; Air Marshal Sir Charles Burnett, RAAF (with his back to the camera); Rear Admiral J.J.A. van Staveren, RNN; Rear Admiral A.F. Palliser, RN (hidden by van Staveren); Vice Admiral Sir Geoffrey Layton, RN; Vice Admiral C.E.L. Helfrich, RNN; Hart; Rear Admiral W. R. Purnell, USN; Lieutenant General Hein ter Poorten, KNIL; Lieutenant Colonel P. G. Mantel, KNIL. Military History Section, Royal Netherlands Army

After a series of hurried consultations aimed at securing cover during his absence, Wavell left India on the fifth. Lieutenant General Sir Alan Hartley, G.O.C-in-C the Northern Command, temporarily took over from Wavell as commander in chief, India. Wavell stopped over at Singapore, where the situation was deteriorating with alarming rapidity, before travelling on to Batavia, which he reached on 10 January. Immediately on arrival Wavell began a series of talks with a galaxy of senior officers from the four Allied nations in order to set up the headquarters and commands for the theater. After yet another visit to Singapore (13/14 January), when Wavell made the cardinal error of not insisting upon the dismissal of the incompetent governor and his colonial secretary, Wavell returned to Java to assume command of the ABDA theater at noon (local time) on 15 January.

In the first days of the command Wavell as bedevilled not only by a series of distinctly unhelpful and increasingly anxious signals from London (normally about Singapore) but by two of the "loose ends" that really should have been settled before the command was activated. As it was, with his command beginning to slither with increasing speed towards defeat, Wavell was forced to turn part of his attention to matters of marginal importance when set against emerging threats to the integrity of his command.

The first of the loose ends concerned Australia. The very first signal that Wavell sent on 10 January concerned the status of Darwin and northern Australia, Wavell's original instructions being ambiguous on this matter. Since Darwin was the command's main port and no conceivable threat to it could be mounted except across the ABDA area, it was illogical not to have the port within Wavell's command. Wavell's line of reasoning was accepted, and on the advice of their Chiefs of Staff the Australian authorities, with a generosity that was uncharacteristic at this somewhat fraught time, assigned northern Australia north of a line between Onslow (Western Australia) and the southeastern tip of the Gulf of Carpentaria to ABDA Command with effect from 24 January. This gain was the only one registered by ABDA Command in its brief and ineffective existence.

The status of Burma was the other residual problem that affected Wavell. Apart from Malaya it was the only part of the Asian mainland included in the ABDA area. Just as political factors had precluded any part of China from being included within Wavell's command, so nonmilitary considerations had led to the inclusion of Burma.

The Americans regarded Burma as vital if China was to be kept in the conflict. For much of the war the Americans placed great store on Chinese participation in the struggle against Japan, believing that the Japanese commitment in China was a debilitating one, without which substantial Japanese forces would be diverted to the Pacific. This was never the case, and the Americans failed to realize both the passivity of Chiang Kai-shek's forces and the generalissimo's willingness to let foreign powers fight one another rather than becoming too involved himself. Chiang was more interested in consolidating his position inside China against internal enemies, particularly Mao Tse-tung's communist forces, than in expelling the Japanese. The Americans never appreciated that their massive wartime investment in Nationalist China was never to show a commensurate return.

In 1941/42, however, it seemed vitally important to keep China in the war. This meant retaining Burma, which represented, through the Burma Road, the only means of supplying China. Burma's retention was considered essential if for no other reason than its loss would present the Americans with all kinds of problems if they were to insist on trying to keep China going. Despite its physical separation from the rest of the theater, Burma was included in the ABDA area in order to show American resolve to maintain the China connection. This, in effect, was the Americans' chief concern in the war against Japan after Pearl Harbor, Australia, and the Philippines. Yet as soon as the British accepted the argument in favor of including Burma in the ABDA area, the Americans began to press for special command arrangements in Burma. At the 10 January meeting of the British and American staffs in Washington, the Americans suggested that they should assume control of communications from Rangoon to China and that an American officer should command American and Chinese aircraft that would have to be deployed from China if the inevitable Japanese invasion of southern and central Burma was to be forestalled.

The British were in an awkward position. They were sceptical of the value of Chiang Kai-shek to the Allied cause and had no faith in Chinese forces or security. But they needed help in holding Burma. There was never any question of the British accepting a divided command in Burma at a time when the country was undergoing its second command change in a month. Disaster was already threatening, but the British saw no reason to make it certain by creating a faulty command structure. Yet with Britain dependent on American supplies and the Americans of the unshakeable belief that they, unlike the imperialistic British, were politically acceptable to the Chinese, the British had to compromise. It was subsequently agreed that a U.S. liaison officer was to be appointed to China in a semipolitical, semimilitary role. He was to represent his country on any international war council that might be established in China, and he was to supervise and control all American aid to China. As part of his latter duties he was to assume responsibility for the control and maintenance of the Chinese section of the Burma Road, while British officers and officials were expected to comply with his views on matters affecting their part of the road. The American officer was also to command all American forces in China and any Chinese forces that Chiang Kai-shek cared to place under him. If such forces were deployed in Burma they would come under ABDA Command, Wavell being directed to ensure close coordination with British forces.

Much time was spent in the various exchanges that led to these arrangements, though they quickly fell apart under the weight of a Japanese attack far beyond Allied power to parry. But the arrangements did enrich military folklore by bringing onto the scene one of the most colorful commanders of the war, Major General Joseph W. Stilwell, who earned and consistently lived up to his dubiously endearing nickname Vinegar Joe. Among his least attractive traits as far as Chiang Kai-shek was concerned was that Stilwell saw through Chiang's posturing in no time at all. Stilwell's dubbing of Chiang as "the Peanut" is well known and is probably the single point by which Stilwell is remembered. Stilwell was a first-class soldier, and a disaster in China.

Wavell's first priority on arriving at Batavia was to organize commands and operational areas. Despite the evident goodwill on all sides, this task was not an easy matter, partly for political reasons and partly because there were few Allied officers in the Far East with established international reputations that would make them immediately acceptable to Allies. Only two officers in the general area, Wavell and MacArthur, enjoyed a standing that transcended national and service boundaries. It was obviously both unwise and undesirable to try to put these two together in a team, particularly since the increasingly delicate situation on Luzon meant it hardly would be possible to recall MacArthur at this time. Command appointments had to be filled by officers who were not only unknown to one another but virtually unknown outside their own national services. There was so little time available to the Allies that appointments had to be made from the ranks of officers who were already in what had been nonoperational commands rather than waiting for specially selected officers to be sent out to the theater.

Wavell's two most important subordinates were obviously his deputy and his chief of staff. Lieutenant General George H. Brett, USAAF, was chosen as Wavell's deputy. He had been en route to Chungking at the start of the war and had been ordered to take up the post of commander of U.S. Army Forces in Australia. He relinquished this post when he became deputy supreme commander, though he was to return to it when ABDA Command was dissolved. Lieutenant General Sir Henry R. Pownall, the British commander in chief, Far East, was appointed Wavell's chief of staff. In recognition of what was by then an established fact, Pownall's command was dissolved on his appointment to the ABDA staff. Admiral Thomas C. Hart, commander of the U.S. Asiatic Fleet, retained his national command but assumed the post of commander, ABDA naval forces (ABDAfloat), while another survivor of the Philippines debacle, Major General Lewis H. Brereton, USAAF, took on the role of commander, ABDA air forces (ABDAair) pending the arrival in Java of the ABDAair-designate, Air Chief Marshal Sir Richard E. Peirse, RAF. Lieutenant General Hein ter Poorten, Netherlands East Indies Army, the commander of Dutch military forces in the Indies, took up the appointment of commander, land forces (ABDAarm).

The Americans and British balanced command appointments between themselves, with only the merest nod in the direction of the Dutch and Australians. As in the case of Wavell and Brett, they ensured that every commander had a deputy of different nationality. In addition, all three nations immediately involved in the theater of operations retained their own service commands.

Hart's deputy and chief of staff was Rear Admiral A. F. Palliser, former chief of staff to Phillips and Force Z. The senior British naval officer in the Far East, Vice Admiral Layton, reassumed his old post of commander in chief, Eastern Fleet, on the death of Phillips and shifted his headquarters from Singapore to Batavia. There he took part in the preliminary confer-

Three faces of impending defeat. General Sir Archibald Wavell, supreme commander of ABDA forces; his deputy, Lieutenant General George H. Brett, USAAF (right); and his naval commander, Admiral Thomas C. Hart, USN (center). Military History Section, Royal Netherlands Army

ences that actually established the command, but after ABDA Command began to function he transferred his flag to Ceylon, since his responsibilities with the Eastern Fleet embraced the Indian Ocean and the defense of Indian waters as well as the ABDA area. He retained his post until March, when he made way for Vice Admiral Sir James Somerville, who had moved eastwards with the nucleus of a new Eastern Fleet; Layton took over the crucially important task of commander in chief, Ceylon, then obviously under threat of Japanese attack. As commander in chief, Eastern Fleet, Layton nominally remained in command of British naval forces that were in the ABDA area because they were part of the Eastern Fleet. In reality, however, British warships were under the command of Commodore John A. Collins, RAN. Vice Admiral Conrad E. L. Helfrich remained commander in chief of Dutch naval forces, with tactical command of Dutch forces being invested in Rear Admiral Karel W. Doorman. Hart's billet as ABDAfloat commander resulted in command of the U.S. Asiatic Fleet devolving upon his chief of staff, Rear Admiral W. R. Purnell, with Vice

Admiral William A. Glassford commanding afloat. Glassford's command, the nucleus of the Asiatic Fleet, was Task Force 5.

From a naval point of view the whole of the ABDA area was treated as a single operational area with no subordinate or area commands within it. Theoretically Hart was in command of all naval forces and he was empowered for specific operations to establish a Combined Striking Force from the ships of all nations. In reality, the creation of ABDAfloat did nothing to ensure unity for there was little change from the previous situation. The British preoccupation with escorting troop convoys into Singapore led them to establish Collins's ships on 20 January as the inappropriately named China Force, and to keep them in the western part of the ABDA area in order to achieve this objective. Glassford's brief was to ensure the security of the eastern approaches to the Indies and to aid the defense of both the Indies and northern Australia. Though Purnell established himself at Soerabaja, Task Force 5 divided its attention and time among Soerabaja, the Lesser Sundas, and Darwin in order to cover reinforcements and supplies being sent into the Indies. The Dutch had the major part of their forces on the Java station.

The Anglo-American arrangements placed the British and the Americans in the fortunate position of being able to count on the Dutch for support without the Dutch being able to obtain any compensatory advantage in facing up to the Japanese thrusts into the northern Indies. One of Wavell's first directives as supreme commander was to instruct the Dutch to support British operations designed to get convoys through to Singapore. Though Doorman was to be appointed commander of the Combined Striking Force when this formation was established on 1 February, against the wishes of Hart and Palliser, these arrangements were a constant source of anger to the Dutch who, after all, had more to lose and contributed more in naval and air terms to ABDA's defense than the British. Helfrich was particularly bitter, and he felt his exclusion from overall command most keenly. His bitterness is understandable when it is realized that the Dutch admiral was native-born and was fighting not merely for queen and empire, but also for homeland. To Helfrich the policy of holding onto the flanks and making major efforts to reinforce Singapore was madness, since the Japanese for the most part were unopposed as they came through the center. His resentment at being excluded from command was not mere pique. His own headquarters at Batavia would have been the ideal location for ABDAfloat headquarters, but that was tucked away miles into the interior at Lembang, virtually out of touch with naval units and certainly with no direct communications with Dutch naval headquarters. Helfrich was virtually ignored by Hart and Palliser, and the only way the Dutchman was kept informed about ABDAfloat intentions was through a Dutch officer on Hart's staff acting in a personal capacity. Problems of command organization were not helped by personal antipathies or by the fact that the one success the Allies enjoyed at sea, the action off Balikpapan, came about as a result of much goading and needling of ABDAfloat by Helfrich. In the end Dutch anger at what seemed to them to be their Allies' dilatoriness in facing up to the real dangers to the Indies could be calmed only by a political sleight of hand that saw Hart relinquish operational direction of ABDAfloat in favor of Helfrich on 12 February because of "ill health." Roosevelt and his senior political advisers were quite prepared to see Hart leave the Indies at this stage of the campaign. With the Indies clearly on the brink of defeat and the Americans having been able to pull back most of their ships to Australia, the Indies were obviously no place to leave a four-star American admiral in command.

The arrangements of ABDAfloat, however, were simplicity itself when compared to those of ABDAair. Brereton, as commander, had a Dutch deputy and an Australian liaison officer with him, but reverted to deputy commander when Peirse arrived in Java towards the end of January. Peirse and Brereton commanded their respective national contingents and Lieutenant General Ludolph H. van Oyen commanded Dutch air units. For operational purposes, however, the ABDA Command was divided into five air subcommands. These were Norgroup, covering Burma; Wesgroup, covering northern and central Sumatra, Malaya, and western Borneo; Cengroup, consisting of southern Sumatra and western Java; Easgroup, comprising eastern Java and the eastern Indies; and Ausgroup, covering the northern Australian subarea after it became part of ABDA area. In addition, ABDAair established a reconnaissance force that was divided among four of the groups, Norgroup being the exception.

The division of the command into groups was inevitable given the size of the theater, but the obvious complexity of the arrangements, which were heavily weighted towards the west in the areas of Singapore, southern Sumatra, eastern Java, and western Borneo, where the immediate threat to the Indies was least apparent, could hardly be expected to work smoothly, given the speed with which the subcommands were constituted. But the cause of smoothness was not aided by three developments. First, Royal Air Force units that were either evacuated from Malaya and Singapore or flown in from the Indian Ocean to Sumatra refused integration into Wesgroup until after the last of the British troop convoys had been escorted into Singapore. It was not until 7 February that ABDAair took over command of RAF and RAAF units in the Wesgroup area. Though on several occasions during the war the RAF obstinately and willfully chose to go its own way in spite of orders, the manner in which a British supreme commander and a British air commander tolerated a freewheeling organization within

Wesgroup smacks of tacit collusion in the pursuit of a national interest at the expense of a wider inter-alliance commitment.

Second, in setting up ABDAair the British insisted upon the command being organized along the lines of British practice. The Royal Air Force was an independent service and there was no army aviation and no naval aviation except on carriers. All shore-based naval aviation was a responsibility of the RAF's Coastal Command, which was the Cinderella of the service. The RAF was supposed to allocate sufficient resources to Coastal Command to enable it to support the navy effectively. In practice it rarely did so, and the division of command was a serious handicap to the British conduct of naval operations between 1939 and 1942. The Dutch (and less importantly the Americans) had air forces directly integrated into their army and navy commands. Because the Dutch had to conform to British practice, Dutch air power, which would not have been strong enough in any case to meet the Japanese challenge, was wrenched away from its parent organizations just at the time when it was desperately needed to carry out the functions for which it had been trained and organized. This was particularly disastrous for the Dutch navy because its ships lost their reconnaissance force, without which the Dutch had no real chance of fighting the Japanese successfully. In an improvised command structure, Dutch aircraft could hardly be expected to perform effectively, unless, of course, the headquarters of ABDAfloat and ABDAair were colocated. Predictably, inevitably, they were not.

The third development was this simple fact. With ABDAair moving its headquarters from Lembang to Bandoeng in the course of the campaign because of lack of sufficient accommodation (the need for more accommodation grew in inverse proportion to the number of aircraft available), after January 1942 the headquarters of the air and naval commands were not even in the same town. Throughout the campaign in the Indies Allied naval movements were plagued by lack of reconnaissance and air cover, a failure that stemmed in large part from the command weaknesses built into the Allied organizational structure at British insistence.

Ter Poorten, ABDAarm commander, had a British deputy and chief of staff, Major General Ian S. Playfair, later one of the official British historians of the war. The obvious physical separation of various land areas dictated a division of the land forces into subcommands. Burma was placed under Lieutenant General T. J. Hutton, who was replaced by General Sir Harold H. Alexander in the course of the campaign. (Hutton was informed of the change on 21 February, in the midst of the Sittang River disaster, and of the reversion of Burma to India Command.) Malaya was under Percival; the Philippines under MacArthur; and U.S. Army Forces in Australia initially under Brereton's command (at one time he held three command appointments simultaneously) and then under Major General Julian F.

Barnes, U.S. Army. Subsequently the Darwin subarea under Major General D. V. Blake, Australian army, became part of ter Poorten's organization. The ABDAarm commander retained his command of Dutch forces in the Indies, but never exercised any form of control or direction over the Philippines. Throughout the lifetime of the ABDA Command the Philippines was treated as an entirely separate theater.

It is hard to think of a command structure that summed up better the collective weaknesses of the Allied nations, but in the circumstances of the time it is hard to see how these arrangements could have been bettered. ABDA Command made mistakes, but the greater mistake was in being organized in days to rectify the errors and omissions of years. It was a hopeless task. The day that Wavell arrived in Batavia the Japanese arrived off Tarakan in their first moves against the Indies. By the time the command was activated the Japanese had secured the first critical breakthrough in the northern Indies. By 15 January the situation in Burma was threatening, the position in Malaya was critical, and the American cause in the Philippines was past recall, even though the defenders on Luzon had weathered the initial assault on their positions on Bataan. The future promised, or threatened, only disaster. The broad outlines of Japanese intentions could be discerned; they were governed by the need to secure airfields built up by the Dutch in order to fight an invader in the outlying parts of the Indies. Yet without massive naval and air reinforcements Wavell could do little to halt or even delay the Japanese advance.

The questions of deploying forces within and of the provision of reinforcements for the ABDA area were obviously critical because in the Indies Wavell faced on a large scale the same problem that Percival had faced in Malaya. This was the time problem between the speed of the Japanese advance and the rate of Allied reinforcements becoming available. In many ways the provision of reinforcements was the acid test of Anglo-American sincerity in defending Southeast Asia, just as the deployment of reinforcements within the theater was certain to be the measure of Wavell's foresight and generalship. There was little the Americans and British could send to the area; what little was available, therefore, had to be deployed in a manner best designed to frustrate Japanese intentions. The paucity of reinforcements, the lack of available shipping, and the speed of the Japanese advance were certain to restrict the Allies to a single reinforcement opportunity. Unless Wavell managed to get his sums right the first time he asked, there was little prospect of his being given a second chance. Even if he did come up with the correct answer, it might not be enough to avert defeat.

The various national governments were responsible for sending reinforcements to the ABDA area. The deployment of these reinforcements once they were within the theater of operations was the prerogative of the supreme commander. Under the complex and cumbersome chain of command established at the Arcadia Conference, Wavell had to answer to two authorities, one in London and the other in Washington. Any proposal, request, or assessment Wavell might make had to be sent to both capitals. London then would signal Washington whether or not the British Chiefs of Staff planned to forward any views on the matter. If the British did not comment the Combined Chiefs of Staff would decide policy before reporting to Roosevelt and Churchill for final decisions. If London acquiesced in the decision, appropriate orders would be issued from Washington.

Explicit in this arrangement and the whole of the Arcadia discussions was the Anglo-American assumption of their unimpaired direction of the Allied war effort against Japan, with what was a de facto division of strategic responsibility between the British in the Indian Ocean and the Americans in the Pacific. Australian attempts to secure a formal inter-Allied body in Washington to settle the strategic direction of the war were thwarted; both the Americans and the British, for their different reasons, were opposed to the demand. The British were prepared to argue with the Australians, but not in front of the Americans. As a means of calming the disgruntled Australians, Churchill on 19 January proposed the establishment of the Far East Council in London. This council, which was to review strategy in the Far East, consisted of the British prime minister; his Chiefs of Staff; and Australian, British, Dutch, Indian, and New Zealand ministerial representatives. Though a similar organization was later established in Washington under American auspices, the British intention in proposing the council was to reinforce their position of primacy among the non-American Allied nations and to give the Dutch and Australians the means of expressing their views.

The first council meeting took place on 10 February, but by that time its meeting had become virtually pointless since the Allies that met in London were by then well on the road to defeat from which, in realpolitik terms, there was to be no recovery. Moreover, by the time the council first met it was becoming clear that the Australians, having been frustrated in some directions and successful in others, had read the fine print very carefully. They had realized that, just as the Americans and British retained the right to decide upon the troop levels they were prepared to make available to the ABDA area, the same right applied to them. And after the beginning of February the only troops that were available to reinforce ABDA Command were Australian. With the position of Singapore becoming ever more precarious and then, after 15 February, hopeless, the Australians were not inclined to fall in with the suggestion of Wavell and the British and American governments that Australian troops from the Middle East, then on their way across the Indian Ocean to Java and Sumatra, should be diverted to Burma. With the Australian refusal to concur with this suggestion, the last slim chance of retaining any part of the original ABDA area vanished.

At the Arcadia Conference the British and the Americans, having agreed on the places that had to be held if Japanese successes were to be stemmed, endorsed one another's initial decisions to reinforce their respective garrisons. They also planned for the garrisoning and reinforcement of a string of bases across the Pacific, bases the Americans needed in order to sustain Australia. The British decision was straightforward and confined simply to Singapore. This was endorsed by the Americans. The British had no means to attempt anything else and, in any case, the only area of real interest to them other than Burma was northern Australia, then beginning to be looked after by the Americans and Australians. On 28 December two convoys left Brisbane for northern waters. The transports *Aquitania* (44,786 tons), *Herstein* (5,100 tons), and *Sarpedon* (11,321 tons), with over 10,000 tons of supplies and nearly 5,000 Australian troops, sailed for Port Moresby in New Guinea in the company of the *Australia, Canberra, Perth*, and *Achilles*. This convoy was preceded by the *Pensacola* convoy making its way to Darwin with troops tasked to secure the port. In theory the movement was the first stage of the support for the Philippines. In reality, though a battalion from the 131st Field Artillery Regiment made its way to Java and defeat, the Americans were establishing themselves at Darwin on a permanent basis. The same day the importance of Darwin was underlined by the arrival in the port of the heavy cruiser *Houston* and the destroyers *Alden, Edsall*, and *Whipple* from Task Force 5 with the invaluable support ships *Otus* (a 6,750-ton destroyer tender), *Pecos* (a 5,400-ton oiler), and *Golden Star* (a transport of 4,860 tons).

But the Americans could do little more for Australia for the moment. They did have troops and transports available to send to the Pacific, but they would take time to cross the Pacific and their numbers would be reduced by the demands of garrisoning the islands of the Pacific needed to maintain Allied lines of communication. These islands were Palmyra and Christmas islands in the Line Group, Canton Island in the Phoenix Islands, Samoa on the direct Pearl Harbor to Australia route, and Bora Bora in the Free French Society Islands on the Panama to Brisbane run. The Americans also recognized the need to support the New Zealand garrison at Suva in the Fiji Islands and the wretchedly equipped Free French at Noumea on New Caledonia. Both the New Zealanders and the Free French reinforced their garrisons in the first week of the war. As with Amboina and Timor (both reinforced by the Australians during December), and Nauru and Ocean Island (garrisoned with half-batteries of artillery in February 1941 to deter German raiders), these islands shared the common characteristics of being so important and so undergarrisoned as to invite attack. The Americans had to be selective because they did not have sufficient troops to hold all these places in strength. The Americans planned to send nearly 40,000 air and ground troops to the Pacific and Australia, and nearly 30,000 set out from the United States in January. But this force, though surprisingly large for the Americans so soon after the start of the war, was small in comparison to needs and the vastness of the combat zone.

As the American convoys moved across the Pacific in early February, their progress was covered by Rear Admiral Wilson Brown's Task Force 11, which left Pearl Harbor on 31 January. This force consisted of the *Lexington*; the heavy cruisers *Indianapolis, Minneapolis, Pensacola,* and *San Francisco*; and ten destroyers. After it had completed its convoy duty, the task force was assigned to the Anzac area, partly to buttress the Anzac Force, partly to reassure the Australians and New Zealanders, but mainly to carry out a raid against Rabaul. Though this raid had to be abandoned when it was compromised, the force stayed in the general area to cover the occupation of New Caledonia by the Americal Division* in March and to join with the *Yorktown* in a raid against Japanese positions on New Guinea in April. The Australians had had their insurance policies paid up for them: the U.S. Navy had arrived in the waters of the Southwest Pacific.

These decisions and actions, of course, had immense repercussions for ABDA Command and particularly the Dutch. The British order of priority was Singapore, India with Burma, northern Australia. The British government saw fit to reinforce Singapore and Wavell was to see no good reason to alter that decision. He therefore sanctioned the effective writing off of two divisions—his last reinforcements—in an increasingly hopeless cause on peninsular Malaya. The last convoy reached Singapore on 5 February and two days later Wavell began the diversion of a British armored brigade to Burma from its intended Javanese destination. On 13 February, just before Singapore capitulated, the supreme commander raised the matter of diverting the 6th and 7th Australian Divisions to Burma. The reaction of Canberra to this suggestion was glacial. If Java and Sumatra were to be conceded then the only place that these divisions would go was to Australia. With the Americans, on the other side of the ABDA area, fixing their priorities as Pearl Harbor, Australia, the Philippines (though written off), and Burma, two implications were becoming obvious. Java, to the Americans and British, was a nonpriority, and the Australians would not be able to fight for the island if their two major allies would not help to defend it to the end. When it came to the crunch, the Dutch in the Indies were on their own. Moreover, reinforcements would not be forthcoming, and without them there was no hope of stopping the Japanese. Not all these events were

*The Americal was formally constituted as a division in May 1942.

obvious before the unfolding of events revealed them to be so, but they did become clear as the floodtide of defeat mounted and overwhelmed ABDA Command. In this situation Wavell, rather then commanding in the midst of defeat, presided over a disaster, and presided in a manner that hastened rather than delayed the end—an end that the hapless Dutch had to face almost alone.

CHAPTER 10

The Breaking of the Dutch, 11 January– 21 February 1942

By the end of 1941, after just three weeks of war, it was clear to the Japanese high command that the way was open for it to begin to strike at the main objective for which Japan went to war—the islands of the Dutch East Indies and, in particular, oil-rich Borneo, Java, and Sumatra. By that time the Japanese, by securing all their primary objectives, had obtained the essential prerequisites for an attack on the Indies. The islands of the central Pacific were secure; the islands to the east of New Guinea were clearly doomed. There was little possibility of any substantial American move in the central Pacific that could deflect the Japanese from operations in the Indies. Thailand had capitulated on 9 December. Northern Malaya had been overrun and the offensive was being developed beyond the Perak into central Malaya with considerable ease and success. The Americans seemed on the brink of defeat on Luzon, while Davao and Jolo had been secured and were in the process of receiving Japanese aircraft on their airfields. The Japanese, therefore, felt free to develop their offensive into the Indies, secure in the knowledge that no real threats to their flanks and rear could present themselves and that they were faced by a collection of enemies decidedly inferior, in the air and at sea, to the Japanese forces available for strikes into the Indies.

The ultimate objective of the Japanese attack on the Indies was the island of Java, the richest of the islands and the site of Batavia, present-day

Jakarta, the capital and largest city in the Indies. The Japanese planned to take Java by a double envelopment from the east and west once two initial requirements were fulfilled. The first was that in the west Singapore had fallen or was poised to fall before operations began against southern Sumatra. These operations were in themselves a prelude to further operations over the Sunda Strait. Second, the Japanese intended to secure certain air and naval bases in the outlying and central parts of the Indies, in particular on the islands of Borneo and Celebes, from which the effectiveness of Java's defenses could be broken prior to invasion.

The plan that the Japanese pieced together for their invasion was a skillful blend of a variety of air, sea, and land forces into a strategically brilliant but tactically cautious mosaic. It was designed to ensure that at every stage of their operations the Japanese ran as little risk as possible and were able to bring a crushing superiority of force, particularly in the air and at sea, against their enemies. At the same time the Japanese planned to synchronize their attacks so that covering forces could provide mutual support, should the need arise. This also ensured that they could catch and keep the Allies off-balance and unable to concentrate to meet any of the threats that developed as the Japanese broke into and through the shell of the outer Indies.

The main cutting edge of the Japanese attack was to be their air power. In support of their operations the Japanese deployed on Jolo the 23rd Air Flotilla and on Davao the 21st. The Japanese planned to mount their seaborne assaults behind a front secured by naval aircraft; at no stage did the Japanese amphibious forces contemplate a move against an objective beyond the range of their air cover. The Japanese planned to fight for and secure air supremacy over Allied air and naval bases that were themselves the objectives of the Japanese amphibious attacks; once these bases were secured by assault the Japanese planned to move their aircraft forward to repeat the process, all the time closing in on Java. The initial Japanese moves were to come in the center, against eastern Borneo, and in the east, against eastern Celebes. The central thrust, backed by the Jolo-based aircraft, was to be mounted from Davao across the Celebes Sea to Tarakan Island off Borneo, and hence via the Makassar Strait against first Balikpapan and then Bandjarmasin. The eastern thrust, supported by the 21st Air Flotilla, also was staged from Davao but moved southwards across the Celebes Sea to attack objectives on three of the four peninsulas that form Celebes. In turn these objectives were Menado, Kendari, and Makassar.

Obviously both thrusts were important and their final success would be interrelated, but of the two, the eastern prong of the attack was more crucial. It was assigned objectives in addition to the opening up of the route for a direct assault on Java and the other islands east of Java that made up the Malaya Barrier. By directing the eastern thrust through the Molucca Sea into the Banda and Flores seas the Japanese not only ripped apart the eastern approaches to Java but also paved the way for securing Amboina Island, off Ceram, and the joint Dutch- and Portuguese-owned island of Timor. The possession of both islands in the course of the campaign came to be considered of critical importance by the Japanese. By taking first Menado and then Amboina the Japanese would cut off the southern Philippines from any means of reinforcement by air from Australia except by long-range bombers, while by securing Timor they would sever the direct air link from Darwin in northern Australia via Koepang to Soerabaja in eastern Java. In order to help secure these islands, where the Japanese might reasonably expect to encounter as strong an Allied resistance in the air as the Allies were capable of mounting, the Japanese deployed parts of Nagumo's carrier task force to help in reducing the Allies. Nagumo's forces were by far the most powerful of the forces available to the Japanese, and they were not to be confined to striking merely at Amboina, where the Japanese knew that soon after the start of the war the Allies had attempted to concentrate a bomber force. Once Kendari and Amboina were secured and handling Japanese aircraft, Yamamoto planned to strike at Darwin, which was fast becoming the key Allied port through which reinforcements and supplies for the Indies had to be channelled. Nagumo's carriers were to form part of the strike against Darwin. Later they were to pass through the Timor Sea in order to deploy to the east and south of Java, thus adding to the process of trying to keep the Allies guessing as to future Japanese intentions, offering distant support as the central and eastern thrusts coverged on Java, and, at all times, checking both the movement and freedom of Allied naval units.

While the plan by which the Japanese intended to break Allied resistance in the Indies was by any standard impressive, no less notable a feature of it was its economy of effort. In carrying out a series of operations of short duration and limited intensity during the invasion of the Philippines, the Japanese had used substantially the same forces repeatedly, while in the South China Sea covering forces had doubled up in supporting the succession of operations in Thailand and Malaya, British Borneo, and the Philippines. Now, there was less need to support forces firmly established ashore in Malaya and the Philippines, and these same naval forces were redeployed forward for operations against the Indies.

The main weight of the Japanese assault was to fall on the central and eastern parts of the Indies. The western thrust was the least important in the sense that it could not be started until the latter stages of the Malayan campaign, by which time the central and eastern thrusts should have secured considerable if not decisive success. The Japanese timetable, however, precluded the closing of Java from the east until the western thrust was developed. The Japanese deployment and concentration of their forces reflected this imbalance between the western and the other two axes of advance. Kondo's heavy force, which had provided distant support for operations in the South China Sea, returned to the Pescadores on 11 January, leaving only Ozawa's light carrier *Ryujo* and her powerful escorting force of five heavy crusiers and a destroyer flotilla to cover subsequent operations in British North Borneo, along the Malayan coast, and subsequently against southern Sumatra. Most of the destroyers used in close cover for forces invading Thailand and Malaya subsequently participated in the latter operation.

Kondo's battle force—two battleships, three heavy cruisers, and six destroyers—was thus at the Pescadores when the first Japanese landings in the Indies took place. Its absence was not missed; there was little need for such a force in the preliminary operations in the Indies. The battle force was needed to cover the deeper advances into the Indies, and as a result it was deployed to Palau. The day after Kondo's ships reached the Marshalls, the sixteenth, they linked up with the 2nd Carrier Division, the *Hiryu* and *Soryu*, in the company of one heavy cruiser and two destroyers. These two carriers had been detached from Nagumo's force, which had been deployed to assist the assaults on New Britain and New Ireland that were to take place at the same time as the Japanese struck beyond the outlying parts of the Indies. The two fleet carriers were to act as the spearhead of the moves against Amboina and into the Banda Sea, while Kondo's heavy ships patrolled an outer ring between Mindanao, Palau, and northern New Guinea, the open flank to the Pacific. Though the 2nd Carrier Division was given additional destroyers as well as a light carrier, a seaplane tender, and heavy cruisers to support its operations, the cautious disposition of the battleships and the forward deployment of the carriers seems very strange. Even allowing for the fact that the carriers had the support of shore-based aircraft and had submarines from the 4th and 5th Flotillas in front of them, this appears to have been a reversal of the natural order of things, with aircraft carriers operating in front of battleships. Admittedly, it was a deployment practiced in the interwar period, but it suggests either a lingering battleship mentality on the Japanese part or extreme confidence in both the ability of the carriers and the weakness of the Allies.*

The other part of the jigsaw involving the heavy forces was the remaining four carriers and their escorts, and they were to fit into the picture after their sortie against Rabaul, 20/23 January, when they returned to Truk.

---

*Two other matters arise from this disposition of forces. It was strange to put two of the most important ships of the navy into the forefront of the battle. Equally, it was strange to put battleships, limited in their effectiveness to horizon range, to guard a flank that the enemy could approach only with carriers. The episode, though small and of little consequence, does seem rather odd and perhaps indicates that the Japanese had not fully absorbed the principles and importance of carrier warfare.

While they were there the American raid on the Marshalls and Gilberts of 1 February was mounted. This drew the Japanese carriers eastwards in a futile chase until the fourth, when they were recalled, the *Shokaku* and *Zuikaku* to Japan to watch the eastern approaches, the *Akagi* and *Kaga* to Palau, where they linked up with the 2nd Carrier Division on 8 February. Nagumo's task force thereafter constituted exactly the same ships, the 5th Carrier Division excepted, as deployed at Pearl Harbor. It was this force that broke through the Banda and Timor seas to attack Darwin on 19 February.

Numerically the strongest part of the Japanese strength in equatorial waters was therefore concentrated at Davao for the central and eastern thrusts into the Indies, the preliminary operation in the center being against Tarakan and in the east against Menado. These forces were composed of most of the ships that had taken part in the preliminary and main-force landings on Luzon and the operations against Davao and Jolo. These ships, with four destroyers transferred after 18 January from Kondo's command once they had escorted a troop convoy from Hong Kong to the southern Philippines, were the workhorses in the invasion of the Indies. They participated in a succession of operations that tore the Allied defenses apart. By staging most of their operations through Davao the Japanese were free to transfer units from one area of operations to another, and it was inevitable that the composition of various task forces should alter in the course of operations. Losses, ships out of service because of marine or war damage, and the need to juggle resources in the light of an objective's importance and the degree of risk involved in an operation all combined to produce considerable variation in force organization during the campaign. Yet the basic composition of the forces involved was established at the outset and remained throughout the duration of the campaign. For the eastern and central thrusts, excluding Kondo's force and the eighteen ships under Nagumo's command, the Japanese deployed a total of one light cruiser, four seaplane tenders, three heavy and three light cruisers, thirty destroyers, and a considerable number of minesweepers, minelayers, submarine chasers, and patrol boats. When all the forces deployed in southern waters—these units plus those of Kondo, Nagumo, and Ozawa—are taken together, one begins to realize both the scale of Japanese operations and the importance to the Japanese of securing the resources of the Indies. The land forces might be small, but the major part of Japanese naval aviation was involved and, excluding the submarine arm, about half the strength of the Imperial Navy was deployed in direct or distant support of these operations.

Hardly a good omen for the Japanese in the invasion of the Indies was the loss of the services of one of their heavy cruisers, the 13,380-ton *Myoko*, as a result of an attack by ten Flying Fortresses on Japanese shipping in Malalag Bay, Davao, on 4 January. The *Myoko*, one of the last of Japan's cruisers to complete a yearlong refit before the start of the war, suffered sixty-four dead and wounded when one of her three forward turrets was struck by a single bomb. Two other Japanese warships, the *Myoko*'s sister ship the *Nachi* and the seaplane tender *Chitose*, were damaged by bomb splinters, but only the *Myoko* had to return to Sasebo for repairs. (She returned to operations on 26 February and was one of only two Japanese heavy cruisers to survive the war, though at the end she had been so damaged by American and British submarine attacks that she was incapable of action.)

Without radar Japanese ships were always vulnerable to an undetected air attack, but on this occasion their luck held. Three days later the Japanese ships involved in the invasion of the Indies began to slip out of anchorages at Davao and Jolo. First to leave were the sixteen transports carrying Major General Shizuo Sakaguchi's *56th Regimental Combat Group* and the *2nd Kure Special Landing Force* to Tarakan. These sailed in the company of three minelayers, six minesweepers, three submarine chasers, and four patrol boats (modified ex-destroyers). A covering force of one light cruiser and seven destroyers under Admiral Shoji Nishimura was in attendance. On 9 January ten transports, carrying the marines of the *1st Sasebo Special Landing Force*, cleared Davao en route for Menado in the company of five mine-sweepers and two submarine chasers. Rear Admiral Tanaka, with one light cruiser and eight destroyers, was in support. Covering the progress of both invasion forces was a task force consisting of the seaplane tenders *Chitose* and *Mizumo*, two heavy cruisers, and escorting destroyers in the Celebes Sea, aircraft from the two shore-based flotillas, and submarines. Despite this air cover the Tarakan force was bombed during passage by Flying Fortresses from Malang Field near Soerabaja in Java, but without result.

Tarakan was rich in oil fields and had an airfield and harbor. These three prizes were what drew the Japanese on the afternoon of 10 January to the island where they were to lose two minesweepers, *W13* and *W14*, to coastal artillery on the twelfth. The destroyer *Asagumo* was also damaged when she touched bottom, but in return the destroyer *Yamakaze* sank the minelayer *Prins van Oranje* as the Dutchman tried to escape to the south. The Dutch fired the oil wells and over 100,000 tons of stored oil and carried out demolitions on the airfield with the approach of the Japanese. The latter came ashore on the night of 10/11 January and forced the surrender of the 1,300-strong garrison on the morning of the twelfth.

Across the Celebes Sea neither Menado in particular nor Celebes in general had mineral wealth comparable to that of Tarakan and Borneo. Menado was an objective merely because of its air base, and its 1,500 defenders, only one-quarter of whom were regulars, could not hope to hold

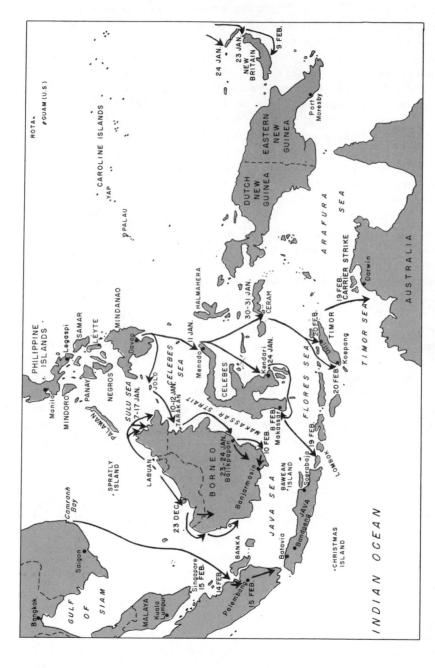

Japanese Strikes against the Dutch, 23 December 1941 through 21 February 1942

off a double envelopment of the tip of the peninsula as the Japanese landed near Menado and Kema in the early hours of the eleventh. These landings were so successful that there was no need for the first-ever Japanese airborne operation later in the morning, when 334 paratroopers from the *Yokosuka Naval Air Landing Force* were dropped all over the northern part of the peninsula. The paratroopers, who were staged through Brunei, were badly dispersed in the drop and played no effective part in the operations. Dutch resistance was slight, but denial was effective and it took until 24 January to bring the airfield back into operation. At Tarakan, on the other hand, despite Dutch air raids on 13 and 14 January, the airfield was handling aircraft from the 23rd Air Flotilla as early as 17 January, partly because the *2nd Base Unit* had been embarked with the Tarakan force for the purpose of speedily bringing captured installations back into service.

Repairing the airfields at Menado and Tarakan and bringing up the 2nd Carrier Division preceded the next phase of Japanese operations. This involved the reduction and occupation of Balikpapan in the center and Kendari in the east with simultaneous air strikes mounted by the 21st Air Flotilla and the carriers against the concentration of Allied air power that the Japanese wrongly believed to be based on Amboina.

Orders for the resumption of the offensive were given on 17 January, the same day as the *Hiryu* and *Soryu* arrived at Palau. Both invasion forces, constituting the same military forces and roughly the same fighting ships that made the initial assaults, left their newly won bases on 21 January. Bad weather shielded the advance on Balikpapan, with the result that the invasion force escaped air attack until after it arrived off the port on the afternoon of 23 January. By the night of the twenty-third the invasion force had come to anchor and was putting men ashore against a background of the fiercely burning town. The Dutch garrison commander, disregarding a Japanese ultimatum not to destroy the installations, fired the oil wells on the approach of the Japanese. The Dutch garrison of 200 men did not attempt to stand and fight for the port but withdrew into the interior, first to Samarinda airfield, some 120 miles from Samarinda itself, and then, when pressed by the Japanese, to Tenggarong and Muaramuntai, where the Japanese finally forced their surrender at the end of the campaign in the Indies.

Arriving off Kendari on the morning of the twenty-fourth, the Japanese also encountered bad weather. This proved providential for the American seaplane tender *Childs*, which was leaving port just as the Japanese came into sight. Two of Tanaka's eight destroyers closed the *Childs*, but she slipped into a rain squall and, despite a subsequent attack by six Zeros, made good her escape. Ashore, events moved more smoothly for the Japanese. Only two men were wounded in overcoming a Dutch resistance that did not merit the description "token." By the evening the airfield was in the service of the 21st Air Flotilla, which in the meantime had been softening up Amboina. Amboina was thoroughly raked over on 24 and 25 January, after which the *Hiryu* and *Soryu* turned for Palau.

The Japanese, however, did not have things all their own way. The American submarine *Swordfish* sank the 4,124-ton transport *Myoken Maru* and damaged another merchantman off Kendari on the twenty-fourth, while one of the four destroyers from Hong Kong that arrived at Kendari as reinforcements for the operation, the *Hatsuharu*, was damaged by U.S. aircraft the same day. By that time, however, far more severe damage had been inflicted on Japanese forces off Balikpapan.

Japanese preparations at Tarakan for the Balikpapan operation prompted the now-activated ABDA Command to try to contest the landings with surface, submarine, and air units. The Japanese ships had not even come to anchor before three B-17s attacked them, damaging but failing to sink two transports. The next Allied representative to arrive on the scene was the Dutch submarine *K-XVIII*, one of eight Allied submarines directed to Balikpapan. Though the Dutchman failed in an attack on the flagship *Naka*, the boat slipped past the screen to sink the 7,000-ton transport *Tsuruga Maru* at about midnight. Immediately the Japanese escorts hauled off to seaward to begin hunting for the submarine, thereby leaving a wide gap between themselves and their consorts.

It was this gap that four American destroyers from Task Force 5 entered shortly afterwards. Glassford's ships had been at Koepang Bay, Timor, on 20 January when they received orders to set course for Balikpapan. In passing through the Sape Strait, between Flores and Saembawa, the light cruiser *Boise* ran aground and was forced to retire to Java, while the light cruiser *Marblehead* developed engine trouble. She was ordered to proceed via the Lombok Strait to take up a covering position in the southern Makassar Strait while the four destroyers of Commander Talbot made their attack.

Talbot chose to advance on a northwesterly course in order to take the Japanese ships when they were silhouetted against Balikpapan's burning oil installations. His force arrived just after the Japanese escorts began their search for the *K-XVIII*, leaving the way clear for Talbot's ships to make a high-speed run against the anchored, defenseless transports. Their run to the north was singularly ill-rewarded. Probably because of excessive haste and certainly because of faulty torpedoes, the Americans scored no successes, but in a more deliberate run to the south they sank three transports and a fast assault boat and damaged two more transports. By the time the Japanese grasped what was happening and realized that they were faced by Allied surface ships, there was only time for the briefest artillery exchange as the American ships headed for home at their best speed. To add insult to Japanese injury, on 26 January an air attack caught and destroyed the valuable aircraft depot ship *Sanuki Maru* the day after she, with other transports and escorts, had arrived off Balikpapan.

For both the Japanese and the Allies the action of Balikpapan was an unsatisfactory affair. With so much strength in the area the Japanese should have been overinsured against such a reverse, but the very nature of their forward movements over widely separated areas always ran the risk of surprise by an enemy force with the tactical advantages of choosing when and how to mount small but damaging raids. For the Americans, the first surface action since 1898 involving U.S. warships should have been more decisive; with the advantages of first sight and attacking out of a dark background against silhouetted targets, the Americans should have exacted a heavier toll of Japanese shipping.

The first Allied naval victory of the war had very little appreciable effect on Japanese operations. The Japanese were made a little cautious by the experience, but in reality they had enough resources at hand to take their losses in stride, and the action did not delay Japanese operations into the Indies by as much as a single day. (In fact at this time the forthcoming invasion of Amboina was brought forward by a week.) The Japanese had too much force in the area and too many advantages of geographical position for their overall strategy to be much affected by losses that, at this stage in the war, could be absorbed easily. Nevertheless, the real significance of the action was that in the long term Japan could not afford a succession of Balikpapans because she lacked the replacement facilities and trained manpower to cover such losses. Yet her plans for conquest and maintenance of a perimeter line condemned her to fight such actions, which were certain to become increasingly difficult as Japanese transports were forced to operate in disputed waters without guaranteed air cover. Within just a year of Balikpapan the Japanese were to abandon the struggle to hold Guadalcanal after suffering, in the Solomons, a series of defeats that were similar in character to the action of 24 January 1942.

One of the most unfortunate aspects of the Pacific war is the manner in which interpretation of events surrounding the eclipse of Japanese power invariably concentrates on the great carrier battles that resulted in the annihilation of Japanese naval air power. There were in fact three quite distinct but related aspects of the destruction of Japanese naval power. The major fleet actions, of which those in the Coral Sea, at Midway, in the Philippine Sea, and in Leyte Gulf were by far the most important; the utter annihilation of the Japanese merchant marine; and the crushing of Japanese light forces in scores of small and savage actions, normally fought at night, among the islands of the South Pacific. Balikpapan was the first of the actions that were to see the breaking of Japanese attempts to sustain their forward forces.

At the time, however, such matters were very much for the future. In the immediate context the situation that was developing was one full of peril for the Allies and promise for the Japanese. The thrusts that secured Balikpapan and Kendari must be seen in two contexts: the immediate theater of operations in the central and eastern Indies; and, more widely, in conjunction with the almost contemporaneous operations against eastern Johore, British North Borneo, and Dutch West Borneo to the west and Rabaul to the east. In the immediate context the seizure of Kendari resulted in the Japanese securing use of what was generally regarded as the finest airfield (completed in 1940) and harbor in the Indies. By securing Balikpapan the Japanese cleared the way for their air power to dominate the southern approaches to the Makassar Strait. By taking Kendari the Japanese secured a springboard for an operation to pocket Amboina and, inevitably, Timor; by capturing Balikpapan the route to Java itself was laid bare. In taking both Balikpapan and Kendari the Japanese secured the means to break the whole of the Allied position in the eastern Indies, thereby cutting off Java from possible sources of succor from that direction. In the wider context the Japanese successes were rather like a wet blanket being brought down on the glowing embers of Allied resistance: burn marks were to show through but only briefly and ineffectively. The results of the Japanese gains were stifling. Their successes unmistakably pointed to the complete isolation of Singapore and to total Japanese domination of the South China Sea, the baring of southern Sumatra to invasion, Japanese domination of the Java Sea, the rupture of the Allied positions in and around Timor and the Lesser Sundas with the subsequent exposure of northern Australia to attack, the isolation of New Guinea, and the menacing of Allied positions in the islands of the Southwest Pacific. And the Japanese attack in the Indies was only beginning.

The forward impetus of the Japanese invasion of the Indies was checked after the capture of Balikpapan and Kendari not because of the losses the Japanese suffered off these ports but because the Japanese chose to advance their timetable and secure their left flank before developing their offensive against the Lesser Sunda Islands. The cause of their immediate concern was the island of Amboina, which was held by a regimental group of 2,600 Dutch and native troops and an Australian infantry battalion. After the start of hostilities a squadron of Australian Hudson bombers was stationed on the island. Though this force was small, it was enough to worry the Japanese. They were not to know that after the fall of Menado the bombers had been withdrawn and that Amboina could no longer impose any real delay on or loss to the Japanese advance.

To reduce Amboina the Japanese planned and executed what was, in effect, a triple envelopment. The Japanese planned for their normal nighttime landings in the early hours of 31 January. Accordingly, on the twenty-seventh five transports, in the company of two destroyers and two submarine chasers, nosed their way out of Davao. The transports carried the *228th Infantry Regiment*, fresh from its triumph at Hong Kong; the two destroyers, the *Arashio* and *Michishio*, had been part of the force that had brought the regiment across from the Asian mainland on 18 January. The *228th* was to land on the southeastern coast of Amboina with the aim of securing Ambon. On the twenty-eighth six transports carrying the *Kure 1st Special Naval Landing Force* left Menado in the company of a light cruiser, six destroyers, and some minesweepers, with two of the destroyers and two of the minesweepers doubling as transports. The marines were to land on the northwestern coast of Amboina with the aim of securing the airfield near Laha. Close support was provided from Kendari by the ubiquitous seaplane tenders *Chitose* and *Mizumo* and an assortment of destoyers and lighter craft. A heavy cruiser force provided distant cover from the Celebes Sea.

The transports arrived off Amboina late on the thirtieth and began to put men ashore exactly on schedule; one minesweeper-transport was lost in the process on a minefield. The Japanese quickly secured the surrender of the encircled Dutch garrison at Paso, captured the airfield on 2 February, and forced the capitulation of Ambon on the third. By the next day virtually the whole of the island was under effective Japanese control.

Though Allied resistance on Amboina was as unavailing as it had been elsewhere, it was certainly more substantial than anything the Japanese had encountered to date. There was even an attempt by some isolated infantry sections to remain in the field after the surrender of the main forces, but this fell apart within a week. In a sense, however, Amboina was a sign of the shape of things to come. As the Japanese broke through into the inland seas they were certain to encounter growing, if still ineffectual, Allied resistance. The Dutch, fighting on what was to them virtually the only home soil not under enemy occupation, would make their stand in the defense of Java. The Americans were beginning to become more organized though their supply services, particularly for their submarines, remained very weak. The British, too, could be expected to devote growing resources to the struggle to save the Indies. The decision to withdraw from the Malayan peninsula to Singapore Island, plus the safe escorting of the troop convoys carrying the 18th British Division into Singapore at the end of January, spelled a lessening of British naval commitments to Malaya and Singapore.

On 1 February Admiral Hart constituted the Combined Striking Force. In doing so he faced three major problems, even though on paper his force of heavy and light cruisers and destroyers seemed substantial. First, for the immediate future there was little prospect of any major British participation in the force, and it was utterly essential to deploy the force quickly if it was to be effective at all. British responsibilities had lessened after the Singapore decision, but nevertheless remained great, especially in the Indian Ocean. Second, while for the immediate moment the Combined Striking

Force was confined only to Dutch and American ships, the force itself was not concentrated. Indeed, on 1 February when the force was instituted, Dutch ships were searching the Karimata Strait (between Borneo and Sumatra) for what Hart knew to be a nonexistent Japanese force. Clearly there were major command and organizational problems on the Allied side; these were inevitable given the fact that ABDA Command and the Combined Striking Force were scratch formations. The striking force had no experience of working as a formation. Crews of the various nations had no knowledge of their allies' personnel, methods, communications, and battle procedures; while both ships and men of all three services were beginning to feel the strain of two months of intensive and continuous service without proper maintenance and rest. Third, and most critical of all, whatever Hart did manage to scrape together, he did not have air superiority or the initiative. Both were held firmly by the Japanese. However powerful Hart's formation might become in terms of artillery, it would not have sufficient aircraft either to protect it or to strike hard at the enemy. At every stage the Combined Striking Force could at best only try to respond to events—without air cover.

The Balikpapan setback, while it did not delay the Japanese, did force them to recast their plans. Originally the Japanese planned to move with their naval forces directly against Banjarmasin, even though the town was many miles from the coast and the river on which it stood was too shallow for the transports to navigate. The Japanese had planned to make their move at the same time as their forces at Kendari moved against Makassar. After the Balikpapan action, it obviously was dangerous to leave anchored transports at the mouth of the Barito, where they were easily within range of Allied aircraft on Java and possibly subject to another destroyer raid. These factors led the Japanese to modify their plans for an assault for which they believed they had an inadequate number of escorts. The Japanese divided their forces in order to continue their operations. While a small detachment remained in control of Balikpapan and forces harried the Dutch garrison in the course of its thirteen-day withdrawal northwards to Samarinda II airfield, the Japanese planned to advance on Banjarmasin from two directions. The main force would advance overland while a small force moved around the coast of Borneo, the two arms of the pincers coming together at Banjarmasin and its airfield at Ulin. Accordingly, on the twenty-seventh a group began to move by barge slowly and cautiously southwards down the coast, occupying Kota Baru in order to pass safely between Borneo and Laut Island. It then landed on Borneo some 50 miles southeast of Banjarmasin and began an overland advance. This group reached Banjarmasin on 10 February, when it linked up with the main force, a battalion group drawn from the *146th Infantry* that had set out from Balikpapan on 30 January. This group had made the short sea crossing to Tanahgrogot, after which the transports had been withdrawn to Palau for refuelling. The unit moved directly across the mountains, securing first Mura Uja and then, on the morning of 10 February, the Ulin airfield. By the evening of the tenth the town of Banjarmasin itself had been fully occupied and the reconcentration of the Japanese forces had been completed, but it was not until the twenty-fifth that the Japanese were able to put the airfield back into service. The Dutch had effectively demolished the major installations in the area before the garrison of about 470 men had pulled back to Kotawaringin airfield, from which it had been withdrawn to Java.

To cover the initial movements on 31 January the Japanese used some of their naval forces in a demonstration in the southern part of the Makassar Strait. This, plus the knowledge of Japanese shipping concentrations at Balikpapan and Kendari, served to convince ABDA Command that the Japanese were making their next move, though it was not exactly clear whether Banjarmasin or Makassar was to be the Japanese objective. To deny the Japanese access to the southern part of the strait, Hart ordered the Combined Striking Force to sea under Doorman.

Doorman slipped out of the Bunda Strait at about midnight, 3/4 February, with a force of one heavy American cruiser, one American and two Dutch light cruisers, and seven destroyers, three of them Dutch. With the mountains of Bali still visible in the morning sunlight, this force was set upon by thirty-seven twin-engine bombers, plus a fighter escort, from Kendari. The Japanese aircraft were on a mission against Soerabaja when they came across the Allied force, which had only four flying boats in company. Japanese fighters accounted for these. When the ships were attacked they scattered in an effort to break up the attackers and allow the antiaircraft guns a clear selection of targets. While these tactics were successful initially, it was inevitable that at some stage the warships would begin to suffer. The flagship *de Ruyter* was hit and her antiaircraft control knocked out, but it was the American cruisers that took the brunt of the attack. The heavy cruiser *Houston* was struck on her main deck aft and lost her rear turret with almost its entire crew burned to death. The *Marblehead* fared even worse, taking a series of near-misses that jammed her rudder to port, causing a starboard list and flooding fore and aft, and threatening to break the ship's back. Two bombs on board did massive damage, including tearing back the after deck like the opened lid of a gigantic sardine tin. Doorman had little option but to abandon his mission. Forming a protective screen around the *Marblehead*, which could be steered only by her screws, he set course via the Lombok Strait for Tjilatjap, a port beyond the range of Japanese aircraft. The second Allied naval attempt to meet the Japanese challenge with surface warships had thus ended in defeat with the loss of the services of two cruisers.

The defeat augured ill for the Allies not just because future naval

Rear Admiral K.M.F. Doorman, RNN, commander of the Allied strike force established in the Indies. He was lost in the *de Ruyter* at the Battle of the Java Sea, 27 February 1942. Naval Historical Department, Royal Netherlands Navy, The Hague

operations were almost certain to take place under similar conditions but also because from 4 February onwards the tempo of Japanese operations increased dramatically. Air operations against Allied airfields and installations were stepped up considerably, with the Japanese significantly electing to hit the Darwin to Koepang to Soerabaja air ferry route with a damagingly successful strike against American aircraft on Timor on 5 February. But the real rise in tempo was best expressed in amphibious operations. In the course of a little more than two weeks the Japanese were to undertake four more landings, fight one light force action, and commit their carrier forces in a series of hammer blows that reduced the Allied position to near-debris. It was this series of operations that effectively doomed Java even before the battles for the actual island took place.

The characteristic symmetry and synchronization of the initial thrusts through the Makassar Strait and Molucca Sea were to be maintained, even though the Banjarmasin operation was scaled down in naval terms. But the thrusts were also expanded by the development of the western lunge from the South China Sea via the Karimata Strait against southern Sumatra. The attacks were not quite in phase, but this was of small account; the Japanese advantages of position, timing, and air supremacy were enough to paralyze any Allied response.

The first operation to get under way was that directed against Makassar. Six transports carrying the Sasebo marines cleared the new base at Staring Bay, Kendari, on 6 February. The Balikpapan episode and the obvious risks of breaking into the central Indies were reflected in the scale of protection the Japanese afforded this force. With the seaplane tenders and heavy cruisers back beyond the horizon in support, the Japanese provided three fast patrol boats, two submarine chasers, two minesweepers, a light cruiser, and no less than eleven destroyers for the close escort. Four more destroyers and four minesweepers came across from Balikpapan to support the landings on 8 February. For the loss of ten men killed and wounded the marines secured Makassar. The only real opposition to the operation came from the American submarine *S-37*, which torpedoed the destroyer *Nat-sushio* late on the eighth. The destroyer foundered in a gale the next day. Doorman raised steam with two cruisers and two destroyers when news of the invasion came in, but quickly abandoned his sortie when it became clear that he was too weak and too late to affect the issue on southern Celebes.

On the night of 8 February, too, the Japanese began their crossing of the Johore Strait against Singapore Island. This was the signal for unleashing the western thrust into the Indies in the pursuit of three immediate aims. These were to secure first Banka Island, which was responsible for 10 percent of the world's tin production, and second Palembang, the center of the Sumatra oil industry and the only major source of oil in the Indies still remaining in Allied hands. Only after these areas were reduced and the Japanese position in southern Sumatra was consolidated could the Japanese turn their attention to their third objective, the move against Java itself.*

The forces that the Japanese assembled at Camranh Bay for these operations were considerable. The army element consisted of two infantry regiments, the *229th* and *230th*, from the *38th Infantry Division*, which arrived in Indo-China from Hong Kong on 20 January. An advance guard, drawn from two battalions of the *230th*, sailed on 9 February in eight

*During the Malayan campaign the Japanese high command became convinced that, rather than wait for the fall of Singapore before starting their move against southern Sumatra, it was in their interests to seal off Singapore from the outside world by beginning their operation against Palembang before Singapore was assaulted or fell. In fact, the Japanese had to delay their operation against southern Sumatra, putting it back from the tenth to the fifteenth, because Kuantan airfield could not be readied in time.

transports in the company of one light cruiser, four destroyers, five mine-sweepers, and two submarine chasers. The main force, all the *229th Infantry Regiment* and the remaining battalion from the *230th*, sailed on the eleventh in thirteen transports with an escort of a light cruiser, four destroyers, one general-purpose frigate, and a submarine chaser. The small size of the close escort for both convoys was offset by Ozawa's covering force of one light carrier with its forty-eight aircraft, one light and five heavy cruisers, and five destroyers, which sailed on the tenth.

Ozawa's force, especially when backed by shore-based aircraft from Kuantan, was more than strong enough to deal with any force that could be pitted against it, but in moving southwards it happened upon a host of ships carrying refugees from Singapore to Sumatra and Java. The outcome was predictable as upwards of forty ships, ranging from 8,000-ton tankers to the meanest motor vessels and yachts, were dispatched by gunnery and air-craft, with unknown hundreds of Allied personnel killed in the process. Among the ships lost was the patrol ship *Li Wo*, which took on one of the invasion convoys with its single 4-inch gun and rammed one of the trans-ports in a vain attempt to "take one with her." For this act her captain, on the word of a beaten enemy after the war, posthumously received the Victoria Cross.

The slaughter of shipping from Singapore did not go unnoticed by the Allies, even though they could do nothing to prevent it. Japanese prepara-tions were known to the Allies, who discovered the convoys in the South China Sea and noted that they were joined en route by a variety of craft, particularly small and shallow-draft vessels from Indo-China and Borneo. Allied aircraft discovered that Japanese shipping was congregating near the Anambas—and becoming disorganized as the warships fell in with fleeing Allied ships—and guessed that Palembang was the intended Japanese destination. This was confirmed on the thirteenth when a single Allied reconnaissance aircraft found that the Japanese ships were clear of the Anambas and heading south.

There could be no question of the Allies not seeking to contest the invasion of southern Sumatra. Withdrawing to fight battles in areas of one's own choosing on shorter lines of communication is an obvious and essential feature of the defense, but in Malaya this feature of warfare had become virutally synonymous with not fighting at all. There was nothing at all to be gained by withdrawing into an area that the enemy could dominate both geographically and in terms of concentrated firepower. As it happened, one of the most regrettable features of the Indies campaign from the point of view of the Allies was that when they came to fight the battles for Java, they had ceded too many advantages to the Japanese to have any real chance of success. But for southern Sumatra the Allies had to fight. Palembang was the center of the rich Sumatra oil industry, while the southern part of the island was the shield of Java in the same way as the north was the shield of

Singapore. If the south was lost Java was as good as written off. Resistance had to be offered if for no other reason than because the Dutch demanded it. Dutch tempers were beginning to fray as a result of Japanese success, their own powerlessness, and the apparent American and British tendency to regard the Indies as ultimately expendable. The Dutch wanted to fight.

Thus, when the Japanese progress beyond the Anambas was discovered, Wavell ordered Doorman to take the Combined Striking Force to meet the Japanese. This was no easy task because Doorman's units were scattered; a major part of his force was south of Bali on escort duties, while the *Exeter*, the only heavy cruiser available, was south of the Sunda Strait. By late on the fourteenth Doorman had assembled north of Sunda Strait a force consisting of the *Exeter*; the Dutch light cruisers *de Ruyter*, *Java*, and *Tromp* and the Australian light cruiser *Hobart;* the Dutch destroyers *Banckert*, *Kortenaer*, *Van Ghent*, and *Van Nes*; and the American destroyers *Barker*, *Bulmer*, *John D. Ford*, *Parrott*, *Pope*, and *Stewart*. By that time Doorman knew that the advance Japanese echelon had reached Banka Island and was either off or in Moentok harbor, ready for an assault up the Moesi River on Palembang.

The problem for Doorman was that he had to decide from which direction to approach Moentok. The direct approach was the narrow Banka Strait, but lacking air cover and faced by the possibility of the Japanese having mined its waters, the strait presented hazards that would have made most commanders hesitate. The alternative was to sweep east of Banka and come into Moentok from the northeast, thus falling on the enemy rear. The danger of this course for a force that had to remain intact was that it came close to Ozawa's force. Even excluding the *Ryujo*, this force was vastly superior to the one under Doorman's command. Any one of the five Japanese heavy cruisers—the *Chokai* and the whole of the *Mogami* class—outgunned the *Exeter*.

Ozawa had his problems as well; though they were not those of mere survival, as was the case with Doorman, they remained very real. Ozawa had a very tight schedule to meet. The Japanese wanted to capture Palembang's two airfields, P. 1 and P. 2, and the oil installations at Pladjoe and Soengai Gerong intact. To this end they mounted a series of small airborne operations near these objectives on the morning of the fourteenth. For their operations the Japanese used about 360 paratroopers. The Dutch deployed seven battalions throughout Sumatra, mostly in the south.* The Japanese therefore planned to get their amphibious forces up to Palembang by or on

---

*To put matters in their correct perspective, one must note that seven battalions were lost in so vast an area. Sumatra, with an area of about 165,000 square miles, is larger than Japan and almost as large as Britain and West Germany combined. In the area of Palembang the problems of numbers-to-space reflected the wider Sumatra situation. P. 1, Soengai Gerong, and Pladjoe were within 10 miles of Palembang, but P. 2 was 50 miles away from Palembang with virtually no major or even minor settlements between the two.

Vice Admiral Jisaburo Ozawa, commander of the carrier and cruiser support force during the invasions of Malaya and the western Indies, and during Operation C, the raid in the Indian Ocean. The last carrier commander, he led the surviving Japanese carrier forces at the Battles of the Philippine Sea and Leyte Gulf. U.S. Navy

the fifteenth; the airborne troops could not reasonably be expected to hold beyond that date. Ozawa therefore had to get his convoys to their landfall in time to be effective, but his primary concern was obviously the safety of the convoys themselves, particularly the main-force convoy bringing up the rear. Yet the aggressive and astute Ozawa, who with fatalistic brilliance was to play the part of sacrificial carrier admiral at the Battle of Leyte Gulf in 1944, would never forego the chance to annihilate the only substantial Allied naval force operating between Japan and Australia.

When Ozawa received warning on the fourteenth that Doorman's force was approaching by the main channel, he ordered his advance force to move up the Moesi beyond the river bar, where it would be safe from attack, and instructed the main-force convoy, then east of Lingga Island, to double back northwards and await developments. Ozawa then stood southwards to meet the Combined Striking Force, which by this time had lost the service of two of its destroyers. In coming north the *Van Ghent* had been lost when she struck an uncharted reef off Banka and the *Banckert* was detached to pick up survivors. Ozawa intended to use his aircraft to destroy the effectiveness of the Allied force and to close with his cruisers, but his aircraft were too few in number to be effective. They were all high-level bombers, and there were no dive-bombers or torpedo-bombers to add variety to a repertoire that Allied seamen were becoming used to. The bombers used the same routine to the extent that Allied ships could anticipate their point of release and take evasive action accordingly. By putting the rudder hard over and then coming back amidships in order to prevent the steering gear being jammed when hard over, the Allied ships, which stayed concentrated in order to combine their firepower, escaped being hit.

Nevertheless, by early afternoon Doorman abandoned his mission. His ships were becoming dispersed and ammunition was running low. Doorman's position, without air cover, was as unenviable as his decision was ultimately inevitable. Even though Ozawa's aircraft had been found tactically wanting, they had proved to be strategically adequate. The Allied force, with only two destroyers damaged by near-misses, had been repelled and then harried in the course of its withdrawal; with the turn of the Allied ships to the south the security of the Japanese convoys had been assured and the path for the approach on Palembang had been cleared. This was just as well for the Japanese because the airborne forces ashore were being given a rough time.

At the time when Ozawa's ships were indulging themselves on the evacuation fleet from Singapore and shaping up to deal with Doorman, the Japanese paratroopers were encountering a fiercer resistance from the Allies around Palembang than might have been expected from the experience of previous actions. At the end of the fourteenth the Japanese held only P. 1, the Allies having evacuated the base after a hard day's fighting. P. 2 and Soengai Gerong had been held throughout the day by the Dutch with no major difficulty. At Pladjoe the initial Japanese onrush had secured the oil installations, but a determined counterattack had driven out and dispersed the Japanese. The damage done to the installations in the course of the fighting proved too great for a proper demolition program to be put into effect.

By the morning of the fifteenth the Dutch had regrouped and there seemed little to prevent the annihilation of the Japanese force on P. 1. But two factors served to swing the balance the Japanese way. First, the force on P. 1 was augmented by another airborne company that was dropped in. It was not much, but it was just enough to hold. Second, at the time when Ozawa's aircraft were attacking Doorman's ships, the Japanese advance up the Moesi began to materialize. On the previous night the advance echelon shed one company to garrison Moentok and then transshipped into barges and various assault boats for an advance by river on Palembang. Throughout the day (the fifteenth) Allied aircraft on Sumatra (thirty-eight bombers and twenty-two of the Hurricanes flown in by the *Indomitable*) carried out a series of attacks on the advancing Japanese units. During these operations the advancing Japanese lacked air cover; Ozawa's aircraft were already committed and the Japanese simply did not have enough aircraft to contest Allied air superiority. Though the Allied aircraft sank one small transport and imposed losses and delays on the Japanese, they could not halt the offensive. It was this thrust up the river that checked any Dutch attempt to deal with P. 1 and, indeed, in the long run made the defense of the whole Palembang area untenable. As the Japanese advance up the Moesi took shape, the Allied evacuation of Palembang began, and on the night of 15/16 February Japanese amphibious forces and the paratroopers at P. 1 linked up. The Japanese main force arrived at Palembang on the seventeenth at a time when the advance echelon set off towards Oosthaven on the Sunda Strait in pursuit of the Allies.

By 17 February, however, virtually all the Allied forces in southern Sumatra had been evacuated across the Sunda Strait. The premature nature of the withdrawal was indicated not merely by the masses of equipment abandoned in the chaos of the retreat but also by the fact that on the nineteenth, with Oosthaven still unoccupied by the Japanese, a British landing party returned to the port and salvaged a great deal of aircraft equipment before returning to Java unmolested. In reality, however, it did not matter very much whether the withdrawal from Palembang and southern Sumatra was premature or not; the unpalatable and simple fact was that Sumatra had been lost to the Allied cause within three days. By their evacuations of 16/17 February the Allies tacitly recognized that the Japanese had secured a vice-like grip on Java from the west. On 17 February, moreover, three operations in the eastern Indies were launched that in the space of three or four days reduced to zero the chances of retaining Java. By these actions the Japanese secured from the east a grip on Java as strong as the one they had already secured on the island from the west.

These three operations were the strike by carrier and shore-based aircraft on the northern Australian port of Darwin, the invasion of Bali, and the landings on Timor. All three took place roughly within twenty-four hours of one another, between the morning of 19 February and the early hours of 20 February. The Bali operation provoked an engagement in the Badoeng Strait on the night of 20/21 February. Bali itself was secured by the Japanese with little difficulty, but it was not until the twenty-fourth that the Japanese managed to overcome resistance on the divided island of Timor.

The main aim of all three operations was to cut off Java from the east. The Japanese motive in attacking Bali was to secure the island as a forward base for subsequent operations against Java. Possession of the island would give the Japanese an air base at Den Passar that was both more serviceable than that at Makassar and within one hundred miles of Soerabaja and major Dutch installations in eastern Java. The reasoning behind the Timor attack

KNIL troops returning to Batavia, Java, after the fall of Palembang, southern
Sumatra. Military History Section, Royal Netherlands Army

was that Japanese possession of Koepang would sever the fighter air link
between Java and Australia. The logic behind the Darwin operation was
that it would deal at the source with the problem of Allied supplies to the
Indies.

The Darwin operation was the first of the expeditions to get under way,
the initial orders for the raid having been issued on 8 February with the
carrier force leaving Palau a week later. On 17 February it put in at Kendari
before beginning a high-speed night passage across the Banda Sea to be in a
position to launch its aircraft from the Timor Sea on the morning of the
nineteenth. For the attack the four Japanese carriers launched a total of 188
aircraft—36 fighters, 71 dive-bombers, and 81 level-altitude bombers—
while the 21st Air Flotilla joined in with about 50 bombers from Amboina
and Kendari.

Though Darwin received from coast-watchers on the island of Bathurst
a last-minute warning of an impending air strike that was only one aircraft
less than the 7 December first-wave attack on Pearl Harbor, the Japanese
achieved as complete a surprise at Darwin as they had over Oahu some ten
and one-half weeks earlier. But in several significant ways the attack on
Darwin differed from that on Pearl Harbor. There were few warships in
the harbor at Darwin at the time of the attack and, though they were given
special treatment by the attacking aircraft, they were not the main objective
of the Japanese attack. In contrast to Pearl Harbor, at Darwin the Japanese
spread their efforts, attacking the dockyard installations, the oil depot, the

airfield, and the town as well as shipping in the harbor. In the Pearl Harbor operation, as we have seen, the Japanese concentrated against military targets but neglected critically important port facilities.

Darwin was totally ill-prepared to meet the demands of becoming a major military base for operations in the Indies. Its air defenses were minimal and there were virtually no antiaircraft guns ashore. Its single wharf allowed the handling of just two ships at a time, and some ships in the harbor on the nineteenth had been there since the sixth without having been fully unloaded. A cyclone had shut down the port from the second to the tenth, but its effect was minimal compared to what hit Darwin on the morning of the nineteenth. The wooden town was savaged and set on fire and the airfield was mercilessly strafed. About twenty aircraft were destroyed, at least four of them in the air when they were caught returning to Darwin after abandoning an attempt to fly to Koepang because of bad weather. The wharf and dockyard installations were wrecked in the very first blows, which severed the oil and water pipes. Burning oil poured into the sea, licking around an increasing number of sinking and damaged ships. Eleven warships, transports, merchantmen, oilers, and auxiliaries, the *William B. Preston* included, suffered various degrees of damage though the *Preston* herself managed to get to sea and escape to Broome in northern Western Australia. The American destroyer *Peary* and nine merchantmen and auxiliaries were sunk or beached. Perhaps the most unenviable fate suffered that day befell the Chinese crew of the Australian merchantman *Neptuna*, whose cargo included depth charges. As the burning oil from the fractured mains engulfed the ship, the crew had the choice of jumping to certain death in the burning sea or waiting for death either in the fires on the ship or when the cargo exploded. About 550 Allied personnel were killed and wounded in the course of an attack that effectively wrote off Darwin for some time. The Japanese are reported to have lost five aircraft, though only two were lost by the carriers that reached Kendari on 21 February, the same day as Kondo's heavy force, which had come down from Palau, put into the port.

Both the Bali and the Timor invasion convoys sailed on 17 February, the Bali force from Makassar, the Timor force from Amboina. The Timor force comprised parts of the *228th Infantry Regiment* and the *Yokosuka Naval Air Landing Force*, the paratroopers being used in a marine role. For the invasion the Japanese had to plan for two quite separate operations to take the only places of any value on Timor. These were Koepang, capital of Dutch Timor, in the extreme southwest, and Dili, capital of Portuguese Timor, on the northeast coast. The invasion force that sailed on the seventeenth was directed to Koepang. It consisted of nine transports in the company of the light cruiser *Jintsu* and her eight destroyers. A second convoy, sailing the following day, consisted of five transports, two destroyers, two minesweepers, and a number of submarine chasers. This invasion force was destined for Dili where, since 17 December, 400 Australian and Dutch troops had been stationed, much to the annoyance of the Portuguese authorities. The Allied nations had been concerned for the safety of Portuguese Timor because the Japanese had shown considerable interest in it before the start of the war. The Portuguese feared that the uninvited presence of the Allied force would induce an attack that otherwise might be avoided, and they guessed that, in the event of such an attack, the Dutch-Australian force would be too weak to resist the Japanese successfully. The only attempt by the Allies to send further reinforcements to the island was mounted on 15 February from Darwin, but the attempt was abandoned the next day when the troop convoy was ineffectually attacked by Japanese aircraft. The Portuguese were right on both counts. The Japanese had not originally intended to move against Dili, yet the Allied occupation of Portuguese Timor did in fact provoke an invasion that the Allies could not hope to defeat.

The Japanese synchronized their convoy movements across the Banda Sea in order to arrive off Timor during the night of 19/20 February. The landings took place in the early hours of the twentieth. In the south two infantry battalions, plus a light tank detachment, made the assault and advanced on the heavily bombed capital, while airborne forces from Kendari were dropped well behind Koepang, near the airfield, in order to encircle the garrison. The Allied forces were unable to break through the encirclement on February 21 and 22, and on the twenty-third most of the Allied forces that had not capitulated on the twenty-first, after the first Allied failure to break out, laid down their arms. In the north Dili was taken by the Japanese after token opposition.

The odd feature of the Timor episode was that, unlike most operations in the Indies, except at Balikpapan and in northern Celebes, enough Allied forces to prove significant evaded capture and took to the interior. Timor was small, but it was large enough to support a guerrilla struggle because the terrain was difficult enough to impede motorized formations but not so difficult as to hinder fast movement by guerrillas. Unlike the situations at Tarakan, Balikpapan, and northern Celebes, routes in Timor were not so limited as to impose severe restraints on forces in the hills. In short, Timor was ideal country for guerrilla warfare. Unlike the people in most parts of the Indies, whether in Dutch or Portuguese territory the population of Timor was well disposed towards the Allies. With few Japanese left to occupy Timor, about 420 Allied personnel, roughly divided equally between the Dutch and Australians, carried out a guerrilla campaign that grew in intensity after April as the Allied forces began to get food stocks organized. For the best part of six months these forces enjoyed some success, but their position became increasingly precarious after November, when the Japanese set about a systematic destruction of villages and food stocks in Allied-controlled areas. The evacuation of most of the Allied forces took place in December 1942 and was completed, by American submarines, in February 1943—almost a year to the day after the Japanese landed on Timor. Nevertheless, the simple fact was that by 24 February 1942 all the places of major importance on Timor were in Japanese hands and on that day the Japanese transports and warships that had taken part in the operations sailed for Makassar.

It had been from Makassar on the night of 17/18 February that the advance echelon of the Bali invasion force sailed. The whole Bali operation was in fact an afterthought on the part of the Japanese. The operation was decided upon in late January when the limitations of the airfield at Makassar became apparent. Makassar airfield was frequently closed in by bad weather, and Bali was considered the best alternative. The unit earmarked for this operation was an indication of the somewhat improvised nature of the invasion. An infantry battalion from the *14th Army's 48th Infantry Division*, pulled out of Luzon after the fall of Manila and sent down to Makassar, was made the advance party. The main force was scheduled to reach Bali on 24 February.

The single battalion needed just two transports, the *Sagami Maru* and *Sasago Maru*. They were escorted by four destroyers, with a force of one light cruiser and three more destroyers providing distant cover for an operation that was certain to run some large measure of risk. The very closeness of Bali to Dutch bases on Java was what made Bali so attractive an objective to the Japanese. But the proximity cut both ways: the Japanese were carrying out an operation close to Allied air and naval bases in waters that were still disputed. The Japanese knew that they had to be quick in carrying out their landings at Sanur in the Badoeng Strait.

The Allies knew of Japanese intentions as early as the first week of February and were determined to try to deny the Japanese control of Bali. ABDA Command intended to concentrate Doorman's force to protect Bali as it became aware of Japanese preparations at Makassar. But at every turn events conspired to prevent the Combined Striking Force from assembling in time to contest the landing. Ozawa's thrust on Palembang drew Doorman westwards in a vain attempt to protect Sumatra at the very time when Doorman needed to stay in eastern Java to counter the threat to Bali. The need to disperse his force in order to refuel his ships after the Banka sortie meant that as the Japanese invasion force crossed the Java Sea Doorman was at Tjilatjap with two light cruisers and four destroyers. The light crusier *Tromp* was at Soerabaja and four American destroyers were refuelling at Ratai Bay in southern Sumatra against a somber backdrop provided by the Dutch destroying their oil dumps.

The Japanese invasion force reached Bali on the evening of the eighteenth and landings began on the following morning. A raid by Flying Fortresses resulted in the *Sagami Maru* being badly damaged, but during the afternoon she raised steam and with two destroyers as escort set course for Makassar. The *Sasago Maru*, in the company of the *Asashio* and *Oshio*, was preparing to sail for Celebes late that night when Doorman broke into the Badoeng Strait with two light cruisers, the *de Ruyter* and *Java*, and three widely separated destroyers, the *Piet Hein*, *John D. Ford*, and *Pope*. Doorman's force was spread over a distance of about 7 miles.

Doorman chose to make virtue of necessity and planned not to concentrate before a night action but to steam through the Badoeng Strait in three successive waves, first with his Tjilatjap force (less the *Kortenaer*, which ran aground leaving the harbor), then with the *Tromp* and the four American units, and finally with eight Dutch motor torpedo boats, which were to finish off anything left in the strait. He planned to use gunfire as the primary means of attack. Either of his first two echelons should have been powerful enough to deal with any Japanese force in the Sanur Roads, but the obvious weaknesses of Doorman's plan were its lack of concentration and reliance on gunfire in what was certain to be a high-speed night action in which the initial encounter would be against an enemy hidden against the black background of Bali.

The ensuing action in the Badoeng Strait was thoroughly confused, but the outcome was clear enough. Doorman's force and the Japanese sighted one another virtually simultaneously, and the two Japanese destroyers left their transport in order to gain sea room. Heading eastwards they crossed the *T* of the Allied cruisers, probably more by accident than design, and the two sides exchanged salvos at a mile's range. No hits were registered by either side. As the courses diverged fire was checked, the Dutchmen carrying on up the strait as planned, the Japanese destroyers steering east and then south, thereby falling in with the three Allied destroyers bringing up the rear. In a furious exchange of gunfire and torpedoes the Japanese sank the *Piet Hein* and forced the retirement of the *Ford* and *Pope* to the southeast. Such was the confusion surrounding this phase of the action that, as the American destroyers disengaged, the *Asashio* and *Oshio* (which had become separated) mistakenly engaged one another, fortunately for themselves ineffectively. Realizing their error, though neither ever admitted it, the destroyers took up formation and returned to the *Sasago Maru*.

Hardly had they done so when the second Allied force entered the strait, the four American destroyers leading the *Tromp* in a ragged line-ahead formation. Though the Japanese ships could not be identified with any certainty, the American destroyers fired torpedoes into the roadstead, whereupon the *Asashio* and *Oshio* came out to challenge a force that they in turn could not identify. When firm contact was made the two Japanese destroyers badly damaged the leading destroyer, the *Stewart*, and forced the Allied ships away to starboard, clear of the *Sasago Maru*. As the ships ran through the strait their tracks crossed, the Japanese taking up station next to Nusa Besar. As the Allied ships turned to the east to get clear of the strait, ranges shortened and a fierce action between the *Tromp* and the two Japanese destroyers took place. The *Oshio* was hit and the Dutch warship received such heavy damage to her superstructure that subsequently she had to retire to Australia for repairs. Immediately afterwards, with the Allied ships spread across the strait, the *Asashio* and *Oshio* turned back to their transport. Just afterwards the *Arashio* and *Michishio*, having been ordered to leave the *Sagami Maru* to make her own way back to Makassar, arrived on the scene. Their intervention, had it come a little earlier, might have been interesting, but in fact they blundered into the center of the Allied line. The *Michishio* was raked by Allied gunfire and stopped dead in the water, but the Allied ships showed no inclination to turn back and complete her destruction. The torpedo boats, coming through the narrows some time after these exchanges, failed to make contact with the Japanese.

Thus ended a series of actions known collectively as the battle of the Badoeng Strait. It was a dismally fought action on the Allied part, just one more defeat to set alongside the disappointments and failures at the Makassar Strait and Banka. In a series of actions a total Allied force of three light cruisers, seven destroyers, and eight torpedo boats failed to register even minor damage on two destroyers and a transport. Their only success was in badly damaging but not sinking a destroyer that came up late in the action. The cost to the Allies was a destroyer and a torpedo boat damaged on leaving the harbor, a destroyer lost, and a light cruiser and an American destroyer badly damaged. Undoubtedly the aggressiveness of the *Asashio* and *Oshio*, two destroyers that individually were more than a match for any single destroyer on the Allied side, was decisive in frustrating Allied intentions. But nothing could hide the fact that an operation that should have resulted in a comfortable Allied success ended in an unfortunate, if minor, tactical reverse.

But the failure to prevent the landings on Bali was the real defeat, one much more significant that the inability to deal with three Japanese ships. The implication of this failure, when taken in conjunction with the Darwin and Timor operations, was that the Japanese secured the pin on eastern Java just as effectively as they had already secured a pin on Java in the west. From the time that they secured their landing on Bali the Japanese achieved a position of overwhelming geographical advantage, overlooking the Bali and Lombok channels just as they did the Sunda Strait after their occupation of southern Sumatra. For the defenders of Java itself it must have seemed that with the fall of Bali the stone was being pushed across the mouth of the tomb. Their position, indeed, was hopeless, and perhaps it always had been. The Allied position in the Indies may have been hopeless from the outset, but after the fall of Bali it was evident that Allied resistance in the Indies had only a matter of days to run its course. The ground forces were too few to have any chance of holding any landings. All the time Allied naval power was being nibbled away in a series of unnamed actions. The destroyer *Van Nes* succumbed in the Banka Strait on 17 February and the following day the submarine *K-XII* was lost. Both were sunk by air action. By the time the Japanese main forces landed on Bali on 24 February ABDA Command had already estimated the life expectancy of its remaining air power at just two weeks. This assessment by Peirse was a correct one, though perhaps a little overgenerous: two weeks was the length of time left to the Allies on Java. Just twenty-two days were to separate the capitulation of Singapore and the Dutch decision to surrender in the Indies.

CHAPTER 11

Sunset for an Empire

WHEN WAVELL INTERVENED in the conduct of operations on the Malayan peninsula it was clear that the defeat on the Slim River removed any possibility of the British either retaining central Malaya or delaying the Japanese in that area for any appreciable time. As Percival and his subordinate commanders realized as well, Wavell was of the opinion that, while the Japanese still had to be delayed in central Malaya for as long as possible, if the British were to hold Singapore, they would have to stand in Johore. The battle there could not be long delayed, and extricating the mauled and dispersed British forces in central Malaya was an immediate priority. However disorganized these forces were, they had to be made available for the effort to hold Johore because, of the reinforcements promised Malaya Command, only the 45th Indian Brigade had arrived by 7 January. The state of training of this formation made even this a dubious asset. Johore, in effect, had to be held with what was already in Malaya in order to allow more battalions to enter the line as effective fighting units. In this Wavell and Percival were in complete accord.

These points were so obvious and critical to Wavell as to countenance no argument. Though he had yet to arrive in Java to take up his unenviable post as supreme commander, Wavell was well aware that he was involved in a race against the clock if he was to be successful in denying the Japanese mastery of Southeast Asia. Though the war was but a month old, the

Japanese had already secured so many advantages—in geographic position, concentration, and in air and sea supremacy—that their overall position was nearly overwhelming. They held the strategic initiative and could impose their will on an enemy whose land forces were dispersed and whose sea and air forces were considerably inferior to their own. Wavell was thus faced with awesome and daunting problems, "an option of difficulties," in his own and his biographer's words. He had to try to buy time for the Allies to bring reinforcements to the theater; without substantial reinforcement there was little prospect that ABDA Command could stem the tide of Japanese conquest.

In order to buy time and hold his command together, Wavell determined to hold the line of air and naval bases linking Singapore, southern Sumatra, Java, Bali, Timor, and Darwin. The main artery for ABDA Command between Singapore and Darwin was the bases through which reinforcements would be pumped into the command as (and if) they arrived from the Indian Ocean and northern Australia. This was the main reason for Wavell's immediate concern over the security of Singapore. Singapore was the sheet anchor in the west for Wavell's whole plan to hold the ABDA area, not just because it was the point of entry from the Indian Ocean but also because the whole campaign on Malaya tied down substantial Japanese land, air, and sea forces that otherwise would be directed against the western Indies with an all-too-predictable outcome. Even if Singapore proved unable to withstand assault, it was absolutely essential that it be held for as long as possible in order for the command to have any chance of retaining a grip in the western Indies.

The whole of the Wavell approach is open to censure, though it must be readily admitted that in the absence of adequate air and naval forces Wavell's position was almost certainly an impossible one; it is unlikely that any course would have substantially affected the outcome. But at this stage in the proceedings three major criticisms can be levelled against the Wavell approach. First, the concern he showed for Singapore involved such expenditures of resources, particularly of ground forces, that his approach almost certainly could never show an adequate return in a situation where the enemy held air and sea supremacy. Second, the emphasis placed on Singapore necessarily involved abandoning other areas. His American and Dutch colleagues and subordinates wanted to meet the Japanese challenge as it developed in the northern Indies. This Wavell rejected. He took the view that there was little point in trying to meet the Japanese in the north with the few aircraft that the command had at its disposal. Hence, the British abandoned Amboina and failed to contest the Tarakan, Menado, and Kendari landings with concentrated air power. Wavell preferred to hold Allied air strength in the center and rear for later battles. This was certain to condemn it to fighting for a battle already lost. Wavell chose to rely on submarines to contest Japanese moves in the northern and eastern Indies, even though they had proved singularly ineffective in inflicting losses or preventing landings in Malaya and the Philippines up until that time. Wavell was determined to use British surface units and part of the Dutch fleet to keep open communications with Singapore via the Sunda Strait—a policy of trying to repaint the front door when the back of the house was falling down.

But the third criticism of the Wavell approach is the relevant one from the point of view of developments on the Malayan peninsula. While Wavell's intentions in intervening in the battle were justifiable and indeed welcome after the tepid British generalship of the previous month, the manner in which he did so was disastrous. The instructions he gave Percival were detailed and extensive, and contained virtually every conceivable failing.

It was evident that by 8 January Wavell retained little if any confidence in Percival and his commanders, who had fought the previous month's battles. But even this cannot excuse the manner in which Percival that evening was summoned, kept waiting in an anteroom for more than an hour, and then given his orders without any chance of expressing an opinion or offering advice. Wavell, who had met Gordon Bennett earlier in the day, gave orders that were essentially Bennett's plan of campaign—a plan Percival already had rejected, of course, on very good grounds. The conduct of the battle for Johore was to be entrusted to Bennett, who was to command a new formation called Westforce. This was to consist of the 27th Australian Brigade, the 22nd Australian Brigade (as and when it could be relieved from its watch on the South China Sea), the two brigades of the 9th Indian Division, any units from the 11th Indian Division that might quickly be retrieved from the central Malaya debacle, and the 45th Indian Brigade. Wavell ordered Westforce to give battle on the Segamat, Mount Ophir, Muar line, thereby allowing what was left of the 3rd Indian Corps to pass into southern Johore in order to reorganize.

Of all the weaknesses involved in Wavell's decisions, the most serious involved Bennett himself. It would be easy to be contemptuous of people like the Australian general. Some at the time commented that, as a well-balanced Australian, Bennett had a chip on each shoulder. In fact, despite a sound tactical ability, he had been promoted beyond his level of competence and had no awareness of his inadequacies. (Neither had Wavell.) Bennett had been promoted to commander of the 8th Australian Division primarily because of the untimely deaths of more senior officers and in spite of an ostentatious self-publicity campaign he had waged against the Australian military hierarchy. He was rude, abrasive, meddling, and detested by certain of his subordinates. One of his brigadiers, Taylor of the 22nd Brigade, deliberately placed as much distance as possible between himself and his commander after an incident during training when Bennett tried to take over the brigadier's command. Bennett was not without aptitude; his promotion from an officer of the reserve to acting brigadier during the First World War was proof that he was able, but he was hardly up to a divisional command and certainly not up to a corps command, and Westforce, in effect, was a corps. To make matters worse, Westforce had only Bennett's command headquarters, and this was not adequate to control a corps battle.

The corps battle that Wavell had in mind in selecting the Segamat-Muar line was, furthermore, a larger battle than was strictly necessary. The line was over 40 miles wide, with no less than two major and one minor roads that could accommodate Japanese advances. Wavell chose the wrong ground on which to fight for Johore because he ignored or was ignorant of claims that the Tampin-Malacca line should be the site of the British effort. This line was much shorter, only 15 miles across, and would have been much easier to defend because the terrain forced rail and roads into a relatively narrow bottleneck. Moreover, the Wavell arrangement incorporated all the problems of movement, lines of communication, and routes of withdrawal that had led Percival to reject Bennett's suggestions on the fourth.

Nevertheless, it must be admitted that Bennett, even if he had an overinflated view of his own ability, brought aggressiveness and a touch of decisiveness to the defense, and he had clear and sensible ideas on the tactical deployment best suited to hurt the Japanese. He correctly saw that what was needed to slow the Japanese was a series of in-depth positions, held in strength, with counterattacking forces held close to smother any Japanese attempt to work their way around the flanks. These were the tactics that should have been employed in northern and central Malaya, but now, as Percival became convinced of their worth, it was too late for them to be fully effective. The balance of forces had in fact shifted too much for these tactics to have any real chance of success, and what success was to be registered in the initial encounters under Bennett's direction was to be dissipated by a single error of disposition.

As the British withdrew from central Malaya through Kuala Lumpur, occupied by the Japanese on the eleventh following an amphibious assault on Port Swettenham, Gordon Bennett moved his Westforce units in order to give battle on the Segamat-Muar line. Taking command of the 9th Indian Division on the thirteenth, he used the 8th Indian Brigade to secure the rear of his 27th Australian Brigade, which he deployed in and in front of Gemas, while he moved the 22nd Indian Brigade to Jementah to secure the Australian left flank along the minor road from Ayer Kuning to Segamat. On the coast road Gordon Bennett deployed the 45th Indian Brigade along the line of the Sungei Muar.

By this deployment Bennett intended to fight a series of defensive actions on the main road from a position of concentrated strength. The first two days of action, the fourteenth and fifteenth, provided good pickings for

the Australians. On the fourteenth the Australians carved up a reconnaissance detachment in a well-planned and efficiently conducted ambush
before Gemas, the only failure being a total lack of artillery support because
of a communications breakdown. On 15 January the Japanese, attacking
with two regiments, failed to make any impression on the Australian
positions, and they lost a number of their scarce tanks in the course of the
day's fighting. During that evening, however, Bennett withdrew his forward battalion to the next defensive line just behind Gemas, and during the
next two days the Japanese again tried unsuccessfully to force their way
through to Batu Anam and Segamat. Thus on the main road Bennett's
tactics worked well, but Australian success there was confounded by a
disaster on the coast road, where Bennett had been singularly careless both
in deployment and in supervision.

Though the 45th Indian Brigade was a low-caliber formation, it was
deployed on the coast in what was potentially the most vulnerable part of
the line. If the battle went badly, this would be the most critical part of the
front. The peculiar topography of Johore forced the main road from Gemas
to Johore Bahru to sweep northwards after Segamat to take it clear of the
sources of the Sungei Muar before it turned towards the Malacca coast. It
then passed through the villages of Yong Peng and Ayer Hitam, both less
than 20 miles from the sea, before running the 60 miles to Johore Strait. But
whereas Gemas was some 65 miles from Yong Peng, Muar was only about
40 miles away. The simple facts of geography meant that if the British
defense on the Sungei Muar was broken, the Japanese would be closer,
appreciably closer, to the Yong Peng bottleneck than the three brigades
standing near Gemas. These brigades, moreover, had to negotiate the
problematic Segamat junction because all three brigades had to pass
through the town.

Bennett made the classically correct staff officer's deployment on the
Sungei Muar, with two units holding both banks of the river and with one
battalion, less a company watching the coast, held in reserve at Bakri. The
deployment manifestly failed to take account of the terrain or the weaknesses of the formation. By ordering the 45th Indian Brigade to deploy the
length of the lower river, Bennett condemned two battalions, each less one
company deployed forward, to hold a 25-mile front. At the very most only
the last 9 miles of the river needed watching and defending. Deployment
upriver from Jorak served little purpose. The road beyond Lenga led
nowhere, and any Japanese attempt to negotiate the watery maze of the
streams and swamps in the Muar basin was certain to produce the same
result that had befallen the *42nd Infantry Regiment* at Kampar. To compound the problem of defending Muar was the open flank presented by the
Malacca Strait and the fact that the whole of the Muar-Bakri position could
be encircled by a Japanese landing at Batu Pahat, a coastal settlement 30

miles behind Muar but only some 12 miles from Bukit Pelandok on the Bakri to Yong Peng road. This village was only 10 miles from Yong Peng itself. The whole deployment of the 45th Indian Brigade constituted an open invitation to disaster, and Yamashita was never one to let the grass grow beneath his feet. When he grasped the possibilities presented by British deployment and weakness he was to pursue them ruthlessly.

After having secured central Malaya, Yamashita was able to take stock of his situation, which, oddly enough, was a neat reversal of the traditional Clausewitzian dictum of the diminishing force of the offensive. As the *25th Army* moved southwards it was actually growing stronger. Yamashita's initial moves against Thailand and northeastern Malaya had been made with elements of four infantry regiments, the *11th, 41st, 42nd*, and the *56th*, plus supporting arms. The second echelon of these formations had been brought ashore on 16 December and the main drive to the Perak had been accomplished by just the three regiments of the *5th Infantry Division*. At Taiping on 23 December the *4th Guards* had joined up with the advance and on the thirtieth the two-battalion-strong *55th Infantry Regiment* landed at Kota Bharu and followed the footsteps of the *56th* down to Kuantan. Thus Yamashita had secured eastern, central, and northern Malaya with just six regiments, one of which was not engaged. The day after the Slim River action the *21st Infantry Regiment* arrived in Thailand and on the tenth the *5th Guards* reached Ipoh. These formations were therefore on hand to add weight to the drive into Johore while two more formations, the *114th Regiment* and the *3rd Guards*, had still to deploy.

Yamashita, therefore, had eight regiments—just over two divisions—available for his assault on Johore, and naturally he chose to follow up success. The simple formula of using the main force down the trunk road and mounting flanking attacks down the Malacca coast had served Yamashita well, and there was no reason to depart from it. In fact Yamashita had good reason to reinforce this assault by scaling down operations in eastern Malaya. It had been part of the Japanese plan to land the uncommitted part of the *18th Infantry Division*[*] at Endau after the two regiments of the *23rd Infantry Brigade* had secured the port. But by the time Yamashita was considering his future intentions his air forces had not established sufficient control of the skies to warrant the risk of sending heavily laden transports, full of combat troops, as far south as Endau. Between them the *Southern Army* and the *25th Army* agreed that, while divisional troops and equipment should be put ashore at Endau on 26 January,[†] after the port had been secured by the *55th Infantry Regiment*, the *114th* should come ashore in

---

*The *18th* included the *114th Infantry Regiment* and divisional and supporting arms troops only. The division's other regiment, the *124th*, was in Borneo and did not see service in Malaya.

†At the same time the navy intended to occupy the Anambas as a base for its light forces.

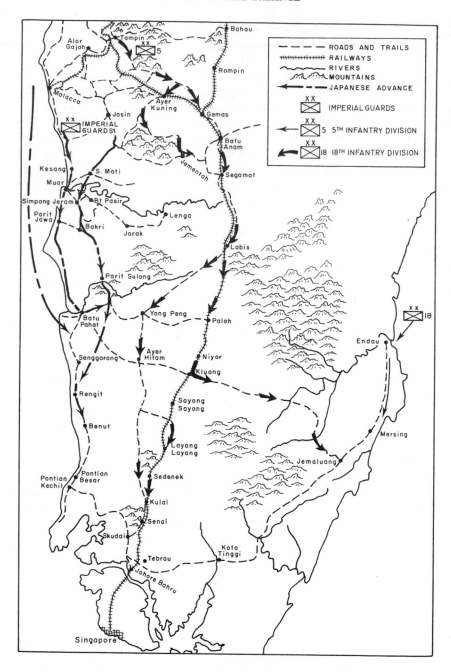

The Campaign in Johore, Southern Malaya

southern Thailand in the company of extra lines of communications troops and equipment. The *56th Infantry Regiment*, having secured Kuantan, was to be deployed away from the east coast, to Kuala Lumpur, ready for a reserve role. Yamashita wanted it fresh for the Singapore assault. He was prepared to let the attack along the east coast be developed by the *55th* alone, the regiment being ordered not to press on to the Johore Strait but to strike across country against Kluang. Thus, in the center, striking along the main road against the three brigades Gordon Bennett deployed at Gemas and Segamat, Yamashita had three brigades with three more coming up in support. But in the west, along the Malacca Strait, the *25th Army* deployed two guards regiments against the hapless and woefully prepared 45th Indian Brigade.

There are no prizes for guessing the outcome of the Muar encounter. The 45th Indian Brigade was simply ripped to pieces. The forward companies were wiped out to a man and the Rajputana battalion, holding Muar, was reduced to company strength during the sixteenth. The Jat battalion, holding the river above Jorak, was cut off; and the Garhwali battalion, at Bakri, was repulsed with losses when it tried to break through to Muar and seal off the Japanese breakthrough across the river.

At first Gordon Bennett did not seem to have grasped the seriousness of the situation on the Sungei Muar. He did send the reserve battalion of the 27th Australian Brigade from Gemas to Bakri to boost the defense, but with the defenders of Gemas doing well and no challenge developing along the Jementah road, he saw no cause for immediate concern. Percival, however, was more alert to a situation that rapidly assumed very threatening proportions. He was aware that the Japanese thrust along the coast was more powerful than anticipated, and on the eighteenth was told by intelligence that a full Japanese division was deployed there—not quite accurate, but the assessment was near enough. It was evident that the 45th Indian Brigade faced annihilation, particularly because during the morning of the sixteenth a single battalion from the *4th Guards Regiment* came ashore at Batu Pahat.

The threat to the lines of communication of the Gemas defenders suddenly became very real because the Japanese, having forced the Muar line, intended to push along the coast with the *4th Guards* to Batu Pahat while the *5th Guards* struck inland towards Yong Peng. With at least two units of the 45th Indian Brigade either destroyed or cut off there was little in the area to hold the Japanese advances, while the extrication of what remained of the Jats and the Garhwalis obviously became extremely important. On the seventeenth Percival made the critically important decision to put everything that could be scraped together into an effort to retain the crucial area bound by Yong Peng, Bukit Pelandok, Muar, Batu Pahat, and

Ayer Hitam. In order to prevent the disintegration of his left flank, which would threaten to collapse the whole of the Gemas position, Percival ordered an Australian battalion from the 22nd Australian Brigade at Mersing to move to Bakri when it was relieved by a battalion from the 53rd British Brigade, while the major part of the newly arrived British formation was ordered forward to Ayer Hitam.

Percival's problem was a delicate one. The only possibility of holding around Muar and Bakri lay in the immediate concentration of the 22nd Australian and 53rd British Brigades along the roads from Yong Peng and Ayer Hitam to the west coast. But the thrust of the *55th Infantry Regiment* along the South China Sea coastline on Endau began to pay dividends for Yamashita because Percival did not dare loosen his grip on the east coast in order to try to prevent the crumbling of his position in the west.

If the British were to have any chance of holding in and around Muar and Bakri, they had to retain a grip on the latter settlement. This would allow the Jats to rejoin and deny the Japanese unimpeded use of the direct route to Yong Peng. The British reinforcements in the meantime would lead an assault down the road in order to smother the Japanese offensive at its source. The weakness of the British plan was that the Japanese were not going to sit on their hands after Muar and Batu Pahat. Japanese countermoves, because they could be mounted more quickly than the British could move into the area, would in any likelihood frustrate the whole of the British plan. So it proved.

While the defenders of Bakri hung on and were rejoined by just two Jat companies from the middle reaches of the river Muar, the Japanese *5th Guards Regiment* launched a series of holding and close flanking attacks on Bakri and the *4th Guards* launched a deep flanking movement that secured Parit Sulong and Baukit Pelandok by the eighteenth, thus trapping the 45th Indian Brigade and blocking the route along which any relief attempt would have to be made. Moreover, as Percival correctly foresaw, the Japanese occupation of these two villages posed a direct threat to Yong Peng. This village had to be held at least until the twenty-fourth because the three brigades around Segamat (already under mounting pressure both on the main road and along the route from Ayer Kuning as the Japanese pushed their *21st Infantry Brigade* along it in an outflanking movement) could not possibly get clear of Yong Peng before that date. Percival thus ordered the 6th/15th Indian Brigade* to secure and hold Batu Pahat on the coast (a little late in the day) and the 53rd British Brigade to secure Bukit Pelandok, while the 45th cut its way out of Bakri. But on the nineteenth the vanguard of the British formation was roughly handled short of Bukit Pelandok and an attack to secure the vital defile near the village was beaten

*In fact this brigade consisted of three reinforced British battalions and is generally referred to as the 15th Brigade.

back by a Japanese counterattack the following day. From this reversal Percival drew the correct and only conclusion—that the battle on the coast roads, and with it the whole of the battle to hold northern Johore, was lost.

Despite the success around Gemas there was nothing the British could do to retain their positions along the line Wavell had given Percival to defend. All that remained was for the British to await the inevitable: the destruction of the 45th Indian Brigade as it tried to break out of Bakri and the defeat of a belated and essentially irrelevant attempt by the 53rd British Brigade to break through the Japanese position at the Bukit Pelandok defile on the morning of 22 January. The Indians, with the Australians from the 27th Brigade, did manage to cut their way through the roadblocks established by the *5th Guards* behind Bakri on the twentieth, but, encumbered as they were by their wounded, they were hounded as they withdrew. The formation found its retreat blocked at the bridge at Parit Sulong by the *4th Guards* and there the Japanese annihilated it, disgracefully murdering captives and the wounded, who had to be abandoned when the last elements of the formation attempted an independent breakout. The 45th Indian Brigade suffered 80 percent losses during their nine days in the line; some 900 men from Indian and Australian units finally reached the temporary sanctuary of Yong Peng on the twenty-third.

In the course of the Malayan campaign it is possible to identify three crises for the defenders: the debacle at Jitra; the Percival decision not to move the 9th Indian Division west of the mountains on 18 December; and the loss of the battle on the Segamat-Muar line. The latter crisis, however,

Japanese engineers form an improvised bridge to keep the advancing infantry moving. Note the presence of cold steel with the infantry—five bayonets and one sword. Robert Hunt Library

was not merely one for Malaya and the British; it also directly affected Wavell and ABDA Command. It did so because it immediately called into question Wavell's intention of trying to hold Singapore as a bulwark against the Japanese in the west. It also threw into the melting pot the whole issue of continuing to send reinforcements to Singapore.

The disaster on the Sungei Muar threatened to undermine the whole of Wavell's strategic plans for the defense of the ABDA area because, as Wavell himself realized on the twentieth when he was in Singapore, a retreat to the Batu Pahat, Kluang, Mersing line was now inevitable and there was the distinct probability, not to say certainty, that a withdrawal to Singapore Island itself would be forced upon the British. Wavell also knew that no plans for a withdrawal to the island had been prepared and that no orders for the defense of the island had been issued. No defensive works had been started on the island by the twentieth for the usual "bad for morale" reason.

It is inconceivable that Wavell could have retained any illusions about Singapore holding out for very long. Yet in this crisis he made no move to divert reinforcements being sent to Singapore to other areas where they might prove useful. In Singapore, at the very best, they could only swell the numbers of those forced to capitulate at the end of a miserable, contemptible campaign. The events in northern Johore prompted the crisis in London already dealt with in earlier pages, but Wavell was even more immediately affected. The British official historian summarized Wavell's "option of difficulties" succinctly.

> He had therefore to decide whether to try to hold Singapore Island or whether to put up a purely token resistance and divert to the Netherlands East Indies or to Burma the reinforcements on their way. There were four questions to be considered: the first, would the available formations withdrawn from Johore and reinforced by those arriving at the end of January enable the island to be held for a reasonable length of time; the second, if the island could be held for a reasonable length of time, would its retention help in the defence of the ABDA area; the third, if the island could be held for only a few weeks, would it not be better to divert elsewhere the reinforcing formations and units; and lastly, if he did decide in the interests of the ABDA area to divert the reinforcements, what would be the effect on world opinion and on the morale of the Singapore garrison.*

Wavell's immediate difficulty was that, apart from those forces already en route to Singapore, he could not expect reinforcements to reach the ABDA area until the end of March. Somehow or other Wavell had to prolong the defense of the ABDA area until that time; the reinforcements then making their way to Singapore probably represented Wavell's last assets, and their disposition was of the highest possible importance. The

*Kirby, *Singapore: The Chain of Disaster*, p. 214.

question he faced was thus whether or not sending forces into Singapore would allow the garrison to hold out until that time. It is impossible to conclude that Wavell really believed that Johore and Singapore could hold out for another seventy days if supported by an extra four brigades when Malaya, from Jitra to Gemas, had been lost by nearly 90,000 troops in just forty-four days. Yet Wavell saw no reason to divert the reinforcement convoys that arrived in Singapore on 22 January, 29 January, and, incredibly, on 5 February.

Wavell, it would appear, was a supreme commander whose commands applied only to the Dutch and their forces; general direction and supervision seem to have been his watchwords in dealing with the Americans in the Philippines and Australia or British government policy with regard to Singapore. Wavell's reason for not interfering with the British decision to continue to send forces into Singapore was precisely the same as the reason for London's continuing to send reinforcements. It was politically expedient to allow events to continue on their own to an end that everyone concerned clearly foresaw. The soft option of doing nothing was more acceptable than making a decision that was an admission of defeat. By any standard Churchill, the British Chiefs of Staff, and Wavell were guilty of criminal dereliction, not least to the men they allowed to sail into the hell of Japanese captivity. In Wavell's case the dereliction was compounded by the fact that these forces were his very last hope of holding his command together.

Wavell was later to claim that if Singapore had been able to hold out for another month—until the reinforcements began to arrive—this would have made all the difference for his command. It is difficult to see the basis of such a comment. The only thing that could have saved ABDA Command would have been a massive infusion of Allied air power and then a substantial reinforcement of Allied naval power in the Indies by the U. S. Pacific Fleet. Neither could have been forthcoming. The Allies simply did not have the available aircraft, and the Americans were not willing to deploy their naval power to the Indies. It was not until 25 February, the day when ABDA Command was dissolved and Wavell left Java, that the American carriers first went so far eastwards as to pass between the Solomons and the New Hebrides into the Coral Sea. The only reinforcements Wavell could expect were Australian ground forces from the Middle East and, in the last analysis, land forces were incapable of denying the Indies to an enemy with the advantages of mobility and concentration invested by air and sea supremacy. This is not to argue that as a result the final destination of the Singapore troop convoys was essentially irrelevant; in Burma or northern Australia they might have been invaluable, in the Indies less so. In Singapore they were useless, and this was known, not least to Wavell. The same element of intellectual dishonesty that characterized British deliberations about Singapore was maintained right up until the end; Britain and her generals at least merited full marks for consistency.

When Percival accepted defeat in northern Johore on 20 January he gave orders for the reorganization of his forces in order to place a single formation on each of the three axes of the Japanese advance. These formations were Eastforce, the 22nd Australian Brigade, at Mersing; Westforce, the 27th Australian and 45th Indian Brigades and the 9th Indian Division, in the center; and the 11th Indian Division, the 15th Indian Brigade, and the 28th Indian and 53rd British Brigades, on the Malacca Strait coastline. Command of the next phase of the battle was to be vested in the 3rd Indian Corps and Heath.

This regrouping was essential. With the Japanese clearly pressing on all three fronts, the arrangement whereby Bennett, with his divisional staff, had to command forces on the two major axes was obviously unsatisfactory. But Percival's intention was to stand and fight on the Mersing, Kluang, Ayer Hitam line, with the 15th Brigade left forward holding Batu Pahat. Such a plan was fraught with peril, particularly because even before Heath assumed command of the battle the 45th Indian Brigade had been eliminated, and the 53rd British Brigade had been ravaged by having to send its units to other formations and by a bad reverse around Bukit Pelandok. The real weakness of Percival's plan, however, was that it paid insufficient attention to inadequacies of the left flank defenders. There a rampant *Imperial Guards Division*, having already shattered the defenders of Muar and Bakri, was opposed by two reconstituted brigades and a worsted British formation, none of which were in contact with one another. It was on this very flank that the British encountered their initial disaster, which, in turn, triggered a debacle in the center.

The withdrawal of Bennett's formations from their exposed positions around Segamat was well conducted. The Australians fell back slowly on Yong Peng and Ayer Hitam by the road; the 8th and 22nd Indian Brigades used the railroad track to get back to the Niyor-Kluang position. The *5th Infantry Division*, using the *21st Infantry Brigade* along the road and the *9th Infantry Brigade* to pursue the Indians, followed up hard but proved incapable of catching and dealing with either part of Westforce. The Indian brigade at Batu Pahat, on the other hand, did less well than its colleagues in the center. It had been left as badly isolated by the Japanese securing the coast roads from Yong Peng and Ayer Hitam as the 45th Indian Brigade and its two Australian battalions had been at Muar and Bakri. The fact that the *4th Guards Regiment* severed the Ayer Hitam to Batu Pahat road on the afternoon of the twenty-first forced the 53rd British Brigade, which was down to one British and one Indian battalion, to take the long way around once it broke clear of Bukit Pelandok. The brigade was forced to detour 102 miles, through Kulai, Skudai, and Pontian Kechil in order to come up to the

Benut position in support of the 15th Brigade. Yet even this was a dubious benefit to the defenders of Batu Pahat. The battalion of the *4th Guards Regiment* that had landed behind Batu Pahat on the seventeenth was in a lying-up position in the plantations between the river and Senggarang; in effect the 15th Brigade was surrounded.

Because of a pause for the Japanese to reorganize and prepare for the next phase of their operations, the position of the 15th Brigade was not immediately challenged. The brigade's commander, P. S. Challen, became increasingly aware of his vulnerability, and on the twenty-fourth requested permission to withdraw to Rengit. This request was rejected, as were two further requests the following morning. Heath's attitude was that a decision to withdraw the 15th Brigade had to await a commanders' conference on the afternoon of the twenty-fifth. Underlying his refusal was the very real fear that if the British started to pull back they would not be allowed to stop, as had been the case in northern and central Malaya. By that afternoon, however, the 53rd British Brigade, advancing from Benut, found that the Japanese had moved their battalion from its sanctuary among the trees into a series of blocking positions along the road between Rengit and Senggarang.

When Percival learned of this situation he immediately realized the threat to his whole position. The policy of having a strong center and two weak flanks was beginning to reveal its inherent shortcomings. If the Japanese broke through the three weakened formations along the coast, as they seemed quite capable of doing without too much difficulty in the light of the Muar-Bakri action, they would be in a position to get to the Johore Strait and around the back of Westforce before Bennett's formations had a chance of getting back to Johore Bahru. Because of the short distance from the Sungei Batu Pahat to Johore any faltering by the 11th Indian Division threatened Westforce with encirclement. Percival had to get the 15th Brigade back from Batu Pahat as quickly as possible and in good order. If he failed to do so the battle along the coast, and with it the battle for southern Johore, would be lost.

Inevitably the Japanese were not prepared to let opportunity slip away. The two guards regiments were too experienced and professional to be second best to two scratch formations mounting improvised attacks. But they were not good enough to annihilate either brigade, so the Japanese had to be content with another partial victory with the enemy slipping away once again. First the thrust by the British brigade to open the road for the 15th Brigade was beaten back with losses, as the Japanese secured Rengit. Then the 15th broke out of Batu Pahat and was surrounded north of Senggarang, though nearly 4,000 men from the brigade managed to get back to British lines. Just over 1,000, led by Malay policemen, made their way through the streams, plantation, and jungle back to Rengit. They reached friendly forces late on the twenty-seventh in an utterly spent state. The remainder were evacuated by sea between 28 January and 1 February, one of only two occasions during the entire campaign on which the British made satisfactory use of what little sea power remained to them.

The Japanese failure—on land and in the air—to deal with the evacuation of the 15th Brigade is striking. With such overwhelming superiority the Japanese should have totally destroyed the brigade. The failure, however, was not very serious because the formation lost, besides its cohesion, all its artillery, heavy equipment, and transport. Even if it escaped annihilation, it had to be written off for the purposes of the defense of Singapore—a fate it shared with the 22nd Indian Brigade in the center, though this formation was to experience almost total physical annihilation.

When on the twenty-fifth Percival ordered the breakout of the 15th Brigade from Batu Pahat, he also recognized the inevitability of a withdrawal to Singapore Island itself, a tacit admission of defeat and the loss of Singapore. He therefore ordered Westforce to begin to pull its formations back from Kluang and Ayer Hitam. In order to allow Eastforce to get back to Johore Bahru before Bennett's force, Heath gave orders for Westforce to conduct a phased withdrawal to Kulai on 31 January while the two remaining brigades from the 11th Indian Division drew back to hold Skudai, thereby ensuring the security of Westforce's flank and rear.

Success in carrying out these orders depended on very careful timing and the closest coordination of the forces involved. This was particularly true of Westforce, which was in the unenviable position of having to conduct its withdrawal slowly enough to allow Eastforce to slip through the potential Tebrau, Johore Bahru, Skudai, Senai bottleneck without causing a massive pileup of retreating formations. But at the same time Westforce had to withdraw quickly enough to avoid any of its three brigades being caught by the Japanese. The latter was difficult enough because the Japanese at this stage could be relied upon to give the retreating defenders no respite, but to make matters worse all three brigades had to be channelled through the road and rail center at Kulai. Unless Westforce was very careful, the converging of all three formations at one junction could produce unfortunate results. To compound the problems of Westforce during its withdrawal, the two Indian brigades had to shed their artillery, transport, and heavy equipment before they reached Layang Layang, where the road turned eastwards, away from Johore Bahru. The 8th and 22nd Indian Brigades, as they drew back from Kluang, had to send their transport to the main trunk road not later than the time when they reached the trail between Rengam and the Namazie Estate, the last east-west route before Layang Layang. The Indians, therefore, had no artillery support, no transport, no heavy equipment, and no communications, other than by civilian telephone line, for the major part of their planned withdrawal.

The 27th Australian Brigade on the road and the 8th Indian Brigade alongside the railway line broke contact with the Japanese on the twenty-seventh; the Australians fell back to a position near the Namazie Estate, the Indians to Layang Layang. The 22nd Indian Brigade, therefore, was left to hold a position between Layang Layang and Rengam for nearly two days, yet because of the myriad estate roads and paths east of the railway line the Indian formation, bereft of its transport and guns, could not hope to hold its position. It could easily be outflanked if the Japanese worked their way around the brigade's right flank—a possibility suspected by the brigade commander, Gordon W. A. Painter, and quickly confirmed by the Japanese themselves. Permission to withdraw to Layang Layang, which would be secure against such outflanking movements, was sought but refused. The 22nd, moreover, had been left needlessly vulnerable by the 8th Indian Brigade's withdrawal to a position well south of Layang Layang and its failure to control the village as it had been ordered. As if to prove that with such friends Painter had no need for an enemy, on the night of 27/28 January the only bridge at Layang Layang was blown, without the authority of the 9th Indian Division and with, naturally enough, the 22nd Indian Brigade on the wrong side of it. The demolition also brought down the telephone line. When the divisional commander, Barstow, went forward to find out what was happening he was killed in a Japanese ambush near Layang Layang. What was happening of course was that the Japanese *9th Infantry Brigade* had made full use of the estate roads and had come around the right flank of Painter's forces, establishing the all-important roadblock where the 8th Indian Brigade should have been. After an initial failure at forcing the roadblock there was little option but to attempt a breakout through the jungle in an effort to regain contact with Westforce, but with the other two brigades themselves moving back to Johore Bahru this was obviously out of the question. For four days the 22nd Indian Brigade forced its way southwards, all the time its strength draining away until on 1 February its remnants, some 400 men with Painter, were surrounded east of Senai and forced to surrender. Just 60 men reached the Johore Strait and were rescued by snatch parties from Singapore Island.

Thus ended the battles for Johore, and with them the last British hopes of holding Singapore for any length of time. From the defenders' point of view a dismal and disastrous series of actions that began among the carnage of the Slim River battle witnessed, in the space of two short weeks, the utter destruction of three brigades, the 15th Brigade and the 22nd and 45th Indian Brigades, and the wrecking of two Australian battalions in the defense of Muar and Bakri. The 53rd British Brigade, in its first battles, had suffered severe losses, and all units had been affected to some degree. Some were down to 30 percent of their effective strength and to all intents and purposes were useless; most were at about half-strength. Morale was virtually at zero. And, the ultimate battle in defense of Malaya and Singapore still remained to be fought. This last and most crucial engagement was fought on the British side by ground forces that had been ruined beyond recall, fought almost without air support because by now British air power was all but extinct, fought without naval support, fought without intelligent direction, and fought without hope.

Already the first ugly signs of a breakdown of discipline among rear-echelon troops and units just arrived in Singapore were beginning to come to the surface. Against a background of burning docks and oil dumps and the thud of demolitions as the British began to lay waste installations no longer essential to the defense (including, significantly, the naval base that the Royal Navy had abandoned without first having carried out a proper demolition program), Singapore, a city swelled by refugees to twice its normal size, waited mutely for the end. As the troops crossed the causeway to the island, the last leaving the peninsula on 31 January, they were moved straight to locations along the coastline, which they were called upon to man. There they found a situation that had become depressingly familiar during the previous eight weeks—nothing. They had to dig their own defensive positions because none had been prepared; that would have been bad for morale.

As it arrived at Johore Strait the *25th Army* had to consider how it was to mount its assault crossing. Prewar consideration of this problem had concluded in favor of an assault on the island's northwest coast, between the Sungei Kranji and the Sungei Berih, from positions in Johore west of the Sungei Skudai. The great advantage of a successful attack in this sector was that it would carry into central Singapore Island on the direct line of approach to Singapore City, cutting off the causeway, securing an area where many defense installations were established, and quickly gaining control of Tengah airfield. Forewarned by intelligence that the British had concentrated the brigades of the 18th British Division on Singapore's northeast coast and recognizing that these formations, only one of which had been employed on the mainland, were likely to be the best available to the defenders, Yamashita decided to act upon the prewar conclusions. The *25th Army*, therefore, planned an assault with two divisions between the Kranji and the Berih; it then would follow up a day later with its third division east of the Kranji. In order to pin down and divert the attention of the defenders in the east of the island the *25th Army* planned a battalion attack on Pulau Ubin Island, in the eastern end of the Johore Strait, twenty-four hours before the main assault took place late on 8 February.

For his major effort Yamashita selected the *5th* and *18th Infantry Divisions*, a decision that can be explained by the fact that before the war these divisions, particularly the *5th*, had received specialist training for amphibious assaults. The decision also can be explained in terms of Yamashita's

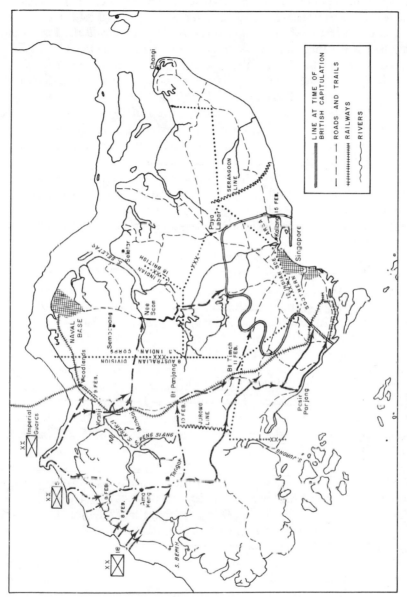

The Singapore Campaign, 8 through 15 February 1942

bitter contempt for the *Imperial Guards* in general and their commander, Nishimura, in particular. The decision, however, could not be explained in terms of maintaining the order of battle that the Japanese had used down the length of the Malayan peninsula since the start of hostilities. On the extreme right flank of the assault the *25th Army* deployed the formations that had made their way down Malaya's eastern coast, the *55th Infantry Regiment* and one battalion of the *56th*; for the left flank of the *18th Infantry Division*'s assault the newly arrived *114th Infantry Regiment* was deployed. The *5th Infantry Division*, on the *18th*'s left flank, employed a strong right, the *21st Infantry Brigade*, and a weak left, the *11th Infantry Regiment*. The *Imperial Guards Division*, having made its effort down the west coast of Malaya, was switched to the east flank for the secondary attack. Its single assault group consisted of the *4th Guards Regiment* reinforced by a single battalion from the *3rd*. All three divisions were supported by about a regiment of artillery and a sapper unit, the *5th* and *18th* being given considerably more specialist support for their crossings. The *5th* and the *Imperial Guards Divisions* held a full regiment in reserve, the *18th* two battalions.

Obviously Yamashita would have liked to have pressed ahead with an assault as soon as possible; he had no desire to allow the defenders time to reorganize, even if they were so disorganized that no amount of time would have been enough for their salvation. But the *25th Army* had its problems. It had to sort out its divisions and ensure no congestion behind the coastline and it gave the assaulting units of both the *5th* and *18th Infantry Divisions* a "refresher" course on the Sungei Muar for a couple of days. With only enough assault boats for these two divisions, the *Imperial Guards*, which needed the training most, had to do without; all the training they received was on the morning of the ninth with the assault boats that were returned to the northern coast after the main assault had been carried out. The supply problems for the operation, however, remained serious. These had been eased by the *55th Infantry Regiment*'s capture of Endau on 21 January, which meant that the supply and reinforcement convoy scheduled to come ashore on the twenty-sixth could proceed on time. That operation was not uneventful. The Royal Air Force spent virtually the last of its strength and the Royal Navy lost the destroyer *Thanet* in unavailing attempts to sink the thirteen small craft and two transports that arrived at Endau in the company of Ozawa's *Ryujo*, four heavy cruisers, and six destroyers. Though the two transports were damaged by bombs, neither was lost. The forces and equipment that came ashore proved, in fact, decisive in the attack on Singapore. By the time that Singapore finally surrendered, the attacking Japanese units were virtually out of ammunition. Without the Endau convoy of the twenty-sixth Yamashita would have been forced to abandon the attack or wage it with great difficulty.

Across the strait on Singapore Island farce rubbed shoulders with pathos. The civil administration had been so obstructive and underhanded during the campaign that Percival resorted to not leaving meetings until the governor had signed the minutes. Among the many tribulations the army suffered at the hands of these incompetent administrators, who simply could not see that defeat was imminent, was an initial refusal to sanction the siting of defenses on the greens and fairways of the local golf club. But military incompetence ran a close second in the defense of Singapore. Though Wavell, the British Chiefs of Staff, and his own intelligence had warned him that the Japanese would make their main effort against northwest Singapore, Percival persisted in believing that the northeast would be the location of the Japanese main effort. Accordingly, he deployed his stronger formations in the east and his weaker units in the west, the exact reverse of the Japanese deployment. To add to this error of judgment Percival made the unforgivable blunder of hopelessly mismanaging arrangements for the boundaries of the various formations, thereby ensuring that units whose only hope lay in rapid movement and clarity of administration and command had to face their final ordeal in administrative chaos.

The British should have bared the southern part of the island because the possibilities of an assault from the sea were so remote. Instead of trying to provide all-around defense the British should have concentrated in order to hold the area between the Sungei Berih in the west and the Sungei Seletar in the east, taking advantage of the natural line presented by the Sungei Kranji to divide the front into two parts. This course Percival rejected, placing in the western part of the island the 8th Australian Division, with the 22nd and 27th Australian and the 44th Indian Brigades under its command. Each of the three formations had three battalions, a machine gun company, a field artillery regiment, and an antitank battery. This division was entrusted with the area that lay west of a line that ran slightly east of Woodlands-Bukit Timah village and from there to the Sungei Jurong. Covering the northern part of the remainder Percival deployed the 3rd Indian Corps, with the 11th Indian and 18th British Divisions under its command; the 9th Indian Division was dissolved. The 11th Indian Division had under its command the 8th and 28th Indian Brigades along with the 53rd British Brigade, which was to revert to the 18th British Division when the 15th (Indian) Brigade was reconstituted. The British brigades were all up to full strength with three battalions, a machine gun battalion (absent from the 53rd), an antitank battery, and the best part of two field regiments each. On paper the 28th Indian Brigade was almost at this strength, but the 8th was down to just three weakened and uncertain infantry battalions, which in fact fought far better than certain other units. The corps reserve consisted of the re-forming 15th Brigade. The southern part of the island was divided between Singapore Fortress, with three brigades of Malays and coastal artillery, and the command reserve, Paris's 12th Indian Brigade.

Besides the failings of deployment and boundaries that placed the weakest formations in the most threatened sectors, there were many flaws in the arrangements. While one could make an endless list, including such matters as morale, communications, exhaustion, and wanting leadership, two flaws were critical. The first was obvious. There were no reserves worthy of the name. The command reserve, five shattered battalions, was more nominal than real; the 3rd Indian Corps had the weak 8th Indian Brigade; the 8th Australian Division had none and its units had to shed one of their companies in order to provide for their own support. Yet reserves were vital because the second weakness of the defense was that the units deployed forward could not hope to hold an assault on the heavily indented swampy coast or on the difficult terrain inland. Given the thin veneer that constituted the British defense, the nature of the ground and the precariousness of their own supply lines promised to be greater obstacles to Japanese success than any counterattacking reserve.

Because of Percival's errors and the weaknesses of the forces involved, the British defenses appeared to be mainly gaps, held together (or apart) by occasional groups of soldiers. At the very best it was a sieve through which the Japanese *5th* and *18th Infantry Divisions* passed, albeit not without some difficulties, on the night of 8/9 February. A day-long artillery bombardment softened up the 22nd Australian Brigade in preparation for a major assault astride the Sungei Murai and the lesser assault north of the Sungei Sarimbun. Even though the Australians inflicted quite severe losses on the first two waves of the attack, sheer weight of numbers swamped defenders who for the most part were unsupported by their artillery and were not relieved quickly enough by reserves sent up by both the 8th Australian Division and Malaya Command. The division sent a battalion from the 27th Brigade, the command its own and the 3rd Corps's reserve, but these formations were certain to arrive on the scene too late and in too little strength to help a command that by midmorning on the tenth had virtually ceased to exist. A series of desperate close-quarter battles with a relentless Japanese enemy and withdrawals over difficult country ruined all three of Brigadier Taylor's battalions, particularly the 2nd/18th (on which the brunt of the assault fell) and the 2nd/20th.

In order to try to hold a line, Taylor attempted to use what he could salvage from the wreck of his brigade and from the reserves to defend a position between the north of Tengah airfield and Choa Chu Kang. It quickly became obvious to him that if he was unable to counterattack and defeat the Japanese, his best course would be to withdraw his force, the reserves, and the flanking 44th Indian Brigade into the line of defenses prepared long before the war between the Sungei Peng Siang and the

Sungei Jurong. By the evening of the tenth he had been successful in manning this position, the Jurong line, with a spare reserve battalion and the 12th and 44th Indian Brigades; the 15th Indian Brigade was in reserve, with the remnants of the 22nd Australian Brigade forward in a covering position.

There is little doubt that even with this effort the Jurong line could not be held for very long; there was no real chance that ad hoc units could withstand a serious assault. By crushing the 22nd Australian Brigade the Japanese had obtained so secure a beachhead on the island that they could quickly have moved the major part of their forces into a position to smash through the Jurong line. This did not prove necessary; with everything falling apart by this stage three failings wrecked any possibility of the British holding the Japanese away from Singapore for more than a matter of hours or days.

The first disaster was the collapse of the resistance by the 27th Australian Brigade, a failing caused by less hard fighting on the part of the *Imperial Guards Division*, which came ashore on the ninth, than by total and unmitigated incompetence on the part of Bennett and his brigade commander, D. S. Maxwell. The second failure was Percival's neglect in sweeping everything out of quiet sectors of the front into a reserve, ready for an immediate counteroffensive. This move was essential from the time he brought his reserves forward to help the 22nd Australian Brigade on the morning of the ninth. After that time, with the main Japanese effort obviously made, there was nothing to be gained by leaving forces in the east and south of the island; unless the Japanese were halted the battle for the island was over, so there was absolutely nothing to be gained by maintaining the preinvasion deployment. The third failing was Percival's confidential warning to his most senior commanders of his intention to hold a close perimeter defense around Singapore if he was forced out of the Jurong line and the northern part of the island. Bennett circulated these intentions to his subordinate commanders, but he did so in such a manner that they interpreted intentions as orders and began to pull back from the Jurong line even though the position had not been subjected to a serious assault.

For this debacle Bennett must take full responsibility, as he must for his total lack of supervision of Maxwell's conduct of operations in the Kranji-Woodlands area. Maxwell's ambiguous orders and changes of command led to the *Imperial Guards*, after a very bad time during the assault phase, establishing themselves ashore and advancing towards Kranji itself. The pulling back of Maxwell's forces from the coast and away from the road and railway not only opened up the flank of the 11th Indian Division but also bared the direct route from Woodlands to Singapore—and the rear of the Jurong line. This was the main error, after which any faint hope of recovery was gone. By late on the tenth the *5th Infantry Division* was closing in on

Bukit Panjang village with the *18th* a little to the south on the road to Bukit Timah village. By this stage an alarming gap was beginning to open up along the Sungei Peng Siang, between units of the 27th Australian Brigade and the llth Indian Division in the north and the units coming back from or still on the Jurong line. The subsequent events were chaotic, with unavailing British efforts to throw units into the path of the Japanese advance in an effort to slow them down. The Japanese, more troubled by their failing ammunition supplies than by the efforts of the defenders, were never denied for long.

Though resistance increased in bitterness as is so often the case when the end of a battle is clearly in sight, this was the last splutter of the flame before it flickered and died. The British could not avoid capitulating and on the evening of 15 February Percival signed the instrument of surrender. By then it was clear that no further purpose would be served by prolonging resistance in a city crammed with refugees, a city where the dead lay unburied in the streets, the water supply had been failing from the time the Japanese secured the city's reservoirs and pumping stations, and where drunken and sullen mobs of soldiers roamed the streets. Fearful of the retribution that the Japanese might exact on civilians and soldiers alike if he attempted to fight on, Percival at least tried to spare Singapore the final ordeal of an assault. He was only partly successful; the Japanese committed

The Ford Car Factory, Singapore Island, on "Black Sunday" 15 February 1942. The negotiations for the surrender between the victor, Yamashita (far side of table, third from left), and Percival (near side of table, second from the left). Imperial War Museum

Perfectly disciplined Japanese soldiers during their victory parade in Singapore after the city's fall. Indiscipline came later. Orbis Collection

horrible excesses against the Chinese once the surrender was complete, but at least that was after the battle was over. Retribution could be exacted later.

So ended a campaign that cost Britain two capital ships and several other ships, perhaps as many as 200 aircraft, and 138,708 men, more than 130,000 of whom were taken prisoner. In Hong Kong, Malaya, Singapore, and in the Indies combined the British lost a total of about 166,500 men to set against the 9,824 Japanese killed and wounded in Malaya and Singapore and the total of about 15,000 lost in the general area of Malaya and the Indies. Nothing in any way can diminish the humiliation explicit in these losses. A garrison that outnumbered the attackers by more than five to two at all stages of the campaign was hounded to utter destruction in seventy days—thirty days less than the Japanese themselves had anticipated.

Much ink has been spilled during the inquests that have been held into the campaign in Malaya. Regarding Singapore's untimely end three general conclusions recommend themselves in explaining Britain's failure to hold the island. These are that the loss can be traced back to the muddled strategic thinking of the interwar period; the definition of Britain and the Middle East as priorities ahead of Singapore in the period 1939–41; and the extremely poor performance of the army in the field in the course of the campaign. There can be no doubt that these conclusions do much to explain why the British failed to hold Singapore.

The unreality that permeated so much of Britain's strategic thinking before the war lies at the root of the disaster. So, too, does Churchill's persistent misreading of Japanese intentions and capabilities in the course of 1940 and 1941. Churchill's denunciation of the Naval Intelligence Division for the latter's alleged tendency to overstate Japanese strength and effectiveness clearly points to the fact that Churchill did not see the emerging threat. In February 1941 he wrote to Roosevelt to the effect that though the British could not deal with a spread of war into the Pacific, he did not believe that the Japanese would lay siege to Singapore. In a sense he was correct. The Japanese did not intend to besiege Singapore; they intended to take it. But the whole of Churchill's argument that the battle was lost before it began ignores three simple facts. First, Churchill's case that before the war nothing could be spared to send to Malaya and Singapore is belied by the large number of forces sent there after 8 December. Before that date they were available. The error was one not of inadequate strength but of strategic perception and direction at the highest level.

Second, there is no getting away from the fact that, even without the reinforcements sent to Singapore in 1942 and notwithstanding the material weaknesses of the garrison in Malaya, the forces already on the peninsula should have been able to defeat, hold, or substantially delay and inflict far heavier casualties on the Japanese. There can be no extenuating circumstances to explain away the fact that three Japanese divisions, only one of which ever deployed its full infantry component, handed out a hiding to a force more than twice its size. This leads directly to the third point.

What is either forgotten or ignored about the fall of Singapore is that it was not so much lost by the British as taken away from them by the Japanese. Focusing so much attention on British failings has served to deny the Japanese proper recognition and acclaim for what was by any standard one of the most brilliant feats of arms in the war, perhaps in modern military history. At every level—strategic direction, tactics, command, equipment, in the air, at sea, and on land—the Japanese decisively outscored a British force that, when it had divested itself of notions of Japanese racial inferiority, built up a picture of Japanese omnipotence and invincibility in the jungle. This image had an immediate impact on events in Malaya; at every stage forces were looking over their shoulders for a shorter line in the rear. The first, and in many cases only, tactic in response to contact with the enemy became withdrawal. The myth of the Japanese supersoldier took a long time to die; it was not until 1943–44 that it was laid to rest in Burma, and by then the Americans and Australians had ripped more than a few holes in the myth through various actions in the Pacific. Not until late in the war did the British realize that, just as the Japanese had used Western techniques to defeat Western powers, they in their turn could use the methods that the Japanese had so successfully employed in 1941–42. The Japanese had pieced together realistic training, good equipment, sound tactics, and high morale, but they forgot to apply for a patent. All this, however, lay in the future. The return of the British to Malaya and Singapore in September 1945 was a long way off in February 1942, when Japan's victory and Britain's prostration were complete and total. At Singapore the British had to endure a defeat not a little of which was of their own making. Such defeats are the hardest to endure because they are the ones that are deserved.

CHAPTER 12

The End in the Indies

By THEIR SUCCESSFUL OCCUPATION of Palembang and southern Sumatra the Japanese snuffed out the faint possibility that the Allies could fight either effectively or for a long period in the defense of Java. By taking southern Sumatra in the west and then Bali and Timor in the east, the Japanese established a semicircle of air and naval bases around the richest island in the Indies. In doing so they shattered what had been a command covering thousands of square miles into four small pockets of local Allied resistance—northern Australia, Burma, Java, and the Philippines—resistance the command itself was unable to direct, coordinate, or reinforce. The ease with which the Japanese crushed Allied opposition in the eastern and western Indies was an unmistakable sign that the final Japanese conquest of the area that ABDA Command has been formed to defend was but a matter of days away.

All this was patently obvious to both Allied and Japanese commanders, and naturally the emotions and plans of the two sides differed greatly. On Java helpless resignation reigned. Among the Japanese the natural elation of being on the brink of achieving the conquest of Southeast Asia buoyed up the forces involved and led Yamamoto on 20 February to amend the plans for the reduction of Java. With all the opportunism of the gambler that he was, the commander in chief of the Combined Fleet planned to push the carriers and Kondo's Battle Force through the chain of islands that formed the eastern Indies in order to rampage in the Indian Ocean south of Java (and against the Australian coast). In effect he planned a fourfold envelopment of Java, with the most powerful part of the Imperial Navy being deployed to annihilate any forces fleeing or reinforcing the island. Even as Yamamoto made these amendments, however, the Allies conceded defeat in the Indies. When on 25 February Nagumo's carriers and Kondo's battleships cleared Kendari to take up their positions in the waters between Java and Australia, they sailed against an ABDA Command that no longer existed.

It can be argued that the process of winding up ABDA Command predated its creation by more than a month or, if one is more charitable, that the process began on its creation. There is much to be said for the argument that ABDA Command never had a chance of denying the Japanese Southeast Asia, that all it could hope to achieve was to buy time. Even this it failed to do because the Japanese were too good for a scratch force that had to pay the price not only of its own weaknesses and mistakes but also for years of illusions. Be that as it may, by the time of the moves against Bali, Darwin, and Timor, the hopelessness of the Allied cause in the Indies was beginning to be recognized not merely within ABDA Command itself but also in London and Washington. The fragmentation of the command led the Combined Chiefs of Staff in Washington on 18 February to ask Wavell if he thought that Burma should revert to India Command. Wavell had never fully approved of Burma being in ABDA Command in the first place, and the following day urged that Burma should be returned to his former command. Two days later, on the twenty-first, Burma passed from the ABDA theater back to India—yet another command change at a time of disastrous defeat, this time on the Sittang River.

ABDA Command thereafter comprised just the Philippines, where its authority had never been even nominal, and Java and northern Australia. In effect, from the time Burma was moved out of ABDA Command the command itself was dead. There was no need for a command to conduct the local defense of Java, a fact that Wavell was not slow to appreciate.

While the decision was being made to remove Burma from Wavell's command, Wavell advised the Combined Chiefs of Staff of the Peirse report of 19 February that Allied air power on Java had a life expectancy of about two weeks. On the twentieth Churchill signalled Wavell that he should consider the future location of his headquarters, and he told the ABDA commander that he anticipated that MacArthur would be evacuated from the Philippines in order to take up a command in Australia. Churchill also expressed a desire to see Wavell back in his post as commander in chief, India. The following day a series of telegrams crossed one another. In a signal to Wavell the Combined Chiefs of Staff expressed the view that "Java should be defended with the utmost resolution. . . . Every day gained is of importance." But the ABDA commander was informed that, while he might redeploy forces within his command for the defense of Java, he could not expect to receive any reinforcements from outside the theater. Burma, Ceylon, and northern Australia were being given priority ahead of Java. This effectively answered the Dutch pleas that naval forces from the British Eastern Fleet in the Indian Ocean and units from the Anzac area should be moved to support Java. In a second message the Combined Chiefs of Staff suggested that Wavell move his headquarters; the following day they specifically suggested that Wavell move to Australia. By that time, however, Wavell had wired his own recommendation to Churchill. On the twenty-first he signalled London to the effect that the defense of Java had broken down and that Allied air power, then down to just eighty aircraft, had passed below the point where it could hope to be effective and where it could only expect to suffer increasingly heavy losses for no return. Wavell told Churchill that Allied air power could only hope to survive for a few more days. The supreme commander went on, "Anything put into Java now can do little to prolong [the] struggle. It is more [a] question of what you will choose to save." Wavell was certainly learning quickly. There was no question of his repeating the error of reinforcing Java long after its fall was inevitable as he had Singapore, but then, Java belonged to the Dutch.

Wavell was quite decisive in his view of the future location of his headquarters. He expressed the view that there was "little further usefulness" in maintaining ABDA Command. With the only task of the command being the defense of Java, Wavell proposed to wind up his command, leaving the defense of Java in the hands of the local Dutch commanders. On the twenty-second Wavell went with Brett to confer with the Dutch governor-general of the Indies, Jonkheer Dr. A.W.L. Tjarda van Starkenborgh Stachouwer, in what Wavell's biographer described as a "dignified, frank and painful" discussion. Undoubtedly the combination of Dutch stoicism and good manners prevented van Starkenborgh from making some pertinent and pithy observations. In effect, the Americans and British, after creating ABDA Command without consulting the Dutch, taking for themselves all the major command appointments, and having contributed very little to the attempt to hold the general area, while securing what Dutch help was available for the vain defense of Singapore, were intent on abandoning the Dutch before the last battles for Java were fought. The Dutch, fighting not simply for an empire but, in many cases, for their homes and families, were to be left on their own, unsupported except for the 5,500 British and 2,900 Australians (servicemen and civilians) and the one American artillery battalion already on the island.

Of all the unpalatable aspects of the campaign in the Indies the most distasteful surely must be the rapidity and totality with which Wavell,

London, and Washington recognized Java's indefensibility after so long and stubborn a refusal to abandon Singapore. Admittedly, the circumstances were different. There were no reinforcements left to send to Java; these had been wasted at Singapore. The linchpin of Wavell's strategy to hold the Indies had been the retention of Singapore; once the British base had surrendered, the western Indies became indefensible and hence Java was left exposed. There is no doubt that at the time Wavell, London, and Washington were correct in regarding the Allied cause in the Indies as hopeless. But their views seem to sit ill beside the prodigal waste of resources that had been the chief characteristic of the Singapore effort.

Van Starkenborgh had little real option but to concur with Wavell's views. Though these views had not been formally approved by the Combined Chiefs of Staff, it was evident that they had Washington's support and there was nothing the Dutch could do about it. The governor-general accepted that Java should revert to Dutch command, as part of the process whereby each of the different parts of the ABDA Command reverted back to its original national command. Van Starkenborgh accepted Wavell's argument in favor of winding up ABDA Command immediately on the ground that to wind it up after either invasion or heavy air attack was certain to be disastrous for morale. Both men agreed that, if ABDA Command was to be dissolved, then the sooner the better. Wavell told the governor-general that he would urge the Combined Chiefs of Staff to continue to send reinforcements to Java in order to show the Dutch that the dissolution of the command did not imply they were being abandoned. In view of what Wavell had previously signalled about the pointlessness of attempting to send reinforcements to Java and the decision of the Combined Chiefs of Staff to place other theaters before Java in the list of priorities, this sweetener on Wavell's part seems little more than a shallow and dishonest deception. Whether the Dutchman saw through it is unknown. He accepted Wavell's points, and with Dutch agreement the supreme commander signalled the Combined Chiefs of Staff, recommending not to move but to dissolve his command. Washington accepted the logic of the argument and, after an existence of just forty-one days, ABDA Command passed into history at 0900 (local time) on 25 February 1942.

Even before the Japanese forces involved in the Bali, Darwin, and Timor operations began to move to their battle stations on 17 February, hundreds of miles in the rear final preparations were being made for the main-force landings on Java. The Japanese planned for two sets of landings, one in eastern Java and the other in western Java in the general area of Batavia. In western Java the Japanese landings were divided among three areas. The *2nd Infantry Division* divided its attention between Merak and Bantam Bay, at the northern exit of the Sunda Strait; while the *Shoji Detachment* and the *230th Infantry Regiment*, less one of its battalions but with a mountain

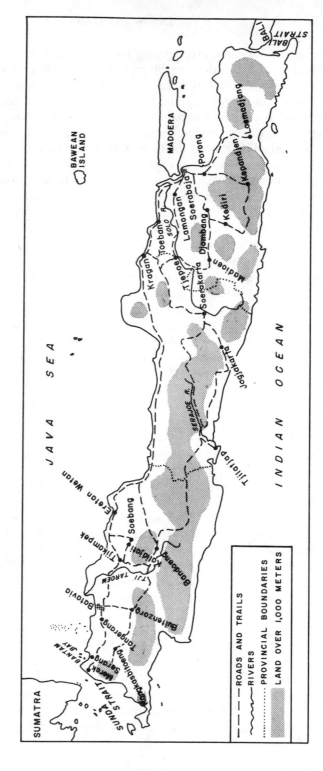

Java

artillery unit, a light tank company, and signals troops in support, was detailed to land some 120 miles east of Bantam Bay at Eretan Wetan. Among them, these forces were to secure Batavia and the general area of western Java. To the east the *48th Infantry Division* plus the *Sakaguchi Detachment*, the *56th Regimental Group* less the detachment it had left behind on Borneo, were to land at Kragan, a port on the north Java coast some 90 miles west of Soerabaja. The detachment was given the task of forcing its way through the mountains of central Java in order to take the southern port of Tjilatjap, while the *48th Infantry Division* was allocated the task of securing the major prize in eastern Java, the port of Soerabaja itself. As a preliminary to the two invasions a small detachment was to secure Bawean Island, about 100 miles north of Soerabaja in the Java Sea, in order to establish a radio relay station for the main-force operations.

Even before the islands of Bali and Timor were assaulted, the major part of the forces involved in the Java operation sailed from their ports of embarkation, the western invasion force leaving Camranh Bay on 18 February in no fewer than fifty-six transports. The *48th Infantry Division*, having completed its movement down from Luzon during the early part of February, sailed from Jolo on the following day in forty-one transports. This force put in at Balikpapan to embark the *56th Regimental Group* and sailed from the port for Java on the twenty-third.

The naval forces that were deployed for the Java operations were substantial and, being large in number and formed into various groups that linked up with one another at different times, unclear in their exact composition. There were four main groups of forces: those deployed to the south of Java, those deployed as escorts and cover for the eastern landings, those attached to the invasion operations in western Java, and the small force in the Java Sea that gave distant cover to both the western and the eastern landings.

The forces deployed to the south of Java consisted of three groupings: fourteen submarines; Nagumo's carrier task force of four carriers and their escorts; and Kondo's Battle Force of two battleships, three cruisers, and a number of destroyers. The western force consisted of a close escort of the light cruiser *Natori* and eight destroyers, which sailed from Indo-China with the transports. As this convoy entered the combat zone from the South China Sea it was joined by minesweepers and submarine chasers that had taken part in the southern Sumatra operation as well as by another destroyer flotilla and the *Ryujo*, two seaplane carriers, four heavy cruisers, and a division of destroyers. The eastern invasion force was convoyed on its way from Balikpapan by eight destroyers and their leader, the *Naka*, with some six chasers and two minesweepers and other units in attendance. As this force entered the Java Sea from the Makassar Strait it was given support by the light cruiser *Jintsu* and her destroyers, which had sailed from

Koepang, Timor, on the twenty-fourth. Two heavy cruisers, the *Haguro* and *Nachi*, with a destroyer escort, provided support. Sailing from Kendari as general cover for both sets of landings were the heavy cruisers *Ashigara* and *Myoko* and their escorting destroyers.

The Japanese plan of invasion basically relied on the powerful escort forces and the simultaneous nature of the twin thrusts on Java to frustrate the possibility of Allied intervention. But it would appear that in ordering their deployments the Japanese, particularly Yamamoto, who had ordered the plans changed, were either singularly confident or unduly contemptuous of Allied strength on Java. The deployment of Nagumo's carrier forces and land-based aircraft to the waters south of Java contributed to the considerable Allied losses in the area. Yet the deployment shows that Yamamoto, thousands of miles from the scene of the action, either exhibited genius in being able to gauge Allied weakness in the area after weeks of war or, more likely, accepted far too willingly exaggerated combat reports, which claimed that the Allies were effectively written off. There is no denying that the Allies were extremely weak in the air, but hardly weak enough to justify stripping the eastern invasion force of its air support. Though defeat and disaster were avoided, a more conservative and cautious deployment of air strength would have been prudent in view of the importance of the merchantmen and troops earmarked for this operation.

The scale of the escort and the way in which the eastern invasion force was deployed also give rise to comment, for it was formed into two columns over a length of 20 miles. With only one flanking destroyer on either side and many submarines remaining to the Allies, this formation ran risks that were really unacceptable but that, fortunately for the Japanese on this occasion, failed to materialize. Moreover, at one stage on the twenty-seventh, as this convoy entered dangerous waters, the heavy cruisers *Haguro* and *Nachi* were nearly 200 miles astern of the convoy, while the *Jintsu* and her destroyers were not in immediate support. This scattered deployment could well have ended in disaster on the twenty-seventh had the Allied forces available to meet the invasion made contact a couple of hours earlier than was in fact the case. The Japanese tendency to move forces in separated groups over vast distances against a single objective always threatened to leave the groups exposed to defeat in detail because they were invariably too widely spaced to be mutually supporting. As long as the Japanese could move behind a secured air front (and Japanese naval aircraft outranged Allied naval aircraft throughout the war), this tactic was reasonably sound, but stripping air support from the eastern invasion force in fact brought that force uncomfortably close at least to embarrassment. What subsequently proved to be an overwhelming victory for the Japanese in the Battle of the Java Sea obscured this, but the Americans brought the lesson home to the Japanese with a vengeance at Midway. Even then, however, the Japanese were slow to absorb the lesson.

Allied intelligence and reconnaissance quickly revealed the emerging Japanese intentions and the local Dutch naval commander, Conrad E.L. Helfrich, began to try to redeploy his pitifully inadequate and dispersed forces to meet the threats that were developing. By 25 February the means he had at hand were totally inadequate to his needs. The Allies had suffered a continuous rate of loss that had drastically reduced their numbers, while their effectiveness had been greatly lowered by torpedo shortages and the overworking of ships and men.

During the campaign the Americans deployed in the Indies one heavy and two light cruisers and thirteen destroyers, the British one heavy and four light cruisers and seven destroyers, while the Dutch had the same number of destroyers as the British but only three light cruisers. By 25 February, accidents, enemy action, and overwork had made massive inroads into these numbers. Both of the American light cruisers had been

Vice Admiral Conrad E. L. Helfrich, RNN. The last Allied naval commander in ABDA Command, he saw the defense of the Indies downgraded to the point where, when he took command, the Dutch possessions could no longer be defended. Naval Historical Department, Royal Netherlands Navy, The Hague

detached because of damage, while the *Houston* should have been. Helfrich, however, could not afford to part with a heavy cruiser that, even without her rear turret, represented nearly half of his 8-inch ordnance. Two American destroyers, the *Peary* and *Stewart*, had been lost, the former at Darwin, the latter in a dockyard accident. The *Pope* was in drydock at the time of Helfrich's need, while the *Bulmer* and *Barker* were escorting the destroyer tender *Black Hawk* to Australia. The *Parrott* and *Pillsbury* had had to be detached because their torpedoes were all but expended, while two more destroyers, the *Edsall* and *Whipple*, were put out of the fight because of damage sustained in accidents. That left only four American destroyers, the *Alden*, *John D. Edwards*, *John D. Ford*, and *Paul Jones* under his command and fit for action.

The British had not suffered losses in the Indies but two of their destroyers, the *Express* and *Vampire*, had been detached for escort duties in the Indian Ocean. In any case, the British contribution to the defense of Java was exaggerated by the presence of such light cruisers as the *Danae* and *Dragon*. Their effectiveness can be gauged by their having spent most of the time since 1939 on nonactive stations. They were World War I vintage, very fine in their day but totally outclassed by their Japanese opposite numbers in 1942. The Dutch, however, had taken losses that were grievous because there was no possibility of their being replaced. The *Tromp*'s services had been denied as a result of the Badoeng Strait engagement, while four of the destroyers had been lost: the *Van Ghent* off Banka, the *Van Nes* at the Sunda Strait, the *Piet Hein* off Bali, and the *Banckert* at Soerabaja. In all, three light cruisers and fifteen destroyers that had served the Allies in the Indies had been lost, to a variety of causes, by the time the Japanese invasion forces neared Java. What was left to Helfrich was a total of two heavy cruisers, one of which had been badly damaged, while the other stood in urgent need of a refit; six light cruisers, two of which were no more than floating coffins; and twelve destroyers, all of which badly needed overhauling.

On 21 February, in order to meet what would obviously be a two-pronged invasion of Java, Helfrich constituted an eastern and a western striking force from the few ships that he had available. With the threat from the east developing slightly before that in the west, Helfrich decided to concentrate Allied warships under Doorman's flag at Soerabaja. Doorman had with him his two light cruisers, *de Ruyter* and *Java*; his destroyers *Evertsen*, *Kortenaer*, and *Witte de With*; and the four American destroyers. The *Houston* was en route to Soerabaja, but the British forces were at Batavia. The shortage of fuel, even in oil-rich Java, meant that the Allied warships had to be dispersed so they could obtain sufficient fuel from a variety of sources, thus increasing the wear and tear on men and machinery. Helfrich ordered the better ships at Batavia to join Doorman, leaving only a token force of the *Danae* and *Dragon*, plus the antiquated *Scout* and *Tenedos*, to oppose the Japanese in the west. Because of refuelling difficulties the Australian light cruiser *Hobart* had to be left behind when the heavy cruiser *Exeter*, the light cruiser *Perth*, and the destroyers *Electra*, *Encounter*, and *Jupiter* set course for Soerabaja.

The Dutch plan was to try to concentrate to meet the Japanese thrust in the east and to leave minimal forces in the west. Without waiting for either the *Houston* or the British to join him, Doorman took his force to sea in a dusk-to-dawn sweep of the waters to the north of Madoera (25/26 February), in the belief that he might intercept transports coming south of Bawean Island. Just before midnight the forces at Batavia (the *Hobart* and her four elderly companions) similarly set off on a night sweep of the western approaches to Java. Neither force encountered the Japanese, who at that time had not advanced as far south as the Dutch believed and were not within range of Allied warships. By midmorning of the twenty-sixth the Batavian contingent was back in the harbor, where it was joined by the *Evertsen*, detached from Doorman's command in order to top up at Batavia. The following day this combined force of three light cruisers and three destroyers received orders to make another sweep of the Banka area during the night but, if no contact was obtained by 0430 on the twenty-eighth, to make for Ceylon via the Sunda Strait. With all the advantages of scouting that air superiority conferred on the Japanese, the western invasion force had no trouble in retiring from the area when the Allied ships approached. Japanese aircraft failed to sink any of the Allied ships. The Japanese were not prepared to press into the Java Sea unless and until they were sure that they faced no opposition, no matter how insignificant. With the failure to obtain a contact, the Allied force began its withdrawal through the Sunda Strait. The five British ships reached Ceylon safely. The *Evertsen*, on the other hand, became detached during a storm and remained in the area of the strait.

The Batavian force therefore was spared an encounter with an enemy that, without doubt, would have destroyed it. Helfrich was well aware that sacrifice was called for, but his orders at least spared the British ships from having to make a pointless sacrifice. His decision has been criticized by the official American naval historian on the grounds that Helfrich's orders for separate forces and for the Batavian force to withdraw if it failed to obtain a contact prevented the Allies from meeting the Japanese with their full strength. The charge is superficially reasonable, but it is utterly irrelevant. The ships that swept the Banka area for Japanese transports would not have added anything to the strength of Doorman's force. In any case, by the time these ships slipped through the Sunda Strait on their way to Ceylon Doorman was dead, one-third of his force had been sunk, and another third of his ships had but hours before meeting their end.

Events in the east unfolded with alarming rapidity. After his sweep
south of Bawean on the night of 25/26 February, Doorman returned to
Soerabaja, where he was joined by British ships coming up from Batavia.
Doorman intended to sail immediately to the north to meet the Japanese,
proposing that his cruisers should deal with the Japanese warships while
the British and Dutch destroyers should seek to break into the lines of
transports and wreak havoc with guns and torpedoes. Because of the danger
of pressing too far to the north and thus allowing the Japanese force to slip
through to Java unmolested, Doorman intended to conduct a sweep relatively close to Java in the southern part of the Java Sea. Accordingly, just
before midnight on the twenty-sixth Doorman led his forces out of Soerabaja. Throughout the night the Allied force sought in vain for the Japanese
invasion force. Doorman had been unlucky in that he had been too quick for
the Japanese. The latter, having planned to make their landfall on the
twenty-eighth, were still many miles to the north.

Soon after dawn Doorman's forces were discovered by Japanese aircraft,
which throughout the day proved a crippling handicap to the admiral.
While many aspects of the Japanese performance on the twenty-seventh
were far from satisfactory, the contribution of the scouting Japanese aircraft
was an outstanding exception. Every turn, every change of speed that
Doorman made was faithfully reported by the Japanese reconnaissance
aircraft and the Japanese admirals moved their forces to accommodate
changing Allied intentions. The transports were turned away when it
seemed danger threatened, back towards Java when it appeared that it had
passed; the escorts closed up when an action appeared imminent. Even after
dark on the twenty-seventh the Japanese aircraft, using extremely powerful
flares, continued their task of relentlessly shadowing the Allied force. In
view of the good performance of Japanese aircraft and the difficulty that the
Japanese encountered in dealing with Doorman's force, one is left with the
unanswerable question of what Nagumo's carriers might have achieved had
they been in support of the invasion force and not scourging the seas south
of Java. Doorman, on the other hand, with one critically important exception, enjoyed no comparable service. He fought this action, metaphorically
and at the end literally, in the dark.

At midmorning, after having survived with little difficulty a weak and
poorly conducted air attack, Doorman set course for Soerabaja. The need
to refuel the destroyers, the failure of the search, the lack of air reconnaissance, and the depleted state of antiaircraft ammunition stocks all were
factors that prompted this decision. Despite orders from Helfrich to resume
the search for the Japanese, Doorman persisted on his course. His leading
destroyers had just entered the swept channel through the minefields that
guarded Soerabaja when Doorman received reliable and confirmed sighting
reports that placed the Japanese transports to the west and northwest of

Bawean. Doorman immediately altered course and raised speed in order to close the enemy.

The Japanese escorts had followed the various changes of direction made by the Allied force and had closed up their forces a little in the course of the morning. But Doorman's obvious abandoning of his return to Soerabaja seriously alarmed the Japanese. It was evident that Doorman was making for the convoys and that he might be able to reach them before the heavy cruisers *Haguro* and *Nachi* came on the scene. One of the great ironies of the Battle of the Java Sea was that by discontinuing his search in midmorning and setting course for Soerabaja, Doorman unwittingly let slip his only chance of coming across the Japanese invasion force when he had a definite superiority over its escorts. Though the Allied force would have been outnumbered in destroyers, the presence of the *Exeter* and *Houston* and three light cruisers would have given it a definite edge in gun power if it had been able to make contact sometime around noon. By the time that contact was made, however, the balance of force had swung decisively against the Allies. By the time Doorman's ships sighted the masts of the *Jintsu* and her destroyers, the *Nuku* and her escorts were on hand to support the threatened Japanese force. They were some 20 miles to the west, having come south from the transports. The *Haguro* and *Nachi*, having steamed at full speed to put the miles behind them, sighted the *Jintsu* and her escorts at about the same time as Doorman, and thus were within a matter of minutes of providing support. With the three Japanese forces standing between the Allies and the transports, the Japanese thus held not just the advantage of position but, by a very fine margin, a five to three advantage in heavy guns.

The Allied force approached from the southeast in three parallel columns, the center column consisting of the cruisers led by the *de Ruyter*. On the port beam were the two remaining Dutch destroyers, *Witte de With* and *Kortenaer*, while the four American destroyers, headed by the *Edwards*, took up station on the port quarter. The British destroyers, led by the *Electra*, were on the starboard beam, where the Allies might reasonably expect to make their first sighting of the enemy. The Japanese dispositions resulted in the *Jintsu* and her destroyers being the first Japanese force to obtain contact with the Allied ships. Close to the west were the *Haguro*, *Nachi*, and their destroyers. The light forces attached themselves to the *Jintsu* column as they came up, thereby allowing the heavy cruisers to maneuver together but independently. Some 10 miles beyond the heavy cruisers at the time of the first contact were the *Naka* and six destroyers. Beyond these forces to the northwest were the precious transports and a minimal escort.

The course of the battle was dictated by the Allied need to outmaneuver or outshoot the Japanese escorts in order to get at the transports. The Japanese objective was primarily to frustrate the attempt, secondly to destroy Doorman's force. Two factors served to ensure that the Allied aims were not achieved: Japanese control of the air and the initial Japanese advantage of a position between the transports and the enemy. These were handicaps the Allied force proved incapable of overcoming.

Indeed, the initial position of the combatants threatened that the Japanese would secure at the very outset the immense tactical advantage of crossing the Allied *T*. With twenty 8-inch guns to play on the Allied line, to have been able to cross the Allied *T* would have placed the Japanese in a position of very great, perhaps decisive, advantage. It was not surprising, therefore, that Doorman chose to turn away on a roughly parallel westerly course, but this line of action in fact was the one least suited to secure Allied aims. First, it forced the Allies away from the transports, allowing the Japanese in part to secure their primary objective virtually without trying. Second, it was essential for Doorman to close the range as quickly as possible in order to get into action the only advantage that remained to the Allies, their superiority in the numbers of guns on their light cruisers. A long-range duel fought beyond the range of 6-inch and 5.9-inch guns could only result in either decisive damage being inflicted on the Allied ships or the latter being forced to break off the action. If the Allies were to close the range, then Doorman had to accept the Japanese crossing his *T*.

Perhaps the most remarkable feature of the action that developed as the two sides settled down to an artillery and torpedo duel was that, even with the overwhelming advantage of spotting aircraft, the two Japanese heavy cruisers fired for just over sixty minutes and achieved only two hits, one of which was a dud. The Japanese shot brilliantly, but unluckily. Straddles followed one another with almost monotonous regularity. (It is believed that the *Perth* steamed through eight in succession.) Very close groupings characterized all of them, but somehow the Allied ships led charmed existences until 1638, more than fifty minutes after the first exchange of fire. Then the *Exeter* was hit by an 8-inch shell that penetrated to the boiler room before exploding, putting six of the ship's eight boilers out of action. With the immediate loss of power, the *Exeter*'s guns failed to reply as the ship's speed fell to 11 knots and she pulled out of the line away from the enemy in an effort to avoid being run down by the next astern, the *Houston*.

This one hit effectively decided the battle because as the *Exeter* hauled out of the line chaos engulfed the Allied force. Of the many weaknesses that plagued Doorman's force, the most serious was communications. There was no common code for the ships of three navies and Doorman had to carry a British liaison officer with him in the *de Ruyter* in order to pass orders to the *Exeter* for her to relay them to the English-speakers. The system was slow and inefficient but the best that could be arranged under the circumstances. As the *Exeter* staggered out of the line the *Houston* assumed that a turn had been ordered and followed the British cruiser; the *Perth* and *Java*, acting on the same assumption, conformed, until all four ships were more or less in line abreast. The *de Ruyter*, with the three British destroyers, momentarily steamed on the original course in an isolation that rapidly threatened to become precarious rather than splendid. Within five minutes of the hit on the *Exeter* the Allied line had virtually ceased to exist. To compound the chaos during that time a torpedo, probably fired from the *Haguro*, found its mark on the *Kortenaer*. The Dutch destroyer broke her back almost immediately.

The Japanese initially believed that the Allied turn away was deliberate, being aimed at avoiding torpedoes, which the Japanese had used on a lavish but ineffective scale since shortly after the action was joined. Most of these attacks had been mounted by the *Naka* and her escorts as they moved around the rear of the two main Japanese columns engaging Doorman. These attacks met with fierce but generally ineffective fire from the Allied line and, until the *Kortenaer* was struck, none had achieved any result. Ranges of about 8 miles proved beyond the Long Lance torpedo on this occasion. But aided by the reports of the spotting aircraft, the Japanese rapidly came to the conclusion that the turn away had been forced upon the Allies by reasons more serious than the desire to dodge torpedoes. When it became clear that, amid the chaos of the Allied line, some form of reasoned order was being restored as ships settled on a southeasterly course away from the enemy, the Japanese swung around to the south and southeast, naturally reversing their order of battle in the process. From being the most southerly and closest of the Japanese forces to the Allies, the *Naka* and her destroyers became the most westerly and distant. The two heavy cruisers for the moment came inside the destroyers to take a station most likely to regain contact with an Allied force then withdrawing under cover of smoke.

With the Japanese working their way westwards to get around the Allied flank in an attempt to continue the battle, Doorman began the task of reorganizing his forces. This was achieved surprisingly quickly. The lone *Exeter*, as she limped eastwards, was afforded cover on her starboard side by the sole surviving Dutch and three British destroyers. Further west, after a series of circles and violent turns, the four Allied cruisers regrouped in a line-ahead formation, with the *de Ruyter* in the vanguard and the four American destroyers taking station on the disengaged port side.

The *Exeter* naturally lagged behind and the Japanese, as they swung eastwards on a course that took them across the Allied wake, logically concentrated against her. A series of confused skirmishes followed, with the Allied warships maneuvering to draw fire and thus facilitate the *Exeter*'s escape. In the course of the initial exchanges the *Electra* hit and badly damaged the *Asagumo*, causing the Japanese destroyer to go dead in the water for some minutes. But the Japanese ship managed to get under way and reached Balikpapan the next day. The *Electra*, however, did not long enjoy her partial success. As it became obvious through the smoke-strewn battle area that the Japanese were preparing for an onslaught in full strength on the *Exeter*, the *Electra* led her two sisters through the smoke screen to attack the Japanese forces. Because of her distance from the other two destroyers, she entered the screen alone and emerged on the other side equally alone to face two light cruisers and fourteen destroyers bearing down on her. Very briefly the one-sided action flared, and the British destroyer was shot to pieces within seconds.

The sacrifice of the *Electra* was not altogether in vain because neither the *Jintsu* nor the *Naka* was prepared to lead its formation into too close an action. Both they and the two heavy cruisers reversed course westwards in order to retain their positions between the transports and the Allies. They were not prepared to indulge in a stern chase with the Allies to starboard on the flank nearer the transports. The Japanese were in an awkward position. Their failure to destroy Doorman's force left them as night drew on having to guess whether Doorman would attempt to repeat his efforts to work around the flank to get at the transports or whether he would set a course for Soerabaja—and possibly encounter the distant support force then coming into the waters that washed Madoera Island. After the respite afforded by the *Electra*, Doorman had made two efforts to work his way around to the east, one with just the American destroyers, the other with his cruisers. After contact was broken off, with the Japanese steering westwards and the Allies heading towards Soerabaja, he made one more attempt to get around what he hoped would be the unguarded eastern flank. He was unfortunate in that the Japanese had guessed his intention. As he steamed northwards, therefore, Doorman encountered first the *Jintsu* and her destroyers and then the *Haguro* and *Nachi*. A desultory exchange at long range and in poor light inflicted no damage on either side. The Allies broke off the action by turning to the east and then to the south to make a landfall on the north Javanese coast. Throughout the hours of daylight, therefore, the Japanese had been successful in frustrating Allied attempts to get among the transports; it was now a question of what the night would bring.

On reaching the coast Doorman had to choose between resuming his effort against the transports and returning to Soerabaja. For the American destroyers there was no such choice. Out of torpedoes and low on fuel, they had to steer a course for port. Doorman chose to resume his foray, but in following the flagship the *Jupiter* struck a mine that had strayed from a field laid that day by the Dutch. The British destroyer sank slowly. As Doorman headed north in one final, stubborn attempt to locate the transports, his ships steamed through the survivors of the *Kortenaer*. The *Encounter* was detached to rescue survivors, while Doorman maintained his course with his four cruisers, now devoid of escorting destroyers.

As Doorman steamed northwards he again met first the *Jintsu* force and then the two heavy cruisers coming roughly south; once again the Japanese had managed to frustrate the Dutchman's attempt to evade their warships and get among the merchantmen. But this time the Japanese were to be rewarded not merely with forestalling the Allies but with decisive success. After the *Haguro* and *Nachi* reversed course and engaged in an indeterminate exchange of gunfire with the Allied ships, they launched torpedoes that crashed into the *de Ruyter* and *Java* at either end of Doorman's line. Both Dutchmen sank almost immediately, but not before Doorman had the time and presence of mind to issue his last orders to the *Perth* and *Houston*, to make for Batavia and not to attempt the rescue of survivors.

Thus ended the Battle of the Java Sea, the first major engagement between fleets since the Battle of Jutland, a quarter-century earlier. In terms of sea battles it was rare in that it was fought by combatants both of whom sought battle; most naval battles have been fought with one side reluctant to stand and fight. The Battle of the Java Sea was different. The Allies, despite their inferiority, had to give battle if they were to prevent the invasion of Java from the east. There was nothing to be gained by adopting a passive role as Japanese forces closed in for the kill because Allied inferiority was such that there was no threat, no check on Japanese movements, presented by trying to preserve "a fleet in being." To do nothing would be to lose Java and invite destruction. The Japanese, on the other hand, did not have the same overwhelming reasons to seek battle for the very good reason that they enjoyed virtually all the advantages of command of the sea even before the action. They were prepared to give battle, particularly when the heavy cruisers came up, as the best means possible of securing the absolute safety of their transports. Of course, with so much of Japanese naval doctrine built around the desirability of battle, it was natural that the Japanese should welcome the engagement as a means of reducing enemy power in the most effective manner possible. But in reality the Japanese had little to gain even from a successful encounter; after the battle they enjoyed very little more in terms of freedom than they had before the action.

The battle was also unusual in one other respect: it was fought to a decisive result. It was the first such battle since the action off the Falklands in 1914. The Allies lost two light cruisers and three destroyers; one heavy cruiser was badly damaged. Only one Japanese warship suffered any appreciable damage and only two or three Japanese ships suffered hits and casualties. The most overwhelming human losses were inflicted on the Allied nations. The defeat was decisive, and everyone involved in the action knew it at the time. The Allies had not been in a position to offer Java effective defense even before the battle; after it the position of the surviving Allied warships and Java alike was hopeless. What was left to the Allies was a broken force consisting of one heavy cruiser and seven destroyers (the four American destroyers that had fought on the twenty-seventh, the *Pope*, *Witte de With*, and *Encounter*) at Soerabaja in eastern Java; the *Evertsen* and the five British warships from Batavia in western Java (within hours after the loss of the *de Ruyter* and *Java* all but the Dutch destroyer cleared the Sunda Strait on a course for Ceylon); and the *Perth* and *Houston*. These were to the north of Java, unwittingly on a course that was to lead them to destruction—a fate they shared with other Allied ships south of Java at this time as they too ran into an enemy they were trying to evade.

The carnage so evident in the Java Sea on 27 February was beginning to be repeated with a vengeance south of Java on that same day as Allied warships, auxiliaries, and merchantmen attempted to flee via the Sunda or Badoeng straits or from Tjilatjap for the safety of Ceylon or Australia. They had to run the gauntlet of fourteen submarines, Nagumo's carrier force, Kondo's Battle Force, and land-based aircraft reaching into the Indian Ocean from Kendari and Banjamasin. In the last six days of February and the first four days of March the Japanese submarines accounted for just over 73,000 tons of Allied merchantmen, but the first really significant loss south of Java took place at the time the Battle of the Java Sea was being fought to the north. The old tender *Langley*, the first carrier ever owned by the U.S. Navy but long since reduced to seaplane tender status, was caught by land-based aircraft and sunk, along with her cargo of forty American aircraft destined for Tjilatjap. On 1 March five merchantmen succumbed, while the *Edsall* was sunk with all hands. The American destroyer was chased and caught by the two battleships and two heavy cruisers from Nagumo's command, while aircraft from the carriers destroyed the fleet oiler *Pecos*, which had the misfortune to be carrying the wounded from the *Houston* and *Marblehead*, the crew of the *Stewart*, and some of the survivors from the *Langley*. Loss of life when the *Pecos* went down was therefore heavy, but the *Whipple* picked up what survivors there were. The following day Kondo's forces muscled in on the action, accounting for the British destroyer *Stronghold* and the American destroyer *Pillsbury*, while two more merchantmen and the old U.S. gunboat *Asheville* also were lost, the latter to Nagumo's destroyers. Kondo's escorts on the fourth annihilated a small British military convoy led by the sloop *Yarra*, while air raids on Tjilatjap accounted for three small merchantmen. On the fifth, however, Nagumo's aircraft cut loose with raids on air bases at Broome in northern Australia and against Tjilatjap, destroying or causing to be scuttled over the next forty-eight hours twenty-one small ships totalling 20,000 tons. A few captures supplemented the Japanese haul, but for the most part the Japanese were more intent on sinking ships that would have been more than useful to them if they had taken the trouble to try to take prizes. Overall, between 22 February and 5 March, the Japanese accounted for about 175,000 tons of Allied warships, auxiliaries, and merchantmen either at Tjilatjap or in the waters south of Java.

With so many warships and submarines working supposedly interlocking sectors of ocean and Japanese aircraft operating without opposition, it seemed impossible that any Allied ships could evade the Japanese net. Yet it would appear from the number of sailings from Javanese ports that as many reached safety as fell foul of the enemy. Among the most ironic of the evasions was that of the *Sea Witch*, which arrived in Tjilatjap on the twenty-seventh with a cargo of twenty-seven crated fighters. Tjilatjap had no airfield and the aircraft, brought in at such risk, had to be destroyed in their crates on the dockside when the port was abandoned by the Allies. The Japanese forces failed to intercept the *Hobart* and her companions after their sortie towards Banka on 27/28 February; these escaped to Ceylon after stopping at Padang to pick up refugees. More seriously, the Japanese failed to locate the military convoy (S.U.1) with twelve transports totalling 97,741 tons, which was bringing 10,900 Australian troops back home from the Middle East. This troop convoy was under the protection of the battleship *Royal Sovereign*, the heavy cruiser *Cornwall*, and five escorts. The convoy moved a little too far to the west for it to be detected by the Japanese. Had it been found and annihilated (the fighting value of the British R-class battleships was very low), then the Japanese would have secured a return commensurate with the effort they made south of Java. They would certainly have carried out an action that would have done little to restore Anglo-Australian relations, which were more than slightly strained as a result of the Singapore disaster. But this convoy escaped unscathed, as did the *Edwards* and her three compatriots from the Java Sea, as they fled southwards from Soerabaja. For the other survivors of the battle, plus certain ships in northern Javanese ports, there was to be no escape.

The *Perth* and *Houston* were the first of the Allied ships north of Java to be lost, but their loss involved a tragic irony for the Allies. They alone of the Allied warships, except for the American destroyers at Balikpapan, actually managed to get among the Japanese transports and sink some of them before they themselves were destroyed. After weeks of striving vainly for such a chance, when the elusive opportunity finally presented itself, the Allied force was numerically and qualitatively too weak to take advantage of it.

The *Perth* and *Houston* refuelled at Batavia on the twenty-eighth, receiving orders to sail that night via the Sunda Strait to Tjilatjap, from where Helfrich, with more determination than realism, intended to carry on the fight. The danger of trying to pass through the strait was obvious. The western invasion force arrived off its objectives on the twenty-eighth and throughout the latter part of the day was involved in putting forces ashore at Bantam Bay and Merak. In order to reach the strait the two cruisers would have to steam through waters infested by Japanese transports and warships.

The promise inherent in meeting the former was more than offset by the perils of a probable encounter with the latter.

The two Allied cruisers anticipated action when they left Batavia after dark. Given their deployment, the Japanese forces in Bantam Bay clearly did not, though this seems surprising since the cruisers had fled during the Battle of the Java Sea to Batavia, where they refuelled while under air attack. The Japanese had the *Ryujo* force well to the north, out of harm's way, and three cruisers and ten destroyers in a wide screen around the transports in the bay. Most of the warships were either in the strait or in the north of the bay. Only the destroyer *Fubuki* was on station to the east on the direct route from Batavia and only two destroyers, the *Harukaze* and *Hatakaze*, were in direct support of the transports when the *Houston* led the smaller Australian cruiser into the anchorage.

The Allied cruisers therefore faced extremely weak opposition as they sighted the Japanese transports, but any advantage they enjoyed was certain to be fleeting as Japanese forces converged on the two ships in response to the *Fubuki*'s calls for assistance. Just what happened in the two hours either side of midnight (28 February/1 March) is impossible to disentangle as warships clashed at high speed amidst the shoals. At least for the early part of the action identifying the sources of damage inflicted on various ships is simply guesswork, but at the end of the action four Japanese transports and a minesweeper had been sunk or damaged and beached, and five Japanese warships had been damaged. Much of the loss and damage suffered by the Japanese forces may well have been self-inflicted. It appears that the minesweeper and two of the transports were lost when the *Fubuki*, resorting to a foolhardy expedient in an effort to nail the *Houston* and *Perth*, fired torpedoes at the two Allied cruisers when they were standing out against a background formed by the transports. When the cruisers combed the tracks the torpedoes smacked into the helpless Japanese ships off the coast. For the *Perth* and *Houston*, however, in the end there could be no escape from the concentration of force that quickly came up to oppose them. First the *Perth* succumbed to a flurry of shells and torpedoes and then the *Houston*, crippled by an explosion that scalded to death all those in the engine room, slipped beneath the waves. Early the next morning the *Evertsen*, coming up astern, was caught and crippled by Japanese warships still prowling the area. She ran herself aground in the Sunda Strait in order to avoid foundering, and she became a total wreck.

On the twenty-eighth the *Exeter*, *Encounter*, and *Pope* in Soerabaja received the same orders as the *Perth* and *Houston*. Palliser, the senior British naval officer on Java, confirmed that the ships should proceed via the Sunda Strait as opposed to the nearer Bali or Lombok passages. These orders condemned the three ships to a long approach in the course of which they could scarcely hope to remain undetected by a rampant enemy. In order to evade detection the ships headed east of Bawean Island in the hope that by hugging the south Borneo coast they might somehow be overlooked by the Japanese, but this faint hope proved illusory. The Allied ships were trapped on the morning of the first by a collection of Japanese warships and flight proved unavailing. The two British warships were sunk by gunfire and torpedoes from Japanese cruisers and destroyers. The *Pope* was caught by aircraft from the *Ryujo*. Japanese warships and demolition charges between them administered the coup de grace. Japanese aircraft that same day badly damaged the *Witte de With* in Soerabaja. The next day she (along with the *Banckert*; the submarines *K-X*, *K-XIII*, and *K-XVIII*; the mine-layers *Soemenep*, *Bangkalen*, and *Rigel*; the gunnery training ship *Soerabaja*; the accommodation ship *Konig der Nederlanden*) and various other ships were scuttled in the port by their Dutch masters. The *Soerabaja* and *Konig der Nederlanden* must have been among the oldest warships to see action in the war. The *Soerabaja* had been involved in troop convoying in the southern Indies during December. She had been launched in 1909 as the *Zeven Provincien*, a protected cruiser, and had been renamed in 1937 when she was recommissioned some four years after a mutiny on board. The *Konig der Nederlanden* was even older, having been launched in Amsterdam in 1874 as a ram battleship. Venerable age, however, was no guarantee of immunity from destruction; modern naval warfare leaves no room for sentimentality, no allowance for the obsolescence of design.

Thus the Japanese landings on Java predated by a matter of hours the total demise of Allied naval power in the Indies. Of course, a matter of hours was no more than Allied resistance had been able to buy at any stage of the campaign in the Indies. Throughout the islands the Dutch and Allied resistance had been unavailing and short-lived; only on Amboina and Timor had the Japanese been denied for any length of time and in these instances resistance was measured in terms of a few days rather than hours. Even the two Allied naval efforts at either end of Java delayed the Japanese by no more than a day or so.

What the Allied naval forces had been unable to prevent, neither the weak air forces nor the dispersed ground forces available to the local Dutch commander could hope to frustrate for very long. On paper Hein ter Poorten had substantial ground forces at his disposal, but in reality the sheer size of Java meant that the Allied ground forces were very thinly spread and could not hope to react to Japanese landings quickly and in a concentrated manner. Moreover, all the Allied forces, but particularly the Dutch, were low on morale, and all were aware that local feeling for the Allied cause ranged from the uncertain and indifferent to the actively hostile.

For the ground defense of Java the Dutch had three regional commands covering western, middle, and eastern parts of the island. In eastern Java

Mountain artillery. Because of the rugged terrain of much of the Indies, light mountain artillery constituted a large part of the KNIL's strength. Often more useful than field artillery, a pack howitzer battery formed an organic part of a column, normally about 800-strong. Six horses were needed to carry the 75-millimeter guns with which the artillery fought. Here a gun cradle is being transported across a stream. Military History Section, Royal Netherlands Army

Major General G. A. Ilgen had under his command the Soerabaja Detachment, which was given as its main task the defense of the now-useless naval base. Ilgen also commanded the 6th Infantry Regiment, one marine and two reserve battalions, one artillery regiment, an antiaircraft battalion, a mountain artillery battalion (deployed to cover the harbor channels at Soerabaja), and various other units and subunits, some indigenous and others from the retired lists. Certain of these units were on Madoera. In middle Java was the very weak 2nd Infantry Division of Major General P. A. Cox. In effect this formation was no more than a weak brigade with Group South (three infantry battalions) and two cavalry squadrons under Cox's command.

The bulk of Dutch and Allied field forces on Java was deployed in western Java for the very obvious political reason that the Dutch had to attempt to hold Batavia and Bandoeng. Western Java was divided into two districts for the purposes of command, the boundary line between the two districts being the Tji Taroem. West of the river was Major General W. Schilling's 1st Infantry Division. Under his command were the 1st and 2nd Infantry and the 1st Artillery Regiments and Black Force, a composite

Allied force under the command of an Australian officer, Brigadier A. S. Blackburn. This formation consisted of the Australian 2nd/3rd Machine Gun and 2nd/2nd Pioneer Battalions, two British antiaircraft units and a light tank squadron, and two American field batteries, the third being in the east. East of the river the Dutch deployed Major General J. J. Pesman's Group Bandoeng, consisting of the 4th Infantry Regiment and the 1st Mountain Artillery Battalion. In addition to these field forces were various garrisons, the most important being those at Batavia, Bandoeng, Tjimahi, and Tjilatjap. There were also various home guard units of very dubious value.

In making these dispositions the Dutch attempted to provide the three towns of major strategic importance in Java, Batavia, Bandoeng, and Soerabaja, each with a single mobile regimental group, complete with supporting arms and services. Cox's 2nd Infantry Division was envisaged as a general reserve but it was earmarked for support of the forces in western Java when it became clear that no substantial Allied forces would arrive to aid the defense. In western Java itself Schilling anticipated that the Japanese would make their main effort at Bantam Bay. To meet this challenge he deployed a covering force made up of local forces with a stiffening of regulars and held the main part of the 1st Infantry Regiment deployed around Tangerang to block a Japanese advance from Bantam Bay to Batavia. The Dutch hoped that the 1st Infantry would be able to hold a Japanese attack for long enough to allow Black Force and the 2nd Infantry, held in reserve at Buitenzorg, to counterattack the Japanese flanks.

All three Japanese invasion convoys (at Merak-Bantam, at Eretan Wetan, and at Kragan) were attacked by aircraft. Damage was inflicted on transports and landing craft at all three places, but the scale of these attacks was so small that the damage suffered by the Japanese amounted to no more than pinpricks. The invasion forces were able to establish themselves ashore on all three fronts by dawn on 1 March. Only at Kragan did the Japanese encounter any real opposition and this was quickly overcome. The Japanese pressed well inland as quickly as possible. As at Lingayen Gulf where, of course, the *48th Infantry Division* had come ashore, the Japanese did not attempt to consolidate their beachheads. Rather, they sought security for their landing sites by moving well inland to take communication centers that an enemy would have to move through in any attempt to counterattack the beaches. By nightfall on 1 March the *2nd Infantry Division* had taken Serang, the *Shoji Detachment* had secured Kalidjati airfield and Soebang, and the *48th Infantry Division* was in possession of Tjepoe.

The eastern invasion force experienced very little difficulty in securing its objectives, though inevitably the Dutch were able to put into effect a thorough demolition program at Soerabaja before the port fell. The *48th Infantry Division* conducted a threefold envelopment of Soerabaja, its main effort being made not along the coast road but inland along the main line of communication via Tjepoe, Ngawi, Madioen, Ngandjoek, and Djombang. Just one regiment was directed along the northern roads that converged on Gresik via Toeban (on the coast) and Bedjonegoro.

With the Japanese landing at Kragan all but unopposed, Ilgen had no chance of inflicting any substantial damage on the invaders. From the very start, therefore, the Dutch aim was to secure time for the extensive demolition program at Soerabaja to be put into effect. To achieve this Ilgen pulled his forces back to the line of the Solo River, where he intended to conduct his major defensive battle. But with so many routes to Soerabaja available to the Japanese, the Dutch deployment was fragmented and weak. The 6th Infantry was used to block the Tjepoe to Lamongan road at Babat, while a cavalry company was deployed around Tjarobban as a light covering screen for the artillery, which was concentrated at Djombang on the main Madioen to Soerabaja route. The marines at Soerabaja on 4 March were ordered forward to Djombang to spearhead a converging attack on Tjepoe from Djombang and by the 6th Infantry, but even before the marines ran into the advance guard of the main part of the *48th Infantry Division* near Kertosono, just west of Djombang, on the morning of the fifth, it was obvious that the attack would fail. The 6th Infantry could not hope to carry out its part of the offensive because its right flank was being turned by the Japanese forces moving down from Toeban to Lamongan, while the attack from Djombang was made in insufficient strength for it to have any chance of success. The simple fact was that the dispersal of the defenders over so wide a front, against an enemy with so many options in mounting assaults, could end in only one way. By the afternoon the marines had been shouldered aside and the Japanese had secured Kediri. On the following day the Dutch forces at Porong, just to the south of Soerabaja, came under heavy attack. In this situation the Dutch commander attempted to activate his plans to start guerrilla warfare in southern Java in the Kepandjen, Djember, and Loemadjang areas, but by the time any number of Allied troops had managed to gather together in the Loemadjang area, the campaign was all but over. By the evening of the seventh Japanese forces stood on the outskirts of Soerabaja, but they were too late to prevent the garrison from completing its work of destruction before it withdrew to Madoera.

In middle Java the *56th Regimental Group* experienced equally little difficulty in its operations. Almost at the outset of the Japanese offensive, Group South lost one of its battalions to the West Java Command, with the result that the Dutch only had a battalion group to oppose each of the two thrusts the Japanese mounted against Tjilatjap through the mountains. Though the Dutch and Japanese were closely matched in terms of numbers, the Japanese encountered very little effective resistance in advancing first to Soerakarta and then to Tjilatjap by the coast route. The Japanese advance along the inland axis was more hampered by Dutch resistance but this did not prevent Japanese forces from entering the devastated port of Tjilatjap at the same time as the columns of the *48th Infantry Division* closed in on Soerabaja.

In western Java, too, the week-long timetable of victory and defeat was to be observed, with the Japanese reaching the outskirts of Bandoeng by the evening of the seventh. Events in western Java were somewhat more resolute than in eastern and middle Java, though the result was the same. Allied resistance, although more substantial than elsewhere in Java, was brittle, and the Japanese had relatively little difficulty in shattering a resistance that the defenders themselves quickly recognized to be futile.

The Japanese encountered no difficulty in establishing themselves ashore at both Merak-Bantam Bay and Eretan Wetan, but they found that their converging attacks towards Batavia, the very symbol of Dutch authority in the Indies, made relatively little progress at first in the face of methodical and extensive Dutch demolitions on the coastal roads leading to the city. The *230th Infantry Regiment*, for example, quickly secured Djatisali, but an attempt to work round the Dutch flank at Tjikampek failed to make any headway and the Japanese chose instead to reinforce the formation's successes further inland. A reinforced infantry unit, with light armor in support, surprised and overran the British garrison at Kalidjati Air Base on the morning of 1 March and then consolidated its position by moving on to take Soebang.

To the west the *2nd Infantry Division* similarly had to direct its main effort inland as a result of Dutch demolitions and defenses along the Merak to Tangerang to Batavia route, but one regiment was left to advance along this axis. It proved sufficient to overcome weakening Dutch resistance and it entered and captured Batavia on 5 March. The main effort of the *2nd Infantry Division* was directed along the Rangkasbitoeng to Buitenzorg road, but any hope Schilling had of holding the Japanese on this road, essential if the defenders of Batavia were to get clear of the city, had evaporated as a result of the activities of the *230th Infantry Regiment*.

The threat of a double envelopment of Batavia made the defense of the city impossible. The developing menace of the *230th Infantry* forced the slackening of Dutch resistance around Tangerang as the Dutch attempted to pull the 1st Infantry Regiment and the Batavia garrison out of the coastal area into the Bandoeng plateau in order to continue the fight. But the Dutch saw the fall of the base at Kalidjati as a threat to the whole attempt to stand inland, and they were resolved to retake the airfield. It was this decision that undermined Schilling's original intention to counterattack the Bantam Bay invasion force with the 2nd Infantry Regiment and Black Force.

Instead, he was obliged to give up a battle group (the 2nd Infantry Regiment, a cavalry company, and two artillery units) in order to facilitate the recapture of Kalidjati.

The 2nd Infantry was ordered to move via Bandoeng and Poernakarta to Soebang, leaving only Black Force in the Buitenzorg area to face the bulk of the *2nd Infantry Division*. The Dutch attempt to counterattack at Kalidjati on 3 March ended disastrously; however, the reason for this in large part stemmed from the partial success of the only major Dutch counterattack during the whole of the short-lived Java campaign. This took place on 2 March when twenty light tanks from the Dutch army's Experimental Battalion, based at Bandoeng, spearheaded a drive to retake Kalidjati. The counteroffensive retook Soebang (hence the orders to the 2nd Infantry Regiment to form up for its attack at the town) and reached the edge of the Kalidjati airfield. But lack of infantry support for the armor and the approach of night forced the Dutch to pull back from Kalidjati and consolidate overnight, while the 2nd Infantry came up to support a resumption of the offensive the following day. The Japanese, however, had been alarmed by the developments of the second, and from the morning of the third they began to bring in aircraft to Kalidjati in order to deal with the Dutch. These aircraft caught the 2nd Infantry on its forming-up position and for five hours on the afternoon of the third subjected the Dutch units to incessant attack. By nightfall the Dutch had been reduced to debris. Morale had been shattered, and the Dutch were in full retreat back to Poerwakarta. With the defenders broken beyond redemption, there was virtually nothing to oppose a Japanese advance southwards from Soebang. This was resumed on the fifth and by the evening of the seventh the Japanese had secured Lembang, just a few miles north of Bandoeng.

Around Buitenzorg the Allied position did not deteriorate with the same rapidity and totality as it did in the Soebang-Kalidjati area, mainly because Black Force held the Japanese on the Leuwiliang position from the second to the fourth. By its successful delaying action Black Force ensured the escape from Batavia of its garrison and the 1st Infantry Regiment, but to no real purpose. Black Force conducted a well-organized withdrawal on the fourth to behind Buitenzorg, which the Japanese, following up hard, secured during the late evening. The overall Allied position was hopeless. The defenders were being pushed back towards Bandoeng by the advances of the *2nd Infantry Division* from both Batavia and Buitenzorg and the *230th Infantry Regiment* from Soebang, while they could not concentrate to deal with any of these threats. Furthermore, the Allies had no counter to Japanese air supremacy, the danger from which became ever more acute and agonizing because of the presence in Bandoeng of thousands of civilian refugees. With all the major towns either lost or on the point of falling, there was little to be gained by trying to prolong a resistance that might easily give the Japanese the pretext to bomb Bandoeng and to take reprisals against both the civilian population and the military.

Pesman, the local commander whose responsibilities included the defense of Bandoeng, and van Starkenborgh favored the early surrender of Bandoeng precisely in order to spare the city and its population from such ordeals. When Japanese emissaries arrived bearing an invitation for the governor-general to proceed to Kalidjati for talks, van Starkenborgh was ready enough to do so. It was ter Poorten who realized that the enemy would not be interested in talking about anything less than the total and unconditional surrender of the Allies in the Indies. The governor-general, in his concern with Bandoeng and the civil administration, had not realized this. What complicated the picture was the fact that the governor-general was no longer the Dutch commander in chief. The Dutch government-in-exile in London on 4 March had divided civil and military responsibilities. Van Starkenborgh had appointed ter Poorten as head of the military forces and Rear Admiral J. J. A. van Staveren as commander of the naval forces left to the Dutch. The Japanese were unaware of this development, and when van Starkenborgh and ter Poorten met with Imamura on 8 March, this matter had to be explained to the Japanese. When it became clear that ter Poorten's anticipation of Japanese demands had been correct, the governor-general was excluded from the talks, and ter Poorten was left to conduct the surrender negotiations by himself.

The Dutch general had no option but to accept a surrender and Imamura's demand that he broadcast his decision to his forces. This ter Poorten did on 9 March. The Japanese insisted on this so that the surrender would be known to all Allied forces, since Imamura had no intention of having to deal with each of the Allies in turn, and radio broadcast was the only method by which ter Poorten could contact many of his forces. Black Force, for example, had withdrawn from its positions on the seventh without as much as informing ter Poorten of its intentions or reasons for doing so. The American, Australian, and British forces on Java surrendered reluctantly, and only when it became obvious that everything was against trying to continue the struggle from the interior. The Allied forces on Java surrendered on the twelfth, the same day as the *Imperial Guards Division* landed at Sabang and Iri in northern Sumatra, after having made the short sea crossing from Singapore in the company of seven cruisers and ten destroyers. No instrument of surrender was ever signed in the Indies, but the campaign was over, just sixty days after the first landings at Menado and Tarakan.

Thus ended a campaign that for the Allies was nothing short of a total, humiliating disaster. For the Dutch, if it is possible to have a degree beyond totality, the result was worse. For the Japanese the operations in the Indies triumphantly vindicated their decision not to await the fall of Luzon and the

Philippines but to press ahead with the subjugation of the Indies.* By their action, and at the cost of some 6,000 killed, wounded, and missing, the Japanese drove a wedge between the British in the Indian Ocean and the Americans in the Pacific, ensuring in practical terms the utter isolation of the Philippines and capitalizing on all the advantages of timing, concentration, surprise, and initiative that their initial operations had conferred upon them. Though the Americans remained in the field on Luzon and none of the major islands in the Philippines had been reduced, the Japanese had secured all the objectives for which they went to war. With the fall of Java the Japanese secured the last part of the Sumatra, Java, Lesser Sundas arc, which in turn was but one link in a great chain that, within six more weeks, was to run from northern Burma via the Indies and Oceania to Kamchatka. Amidst all these gains Java was the great prize that really counted above all the others. With a population roughly equal to that of France (about 41,000,000), Java possessed resources and wealth that, given time and in association with resources taken from other conquests, would enable the Japanese to withstand American power. Or so it was believed and hoped.

For Britain and the Netherlands the defeats were catastrophic. The loss of Singapore came in the same week as the Channel Dash, when German battle cruisers passed through the channel to Germany from Brest without effective interference from either the Royal Navy or the Royal Air Force. National mortification and the sense of outrage at this German coup were profound, yet really there was very little cause for this, since Britain had very few means to oppose such a move. Just as British naval and commercial movement around the south coast of England went on throughout the war with relatively little interference from the Germans, so a well-planned and carefully protected naval movement by the Germans ran relatively few risks of being frustrated. British feelings of offended dignity would have been better directed towards the events in Southeast Asia, for the latter marked a watershed in British imperial history. The loss of Singapore in 1942 was a profoundly shocking event to the British. It was a humiliation after which things could never quite be the same again. The easy, almost casual, arrogance of Britain, based upon a sense of massive security that had been built up over generations of success, was swept aside by a brutal

---

*Of course in a very narrow sense the fact that the Philippines were effectively bypassed and the Indies conquered before the American defeat in the Philippines was an accomplished fact, does raise the point that perhaps the Japanese plans to develop their attacks southwards through the Philippines into the Indies were misplaced. It could be argued that events showed that the Japanese could have secured the Indies without having had to bring the Americans into the war at all. It was certain that the Indies had been conquered without the Japanese having accomplished either of the two objectives that they considered absolutely essential to their plan: the destruction of the U.S. Pacific Fleet and the conquest of the Philippines. On the other hand, the Philippines had been effectively conquered by March, and Mindanao was used as the Japanese staging post for their operations against Dutch territory.

conquest at the hands of a despised and undervalued foe. A genteel society, whose nineteenth-century pace and ethos had been portrayed so well by such writers as Somerset Maugham, was totally unsuited to meet the challenge of modern war. Furthermore, the basis of this society—the myth of white supremacy and the unchallenged position of Britain—could never be reasserted even by ultimate victory.

But if the British Empire was shaken to its foundations by the revelation of its weakness and failure, Britain did remain unconquered, still was involved in a global war, and continued to have substantial resources and forces at her disposal. She did have the means and opportunity for recovery, if only as *minor inter pares* in an alliance that was to bring about the defeat of the Axis in Europe and Asia. For the Dutch this chance of recovery did not exist. The third greatest of the colonial powers, already occupied by the Germans, lacked the means to reassert her old authority, mainly because even in defeat the Japanese helped to shape and direct forces far too powerful for the Dutch to overcome.

For many Dutchmen perhaps the saddest fact about the fall of the Indies was that ter Poorten's decision not to try to wage guerrilla warfare on Java was made because of the uncertain attitude of the natives towards their defeated Dutch masters. It was a sad commentary on three centuries of Dutch rule, and particularly on the ethical policy, that for all their good intentions the Dutch went down to defeat amid a combination of indifference and joy on the part of most sections of native opinion. Though certain parts of society tried to keep their distance from the Japanese and there were many native intellectuals who had no time at all for what they saw as Japanese fascism, the Japanese were welcomed as liberators by most parts of native society. Within weeks the Japanese made the cardinal error of alienating much of the potential goodwill they commanded by showing that they were as rapacious as the Dutch in the bad old days of the Culture System, and far more brutal.

In defeating the Dutch the Japanese unwittingly helped to give new impetus to the twin forces of Indonesian nationalism and communism that were to dominate the Indies in the two decades following their own capitulation in September 1945. These forces, naturally, had been growing throughout the previous forty years and explain why the defeat of the Dutch caused so little sense of loss in the Indies in 1942. Unlike the British in Malaya but like them in India, at the time of their defeat in the Indies the Dutch were under notice to leave. In the Dutch case the events that led to the emergence of a vehement local nationalism were in large part of Dutch making.

Certainly, various factors in the emergence of Indonesian nationalism were beyond Dutch control, for it was part of the Oriental awakening in the early years of the present century, an awakening that was obviously and openly centered upon a strong xenophobic desire to remove foreigners from their positions of dominance. Indonesian nationalism was part and parcel of the process that saw the development of Indian, Chinese, and Japanese nationalism, the most powerful spur of which came with Tsu-shima and the defeat of Russia in her war with Japan. Moreover, the Islamic revival in the Indies at the turn of the century (and the example set by the Young Turks in the crumbling Ottoman Empire) helped to create the cultural, ethnic, and social basis for opposition to Dutch rule. Later, the example of the Russian Revolutions of 1917 and the success of the Bolsheviks were important in sharpening class and racial divisions in the Indies and provided the background for the emergence of a communist party that was to be the largest single party in the Indies until 1965.

Nevertheless, it was the Dutch who really provided nascent Indonesian nationalism with its chance by virtue of their crowning achievement, the pacification of the Indies. In the course of the nineteenth century the Dutch fought a series of wars to put down regional rebellions and extend their control to areas that hitherto had been beyond the writ of Batavia. Throughout the Indies the diversity of tongues, cultures, ethnic and tribal groups, social and political organization served to prevent any emergence of a national consciousness until the Dutch actually created a nation. In breaking the back of resistance to their rule, the Dutch welded the disparate islands of the Indies into a single political identity, giving the Indies a singular coherent form. Just as they reach the peak of their efficiency, many machines slither into obsolescence; so the Dutch, in finally subjugating the Indies, created a political form that was certain to become too strong for them to control.

It is possible, of course, that matters need never have turned out this way. The Islamic revival that did so much to provide the basis for emergent nationalism coincided with van Deventer's championing of the ethical policy and the start of its implementation by the Dutch authorities. This, however, never really worked. Far from creating the atmosphere whereby the Indies and the Netherlands worked towards a relationship akin to a federal idea, it produced circumstances that were destructive of Dutch-Indonesian cooperation. The essence of van Deventer's notions was the development of a native elite that would be assimilated into Dutch political life; the means by which this was to be achieved was education. The weaknesses of the concepts are twofold and obvious. First, being elitist, this vision had little for the ordinary person; there was nothing that the Dutch could offer the majority of the population other than a continuation of old ways. Even if the rigors of the old systems abated, there was no positive incentive for the people, most of whom lived at subsistence level, to give positive support to their colonial masters. Second, the process of education, as has often been the case in colonial settings, helped fire aspirations that could not be met by the Dutch political system.

When actually put to the test, the Dutch, despite their professed belief in the ethical policy, would not share power. Though the policy of extending European education touched but a small part of the native population, the part that was affected naturally saw itself as a group that represented the new "nation" and identified its own interests and those of the "state" as one and the same thing. The more insistent nationalist demands became, the less the Dutch could accommodate them. Just as the Dutch adopted a policy of firmness when dealing with the ever-growing menace of Japan, so too did they adopt a policy of refusing to make concessions of any real substance when it came to dealing with Indonesian nationalists.

Naturally enough, when the nationalists found the legal channels to power denied them, they were inclined to use more direct methods. In fact, in 1941–42 matters never reached that point, but had it not been for the Japanese invasion and conquest it is inevitable that some form of major confrontation would have broken out sooner or later. This was why so many sections of society welcomed the Japanese as liberators but then in turn repudiated the conquerors. The Japanese had nothing that could satisfy local nationalism. Those nationalists who opposed the Dutch were not to know this at the time. Only the rapid unfolding of events was to reveal the shallowness of Japanese claims to the leadership of a genuine Pan-Asiatic liberation movement. For the Dutch there were elements of tragedy in this situation. There was the deep and genuine tragedy of their idealism and good intentions having gone sour on all concerned, that despite their efforts little real enthusiasm for Dutch rule existed among the ordinary people. There was the tragedy for the Dutch in that this brave and stoic people fought their last battles in defense of their homes and empire with precious little support from their Allies. But this pales beside the greater tragedy that they fought their last battles in an atmosphere of indifference on the part of a population they had ruled for generations.

CHAPTER 13

Sobering Reality on Bataan, 7 January– 9 April 1942

FOR THE AMERICANS the defense of the Bataan peninsula officially began on 7 January. At the outset both the Japanese and the Americans were sanguine about the outcome of the impending battle. The Japanese had seen nothing to indicate anything other than a speedy conclusion to the Luzon campaign. They had savaged several enemy formations and they knew that many Filipinos had deserted. The momentum and exhilaration of an army on the offensive concealed certain matters that should have been food for thought. Yet with success crowning Japanese endeavors throughout the Far East and with the whole of Luzon, except Bataan, cleared of the Americans, everything seemed set for a short, sharp action to wrap up the campaign. On the other side the Americans, perhaps surprisingly, were confident. Though mauled, their units had generally fought well, and none had been destroyed in the course of some quite successful rearguard actions. Now, on Bataan, there could be an end to disheartening retreat, and morale revived as a result. The Bataan position was a strong one, and the defenders could look forward to fighting actions without having to think of moving to a shorter line or back through rear positions. To the troops Bataan offered security and the end of withdrawals. The ordinary soldier took comfort from the belief, fostered by officers, that help from the United States would be forthcoming. The hopelessness of their strategic situation had yet to dawn on the troops. Even though American commanders believed that they faced a greatly superior enemy, there was a general confidence that the Japanese could be held on the defense lines that straddled the peninsula.

Even though the Americans held exaggerated views of their enemy's strength and of their own chances of relief, there was no denying that the selection of Bataan as the site for their main defensive effort was astute. The peninsula lent itself naturally to defensive warfare. The roughness of the terrain was a fierce impediment to movement and to the deployment of armor, which was confined primarily to the eastern coastal plain. The thick jungle that covered the peninsula, moreover, was not just another factor that hampered movement; it also provided effective cover for the defenders. This went some way to cancel the effectiveness of the one clear-cut advantage that the Japanese retained over the Americans after the withdrawal of the *48th Infantry Division*—air supremacy.

The Americans had selected two battle lines on which to conduct their defense of Bataan. These were the Main Line of Resistance (M.L.R.) between Mauban and Mabatang, and the Rear Battle Position (R.B.P.), which straddled the direct route between Bagac and Orion. These two lines followed natural obstacles, the M.L.R. being anchored in the center on one of the two dominating features of the peninsula, the 4,111-foot-high Mount Natib. To the south was the massif of the Mariveles Mountains, of which Mount Bataan, at 4,554 feet, was the highest point. Along the latitudinal saddle between these two extinct volcanoes ran the boundary between the two corps charged with the defense of the peninsula. West of the boundary, along the jagged coast washed by the South China Sea, was Wainwright's 1st Philippine Corps with (on 7 January) the 1st, 31st, and 91st Infantry Divisions and the reconstituted 26th Cavalry under its command. On the Manila Bay side of the peninsula Parker, until this time Bataan Defense Force commander, had under him the 11th, 21st, 41st, and 51st Infantry Divisions and the 57th Infantry Regiment. These five formations made up the 2nd Philippine Corps. In the 2nd Corps area was MacArthur's strategic reserve, the Philippine Division, less its 57th Infantry Regiment and one battalion of the 45th Infantry, which was with Wainwright. South of the Mariveles Mountains was the Service Command area under Brigadier General Allen C. McBride. The area was divided into Western and Eastern Sectors that corresponded to the intercorps boundary. In the Western Sector were service elements from the broken up 71st Infantry Division and an assortment of air force, marine, and naval personnel pressed into service as infantrymen. The Eastern Sector was held by the newly raised 2nd Infantry Division, which was made up of drafted policemen. The total American and Filipino military strength on Bataan was about 83,000 men, of whom some 48,000 were with the two corps. About 25,000 troops were with the 2nd Philippine Corps.

The presence of the Philippine Division in the 2nd Philippine Corps

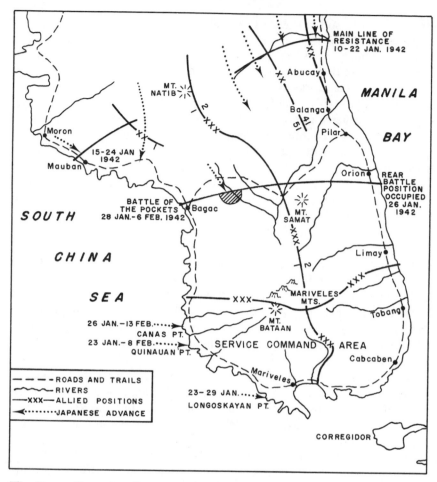

The Bataan Campaign, January and February 1942

area—plus the fact that one whole regiment from this all-regular formation had already been attached to Parker's command—was a clear sign of the relative importance of the 1st and 2nd Philippine Corps. The natural route into the peninsula from San Fernando and Layac was by the all-weather single-lane road that ran down the length of the east coast. It was on this side of the peninsula that Honma chose to make his major effort and where the Scouts of the 57th Infantry were deployed (in the Samal, Calaguiman, Mabatang, Abucay area) precisely to deny the *14th Army* commander control of this vital coastal road. On 7 January, while the 52nd Infantry Regiment covered the coast southwards from Balanga to Limay (thereby securing the 57th Infantry's rear), the 57th was joined on the M.L.R. by five other regiments from two divisions. Immediately on the left was the

41st Infantry Division with all three regiments in the line. The number regiment of the division tied in with the 57th, while the 43rd reached inland to the 51st Infantry Regiment. On the extreme left of the American position was the 53rd Infantry, whose left flank was unsupported and covered only by the ravines and jungled slopes of Mount Natib. The narrowness of this front, roughly along the Batantay and Calaguiman rivers, allowed the equivalent of three artillery regiments in and around Abucay to give support to all six front-line regiments. The 21st Infantry Division was constituted as corps reserve while the 11th, after its exertions on the Guagua to Layac road, was in the process of reorganizing when battle began on the afternoon of 9 January.

What was to be the spearhead of Honma's drive into Bataan, the *65th Infantry Brigade* of Lieutenant General Akira Nara, arrived at Angeles only on 6 January after a series of forced marches from Lingayen Gulf. Originally this formation had been designated for mopping-up and occupation duties, but the premature withdrawal of the *48th Infantry Division* resulted in its being deployed for what turned out to be a set piece battle, a battle for which it was singularly ill-suited. The *65th* had three two-battalion regiments, the *122nd*, *141st*, and *142nd*, each of which had only three as opposed to the normal four rifle companies. The formation lacked its artillery arm and most of the supporting services, while few of its 6,500 men had much more than one month's basic training.

Japanese field intelligence credited the Americans on Bataan with a strength of about 45,000 men, but the imbalance between the forces (much greater than was believed at the time of course) and the state of the *65th Infantry Brigade* seem to have caused the *14th Army* no second thoughts about the coming operation. This was partly because of the persistent belief that the Americans were already a defeated enemy and partly because other formations and units were available to support Nara. From the *16th Infantry Division* came the dubiously rated *9th Infantry* and an artillery unit, while the *48th Infantry Division* loaned two field artillery units on a temporary basis. The *14th Army* was able to provide the *7th Tank Regiment* and four battalions of heavy field artillery.

Because the *14th Army* envisaged forthcoming operations as little more than a pursuit punctuated by short but intense actions, Honma ordered the attack to be conducted down both sides of the peninsula. The *14th Army* anticipated that any advance down the west coast from Moron was unlikely to encounter resistance north of Bagac, and possibly not even there. Accordingly, only the *122nd Infantry*, with token artillery support, was ordered to move along Route 7 to Olongapo and hence to Moron. Its initial objective was Bagac and its main objective was to link up with the forces coming down the east coast in the general area of the town of Mariveles. On the east coast the Japanese expected to meet resistance, but they did not expect it to be substantial. To overcome it they deployed four regiments for two two-echelon attacks. Along the coast road the *141st Infantry* was to make a breach through which the *7th Tank Regiment* was to pass, while inland the more experienced *9th Infantry* was to come around the flank of the main American positions by attacking across the lower slopes of Mount Natib. The *9th* was to open up a breach; the *142nd* was to exploit. In their operations against the 2nd Philippine Corps the Japanese were employing the same basic tactic as Yamashita was using in Malaya and Iida was to employ in Burma. This was to advance with the main force along the direct route and to grip the enemy frontally while flanking movements through the jungle brought forces across the enemy's line of supply and retreat. Reliance for the decisive breakthrough was vested in the *9th Infantry* because the Japanese plan envisaged the American defenders being rolled up by an advance by the *9th* and *142nd* to the coast.

On the afternoon of 9 January the Japanese offensive on the east coast opened with a vicious artillery bombardment, and the Japanese infantry made unopposed progress towards the Calaguiman. An initial lack of infantry resistance was taken as a sign of American weakness, but in fact the Japanese had placed the American defensive positions some 3 miles north of their actual location and virtually no contact was made between the rival infantry units on the ninth. The heaviness of the American counterbombardment should have alerted the Japanese to the fact that the Americans were resolved to stand and fight, but it was not until the following day, when the *141st* began to run into resistance from the 57th Infantry, that the Japanese began to realize something was amiss. The attack along the coast road stalled, while the offensive inland never even began. The *9th Infantry*, far from making the decisive breach in the enemy line, was languishing far behind the front as it struggled through extremely difficult country—the antithesis of a mobile, hard-hitting assault force. Slowed by terrain and vegetation to the extent that it barely averaged 1 mile a day and hampered by hopelessly inaccurate maps, the *9th Infantry Regiment* did not come up to the American front-line positions until 16 January—six days late.

It was just as well for the Japanese, therefore, that in Nara they had a commander who was not afraid to recast his plans when operations failed to develop along the lines intended. When the attack along the coast road stalled he switched all but two companies of the *141st Infantry* inland, first against the 42nd Infantry and then, when repulsed, further west to hammer away at the 43rd. By the eleventh, moreover, Nara had modified his original plan still further. It was evident that the *9th Infantry* could not be relied upon to make any impact on the battle in the immediate future. The *142nd*, therefore, was ordered to come around the rear of the *141st* and attack the 42nd and 41st Infantry Regiments. Thus, within three days of the start of the battle, Nara had abandoned an attack by four regiments on

two separate axes in favor of a simple linear attack by three formations over
the greater part of the American front. It was a substitute of brute force for
guile and maneuver, implemented in the belief that if the attack was pressed
home with sufficient force and determination, somewhere along the line the
enemy would break. The plan was not particularly subtle or original, but it
was the best that Nara could attempt in light of the unexpectedly strong
resistance put up by the defense and the failure of the *9th Infantry* to come
into the battle.

By the thirteenth the Japanese had barely dented the American position.
The deepest penetration was achieved, incredibly, by the two companies of
the *2nd/141st Infantry Regiment*, left on the road to face the 57th Infantry.
Such was the élan of these companies that they managed to establish
themselves over the Calaguiman; as a result two battalions from the 21st
Infantry Regiment had to be sent to steady the Scouts. Between them the
21st and 57th managed to eliminate most of the Japanese toeholds over the
Calaguiman during the thirteenth. That day also proved a singularly
unrewarding one for the Japanese on the other parts of the line. The *141st
Infantry* moved further inland to attack the sector of the front held by the
51st Infantry Division but without any obvious success, while the efforts of
the *142nd* against the 41st Infantry Division proved equally fruitless.
Clearly, after four days of strenuous exertions, things were going badly for
the Japanese, and on this day Honma chose to intervene in the conduct of
the battle. He obviously believed that the most intelligent method of
waging war was to attack in areas where the enemy was not present, to go
through gaps rather than fight through defensive lines, because he decided
to try to force a decisive result along the west coast, where his forces had not
encountered resistance. Honma therefore ordered Nara to keep the 2nd
Philippine Corps tied down by frontal assaults while reinforcements were
moved to the west coast to join the *122nd Infantry*. These forces were given
orders to secure Bagac and then to move across the peninsula along the road
that led to Pilar in an effort to carry out the encirclement that had proved
beyond the capacity of the *9th* and *142nd Infantry Regiments*.

Control of the battle in the west was therefore taken away from Nara,
who was free to concentrate simply on the battle against Parker's forces.
Honma placed Major General Kaoki Kimura, the infantry group commander of the *16th Infantry Division*, in charge of the operations on the west
coast. Kimura took with him to western Bataan his group headquarters,
two battalions of the *20th Infantry*, and two artillery subunits. There forces
brought Japanese strength in the area to about 5,000 men, the equivalent of
a weak brigade.

Kimura arrived at Moron on 18 January, the day after the town was
secured by the *122nd* in the face of resistance from six battalions, four of
them regular. Though the main reason for the Japanese success at Moron

was the American refusal to stand and fight a prolonged action in front of the M.L.R., nothing could disguise the fact that the American performance at Moron was dismal. The Japanese had every reason to be pleased with themselves. Kimura immediately gave orders for this spectacular success to be followed up by the *122nd* carrying out an advance directly along the rough Moron to Bagac road, while a battalion from the *20th Infantry* was to attempt to move around the lower slopes of Mount Silanganan and take the Americans on their open right flank.

The Japanese advance ran up against the M.L.R. on the eighteenth, and within a matter of two days precipitated a major crisis for the 1st Philippine Corps. In fact this was merely one of three crises, one in each of its three areas, that shook the command in the course of a week. The period 15–22 January really was the critical juncture in the battle for Bataan, the time when the outcome was quite literally in the balance. These crises, following hard after one another, were: the 15/16 January Japanese breakthrough on the front of the 2nd Corps and the subsequent failure of the Philippine Division to seal off the breach; the 1st Corps' forced abandonment of its M.L.R. position after the *3rd/20th Infantry* established a roadblock on the Mauban to Bagac road behind the M.L.R. on 21 January and resisted all efforts to reduce it; and the start of the "Battle of the Points" in the Service Command area as a result of Japanese landings at Quinauan and Longos-kayan points on the night of 22/23 January.

Inevitably the first and gravest of these crises affected Parker's 2nd Philippine Corps, against which the Japanese were making their main effort. After 13 January the weight of the Japanese offensive along the whole length of the front forced the Americans to start to deploy their reserves in order to steady the line. With the Americans becoming increasingly stretched, the decision was made to release the Philippine Division from the reserve to support Parker's formations. Simultaneously Wainwright was ordered to release his own reserve, the 31st Infantry Division, for use in the 2nd Corps area. This highly undesirable move was ordered because late on the fifteenth the Japanese finally managed to break into the American line in the sector held by the 51st Infantry Division. The penetration, however, was not a clean one. The 51st Infantry Regiment was pushed out of its positions in considerable disorder, but managed to keep in touch with its flanking formations. With a battalion from the 21st Infantry Regiment moved up in support, the 51st Infantry Regiment was ordered to carry out a counterattack the next morning in order to regain the ground it had lost. The protests of the divisional commander were overruled, and the counterattack was carried out with predictably disastrous results. The Japanese had anticipated just such a move, and while the counterattack actually managed to gain all its objectives, the Japanese defensive measures took such a toll that the 51st spent itself during the operation. It was in no state to meet the immediate Japanese reply to its success—a full-blooded drive by the *141st* against its right flank and an assault on its left flank by the *9th Infantry*, which at last came into the action. Under attack on both flanks by two Japanese regiments, the 51st Infantry Regiment broke.

For the Americans and the Japanese alike this was the decisive moment of the battle. After a week of continuous fighting the Japanese had managed to make a clean break, about 1,000 yards across, through the American defensive position. The 51st had been destroyed as an effective fighting unit, while the 53rd was lost to the defense because it was trapped on the slopes of Mount Natib without any means of extricating itself. In the course of the next few days the 53rd literally fell to pieces as its scattered subunits moved in every direction, except to the north, in an effort to get back to friendly lines. The collapse of the 51st Infantry bared the flank of the 43rd while, more seriously for the Americans, continued attacks by the *142nd Infantry* during 16 January on the 42nd and 41st Infantry Regiments forced the 23rd and 32nd Infantry to send battalions to these regiments in order to prevent a breakthrough in this area. Thus, just when the Americans needed to keep all their reserves concentrated in an effort to remedy the situation brought about by the collapse of their left flank, they were forced to divide their reserves so that only two regiments of the Philippine Division, the 31st U.S. Infantry and the 45th, were available to try to stem the Japanese advance.

For the Japanese, a single fresh infantry regiment probably would have been sufficient to roll up the American position from the west, but such a formation simply was not available. It was at this point that the Japanese began to pay the inevitable price for beginning an operation without proper preparation in the belief that the opposition was weak. Where the quality and strength of the enemy is unknown it is always prudent to presume the strongest rather than the weakest possible resistance, but the Japanese could do nothing about that fundamental error at this stage. They had only the *9th* and *141st Infantry* with which to exploit success. The *141st*, having made the breach, hesitated to plunge too far in pursuit of the 51st while the hard shoulder formed by the 43rd Infantry remained intact. As the 43rd drew back its exposed flank, the *141st* followed it, thereby failing to move against the rear of the 41st Infantry Division and failing to follow the 51st down the Salian valley, a move that could have turned the whole of the M.L.R. The latter task should have been carried out by the *9th Infantry*, but to complete a disastrously inept performance during this battle, this formation came too far to the west and passed above the source of the Salian. Because of the vagaries of its maps, the *9th Infantry* moved southeast and then east down the Abo-Abo River valley rather than eastwards down the Salian, with the result that it passed out of the battle area at the very time that the Americans were at their most vulnerable.

The *9th Infantry*, therefore, posed no immediate threat to the American position as the defenders prepared for the counterattack that would decide whether or not they could maintain the M.L.R. With less than two full regiments available to try to seal the breach, there was little chance that a counterattack would be successful. It was almost certain to be conducted too slowly and in too little strength to turn back the Japanese. The attacks of the 31st U.S. Infantry and the 45th Infantry, moreover, were fragmented and poorly coordinated, with neither regiment making a serious impression on the *141st Infantry* despite three days of attacks. By the third day, the nineteenth, the American position had deteriorated sharply. The two regiments of the Philippine Division had run out of momentum and were in a potentially vulnerable position as the tide of battle turned against them. Nara made preparations to exploit their weakness, caught as they were in forward positions with strengths that were inadequate to resist a serious assault. Nara began on the nineteenth to thin out his front opposite the 41st Infantry Division and the 57th Infantry Regiment. Infantry and artillery alike were directed westwards to take part in a major effort set for noon on the twenty-second. Nara intended to pin down the 57th, 41st, 42nd, and 43rd Infantry Regiments with a series of attacks using the least number of troops necessary, while his artillery pulverized the American units in the area of the breach. His reinforced infantry was then to make the decisive breakthrough into the Salian valley.

Before this attack was launched, however, the *9th Infantry Regiment* at last began to exert an influence on the battle. By the nineteenth its leading patrols began to near Guitol, and by the twenty-first the regiment was concentrated near the village in a manner that began to assume ominous dimensions for the Americans. Not only was the *9th* in a position that controlled movement up and down the Abo-Abo valley, it also was uncomfortably close to the Salian and the American line of withdrawal from the M.L.R. Though units from the 21st, 31st, and even the 51st Infantry Divisions were scraped together to try to push the Japanese back, they registered no success. The American position, therefore, was becoming precarious even before Nara's main blow fell on the twenty-second against the 31st U.S. Infantry. After six days of continuous action, the American troops had to give ground; by nightfall they were back on the line from which they had set out on the seventeenth. In a matter of six hours the Japanese wiped out the gains that the Americans had taken six days to secure. Though the Philippine Division had not been broken and the Japanese advance had been slower than what might have been expected— and what Nara had demanded—the American position was beyond recall.

The whole left flank had crumbled away and the Americans had to face the very real danger of a double envelopment by the *9th* and the *141st Infantry*. With the Philippine Division having been committed and having failed, there was no possibility of halting the Japanese, while any attempt to maintain the present positions could only result in the complete disintegration of the entire 2nd Philippine Corps. Late on the twenty-second MacArthur, acting on the advice of his chief of staff, who had inspected the front during the day, gave orders for the 2nd Corps to begin a withdrawal to the Rear Battle Position. The Americans had lost the battle on the M.L.R.

The Japanese breakthrough on the interior flank of the 2nd Philippine Corps automatically made untenable the 1st Philippine Corps' M.L.R. position on the other side of Mount Natib. When Parker was given instructions to pull his men back to the R.B.P., Wainwright was ordered to do the same. In fact Wainwright had no choice in the matter, not because of events in the east (events that in any case would force him to conform to Parker's movements), but because his battle against Kimura had started badly and deteriorated rapidly. Events in western Bataan hinged on the activities of just one Japanese unit, the *3rd/20th Infantry*, which somehow managed to get behind the American front-line positions between 18/21 January at the time when the *122nd Infantry* was making a series of frontal attacks on the M.L.R., with not very marked success. By the twenty-first the *3rd Battalion* had established itself some 3 miles beyond Mauban on the main road over which American forces on the M.L.R. drew their supplies and down which they would have to retreat. The presence of a single battalion on the road should not have been decisive, but the 1st Philippine Corps had just the 1st and 91st Infantry Divisions, plus elements of the 71st under the command of the latter, in the line. The corps had had its reserve taken away from it and had only the forces immediately at hand to try to eliminate the Japanese roadblock.

Wainwright realized almost as soon as the Japanese established their roadblock that his continued presence on the M.L.R. was all but impossible. His problem was that he could not hope to begin withdrawing his formations and their equipment unless and until the roadblock was cleared. Three quickly mounted attacks on the Japanese position on 21 and 22 January, the second attack including armor, failed to dislodge the Japanese. On the twenty-third a general attack from virtually every direction by a force that nominally totalled five battalions similarly failed to reduce a Japanese position that seemed to harden rather than wilt under pressure. No other single action of the Philippine campaign better illustrated the superiority of a Japanese unit over its American or Filipino counterpart at this stage of the war. The Japanese on the roadblock had no supply line and no equipment except what the infantry had carried over country similar to the type that had ridiculed the *9th Infantry*'s attempts to play the role of assault force east of Mount Natib. On the roadblock itself Japanese camouflage and fire discipline must have been phenomenal to withstand more than four days of attack. By any standard the achievement of this battalion was remarkable.

With the Japanese roadblock holding firm despite all efforts to destroy it and the *122nd Infantry* pressing its assault on the M.L.R., the overall American position by the twenty-fourth was so bad that there was no alternative but to attempt a withdrawal. For the infantry on the M.L.R. this meant withdrawing progressively to the coast and then along the open beaches back to safety. With the Japanese on the road there was no alternative to this course of action, which involved destroying and then abandoning the equipment, guns, and vehicles of the 1st and 91st Divisions. Most of the infantry did manage to withdraw successfully. Though the Americans must be given credit for careful planning and execution of the withdrawal, the main reason why they were able to extricate themselves safely was the same as the reason why the 2nd Philippine Corps managed to survive the initial breakthrough of 15 and 16 January at the hands of the *141st*. The Japanese had no reserve force with which to press home their advantage. Once more, if the Japanese had had a single fresh formation available for the attack on or about 23 January, they might well have been able to wrap up the whole 1st Philippine Corps. As it was, Kimura had started his operations against the M.L.R. with just one unit, the *2nd/20th Infantry*, in reserve. In the course of the battle around Mauban he had committed it in what was either a foolhardy and impetuous attack that showed the Japanese at their reckless worst, or a brilliantly imaginative move that revealed Japanese opportunism and willingness to take risks. This effort resulted in a series of actions that became known as the Battle of the Points.

The Battle of the Points arose out of Honma's suggestion that landings be made behind Mauban to secure Bagac and control the roads from Pilar and Mariveles before the Americans had a chance either to fall back to the town or to move reinforcements into the area. Kimura decided on a landing by the *2nd/20th Infantry* at Caibobo Point, south of Bagac. What was initially a limited and small-scale operation quickly became a significant attempt to tear open the rear of the 1st Philippine Corps position.

The *2nd/20th* embarked at Moron on the night of 22 January at the very time when Wainwright and Parker were receiving their instructions to withdraw from positions on the M.L.R., where the Japanese stood poised for simultaneous victories over both their corps. From the very start there were problems with the landing, which appears to have been desperately understrength in relation to the objectives that were being pursued. If nothing more, the operation was certainly poorly prepared. The attacking troops were equipped with only 1:200,000 maps, which were useless in this area, and they had no knowledge of the coast and terrain on which they were to land.

Rough seas and an unfortunate chance encounter with one of the few American patrol boats still operating out of Mariveles resulted in the *2nd/20th* being scattered as it moved through the night towards Caibobo Point. Fierce but unknown tide races and the heavily indented coast, featureless against the dark sky, led the Japanese far to the south of their intended landing place. Some 600 men came ashore at Quinauan Point and about half that number landed at Longoskayan Point. The latter landing remained unknown to the Japanese command until after the final surrender of Bataan. But both landings were very quickly known to the Americans, who had placed small detachments, lookouts, and patrols in the general area to guard against the possibility of Japanese landings behind the M.L.R. and R.B.P.

The landings were obvious and dangerous threats to the security of the 1st Philippine Corps, and in strategic terms the Japanese could scarcely have improved upon their move if they had deliberately set out to land on these points. But tactically the Japanese move was less sound. Unless the Japanese quickly and firmly established themselves ashore, secured road-blocks, and, with reinforcements and supplies, took Bagac and linked up with the rest of Kimura's forces, they were doomed to defeat. The attack, begun without sufficient resources, was certain to fail unless the Japanese could exploit their initial advantages of surprise and concentration to triumph over the odds. The Americans were certain to be able to bring superior forces against any landing reasonably quickly, and the only justification for the Japanese using a force as small as a single battalion—and emptying their reserve as a result—was if the Americans were already in the process of disintegration. By the twenty-second this was not the case. Two weeks of American resistance on the M.L.R. should have been sufficient warning that the Americans were not yet finished. By opting for an ambitious amphibious assault Kimura may have deprived himself of the very force that meant the difference between success and frustration during the pursuit phase of the operations on the Mauban to Bagac road.

A decisive result eluded the Japanese both at Longoskayan and at Quinauan points, for at both places they were confined to relatively shallow beachheads. Very quickly a stalemate was established at each point, since neither side had the strength to overcome both the enemy and the demands of a rough and heavily jungled terrain. American counterattacks initially proved unavailing, but there could be only one outcome when the Americans began to deploy units from the Philippine Division and the regular artillery (released as the Americans drew back from the M.L.R.) against the beachheads. On the twenty-seventh the 57th Infantry arrived at Longoskayan Point to find that the local forces in five days had pushed the Japanese almost to the end of the point. On Lapiay Point they had already eliminated a small pocket of resistance by a group that had become detached as the Japanese were pushed off the lower slopes of Mount Picot. In less than three hours on the twenty-ninth the Scouts, aided by the infantry already there and by heavy artillery support from Corregidor, wiped out the Japanese force. The total cost to the Americans from the eight days of fighting was about 100 killed and wounded; the Japanese, with no line of retreat, died to a man.

The more substantial Japanese force at Quinauan Point, however, proved a much tougher nut to crack. Counterattacks by Philippine constabulary forces almost immediately after the landings stabilized the front before the 3rd/45th Infantry arrived to begin a set-piece assault on the twenty-eighth. In extremely difficult country the American offensive quickly stalled, with advances of only 15 yards a day being recorded by some companies over the next five days. Such were the difficulties of the attackers that armor had to be committed on 2 February in terrain where no self-respecting tankman would have gone on leave, much less into action. But tanks had to be used in order to cover the otherwise hopelessly vulnerable infantry. By a combination of artillery and armor support and heavy saturation fire from the infantry, the Americans were able to press the Japanese back into an area 100 by 50 yards by the late afternoon of 4 February. Then the Americans and Filipinos looked in amazement on a spectacle that was to be repeated on many occasions later in the Pacific war. With all hope gone, the Japanese defenders, like lemmings, began to throw themselves over the cliffs, seeking death either on the rocks or in the sea. A few did not seek death in this manner, and for the next four days the opposing infantry played a deadly game of hide-and-seek among the caves rocks, and pools along the beaches. Japanese resistance was brought to an end by the Americans, who incarcerated the last defenders in the caves by dynamiting the entrances. The bodies of tortured and mutilated prisoners, discovered behind the Japanese lines, did not make the Americans inclined to try to take the Japanese alive. As in the case of Longoskayan Point, all the troops the Japanese committed at Quinauan Point were lost, but they had fought for eighteen days and inflicted about 500 casualties on their attackers.

This was not quite the end of the Battle of the Points because for three brief days three, not two, points were held by the Japanese. The third location was Canas Point, or, more accurately, the twin promontories of Anyasan and Silaiim points just around from the Canas headland. The Japanese landed in this area in the early hours of the twenty-seventh with one company from the *1st/20th Infantry*.

Responsibility for this attack lay with General Morioka of the *16th Infantry Division*, who on the twenty-fifth took over from Kimura command of operations in western Bataan. Morioka sought to reinforce the *2nd/20th Infantry* on Quinauan Point and to press the issue there to a successful conclusion, but his initial attempt to support the *2nd Battalion* merely resulted in the establishment of another beachhead as the 200 men of the *1st Battalion*, like their predecessors, were put ashore on the wrong headland.

For the third time, therefore, Japanese forces came ashore only to be caught in a narrow beachhead from which there could be no escape. After the 2nd/45th Infantry, supported by units from the 12th Infantry and the constabulary, began to counterattack in strength on the twenty-ninth, Morioka, rather than accepting defeat and cutting his losses, stubbornly and unimaginatively tried to reinforce his isolated company by sending the rest of the battalion to its support. Unfortunately for the Japanese their security, not for the first time in the Battle of the Points, was poor. The Americans discovered Japanese intentions from documents recovered from the body of a Japanese officer, and on the night of 1/2 February the *1st/20th Infantry* ran into a rough reception as it approached its intended landing beaches. Despite the opposition, the Japanese managed to get ashore with very little loss. Once ashore they were doomed as surely as the defenders at Longoskayan and Quinauan points had been, even though they were to survive a few days longer. Once again superior American forces moved with decisive results against Japanese forces that could be neither augmented nor withdrawn, but it was not until 12 February that American infantry, with armor support, moved in for the kill. After more than two weeks of continuous action to weaken and reduce the Japanese, the Americans laid on a massive artillery bombardment that was confidently expected to put an end to Japanese resistance. As the Americans advanced behind the barrage they found that the Japanese were not merely fighting but actually counterattacking. The Japanese lost heavily and their positions around Salaiim Point were wiped out during 12 and 13 February, but eighty Japanese soldiers somehow managed to escape from the caldron. Amazingly, they reached a position 1 mile south of Bagac before they were discovered and annihilated between the sixteenth and eighteenth, though it took units from the 26th Cavalry and the 72nd and 92nd Infantry to do so.

The end of the Battle of the Points came at roughly the same time as the *14th Army* was forced to admit overall failure in its attempt to overrun Bataan. When the various battles of the beacheads were at their fiercest, Japanese main forces attempted to "bounce" the R.B.P. as they followed up the American withdrawals from the M.L.R. These attempts were unsuccessful, badly so in the 2nd Corps area, narrowly so on the front of the 1st Philippine Corps. On Wainwright's front Morioka's forces managed to make a breach in the R.B.P. before the Americans could man the line properly after they retreated from the Mauban area, but the Japanese proved too weak to consolidate and then exploit their success. The Americans were given enough time to knit their line together, thereby trapping and then annihilating the very Japanese forces that had made the breach and given the *14th Army* its fleeting chance of decisive victory. The reason for the initial Japanese failure on the R.B.P. was simple and obvious: lack of strength. Japanese units that had gone into action at Mauban on 18 January lost one-third of their strength in a week, and what remained was near exhaustion. The forces that might have tipped the balance against the 1st Philippine Corps had been destroyed at the Battle of the Points. All but thirty-four men who were plucked from various beaches and coves were lost at Longoskayan, Quinauan, Salaiim, and Anyasan points in actions that saw the total annihilation of two of the twelve infantry battalions that the *14th Army* had deployed for the assault on Bataan.

It may seem strange to refer to one or two battalions as crucial in the difference between victory and defeat, but in a sense the decisive break is always secured by a section, platoon, company, or unit at a given point. In the case of the battle for the R.B.P. this really was the case. Like two boxers who were out on their feet, both sides attempted to summon up the last dregs of their strength in one final effort; while they smothered one another with punches, neither could land a telling blow. The Japanese were in bad physical shape, but so too was the 1st Philippine Corps, which lost twenty-five artillery pieces at Mauban. This may not sound like much, but it left the corps with just six guns with which to support the R.B.P. American infantry losses also were heavy, but the most serious loss was that the cutting edge of the American forces was being blunted remorselessly by hunger and sickness. Three weeks of half-rations, debilitating heat, and rising rates of sickness for which there was no counter, were wearing down the Americans just as effectively as Japanese shells and bullets. By January/February the combination of enemy action, hunger, and illness had not eroded American strength to the point where the Japanese—beset by their own supply problems—could secure victory. Yet in denying the Japanese victory in the first six weeks of 1942, the Americans only condemned themselves to a lingering end that was probably worse than the one they so narrowly averted on the M.L.R. and R.B.P.

The margin by which the Americans avoided defeat on these two occasions was very narrow indeed. During the period of movement between the M.L.R. and the R.B.P. the Americans enjoyed the protection of neither front and were thus at their most exposed. But amid the confusion that seemed to dog American movements throughout the Luzon campaign, the covering forces, with armor support, ensured that no sizable disaster (other than the unavoidable loss of its guns by Wainwright's force) overwhelmed the defenders. Unfortunately for the American soldier what the Japanese had so signally failed to do—produce a decisive break in the line—was almost achieved by the American command itself.

The R.B.P. was a shorter and stronger position than the M.L.R., and, unlike the Mauban-Mabatang line, it was continuous. Its weakness lay in its lack of depth and of a fallback position, and MacArthur knew that his army would have to fight to destruction on this position. To hold the 16-mile front MacArthur still deployed the 1st and 2nd Philippine Corps, with Wainwright's forces holding a 7-mile front between Bagac and the Pantingan River. The 1st Corps front was divided into two sectors, both of which were held by reinforced divisions. On the left was the 91st with the 45th Infantry Regiment, less troops on the points, in support; on the right was the 11th, supported by an understrength constabulary regiment. The 1st Infantry Division was re-forming behind the front, while the 26th Cavalry was in reserve. On the front of the 2nd Corps the order of battle was more complicated. Tying in with the 1st Philippine Corps were the 21st and 41st Infantry Divisions and the 57th Infantry Regiment in one command sector on the extreme left; in the left center were the weakened 31st Infantry Division and a regimental group made up of the debris from the 51st Infantry Division. In the right center, behind a virtually impassable swamp, was the 1,400-strong Provisional Air Corps regiment, made up of air personnel pressed into service as infantry, while the 31st U.S. Infantry Regiment was on the right. The 1st/33rd Infantry constituted the corps reserve.

This was the *intended* order of battle, according to instructions issued when the M.L.R. was abandoned. As the evacuation from the Mauban-Matabang position was being carried out, the U.S. command, having previously decided to dispense with a strategic reserve, changed policy and ordered the three regiments of the Philippine Division out of the line. By 26 January, when most of the American forces were back in the R.B.P., Murphy's law began to run its inexorable course. Some of the sector commanders affected by the revised decision could not be informed. For the 1st Corps the situation was serious. The pathetic flotsam from the 1st Infantry Division had to come forward alongside the 91st and take over from the 45th Infantry Regiment, and the 1st, with about two battalions worth of troops, was no substitute for the Scouts. For the 2nd Corps the changes were disastrous because the corps lost regiments at either end of its front and had to replace them with formations taken out of the center. The 31st Infantry Division lost the two battalions of the 33rd that it had as the replacement for the 57th Infantry, while the 2nd and 3rd Battalions of the 31st Infantry replaced the 31st U.S. Infantry on the coast. In the left center of the 2nd Philippine Corps front, therefore, the sector commander, Bluemel, was left with the 32nd Infantry Regiment, the 1st/31st Infantry Battalion, and the 51st Regimental Group to hold a 2½-mile front. Obviously Bluemel was the commander most affected by the changes, and he was not informed of them. He discovered that half his formation was leaving or had already left its positions only when he toured his front and found units missing. As if this potentially disastrous situation was not bad enough, inevitably when the Japanese launched their attack on the R.B.P. they did so on two fronts, one in the west, the other in the east. The attack in the west fell on that part of the line held by the 1st Infantry Division, in the east it fell on the front held (or not held) by Bluemel's forces. The choice of axes was providential because the Japanese obviously did not know of the confusion that engulfed the American line, but the choice could not have been bettered.

The Bataan campaign almost becomes predictable at this point because the Japanese attempt to break through the R.B.P. was virtually a carbon copy of the fight for the M.L.R. The main Japanese effort was against the 2nd Philippine Corps, but the attack was underprepared (the artillery had no time to come up in support) and a failure, despite the fact that for nearly twelve hours there was a yawning gap in Sector C before the 41st Infantry Regiment could come across to hold the line. Predictably, the formation entrusted to break through the 2nd Philippine Corps front at this very gap was the *9th Infantry Regiment*, which added yet another mediocre failure to its impressive list. Once again there were mitigating factors, and it would be wrong to blame the *9th* entirely for its lack of success in battle, but its persistent failure to make anything of its chances certainly did nothing to endear it to Nara. Despite an initial attempt on the twenty-seventh to rush the R.B.P. and a set-piece attack on the thirty-first, an attack met and defeated primarily by massed American artillery, a breakthrough on the 2nd Philippine Corps front eluded the Japanese. On 2 February Nara called off his attack in the face of mounting losses and an obvious faltering on the part of his units.

On their right flank the Japanese had done better, just as they had on the M.L.R. Perhaps predictably, the unit that made the potentially decisive breach in the 2nd Corps front was the *3rd/20th Infantry*; just like its two sister battalions, it was to suffer effective annihilation as its reward. After having been repulsed by the 91st Infantry Division on 26/27 January, the *3rd/20th* broke through the 1st Infantry Division's sector during the night of 28/29 January and established itself in wild country a mile or so behind the front line. Because no other units pushed through the gap in the R.B.P. to support it, the *3rd/20th* found itself trapped after 31 January, when the 1st Infantry Division managed to reestablish itself along the R.B.P. and link up with the 91st and 11th Divisions on either flank. From that time on the *3rd/20th* was doomed as an effective fighting unit because the American forces on the R.B.P. held increasingly heavy and desperate Japanese attempts to break through in order to extricate the battalion. The Battle of the Pockets, as it became known, was slowly but remorselessly won by the Americans as they threw a cordon around the Japanese and gradually exerted increasing pressure, just as the Americans were doing successfully at exactly the same time at Quinauan and Canas points. But in this case the difficulty of the country made it virtually impossible to complete an encircling attempt, and when the Americans inadvertently left one gap in their line the Japanese were through it without waiting for a second invitation. The *3rd/20th* managed to break out of the encirclement and then through the R.B.P. to reach Japanese lines on 15 February with 378 men after nearly three weeks of action during which they received neither supplies nor support. The achievement of the *3rd/20th* was no less impressive than it had been around Mauban and its escape was remarkable, but this could not disguise the facts that the Americans had weathered the storm and that the Japanese had failed in their attempt to force the R.B.P. before the American defense had time to harden. Honma admitted as much when on 8 February he ordered the indefatigable Nara to cancel his proposed renewal of the attack on the 2nd Philippine Corps.

As the battles along and behind the R.B.P. raged during the first week in February, Slim's observations on the Japanese army could never have seemed more appropriate. Inflexibility, blind obedience to orders that flouted reality, dangerous overconfidence, narrow administrative margins, and a total unwillingness to admit failure had conspired to all but ruin the *14th Army*. The forces that had overrun almost the whole of Luzon with minimal losses had been brought to the brink of disaster—and one regiment over it—by a persistence that was as wasteful as it was unnecessary. It was unnecessary because by any rational standard the Japanese were assured of victory with very little effort. The *65th Infantry Brigade* could have beaten the 1st and 2nd Philippine Corps without the help of any other Japanese formation—if Imperial General Headquarters, *Southern Army*, and the *14th Army* had been prepared to allow its positional advantage to destroy the Americans not by action but by starvation and disease. In the tactical situation that prevailed on Luzon time meant nothing to the Japanese. Unfortunately for all concerned, this was not the Japanese method of waging war. Psychological necessity demanded that the Americans be defeated in the field, but by the time its attacks on the R.B.P. had been repulsed, the *14th Army* had seen enough to doubt the wisdom of the course it was pursuing.

By 8 February the Japanese forces had suffered losses and privations that any Allied command in the same situation would long since have found impossible. The Japanese command, however, was always prepared to fight its divisions to absolute destruction, and by this time that was not very far off. Honma later estimated that his total effective strength at this time was three battalions. The total strength of the *16th Infantry Division* was about 700 men; the *65th Infantry Brigade* mustered about 1,000 men. In a little more than two weeks 11,000 Japanese soldiers had become nonbattle casualties; obviously, the slenderness of Japanese medical facilities had long since been revealed. Among the battle casualties mortality rates were rising because of infection and complications that need never have arisen. At this stage of the campaign the Japanese were probably suffering more than the Americans from the shortages of food and medicine, and the Americans were on half-rations and fast exhausting their supply of drugs.

In this situation Honma called off his attacks while he considered his position. He was very awkwardly placed. On one side were the massed ranks of Japanese military orthodoxy, the *attaque à outrance* school that placed moral force above every other consideration and that would argue for the attack being pressed at all costs. Such military doctrine, seen at its worst in some of the more ghastly episodes of World War I, held in esteem the notion of imposing one's will on the enemy, and nothing could withstand the fury of the Japanese army in the attack. The old fallacy of the last battalion deciding the issue if an attack was pressed was as strong in Japanese minds as it had been in the thoughts of Falkenhayn, Haig, and Joffre a quarter-century earlier. Honma knew that Imperial General Headquarters and *Southern Army* would not consider their having taken the *48th Infantry Division* away from him and their having altered the timetable of conquest as sufficient reasons for his failure to defeat the Americans. Honma knew what was demanded of him. On the other side was reason and reality, summarized for him by his chief of staff, Lieutenant General Masami Maeda. Maeda considered what already had been achieved on Luzon a victory. He believed that to persist with an attack on Bataan would yield no commensurate return. Maeda thought that the rest of the Philippines should be occupied (the deployment of the *16th Infantry Division* to Bataan meant that the islands outside Luzon were virtually untouched) while starvation reduced the Bataan defenders to surrender. Maeda was after as cheap and as economical a victory as possible.

Honma's position was unenviable, and needless to say he compromised. It was physically impossible to continue the attack, despite Nara's determination, and Honma ordered his army to cancel all offensive operations. In what was a monumental admission of failure and a loss of prestige for Honma personally, he ordered his army not only to go on to the defensive but also to withdraw to more easily defended positions along the Bagac-Balanga line. This was a withdrawal made out of choice, not one imposed by the Americans, but it was still a withdrawal, the first Japanese retreat of the war, from ground that had been paid for with blood. To the defenders of Bataan must go the credit for achieving something they had failed to achieve elsewhere on Luzon, something the British and Dutch had lamentably failed to achieve elsewhere in Southeast Asia. Honma opted for a waiting game. He wanted time for starvation and illness to eat away at American strength and he wanted time to make the blockade of Bataan total by securing absolute control of southern Luzon and Mindoro, thereby ending any possibility of supplies being smuggled into Bataan. He wanted time in order to get Imperial General Headquarters to release more forces so that a properly organized set-piece battle could be mounted in adequate strength. Honma still wanted a military solution to the Bataan problem. He was not prepared to wait for a meek American surrender when the enemy's supplies were exhausted. He, and the entire Japanese command, wanted to bring about something never previously recorded in history: the military defeat and surrender of an American army in the field in a foreign war.

After 8 February, therefore, both sides settled down to prepare for the next round; or rather, the Japanese did so. There was very little the Americans could do but await an assault that they increasingly realized would bring about their utter ruination. Yet at this point in the campaign the American side naturally divides into two parts: what was happening on Bataan itself and what was being decided in Washington regarding the higher direction of the war. The latter, naturally, was bound up with MacArthur's personal fate and conduct of the battle.

On Bataan the euphoria of having held the Japanese on the R.B.P. quickly wore off, with the inevitable reaction setting in quickly. Among the troops and junior officers there was a widespread desire to pursue the Japanese and undertake a general offensive. But Parker had no intention of using his corps offensively, and he never seriously considered the possibility of following up the Japanese as they drew back to the Bagac-Balanga line. Such an advance was beyond the physical capabilities of the troops and administratively impossible. The demands of static warfare were less than those of an offensive that, in the end, could achieve nothing. Parker knew that in these circumstances a second retreat into Bataan was unavoidable, and he never even bothered to ask for guidance from MacArthur's command on the question of following up the enemy's retreat. Strategic necessity had to prevail over tactical and psychological considerations, but enforced idleness only brought home to the ordinary soldier the hopelessness of his situation.

Most of this hopelessness stemmed from the slow breakdown of administration. From the very start of the campaign action reports and quartermasters' returns were equally important to American commanders, and in the end the weakness brought about by lack of food and medicine was chiefly responsible for destroying the cohesion and morale of the defending forces. Food was a concern that ultimately took precedence over everything else as the average ration allowance (72 ounces per day for the American soldier before the war) fell to 13 ounces (18 percent) by late March. Troops had to operate in blistering heat, in scarecrow uniforms, on hopelessly inadequate diets. Their increasing enfeeblement left them too weak to withstand the ravages of illness. By the beginning of March 500 new malaria cases were being admitted to field hospitals every day, and during the month this figure doubled. Amoebic dysentery and a whole host of diseases related to vitamin deficiency, including sight problems that were particularly serious for the gunners, ravaged the garrison. By the time when the Japanese were ready to begin their final offensive in early April the garrison was too weak to offer serious and effective resistance.

But malnutrition and sickness were not alone in destroying the fabric of the American defense. Equally important was the despair brought about by the realization that the Philippines had been abandoned to defeat because help was not on its way. This feeling of hopelessness and bitterness assumed vicious proportions when it was learned that MacArthur had left his headquarters on Corregidor for Australia via Mindanao on 12 March.

By the beginning of February Washington had to face up to the problem of what to salvage from the disaster that was certain to overwhelm the Allies throughout Southeast Asia in the next few weeks. It really boiled down to who rather than what, and in this situation only one man was absolutely indispensable and had to be brought to safety at all costs. This man was not MacArthur but Manuel Quezon, president of the Philippine Common-wealth. As the symbol of the people the Americans had intended to lead to nationhood, Quezon could not be allowed to fall into Japanese hands. Scarcely less important, and to the American public infinitely more so, was MacArthur, despite the fact that his overall performance on Luzon had been insipid. He had spent six years in the Philippines (1935–41) and had boasted of his intention to defeat any Japanese invasion of the islands. The performance of the defenders showed that far less had been achieved during MacArthur's command than anyone had the right to expect, while the troops involved in the defense of Luzon from December onwards had the right to expect better leadership than they received. Perhaps the Filipino troops were less than first rate, but they were certainly better than a generalship that led them to Bataan without the means to survive and fight. They had the right to expect more than just one visit to Bataan from a general who mentioned his own name in virtually every dispatch he issued and who finally left them when their defeat was assured.

MacArthur received much abuse from the soldiers he led so dismally on Bataan, partly for his alleged inactivity on Corregidor and then for his escape to safety. Much of the abuse was naturally tinged with the subse-quent bitterness brought about by the horror of three and one-half years in Japanese prison camps. But in the matter of his move to Australia, MacAr-thur was not a free agent. He was ordered to Australia on 23 February by a Roosevelt administration that valued his abilities as a commander of forces to be assembled for the eventual counterattack and as a symbol of American determination to stand by Australia. Washington accepted MacArthur's request that he be allowed to determine the timing of his departure, but on 6 and 9 March, as the Indies campaign drew to a close, the Roosevelt administration urged speed on MacArthur. After eventful sea and air passages, MacArthur arrived in Australia on 17 March.

MacArthur expected to find substantial American forces in Australia when he arrived, and he expected to be able to launch some relief attempt to Bataan almost immediately. He was amazed to find Australia virtually bereft of American forces. It was not until 6 April that the first American combat troops to be dispatched from the United States after the outbreak of the war arrived in Australia, and it was not until 18 April—a day more famous for one of the smallest but most momentous operations of the entire war—that MacArthur received instructions and a designated command from the Combined Chiefs of Staff. MacArthur openly fumed at the delays that kept him in relative idleness for a month. He assumed malevolence towards him personally was the real reason for his being becalmed at this critical stage of the war, and he blamed Marshall and the navy for his "unemployment." In part he was correct: the U.S. Navy, after what he had said about it and Hart, was not among his keenest admirers. But MacArthur failed to understand the complexities of inter-Allied and interservice

Time not on their side but obviously on their hands. Exercising command on Corregidor, MacArthur and his chief of staff, Brigadier General Richard K. Sutherland. U.S. Army

arrangements; he also failed to realize just how far the arrangements he had put into effect in the Philippines on his departure contributed to the delays in redefining command boundaries and responsibilities.

The withdrawal of MacArthur from Corregidor in no way diminished Washington's determination to fight on in the Philippines. This had been made clear when Washington rejected Quezon's 8 February appeal to Roosevelt that the United States grant immediate independence to the Philippines as the first step in both the Americans and the Japanese withdrawing their forces from the islands and guaranteeing the new state's neutrality. MacArthur rather tentatively gave his support to Quezon's scheme, which was totally unrealistic and born out of Quezon's smoldering resentment at the American "betrayal" of the Philippines. MacArthur shared Washington's determination not to capitulate, but when he went to Australia he created a command structure for the Philippines that allowed him to control the campaign there. He created four commands—for Bataan, the Manila Bay fortresses, the Visayans, and Mindanao—with his own tactical headquarters kept on Corregidor. It was amazing that MacArthur, sent to command in an Allied rather than a national theater, should have presumed that he could maintain his previous command while 3,000 miles from the battle. It was equally amazing that he did not inform Washington of these arrangements. Marshall, when he discovered them, tersely told MacArthur that they were "unacceptable." On 26 March MacArthur received the Medal of Honor for his conduct of the defense of Bataan (though he refused to write a citation for Wainwright for the same award), but he lost his Philippine command. A new command was created on Washington's instructions in order to fight the last battles on the island.

MacArthur's arrangements for the Philippines were unacceptable to Washington and the general personally was scarcely less so to the U.S. Navy, which was determined to keep the Pacific war a naval affair. In an area perhaps as much as 98 percent sea, this attitude was not unreasonable, but it made no sense politically. MacArthur was too senior to be turned out to pasture, and Nimitz, the naval commander in chief in the Pacific, was his junior. After weeks of argument between the services an arrangement was made that broke the cardinal rule of unity of command but that worked superbly. MacArthur was to be given command of the Southwest Pacific, Nimitz the rest of the ocean, with the result that in time the two were to become the arms in a gigantic pincer movement that was to grip the Japanese and crush the life out of them. In this situation Japan's supreme geographic advantage was to avail her nothing because her central position prevented her from turning to deal with either threat for fear of the other. By the time the Japanese were able to turn and fight, at the Philippine Sea in mid-1944, the war had been lost because their strength had been eroded and the Americans had too many advantages—in the air, at sea, in initiative, and in position—for resistance to be availing. It was the precise reversal of the situation in which the Philippines found itself in December 1941, but in March 1942 such events were nearly thirty months hence, and what was important was what was happening on Bataan.

While American forces on Bataan were weakening daily and the American supreme command was undertaking its various local command arrangements, the Japanese were pressing ahead with arrangements that even the doleful Honma was sure would being the campaign to an end. These arrangements involved replacements for the losses suffered by the formations already on Luzon and the dispatch of more formations to aid the *14th Army*.

Reinforcements for the two formations that had undertaken the original attacks, the *16th Infantry Division* and the *65th Infantry Brigade*, came from two sources. First, as the Japanese offensive was allowed to die away, the supporting services, particularly the hospitals, could begin to come to grips with problems that previously had overwhelmed them. Men who had been put out of action by minor wounds or illness began to return to their units as Japanese field hospitals began to function properly. Second, in March 3,500 fresh drafts were sent to each of the formations so that they could begin to approach their established strengths. Neither was able to cover its officer losses, but in its overall strength the *65th Infantry Brigade* by the end of March was slightly stronger than it had been in early January. The *16th Infantry Division*, on the other hand, never recovered despite being reinforced. It had only the *9th Infantry* as a complete regiment under its command. The *20th Infantry* had been annihilated, while only one battalion from the *33rd Infantry* was with its division. One battalion was deployed on occupation duties in southern Luzon while another was used to occupy northern Mindoro of 27 February as part of the process of drawing the noose tight around Bataan. Even with its reinforcements the *16th Infantry Division* played only a minor diversionary role against the 1st Philippine Corps when the Japanese began their final offensive on Bataan.

Most of the reinforcements that found their way to Bataan were directed down the east coast against the sector held by the 2nd Philippine Corps. The first of the infantry to arrive was the *61st Regimental Group*, which consisted of the *61st Infantry*, a mountain artillery unit, and a sapper company under the command of Major General Kameichiro Nagano. This 4,000-strong force was part of the *21st Infantry Division*; it had been detached for service in the Philippines when the division was moved into French Indo-China in mid-February. On 27 February, the day after the *61st Group* arrived at Lingayen Gulf from China, the leading elements of Lieutenant General Kenzo Kitano's *4th Infantry Division* reached Luzon from Shanghai. Honma subsequently described the division as the worst equipped in the entire Japanese army, but it was all that was available and it was better than nothing. The *4th Infantry Division* was drastically under-strength in every respect. Its supporting services were weak, even by the dubious standards of the Japanese army, and it had no antitank component. Its two regiments, the *8th* and *37th Infantry*, had battalions of three and not four rifle companies, while the division's muster of about 11,000 men meant that it was at little more than half-strength.

But if the Japanese were hard put to find infantry to support the *14th Army*, the same cannot be said about the artillery. After 8 February two regiments and three battalions of artillery and three mortar battalions (with artillery pieces that ranged in size from 300 millimeter mortars to 75 millimeter mountain guns) were brought up to support the *1st Regiment* and *9th Battalion* of heavy field artillery already in the line. Two air regiments of bombers also were deployed to support the *14th Army*'s endeavors.

Honma's plan of attack was little more than a repetition of his original assaults on the M.L.R. and R.B.P., with the very important difference that this time he had a sufficient margin of superiority over the Americans to avoid the prospect of yet another reverse. He planned to make his main effort in the center of the peninsula against the left-center of the 2nd Philippine Corps. For this purpose he concentrated the *65th Infantry Brigade*, *61st Regimental Group*, and *4th Infantry Division* on a 3½-mile front opposite Mount Samat, the first objective of the attack. The *14th Army* planned to follow three lines of advance. The *65th Infantry Brigade* was to attack along the line of the Pantingan River, the boundary between the 1st and 2nd Philippine Corps. The *61st Infantry Regiment*, with a battalion from the *8th Infantry* and armor, artillery, and engineers in support, was to follow the Catmon River and secure the western slopes of Mount Samat. The remainder of the *8th Infantry* was to form the third thrust. It was to advance down Trail 4 to secure Mount Samat itself. The *37th Infantry* was held in reserve, while the *16th Infantry Division* and detachments from Nagano's *61st Infantry Group* were to mount feigned attacks on both flanks in order to tie down American forces.

The emphasis of the attack was clearly placed on the *65th Infantry Brigade* and the reinforced *61st Infantry*; the attack by the half-strength *8th Infantry* was secondary to the main efforts to its right. But to make the decisive breach Honma was depending on his artillery, reformed and massively concentrated under Lieutenant General Kishio Kitajima, who was sent to Luzon specially to organize artillery support for the operation. In fact, Honma's plan of attack was little more than an artillery exercise, with live ammunition and targets. The aim was to blast a breach in the R.B.P. through which the infantry were to pass. This was considerably different from previous attacks, which had relied primarily on the infantry to make, consolidate, and then exploit a breach. On this occasion Honma intended to preserve his infantry as far as possible and rely on materiel to achieve results. The infantry were to advance in short bounds; the artillery then would come forward to repeat the process of destroying enemy resistance by short but very intense bombardments. Such a systematic approach was certain to be slow, but this was no real concern to Honma. Given the tactical situation on Luzon and the fact that Honma's forces were not urgently required for service elsewhere, time was of no consequence. In fact, Honma allowed significantly longer for this attack to be successful than he had for previous operations. He anticipated strong American resistance around Mount Samat because this mountain provided the 2nd Philippine Corps with an unrivalled artillery observation post, and Honma expected the Americans to fight hard for its retention. Honma thought it would take a week to make a clear breach through the R.B.P. and secure Mount Samat, and he allowed another two weeks for the reduction of a defensive position he wrongly believed covered Limay. He anticipated that another week would be needed to mop up. Certain of his commanders believed that the attack would be a walkover, but Honma, having been proved badly wrong on two occasions, was evidently intent on overestimating rather than underrating the effectiveness of American resistance.

As the Japanese perfected their plan of attack, the last hours of life left to the American army on Bataan slipped away. In the line opposite the assembling Japanese forces was an impressive number of units. Any assessment based simply on ration strengths would have given an arriving American general confidence in the ability of his forces to withstand assault. The 2nd Philippine Corps alone had a strength of nearly 30,000 men, more than it had in January during the battles on the M.L.R. But numbers belied strength, and no one was misled by the pins on the maps. By the end of March the Americans had reached the breaking point. The crippling effects of the blockade, the inability to rest units away from the congested battle area, the decline in morale caused by the realization that help was not coming and that their commander had left, plus an increased Japanese patrol activity signalled a forthcoming assault, the natural tightening of nerves on the part of men who knew they were to be attacked, all conspired to ensure that the 2nd Philippine Corps was defeated before the final battle began. Parker's command might have 30,000 men in the line, but in effect his corps had little more than one-third that number. Divisions were little more than regiments, regiments no more than battalions, and battalions were effectively no more than a couple of companies. Those Japanese generals who expected an easy battle were right: the defenders were no longer capable of a sustained effort.

On the front where the main Japanese effort was to fall was Parker's 2nd Philippine Corps between the Pantingan River and Manila Bay. On the left, linking up with the 1st Philippine Corps, was the 41st Infantry Division with all three of its infantry regiments in the line. On its right was the 21st Infantry Division, again with all three formations forward. Neither division had the strength to hold a reserve. On the right of the 21st Infantry Division, manning the sector where the Japanese had come to grief in the initial assault on the R.B.P. some two months earlier, was the 51st Infantry Division. It had been so ravaged by losses, however, that it was no more than a relatively weak regimental combat team made up of various elements from the whole division. The 32nd Infantry extended the line westwards to where the Provisional Air Corps Regiment was deployed. The coast road from Orion to Limay was held by the 31st Infantry Regiment. The constabulary from the 2nd Infantry Division was deployed behind the 31st Infantry in position to meet any Japanese landings in the rear, but this task was to be entrusted to the corps service elements in the event of a serious Japanese effort on the R.B.P. In this eventuality the 2nd Infantry Division was to pass into corps reserve, ready for the counterattack. In the meantime the 2nd and 3rd Battalions, 33rd Infantry, constituted the corps reserve. The small size of the area remaining to the Americans allowed the force reserve, which consisted of the three regiments of the Philippine Division, what was left of the Provisional Tank Group, and two engineer battalions, to come up in support very quickly. The 31st U.S. Infantry Regiment was in the immediate area of the front, but the 45th Infantry, in the 1st Philippine Corps area, was moved up to the intercorps boundary to be in a position to support the 2nd Corps. In more immediate support of the 2nd Philippine Corps were two-thirds of the 150 guns left to the Americans on Bataan.

From this recounting of the American order of battle in the 2nd Corps area it can be seen that the sector where the Japanese planned to attack was precisely the one where the Americans were weakest. The 41st and 21st Infantry Divisions were both fully stretched across wide frontages with no reserves at hand to guard against the possibility of the battle going badly.

Honma's offensive began in mid-morning on 3 April, a date deliberately chosen not only because was it Good Friday but also because it was the anniversary of the death of the first emperor of Japan. The preliminary Japanese bombardment lasted five hours and was augmented by bombers, which had spent the previous days attacking opportunity targets in the rear. American officers compared the ferocity of the Japanese artillery attack to the worst they could remember on the Western Front in France in 1917–18, and this bombardment did its job. Relatively few of the defenders were killed, but the demoralizing and disruptive effects of the bombardment were intense. For troops already at the end of their endurance a prolonged artillery bombardment was simply too much. The 41st Infantry Division, against which the greatest weight of the bombardment was directed, was crumbling before the Japanese rose from their jumping-off positions.

The advancing Japanese infantry and armor, initially from the *65th Infantry Brigade* and *61st Infantry Group*, therefore encountered only sporadic opposition. Only the left flank of the 41st Infantry Division, the 41st Infantry Regiment, remained reasonably secure. The 42nd and 43rd Regiments, along with the left flank of the adjoining 21st Infantry Regiment, had given way under the initial impact of the attack. Encouraged by the unanticipated extent of the success, Honma seized the opportunity for forcing a quick decision and gave orders for the scope of the attack to be broadened immediately. In the course of the next day's fighting (4 April) the Japanese effectively destroyed the 41st Infantry Division as a fighting formation and began to batter both the right and left flanks of the 21st Infantry Division into ruins. By the end of the day the 41st Infantry Regiment had been pushed clear of the Pantingan line and away from the trail that ran parallel to the river to the American rear. The 42nd had ceased to exist while the battered 43rd, even when supported by the 2nd and 3rd Battalions, 33rd Infantry, which were sent up to hold the line, had no chance of imposing the slightest check on the *65th Infantry Brigade*. The division's entire main defensive line had been lost, while the 21st Infantry Regiment was in desperate straits against the *61st Infantry Regiment*. The 21st Infantry Division's other two regiments, the 23rd and 22nd, were also beginning to wilt as Japanese pressure on them intensified.

Though the battle still had a few more days to run its course, the issue had already been decided, if not on the third then certainly on the fourth. Though the main American counterattack was still to come, it had no chance of success. The breach that the Japanese had made in the center of the R.B.P. (thereby separating the 1st and 2nd Philippine Corps) was too wide for the physically and numerically weak American forces to seal. Having failed to hold the Japanese with their full strength, the Americans could not hope to defeat them with the wretchedly inadequate forces they had left. With the collapse of the 41st Infantry Division and the buckling of the 21st, no formation from either division could be made available to support a counterattack that by definition would be too slow in execution and made in insufficient strength to reverse the verdict of 3/4 April. With depleted units moving up to hastily designated jumping-off positions, fragmentation was certain to attend any American effort to counterattack, and this could only result in the further disintegration of the whole 2nd Philippine Corps.

In fact, the American counterattack on 6 April was overshadowed by simultaneous Japanese attacks through the vacant 41st Infantry Division area and the right flank of the 21st Infantry Division. The American attempts to parry the initial Japanese breakthrough met with some local successes, but overall the attack was irrelevant. There was nothing that the

Americans could do to disturb the equilibrium of the Japanese because the battle was running too fiercely against the defenders. By nightfall on the sixth the American position had worsened dramatically, despite the attempted counterattack. The Japanese commitment during the day of their immediate reserve, the *37th Infantry Regiment*, against the 51st Regimental Combat Team, caused the crumbling of the left anchor of the American defense on the R.B.P. With that position gone, units to the west, in the area of the breach, were like sandcastles facing the incoming tide. By the night of 6/7 April the Japanese had managed to drive a salient 3 miles deep and 3 miles across at its base through the center of the R.B.P. For the moment there was no danger to the 1st Philippine Corps, which was secure along the R.B.P. and the Pantingan River, but the total collapse of the 2nd Philippine Corps could not be delayed for more than a matter of hours.

On 9 February Roosevelt had prohibited surrender, and this order remained unchanged. Yet by 7 April, with the Japanese approaching Limay and the last reserves having been thrown in to no effect, surrender was inevitable. The 2nd Philippine Corps was fast falling to pieces and the 1st Philippine Corps was in full retreat as it attempted to guard against the possibility of its right flank being turned. In the rear areas were stores that had to be denied to the Japanese and the hospitalized, who had to be protected.

The two senior American commanders, Wainwright for the Philippines and Major General Edward P. King on Bataan, were thus caught in the classic dilemma of obedience to orders from above and loyalty and concern for their men, who could do nothing more than die uselessly. Wainwright had no option but to try to continue the struggle. He had forces other than those on Bataan under his command and still in the field, and it was impossible for him to consider surrendering part of his force. In any case the Japanese would never accept a partial surrender while Wainwright remained on Corregidor to thumb his nose at them. King, on the other hand, had a narrower field of responsibility. On his shoulders fell the responsibility for disobeying Roosevelt's and Wainwright's direct orders not to surrender. By the eighth it had become clear that nothing could prevent the Japanese from reaching Mariveles in the next twenty-four hours and that only an immediate end to the fighting could avert a bloodbath. With some 78,000 troops and 26,000 civilians on Bataan, King probably had no more than a couple of battalions under effective command as his force fell apart. Without informing Wainwright of what he was doing (thus absolving Wainwright of the responsibility for surrender), King on 8 April sought negotiations to end the hostilities on Bataan. King found the Japanese unresponsive and angered by the fact that a general surrender in the Philippines still eluded them. The Japanese refused to accept anything but unconditional surrender and King was unable to extract any concessions from the victors. King therefore had to surrender without having secured from the Japanese any undertaking that they would respect the terms of the Geneva Conventions, and without signing any formal document. King had to trust to the magnanimity of the Japanese in their hour of victory, and little, if any, was forthcoming as American forces began to lay down their arms on Bataan from 8 April onwards.

The campaign in the Visayans, on Mindanao, and on Corregidor had almost a month to run its course, but the campaign on the Philippines was over from the time the Americans surrendered on Bataan. Luzon was the key to the islands in 1941–42, and all Luzon was under Japanese control as a result of King's capitulation. Apart from the bravery and endurance of the troops, the campaign had been a disaster for the Americans from beginning to end, with just one important exception. The Americans believed that they had done well on Bataan, and this was as important as actually doing well. In stark terms the Americans had survived the more substantial British in Malaya by almost two months and the Dutch by four weeks. American forces were still in the field, denying the Japanese undisputed control of the islands at the end. In the midst of total disaster throughout the Pacific and Southeast Asia, as well as in the Indian Ocean since the last rites on Bataan coincided with the carrier raid on Ceylon, the continuation of American resistance on Bataan was inspirational. The British were shamed

The end on Bataan. American and Filipino soldiers begin the infamous march that cost many their lives before the survivors reached Camp O'Donnell, near San Fernando in central Luzon. U.S. Army

by their failure in comparison to what was happening in the Philippines, and the Americans, naturally, took pride in what they believed to be happening on Luzon.

But any serious examination of the campaign on Bataan must quickly come to terms with two matters: MacArthur and his conduct of the battle, and the nature of the campaign itself. MacArthur was given his nation's highest award for his conduct of the battle. In some armies a general who allowed his air force to be destroyed on the ground after nine hours' warning time and who led his army into an area he had neglected to stock (after having failed to honor his promise of defeating the enemy) would have been shot. MacArthur, in fact, became a national hero, and his subsequent triumphs eclipsed the wretchedness of his performance in the dark days of 1941–42. It was right that his victories should outshine the defeat because his triumphs were achieved with remarkable economy of life, and his operations were conducted with verve, imagination, and ingratiating conceit. But MacArthur must be considered one of the most fortunate generals of the war in that he was given a second chance. The hapless Kimmel, who lost his fleet at Pearl Harbor, was never employed again, though he was less blameworthy for the disaster that overwhelmed the U.S. Pacific Fleet than MacArthur was for the debacle in the Philippines.

An examination of the campaign itself shows that the real reason why the Americans evaded defeat for so long on Bataan was less the effectiveness of their resistance than the weakness of the Japanese. The Japanese committed no more than nine infantry regiments to the Philippines campaign, and when the Americans stood at the M.L.R. on Bataan they opposed just nine infantry battalions. At the very height of the battle for Bataan the Americans were opposed by no more than a reinforced division and brigade, and the Japanese really had to scrape the bottom of the barrel for the forces they did finally deploy on the peninsula. However great the sacrifices of the defenders were, the harsh truth was that they failed either to inflict substantial losses on the attackers or to tie down disproportionate enemy resources and disrupt the Japanese timetable.

The final reduction of the Philippines was delayed not because of American resistance but because the Japanese decided to alter their priorities. No delays were imposed on the various arrangements the Japanese were making to extend the struggle into the Southwest Pacific; Japanese forces were not diverted to the Philippines on any major scale from other more important theaters. The Indies were not afforded any relief or respite because of the events on Luzon, and Japanese losses in the Philippines were light. The Japanese lost just under 3,000 killed and 5,000 wounded in taking Luzon (the final assault between 3 and 7 April cost them 227 killed and 402 wounded), a very light cost when it is recalled that about 1,800 Japanese soldiers were killed in the Battle of the Points. In its widest strategic sense the American defense of the Philippines achieved nothing of significant value. The real tragedy of the Bataan force was not merely in the appalling treatment it received at the hands of its conquerors but that, through no fault of its own and despite its privations and sufferings, it achieved so very little. For the Japanese, however, the senseless stubbornness of the enemy had been broken in yet one more confirmation of the irresistibility of Japanese arms. A few fights remained, but no one doubted that the other islands, and the famous island fortress of Corregidor, the Gibraltar of the East, would fall. Indeed, for the Japanese the fall of Corregidor was less than a month away—but so, too, was the Battle of the Coral Sea.

CHAPTER 14

From Victoria Point
to Yenangyaung

THERE ARE SEVERAL AREAS of the world that could vie for the unenviable title of the worst theater in which men had to do battle during the Second World War. Burma's claims for this dubious distinction are particularly strong because the country's combination of terrain, climate, relief, and natural vegetation create fearsome obstacles to the conduct of war.

Location and, to a lesser extent, size were the key factors in turning Burma from a backwater into a front line state during the war. Burma is a large country, extending over nearly twenty degrees of latitude, and it is larger than any single country solely in Europe. With an area of about 262,000 square miles, Burma is roughly the same size as Texas or three times the size of Britain. It is larger than any of the present-day states with which it shares the greater Indo-China peninsula. It occupies the north-western part of the peninsula, bordered in 1941 by British India to the north; China, French Indo-China, and Thailand to the east; and by the Indian Ocean and Bay of Bengal to the west. Though in 1941 Burma possessed a flourishing rice industry and substantial oil and tungsten deposits, her real value to the Allies and the Japanese alike was not economic but strategic. The Japanese coveted the country as a buffer zone, a shield for the gains they intended to make in the Indies. By securing Burma and the Andamans and Nicobars the Japanese would obtain defense in depth for Singapore, Sumatra, and Java against any British assault on the direct routes from Ceylon and the Bay of Bengal. The British, on the other hand, valued Burma not only for the protection that it naturally afforded northeast India and the sea communications of the Bay of Bengal, but also because it was a vital link in the communications chain that led southwards to Malaya and northwards to China. The four major airfields along the Tenasserim coast (Moulmein, Tavoy, Mergui, and Victoria Point) formed a vital imperial lifeline for the British, who needed them in order to fly aircraft from India to Malaya and Singapore. The Burma Road, running from the railhead at Lashio in eastern Burma to Chungking, was equally vital to Chiang Kai-shek's Nationalist China because without this road China would have been isolated from the outside world.

The size and location of Burma explain more than just the importance of the country in 1941; these factors lay at the heart of the problems that surrounded the organization of Burma's defense. Before 1937 Burma was one of the provinces of British India, which at over 2,914,000 square miles was almost as large as the continental United States, Alaska excepted. Burma, therefore, was a small concern to any commander in chief for India. From his Delhi headquarters, the commander's attention naturally turned at various times to the north, the northwest frontier, and the Middle East, not to the east and south. Those areas were the preserve of the Royal Navy, and as long as the Royal Navy was unchallenged in the Indian Ocean there was no conceivable threat to Burma. Even after Japan began to emerge as a potential threat in the early thirties, Burma was sheltered behind a seemingly hard outer crust of defenses formed by the vastness of China, French power in Indo-China, and the British presence on Singapore. Japan was several thousand miles away, and between Japan and Burma were countries that protected her in the same manner that she protected India. Even after Burma was separated from India in April 1937, just before the start of the Sino-Japanese war, there was no real change in this situation. In the grandest of strategic terms, the Maginot Line was the guarantee of Burma's security, because the French fortress system was the underwriter of all French, Dutch, and British possessions in the Far East. As long as French power in Europe remained intact, French Indo-China was secure, and with French Indo-China secure Burma was safe.

Both distance and the existence of more powerfully defended colonies served to defend Burma without the colony having to exert itself very much in its own defense. With no real external threat to face, the Burmese military commitment and establishment, despite the presence of a general officer commanding, was small and mainly concerned with internal security. The military interest in Burma was bound up with maintaining public order, controlling the frontiers, and guarding the Syriam oil refineries, Rangoon's port facilities, and various airfields. To discharge these duties there were two regular British battalions, four regular and two reservist

battalions of the Burma Rifles, and the nine battalions of the Burma
Military Police, six of which were organized along paramilitary lines as the
Burma Frontier Force. Neither the Frontier Force nor the three remaining
battalions of the Burma Military Police were under military command; they
were under civilian control. In addition, there was the part-time Burma
Auxiliary Force, recruited from the British, Anglo-Indian, and Anglo-
Burmese communities. The auxiliary force was used mainly to guard the oil
refineries, where many of its members were employed. Supporting arms
and services were virtually nonexistent, while the colony had neither air
nor naval defenses.

The small size of the military forces in Burma made expansion extremely
difficult because the basic cadre of officers, noncommissioned officers, and
specialists, particularly in the artillery and engineer arms, was too small to
man the existing units and depots and provide the nucleus of fresh battalions. After the war in Europe began the Burma Rifles were doubled in
strength by raising four regular and two part-time volunteer units drawn
from the ethnic Burmese as opposed to the hill tribesmen on whom the
British hitherto had relied to provide the soldiers of Burma. But this did
nothing to cure the basic weaknesses of supporting arms and administrative
services, or the shortages of all forms of military equipment, ranging from
weapons, clothing, and personal-issue kits to artillery and reserves of
ammunition. All of this, of course, reflected the fact that, in the list of
British defense priorities, Burma preceded only the Caribbean. Burma's
long-standing immunity from outside threat made it impossible to convince
the authorities that Burma would become hopelessly vulnerable if, for some
reason, parts of the protective shield that guarded her proved wanting.
When France was overrun by the Germans in the summer of 1940 the
cornerstone of Burma's defenses, French power in Indo-China, collapsed.
Thereafter, with Thailand brought increasingly under Japanese influence,
Burma's position became increasingly serious because a large part of her
eastern border suddenly became potentially hostile. Even in these circumstances there could be no question of giving Burma special help to
prepare herself for possible invasion, although such help was not merely
desirable but essential. The threat against Burma was also directed against
Malaya and Singapore, and these naturally had priority over Burma. What
resources were available for the Far East were directed either to Singapore
or to India as the main bases from which the British would have to operate.
Thus, even when a threat to Burma was perceived, there was little that
could be done to counter it.

The command arrangements for Burma were a further source of weakness. Burma was separated from India in April 1937 partly in response to
the growing force of Burmese nationalism. Setting up a separate Burma
command was the logical extension of the political divorce, yet the new

command could never function effectively. Though called a command, Burma was given what was effectively a brigade staff. The headquarters had to function as a defense department, a general headquarters, an operational command, and the controlling headquarters for a massive lines of communication area. Performing all of these tasks was far beyond the capacity of Burma Command, but there was no question of adopting the one solution that at least in part could have redeemed this hopeless situation—a reversion to India Command. This was what Delhi wanted. India Command was not blind to the fact that in strategic terms Burma was part of India, that Burmese lines of communication stretched back to northeastern India, and that any reinforcements for Burma would have to be provided by Delhi.

In November 1940, when the British established the Far East Command in Singapore, Burma was allocated to this new command. Seemingly good reasoning dictated this move. Burma and Malaya were both on the Indo-China peninsula, and any threat to one would be a threat to the other; close coordination of the efforts in both countries was therefore essential. Malaya was dependent on southern Burmese airfields, and the Burma Road bestowed on Burma an international importance that seemed to accord better with a Far East Command that stretched out to the Americans and the Dutch than with an India Command that at this stage of the war was more inclined to the Middle East and the gulf. Moreover, of course, unless Burma was included in the Far East Command there was little point in having such a command in the first place. Without Burma, Singapore and Malaya had only Hong Kong and British Borneo, and these hardly justified the creation of a command in the Far East. Yet the arrangement was manifestly faulty. Any commander in chief, Far East, was certain to be so concerned with Malaya and Singapore that Burma was bound to be neglected, and there was never any question of a commander in chief exercising direct and effective control of the situation in Burma from far-away Singapore. Admittedly, in certain respects India Command was no better placed, but in effect it was administratively responsible for Burma, and the separation of administrative and operational control is one of the cardinal errors of war.

Not unnaturally, Far East Command defended its retention of Burma with partisan intensity in the face of efforts by two successive commanders in chief for India, General Sir Claude Auchinleck and Wavell, to regain control of the colony. The British Chiefs of Staff conceded the force of Delhi's argument in November 1941, when they decided in principle to return Burma to India, but the final decision was deferred until the arrival in the Orient of the new commander in chief for the Far East, Pownall. On 11 December, however, three days after the start of the Pacific war, the Chiefs of Staff decided to transfer Burma to India forthwith. The next day

Wavell assumed responsibility for a country against which the threat was becoming obvious. The snag in this transfer was that there was very little India Command could do to affect the situation at this stage.

The reason for this was twofold. First, in the second half of 1941 there was not a single fully trained complete division in the whole of India. Thus India could not send sufficient numbers of trained units and formations to Burma to secure the colony against attack. Second, even if forces had been available on a scale sufficient to defend Burma, the colony lacked the administrative infrastructure that would have enabled these forces to be maintained. There was an almost total lack of stockpiles and depots, which would be needed to sustain major forces in Burma. This situation arose mainly out of prewar neglect and penny pinching, but geography also had imposed its own limitations.

Despite the fact that Burma has an extreme length of some 1,200 miles and then bordered four countries, she was almost island-like in her isolation from her neighbors because of the high mountains to the north and east. These mountains, part of the Indo-Malayan chain, are offshoots of the Himalayas as they fall away from the high Tibetan plateau towards the southeast. They fall away slowly enough to stand at 19,296 feet at Hka-Koba Razi (Burma's highest point) in the extreme northeastern part of the country; though they fall away more quickly thereafter, they remain formidably high. From Hka-Koba Razi to the Bay of Bengal they sweep down in an arc up to 100 miles wide, falling as they approach the sea from up to 12,000 feet in the Naga Hills in the north to the 10,000-foot peaks of the Chin Hills in the southern-center and thence to the Arakan Yoma, which form a 3,000-foot barrier between the narrow Arakan coast and the central inland basin. To the east the high uplands of western China give way to the lower Shan Plateau, which stands at about 3,000 feet above sea level. Both the uplands and the plateau, however, are heavily dissected by a multitude of torrents and rivers that have cut deep gorges through the landscape by the speed of their flow to the sea. In most cases these rivers cannot be navigated or bridged.

Nestling between these high regions is Burma's central basin, which is drained by many rivers, the chief of which are the Irrawaddy, its major tributary the Chindwin, and the Sittang. The latter is subject to tidal waves and is ill-suited to navigation, but the Irrawaddy is the country's major line of communication, with over 2,000 miles of commercially used waterway in its delta area alone. The Salween River to the east separates the massive central basin (approximately 750 miles from north to south and 450 miles from east to west) from the fourth major geomorphological region of the country, its tail. This tail is the 500-mile-long Tenasserim coast that reaches southwards to within 270 miles of northern Malaya. Though it shares the Kra Isthmus with a more substantial area of Thailand, in the east the Tenasserim area is well defended by a formidable chain of mountains running southwards from the 5,500-foot-high Dawna Range to the Taung-nyos and the Baliauktaung Range.

What elevation has established, climate and natural vegetation have improved, thereby bestowing on Burma an impressive line of natural defenses. Burma is partly within the tropics. The average temperature is 82°F (27°C), and the annual temperature range widens as one moves both northwards and inland. There are, however, three distinct seasons: the cool dry season between October and February, the hot dry season between March and May, and the rainy season, between June and September, during which Burma is assailed by the southeast monsoon. Inland Man-dalay, the old royal capital, receives about 33 inches of rain a year; the Sian Plateau, being higher, attracts about twice as much precipitation. Rangoon, the Irrawaddy delta, and the Tenasserim coast have about 100 inches of rainfall annually, while the Arakan coast, where the full blast of the monsoon strikes, receives upwards of 200 inches of rain a year. In such conditions of rain and heat, an abundant tropical rain forest covers nearly two-thirds of the country. Even on the upper slopes of the mountains, where frosts and mists are not uncommon, vegetation is profuse—and overland communications inevitably are scarce.

Communications lay at the heart of the problems in ordering Burma's defenses. Transportation was largely confined to coastal and river traffic, supplemented by about 2,000 miles of meter-gauge railway. There were probably only about 1,500 miles of reasonably passable roads in the whole country, and these were subject to flooding and landslides. Most com-munications by land were confined to trails that were impassable during the monsoon. To compound the problem of movement within Burma, the rivers and mountains run longitudinally, with the result that communica-tions across the country are virtually nonexistent.

From these geographic factors three important facts emerged. First, the key to the whole of Burma was Rangoon; second, any Japanese movement into Burma from Thailand had to be across the grain of the country; third, there was no decent overland route between central Burma and India. Because sea communications were superior to those by land, the over-whelming advantage of geographic position was in British hands as long as two places were held. The first was Rangoon itself, the second was Singa-pore. The British used this advantage extensively in the first ten weeks of war to bring in fresh troops, but they could never exploit it fully because they did not have enough forces available. Once Singapore was lost, however, it was only a matter of time before the Japanese chose to make their way through the Strait of Malacca in order to operate against those parts of Burma's 2,000-mile coastline that remained in British hands—in effect, just the Irrawaddy delta and Rangoon. If and when Rangoon fell to the Japanese the defenders would be forced northwards into an area that was inadequately stocked for military operations and that lacked routes to and from India, which alone could provide sanctuary or support. A retreating army, therefore, would have to move back to India along a nonexistent communications system, with no depots, and across an area where malaria and many other tropical diseases were endemic.

To complete the communications picture two points, one obvious and the other less so, must be considered. Burma's line of communications with India was routed through Rangoon because sea communications were cheaper, faster, and easier than moving along the existing overland routes through the mountains and valleys. Therefore the British logistics system was dangerously dependent on Rangoon's port facilities. Not only was there no provision for military control of the docks, but there was no means of ensuring military direction of rail and river traffic. Utterly inadequate provision had been made for the army to take control and feed the civilian work force, without which these facilities would collapse. With the Rangoon water table uncomfortably high, there could be no provision on a large scale of underground storage depots and air raid shelters, and Rangoon was comfortably within range of Japanese bombers in French Indo-China. The very real danger that the British faced, therefore, was the wholesale flight of the civilian population, including of course the workers in the dock, railway, and river trades, in the event of Japanese air attacks. Needless to say, the provision against air attack was largely in the form of paper directives. The whole situation involving British lines of communication was precarious.

The deployment of British forces for the defense of Burma was determined by a host of factors, among which were the size and complexity of the country, natural obstacles, political considerations, and the nature and scale of any Japanese attack. For most of the period between 1937 and the start of the war the British anticipated that the main threat to Burma was from the air, and they expected that the main target of Japanese attention would be Rangoon's port and oil refineries. To counter this threat the British had virtually no antiaircraft guns and only a rudimentary early warning system at Rangoon, while the sixteen major airfields in the colony enabled each of the Royal Air Force's aircraft in Burma in December 1941 to have one complete airfield all to itself, if so desired. British air strength, if such is the phrase for it, was just one squadron of Buffalo fighters.

Though the British expected that the main Japanese effort would be in the air, in the course of 1941 they became convinced that the Japanese could use two divisions in an attack on Burma from Thailand. To this very realistic assessment the British added the more or less correct assumption that the Japanese would not make a major effort in Burma before an attack on Malaya was under way. The major objective, Singapore, would take precedence over the secondary objective, Rangoon. But, the British guessed (again accurately), the Japanese might well attempt to overrun the Tenasserim area as part of any initial move in Southeast Asia. In doing so the Japanese could invade Burma by one of two routes or even by both. The Japanese had the option of developing an offensive from northern as opposed to central Thailand. They could attempt to secure the routes from Chiang Mai and Chiang Rai directly into the Shan Plateau, with the objective of advancing along the Kentung-Taunggyi axis to Meiktila on the vital Rangoon to Mandalay route. Alternatively, they could attack along the more obvious route from Rahaeng, now called Tak, in central Thailand, over the Dawna Ridge on the direct route over the lower reaches of the Salween and Sittang towards Rangoon. The British decided, again correctly, that the latter was the more likely Japanese invasion route.

The overall British assessment of Japanese strength and intentions, therefore, was quite accurate, but that had been equally true in Malaya, and the portents of that campaign were hardly encouraging. There were several other parallels between the Burma and Malaya campaigns. On the Japanese side there was the same brilliant exploitation of all the advantages of planning, preparation, and holding the strategic initiative; the tactical mastery the Japanese quickly and obviously imposed on the British; the flexibility, initiative, and opportunism that characterized Japanese army operations when things were going well; and of course the totality of Japan's victory. On the British side many of the errors and omissions of Malaya were repeated: the dispersed initial deployment; the failure of the defenders to concentrate to meet the main threat; initial defeats in detail and a series of small reverses and withdrawals from which there was to be no recovery; belated and vain attempts to stem the tide of defeat by dispatching semi-trained and ill-prepared formations and units to the theater of operations. There were points of difference as well, but attention must be turned first to British deployment and forces.

The weakness of the forces in Burma led the British to reinforce the garrison in the course of 1941. In February the decision was made to send to Burma the 13th Indian Brigade, commanded by Brigadier C. Curtis, and by April this formation had been concentrated as army reserve at Mandalay. In July Burma Command, under Lieutenant General D. K. McCleod, divided the units previously in the country into two formations, the 1st Burma Brigade under Brigadier G. A. Farwell and the 2nd Burma Brigade under Brigadier A. J. Bourke. These two brigades were under the command of Major General J. Bruce Scott's 1st Burma Division, with its hastily established and improvised headquarters at Toungoo. A small force that included two badly depleted British battalions was kept in Rangoon, mainly with the needs of internal security in mind.

In August 1941, as the situation in the Far East deteriorated, the Allies became aware of the withdrawal of Japanese merchantmen from the oceans of the world and of Japanese coastal shipping from the Indies and Malaya. It was then that the British decided to send the 16th Indian Brigade (Brigadier J. K. Jones) to Burma. The move began in November and was being completed when war began. After the start of the war Wavell, as commander in chief for India, was ordered by London to make available formations for the defense of Burma. He was told that he could retain the 17th Indian Division, scheduled to move to the Middle East, and that he could expect to receive the 18th British Division, then rounding the cape en route for North Africa. However, the situation in Malaya deteriorated so rapidly that the whole of the 18th and two brigades from the 17th (the 44th and 45th Indian Brigades) were removed from Wavell's sphere and allotted to Singapore. All that Burma received from the intended initial allocation was the headquarters element of the 17th Indian Division, commanded by Major General John G. Smyth, and its 46th Indian Brigade (Brigadier R. G. Ekin). The former arrived at Rangoon on 9 January and was activated almost immediately; its brigade arrived a week later.

These were the forces that either were in Burma at the start of the war or arrived there before the start of major operations in the country. For the sake of simplicity, however, it is convenient to recount the additional reinforcement and command changes that took place after this time. The diversion of the best part of two divisions from Burma to Malaya led the British Chiefs of Staff to authorize the further dispatch to Burma of formations and units then in India. The British also intended to send two brigades of the King's African Rifles, but these would not arrive in Burma until March or April and in fact were diverted to Ceylon. Other forces did arrive to fill the gaps left by the diversion of reinforcements to Singapore. Three Gurkha battalions of the 48th Indian Brigade (Brigadier N. Hugh-Jones), part of the 19th Indian Division, arrived on 31 January; and between 28 January and 21 February three unattached British units arrived from India, the last in the company of the 7th Armored Brigade (Brigadier J. H. Anstice). The last reinforcements to reach Burma before the fall of Rangoon were Brigadier J. Wickham's 63rd Indian Brigade, part of the 14th Indian Division, which arrived on 5 March.

There were many important changes in command and organization in the course of this short campaign. The most important involved the various transfers of Burma from one command to another: from Far East Command to India Command on 12 December, to ABDA Command on 15 January, and then back to India Command on 25 February. Wavell, in three separate capacities, had command of Burma: as commander in chief, India, between 12 December 1941 and 15 January 1942; as supreme commander of ABDA; and then, after 28 February, when he returned to India. During Wavell's absence in the Indies, General Sir Alan F. Hartley assumed the role of commander in chief, India, and stayed as Wavell's deputy after the latter's return. At the start of the war McCleod was general officer commanding in Burma, but one of Wavell's first actions when Burma came within his sphere of command was to dismiss him and appoint his own chief of staff in Delhi, Lt.General Thomas J. Hutton, in his place. Hutton took command on 27 December, but was dismissed and publicly humiliated by Wavell before General Harold Alexander was appointed in his place. Hutton stayed on as Alexander's chief of staff until mid-April, when he was replaced at his own request. At the same time as Hutton was dismissed, Smyth was also removed from the command of the 17th Indian Division. His place was filled by his brigadier general staff, David T. Cowan. It was not until 19 March that the various British formations in Burma were accorded a corps organization. On that day Lieutenant General William J. Slim took command of the newly constituted 1st Burma Corps, the command being dissolved two months later after the end of the retreat into India. On appointment, Slim had the 1st Burma and 17th Indian Divisions and the 7th Armored Brigade under his command.

Before the start of the war the British deployed the 2nd Burma Brigade in the Tenasserim region while the much weaker 1st was in the Shan area. The 13th Indian Brigade was in reserve. These three brigades formed the original 1st Burma Division. The 2nd, along with the 16th Indian Brigade when it arrived in Tenasserim on 14 January, was placed under Smyth's 17th Indian Division when that division was activated. When the 46th and 48th Indian Brigades became available these were placed under Smyth's command. To add to the confusion various units were moved between formations at various stages in order to "stiffen" suspect battalions and brigades. This was particularly true of British and Gurkha units, which were widely used to buttress the Burma Rifles.

Three brigades was a totally inadequate force with which to attempt to defend Burma. The British knew this, and hence their moves that added five more brigades to the defense between December 1941 and March 1942. But others also knew of the British weakness and, except for the Japanese, the most important of these parties was the Chinese. The Chinese interest in Burma was obvious. American lend-lease equipment could reach China only by way of Rangoon, Mandalay, and Lashio; without this route China would be isolated. Thus, there was strategic justification for Chiang Kai-shek's observation that an attack on Burma was tantamount to an attack on China itself. The problem of such a statement was that the Chinese claimed Upper Burma as part of China, and the British were not so stupid as to ignore the ambiguity in Chiang's seeming generosity.

On 8 December Chiang told the British ambassador at Chungking that all of China's resources would be placed, without conditions, at the disposal of Britain and the United States in the prosecution of the war against Japan.

Given the special Chinese interest in Burma, Chiang intimated, specific forces could be made available immediately to Burma (and further unspecified forces could be sent quite quickly), if Burma would accept the responsibility for feeding these troops. On 14 December the British government informed Chiang that Wavell had been instructed to arrange with him how Anglo-Chinese cooperation could best be assured.

As the British saw it, the Chinese could provide three things for the defense of Burma: American lend-lease equipment, particularly some 620 vehicles bound for China but at the outbreak of war still in Rangoon; aircraft from the American Volunteer Group that had been at Toungoo; and ground troops. The preparatory discussions in Chungking before Wavell's arrival showed that the British were very much interested in securing the equipment and aircraft. The Chinese in turn were somewhat surprised to find the British seemingly not interested in their offer to allocate China's 5th and 6th Armies to the defense of Burma. The only reservation the Chinese then placed on their promise was that their forces be given a separate area or line of communications to defend: they did not want their forces mixed up with other nationals. Such was the situation when Wavell arrived at Chungking for two days of talks with Chiang Kai-shek.

The talks were at best inconclusive, mainly because Wavell and Chiang appear to have been talking at cross-purposes and pursuing totally different objectives. Chiang emerged with the belief that Wavell had rejected his offer of combat troops, Wavell with the notion that Chiang was more interested in geopolitics and in impractical visionary schemes than in hard facts. Wavell had secured Chiang's agreement in principle for British use of Chinese lend-lease equipment and for the retention in Burma of at least part of the American Volunteer Group. But, as Bismarck once observed, agreement in principle invariably means a complete refusal to do anything in practice—and the British were sceptical of Chiang's long-term reliability in these matters. Wavell believed that he had indicated a willingness to accept one Chinese division at once, with two more deployed along the border in support. It is unclear just how this vast discrepancy between the British and Chinese accounts of the meeting arose, but in their independent reports to Washington American observers at the exchanges endorsed Chiang's view of the proceedings. In the weeks to come these reports went some way in reducing British stock, and that of Wavell personally, in the eyes of the Americans, while the feeling of being slighted by the British at the very start of the war naturally offended the Chinese deeply. The upshot of the misunderstandings and mutual suspicions therefore helped to keep the British in Burma weak during the early stages of the war; when the various problems were sorted out and the Chinese moved into Burma it was too late for them to affect the outcome.

It is difficult to resist the notion that in December 1941 the British were not too displeased to see Chinese troops kept out of Burma, at least for the moment. Chinese armies had a reputation for acquisitiveness that placed them second only to locusts, and the British were understandably fearful of exposing central and northern Burma to the "liberating" proclivities of the Chinese. Moreover, in the first two or three weeks of the war the British had reason to hope that sufficient reinforcements for Burma could be found without having to go to the Chinese. Certainly British calculations took into account the unspoken realization that it was asking for trouble for Britain to try to hold Burma with the help of a strongly antiimperialist ally with its own claims on part of Burma. It was a grim type of logic, but there was much to be said for the argument that in political terms it was better to lose Burma unaided than to retain the country with Chinese help. Wavell, in effect, admitted this after the war.

McCleod, and after him Hutton, therefore had to tackle the problem of defending Burma not only with totally inadequate forces but also without any hope of sufficient forces arriving in the short time left before the Japanese showed their hand. Their slight hopes of holding Burma were reduced still further by a deployment that was dictated by political as opposed to strategic and tactical factors. London and Delhi were intent on preserving the territorial integrity of Burma, and this involved holding any Japanese attack in the border areas. In this they were motivated by considerations of Burmese morale and world opinion. In fact, it was a matter of profound indifference to everyone whether or not the British held Myawadi on the Burmese side of the border with Thailand, but this was not how British authorities viewed the situation. As a result, the initial British deployment involved scattering the 2nd Burma and 16th Indian Brigades around the Tenasserim airfields and along the Moulmein to Kawkareik to Myawadi trail over the Dawna Range.

When Smyth took over this sector (his division had a frontage of a mere 400 miles), he appreciated immediately that his specific assignment, to hold Moulmein, was an impossible one. He restrained himself in replying to Wavell's exhortation to undertake an offensive into Thailand and applied himself instead to the problem of trying to hold Moulmein, the key to Tenasserim. The two immediate problems were that Moulmein had a frontage of some 6 miles and there was no bridge over the Salween to Martaban. Moreover, Moulmein could be outflanked, either by a close movement against Paung or by a deep encircling movement through Pa-an and Kuzeik on the Salween and hence to Thaton on the route between Bilin and Martaban. Smyth knew that to defend Moulmein successfully he would need not three brigades but three divisions, well supported by artillery, armor, and aircraft. Smyth's own view was that, with no bridge over the Salween, only one good bridge over the Bilin, and just one bridge

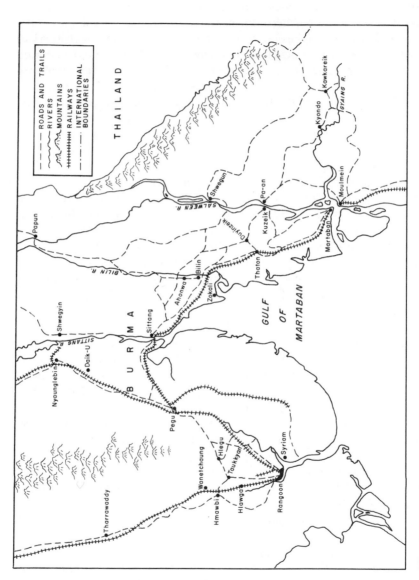

The Southern Burma Theater of Operations

across the Sittang, it was near-madness to try to stand at Moulmein. Ideally he would have liked to have left a small harrassing force in southern Burma and to have concentrated his forces in order to fight the main defensive battle on the Sittang. Hutton, partly because of conviction and partly because of his orders, insisted on the forward policy.

In strategic terms the Japanese were well placed to take advantage of the unbalanced and dispersed British deployment. Their initial assaults on Burma were mainly in the air, though on 16 December one battalion from the *143rd Infantry Regiment*, pushing across the Kra Isthmus from Jumbhorn, secured the airfield at Victoria Point without encountering opposition. Thus the first Japanese objective, to sever the British air link between Burma and Malaya, was secured. Gaining air supremacy over southern and central Burma was much more difficult because Japanese bombers from Indo-China had to operate without fighter cover. The Japanese had suffered heavy casualties in China at the hands of the heterogeneous Chinese air force back in 1937–38, when they tried to bomb targets beyond the range of their fighters. (The experience, incidentally, was critical in the development of the Zero-sen fighter between 1937 and 1940.) In Burma, too, the Japanese took heavy losses at the hands of the Royal Air Force and particularly the American Volunteer Group. The balance of losses in the first six weeks of the war strongly favored the Allies, but the codicils were obvious.

In the narrow tactical sense, the Japanese could absorb their losses; the Allies could not. Japanese raids on Rangoon, beginning on 23 December, brought very heavy civilian casualties and extensive flight from the city. From Christmas onwards the vital port and communications system began to break down because of lack of labor, while it became increasingly difficult to maintain public services and order. By the end of January the port was very nearly at a standstill. Troops arriving in Rangoon from mid-January onwards literally had to unload themselves and their equipment. To add to the Allies' problems in early to mid-January the Japanese made two significant moves. First, with the fall of Manila, they deployed an extra air brigade from the Philippines to Thailand, thus doubling the Japanese strength in the air. Second, on 15 January the Japanese moved against Tavoy, an airfield the British (who had accepted the loss of Victoria Point and Mergui) sought to maintain. The Japanese moved too quickly, however, and overran the airfield's defenders on the nineteenth. With Tavoy lost, the British evacuated Mergui between the twentieth and the twenty-third. By the following day the three most southerly of Burma's airfields were in Japanese hands, and Tavoy already was operational. Thus, the Japanese had secured airfields from which their fighters could support bomber strikes against southern and central Burma.

The air strikes on southern Burma and the Tenasserim offensive were merely the overtures for a major offensive that could not long be delayed. The Japanese knew that every day that passed threatened to make the conquest of Burma a bit harder because it gave time for reinforcements to arrive. Their own concentrations and preparation in Thailand took time, but on 20 January their main strength crossed the border on the main track running from Thailand via Kawkareik to Moulmein over the Dawna Range.

For this invasion Lieutenant General Shojiro Iida's *15th Army* deployed the *33rd* and *55th Infantry Divisions*. It planned to conduct its offensive over a wide front, each division being given its own axis of advance once Kawkareik had been taken. A series of orders from *Southern Army* to the *15th Army* and from Iida to his divisional commanders in the period up until 9 February reveals that the Japanese were prepared to improvise their operation in the light of developments. The Japanese certainly needed to be flexible because both their divisions were badly understrength. The *55th Infantry Division* consisted of two regiments, the *112th* and *143rd*, each of them one battalion short. The *112th* had lost its unit to *Southern Army*'s general reserve; the *143rd* had to leave one battalion in the Tenasserim area when it moved into central Thailand to prepare for the invasion across the Dawnas. The division's third regiment, the *55th*, the regimental group headquarters, and detachments from all the supporting arms had been removed from the division and constituted as the force used to reduce various islands in the central and southwestern Pacific in the first week of the war.* Similarly the *33rd* had only two regiments at the start of the campaign, since the *213th* joined the *214th* and *215th* only during the battles for central Burma. The *33rd*, unlike the *55th*, had its full quota of supporting arms.

In the first phase of their operations the Japanese planned to advance to the Salween line, which was recognized as a difficult obstacle. Lieutenant General Shozo Sakurai's *33rd Infantry Division* was ordered to secure Pa-an, while Lieutenant General Yutaka Takeuchi was to use his *55th Infantry Division* for the more difficult task of taking Moulmein. Thereafter the *55th* was to develop its offensive across the Salween and then along the coast, while the *33rd* was to secure Kuzeik, on the west bank of the Salween, and then Duyinzeik, from where it could divide its attention between Thaton and Ahonwa. By moving the *33rd* along the trails well inland from the coast, where the *55th* was operating, the Japanese could hope to keep any defending force off-balance while retaining the options of encircling the open inland flank or bringing both divisions to the Bilin and Sittang rivers at the same time. After these rivers the Japanese objectives were not defined,

---

*This arrangement probably resulted in the Japanese *55th Infantry Division* becoming the most far-flung division of any army during the course of the war.

but depending on the course of the battle they would have the options of moving either westwards against Rangoon or northwards up the river valleys into central Burma.

The primary Japanese objective was to destroy enemy forces in the field rather than to secure specific geographic objectives, but certain places were obviously important, and in part the campaign would be decided by their possession. The Japanese considered the capital and port of Rangoon, Prome on the Irrawaddy, Toungoo on the Sittang, Yenangyaung, and Mandalay to be critically important. The significance of Rangoon was obvious. Both Prome and Toungoo were vital communications centers in their respective river valleys, while Yenangyaung was the center of the oil industry in Burma. Mandalay's importance was as the hub of the central plain area. Burma's geography naturally pointed to the Japanese making their effort against central Burma up the Irrawaddy and Sittang. The tentative arrangements were for the *33rd* to move against Prome after it took Rangoon, while the *55th* was directed up the Sittang valley. Naturally both divisional commanders wanted the honor of taking a capital city and there was something of a race to take Rangoon. This flexibility provided both divisions with roughly equal chances, but in fact it was the *33rd* that occupied Rangoon. The flexibility of Japanese plans and the lack of an administrative tail for Japanese divisions allowed the army command to switch the divisions without the sort of movement problem that would have beset any Western army in a similar situation.

With the equivalent of 1½ divisions (11 battalions) in the line and a total of 35,000 men when fully deployed, the *15th Army* was small, but it enjoyed a marked numerical advantage over defending forces whose initial deployment played into Japanese hands. With the *55th* leading, the Japanese overran a Gurkha company at Myawadi and worked around the 16th Indian Brigade's main position at Kawkareik, forcing it to withdraw before serious contact was obtained. Even this retirement was chaotic. Many of the brigade's mules stampeded and were lost with their equipment, while nearly all the formation's transport and support weapons had to be abandoned and destroyed when the only means of getting back across the Gyaing River, the local ferry, sank under the weight of an overloaded vehicle. The Japanese, distracted by their own deployment after Kawkareik, let the 16th escape back to the west bank of the Salween. There the brigade had to man an 80-mile front between Martaban and Kuzeik, being deployed to a similar depth back as far as Thaton. The 2nd Burma Brigade, with its high proportion of uncertain Burma Rifles, was reinforced by and placed under the command of the 46th Indian Brigade. It was ordered by both Wavell and Hutton to deny Moulmein to the Japanese for as long as possible.

Hutton's position was a difficult one. He was under direct orders from both Wavell and Hartley to hold well forward, but he knew that Smyth and Cowan had little enthusiasm for this strategy, and no desire to stand and fight at Moulmein. His orders to Smyth's forces during the retirement from Kawkareik reflected his ambiguity and uncertainty. Units were ordered to obtain contact but not to become too closely engaged; they were given permission to retire but not to cede more ground than necessary. He felt that he had to hold well forward in order to secure Rangoon and allow reinforcements to arrive at Rangoon without having to move directly from the docks onto a battlefield lost metaphorically at the dock gates. But a forward deployment was weak, for it meant tying isolated and unsupported units to villages that could be either outflanked or reduced by a concentrated enemy. This was precisely what was to happen, but Hutton took one precaution that was to have profound repercussions on the course of the subsequent campaign. On 22 January, with Burma's communications system beginning to dissolve, he ordered three-quarters of the military stores in Rangoon to be loaded up and moved back to Mandalay and central Burma. Despite all the difficulties it involved, the move was completed successfully, and it proved a major factor in saving the British divisions as they retreated from southern Burma during March and April. Had it not been for Hutton's foresight, these two divisions would have been without supply during their withdrawal. Even with these supplies, their position became desperate, but the stockpiling in Mandalay helped to avert total defeat.

Defeat for the Moulmein garrison, however, could not be averted. On 30/31 January the Japanese *55th Infantry Division* took the town after a desperate resistance on the part of its garrison. Though certain units of the Burma Rifles wavered, the garrison as a whole fought far better than the Brtitish had any right to expect, given the training and experience of the units involved, while the successful evacuation of the garrison in the face of enemy air supremacy and heavy artillery fire was little short of miraculous. Nevertheless, the grim truth was that the 2nd Burma Brigade lost about one-quarter of its strength, virtually all its equipment, and much of its cohesion and confidence. It fared still worse when the Japanese forced the Salween line in the second week of February.

On 9 February the reinforced battalion at Martaban found that the enemy was crossing the river and bypassing the town in considerable strength. Without the means either to counter the enemy's move or to hold on, the local commanding officer on his own initiative destroyed his transport and broke out of the encircled town. His badly exhausted and depleted unit reached Thaton on the eleventh. Up river, however, the 7th/10th Baluch was all but annihilated on 11/12 February at Kuzeik. Just seventy-three officers and men survived a pulverizing attack by the three battalions of the *215th Infantry Regiment*. The Japanese then moved against the

5th/17th Dogras at Duyinzeik, but after a preliminary artillery bombardment declined to press their attack. Bypassing Duyinzeik the *215th* made for Thaton in order to reorganize, while the *214th* maintained the tempo of operations by moving against Ahonwa.

Faced by two Japanese divisions, Smyth on 14 February decided to pull his 17th Indian Division back behind the Bilin River line. He did so in spite of orders to hold in front of the river. Wavell, who throughout the Southeast Asia campaign regarded the Japanese as a second-class enemy, was hounding Hutton with condemnations of withdrawals, allegations that the troops lacked fighting spirit, and exhortations to mount a "bold counteroffensive." The hapless Hutton in turn hounded Smyth, insisting that he conduct a defensive battle in front of the river. Smyth was anxious only to get back behind the Sittang, which unlike the Salween and Bilin was wide, fast, and not fordable. There he could give his units perhaps a week's grace to prepare a position that could be reinforced by the 48th Infantry Brigade and the 7th Armored Brigade. Because the land west of the Sittang was cleared and cultivated, it formed a natural killing zone, and Smyth hoped that two armored units could be deployed in this area to full effect. With the units of the 17th already somewhat the worse for wear, Smyth and Cowan believed it was unrealistic to attempt to stand in front of the Bilin. But given his orders, Smyth felt that he had to compromise and chose to fight a major defensive action on the line of the river itself. The catch in the situation was that the *214th Infantry Regiment* managed to get across the Bilin before Smyth's forces could get into position—a condemnation of Wavell's unrealistic and insipid generalship from far-away Java.

The Bilin action proved disastrous for the British, who never managed to shift the Japanese from the positions they secured around Ahonwa in their first rush of the river. The Japanese made their main effort on their right flank just as the British did on their left. The first encounters strongly favored the British, and the Gurkhas of the 48th were decisive in repelling the Japanese attacks. But even the Gurkhas could not throw the Japanese back across the river; the simple arithmetic of the situation was that the British, by starting with fewer resources, were certain to be exhausted more quickly than the Japanese. Position, moreover, told against the defenders, whose right flank on the coast could be turned if the Japanese *55th Infantry Division* mounted amphibious operations into the British rear area, which was all but defenseless.

The British units fought to near-exhaustion in an effort to hold the Bilin line and to eliminate the Japanese bridgeheads. After three days of heavy hand-to-hand fighting during which bayonet, Gurkha kukri, and samurai sword all left evidence of their gruesome handiwork over the battlefield, the British position was critical, with the Japanese exerting increasingly intolerable pressure on both flanks and in the center. On the British left, the reinforced three battalions of the *214th Infantry Regiment* threatened to break through and roll up the whole of the British position on the river from the north; while in the south the *143rd* (part of the *55th Infantry Division*) threatened to cross the British line of retreat as a result of its landing on 18 February at Zokali, some 5 miles behind the Bilin. In the center at Bilin itself, the 8th Burma Rifles was proving the exception rather than the rule among the rifle units, but it was weakening and had to give ground to the attacking *215th Infantry*. It was able to hold only as a result of Gurkha support.

Smyth had only one depleted battalion in reserve, other units from the 2nd Burma Brigade that were re-forming at the Sittang bridge, and on the nineteenth he ordered this unit forward to take the pressure off the British left flank. Even Hutton, when he came forward to see for himself what was happening, conceded that the defenders could do no more and that to leave them where they were would only result in the annihilation of the division. He therefore sanctioned the withdrawal to the Sittang. The British broke contact on the night of 19/20 February and began the 30-mile trek back to the next river. The obvious difficulties in withdrawing were that the British forces were absolutely played out and that the Japanese started the race to the Sittang from positions that were nearer the river than those held by the British. Equally obvious was the fact that the 17th Indian Division was no longer in a state to offer either prolonged or effective resistance on the Sittang.

In the race to the Sittang the British had one advantage over the Japanese. They could use a poor road, whereas the Japanese were restricted to very rough trails. But this was not enough to offset weariness, disorder, and frequent air attack, including one very punishing Royal Air Force raid on the retreating British formations. The 48th Indian Brigade reached the bridge before the Japanese, but the 16th and 46th were caught during their withdrawal. They extricated themselves from the Japanese pincers with difficulty and heavy losses. To compound British problems at a time when every minute was vital, a vehicle became entangled in the railway bridge's girders, blocking the bridge for more than two hours. A massive traffic jam built up in the early hours of the twenty-second at the very time when the leading Japanese patrols approached the hopelessly congested bridgehead. The Japanese immediately attacked, and assaulted the most weakly defended part of the perimeter defense. The depleted 3rd Burma Rifles melted away under the impact of the assault, though prompt counterattacks restored the situation. For the rest of the day a furious battle raged on the east bank of the Sittang. The Japanese, now within an ace of annihilating the 17th Indian Division before it could get back to Rangoon, fought to break through to the bridge and secure the high ground that overlooked the river. The British, in turn, tried desperately to get the 16th and 46th Indian Brigades back to the bridgehead, where they had to hang on in order to conduct an orderly withdrawal to the west bank. No other form of withdrawal was possible across the 1,000 yards of water because the British had thoughtfully and properly destroyed all the local boats and river craft before the battle started in order to deny them to the Japanese.

For nearly twenty-four hours the assortment of British units withstood successive Japanese assaults, but in the chaos of the night's action the inevitable overwhelmed the defenders. There was no guarantee that reserve demolitions could be fired if the bridge was taken during daylight, and it was not certain that the bridge could be held for the duration of the next day. The British could not afford to allow the bridge to fall into Japanese hands intact. To do so would have been even worse than the annihilation of the 17th. Smyth, therefore ordered the demolition of the bridge, leaving on the far bank the best part of three brigades, surrounded and assailed by an enemy that had shown a very marked disinclination to take prisoners.

Smyth's decision completed the annihilation of his division. It also ended the last British hope of holding Rangoon, and hence Burma itself. Immediately available on 24 February were a mere 1,516 men from the 48th Indian Brigade and 1,170 men from the 16th, while the 46th could muster a total of only 798, a mere battalion's worth of troops. Even worse was the fact that apart from the 1st/4th Gurkhas, who fortunately crossed before the bridge was blown, only one man in four retained his personal weapon. Of course, many guns, most of the transport, and nearly all the divisional equipment, particularly the signals, had been lost. Not even the arrival of the 7th Armored Brigade and several British battalions could hope to restore the situation. Had Smyth been allowed to fight the battle he wanted instead of being forced to deploy and fight in a series of impossible positions, he might have been successful. As it was, the action imposed on Smyth by a curious combination of Iida, Hutton, and Wavell resulted in an irredeemable calamity for British arms.

The destruction of the 17th Indian Division as an effective fighting force more or less coincided with four other developments on the British side. These were the ordering (20 February) of Alexander to Burma as Hutton's replacement, effective from 5 March; Burma's move from ABDA to India Command (21 February) and Wavell's resumption of overall responsibility for Burma after 28 February; the refusal of the Australian government (20–22 February) to allow the 7th Australian Division to proceed to Rangoon and its insistence that the division return to Australia; and the emergence on the battlefield of Nationalist Chinese troops in sufficient numbers to influence the next phase of the campaign. These developments, coming together with the Sittang action, formed a natural watershed in the Burma campaign because they forced the British to pause, reorganize, and consider their next move. The British were afforded just enough time for this by the Japanese, who were beset by their own difficulties.

The *33rd* and *55th Infantry Divisions* in one month had advanced nearly

200 miles over rough jungle trails, without the proper deployment of rear-echelon troops and with little more supply than what the combat troops could carry and scavenge. They had crossed one major river obstacle and several smaller ones, fought and won three major actions and a number of smaller engagements, and stood on the last barrier before Rangoon. By any standard their achievement was remarkable. It is difficult to see why Wavell, with the experience of Malaya and the Indies behind him, persisted in regarding the Japanese as a second-class enemy that could be easily sent scuttling for cover. But the Japanese had to resolve the dispute over future intentions: whether to advance on Rangoon in order to open up a new line of supply from Singapore or to move directly northwards to deal with the Anglo-Chinese forces known to be in central Burma. The time the Japanese spent in sorting out their twin problems gave the British a chance they all but blundered away through command changes that precluded swift and clear decision making. As it was, the British escaped utter defeat in spite of themselves. By a series of half-measures, the British presented the Japanese with a fleeting opportunity of winning a stunning victory around Rangoon, but the Japanese, hell-bent on other matters, unwittingly allowed their chance to slip away.

The crux of the problem for the British after the disaster on the Sittang was deciding whether or not to try to hold Rangoon with the eventual aim of sending to Burma the reinforcements needed to hold the colony and repulse the invader. If they were not prepared to try to hold Rangoon, the British had to accept a withdrawal into central or northern Burma. Given the paucity of overland links between India and Burma, the dangers attached to such a withdrawal were obvious. Whichever way the British decided, there were certain to be considerable dangers. Abandoning Rangoon was politically difficult, but not impossible. It would be a tacit acceptance of defeat, an admission that saving the army in Burma was more important than holding the colony. But any attempt to hold Rangoon in the face of enemy supremacy in the air and at sea was obviously risky. The Japanese had not yet secured supremacy in the air and at sea, but neither could be denied them for very long. If the British decided to try to hold Rangoon, then the city had to be reinforced both quickly and with high quality troops, and all the omens on both scores were hardly auspicious, Moreover, any attempt to hold Rangoon could easily prove to be a mini-Singapore with the British losing the city, its original defenders, and any subsequent reinforcements —all to no effect.

After the Sittang action Hutton and Hartley, along with Burma's governor, Sir Reginald Dorman-Smith, concurred in a realistically simple view. All were convinced that sending brigades to Burma was a waste of time and effort; only good quality divisions or corps could redeem a situation in which the Japanese called the tune on land, at sea, and in the air.

Hutton, having been Wavell's chief of staff in India, was well aware of the state of Indian formations that he might receive as reinforcements. Only the 63rd Indian Brigade, plus certain other undefined units at some unspecified future date, could arrive, and Hutton was under no illusions. He knew when the Australian government banned the use of the 7th Australian Division in Burma that there was no hope left; he was realistic enough to know that even with the Australians there was little cause for optimism. A hopelessly harassed Churchill, grappling with a bewildering galaxy of problems at Britain's lowest point during the war,* on 20 February diverted the 7th Australian Division to Rangoon on his own authority. Though he sought Australian concurrence in this move, which would have seen the Australians arrive in Burma on or about 27 February, an unequivocal Australian rejection was received in London on the twenty-second. The Australians refused to bow to joint Anglo-American pressure to send the 7th to Rangoon, and insisted that the division return to Australia. For Hutton, even though he had been told of his replacement, this Australian refusal to play a part in the defense of Burma was enough to settle his mind. He gave orders on the twenty-seventh for a thorough demolition program at Rangoon, which was to be abandoned on 1 March. He also gave orders for the 63rd Indian Brigade, then on its way to Rangoon, to turn around and not sail on to certain destruction.

Had Hutton's orders been put into effect, they would have been his second major contribution in 1942 to saving the British army in Burma, the first having been transferring supplies back to central Burma, and would have done much to redeem the failures of Sittang and Bilin. Had Hutton been able to carry out his intentions, the overwhelming part of his force would have been well to the north of Rangoon by the time the Japanese crossed the Sittang en route to the capital. But such realism on Hutton's part was altogether too much for Wavell. On 1 March he flew into Magwe airfield and humiliatingly berated Hutton in front of the governor and Hutton's subordinate officers for his alleged mishandling of the defense and for his decision to abandon Rangoon. He ordered Rangoon to be held and the Japanese to be counterattacked, and he insisted that the 63rd Indian Brigade resume its course for Rangoon. The next day he removed Smyth from the command of the 17th Indian Division and replaced him with Cowan. On his return to Calcutta, Wavell met briefly with Alexander, who was on his way to Burma, and gave his new general officer commanding Burma the explicit order to hold Rangoon. These verbal instructions were

---

*Just how bad the British position was is easy to forget. Not only had Force Z, Malaya, Hong Kong, and British Borneo been lost since the start of the war, but other disasters had befallen British arms. In December the British had had two battleships sunk at their moorings in Alexandria by Italian frogmen; in January the battle of Gazala had been lost; and the *Scharnhorst* and *Gneisenau* had slipped up the channel to safety in Germany on 12/13 February.

the only orders Wavell gave to Alexander before 18 April—an amazing state of affairs. So unrealistic were these instructions that they should have resulted in the complete destruction of all British forces in southern Burma. Fortunately for the British, Alexander realized almost as soon as he arrived in Burma that Wavell's instructions could not be put into effect, and he ignored them.

In the meantime, Hutton had no option but to put Wavell's instructions into effect. In the time that had elapsed since the Sittang disaster Hutton had brought what remained of the 17th Indian Division to the Pegu area and had broken up the 16th and 46th Brigades. He had then reconstituted the 16th and re-formed various units from the 48th. On Wavell's departure he ordered the 48th, with two recently arrived British battalions and an armored unit, to reoccupy the various villages near the west bank of the Sittang. These had been abandoned by the British as part of Hutton's intention to withdraw his forces up the Irrawaddy valley in the direction of Prome, but the Japanese had been too quick for Hutton. On 2 March the leading elements of the *15th Army* crossed the Sittang and established themselves on the west bank before the British could reoccupy their old positions. The British units, as they moved forward, immediately began to be drawn into a series of engagements in and around Pegu.

It rapidly became clear that, even with a good armored unit in support, the British battalions were in serious trouble. Virtually the entire strength of the *15th Army* threatened to flow around and over the Pegu defenders because Iida had resisted the demands of *Southern Army* to move immediately into central Burma. Iida concentrated the major part of the *33rd* and *55th Infantry Divisions* for an assault on Rangoon because he wanted to free his army from its dependence on overland communications before he began to move northwards. He therefore ordered a very strong battle group from the *55th* to form a hard shoulder in the Daik-U area to guard against an attack coming from the Toungoo area. He also ordered a smaller force from the *33rd* to perform a similar function on the Rangoon to Prome road in the Hmawbi area. With one battalion from the *55th* directed across the lower reaches of the Sittang estuary in order to secure the all-important Syriam refineries, Iida put the main part of his two divisions across the river to advance on Rangoon via Pegu.

This was the situation that Alexander inherited when he took over command on 5 March, and it is hard to think of a more daunting prospect for any commander. His forces in the Pegu area were exposed to the risk of defeat, while the 63rd Indian Brigade had still to arrive and be deployed. As the Pegu defenders were weakening and their position was becoming more desperate, the brigadier and all the unit commanding officers of the 63rd Indian Brigade were killed during a reconnaissance mission on the seventh, the day before the brigade arrived at Rangoon. For the formation to lose all its commanders before it even entered action was little short of disastrous.

Alexander therefore had to face the prospect of losing three infantry brigades, two armored regiments, an assortment of infantry units, and a large assembly of administrative troops still in Rangoon, all within a matter of hours after he took command. On the sixth it was obvious to Alexander that, unless he ordered his forces to abandon the south and to break out toward central Burma immediately, they were unlikely to have a second chance of avoiding destruction. Indeed, it might already be too late to attempt a withdrawal. Wavell's orders to hold Rangoon had allowed the 63rd to come into action, but only at the risk of total defeat for all the forces around Rangoon—a repetition on a smaller scale of the 18th British Division debacle. Alexander's orders to evacuate Rangoon beginning on the seventh indicated that, for the new general officer commanding, preserving his army was more important than holding a town, however prestigious that town might be.

Lieutenant General Shojiro Iida. Commander of the *15th Army* until March 1943, Iida was the conqueror of Burma and then its defender against the first unsuccessful British attempt to invade Arakan. Robert Hunt Library

Alexander had the reputation of being a lucky general, and luck was with him during the withdrawals from Rangoon and Pegu. With the main part of the Japanese forces to the north and east of Pegu but with some roadblocks established to the south and west, the British defenders around Pegu broke contact and began to fight their way southwards. Iida and his divisional commanders naturally assumed that the British were falling back on Rangoon. Japanese battlefield intelligence failed to pick up the fact that the 7th Armored Brigade, the decisive element in breaking through the roadblocks and extricating the infantry, was moving not towards Rangoon but towards Hlegu. The Japanese also remained ignorant of British forces moving northwards from Rangoon towards Taukkyan. Iida therefore ordered the 55th to detach only a harrassing force to follow up the British retirement, while the 33rd, moving on the outer arc towards Rangoon, was ordered to come around the (presumed) British flank. When he received Iida's orders, Sakurai decided to conduct a wide sweep to get around the British, who were supposedly on the Pegu to Rangoon road, and to approach Rangoon from the direction of Wanetchaung, Hmawbi, and Hlawga. By a matter of hours, therefore, his division crossed in front of British forces coming up from Hlegu and Rangoon.

On the seventh, while both the Syriam refineries and the warehouses and port facilities in Rangoon were being destroyed with ruthless efficiency, the leading British patrols ran into a Japanese roadblock at Taukkyan. This position resisted all British efforts to break through on the seventh, but a heavy and deliberate attack the next morning fell on empty air. On the seventh the British had brushed against the flank guard of the 33rd as it passed westwards. The Japanese had failed to grasp that what was to them a minor encounter was in fact a contact with the leading patrols of the whole of the British forces in the Rangoon-Pegu region. As the Japanese moved on, they left the road uncovered and the British escaped. The gap between the British and Japanese widened as the British moved northwards and the Japanese 33rd Division pressed on to Rangoon. The Japanese entered the capital on the eighth and found it nothing more than a ghost town, inhabited only by the lunatics, incurably sick, and the criminals, released from their various institutions when the civil administration broke down. Across the estuary the refineries at Syriam continued to burn until May.

Almost without exception battles, campaigns, and wars obtain a momentum of their own, one that ensures they will be fought for long after their outcome has been decided. The Burma campaign is no exception in this respect. Though for all practical purposes the campaign was decided by the Japanese taking of Rangoon, much of the heartbreak, suffering, death, and the hardest fighting of the campaign were to be concentrated in the period after 8 March as the Japanese overran central and northern Burma.

By taking Burma's capital the Japanese secured the immediate and immense advantage of free use of sea communications. As noted earlier, this advantage previously had been held by the British who, because of their shortage of materiel and trained manpower, had not been able to take full advantage of their asset. The Japanese, on the other hand, by taking Singapore and the Dutch East Indies, were in a position to exploit their success in lower Burma. They had forces available in Southeast Asia that could be sent to Rangoon by sea, thereby saving a wearying overland march. These forces were available in such strength that the British, all but severed from India by the lack of overland communications, could not hope to meet the new threat. British strength, having made its main effort with a force that proved inadequate to the challenge of two weak divisions, could be no more than a wasting asset.

The Japanese were not slow in following up their success. Within seven weeks of the fall of Rangoon the *15th Army* more than doubled in size. The *33rd Infantry Division* was brought up to full strength by the arrival of a mountain artillery unit and its third infantry regiment, the *213th*, both of which were moved to Rangoon by sea from Bangkok rather than being forced to enter Burma overland. The formation that Yamashita had refused to accept in Malaya, Lieutenant General Sukezo Matsuyama's *56th Infantry Division*, put in its appearance when two of its infantry regiments, the *113th* and *148th*, arrived in Rangoon on 25 March after a six-day sea passage from Singapore. The division's third regiment, the *146th*, because it had been the core of the *56th Regimental Group* in the campaign in Java, did not reach Rangoon until 19 April. By that time the overwhelming part of Lieutenant General Renya Mutaguchi's *18th Infantry Division*, fresh from its triumphs in Malaya, had been in Burma for nearly two weeks. The *1st* and *14th Tank Regiments*, various artillery units, and a considerable number of ancillary troops also reached Burma in the first two weeks of April. Within a matter or a month or so after the fall of Rangoon, therefore, the Japanese had the equivalent of about five divisions of ground troops in Burma. Just as the ground element doubled, so did the air component. As a result of the fall of the Indies the *5th Air Division* received two brigades as reinforcements from the *3rd Air Division*, bringing the Japanese total of military aircraft in Burma to just over 400, divided among four bomber and fighter brigades. By comparison, the British were reinforced by only one British infantry battalion, flown into Magwe airfield on 19 March.

The passage of the *113th* and *148th Infantry Regiments* coincided with three actions undertaken by the Japanese. First, as part of moving the regiments to Rangoon, the Japanese sailed base parties to Pukhet and

Mergui in order to make these two places in southern Burma forward fleet bases where minor emergency facilities would be available to Japanese warships. Second, on 20 March a single battalion from the *18th Infantry Division* sailed from Penang for Port Blair in the Andaman Islands. On 7 February Imperial General Headquarters had ordered the Andamans to be taken, and on the twenty-third the islands passed under Japanese control, thereby assuring the security of one more part of the perimeter defense Japan intended to build around herself. Third, between 21 and 27 March the Japanese launched a series of devastating air strikes against the two major Allied air bases in Burma at Akyab and Magwe, and in these operations they effectively destroyed what remained of Allied air power in Burma.

One of the more curious features of the Burma campaign was the manner in which the Japanese failed to concentrate their air power simply and solely for the purpose of fighting for and winning air supremacy. Just as the Americans, until taught by bitter experience, believed that through bombing they could obtain air supremacy, so the Japanese failed to grasp the fact that bombing could not be effective unless and until air supremacy had been obtained. The Japanese lacked four-engined strategic bombers that alone could be effective in a bombing role, and they persisted in providing their bombers with a scale of fighter protection that was slender by any standard. The Japanese normally provided a rough 3:1 ratio of bombers to fighters, and it is worth remembering that during the course of the air battles over southern England in 1940 the Germans were forced to reverse this ratio in order to hold down their losses. Moreover, in Burma and in certain subsequent campaigns where the Japanese had to fight against an alert enemy, they consistently failed in carrying out sustained and intensive operations, thus allowing their enemies to gain a respite and so fight on. This tendency was particularly marked in certain operations carried out by the Imperial Navy in 1942 and 1943 in the island campaigns in the Southwest Pacific.

The result of these errors was very costly for the Japanese, who up to the fall of Rangoon incurred considerable losses not only in their offensive operations but also during Allied attacks on their airfields. Of course, the Japanese did secure forward air bases from which their fighters could protect their bombers, but only at the risk of leaving their fighter concentrations hopelessly vulnerable to attack for the lack of any early warning system. Until Rangoon fell, the Allied airfields in central Burma had a rudimentary but generally effective warning system, and in the various raids on one another's airfields the Anglo-American air forces had the better of the exchanges. Whether in attack or defense, the spearhead of the Allied air effort was the American Volunteer Group, whose members had been recruited as mercenaries for Chiang Kai-shek's air force from officers then serving with the U.S. Army. It was primarily the Americans, with their P-40 Tomahawks, who exacted an unacceptably heavy toll on the Japanese, but, of course, it was the Americans who were most vulnerable to losses and shortage of equipment. Their facilities in Burma were minimal. The British, scarcely better placed at the time, did have the long-term prospect of continuing the war from India. The Americans were almost in the position of having to fight on until final annihilation, one way or another.

After a series of costly Royal Air Force and American Volunteer Group attacks on their airfields, the Japanese for a week concentrated their efforts, now boosted by two extra air brigades, against Akyab and Magwe. Fighter concentration in these attacks was very marked. As a result of these operations the Allied air forces, already beginning to fall below the level where they could hope to offer effective resistance, were all but annihilated. What remained of Allied air power was forced back either to India or to northern Burma, where it played an ever-decreasing role in the Burma fighting. The British, naturally anxious to conserve their air power for the defense of northeastern India, refused to commit significant numbers of aircraft in what was obviously a lost cause. From 27 March onwards, therefore, the Japanese, who already possessed a fair measure of air superiority, enjoyed almost total air supremacy, and they used their advantage to strike at the cities and communications of central and northern Burma. The Japanese expended much of their effort against civil targets such as Mandalay, which suffered heavy civilian casualties, but they paid relatively little attention to Allied troop concentrations and military targets. This was little comfort to Allied forces, which were subjected to all-too-frequent attacks.

The largely unsystematic employment of Japanese air power reflected a lack of a coherent Japanese air doctrine and the practice of the Imperial Army to post generals to command air divisions on the basis of seniority and vacancies. The lack of a clear division between the ground and air elements within the Japanese army created a situation whereby officers without the training, qualifications, and, in some cases, the interest in air operations were placed in command of air units. In Burma these organizational weaknesses were partially responsible for the escape of British forces that otherwise might have been destroyed. Just as the Japanese army's aircraft failed at Singapore to prevent reinforcements from arriving at the base, so they failed in a similar manner at Rangoon, and then they failed to harry and impede the retreating British forces to the extent that their eventual destruction was assured. Allied forces were impeded by the flight of refugees and damaged communications, but they still retained much of their cohesion and power of movement, if only by foot. Various factors, on both the British and the Japanese sides, conspired to frustrate the Japanese intention to encircle and annihilate the British forces in Burma, but poor use of their air power by the Japanese was one of the most important single factors that enabled the British to escape destruction.

After the fall of Rangoon, Alexander and Iida had very different problems. Alexander knew that at best the Japanese conquest of Burma could only be delayed and made costly; there was no possibility that he could deny the Japanese control of the country. Iida, on the other hand, had to try to achieve the physical destruction of the Allies in a stiuation where his intentions were all too predictable because of the geography of the country. Iida had no option but to drive into central Burma via the Irrawaddy and Sittang valleys with the aim of fighting a decisive battle in and around Mandalay.

Iida planned to carry out an immediate and simultaneous offensive, with the *33rd* being directed up the Irrawaddy and the *55th* up the Sittang. He envisaged the *33rd* moving to take the vital Yenangyaung oil fields by mid-April and then to secure Myingyan and Shwebo my mid-May. The latter town, lying between the Chindwin and the Irrawaddy, was some 50 miles to the north of Mandalay. Iida in effect intended to use the *33rd* as the anvil against which the Allied forces would be pounded to destruction by his hammer—the right-flank offensive up the Sittang. Iida planned to use the *55th* as the vanguard of the Sittang thrust and to feed the major part of his reinforcements into the battle on this flank. With the best part of three divisions, the *18th*, *55th* and *56th*, on the right, Iida intended to use the *56th Infantry Division* in a wide outflanking movement through the Karen Hills and Shan area to Hsipaw and Lashio, thus cutting the line of an Allied retreat into China. Simultaneously, the *18th* and *55th Infantry Divisions*, having secured the airfields and major communication centers in the Sittang valley, were to fight and win the main encirclement battle on the east bank of the Irrawaddy.

Alexander's problems were essentially those of fragmentation and divided command. First, after the successful escape from Rangoon and Pegu, Alexander was left with the 17th Indian Division and the 7th Armored Brigade dispersed and regrouping in the Tharrawaddy-Okpo area, while the 1st Burma Division was badly spread with the 2nd Burma Brigade at Nyaunglebin, the 1st Burma Brigade at Kyauktaga, and the 13th Indian Brigade in the Mawchi-Kemapyu area watching the Salween crossings. With the *55th Infantry Division* established at Daik-U and the Pegu Yoma not presenting too great an obstacle to movement between the Irrawaddy and the Sittang, it was obviously important for Alexander to concentrate his divisions, both individually and together. Alexander's intention of bringing the 1st Burma Division across the Yoma by rail from Yedashe to Taungdwingyi would be possible only if Nationalist Chinese forces were present in sufficient numbers to hold the Sittang.

The reason why Iida was so anxious to maintain the momentum of the

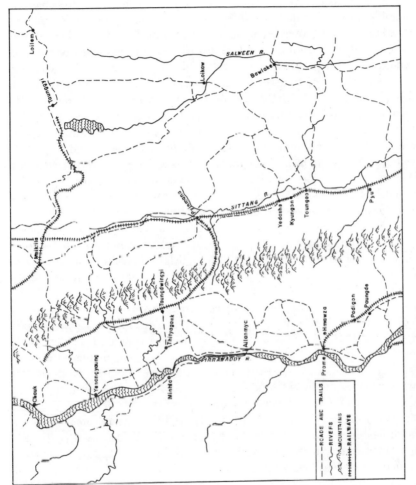

The Central Burma Theater of Operations

offensive and to use the *56th Infantry Division* against Lashio was that the Chinese were present in eastern Burma in some strength. Chinese forces moved into Burma during January in spite of the Chiang-Wavell meeting because men on the spot, aware of the common danger, managed to sort out many of the problems that their leaders had found so hard to reconcile. But the legacy of mistrust and mutual incomprehension remained, and the collapse of British forces in both Malaya and southern Burma made a deplorable impression on the Chinese, who never again trusted the British to stand up to the Japanese. Chiang, despite his professed adherence to the principle of British command of Chinese troops in Burma, did everything he could to retain personal command of his forces, even to the extent of ordering his divisions to ignore arrangements that he had undertaken as a result of deliberations with the British. When Chiang's obstructions ended, his divisional and army commanders could be relied upon to complete the job properly. After 11 March Stilwell was commander of the Chinese forces in Burma. Though this violent Anglophobe cooperated fully and loyally with Alexander, whom he came to admire, he found that his authority was more nominal than real. Stilwell was forced to resort to the full depth of his considerable powers of leadership and personal example to get any response from the majority of his Chinese divisional commanders, who refused to take orders except from the vacillating and incompetent Chiang in Chungking. Such were the problems that Stilwell was to lose one of his best formations, the 200th Division (Major General Tai An-lan) at Toungoo when other Chinese divisions refused to move promptly to its support.

The Chinese in fact deployed three armies in Burma during the campaign, though Chinese armies were the equivalent of a normal infantry division and their divisions were no more than reinforced brigades. Both types of formations lacked proper artillery, armored, and ancillary support. The 6th Chinese Army (Lieutenant General Kan Li-chu) was in eastern Burma covering the Indo-Chinese border with Burma with three divisions, the 49th (Major General Peng Pi-shen), the 55th (Major General Ch'en Mien-wu), and the 93rd (Major General Kuo Ch'uan), under its command. The 5th Chinese Army (Lieutenant General Tu Yu-ming) was the all-important Chinese formation because it held the vital Lashio, Mandalay, Pyinmana area with the 22nd Division (Major General Liao Yao-shiang) and the 96th Division (Major General Yu Shao), while the 200th held the forward position of Toungoo at the time when Alexander ordered the movement of the 1st Burma Division across the Pegu Yoma. The 66th Army (Lieutenant General Chang Chen) was on the Chinese border around Wanting, with the 28th (Major General Liu Po-lung), the 29th (Major General Ma Wei-chi), and the 38th (Major General Sun Li-jen) Divisions in support.

The critical deployment was obviously that of the 5th Army. If the 1st Burma Division was to move across to the Irrawaddy and become part of the 1st Burma Corps, then the 5th Army had to be in a position to hold the Sittang valley, and Alexander had to ensure that its movements conformed with those of the British. The lateral communications across the Pegu Yoma presented the Japanese with the chance to use their infiltration tactics through the mountains. It was therefore inviting disaster to allow a staggered echelon deployment to develop between the Chinese in the east and the British in the west. The immediate problem was that, with only the 200th Chinese Division at Toungoo (though the 22nd was to move first to Pyinmana and then Yedashe), the Chinese were ill-prepared to meet the Japanese *55th Infantry Division*, yet with two armies in the general area, they were no better placed to deal with three enemy divisions. Similarly, with a nominal corps in the Irrawaddy valley, the British were hardly better prepared to deal with the *33rd*.

Since Chiang and his commanders refused to deploy further south than the Toungoo-Pyu area, the British had to concentrate in the Prome-Hmawza region, by ordering the 1st Burma Division to the area around Allanmyo behind the 17th Indian Division. The 1st and 2nd Burma Brigades, however, were caught by the *55th Infantry Division* as they drew back from the Kyauktaga area. Their withdrawal had to be covered by the 200th Chinese Division. From 19 March on, the 200th was in action with the *55th*, and after the twenty-third it was surrounded when the *143rd Infantry Regiment* broke through the Chinese defenses and captured Kyungon. Stilwell ordered the 55th Chinese Division to move from the Shan area and the 22nd to come south to support the 200th. Both divisions refused to obey, leaving the 200th to survive on its own until its few survivors broke out of Toungoo on 30 March and made their way back to Pyinmana and the 22nd Chinese Division. In this eleven-day action the 200th proved that the Chinese knew how to fight and die, for the division gave and expected no quarter. Unfortunately, its gallant though unavailing resistance was blemished by the division's failure to destroy the bridge over the Sittang that led to Mawchi and Bawlake. By securing this bridge intact the Japanese were free to develop their offensive with the *56th Infantry Division* against Lashio.

In an effort to distract the Japanese, the British launched a series of counterattacks south of Prome in the direction of Paungde and Padigon, but in fact the Japanese were far too clever to be held. By moving along both banks of the Irrawaddy the Japanese sidestepped the British effort, and on the night of 1/2 April attacked the main British positions around Prome and Hmawza, with the *215th Infantry Regiment* next to the river and the *214th* coming against the insecure flank. Although they had the 63rd, 16th, and 48th Brigades in the line, with the 7th Armored Brigade in support, the

British were forced to give ground. Alexander settled trying to hold the line linking Minhla, Thityagauk, Taungdwingyi; Pyinmana; and Loikaw. The 1st Burma Corps, the 5th Chinese Army, and the 6th Chinese Army each was given its own sector of front to defend. The problem was that, despite the classical correctness of the deployment, the entire line was likely to collapse if the Japanese moved even weakly against any one part of it. And the Japanese army was hardly noted for its gentle touch. The 1st Burma Corps and the 6th Chinese Army were the major weak spots. The British could not hope to hold a 40-mile front with brigades that numbered no more than 2,000 men, especially when these men were already badly weakened by a retreat across an arid, shadeless area where the temperature reached 46° C and water supplies were minimal. With an open flank that could be turned at Taungdwingyi by an enemy employing infiltration and encircle-ment tactics across the Pegu Yoma, the only hope that the British had of holding their position was if Chiang Kai-shek ordered divisions from the 66th Army into the line. This Chiang promised, but countermanded, and by the time a desperate Stilwell managed to get the tough and ably com-manded 38th Chinese Division west of the mountains, it was too late to be properly effective. The Japanese used all three regiments of the *33rd Infantry Division* to break the British position, then drove on to take Yenang-yaung, but not before the British devastated the oil field on 16 April. In fact the Japanese almost managed to encircle the British, first in the area of Minhla, Thityagauk, and Taungdwingyi, and then at Yenangyaung. The 7th Armored Brigade and the 38th Chinese Division between them proved critical in extricating the defending forces, though at Yenangyaung the 1st Burma Division was effectively ruined beyond recall.*

On the Allied left flank the situation deteriorated with equal rapidity, as the 6th Chinese Army melted away before the advancing *56th Infantry Division*. In the course of its advance the Japanese division shattered the 55th Chinese Division around Loilem so effectively that no part of it was ever reconstituted; the division literally ceased to exist. In fact, the Japanese breakthrough on the defenders' flanks, and the growing pressure the

---

*The oil fields were equally devastated, though exact figures are impossible to substantiate. The official historian of Burmah Oil, Tony Corley, informed the author that, whereas 7,046,351 barrels were produced in 1941 by all the Burmese fields, "reliable estimates" put the total crude oil obtained by the Japanese in Burma from 1942 until 1945 at about 3,000,000 barrels. It would appear that the Japanese managed to get some of the wells at Chauk and Yenangyaung back into service by June 1942. All stocks and various storage tanks were destroyed, but the plants themselves had to be left relatively untouched because of the lack of explosives. Tools and dismantled machinery were thrown down wells and into the river. In the power station the boilers were burned out, while pumping stations were demolished and river crossings plugged with cement. The pipeline was partially filled with water. Wooden derricks and rigs were burned. The total cost of the damage caused by the demolition was subsequently assessed at $78,000,000. The amount was so small primarily because it took equipment depreciation into account.

Japanese exerted against the 5th Chinese Army in the center, began to assume disastrous proportions. On 29 April the Japanese took Lashio and on the following day elements of the *33rd Infantry Division* reached the west bank of the Chindwin opposite Monywa. The Japanese occupation of Lashio ended the possibility of the Allied forces withdrawing back into China, while the *215th Infantry Regiment*'s march toward Monywa threatened to cut off the Allied forces around Mandalay from the shortest overland route to India via Kalewa. These two developments threatened to turn what the Allies had hoped would prove an orderly withdrawal into a hurried and disorganized flight.

There was no alternative for the British and Chinese but to try to get back to the safety of India as quickly as they could, though by the end of April this prospect was a dismal one on four counts. First, the Allies had to contend with the simple fact that in certain places the Japanese were nearer to India than they were. Second, there was very little left in the way of supplies for the divisions as they withdrew. Third, men already exhausted by their efforts over the past few weeks had to move through malaria-infested valleys and then over steep and difficult mountains. Fourth, and perhaps most important of all, they had to get to India across the jungle trails before the monsoon broke sometime during May. Unless the Allied forces managed to keep ahead of the rains, mud threatened to complete the task that the Japanese had begun but thus far been unable to finish. Though ravaged by disease and exhaustion, the Allied forces did manage to keep ahead of the Japanese, the dwindling supplies, and the rains. They did so by a narrow but decisive margin. Though they entered India in deplorable physical condition, the remnants of five divisions arrived in remarkably good order. As Slim remarked, the scarecrows at least were recognizable as soldiers. The Chinese 22nd and 96th Divisions retreated right back into northern Burma before passing through the evil Hukawng valley to Ledo, while Stilwell personally marched the 38th Chinese Division through Wuntho to Imphal. What was left of the 1st Burma Corps fought its way back to Imphal via the Chindwin and Kalewa. Facilities for the Allied forces in India were, predictably, nonexistent. At a press conference in May Wavell and Alexander, putting a brave face on the events of the past four months, referred to the 1,000-mile trek back into India as "a voluntary withdrawal and a glorious retreat." It had begun as a withdrawal forced on the British by a superior enemy, and it was nothing short of a disaster.

For the Allies the Burma campaign was a rout more for the manner of the defeat than for the defeat itself, important though that was. Yet certain features of the situation went some way to mitigate the worst aspects of defeat. Badly beaten though the British and Chinese forces were, they did retain their cohesion. The fact that men identifiable as soldiers staggered into India meant that their fighting spirit remained intact, that here was the nucleus of fresh armies, and that their commanders had been of the highest caliber. This was not the same sort of defeat as those at Malaya and Singapore, where no British general rose to the challenge of defeat. In Burma the various formations were held together by the competence and leadership of Alexander, Slim, and Stilwell, and as a result of the forethought of Hutton. Regardless of the state the troops were in when they crossed into India, the simple fact was that, had it not been for these generals, their mistakes included, the forces would never have made it back to India at all. The British and Chinese forces that reached India were in no state to fight for some time, but the Japanese, for all their advantages of initiative and numerical superiority, had failed to annihilate the forces that had opposed them. In this respect Burma was like many other Japanese victories—only a partial one.

It was also partial in one other respect. Though the Japanese conquest was impressive (in overrunning Burma they lost about 5,000 men and inflicted over 13,000 casualties on the British and unknown losses on the Chinese), securing Burma led them nowhere. Burma was a cul-de-sac in which they were ultimately trapped and crushed. In this Burma reflected the overall Japanese effort during the war, for their initial victories had bought the Japanese a defensive perimeter that they could not maintain. This perimeter was the point of contact at which the balance of forces finally and decisively shifted against the Japanese to an extent that moral and psychological factors could no longer offset. In the final analysis, unless Britain was forced out of India, or the war, or both, Japan could not hope to match the inevitable British buildup in northeastern India. Any British effort against Japan after 1942 was certain to be directed against Burma because there was no other place where the British could attack the Japanese. For the Japanese, however, Burma was just as certain to wither on the vine because Japan's priority was the Pacific, not the Indian subcontinent and the Indian Ocean.

After May 1942 the pertinent question regarding Burma was just how long it would take the British to turn the tables on Japan. In the campaign the British had fought badly. They had been outmaneuvered strategically and trounced tactically, but the Japanese did not have patents on good generals, sound planning, and effective tactical doctrine. Just as Japan had used Western techniques to defeat Western powers, the methods they had used in the jungles of Burma and Malaya were like a weapon lying in the street, a weapon available for either side to pick up and use. Although the British learned their lesson slowly and painfully, in the end they put together a campaign that handed the Japanese army the greatest defeat in its history. But there was one matter that even final success on the battlefield could not reverse.

Wavell (center) and the two commanders who emerged with credit from the disastrous 1942 campaign in Burma, General Sir Harold Alexander (left) and Lieutenant General W. J. Slim. All three went on to become field marshals: Wavell became penultimate viceroy of India, Alexander supreme allied commander in Italy and then the Mediterranean and finally minister of defense, and Slim chief of the Imperial General Staff. Robert Hunt Library

The number of civilian casualties during the campaign is unknown, but such losses were substantial. In this respect Burma was set apart from the other campaigns in Southeast Asia. Wherever armies fight, civilians suffer, either accidentally in the course of battle or as a result of abuse by soldiery. Murder, rape, and looting have always been the prerogatives of victorious armies, and throughout Southeast Asia the Japanese indulged themselves in an orgy of bestiality and excess that can only be understood in terms of a society that did not believe it would have to answer for its actions. As Slim observed, the behavior of the Japanese was a stain on their record that would not soon be expunged. Indeed, there are still signs of anti-Japanese feeling in Southeast Asia as the legacy of the war years.

Burma had its fair share of Japanese attentions in such matters, but it also experienced a full measure of horror fortunately spared most societies in the war. As the Japanese advanced through Burma they were preceded by countless thousands of refugees of all races as the people took to the roads and trails with but the common intention of putting distance between themselves and the conqueror. By the thousands they died of thirst, starvation, and exhaustion; while cholera, dysentery, malaria, smallpox, typhoid, and other no less virulent diseases swept through the columns of refugees, exacting their toll. As the military units passed through the columns of hapless civilians, they stepped over the dead and dying, most of whom simply lay where they had collapsed. When the British army came to clear the road from Tamu to Palel in May 1942, the troops had to use respirators to counteract the effects of decomposing bodies.

One small incident illustrates the full horror and despair that gripped this exodus, an incident as little known in the West as the fact that about 3,000,000 Bengalis starved to death in 1943–44, in large part because the British government did not feel it could divert shipping from military purposes to try to alleviate natural disaster in India. When British troops entered Tamu they found twenty skeletons gathered around the counter of the local post office; one was clutching the broken telephone receiver. Such an incident, perhaps small in itself, nevertheless pointed to the fact that, no matter what happened later in the war, there was never any possibility of the British reestablishing themselves in Burma. It was inconceivable that British authority could survive such a debacle. The only justification for British rule in Burma was the maintenance of order and the protection of the population from external attack; by failing on both counts the British forfeited their right to rule. The many thousands of civilians who died in the course of the Japanese conquest of Burma were the title deeds of Burma's postwar independence and nationhood. Irrespective of what came later (the fact that in 1944 and 1945 the British army inflicted on the Japanese army what until then was the greatest defeat in its history as it reconquered Burma), there was no way in which the verdict of history, delivered in 1942, could be reversed. The mountains and mud, disease and malnutrition, exhaustion and the enemy claimed their victims coldly and impartially—people on the one side, a political system on the other.

CHAPTER 15

The Japanese Options, Spring 1942

By February–March 1942, after less than three months of war, the Japanese stood on the brink of total success in Southeast Asia. Many pockets of Allied resistance remained unreduced, but their days were clearly numbered and for all intents and purposes the outcome of the first phase of the war had been settled decisively in Japan's favor. Japan, by dint of her methodical preparation, audacity, and the prowess of her armed forces, basically achieved all that she had set out to secure in her conquest of Southeast Asia.

As Slim remarked, while things went well the Japanese were ruthless and as bold as ants, but when things went wrong, they were slow to adjust and prone to confusion. This weakness in Japan's strategic direction of the war effort was in no instance more obvious and crucial than during the period of conquest in early 1942. The question that naturally arose as Japan tightened her grip on the Dutch East Indies and the Philippines was what steps she proposed to take in the next critical phase of the war. It was here that Japan, when confronted with a series of very difficult options, made the drastic error of compounding the diffusion of effort over too great an area in the face of an undefeated and potentially superior enemy.

When Japan went to war she was committed to a policy of securing limited objectives that she intended to maintain through a battle of attrition along a defensive perimeter. Despite her easy successes in the initial months

of the war, two matters had become extremely clear by February and
March 1942. First, it had become obvious that the Japanese were involved in
a type of war that differed from the earlier conflicts with China and Russia.
In wars fought around the turn of the century Japan had been opposed by
imperial dynasties that feared defeat in foreign wars less than social revolution at home. In situations where they could never take their wars to the
Japanese homeland, the Manchu and Romanov dynasties were willing to
come to terms with Japan because in the last analysis their defeats were
merely local and could be shrugged off. In the Pacific war Japan made the
fundamental error of supposing that she could limit a naval war against the
two greatest naval powers in the world in the way that she had earlier
limited wars against continental powers. The American reaction to Pearl
Harbor had not been anticipated by most Japanese, and by the spring of
1942 the first inklings of this new strategic reality of being involved in an
unlimited war were beginning to impress themselves upon the Japanese
leadership. Second, the Imperial Navy had manifestly failed to achieve its
immediate objective in the war, and thereby failed to secure the very basis
on which the successes of 1894 and 1904 had been founded. The navy had
failed either to destroy or to neutralize the enemy's main force. Because of
this failure there could be no long-term security for Japan and her conquests.

The question that Japan faced in the spring of 1942 was how best to
consolidate her success and bring the war to an end. Japan's initial plans had
called for waging defensive warfare behind a defensive perimeter until the
enemy's will to continue the struggle was broken. But certain political and
strategic considerations in the first three months of 1942 dictated a switch to
the offensive. Politically, it was impossible for the Japanese to assume a
defensive posture after a series of runaway victories. Strategically, with the
Allies beginning to recover from their initial defeats, it was courting
disaster for Japan to have no definite plan that would allow her to dictate the
direction and pace of the war. Since Japan was in a position of material
inferiority to her enemies, her only compensation was to remain on the
offensive. This retention of the strategic initiative was ever more essential
in light of the navy's failure to destroy the Allied main forces at sea. Japan
therefore had to commit herself to a concentration of force in an effort to
push the issue to a conclusion. She failed to do so, instead choosing to limit
her objectives and to pursue them simultaneously while still adhering to the
principle of using for her operations force that was marginal to requirements. The result was disastrous. But in mitigation it must be pointed out
that the nature of the war in which Japan found herself, and the inadequacies of Japanese resources to the demands that were imposed upon her,
really dictated the nature of Japan's reactions. By definition, therefore, the
nature of her policy—the dissipation of effort over a vast area in the pursuit

of divergent objectives—was an inadequate answer to an almost impossible strategic problem.

Essentially Japan faced three major options. She could extend her operations southwards against Australia, eastwards into the central Pacific, or westwards into the Indian Ocean. There was no question of her attempting a combination of two or all three options. Yet, in a very real sense, a combination of all three, albeit in a modified form, was precisely what the Japanese attempted.

An attack on Australia was impossible. The Japanese lacked the army divisions and the transports needed for such a major undertaking. The Japanese would not have needed too great a force to secure the major cities of eastern Australia, but that force was simply not available. An attack on Hawaii faced immense difficulties, not least because there was no possibility of a repeat surprise attack and the Japanese carriers could not hope to fight for and secure air supremacy against land-based aircraft over so large an area as the Hawaiian Islands. The Japanese were confronted with enormous logistical problems if they attempted sustained operations against the British in the Indian Ocean. Somehow the Japanese had to choose among these options, all of which had inherent drawbacks.

With the advantage of hindsight it is easy to argue that any course of action other than the one they chose would have been better for the Japanese. It was natural in 1942 that Japan should turn eastwards to fight the Americans at one time or another. At some time Japan had to face up to the reality of having to challenge the U.S. Pacific Fleet in the "decisive battle" of the war. It was this battle that had dominated Japanese naval thought throughout the interwar period. But in retrospect it can be argued that in the spring of 1942 there was only one course of action really open to Japan, and that this was the least obvious option since it would have involved securing victory by positional advantage rather than by armed force. It can be argued that the only sensible policy for the Japanese in the spring and summer of 1942 was to have stood on the defensive in Southeast Asia and the Pacific, accepting the possibility of being hit very hard by the Americans, and to have staked everything on a major strategic offensive in the Indian Ocean. Naturally, such an action would have extended still further the commitments of an already overextended Japan, but there was much to recommend such a course of action.

The failure of the Axis powers to coordinate their national strategies was one of the major factors in their ultimate defeat, and coordination was extremely difficult in view of the great distances that separated the Axis partners. But in February 1942 the Japanese knew that in the spring and summer the Germans were planning to renew their offensive in southern Russia towards the Caucasus. The Japanese were well aware of the situation in North Africa, where the issue was in the balance. They knew, moreover, of the desperate British weakness throughout the Middle East, and of the seething open discontent with British rule in India. Had the Japanese risked everything on a major military and naval effort in the Indian Ocean, then both Britain and the U.S.S.R. *might* have been forced out of the war. This move against the only theater where two of the three major powers opposed to the Axis joined hands would not necessarily have involved substantial Japanese land forces. The Japanese would have needed sufficient land forces to secure Ceylon, but India could have been bypassed. The Japanese could have expected that their proximity in Ceylon would bring about the collapse of the British position in India. From Ceylon the British position in the oil fields of the Persian Gulf could have been attacked. The British were very thinly stretched over the vast wastes of Arabia. There was very little in the way of British air power in the area, and there was certainly nothing that could have taken on the Japanese carriers. If such an attack had been made, and if it had been successful, then coming on top of two years of constant defeats it might well have proved decisive in breaking Britain. Moreover, if the British position on the gulf had crumbled, then the way would have been clear for threatening the whole of the Soviet position in southern Russia, and the neutral position of Turkey might well have become untenable. Had these matters come to pass, the Japanese objective in signing the tripartite pact (catching the Americans between more fronts than they could handle effectively) might just have been achieved.

Of course there is a reverse side to the argument. There is no guarantee that Britain in 1942, allied as she was with the Soviet Union and the United States, would have been broken and forced out of the war. Britain might have been able to carry on the war, even after the loss of the Middle East, the Mediterranean, the gulf, and India, though it must remain very doubtful if the Americans, at this stage of the war, could have filled the British need for oil if the gulf had been lost. This line of action leaves aside the very real logistical problems with which Japan was beset, for this operation would have had to be a major undertaking involving the full strength of the Japanese main forces at the end of a very long line of communications in a vast area. Moreover, even if the defeat of Britain could have been achieved, there was no guarantee that Japan's ultimate defeat at American hands would have been averted. A Japanese success on the gulf in the end might have counted for nothing if the Americans, unable to reverse a British disaster in the Middle East, had decided upon a mid-Atlantic defense and an all-out offensive in the Pacific. When, after all the "ifs" have been cleared away, one returns to the situation of early 1942, it seems that the Japanese strategic position was all but impossible. Still, the adoption of the Indian Ocean option could not have produced worse results than the ones the Japanese actually registered in the period March–July 1942.

As commander in chief of the Combined Fleet, Yamamoto was personally convinced that Japan had but one course open to her. That course, he reasoned, was to force an action at the earliest possible opportunity against the Americans in the central-western Pacific. Yamamoto clearly appreciated that the carriers of the U.S. Pacific Fleet presented the only real danger to Japan because these alone could dispute Japanese control of the western Pacific. To this end, in the early months of 1942 Yamamoto became increasingly convinced that Japanese strategy should look eastwards in an effort to neutralize American naval aviation. But in this view Yamamoto had to contend with the problem that had largely brought Japan to the impasse of mid-1941 in the first place: the diffusion of power, responsibility, and decision making within the Japanese high command and the confusion of Japanese objectives. Yamamoto was increasingly obsessed with bringing about a clash with the American carriers because he feared that they might carry the war to the Japanese homeland. American carrier operations against Kwajalein on 1 February, Wake on 24 February, Marcus on 4 March, and Rabaul and New Guinea (17 February to 16 March) gave him considerable food for thought.

Although these attacks achieved very little, the fact that even in the worst of circumstances the Americans could still conduct such operations (if only against the peripheries) boded ill. The attack on Marcus Island, despite its lack of real success, was significant in another way. The island was only 700 miles from Tokyo, and well inside the defensive perimeter supposedly created between the Kuriles and the Gilberts as the shield for Japan and her conquests. For Yamamoto these American operations strongly buttressed his argument for an attack eastwards in order to provoke a final reckoning with the American fleet. Paradoxically, so much of the American carrier activity had taken place among the islands to the south that an equally strong argument could be made for continuing Japan's current actions in order to secure the general area and isolate Australia before the Americans gathered their strength. That American carriers were operating in the area seemed to indicate the presence in the Southwest Pacific of major American strategic interests for which the Americans would be compelled to fight. Thus there were valid arguments in favor of maintaining the tempo of operations in the Southwest Pacific and, indeed, of increasing it by introducing Japanese carriers. Any movement towards the east against the Americans would automatically stretch Japanese lines of communication while shortening those of the Americans. An operation into the Southwest Pacific, on the other hand, was certain to result in an equalization of distance problems as both sides would have to commit themselves far from their main base areas. Many Japanese officers correctly appreciated that any American concentration for a rollback of Japanese conquests would have to be based on Australia, the isolation of which (in the absence of its conquest) was therefore absolutely essential. For Yamamoto the problem of American activity was that it gave support to two quite contradictory arguments.

To make matters even less clear, the third option, the movement into the Indian Ocean, was not unpopular. The Japanese were aware that, despite the disasters of the opening phase of the war, the British had made every effort to build up a major naval force in the Indian Ocean in an attempt to prevent Japanese eruption into that theater. Despite the loss of Singapore, the buildup of British forces in the Indian Ocean by March 1942 had been considerable, at least on paper. By that time the British had assembled one light and two fleet carriers, five battleships, seven cruisers, sixteen destroyers, and seven submarines in order to contest any Japanese offensive from the Indies. In reality, however, the British position was precarious. Their three carriers among them mustered as many aircraft as any one of the larger Japanese fleet carriers, while their aircraft were inferior to their opposite numbers. There was an almost total lack of shore-based long-range reconnaissance aircraft. The overall British ability to mount effective air operations was little more than nonexistent. Their battleships, with one exception, were all old, slow, unmodernized liabilities, and many of the smaller ships were in urgent need of refit and repair. The British had no secure base in the Indian Ocean. Nevertheless, it was significant that, despite the extremely grave situation in the Atlantic and Mediterranean at this time, the British had managed to undertake a massive reinforcement of their forces in the Far East. This could only bode ill for the Japanese in the long term. Therefore, within the Japanese naval hierarchy, many favored an offensive operation against the British in the Indian Ocean at the earliest possible opportunity. The aim of such an operation would be to eliminate any possible threat from the west before Japanese attention was turned to the east against the Americans.

Despite Yamamoto's immense authority and prestige, initially he could not secure his own way regarding the desirability of seeking out the Americans. In the early months of 1942, few shared his view that it was critical to force battle with the Americans as the overriding priority; many of those who opposed him felt that the Japanese had more time than in fact was available. Each of the options had powerful backers and there were good reasons for adopting or rejecting any of the courses open to Japan. Yet all the leading Japanese naval commanders were agreed on one point: offensive action had to be initiated. To use an apt comment made about Germany in her war with the Soviets at about this time, Japan had seized a wolf by the ears and was in no position to let go. The Japanese realized this, but their general failure to appreciate the urgency of dealing with the Americans once and for all led them to choose the British in the Indian Ocean as their initial target before they turned back to the Pacific.

In light of the comment that the Japanese would have been served better by a major operation across the entire Indian Ocean to secure at least the mouth of the gulf, it may seem churlish to criticize the operation of March–April 1942 off Ceylon and in the Bay of Bengal. It may even seem contradictory. Yet in fact there is no real contradiction in such a criticism. The nature and aims of these efforts were ill-considered and totally unrelated to Japan's strategic requirements at that time. The object of these operations was to eliminate the threat that might develop from the west, but two considerations immediately suggest themselves regarding Japanese intentions. First, the British fleet in the Indian Ocean was, to put it bluntly, an impotent irrelevance, the destruction of which would have availed the Japanese little if anything in real terms. The fleet was barely capable of defending itself; its offensive value was minimal, and in any event it could never have an offensive value if the Americans were either defeated or on the defensive. Second, to plan a brief sortie almost by definition implied that there was only the off chance of imposing one's will on the enemy and forcing the British to give battle under conditions of inferiority. Unless a prolonged campaign against vital interests could be sustained there was little or no chance that the enemy would be forced to give battle. Battle could be declined by a fleet whose continued existence was now more important to the British than any single interest that they might have in the Bay of Bengal area. It is ironic that, while overall the Japanese can be criticized for waging war with too few resources over too great an area, in the case of the Indian Ocean operation the reverse was true. In this operation the Japanese were attempting too little with too much: it would have been better to make either an all-out effort or none at all.

The opening Japanese moves in the Indian Ocean began with the successful occupation of the Andaman Islands on 23 March. This island group was of immense importance to the Japanese because its occupation allowed them to secure a shield to Malaya, Singapore, and western and northern Sumatra. By taking the islands the Japanese denied the British what might have proved an ideal base from which to mount operations against their western conquests. The Japanese then moved to secure Pukhet and Mergui, and on 2 April sailed the *18th Infantry Division* from Singapore to Rangoon in forty-six transports. The convoy, which had an escort of one cruiser, two destroyers, and a submarine chaser, reached Burma's capital on the seventh. The escort was so small because the convoy sailed at the time when the Japanese were making their main effort in the Indian Ocean and hence provided direct cover for the forces bound for Burma. The main operation began on 26 March when the major part of the Japanese striking force left Kendari to sortie against Ceylon and the Bay of Bengal. This force, under Nagumo, consisted of five fleet carriers, the *Akagi, Hiryu, Soryu, Shokaku,* and *Zuikaku*; the battleships *Haruna, Hiei, Kirishima,* and *Kongo*; two heavy cruisers; and ten escorts from the 1st Destroyer Flotilla. (This operation was to prove the only occasion when these four fast battleships were deployed under a single flag.) Coordinated with the movement of Nagumo's force—in striking power virtually the same as the force used against Pearl Harbor, Amboina, and Darwin—were two other forces. A weak submarine force was deployed off the west coast of India, while in the Bay of Bengal a carrier raiding force was organized to prey on British coastal shipping. This force, under the command of Ozawa, consisted of the light carrier *Ryujo*, five heavy cruisers, one light cruiser, and never more than four destroyers, though eight were with the force at various times during the operation. With the elite of Japanese naval aviation committed to the attack and strong supporting forces allotted the task of exacting an unacceptable toll of British shipping, everything seemed ready for a Japanese rampage in an ocean where the enemy could offer little more than token opposition. Moreover, considerable numbers of important targets in the area were within range of the Japanese forces. The Indian economy was heavily dependent on the coastal trade of the subcontinent, while harbor congestion in the early months of 1942 was exceptionally severe. It was usual for Colombo, a port capable of handling about forty ships at once, to have upwards of one hundred either being loaded or unloaded or in the roadsteads. Other ports were similarly crowded, while the shipping lanes and the ports themselves were virtually undefended. The scene was set for a British disaster of the first magnitude.

Superficially, the Japanese sortie was indeed a rampage; the British were overwhelmed and humiliated. But, as was so often the case in this initial phase of the war, the reality of the situation was rather different, and there were certain lessons from the raid that the Japanese would have been well advised to consider carefully.

The Japanese advance into the Indian Ocean was known to the British, who ordered the clearing of Colombo harbor as early as 31 March. The British correctly anticipated that the Japanese would advance on Ceylon from the southeast, and they had deployed at Addu Atoll in the remote Aldive Islands, well placed on the unsecured flank of the Japanese advance. The Japanese, despite reconnaissance by the seven submarines assigned to the operation, were unaware of the existence of this base. They were intent on striking Ceylon on 5 April, a Sunday, and for good measure Easter Sunday. The Japanese hoped to catch the British fleet at either Colombo or Trincomalee in exactly the same way as they had caught the Americans at Pearl Harbor. If the British warships could not be located, the Japanese planned to attack merchant shipping and port facilities; they had no intention of repeating the error of 7 December in the latter respect.

The British, on the other hand, were faced with a dilemma. Politically, and in view of the tradition of the service, it was impossible for the Royal

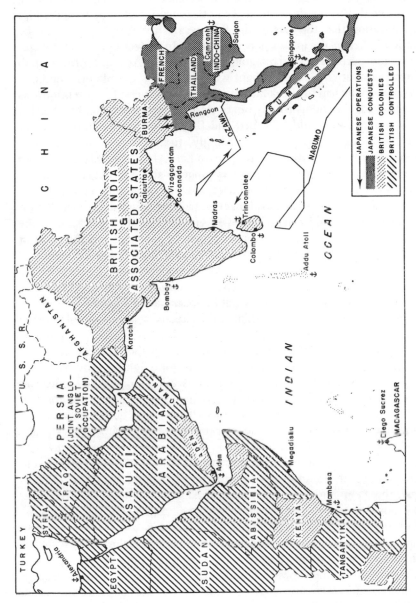

The Indian Ocean Sortie, April 1942

Navy to assume a passive role in the event of a Japanese onslaught. Indeed, the major part of the British Eastern Fleet sortied under the command of Admiral Sir James Somerville once the presence of the enemy main force was detected. But the desire to strike at the enemy had to be tempered by the realization that the loss of the fleet was a luxury that could not be afforded, whereas the loss of port facilities in India would be unfortunate, costly, and perhaps very damaging, but no more. As realists the British appreciated that any stand-up fight with the Japanese could only end one way; Somerville had to check his natural aggressiveness. His intention was to try to evade the enemy by day but to close the Japanese by night when his fleet's weaknesses would be veiled and British superiority in gun power could be brought into play. Accordingly, until 7 April, when he was granted discretion to withdraw his force to East Africa, Somerville's tactics were cautious. These amounted to very gingerly attempts to get around the enemy flank in order to force a night action while remaining undetected by Japanese aircraft. These tactics, however, failed to disguise the fact that for most of the time the British Eastern Fleet was a helpless spectator of the carnage that followed, while even its tentative gyrations ran the greatest possible risks with little or no hope of success. Somerville encountered criticism for taking unacceptable risks in maneuvering his fleet in the enemy's vicinity. In light of the Japanese superiority in ships, aircraft, and battle technique, such criticism would appear well justified.

The initial Japanese carrier strikes were directed against Colombo on the morning of 5 April. Despite the orders to clear the harbor, thirty-four merchantmen and warships were still there when the Japanese attacked. Perhaps surprisingly, this shipping escaped quite lightly. One destroyer and an armed merchant cruiser were sunk, while a submarine tender and one merchantman were quite extensively damaged. Much of the force of the Japanese attack fell on the shore installations and harbor workshops. But in the late afternoon Japanese aircraft located two British heavy cruisers, the *Cornwall* and *Dorsetshire*, some 200 miles south of Ceylon, making their way from Colombo at their best speed. Both ships were subjected to overwhelming attack and sunk in a matter of minutes. In terms of technique, these sinkings have been recognized generally as among the most professional operations carried out by carrier aircraft during the whole war, but the overall direction of the attack left something to be desired. With an inconsistency that characterizes so many actions at sea, the Japanese do not seem to have asked themselves why these cruisers, sighted steaming *away* from the enemy at high speed, should have been in such a position. In fact, the *Cornwall* and *Dorsetshire* were en route for a rendezvous with the rest of the British Eastern Fleet. Had the Japanese extended their search operations in the direction of the cruisers' course, they would certainly have made contact with the British main force. As it was, Somerville's ships followed the action against their compatriots on their radar screens.

After this operation Nagumo led his force well to the east of Ceylon before turning back to renew the offensive on 9 April with a major strike against Trincomalee. Again the Japanese registered successes against harbor installations and ships in port, but once more their major success was against warships at sea. Japanese aircraft encountered the light carrier *Hermes*, minus her aircraft, and conferred on her the dubious distinction of being the first and only British carrier to be sunk by enemy air action during the war. Her solitary escorting destroyer was also dispatched. A corvette, a fleet auxiliary, and a merchantman, which like the *Hermes* tried to regain the safety of Trincomalee after the danger seemed to have passed, were also cornered and sunk. In all, Nagumo's force sank over 56,000 tons of warships and merchantmen. While the carrier force was thus indulging itself, the submarines to the west and Ozawa's ships to the east played havoc with British coastal shipping. The submarines accounted for five merchantmen (32,000 tons), while Ozawa's force sank twenty-three merchantmen (over 112,000 tons), mostly on 6 April. Though the material damage that Ozawa inflicted was considerable, equally important was the fact that his actions virtually paralyzed coastal trade in the Bay of Bengal for weeks. His was the force, moreover, that in attacking Cocanada and Vizagapatam brought the war to Indian soil for the first time.

By the time that Nagumo passed through the Strait of Malacca on the twelfth, the Japanese had good reason to feel pleased with their efforts. In a series of actions the Japanese showed themselves to be considerably superior to their enemy. They had inflicted shaming defeats on the British. The losses incurred by the Eastern Fleet (even without a major engagement) and the damage to its bases were so severe that the fleet obviously could defend neither itself nor British interests in the area. The Royal Navy was forced to withdraw to Kilindi in East Africa, while the merchant shipping losses, and the halting of the coastal trade in the aftermath of the Japanese operations, were exceptionally serious because of the general shortage of shipping in the Indian Ocean at that time. Moreover, the loss of aircraft suffered by the British in trying to counter the Japanese attacks (thirty-seven in all) was heavy given the small number of aircraft available to Britain at this point of the war. In comparison, the Japanese lost twenty-nine aircraft.

One is really left with the unanswerable question of what would have happened if the Japanese had chosen to make a more sustained effort in the Indian Ocean. A sustained operation in the Bay of Bengal could only have reduced British coastal trade to ruins and might have forced the British Eastern Fleet into battle in its defense, though this is unlikely. As it was, news of the attack on Ceylon for a time threw the British war cabinet into utter dismay: it was believed that this indeed could be the beginning of the end. Wavell, writing of experiences that included service as viceroy, referred to this raid as the supreme crisis of the war for India. The fact that the crisis passed and was not the beginning of the end can be attributed not to

successful British resistance but to the enemy's choice not to press matters
to a conclusion.

The Japanese, on the other hand, should have heeded certain features
about the Indian Ocean sortie. Churchill flattered British arms by stating
that in their attacks on Ceylon the Japanese encountered bone, but there
was no getting away from the fact that for the first time in the war Japanese
carriers encountered substantial and organized opposition in the air over
their objectives and, significantly, the Japanese carriers had themselves
been bombed. The five fleet carriers had been very lucky to escape unscathed. Nagumo's grim warning, that along their flight decks carriers were
especially vulnerable to bombing, had not been fulfilled on this occasion,
but Midway was only two months away. Moreover, the quality of the air
operations left much to be desired. The balance of losses favored the
Japanese and seemed to confirm Japanese all-around superiority in every
aspect of naval air warfare. But the results obtained by Japanese high-level
bombers were poor, and for 5 fleet carriers to account for just 9 ships from
about 300 bomber missions was a poor yield for ships with so impressive a
record behind them. In addition, the Japanese air losses were heavy in
terms of the forces available and they were large in relation to the losses
incurred by the Japanese up to that time. The fact that over Colombo the
Japanese encountered opposition from Hurricanes and Fulmars suggested
harder going in the future. The Japanese would have to fight harder and
more carefully if they were to continue to enjoy air supremacy.

Thus, when the first of the Japanese carriers reached home waters on 20
April, there was cause for concern even though the carrier force had good
reason to be pleased with its overall performance. In five months of almost
continual warfare the carriers had ranged over a third of the globe, inflicting
successive defeats on the enemy at relatively little cost to themselves. The
reality of the situation, however, was somewhat different. Despite and
because of their success, the carriers had had to endure inevitable losses of
elite aircrews that, in terms of quality, were irreplaceable. Moreover,
decisive strategic success had eluded the carriers despite the destruction
they had wreaked upon their foes. Even in the Indian Ocean the carriers
had done nothing more than to eliminate for the moment a nonexistent
threat; they had registered a partial victory over a feeble enemy. In many
ways this operation was at best a pyrrhic victory, at worst a crucial defeat in
terms of time and resources that were not Japan's to squander. Thus, a
mixed reception might well have been afforded the carriers on their return,
and, indeed, this was to be their fate—but not quite for these reasons. On
the credit side there was comfort in the humiliation and prostration of the
Allies in Southeast Asia. French power in Indo-China was a broken reed;
the British had been humbled with contemptuous ease both on land and at
sea; the Dutch had been brushed aside with such disdain that they might

never have existed. The Allies stood on the brink of total ruin in Burma and the Philippines, where their days of effective resistance were clearly numbered. Everywhere in Southeast Asia was proof of dazzling Japanese success, prowess, and seeming invincibility and invulnerability. But two days before the first of the carriers tied up in her home port, the Americans had bombed Tokyo.

Few operations have had so little material impact yet so profound psychological and strategic consequences as what has become known as the Doolittle Raid. This raid on the Japanese homeland, the first of the war, marked the effective end of the first phase of the Pacific war, indeed of the whole period of Japanese aggrandizement. Although the tide of Japanese conquest was still to inch its way forward on several fronts over the next few months, and indeed was to do so even as late as 1944, the raid on the Japanese capital coincided with what was effectively the high-water mark of victory and the moment when, for the first time, the unshakeable resolve and consistency of American power, despite defeats, began to impinge seriously on Japanese strategic planning. The Doolittle Raid brought home to Japan's military hierarchy certain fundamental strategic truths that many of the Japanese leaders had never properly considered or had forgotten or ignored in the heady days of triumph after Pearl Harbor. Yamamoto had been one of the commanders who had not been carried away by the momentum of success, and, indeed, almost two weeks before the Doolittle Raid he had been able to secure acceptance of the principle of moving eastwards against Midway for battle with the Americans. Resistance to Yamamoto's ideas had been considerable and lingered on—until the Doolittle Raid. The raid cleared away much of the opposition to Yamamoto's schemes, but, in fact, it had a deeper significance that only became obvious in retrospect. The Doolittle Raid spelled the ruination of all prewar Japanese strategic considerations and assumptions, for it showed that the Japanese could not limit the nature of the war they had initiated. Neither the Chinese nor the Russians had been able to break free of the limitations the Japanese had imposed upon them in wars on either side of the turn of the century: in neither conflict had war been carried to the Japanese homeland. In planning for the Pacific war the Japanese had assumed that they could likewise limit the scope of conflict; the Doolittle Raid showed that the Americans were under no such constraint.

The details of the Doolittle Raid can be related quickly and simply because in themselves they were not particularly important. The determination to strike back at the Japanese homeland was deeply implanted in American hearts long before the fires of Pearl Harbor had been brought under control, but the strategic realities of the Allied defeats and weaknesses in the first three months of war made this impossible. Still, the examples of the Marcus operation and of Pearl Harbor itself beckoned the

American carriers towards the Japanese islands. An attack on Japan became politically imperative as defeat piled on defeat. Such a raid would serve to revive morale and put fresh heart into the United States and her Allies after months of unmitigated defeat and rout. To be seen as carrying the war to Japan was a psychological necessity for the Americans at this time, a small sign that the United States was determined to fight through to victory in the end. Accordingly, with all the ingenuity for which they are noted, the Americans began to prepare for a raid.

They faced two seemingly insurmountable problems in trying to mount a raid on Japan. There were no islands from which to launch such a raid, and if the Americans chose to use carrier-borne aircraft, they ran the risk of exposing their carriers. If carrier aviation was used, the carriers would have to close to a point where they themselves would be vulnerable to counterattack from land-based aircraft that were superior in range to American naval aircraft. Under no circumstances could the Americans afford to put their carriers in peril. The answer to the seemingly unsoluble problem was to embark sixteen twin-engined B-25B Mitchell bombers from the army's 17th Bombardment Group on the carrier *Hornet*. The bombers, commanded by Lieutenant Colonel James H. Doolittle, were specially modified to carry extra fuel, and their volunteer crews underwent intensive training in coaxing heavily laden bombers into the air from very short runways. None of the crews had ever worked from a carrier. It was impossible for such bombers to be recovered on the restricted flight deck of a carrier, so it was planned that they would fly on to airfields in China after having taken off some 450 to 650 miles from the Japanese coast.

The American task force for the operation consisted of the carriers *Hornet* and *Enterprise*, four cruisers, and eight destroyers. The *Enterprise* flew combat air patrol for the force since the *Hornet* was inoperative because of the bombers on her flight deck. But the force's advance to its flying-off position was compromised in the early hours of 18 April when it blundered into a picket line of Japanese fishing boats drawn up some 750 miles east of Tokyo specifically to provide early warning against such an attack. Being compromised, the Americans immediately launched the Mitchells, in wild weather, while the escorts sank four of the Japanese fishing boats. The Americans accepted the inherent risks of encountering an alerted enemy and of the bombers failing to reach their scheduled bases in China. These risks were shown to be well judged because the Japanese, alerted by the warnings sent out by the fishing boat *Nitto Maru*, calculated that if the Americans did not abandon their mission, many hours would have to pass before they came within range to fly off their aircraft. The Japanese never considered the possibility that the Americans would use long-range medium bombers from their carriers on a one-way trip. Therefore, when the sixteen bombers arrived over their objectives they secured complete

The first bomber, piloted by Doolittle, takes off from the carrier *Hornet*, 18 April 1942, for the first raid on the Japanese homeland. Doolittle went on to command an air force, the *Hornet* to a final resting place at the battle of Santa Cruz in October. The white lines painted on the carrier's decks were guides for the Mitchell bombers. By keeping on the lines the bombers had a 6-foot clearance from the island. National Archives, USN 41196

surprise and encountered no fighter opposition and very little flak. Only one bomber was slightly damaged as oil, military, and factory installations were attacked in Tokyo, Kobe, Yokohama, and Nagoya. The carrier *Ryuho*, undergoing conversion in Yokohama Naval Yard, was hit by a solitary bomb. With the Japanese totally confused and not anticipating that the bombers would make for China, Doolittle's bombers made good their escape. Four reached the safety of the airfields in China; one made for Vladivostok. The remaining aircraft crashed as their fuel ran out over China. Except for one man killed during the landings and eight men captured by Japanese patrols, all the crew members were led to safety through Japanese lines by Chinese peasants. Of the eight Americans captured, three were executed by their captors on the spurious charge of having bombed civilians. Inevitably, the losers from the raid were the Chinese peasants, who paid the price for sheltering and helping the American airmen. Japanese vengeance on these people was immediate and savage.

The damage inflicted by the raid was minimal in the material sense. The Japanese tried to dub it the "Do Nothing Raid," as a pun on the name of its leader, but in fact the raid was very damaging to their pride. The real damage inflicted by Doolittle's bombers was in the mockery of Japanese conquests, for the raid revealed for the first time the glaring weaknesses of Japanese strategy and capabilities. Japanese arms, so powerful, so irresistible, could not protect the Imperial capital against an enemy that could choose the time and means of operation. There was no profit for the Japanese in being masters of Southeast Asia and almost the entire Asian mainland between Vladivostok and Johore if they could not defend their homeland. Such gains were irrelevant if Japanese cities were to be subjected to air bombardment. Moreover, this fleabite of a raid, insignificant in terms of damage when compared with contemporary raids elsewhere or subsequent raids on Japan, ridiculed Japanese operations in the Indian Ocean and Southwest Pacific.

The Doolittle Raid clearly showed the absurdity of Japan's limited operations in the Bay of Bengal. Had a full-blooded attack in the Indian Ocean registered strategic success, then the Doolittle Raid would have been tolerable, but the Indian Ocean sortie achieved no strategic gain that could be set against the political loss caused by Doolittle. As it was, the raid showed that in terms of wear and tear on men and machinery the Japanese could not afford such an operation if some 9,000 miles away the American fleet remained intact and undefeated. Likewise, Japanese persistence in operations against the island chains of the Southwest Pacific was no more than chasing the shadow of victory while ignoring the substance. Herein lay the immediate strategic significance of the Doolittle Raid. It made nonsense of a Japanese strategy that could not prevent the Americans from launching an attack, admittedly a small effort, across thousands of miles of ocean, several thousands of miles away from the theaters of operation that the Japanese at that time considered the crucial areas of conflict. The raid made a mockery of Japanese concentration so far to the south, in the Indian Ocean, and around New Guinea and the Upper Solomons, if this bared Japan herself to attack. The irony of this, and the partial nature of Japanese victories to date, must have been very bitter to the tired carrier commanders as their ships tied up in harbor.

It is always dangerous to read too much into a single event or series of events; there is a risk of reading into the contemporary record detail or critical comment possible only in the light of subsequent knowledge. But the Doolittle Raid is a fitting point at which to end the story of the Japanese conquest of Southeast Asia, even though at the time the final conquest of Burma and the Philippines remained to be accomplished. It is appropriate because it allows a thorough examination of the strategic situation as the war moved into a new phase and because the raid called into question the whole viability of Japanese conquests. This allows a reexamination of the realities of the war and the strategy the Japanese hoped to employ.

The quickest and most cursory glance at the map showing the extent of Japanese gains by the time the Americans on Corregidor capitulated on 6

May shows a staggering area of conquest. Yet the reality behind the arrows and the crossed swords of numberless and nameless engagements was that Japan lacked the oil, raw materials, industry, merchantmen, warships, aircraft, and trained manpower to transform these gains into long-term military security. Japan had not had the means to sustain herself and her war in China during the summer of 1941. That, in a very real sense, was why she went to war. But by going to war Japan had drastically increased, not lessened, her obligations and commitments. She had expanded over millions of square miles of water without any commensurate increase in resources, either in the immediate or in the long-term sense. Any long-term increase in military resources to the level needed to ensure the empire's security was impossible because Japan lacked the industrial base to transform raw materials into war production on the scale required to sustain her in a war with the Americans. Even though the Japanese were successful in securing the resources of Southeast Asia, they lacked the means of transport and production needed to make these gains worthwhile. Indeed, as we have seen, Japanese resources actually declined because of the hidden shipping losses sustained by going to war. To Japan this was a loss as serious as a major defeat, as damaging as the failure to sink the American carriers and to destroy the power, repair, and oil facilities at Pearl Harbor. In short, Japan was attempting too much with too little over too great an area. This problem was compounded by her failure to observe the cardinal rule of war: the selection and maintenance of the aim. That aim had to be securing strategic objectives that would force the Americans into accepting a compromise peace. The most effective way this could be achieved was by destroying American naval power. Alternatively, the Japanese could seek to secure a decisive positional advantage that the Americans could not break down. Japan followed neither course of action in the period between December 1941 and May 1942.

Admittedly, Japan had made immense gains that gave her a greatly enhanced buffer zone relative to the Americans, but the gains consisted mostly of sky and sea, with an occasional island to break the monotony. It was an area thousands of miles across, but where economical cruising speeds meant that warships might not steam much more than 300 miles in a day, and where the timely arrival of forces might prove decisive in the defense, in the attack, or in the counterattack. The area had depth, but it also had an extremely long frontage. Its perimeter marked the points where the Japanese intended to hold the Americans, the points of land defense where the Americans were to batter themselves to a standstill. Although psychologically the ordinary Japanese soldier was well prepared for a dogged step-by-step defensive campaign, the notion of perimeter defense was tortuous to say the least. Moreover, it ignored certain possibilities (such as island hopping) that the Americans had considered before the war and were to implement later in the campaign, though the Japanese can hardly be blamed for not having considered such possibilities.

Forward defense, along an extended front, is possible only with super-abundant strength because such a concept demands the dispersal of static forces rather than the concentration of mobile ones. Such a deployment also ties up disproportionately large amounts of resources in maintaining fighting forces. Moreover, dispersal of force, by its very nature, can guarantee neither the timely nor the economical concentration of force to meet an attack. In the Pacific even the timely and economical movement of forces along interior lines of communication cannot be guaranteed. Nor can reliance be placed upon the continued survival, intact and at full fighting effectiveness, of the fighting fleet *once in contact with the enemy*. The Japanese notion of perimeter defense had to be underwritten by the fleet operating along interior lines of communication in order to come to the support of the threatened sectors of the perimeter. The Japanese assumed all these factors—timely and economical concentration, the constant readiness of the fleet, the ability to sustain garrisons—as certainties, whereas at best they could be only imponderables.

As has already been observed, distances posed problems that in part offset the advantages of possessing a central position. It has also been noted that Japanese plans failed to take account of the relative and potential discrepancy of strength between Japan and the United States. The Japanese cannot be criticized for an inability to foresee the sheer scale of American industrial output, which saw the Americans complete 140 Liberty ships during March 1943 alone,* yet the basic idea of waging defensive

*The problem of trying to assess the realism of Japanese intentions is naturally aggravated by hindsight. For most of the postwar period the world has become familiar with the massive reality of American financial and industrial power, and this was not so obvious before 1941. Though there was no denying the fact that prior to 1941 the United States was the most advanced society on earth, American production in 1939 was lower than it had been in 1929, and the awesome extent of the expansion of American wartime production was largely unsuspected.

Since the war many of the more spectacular statistics involving American wartime production have become increasingly well known. For example, it is widely appreciated that one of the major factors in the defeat of the U-boats in the Atlantic was the American ability to build merchantmen quicker than the Germans could sink them. In fact, at the height of the battle of the Atlantic, in March 1943, the Americans launched 140 7,157-ton Liberty ships, each ship having taken fifteen days to build. The record keel-to-launch time for such a ship was a mere eighty and one-half hours. It was impossible for anyone, not just the Japanese, to understand the power of an American economy geared to war.

Japanese leaders feared American power, but they had to make decisions against the background of fitful and sluggish American production in the thirties, a decade when Japanese output doubled. The Japanese had to assess the United States in light of the fact that between 1922 and 1937 the Americans launched just two dry cargo merchantmen, and even the 1937 federal shipbuilding program was small and slow to be put into effect. Given this vast discrepancy between prewar and wartime industrial performance, it is little wonder that the Japanese proved so wildly out in their calculations and estimation of American power.

warfare behind an extended perimeter entailed risks that any Western military organization would have regarded with horror. The Japanese plans envisaged what was in effect a war of attrition against the world's most industrialized state. The United States possessed infinitely greater resources than Japan, yet the original Japanese war plans foresaw the former automatically securing the strategic initiative once the Japanese went on the defensive behind their mid-Pacific shield. The Japanese plans, therefore, accepted the notion of the weaker side (Japan) voluntarily ceding the initiative and passing onto the defensive to await attack by a stronger enemy that would automatically choose the time and place to mount attacks. In a situation of considerable material inferiority, retention of the strategic initiative was essential to Japan: it was her only compensation for material weakness—yet it was a dubious asset. There was no point in the whole of the Pacific where the Japanese could use the initiative in order to force the Americans to give battle under unfavorable circumstances but where the Japanese could hope to register decisive strategic success. Pearl Harbor was out of the question because the Americans had increased army and air strengths on the Hawaiian Islands after 7 December, and the Japanese carriers could not hope to secure air supremacy over so great an area. The Panama Canal was too far away for the Japanese to have any hope of attacking this the most vulnerable point in American maritime communications. Midway was to be fought only because the Americans had broken the Japanese codes, knew their enemy's intentions, and were prepared to fight a defensive battle; it was not fought because the Americans had no alternative but to accept battle. The Americans, not the Japanese, held the options. The notion of the decisive battle in the area of the Marshalls, Carolines, and Marianas, a notion that had been at the heart of all prewar Japanese strategic planning, was equally erroneous because such a battle could come about only when the Americans were ready and not necessarily at a time and place convenient to the Japanese.

The Japanese thus faced a series of dilemmas. They could hardly go over to the defensive, and in any case their defensive plans were thawed, yet to persist in the offensive could only aggravate Japan's already difficult logistics problems and her numbers-to-space troubles. Yamamoto had foreseen if not all the details then certainly the basic framework of Japanese difficulties, and he had warned that the only way that the Japanese could secure their objectives in a war with the United States was to dictate terms of peace inside the White House. In saying this Yamamoto recognized that it was impossible to achieve victory. The problem that he and his colleagues faced in the opening months of 1942 was how to achieve the impossible.

By any rational Western standard the strategy that Japan adopted when she went to war was both incomprehensible and fraught with such dangers as to be positively suicidal. But the strategy is understandable, if not

454   EMPIRES IN THE BALANCE

sensible, when set against the twin realizations that in 1941 Japan believed she had no option but to go to war and that to the Japanese the moral and psychological aspects of war were more important than material considerations. In all her wars since the mid-nineteenth century, Japan had triumphed over material odds. She considered the Pacific war in the same light as her earlier encounters. To overcome material inferiority the Japanese relied, with a confidence that bordered on blind faith, on the one facet of their moral and psychological ascendency over their enemies. This was their acceptance of death, indeed their total willingness to die, in the service of a divine emperor. Events were to confirm the advantages of such commitment, but only within certain limits. During the latter stages of the Pacific war the Japanese resorted to suicide tactics in a desperate effort not to achieve victory but to ward off defeat. In that effort American sailors who fought to live proved more than a match for Japanese airmen who had to die in order to fight. This was proof, if proof was needed, that moral factors cannot hope to compensate for too severe a material deficit—though this evidence, again, was not available to Japan in 1941.

What was evident in 1941, however, was a quite different phenomenon, one identified by Chuichi Hara as "victory disease." This can be defined precisely as the absolute conviction on the part of the Japanese that their own martial prowess was irresistible. It is easy to see from where the Japanese drew their faith. The belief obviously stemmed from the mythology that told of Japan's divine origins and her invulnerability to conquest over two millenia of recorded history. A nation that could trace back through the ages an unbroken history of immunity from defeat could not envisage the prospect of defeat. The part of the national mystique that portrayed Japan as historically destined to lead eastern Asia could not contemplate the limitations that material factors placed upon divine purpose. But if it was easy to see from where the Japanese drew their faith, it is not so easy to see the full implications of this faith and of the "disease" for Japanese thinking in 1941–42.

One can identify three major areas where the blindness caused by "victory disease," with its warping of political and military realities, had a most pernicious effect on Japanese conduct of the war. First, there was the question of the Japanese attitude to the phenomenon of war itself. The Japanese proved utterly incapable of recognizing the totality of war as fought in the present century. To rely completely on armed strength or moral factors to achieve victory is to deny the reality that in war these account for no more than part of the struggle. The totality of war is indivisible, and there are limits on the extent to which any single aspect can prove effective. Japan's historical experience gave rise to the mistaken assumption that war could be circumscribed and its scope limited and controlled through the imposition of Japanese will upon the course of events. With such a fundamental error as the basis of their strategy, the Japanese failed to consider the basic truth, uttered years later by MacArthur but known throughout the years, that "there is no substitute for victory." They failed to realize that the alternative to total war was not limited war but total defeat, that the consequence of failing to secure decisive success would be defeat that encompassed Hiroshima and Nagasaki.

The second and similarly misguided perception was Japan's drastic underestimation of foreign powers. This was particularly marked in the most important decision-making organ of the state, the Imperial Army. The army hierarchy was narrow in its outlook, insular, and lacking in experience with foreigners, except the Chinese. In China, however, the experience of war merely confirmed the army in its contempt for foreigners. The treatment the Japanese army meted out to its Chinese foes was as bad as any of the barbarities practiced by Hitler's forces. It can be explained only in terms of the utter disdain the Japanese felt for foreigners who were weaker and, to borrow a word, *Untermenschen*. This phenomenon was less marked in the Imperial Navy, partly because the navy had more opportunities than the army for contact with foreigners. But Japan as a whole, fed as she was on a diet of fervent martial nationalism, was increasingly contemptuous of foreign powers. Bitterness, humiliation, and a vicious resentment had been bred into Japanese national consciousness as a result of snubs and insults. Whether calculated or unintended, these rankled equally and deeply. This led to a desperate yearning for revenge at any price. It also led the Japanese to underestimate the resolve of foreigners thought to be obsessed with material well-being rather than with political matters. The failure of the democracies in the thirties to match their words with actions contrasted with the Japanese tradition of direct action, and confirmed in Japanese eyes the correctness of their low estimation of Western nations. The fundamental underestimation of American strength and determination stemmed not simply from ignorance of the Americans but from the unrealistic values prevalent in Japanese society at that time. The Japanese regarded the behavior of the democracies in the thirties as the norm, not the exception. They failed to understand that democracies are invariably slow to act but are not inclined to compromise when they do. The effort that is involved in mobilizing a democracy for war makes it all but impossible for it to fight for less than total victory.

The third element was an already powerful nationalist aspiration that claimed for itself the leadership of eastern Asia, with all the brutal insensitivity such a wholesale takeover implied for the subject people of the area. The Japanese saw the "liberation" of eastern Asia from the yoke of white imperialism as their right and duty. They genuinely had no idea why they should encounter resistance from their fellow Asians. The Japanese notions of "Asia for the Asiatics" and the "Southeast Asia Co-Prosperity Sphere" were not mere propaganda devices aimed at deceiving the gullible and feebleminded; the Japanese really believed in these ideas. The very use of the term *co-prosperity* was significant. The Japanese thought they were offering partnership to the peoples of Southeast Asia, and were convinced they would be welcomed by the indigenous populations. They deluded themselves. They believed that people who had lived under white control would accept Japanese leadership and direction in what was clearly going to be a difficult transitional period before the full benefits of cooperation and partnership became obvious. In this the Japanese misjudged the mood of the Asians as badly as they underestimated the resolve of the democracies.

Many Asians, in China, in the Dutch East Indies, in Burma, in India, and even in Malaya, could justify collaboration with the Japanese in precisely these terms. Such people felt that their countries were better served as protectorates of Japan than as playthings of imperialists. But most Asians aspired towards self-determination and independence. There was relatively little enthusiasm for changing one form of foreign rule for another, particularly when the new masters came complete with the *Kempeitai*, the army's secret police that was indistinguishable except by nationality and uniform from such organizations as the Gestapo and N.K.V.D. In the long run this failure to recognize in other Asians the same kinds of nationalist aspirations, the same xenophobia the Japanese themselves felt, was one of the most serious of Japanese shortcomings in the period 1942–45. The Japanese simply could not understand that nationalist feeling could turn against them in exactly the same way that their own nationalism had turned against the Americans and Europeans.

But such matters were reserved for the future, and for the moment the direction of the Japanese war effort was largely being shaped by one man, Yamamoto. The commander in chief of the Combined Fleet was one of the few members of the Japanese high command who retained some form of balanced judgment about the realities of power before the outbreak of the Pacific war and during the first months of victory. His time in Europe, at Harvard, and as attache in Washington had made him aware of the potential power of the democracies. He was as patriotic as the next man but shared none of the commonly held illusions of victory. His prewar prophecy, that on the outbreak of war his forces would run amok for six months or so but that thereafter he could not promise success, was to be grimly confirmed by events. Such a view certainly sets Yamamoto apart from most of his colleagues, but this prophecy has been widely used to show that the man possessed an exceptional ability, strategic insight, and awareness not shared by the overwhelming number of his peers. This is hardly accurate. Yamamoto was more than acute in many of his observations, and he made no secret of his views. Of all his qualities perhaps the most notable was his

moral courage in stating the obvious when so many men of honesty and
integrity were being silenced by fear of assassination. But expressing a view
is not necessarily proof of strategic genius, and some of the acclaim
accorded to him must be questioned.

Yamamoto had one quality that is essential in any commander: confidence in the force he commanded and in his own ability as a commander
and strategist. It must be an open question whether or not his confidence in
these matters tipped over into overconfidence. He was a pioneer of carrier
warfare, but no more so than many others from different nations who have
received none of the accolades he did. It must be doubted, moreover,
whether he grasped the full implications of carrier warfare, especially in
light of his continued emphasis on battleships and his failure to appreciate
the importance of formulating defensive tactics to counter air attacks on
carriers. Had he foreseen any countermeasures to carrier aircraft attack, it
might be possible to prove some of the claims of genius made on his behalf,
but there is no evidence from his actions that this was the case. One must
question, moreover, his toleration of such subordinates as Nagumo, who
was entrusted with the all-important carrier arm. Nagumo was never really
up to the task set him and never showed any real grasp of the strategic and
tactical problems posed by his command; yet Yamamoto, despite his

Admiral Isoroku Yamamoto, commander in chief of the Combined Fleet, 1939–43.
Yamamoto was an organizer and a visionary of genius, but there was little about his
command of operations that confirms his high reputation. He was assassinated in
April 1943 before the final decline of the Imperial Navy became obvious. Naval
History NH 79462

criticisms of Nagumo's conduct of operations at Pearl Harbor, did not remove him from his command.

Moreover, Yamamoto's conduct of the three separate battles he personally directed was questionable by any standard. He also seems to have been incapable of forming a simple battle plan and of adhering to the fundamental principle of war—the concentration of force to achieve the objective. From the Japanese side, the battle of Midway was characterized by a dispersal of force that precluded mutual support and thus exposed the formations to defeat in detail before other units could assist them. The extremely complicated nature of the Midway battle plan, even without the compromise of Japanese security that in fact doomed it, made it prone to disruption and failure. Yamamoto's reaction to the Guadalcanal crisis was at best sluggish. The commander in chief of the Combined Fleet erred by feeding in small forces piecemeal to the battle rather than en masse, thus condemning the Japanese to fight for a victory that was always just beyond their reach. His conduct of the battle of the Eastern Solomons, sometimes called the battle of the Solomons Sea, also left much to be desired. The same dispersal of force that had been at the root of the Midway disaster was repeated, while the complexity of movements almost resulted in defeat. Yamamoto neglected to press his advantage at the end of the battle, thereby failing to secure a significant tactical success that alone would have justified his losses. At one stage in this battle Yamamoto had a strategic and tactical victory within his grasp, but he did not capitalize on the situation, and the chance never repeated itself. His subsequent conduct of the air offensive over the Bismarcks in April 1943 was noteworthy for the lack of a concentrated force equal to the task in hand, the failure to maintain a high tempo of sustained operations in order to achieve the objective, and for Yamamoto's unwillingness or inability to sift tactical analysis thoroughly.

Unlike such commanders as Ozawa, Halsey, Spruance, and Cunningham, Yamamoto seems to have had no "feel" for a situation. He certainly had qualities of genius. The Pearl Harbor attack will always stand as his crowning achievement. The extent of vision, the audacity, the very idea of steaming nearly 4,000 miles to attack an enemy's home base, and the nerve he showed in forcing through the operation against widespread opposition all were cruelly repaid on that day. He was unlucky, but he certainly had his blind spots and his failings; these seem to have been given inadequate consideration in overall assessments of him as a commander.

At least Yamamoto did not lose sight of the reality that the Japanese superiority over the Americans at sea was only transitory, unless the U.S. Pacific Fleet could be annihilated. After the Pearl Harbor debacle the Americans redeployed two carriers from the Atlantic to support the three already in the Pacific. Thus, within days of the outbreak of the Pacific war, there was a rough parity in fleet carriers between Japan and the United

States in the Pacific theater, with the obvious proviso that at the time the Americans could not hope to offer battle because of their inferiority in overall numbers, battleship strength, certain vital equipment, and battle technique, as well as their defensive commitments. But Yamamoto was aware that the American carriers had to be eliminated before new ones entered service. When those new carriers were commissioned, the American superiority of numbers was certain to make the U.S. Pacific Fleet unchallengeable. Yamamoto was aware of the danger even as his forces overran Southeast Asia, and as they did so he hardened in the conviction that immediately after the initial phase of conquest the Japanese fleet would have to turn eastwards to provoke, fight, and win a decisive engagement with the Americans, who alone posed a threat to Japanese security. In fact, what he had to do was finish the job that had been bungled so badly at and immediately after Pearl Harbor.

But even Yamamoto failed to realize how little time was left to Japan and her carriers. He did not recognize that, after its considerable exertions between December 1941 and March 1942, the carrier force needed rest, refitting, and retraining. He also failed to appreciate the qualitative decline of Japanese naval aviation as a result of the losses and accidents of five months of war. He sanctioned the Indian Ocean sortie in the belief that Japan had time to deal with the British before the Americans could make any significant move. Despite the Doolittle Raid, this view was correct; the aim and execution of the Indian Ocean operation were what lacked decisiveness. But even after the raid, Yamamoto and the Japanese high command believed they still had the time and the means to use some of the carriers in the Southwest Pacific before turning to deal with the American main force units in the central Pacific. On tactical grounds alone two errors are discernible in this calculation. If the central Pacific was the main area of operations, it was a mistake to pursue secondary objectives before concentrating on primary objectives, thereby making the achievement of primary aims dependent on the prior realization of secondary goals. Moreover, if the operations in the Southwest Pacific were sufficiently important to justify deploying carriers, then the participation of all and not just some of them was warranted. These errors were crucial, and so was the mistaken assumption that the Japanese had the time to mount a secondary offensive. If the clash with the Americans was the decisive strategic aspect of the Pacific war, as all members of the Japanese high command believed certainly after 18 April, and if the issue had to be forced quickly, then every effort had to be made for that eventuality, not dissipated on secondary or tactical objectives. There was certainly not the time to mount a secondary operation deep in the Southwest Pacific. Such an operation certainly maintained the tempo of the Pacific war, but it did so only at the expense of concentrating on the main aim and preparing forces to execute that aim.

This division of attention and resources between two objectives in May and June 1942 was to be utterly disastrous for Japan, since it left her open to defeat in detail. The concentration of all carrier forces for either operation, at the Coral Sea or Midway, almost surely would have meant such an overwhelming superiority of force for the Japanese that crushing victory in either or both instances would have been assured—if the Americans chose to give battle. The forces that were deployed to the Coral Sea and thereby lost to the Combined Fleet for the Midway operation (the light carrier *Shoho*, which was sunk; and the fleet carriers *Zuikaku* and *Shokaku*, which were badly mauled) were the difference between victory and defeat at Midway. Yet Yamamoto and the Japanese naval command, after having decided upon the Midway operation for June, sanctioned the commitment of carriers to the Southwest Pacific in May. By any standard, the manner in which policy was settled and decisions reached by the Imperial Navy was incredible.

The Doolittle Raid, therefore, forced the Japanese high command to face up to the reality that their conquests could not be secured, that the safety of the homeland could not be guaranteed, and that the peoples of Southeast Asia could not be reconciled to Japanese rule unless and until the Americans were defeated. The Japanese correctly saw the Doolittle Raid as the direct consequence of their failure to account for the enemy carriers either at Pearl Harbor or during the subsequent months of war. They correctly saw that more such raids, mounted in ever-growing strength, would follow unless the Americans were defeated quickly in open battle. But the Japanese, as we have seen, could not respond to this situation effectively, confused as they were by divergent objectives and their inability to comprehend the importance of time. In addition, they could not foresee two further realities: that in shattering American and European power throughout the Far East they had merely released the uncontrollable forces of nationalism and communism throughout eastern Asia; and that the alternative to decisive victory was the total devastation of the empire. Thus, in spite of a series of victories, the Japanese were forced to turn again to the central Pacific—impelled to do so by a single raid that cost the Americans less than 5 percent of the number of aircraft they lost to Nagumo's carriers on that December morning at Pearl Harbor. The Japanese turned eastwards, to reap at Midway the whirlwind of what had been sown with prodigal abandon in the thirties, on 7 December 1941, and in the vast expanses of ocean between Hawaii and Ceylon in the euphoric days of triumph.

Bibliography

OFFICIAL HISTORIES

Bhargava, K. D., and Sastri, K. N. V. *The Official History of the Indian Armed Forces in the Second World War 1939–1945: Campaigns in South East Asia, 1941–1942.* Kanpur: Combined Inter-Service Historical Section, India & Pakistan, 1960.

Butler, J. R. M. *History of the Second World War: Grand Strategy, September 1939–June 1941.* Vol. 2. United Kingdom Military Series. London: Her Majesty's Stationers Office, 1957.

————. *History of the Second World War: Grand Strategy, June 1941–August 1942.* Vol. 3, part 2. United Kingdom Military Series. London: Her Majesty's Stationers Office, 1964.

Cline, R. S. *The United States Army in World War Two: The War Department, Washington Command Post: The Operations Division.* Washington: Department of the Army, 1951.

Craven, N. F., and Cate, J. L., eds. *The Army Air Forces in World War Two: Plans and Early Operations, January 1939–August 1942.* Vol. 1. Chicago: University of Chicago Press, 1948.

Gibbs, N. H. *History of the Second World War: Grand Strategy, Rearmament Policy.* Vol. 1. United Kingdom Military Series. London: Her Majesty's Stationers Office, 1976.

Gill, G. Hermon. *Australia in the War of 1939–1945, Series 2: Navy. Royal Australian Navy 1939–1942.* Vol. 1. Canberra: Australian War Memorial, 1957.

Gillespie, O. A. *New Zealand in the Second World War: The Pacific*. Wellington: Department of Internal Affairs, 1952.

Gillson, D. *Australia in the War of 1939–1945, Series 3: Air. Royal Australian Air Force 1939–1942*. Vol. 1. Canberra: Australian War Memorial, 1962.

Greenfield, K. R., ed. *The United States Army in World War Two: Command Decisions*. Washington: Department of the Army, 1960.

Gwyer, J. M. A. *History of the Second World War: Grand Strategy, June 1941–August 1942*. Vol. 3, part 1. United Kingdom Military Series. London: Her Majesty's Stationers Office, 1964.

Hoogenband, C. van den, and Schotborgh, L. *Nederlands-Indie contra Japan*. Vol. 2. The Hague: Department of Defense, 1949.

Kirby, S. Woodburn. *History of the Second World War: The War against Japan, India's Most Dangerous Hour*. Vol. 2. United Kingdom Military Series. London: Her Majesty's Stationers Office, 1958.

―――. *History of the Second World War: The War against Japan, The Loss of Singapore*. Vol. 1. United Kingdom Military Series. London: Her Majesty's Stationers Office, 1957.

Leighton, R. M., and Coakley, R. W. *The United States Army in World War Two: The War Department, Global Logistics and Strategy*. Washington: Department of the Army, 1955.

McCarthy, D. *Australia in the War of 1939–1945, Series 1: Army. The South West Pacific Area—First Year*. Vol. 5. Canberra: Australian War Memorial, 1959.

Matloff, M., and Snell, E. H. *The United States Army in World War Two: The War Department, Strategic Planning for Coalition Warfare*. Washington: Department of the Army, 1953.

Morison, S. E. *History of U.S. Naval Operations in World War Two: The Rising Sun in the Pacific, 1931–April 1942*. Vol. 3. Boston: Little, Brown, 1968.

Morton, L. *The United States Army in World War Two: The War in the Pacific, The Fall of the Philippines*. Washington: Department of the Army, 1951.

―――. *The United States Army in World War Two: Strategy and Command*. Washington: Department of the Army, 1962.

Prasad, B. *The Official History of the Indian Armed Forces in the Second World War 1939–1945: Defence of India, Policy and Plans*. Kanpur: Combined Inter-Service Historical Section, India & Pakistan, 1963.

Prasad, B., ed. *The Official History of the Indian Armed Forces in the Second World War 1939–1945: The Retreat from Burma 1941–1942*. Calcutta: Combined Inter-Service Historical Section, India & Pakistan, 1952.

Romanus, C. F., and Sunderland, R. *The United States Army in World War Two: The China-Burma-India Theater, Stilwell's Mission to China*. Washington: Department of the Army, 1953.

Roskill, S. W. *History of the Second World War: The War at Sea, The Defensive*. Vol. 1. United Kingdom Military Series. London: Her Majesty's Stationers Office, 1954.

―――. *History of the Second World War: The War at Sea, The Period of Balance*. Vol. 2. United Kingdom Military Series. London: Her Majesty's Stationers Office, 1957.

————. *History of the Second World War: The War at Sea, The Offensive.* Vol. 3, part 2. United Kingdom Military Series. London: Her Majesty's Stationers Office, 1961.

Waters, S. D. *New Zealand in the Second World War: The Royal New Zealand Navy.* Wellington: Department of Internal Affairs, 1956.

Watson, M. S. *The United States Army in World War Two: The War Department, Chief of Staff: Plans and Preparations.* Washington: Department of the Army, 1950.

Wigmore, L. *Australia in the War of 1939–1945, Series 1: Army, The Japanese Thrust.* Vol. 4. Canberra: Australian War Memorial, 1957.

Williams, M. H. *The United States Army in World War Two: Special Studies, Chronology 1941–1945.* Washington: Department of the Army, 1958.

Woodward, L. *History of the Second World War: British Foreign Policy in the Second World War.* Vol. 1. United Kingdom Military Series. London: Her Majesty's Stationers Office, 1970.

————. *History of the Second World War: British Foreign Policy in the Second World War.* Vol. 2. United Kingdom Military Series. London: Her Majesty's Stationers Office, 1971.

STATISTICAL AND REFERENCE MATERIAL

Atlas of the Oceans. London: Mitchell Beazley, 1977.

Statesman's Year Book and *Whitaker's Almanak.* current editions.

The Far East and Australasia: A Survey and Dictionary of Asia and the Pacific. London: Europa, 1976.

The Times Atlas of World History. London: Times Books, 1979.

The Times World Index Gazetteer. London: Times Books, 1965.

The West Point Atlas of American Wars: 1900–1953. Vol. 2. New York: Praeger, 1959.

BOOKS

Acheson, Dean. *Present at the Creation: My Years at the State Department.* London: Hamish Hamilton, 1970.

Agawa, Hiroyuki. *The Reluctant Admiral: Yamamoto and the Imperial Navy.* Annapolis: Naval Institute Press, Tokyo: Kodansha International, 1979.

Alexander, Lord. *The Alexander Memoirs 1940–1945.* Edited by John North. London: Cassell, 1962.

Allen, G. C. *A Short Economic History of Modern Japan 1867–1937.* London: Allen and Unwin, 1966.

Allen, Louis. *Singapore 1941–1942.* London: Davies-Poynter, 1977.

Argyle, Christopher J. *Japan at War.* London: Barker, 1976.

Ash, Bernard. *Someone Had Blundered: The Story of the Repulse and Prince of Wales.* London: Joseph, 1960.

Attiwill, K. *The Singapore Story.* London: Muller, 1959.

Barber, Noel. *Sinister Twilight: The Fall and Rise Again of Singapore.* London: Collins, 1968.

Barker, A. J. *Pearl Harbor.* London: Macdonald, 1970.

————. *Yamashita*. New York: Ballantine, 1973.

Beasley, W. G. *The Modern History of Japan*. London: Weidenfeld and Nicolson, 1963.

Belote, James H., and Belote, William M. *Titan of the Seas: The Development and Operations of Japanese and American Carrier Task Forces During World War II*. New York: Harper and Row, 1975.

Benda, Harry Jindrick. *The Crescent and the Rising Sun: Indonesian Islam under the Japanese Occupation*. New York: Institute of Pacific Relations, 1958.

Bond, Brian, ed. *Chief of Staff: The Diaries of Lieutenant General Sir Henry Pownall, 1940–1945*. Vol. 2. London: Cooper, 1974.

Borg, Dorothy. *The U.S. and the Far Eastern Crisis of 1933–1938*. Cambridge, Mass., 1964.

Boxer, C. R. *The Dutch Seaborne Empire 1600–1800*. London: Hutchinson, 1965.

Braisted, William Reynolds. *The United States Navy in the Pacific 1909–1922*. Austin: University of Texas Press, 1971.

Brereton, Lewis H. *The Brereton Diaries*. New York: Morrow, 1946.

Brice, Martin H. *The Royal Navy and the Sino-Japanese Incident*. London: Allen, 1973.

Bromley, J. S., ed. *The New Cambridge Modern History: The Rise of Great Britain and Russia 1688–1715/25*. Vol. 6. Cambridge: Cambridge University Press, 1970.

Brown, Courtney. *Tojo: The Last Banzai*. London: Corgi, 1969.

Brown, David. *Carrier Operations in World War II: The Pacific Navies December 1941–February 1943*. Vol. 2. London: Allan, 1974.

————. *Aircraft Carriers*. London: Macdonald and Jane's, 1977.

Bruce, George. *Sea Battles of the Twentieth Century*. London: Hamlyn, 1973.

Bueschel, Richard M. *Mitsubishi A6M1/2/-2N Zero-sen*. London: Osprey, 1970.

Burns, James M. *Roosevelt: The Lion and the Fox*. London: Secker and Warburg, 1956.

————. *Roosevelt: The Soldier of Freedom 1940–1945*. London: Weidenfeld and Nicolson, 1971.

Burtness, Paul S., and Ober, Warren U., eds. *The Puzzle of Pearl Harbor*. Evanston: North Illinois University Press, 1962.

Bury, J. P. T., ed. *The New Cambridge Modern History: The Zenith of European Power 1830–1870*. Vol. 10. Cambridge: Cambridge University Press, 1960.

Buss, Claude A. *The Far East*. New York: Macmillan, 1955.

Butow, Robert J. C. *Tojo and the Coming of War*. Princeton, N.J.: Princeton University Press, 1961.

Bywater, Hector C. *Sea Power in the Pacific*. London: Constable, 1921.

Caffrey, Kate. *Out in the Midday Sun: Singapore 1940–1945*. London: Deutsch, 1974.

Callahan, Raymond. *Burma 1942–1945*. London: Davies-Poynter, 1979.

————. *The Worst Disaster: The Fall of Singapore*. London: Associated Universities, 1974.

Calvert, Mike. *Slim*. New York: Ballantine, 1973.

Carew, Tim. *The Fall of Hong Kong*. London: Blond, 1961.

————. *Hostages to Fortune*. London: Hamish Hamilton, 1971.

————. *The Longest Retreat: The Burma Campaign 1942*. London: Hamish Hamilton, 1969.

Carsten, F. L., ed. *The New Cambridge Modern History: The Ascendancy of France 1648–1688*. Vol. 5. Cambridge: Cambridge University Press, 1961.

Chesneaux, Jean; Le Barbier, Françoise; and Bergère, Marie-Claire. *China from the Opium Wars to the 1911 Revolution*. Hassocks: Harvester, 1979.

————. *China from the 1911 Revolution to Liberation*. Hassocks: Harvester, 1979.

Ch'en, Jerome. *China and the West: Society and Culture*. London: Hutchinson, 1979.

————. *Mao and the Chinese Revolution*. London: Oxford University Press, 1965.

Chihaya, Masataka. *I. J. N. Yamato and Musashi*. Windsor: Profile, 1973.

Chihaya, Masataka, and Abe, Yasuo. *I. J. N. Yukikaze*. Windsor: Profile, 1972.

Churchill, Winston S. *The Second World War: The Gathering Storm*. Vol. 1. London: Cassell, 1948.

————. *The Second World War: Their Finest Hour*. Vol. 2. London: Cassell, 1949.

————. *The Second World War: The Grand Alliance*. Vol. 3. London: Cassell, 1950.

————. *The Second World War: The Hinge of Fate*. Vol. 4. London: Cassell, 1951.

Clubb, O. Edmund. *Twentieth Century China*. New York: Columbia University Press, 1964.

Clyde, Paul Hibbert. *The Far East: A History of the Impact of the West on Eastern Asia*. New York: Prentice Hall, 1948.

Collier, Basil. *Japan at War: An Illustrated History of the War in the Far East 1931–1945*. London: Sidgwick and Jackson, 1975.

————. *Japanese Aircraft of World War II*. London: Sidgwick and Jackson, 1979.

————. *The War in the Far East 1941 1945: A Military History*. London: Heinemann, 1969.

Connell, John. *Wavell: Supreme Commander*. Edited and Completed by M. Roberts. London: Collins, 1969.

Cooper, J. P., ed. *The New Cambridge Modern History: The Decline of Spain and the Thirty Years War 1609–1648/59*. Vol. 4. Cambridge: Cambridge University Press, 1970.

Corbett, Julian S. *Some Principles of Maritime Strategy*. London: Longmans, Green, 1938.

Cowan, C. D., ed. *The Economic Development of South East Asia: Studies in Economic History and Political Economy*. London: Allen and Unwin, 1961.

Crawley, C. W., ed. *The New Cambridge Modern History: War and Peace in an Age of Upheaval 1793–1830*. Vol. 9. Cambridge: Cambridge University Press, 1975.

Crowley, James B. *Japan's Quest for Autonomy: National Security and Foreign Policy 1900–1938*. Princeton, N.J.: Princeton University Press, 1966.

d'Albas, Andrieu. *Death of a Navy: Japanese Sea Power in the Second World War*. London: Hale, 1957.

Dening, Esler. *Japan*. New York: Praeger, 1961.

Dulin, Robert O., and Garzke, William H., Jr. *Battleships: U.S. Battleships in World War II*. London: Macdonald and Jane's, 1976.

Dull, Paul S. *A Battle History of the Imperial Japanese Navy (1941–1945)*. Annapolis: Naval Institute Press, Cambridge: Patrick Stephens, 1978.

Dupuy, Trevor Nevitt. *Asiatic Land Battles: Japanese Ambitions in the Pacific*. New York: Watts, 1963.

Earle, Edward Mead, ed. *Makers of Modern Strategy: Military Thought from Machiavelli to Hitler*. Princeton, N.J.: Princeton University Press, 1966.

Endacott, G. B. *Hong Kong Eclipse*. Edited by Alan Birch. London: Oxford University Press, 1978.

Evans, Geoffrey. *Slim as Military Commander*. London: Batsford, 1969.

Falk, Stanley L. *Seventy Days to Singapore: The Malayan Campaign 1941–1942*. London: Hale, 1975.

Farago, Ladislas. *The Broken Seal: The Story of "Operation Magic" and the Pearl Harbor Disaster*. London: Barker, 1967.

Field, Ellen. *Twilight in Hong Kong*. London: Muller, 1960.

Fitzgerald, C. P. *The Birth of Communist China*. New York: Penguin, 1964.

———. *The Concise History of East Asia*. London: Heinemann, 1966.

Francillon, R. J. *Japanese Aircraft of the Pacific War*. New York: Putnam, 1970.

———. *Japanese Carrier Air Groups 1941–1945*. London: Osprey, 1979.

———. *U.S. Navy Carrier Air Groups: Pacific 1941–1945*. London: Osprey, 1978.

Freeman, Roger A. *American Bombers of World War II*. Windsor: Hylton Lacy, 1964.

———. *B-17 Fortress at War*. London: Allan, 1977.

Friedman, Norman. *Battleship Design and Development 1905–1945*. Greenwich, Conn.: Conway Maritime, 1978.

Friend, Theodore. *Between Two Empires: The Ordeal of the Philippines*. New Haven, Conn.: Yale University Press, 1968.

Fuchida, Mitsuo, and Okumiya, Masatake. *Midway: The Battle that Doomed Japan*. London: Hutchinson, 1957.

Glover, E. M. *The Story of the Japanese Campaign in British Malaya*. London: Muller, 1949.

Goodwin, A., ed. *The New Cambridge Modern History: The American and French Revolutions 1763–1793*. Vol. 8. Cambridge: Cambridge University Press, 1968.

Greenfell, Russell. *Main Fleet to Singapore*. London: Faber and Faber, 1951.

Grew, Joseph C. *Ten Years in Japan*. London: Hammond, Hammond, 1944.

Gunston, Bill. *Classic Aircraft—Bombers*. London: Hamlyn, 1978.

———. *The Encyclopedia of the World's Combat Aircraft*. London: Salamander, 1976.

Hagan, Kenneth J., ed. *In Peace and War: Interpretations of American Naval History 1775–1978*. Westport, Conn.: Greenwood, 1978.

Hall, John Whitney. *Japan from Prehistory to Modern Times*. London: Weidenfeld and Nicolson, 1970.

Hargreaves, Reginald, *Red Sun Rising: The Siege of Port Arthur*. London: Weidenfeld and Nicolson, 1962.

Hart, Robert A. *The Great White Fleet: Its Voyage Around the World*. Boston: Little, Brown, 1965.

Hayashi, Saburo, in collaboration with Coox, Alvin D. *Kogun: The Japanese Army in the Pacific War*. Westport, Conn.: Greenwood, 1978.

Hezlett, Arthur. *The Aircraft and Sea Power*. London: Davies, 1970.

———. *The Submarine and Sea Power*. London: Davies, 1967.

Hilson, Norman. *Alexander of Tunis: A Biographical Portrait*. London: Allen, 1952.

Hinsley, F. H., ed. *The New Cambridge Modern History: Material Progress and World Wide Problems 1870–1898*. Vol. 11. Cambridge: Cambridge University Press, 1962.

Hoehling, A. A. *The Week Before Pearl Harbor*. London: Hale, 1963.

Hough, Richard. *Dreadnought: A History of the Modern Battleship*. Cambridge: Patrick Stephens, 1975.

———. *The Fleet That Had to Die*. London: Chatto and Windus, 1963.

————. *The Hunting of Force Z*. London: Collins, 1963.

Hoyt, Edwin P. *How They Won the War in the Pacific: Nimitz and His Admirals*. New York: Weybridge and Talley, 1970.

Hsu, Immanuel C. Y. *The Rise of Modern China*. London: Oxford University Press, 1975.

Hudson, G. F. *The Far East in World Politics: A Study in Recent History*. London: Oxford University Press, 1937.

Hughes, E. R. *The Invasion of China by the Western World*. London: Black, 1937.

Hull, Cordell. *Memoirs* (2 vols.). New York: Macmillan, 1948.

Ienaga, Saburo. *Japan's Last War: World War II and the Japanese 1931–1945*. Oxford: Blackwell, 1979.

Ito, Masanori. *The End of the Imperial Navy*. London: Weidenfeld and Nicolson, 1956.

James, David H. *The Rise and Fall of the Japanese Empire*. London: Allen and Unwin, 1951.

James, D. Clayton. *The Years of MacArthur: 1941–1945*. Vol. 2. Boston: Houghton Mifflin, 1975.

Jentschura, Hansgeorg; Jung, Dieter; and Mickel, Peter. *Warships of the Imperial Japanese Navy 1869–1945*. Annapolis: Naval Institute Press, London: Arms and Armour, 1977.

Jordan, Gerald, ed. *Naval Warfare in the Twentieth Century*. London: Croom Helm, 1977.

Kahin, George McTurnan. *Nationalism and Revolution in Indonesia*. Ithaca, N.Y.: Cornell University Press, 1952.

Kahn, David. *The Code Breakers: The Story of Secret Writing*. London: Weidenfeld and Nicolson, 1966.

Kajuna, Morinosuke. *The Emergence of Japan as a World Power*. Rutland, Vt.: Tuttle, 1968.

Kase, Toshikazu. *Eclipse of the Rising Sun*. London: Cape, 1951.

Kemp, Peter. *Victory at Sea 1939–1945*. London: Muller, 1957.

Kennan, George F. *American Diplomacy 1900–1950*. Chicago: University of Chicago Press, 1969.

————. *Memoirs 1925–1950*. London: Hutchinson, 1968.

Kennedy, Malcolm D. *A History of Japan*. London: Weidenfeld and Nicolson, 1963.

Kennedy, Paul M. *The Rise and Fall of British Naval Mastery*. London: Allen, Lane, 1976.

Khoo, Kay Kim, ed. *The History of South East, South and East Asia: Essays and Documents*. London: Oxford University Press, 1977.

King, Ernest J., and Whitehill, Walter M. *Fleet Admiral King*. London: Eyre and Spottiswoode, 1953.

Kirby, S. Woodburn. *Singapore: The Chain of Disaster*. London: Cassell, 1971.

Lash, Joseph P. *Roosevelt and Churchill: The Partnership that Saved the West*. London: Deutsch, 1977.

Leasor, James. *Singapore: The Battle that Changed the World*. London: Hodder and Stoughton, 1968.

Lebra, Joyce C., ed. *Japan's Greater East Asia Co-Prosperity Sphere: Selected Readings and Documents*. London: Oxford University Press, 1975.

Legg, Frank Hooper. *The Gordon Bennett Story*. Sydney: Angus and Robertson, 1965.

Lenton, H. T., and Colledge, J. J. *Warships of World War II*. London: Allan, 1964.

Lewin, Ronald. *Slim: The Standardbearer*. London: Cooper, 1976.

Lewis, Michael. *The Navy of Britain: A Historical Portrait*. London: Allen and Unwin, 1948.

Li, Lincoln. *The Japanese Army in North China 1937–1941: Problems of Political and Economic Control*. London: Oxford University Press, 1975.

Lindsay, J. O., ed. *The New Cambridge Modern History: The Old Regime 1713–1763*. Vol. 7. Cambridge: Cambridge University Press, 1966.

Lindsay, Oliver. *The Lasting Honour: The Fall of Hong Kong 1941*. London: Hamish Hamilton, 1978.

Lockwood, Douglas Wright. *Australia's Pearl Harbour: Darwin 1942*. Melbourne: Cassell, 1966.

Long, Gavin M. *MacArthur as Military Commander*. London: Batsford, 1969.

Longford, Joseph H. *Japan*. London: Hodder and Stoughton, 1923.

Lord, Walter. *Day of Infamy*. New York: Holt, Rinehart and Winston, 1957.

Lundstrom, John B. *The First South Pacific Campaign: Pacific Fleet Strategy December 1941–June 1942*. Annapolis: Naval Institute Press, 1976.

MacArthur, Douglas. *Reminiscences*. London: Heinemann, 1965.

Macintyre, Donald. *Aircraft Carrier: The Majestic Weapon*. London: Purnell, 1968.

———. *Battle for the Pacific*. London: Batsford, 1966.

———. *Sea Power in the Pacific: A History from the Sixteenth Century to the Present Day*. London: Barker, 1972.

Macintyre, Donald, and Preston, Antony, consultants. *The Encyclopaedia of Sea Warfare*. London: Hamlyn, 1975.

MacIntyre, W. David. *The Rise and Fall of the Singapore Naval Base*. New York: Macmillan, 1979.

McKelvie, Roy. *The War in Burma*. London: Methuen, 1948.

McLaren, Walter Wallace. *A Political History of Japan during the Meiji Era 1867–1912*. London: Allen and Unwin, 1916.

Mahan, Alfred Thayer. *The Influence of Sea Power upon History 1660–1783*. London: Associated Universities, 1965.

Manchester, William. *American Caesar: Douglas MacArthur 1880–1964*. London: Hutchinson, 1979.

Marder, Arthur J. *The Anatomy of British Sea Power: A History of British Naval Policy in the Pre-dreadnought Era 1880–1904*. London: Cass, 1964.

———. *From the Dardanelles to Oran: Studies of the Royal Navy in War and Peace*. London: Oxford University Press, 1974.

Mains, Tony. *The Retreat from Burma: An Intelligence Officer's Personal Story*. South Asia Books, 1973.

Mayer, Sydney L. *The Japanese War Machine*. London: Bison, 1976.

Mehden, Fred. Robert von der. *Southeast Asia 1930–1970*. London: Thames and Hudson, 1974.

Michael, Franz H., and Taylor, George E. *The Far East in the Modern World*. New York: Holt, Rinehart and Winston, 1964.

Millis, Walter. *This Is Pearl! The United States and Japan 1941*. New York: Morrow, 1947.

Millis, Walter, ed. *The Forrestal Diaries*. London: Cassell, 1952.

Morison, Samuel Eliot. *The Two-Ocean War: A Short History of the U.S. Navy in the Second World War*. Boston: Little, Brown, 1963.

Morris, Ivan, ed. *Japan 1931–1945: Militarism, Fascism, Japanism?* Boston: Heath, 1963.

Mowat, C. L., ed. *The New Cambridge Modern History: The Shifting Balance of World Forces 1898–1945*. Vol. 12, 2nd. ed., Cambridge: Cambridge University Press, 1968.

Munson, Kenneth. *Aircraft of World War II*. London: Allan, 1972.

Nicholson, Nigel. *Alex: The Life of Field Marshal Earl Alexander of Tunis*. London: Weidenfeld and Nicolson, 1973.

Nish, Ian. *Japanese Foreign Policy 1869–1942: Kasumigaseki to Miyakezaka*. London: Routledge and Kegan Paul, 1977.

Norman, E. Herbert. *Japan's Emergence as a Modern State: Political and Economic Problems of the Meiji Era*. Honolulu: Institute of Pacific Relations, 1940.

Norwich, Lord. *Old Men Forget: The Autobiography of Duff Cooper*. London: Hart Davis, 1953.

O'Connor, Raymond, ed. *The Imperial Japanese Navy in World War II*. Annapolis: Naval Institute Press, 1969

Okumiya, Masatake; and Horikoshi, Jiro; with Caidin, Martin. *Zero! The Story of the Japanese Navy Air Force 1937–1945*. London: Cassell, 1957.

Oosten, F. C. van. *The Battle of the Java Sea*. London: Allan, 1975.

Owen, Frank. *The Campaign in Burma*. Tiptree: Arrow, 1957.

———. *The Fall of Singapore*. London: Joseph, 1960.

Palit, D. K. *The Campaign in Malaya*. New Delhi: Chowdhri, 1960.

Parkes, Oscar. *British Battleships 1860–1960*. London: Seeley, Service, 1966.

Pelz, Stephen E. *Race to Pearl Harbor: The Failure of the Second London Naval Conference and the Onset of World War II*. Cambridge, Mass.: Harvard University Press, 1974.

Percival, A. E. *The War in Malaya*. London: Eyre and Spottiswoode, 1949.

Pluvier, Jan Meinhard. *South East Asia from Colonialism to Independence*. London: Oxford University Press, 1974.

Pogue, Forrest C. *George C. Marshall*. London: MacGibbon and Kee, 1964.

Potter, E. B. *Nimitz*. Annapolis: Naval Institute Press, 1976.

Potter, E. B., ed. *The United States and World Sea Power*. Englewood Cliffs, N.J.: Prentice Hall, 1955.

Potter, E. B., and Nimitz, Chester W. *The Great Sea War: The Story of Naval Aviation in World War II*. London: Harrap, 1961.

———. *Triumph in the Pacific: The Navy's Struggle against Japan*. Englewood Cliffs, N.J.: Prentice Hall, 1963.

Potter, E. B., and Nimitz, Chester W., eds. *Sea Power: A Naval History*. Englewood Cliffs, N.J.: Prentice Hall, 1960.

Preston, Antony. *Battleships of World War I*. London: Arms and Armour, 1972.

Preston, Antony, ed. *Decisive Battles of the Pacific War*. London: Hamlyn, 1979.

———. *Navies of World War II*. London: Hamlyn, 1976.

Puleston, W. D. *Mahan: The Life and Works of Captain Alfred Thayer Mahan, U.S.N.* London: Cape, 1939.

Purcell, Victor (William Williams Saunders). *The Revolution in South East Asia*. London: Thames and Hudson, 1962.

Reishauer, Edwin O. *Japan: The Story of a Nation*. London: Duckworth, 1970.

Reishauer, Edwin O.; Fairbank, John K.; and Craig, Albert M. *East Asia: The Modern Transformation*. London: Allen and Unwin, 1965.

Richardson, J. O. *On the Treadmill to Pearl Harbor: The Memoirs of Admiral J. O. Richardson*. As told to George C. Dyer. Washington: Department of the Navy, 1975.

Richmond, H. W. *Economy and National Security*. London: Benn, 1931.

———. *Naval Warfare*. London: Benn, 1930.

———. *Statesmen and Sea Power*, London: Oxford University Press, 1947.

Rohwer, T., and Hammelchen, G. *Chronology of the War at Sea: 1939–1942*. Vol. 1. London: Allen, 1972.

Romulo, Carlos P. *I Saw the Fall of the Philippines*. London: Harrap, 1963.

Rooney, D. D. *Stilwell*. New York: Ballantine, 1973.

Roosevelt, Franklin D. *The Roosevelt Letters, Being the Personal Correspondence of Franklin Delano Roosevelt, 1928–1945*. Vol. 3. Edited by Elliott Roosevelt. London: Harrap, 1952.

Rosinski, Herbert. *The Development of Naval Thought*. Newport R.I.: Naval War College, 1977.

Roskill, S. W. *Churchill and the Admirals*. London: Collins, 1977.

———. *Naval Policy Between the Wars: The Period of Anglo-American Antagonism 1919–1929*. Vol. 1. London: Collins, 1968.

———. *Naval Policy Between the Wars: The Period of Reluctant Rearmament 1930–1939*. Vol. 2. London: Collins, 1976.

———. *The Strategy of Sea Power: Its Development and Application*. London: Collins, 1961.

Sansom, G. M. *The Western World and Japan*. London: Cresset, 1950.

———. *Japan in World History*. London: Allen and Unwin, 1952.

Schofield, B. B. *British Sea Power: Naval Policy in the Twentieth Century*. London: Batsford, 1967.

Schurmann, Franz, and Schell, Orville. *Republican China: Nationalism, War and the Rise of Communism 1911–1949*. New York: Penguin, 1968.

Schurmann, Franz, and Schell, Orville, eds. *Imperial China in the Eighteenth and Nineteenth Centuries*. New York: Penguin, 1967.

Seager II, Roger. *Alfred Thayer Mahan: The Man and His Letters*. Annapolis: Naval Institute Press, 1977.

Sheridan, James E. *China in Disintegration: The Republican Era in Chinese History 1912–1949*. London: Collier Macmillan, 1975.

Silverstone, Paul H. *U.S. Warships of World War II*. London: Allen, 1965.

Simson, Ivan. *Singapore: Too Little, Too Late: Some Aspects of the Malayan Disaster in 1942*. London: Cooper, 1970.

Slim, William. *Defeat into Victory*. London: Cassell, 1957.

Smith, E. D. *Battle for Burma*. London: Batsford, 1979.

Smyth, John. *Percival and the Tragedy of Singapore*. London: Macdonald, 1971.

Sprout, Harold, and Sprout, Margaret. *The Rise of American Naval Power 1776–1918*. London: Oxford University Press, 1967.

Stericker, John. *Tear for the Dragon*. London: Barker, 1958.

Stilwell, Joseph W. *The Stilwell Papers*. Edited by Theodore White. London: Macdonald, 1949.

Storry, Richard. *A History of Modern Japan*. New York: Penguin, 1960.

Swinson, A. *Defeat in Malaya: The Fall of Singapore*. London: Macdonald, 1970.

Swinson, Arthur. *Four Samurai: A Quartet of Japanese Army Command in the Second World War*. London: Hutchinson, 1968.

Tainsch, A. R. *. . . And Some Fell by the Wayside: An Account of the North Burma Evacuation*. Calcutta: Oriental Longmans, 1948.

Thomas, David A. *Battle of the Java Sea*. London: Deutsch, 1968.

————. *Japan's War at Sea: Pearl Harbor to the Coral Sea*. London: Deutsch, 1978.

Thompson, Edward, and Garrett, G. T. *The Rise and Fulfilment of British Rule in India*. New York: Macmillan, 1934.

Thomson, D., ed. *The New Cambridge Modern History: The Era of Violence 1898–1945*. Vol. 12., Cambridge: Cambridge University Press, 1960.

Toland, John. *But Not in Shame: The Six Months after Pearl Harbor*. New York: Random House, 1961.

————. *The Rising Sun: The Decline and Fall of the Japanese Empire 1936–1945*. New York: Random House, London: Cassell, 1970.

Tomlinson, Michael. *The Most Dangerous Moment*. London: Kimber, 1976.

Tsuji, Masanobu. *Singapore: The Japanese Version*. London: Mayflower, 1966.

Tuchman, Barbara W. *Sand Against the Wind: Stilwell and the American Experience in China 1911–1945*. New York: Macmillan, 1970.

Walder, David. *The Short Victorious War: The Russo-Japanese Conflict 1904–1905*. London: Hutchinson, 1973.

Warner, Denis, and Warner, Peggy. *The Tide at Sunrise: A History of the Russo-Japanese War 1904–1905*. London: Angus and Robertson, 1975.

Watts, Anthony J., and Gordon, Brian G. *The Imperial Japanese Navy*. London: Macdonald, 1971.

Waung, W.S.K. *Revolution and Liberation: A Short History of Modern China 1900–1960*. London: Heinemann, 1971.

Westwood, J. N. *Fighting Ships of World War II*. London: Sidgwick and Jackson, 1975.

Wheeler, Gerald E. *Prelude to Pearl Harbor: The U.S. Navy and the Far East, 1921–1931*. Columbia: University of Missouri Press, 1963.

Willoughby, Charles A., and Chamberlain, John. *MacArthur 1941–1951*. New York: McGraw-Hill, 1954.

Willmott, H. P. *Sea Warfare: Weapons, Tactics and Strategy*. Chichester: Bird, 1981.

Wint, Guy, ed. *Asia: A Handbook*. London: Blond, 1965.

Wohstetter, Roberta. *Pearl Harbor: Warning and Decision*. Stanford, Calif.: Stanford University Press, 1962.

Woollcombe, Robert. *The Campaigns of Wavell*. London: Cassell, 1959.

PERIODICALS

Bartlett, Donald. "Vice Admiral Chuichi Hara." U.S. Naval Institute *Proceedings*, October 1970, pp. 49–55.

Benda, Harry Jindrick. "The Pattern of Administrative Reforms in the Closing Years of Dutch Rule in Indonesia." *Journal of Asian Studies*, August 1966, pp. 589–605.

Bennett, H. Gordon. "The Conquest of Malaya." (A review of Tsuji, Masanobu.

Singapore: The Japanese Version). *Journal of South East Asian History*, October 1961, pp. 91–100.

Blacker, Carmen. "The First Japanese Mission to England 1862." *History Today*, December 1957, pp. 840–47.

Boxer, C. R. "The Closing of Japan 1636–1639." *History Today*, December 1956, pp. 830–39.

———. "Cornelius Speelman and the Growth of Dutch Power in Indonesia." *History Today*, March 1958, pp. 145–54.

———. "The Dutch East India Company and the China Trade." *History Today*, November 1979, pp. 741–49.

———. "From the Maghgreb to the Moluccas." *History Today*, January 1961, pp. 38–47.

———. "Sakoku, or the Closed Country 1640–1854." *History Today*, February 1957, pp. 80–88.

Brumby, Thomas Mason. "The Fall of Manila: August 13, 1898." U.S. Naval Institute *Proceedings*, August 1960, pp. 88–94.

Buckley, Nora C. "The Extraordinary Voyages of Admiral Cheng Ho." *History Today*, July 1975, pp. 462–71.

Burne, Alfred H. "Japanese and American Strategy in the Pacific." *Military Review*, April 1949, pp. 85–87.

Campbell, Alec. "The Spanish-American War 1898." *History Today*, April 1958, pp. 239–47.

Chen, Edward I'te. "Japan's Decision to Annex Taiwan: A Study of Itō-Mutsu Diplomacy 1894–1895." *Journal of Asian Studies*, November 1977, pp. 61–72.

Clark, J. J. "Sundowner Par Excellence." U.S. Naval Institute *Proceedings*, June 1971, pp. 54–59.

Collier, James R. "Professionals 1920–1940." U.S. Naval Institute *Proceedings*, October 1973, pp. 77–95.

Cook, Charles O., Jr. "The Pacific Command Divided: The Most Unexplainable Decision." U.S. Naval Institute *Proceedings*, September 1978, pp. 55–61.

———. "The Strange Case of Rainbow 5." U.S. Naval Institute *Proceedings*, August 1978, pp. 66–73.

Cooper, Michael. "Richard Cocks: English Merchant in Japan 1613–1623." *History Today*, April 1974, pp. 265–74.

———. "Rodrigues in Japan: A Jesuit Missionary." *History Today*, April 1973, pp. 247–55.

———. "Shipwrecked in Japan 1609." *History Today*, December 1975, pp. 834–42.

Craig, Paul M. "*Lexington* and *Saratoga*: The New Beginning." U.S. Naval Institute *Proceedings*, December 1969, pp. 84–92.

Dartford, G. P. "Malacca: Emporium of the Eastern Trade." *History Today*, December 1960, pp. 856–64.

Delage, Edmond. "Japanese Strategy in the Pacific." *Military Review*, February 1951, pp. 107–9.

Dickens, Gerald. "Why Singapore Fell." *Military Review*, November 1948, pp. 98–100.

Doenhoff, Richard A. von. "Biddle, Perry and Japan." U.S. Naval Institute *Proceedings*, November 1966, pp. 78–87.

Duncan, Francis. "The Struggle to Build a Great Navy." U.S. Naval Institute *Proceedings*, June 1962, pp. 82–88.

Duus, Peter. "Nagai Ryutaro and the 'White Peril.' " *Journal of Asian Studies*, Symposium on Japanese Nationalism, November 1971, pp. 41–49.

Fagan, George V. "FDR and Naval Limitation." U.S. Naval Institute *Proceedings*, April 1955, pp. 411–18.

Farley, M. Foster. "Commissar Lin and Opium." *History Today*, February 1977, pp. 73–81.

Flood, E. Thadeus. "The 1940 Franco-Thai border dispute and Philbuun Sonkhraan's Commitment to Japan." *Journal of South East Asian History*, September 1969, pp. 304–25.

Fuchida, Mitsuo, and Okumiya, Masatake. "Prelude to Midway." U.S. Naval Institute *Proceedings*, May 1955, pp. 505–13.

Fukaya, Hajime. "Japan's Wartime Carrier Construction." Edited by Martin E. Holbrook and Gerald E. Wheeler. U.S. Naval Institute *Proceedings*, September 1955, pp. 1031–43.

Fukuda, Teizaburo. "A Mistaken War." U.S. Naval Institute *Proceedings*, December 1968, pp. 42–47.

Gordon, C. V. "H.M.N.S. *Tjerk Hiddes*—Timor Ferry." U.S. Naval Institute *Proceedings*, February 1960, pp. 31–36.

Hargreaves, J. D. "The Anglo-Japanese Alliance." *History Today*, April 1952, pp. 252–58.

Haight, John McVickar. "FDR's 'Big Stick.' " U.S. Naval Institute *Proceedings*, July 1980, pp. 68–73.

Harris, Richard. "China in the Twentieth Century: Tradition and Revolution." *History Today*, April 1954, pp. 227–35.

Holmes, Wilfred J. "Pearl Harbor Aftermath." U.S. Naval Institute *Proceedings*, December 1978, pp. 68–75.

Hone, Thomas C. "The Destruction of the Battle Line at Pearl Harbor." U.S. Naval Institute *Proceedings*, December 1977, pp. 49–59.

Horie, Y. "The Failure of the Japanese Convoy Escort." U.S. Naval Institute *Proceedings*, October 1956, pp. 1073–81.

Ikei, Masaru. "Japan's Response to the Chinese Revolution of 1911." *Journal of Asian Studies*, February 1966, pp. 213–27.

Johnson, Arthur M., "Theodore Roosevelt and the Navy." U.S. Naval Institute *Proceedings*, October 1958, pp. 76–82.

Johnson, H. K. "Defence along the Abucay Line." *Military Review*, February 1949, pp. 43–52.

Kirchner, D. P., and Lewis, E. R. "American Harbor Defenses: The Final Era." U.S. Naval Institute *Proceedings*, January 1968, pp. 84–98.

Kohno, Shu. "European Military Concepts and 'Sun Tzu.' " *Revue Internationale d'Histoire Militaire*. No. 38, 1978, pp. 117–40.

Kublim, Hyman, "A Century of Port Arthur." U.S. Naval Institute *Proceedings*, May 1957, pp. 505–14.

Lademan, J. U., Jr. "U.S.S. *Gold Star*—Flagship of the Guam Navy." U.S. Naval Institute *Proceedings*, December 1973, pp. 67–79.

Layton, Edwin T. "24 Sentai—Japan's Commerce Raiders." U.S. Naval Institute *Proceedings*, June 1976, pp. 53–61.

Lumby, E.W.R. "Lord Elgin and the Burning of the Summer Palace." *History Today*, July 1960, pp. 479–88.

McAleavy, Henry. "China and the Amur Provinces." *History Today*, June 1964, pp. 381–90.

———. "China under the Warlords." *History Today*, April 1962, pp. 227–33, and May 1962, pp. 303–11.

———. "The Making of Modern Japan." *History Today*, May 1959, pp. 297–307.

———. "The Meiji Restoration." *History Today*, September 1958, pp. 634–45.

Mackay, R. A., Baron. "A Dutchman at ABDA Command and at British Head-quarters in Java, 14 January 1941 [sic]—8 March 1942." *Mededelingen van de Sectie Krijgsgeschiedenis*, 1979.

Merdinger, Charles J.; Shrader, Grahame F.; Eldredge, Michael S.; and Kraft, Carl and Nell. "Pearl Harbor and the *Colorado, Nevada, Taney* and *Utah*." U.S. Naval Institute *Proceedings*, December 1976, pp. 46–54.

Miller, John. "Prelude to Offensive Action in the Pacific." *Military Review*, December 1948, pp. 3–12.

Milner, Samuel. "The Japanese Threat to Australia." *Military Review*, April 1949, pp. 19–28.

Morgan, Gerald. "Minister to Peking." *History Today*, November 1973, pp. 810–16.

Morris, Ivan. "Yoshitsune and the Triumph of Misfortune." *History Today*, July 1972, pp. 490–500.

Morton, Louis. "The American Surrender in the Philippines April–May 1942." *Military Review*, August 1949, pp. 3–14.

———. "The Japanese Decision for War." U.S. Naval Institute *Proceedings*, December 1954, pp. 1325–36.

———. "Japanese Policy and Strategy in Mid War." U.S. Naval Institute *Proceedings*, February 1959, pp. 52–64.

Muir, Malcolm, Jr. "Misuse of the Fast Battleship in World War II." U.S. Naval Institute *Proceedings*, February 1979, pp. 57–62.

Nomura, Minoru. "Japanese Plans for World War II." *Revue Internationale d'Histoire Militaire*. No. 38, 1978, pp. 199–217.

Okmae, Toshikaze, and Pineau, Roger. "Japanese Naval Aviation." U.S. Naval Institute *Proceedings*, December 1972, pp. 68–77.

Okumiya, Masatake. "The Lessons of an Undeclared War." U.S. Naval Institute *Proceedings*, December 1972, pp. 25–31.

Parkes, Oscar. "Japan's War-time Navy." *Naval Review*, February 1952, pp. 47–63.

Parkinson, C. Northcote. "The British in Malaya." *History Today*, June 1956, pp. 367–75.

———. "The Pre-1942 Singapore Naval Base." U.S. Naval Institute *Proceedings*, September 1956, pp. 938–53.

Peattie, Mark R. "Akiyama Saneyuki and the Emergence of Modern Japanese Naval Doctrine." U.S. Naval Institute *Proceedings*, January 1977, pp. 60–69.

Pineau, Roger. "Spirit of the Divine Wind." U.S. Naval Institute *Proceedings*, November 1958, pp. 23–29.

Platonoy, C. "The Battle of Mukden 1905." *History Today*, December 1955, pp. 818–24.

Ramsdell, Daniel B. "The Nakamura Incident and the Japanese Foreign Office." *Journal of Asian Studies*, November 1965, pp. 51–68.

Rice, Richard. "Economic Mobilisation in Wartime Japan: Business, Bureaucracy and Military in Conflict." *Journal of Asian Studies*, August 1979, pp. 689–700.

Sanders, Harry. "King of the Oceans." U.S. Naval Institute *Proceedings*, August 1974, pp. 52–59.

Silberman, Bernard S. "Bureaucratization of the Meiji State: The Problems of Succession in the Meiji Restoration 1868–1900." *Journal of Asian Studies*, May 1976, pp. 421–30.

Stewart, A. J. "Those Mysterious Midgets." U.S. Naval Institute *Proceedings*, December 1974, pp. 54–66.

Stewart, I. M. "The Loss of Singapore—A Criticism." *Military Review*, February 1949, pp. 100–103.

Stoler, Mark A. "The 'Pacific First' Alternative in American World War II Strategy." *International History Review*, July 1980, pp. 432–52.

Storry, Richard. "Fascism in Japan: The Army Mutiny of February 1936." *History Today*, November 1956, pp. 717–26.

Stratton, Samuel S. "The Tiger of Malaya." U.S. Naval Institute *Proceedings*, February 1954, pp. 137–44.

Swanson, Harlan J. "The *Panay* Incident: Prelude to Pearl Harbor." U.S. Naval Institute *Proceedings*, December 1967, pp. 26–37.

Tanaka, Hiromi. "The Military Significance of Korea in the History of China." *Revue Internationale d'Histoire Militaire* No. 38, 1978, pp. 141–61.

Taussig, Joseph K., Jr. "I Remember Pearl Harbor." U.S. Naval Institute *Proceedings*, December 1972, pp. 18–24.

Tolley, Kemp. "Yang Pat: Shanghai to Chungking." U.S. Naval Institute *Proceedings*, June 1963, pp. 80–94.

Tomblin, Barbara Brooks. "High Noon at Chemulpo." U.S. Naval Institute *Proceedings*, August 1969, pp. 70–81.

Torisu, Kennosuke, and Chihaya, Masataka. "Japanese Submarine Tactics." U.S. Naval Institute *Proceedings*, February 1961, pp. 78–83.

Toyama, Saburo. "Years of Transition: Japan's Naval Strategy from 1894 to 1945." *Revue Internationale d'Histoire Militaire*, No. 38, 1978, pp. 162–82.

Watson, D. R. "The French in Indo-China." *History Today*, August 1970, pp. 534–42.

Watson, William. "The Namamugi Incident." *History Today*, May 1964, pp. 318–25.

Weller, Donald M. "Salvo—Splash !" U.S. Naval Institute *Proceedings*, August 1954, pp. 839–50, and September 1954, pp. 1011–22.

Wheeler, Stanley. "The Lost Merchant Fleet of Japan." U.S. Naval Institute *Proceedings*, December 1956, pp. 1294–99.

Wilds, Thomas. "How Japan Fortified the Mandated Islands." U.S. Naval Institute *Proceedings*, April 1955, pp. 401–7.

Wilson, George M. "Kita Ikki's Theory of Revolution." *Journal of Asian Studies*, November 1966, pp. 89–99.

Woodcock, George. "Malacca, the Key to the East." *History Today*, April 1965, pp. 221–31.

————. "Penang, Britain's First Settlement in Malaya." *History Today*, December 1969, pp. 832–39.

Woodman, Dorothy. "Raffles of Java." *History Today*, September 1954, pp. 581–90.

Woodward, David. "The Russian Armada 1904–1905." *History Today*, February 1953, pp. 107–14.

Yokoi, Toshiyuki. "Thought on Japan's Naval Defeat." U.S. Naval Institute *Proceedings*, October 1960, pp. 68–75.

Yoshii, Hiroshi. "Influence of the German-Soviet War on the Japan-United States Negotiations—Particularly Centering on Studies on the Problems of Secession from the Alliance." *Revue Internationale d'Histoire Militaire*, No. 38, 1978, pp. 183–98.

Yoshikawa, Takeo. "Top Secret Assignment." U.S. Naval Institute *Proceedings*, December 1960, pp. 27–39.

Index

TABLE DES MATIERES

* Pour éviter toute confusion avec le numéro I il n'y a pas d'appendice I.

UNIVERSITY OF TORONTO ROMANCE SERIES

This book
was designed by
ELLEN HUTCHISON
under the direction of
ALLAN FLEMING
University of
Toronto
Press